AMERICA'S FINANCIAL APOCALYPSE

HOW TO PROFIT FROM THE NEXT *GREAT DEPRESSION*

No matter where you delve, there are always optimists and pessimists, raging bulls and ruthless bears, whether it is in real estate, collectables, commodities, or the stock market. And due to the overwhelming control of public perception by Wall Street and the financial media, wise investors should always welcome contrarian viewpoints, since perspectives that often oppose the herd help us better assess risk, by objectively viewing the full spectrum.

DISCLAIMER

Preface

Unfortunately, the vast majority of Americans don't understand the real problems facing their nation. In large part, this is due to the media's focus on soap opera-like coverage of meaningless events or trivializing important issues. Rather than providing a realistic and meaningful picture of America's involvement in Iraq, much of the televised media reports the daily body count as a way to impose its liberal, anti-war bias upon voters. America's soap opera-centric media also likes to focus on trivia that will have no impact on anyone, such as who Brittney Spears is dating, which Hollywood stars are in drug rehab, or the latest from the Anna Nicole Smith saga.

In defense of these criticisms, media executives argue that "this is what Americans want to hear about, so that's what we give them." In fact, it is not what the American public wants; not from news broadcasting anyway. Americans want to be educated and informed when they watch news programs. They don't want cheap entertainment. They only become interested in news soaps after having the same trivia thrown in their face on a daily basis.

Show anyone enough of something while providing few if any alternatives and of course they will eventually get hooked. That is precisely why daytime soaps run everyday; what they lack in quality they make for in frequency. These shows enter your life daily, so you become dependent on them, regardless how senseless they are. Give American viewers suitable alternatives and watch the ratings disappear.

Several years ago, when ABC decided to broadcast several hours of the O.J. Simpson chase down Interstate 405, CBS, Fox and NBC also felt the need to do so, as did CNN and other news channels. Why? Because media executives knew it represented the beginnings of a new soap they could turn into a hit reality TV show. This story promised to draw millions of viewers and billions in ad revenues for each network. Best of all, there were no actors to pay. Even before the end of the police chase, network executives already had the first season planned— coverage and analysis of O.J.'s future trial and interviews with the victims' families.

For many months thereafter, all of the networks devoted several hours of daily airtime to the same coverage of the O.J. Simpson murder trial. So viewers had no choice but to watch. Even after the drawn-out trial, the soap continued. Soon, Kato Calin was transformed into a celebrity due to media overexposure.

As a consequence of their "news coverage," broadcast journalists end up glamorizing crime and murder, helping to recruit the next serial killer or martyr. While they wait for the next JonBenet Ramsey or Laci Peterson case to appear, they transform themselves into a televised version of the *National Enquirer*. If it's not something that can be twisted into a longstanding soap opera, they simply aren't interested in covering it, or else they don't cover it adequately. No network is immune from this plague.

Even CNBC has helped transform the stock market into a casino with its drama-filled programming of the NYSE trading floor and other shows that deliver the illusion of value so you will keep watching. And whatever networks can do to get viewers is rewarded with huge ad deals. It's a shame they have allowed the news to be poisoned with the lure of ad dollars.

The media has a moral obligation to provide an objective assessment of events most critical to Americans. Unfortunately, they rarely deliver. Without responsible media coverage, it becomes very difficult for Americans to know what the real problems are. And without knowledge of the problems, there can be no unified force demanding change from politicians.

As a result, irresponsible journalism has allowed political candidates to overlook the real issues facing America. Even if politicians were aware of the nation's biggest challenges, many would do nothing for fear of harsh consequences from powerful lobbyist groups. This is precisely why Americans must understand the real issues. Only then will they pressure leaders for change.

Politicians won't address America's domestic problems—its biggest problems—because voters have allowed the media to determine that Iraq is the only problem. Politicians like this because it gives them a simple way to market themselves for re-election. They either chose to pull out of Iraq or "stay the course." In reality, Iraq is not a problem—not for Americans. The future of America is. And until viewers turn the channel, the media will continue to broadcast trash. Until voters demand solutions, politicians will continue the status quo.

When Americans vote during the next presidential election, most will have no idea what the real issues are. No doubt, for the candidates and much of the voting public, Iraq will continue to remain as America's most difficult challenge. After reading this book, you will be one of the few to understand the complex forces that will most likely send America into a deep depression.

I cannot force Americans to read this book. I can only report my findings and analysis so the reader will understand America's real problems. But still, I cannot force readers to demand change from politicians. I cannot control the stock and bond markets either. I can only provide reasonable investment guidance as a result of America's problems. The rest is up to you.

If there was reliable a way to advise investors with specific securities to buy several years before an economic crisis, this would represent easy money. And there is never easy money; no free lunches and no crystal balls. Things change with time. And those who think they have found a way around continuous reassessment of investment risk usually end up losing it all. Therefore, despite my analysis, investors must appreciate the likelihood of random periods of volatility that will affect investment risk. And they must adjust to these changes.

Investors must actively manage their investments based upon changes in economics, market performance, relative valuation, and indicators of market sentiment. They must learn to think for themselves, scrutinizing reports from Wall Street and the media. Only then will see what is really going on. This is the only way to minimize being fooled by forces that stand to profit from deception. Obviously, this is a very difficult task to take on. It requires a large commitment of time, energy and other resources, but most of all good judgment. I hope this book proves as a valuable resource, serving as a foundation for political change and managing investment risk over the next several years, as America faces a most difficult transition.

Acknowledgements

I would like to express my deepest appreciation to several research organizations for their permission to use numerous charts and data throughout this book:

Economic Policy Institute

Center for Retirement Research at Boston College

The Henry J. Kaiser Family Foundation

Center on Budget and Policy Priorities

The Century Foundation

The use of their data should in no way necessarily indicate that these organizations share similar views as the author. Readers are encouraged to familiarize themselves with the wonderful research and findings of these groups.

Finally, I want to acknowledge the individual efforts of Norma Clavel and Pavan Lall for their editorial work in Chapter One.

Contents

Introduction

For more than two decades, several experts have predicted a major depression in America. While many of these forecasts were written in the early '90s as an aftershock of the '87 crash and the turmoil of the '80s, they were all wrong. On the contrary, America mounted what appeared to be a tremendous rebound, experiencing what most have labeled as its strongest decade of economic growth since the post-World War II period.

By the early '90s, a raging bull market was delivering spectacular returns, causing some to believe that a market collapse and subsequent depression would soon appear. As a result of these fears, some exited the capital markets altogether. Thereafter, the Internet took off causing the market bubble to swell, many high-tech stocks with seemingly limitless valuations.

This bull market period was arguably the greatest in American history. Over the course of its 13-year stretch, the market appreciated by over 600 percent, with average annual returns in excess of 18 percent. Mutual fund managers were thought of as geniuses and treated like rock stars. Even soccer moms thought they were stock gurus. By 1999, with the help of television ads by online brokerage firms, many everyday Americans thought it was easy to make money in the stock market; and many did. Inspired by tremendous investment gains and tacky commercials by online brokers, many younger Americans made plans to retire by age 40. Of course these are just some of the clear signs of the greed, mania and disillusion that occur towards the end of an asset bubble. And we all remember what happened at the start of the new millennium.

Even after the deflation of the Internet bubble, cautious investors who pulled out of the market a decade earlier missed out on spectacular returns since then. Many investors who entered the market near its peak suffered devastating losses. But most who remained invested since the early '90s are still much better off today. While this correction revealed the most recent illusions embedded within the economy, it's only a small part of what will be a larger correction in the coming years. However, the timing of the impending economic catastrophe is critical because mistiming such an event could lead to results that might be equally damaging.

Despite the avalanche of scandals in corporate America and Wall Street, many investors fail to recognize that the post-bubble period is quite different from the Bull Run in the 90s. In fact, many are still clinging to the former "darlings of Wall Street" that performed so well during the Internet bubble. But today, the capital markets have been realigned with authenticity, and economics now control the investment cycle rather than hype generated by Wall Street. Accordingly, Wall Street and the U.S. Government can only hide the realities of America's decline for so long before the truth is revealed.

Since the deflation of the Internet bubble, we have already witnessed a portion of this transition. Subsequently, many of the spectacular performing asset classes and industries of the previous bull market period have performed poorly. But this gives complacent investors incentive to invest in other industries expected to outperform during the massive economic correction that has become a fixture of certainty. Currently, we are in the middle stages of a secular bear market that began in 2001. And if one examines a historical chart of the Dow Jones Industrial Average since 1900, the most reasonable conclusion is that the stock market is trending downward. Therefore, further market corrections or a period of modest returns will be needed in order to compensate for the spectacular appreciation of the '90s.

During the post-war boom, America celebrated its much improved economic position by increasing the size of the average family. As a result, birthrates soared for nearly two decades to produce what has since been referred to as the baby boomer generation. This large group of Americans was responsible for the great bull market of the '90s through massive credit-based consumption, causing a rapid expansion of several industries.

Unfortunately, America entered the free trade paradigm as a losing participant from the start. While America remains as the centerpiece for the global economy, it relies on record debt to maintain its status as the world's strongest consumer marketplace. But this cannot last much longer. Advances in telecommunications and e-commerce have transformed the developing world into a global marketplace, where competitive forces from abroad are much more influential than in the past.

Subsequently, America's vulnerable role in the new economy threatens to erode the strength of its empire. Already, America has witnessed a gradual disappearance of its core citizens; the middle class. As well, poverty continues to grow while America's wealthiest quintile increases their wealth. These trends have been masked by record levels of credit-based spending and manipulation of economic data.

For over two decades, several nations have benefited at the expense of America's job base and living standards. This led to a long period of excessive consumption relative to productivity. When the economic boom from the post-war period began to lose steam in the '60s, consumption began to exceed productivity, as Americans refused to acknowledge a decline in living standards. Up until the '70s, America fueled this consumption-production disparity using the surplus wealth generated during the post-war boom.

During the '80s, America's growing consumption was compounded by massive government spending and a devastating oil crisis. Shortly thereafter, the consumer credit industry grew to meet the demands of a nation experiencing large productivity deficits. And today, America is vastly different than the post-war period. Rather than increases in net wealth, America's "growth" over the past two decades has been fueled by credit spending which has created the illusion of impressive productivity, while serving to mask declining living standards. As a consequence of these changes, America's financial industry is now one of its biggest and most profitable.

Today, America is more dependent on foreign nations than anytime in its history. Declining oil reserves and a foreign-funded credit bubble have positioned the fate of this nation in the hands of the world. Soon, America will soon face the economic burden of 76 million aging boomers. Beginning in 2011, mandatory expenditures for Medicare, Medicaid and Social Security will start to grow rapidly. And by 2025, these expenses will have swelled to unthinkable levels. There is no way America can pull through these transitions using debt, as it has in the past.

Even if America was able to avoid this corrective period in some miraculous way, historical data indicates that the post-bubble correction alone will last until at least 2012, yielding average annual returns of approximately 2 percent unadjusted for inflation. Thus far, these predictions have held. But I expect economic conditions to get much worse beyond 2012.

I cannot tell you with any level of confidence *which* of the major issues detailed in this book will be the triggering event for America's socioeconomic correction. As well, I am not able to tell you with absolute certainty *when* America will slip into economic darkness. It might happen by 2016 or 2025. What I can tell you with full confidence is that a disaster of enormous magnitude and variable duration is going to occur; most likely within the next two decades. The laws of supply and demand dictate that it must.

If all of this sounds uninformative, I remind you that attempting to pinpoint the sequence, timing, and duration of complex events of this magnitude would only result in a misleading level of comfort. One does not need to know precisely when or exactly how a catastrophe will occur in order to profit. Those who are aware of the risks can position themselves to recognize early warning signs and react accordingly. Therefore, the real value in this book is to provide a detailed understanding of the problems and related risks faced by America, the potential interactions of each antagonist upon the others, using this knowledge as a risk management tool.

Regardless of what may or may not turn out to be America's darkest period in at least 70 years, I am not predicting the end to this nation's dominance. This correction period will only represent an oscillation of its socioeconomic cycle. After the disaster is triggered, new reforms will be enacted, providing stability for all Americans, narrowing the wealth and income gap, and diminishing the power and exploitation of Americans by corporate America. Washington will create more opportunities for entrepreneurs. And together, the American people will reclaim the greatness of a once mismanaged nation, facilitating another great economic expansion and bull market period.

As you read through this book, you will notice an enormous amount of data, both in tables and in the text. Some of this data may seem questionable, but I want to assure you that it comes from reputable sources. That is specifically why I took the time to list over 700 references at the end of the book, organized by topic. My insights and opinions are based on my experience on Wall Street, as a business consultant and as an investment strategist for an institutional newsletter.

In summary, I have presented what I feel to be a strong case for America's weakened economic position and competitive landscape by addressing the major issues at hand—the trade imbalance and federal debt, declining social unity and education, adverse effects of free trade, the healthcare and Social Security crisis, the pension crisis, real estate bubble, the war in Iraq, tensions in the Middle East, the global oil shortage, and the effects baby boomers will have as they enter what they expect to be their "Golden Years."

I have also included some alternative investment strategies expected to shield investors or allow them to profit from the economic consequences of America's excessive consumption. In the final two chapters, I discuss those asset classes and industries I expect to deliver the best risk-adjusted performance over the next ten to twenty-year period. Finally, I illustrate how investors should approach risk.

Hopefully, many American voters will view this book as a critical read in order to understand the real issues facing this nation. As you might appreciate, the more comprehensive and detailed a book is, the larger opportunity for potential disagreement among readers due to the number of topics discussed. I have chosen to take this risk of potential criticism because any predictions of a depression mandate a comprehensive treatment, with extensive data, analysis and occasionally even bold assertions. To fall short of this would not do justice to the topic.

Focused readers may notice that I repeat certain concepts in different portions of the book. For instance, I often conclude that many of America's problems are ultimately due to free trade, declining living standards, and its poor healthcare system. The reason for such repetition is to tie together all of the problems since each chapter has been written as a stand-alone that can be read non-sequentially. The reader may choose to read those chapters of most interest first and refer to other chapters as desired.

PART I

AMERICA'S PAST, PRESENT & FUTURE

1

A BRIEF HISTORY OF AMERICA

Although the duration of America's socioeconomic evolution is relatively brief, its existence has been riddled by a flurry of landmark events since its partition from England some two hundred years ago. The *Prima Facie* indicators of its dominant presence can be attributed to the climatic period of inception, as well as its unique alliances with England and Europe.

As history shows, certain colonies of the Empire officially became independent when they broke away from England in the 18th Century. Over the ensuing two centuries, what became known as the United States of America expanded its territorial reach through the addition of 37 new states to an original base of 13, as the nation stretched its wings across the expanse of the North American continent.

This brief but frenetic burst of activity was responsible for the vital changes that transformed America into the epitome of all that is resplendent of developed civilization—Democracy, freedom, and golden opportunity—otherwise known by the entire world as the "American Dream."

To recapitulate American history, post-rebellion from British rule, in 1776 the British Colonies won independence from Great Britain in the Revolutionary War and became recognized as the United States of America following the Treaty of Paris in 1783. This landmark defeat signaled what would be the onset of England's gradual decline and the rise of America as the next world power, a transfer that would materialize over the next 150 years.

However, quiet danger in recent decades in the form of social disarray, political turbulence, economic fluctuations and government mismanagement have poised to cause a severe readjustment of the progress made in America since World War II. As evidenced by the declining economic conditions over the past three decades, the United States of America may well be approaching the nadir of a downward trend from a long post-war period of robust growth and hearty consumption, which by nature must be countered by a compensatory repayment period. Only after these intrinsic scores have been tallied can America refuel and continue its trajectory of dominance. This painful yet unavoidable period of correction and recalibration, while denied by many, is inevitable.

Unlike the post-WWII period which positioned America as the clear world economic and military power, today America's seemingly robust economy has been constructed upon a loose scaffold of consumer and national debt that has served to mask the inherent problems and declining living standards this nation has encountered for nearly three decades. Yet, its mounting reliance on debt was never a condition of the U.S. Constitution, but was implemented within the nation's banking system when the Federal Reserve Act was rapidly passed into law without proper Congressional review in the early 1900s.

Even before their break from the mother country, American colonies were already experimenting with the use of currency notes in-lue of gold and silver coins during military conflicts. The first paper money appeared in colonial America in 1690, issued in Massachusetts as payment for soldiers going to battle in Canada. But when the Constitutional Convention was assembled in 1787 to compose and ratify the U.S. Constitution, it was decided that no currency of the newly formed America would be substituted with any payment other than gold and silver. According to Article 1, § 10, clause 1 of the U.S. Constitution,

"No state shall coin Money; Emit Bills of Credit; make any Thing but gold and silver Coin a Tender in Payment of Debts."

As we shall see later, the abolishment of this law by two former presidents signaled a critical step forward for American economics. Ironically, this change in monetary policy has been largely responsible for America's recent economic decline and growing financial vulnerability.

A Century of Bitter Sweet Transition

After gaining independence from England, European immigrants flocked to America to take part in the opportunities promised by this vast fertile land. In order to develop the Midwestern plains, colonists were offered several acres of land at little or no cost as an incentive to settle this unchartered territory. This period up to the 1840s was the first industrial revolution, which began in the late 18th century in England with the improvement of Thomas Newcomen's steam engine (originally invented in 1712) by James Watt. Ironically, Watt made these modifications in the same year that America won its independence from England. Other notable inventions and the discovery of electricity by Benjamin Franklin actually predated this period.

The early focus of this revolutionary era was on farming and textile production, creating an even greater demand for further industrialization. This prompted much of the southern agricultural regions of the United States to bring in slaves from Africa, which were not hunted down and captured as many believe, but rather purchased at auctions held by powerful African nationals.

By the early 1800s, America was well on its way to gaining the envy of the world. And while most of the nation was still uninhabited, vast railroad lines were being constructed to connect the north and south and the east with the west, which enabled more rapid and safe transportation throughout this new land.

Fueled by a strong sense of freedom, independence and opportunity, the northeastern states enjoyed a vigorous period of manufacturing and political innovation, which served to strengthen the foundation of this new nation. Meanwhile, the southern states benefited from the inhumane slave labor provided by African captives, who helped build the agricultural powerhouse this fertile land provided.

When gold was discovered by James Marshall at Sutter's Mill in 1848, thousands flocked to the California bay area from all over North America and several other nations including Chile and China, all seeking wealth.   This became known as the California Gold Rush and was responsible for the rapid settlement of this state.   The hunt for gold was much more than thousands seeking riches. This movement created numerous entrepreneurial opportunities to support the massive flood of people.   General stores were needed, as were motels and restaurants.   In fact, many more people became rich from supplying the goods and services to prospectors than they did by finding gold.   Today, the entrepreneurial spirit that arose during the gold rush still exists today in California.

A decade later, as America was emerging as a world leader in commerce, an internal bloody war began in 1861, matching the north against the south.   The outcome of the Civil War would determine the next direction America would take as a unified nation.   As America was not yet financially stable, the government made use of currency notes in-lue of gold and silver coinage during this war.

Newcomen's Steam Engine

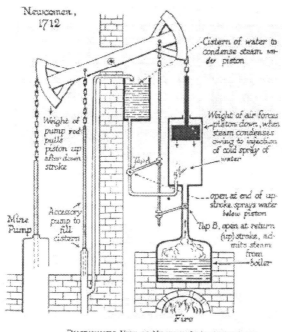

While America still struggled to resolve its civil war, President Lincoln issued the Emancipation Proclamation in 1863, freeing most slaves.   Two years later after the war was over, slavery in America was officially abolished.   But it would take several decades before African Americans would be able to completely sever the bonds of their slavery legacy.   Yet even without the enslavement of Africans, America continued to fuel its successes by offering opportunity and freedom, and this created an entrepreneurial drive that would take the world by storm.

The second industrial revolution began in the late 1800s and was signaled by the birth of the steel industry which catalyzed the formation of large corporations. It was during this period that some of the most innovative creations appeared by early Americans. Most notable were the inventions of Thomas Edison (light bulb) and Alexander Graham Bell (telephone). Finally, electricity discovered by Benjamin Franklin over 100 years earlier would be used for much more than the telegraph.

Monetary Reform

America entered the twentieth century as a young adult, having passed two difficult tests of preserving its freedom through its victorious transition into an independent and productive nation and by the successful although bloody resolution of the Civil War. However, its banking system was still in infancy and was therefore subject to periods of vulnerability. When international gold shipments were delayed in 1907, bank reserves were stifled. This created a "money panic," prompting American and political outcries for monetary reform.

Some feel that these delayed shipments were the result of deliberate actions by Washington in attempt to alter America's currency policies. Regardless of the catalyst, its consequences led to the mysteriously rapid passage of the Federal Reserve Act on December 23, 1913 which created 12 privately owned Federal Reserve Banks, whose stock would be owned by member banks that were themselves to be privately owned. This new monetary system was to be controlled by a 12-man Board of Governors, 7 to be appointed by the President of the United States.

The currency issued by the Federal Reserve were known as Federal Reserve Notes, and were to be "redeemed in lawful money," in keeping with the U.S. Constitution, which as we have seen was defined as gold and silver coinage. However, the Federal Reserve Banking System was also afforded the power to borrow money and expand or contract the number and amount of outstanding bills of credit, despite the original mandates of the Constitution. This drastic change in monetary policy would alter America's economic infrastructure for better and for worse.

WWI and the Roaring '20s

During this same time period, England was still viewed as the world power, and rightly so, as it continued to exert dominant and aggressive military power throughout the world. However one of the first signs of a shift in power would be demonstrated when the newly formed Federal Reserve Banking System of America used its new monetary authority to borrow lines of credit during WWI. This proved to be a successful tactic in financial warfare and was largely responsible for victory by the Allies.

Continued expansion and utilization of government credit by America led to a decade-long period of impressive post-war expansion. By the early 1920s, America's capital markets were showing signs of maturity, as the first great bull market had commenced. America had finally arrived and was now challenging England as the new world economic power. Throughout this period, the Federal Reserve Banks continued to experiment with their manipulative powers of monetary control by expanding and contracting the currency supply for the purposes of controlling the economy.

Subsequently, it was the Federal Reserve's inflationary policy during the 1920s that ultimately led to what became known as the "Roaring '20s;" a period remembered as the first unified celebration of wealth, happiness, freedom, and hope for America's future. The stock market had already commenced its bull run just after the end of the war, and by the mid-1920s everyone seemed to be invested in the stock market. Consequently, widespread participation led to the formation of a stock market bubble, while everyone thought there was no limit to stock prices. Americans felt great and life was good.

Soon, everyone was giving stock tips—bell-hops, caddies, delivery boys...everyone. However, like all bubbles, this one would burst without warning, serving as a triggering event to unmask the political and economic disparities that had accumulated since the post-war period. On October 29, 1929 (known as "Black Tuesday") the stock market began its long and painful correction with an initial market crash. This market sell-off would be the first of many more to come over the next several years, serving to catalyze a series of catastrophic events unlike anything ever witnessed in America.

Box 1-1: An account about the Great Crash from Craig Mitchell

"When the Depression came, after the crash and when we got into 1930, Father received a letter from his good friend Reggie saying... 'Dear Charlie, I will always revere our friendship and remember the great times we've had together, but I know that a new world is coming and I'm not prepared to live in it and I'm dropping out. Please don't have me followed, you will never see me again. I send you all my dearest affection...Reggie.' And indeed, he would go from town to town one step ahead of the detectives my father would send to try and find him. And he was never again located and he was never able to make that transition."

The Great Depression and the New Deal

The Great Depression remains in history books as the most challenging socioeconomic period faced by America. While many wealthy Americans suffered from the catastrophic remnants of this dark correction period, it had an especially devastating affect on the lower class. This decade-long period witnessed two recessions, with unemployment rates of over 25 percent at its peak. Low morale spread throughout the nation, causing many to regard suicide as the only way out.

There are many theories pertaining to the causes of the Great Depression. However it appears that the consensus of historians and economists attributed this disaster to the speculative nature of the stock market created by the lack of controls, loose and irresponsible margin policies by brokerage firms, Wall Street deceit, a huge money supply created by the Federal Reserve, and Washington policies that hurt the agricultural sector. All of these factors led to an overbalance of power within corporate America and a wide income and wealth disparity between the rich and poor, with America's wealthiest 1 percent having gained ownership of more than 80 percent of the nation's wealth. As many Americans struggled to make ends meet during this period, some actually did quite well. But even many of America's wealthiest individuals lost everything.

During the midst of the depression, the commercial oil industry began, yet most did not seem to notice. But this new industry would soon change the world, with America as its number one benefactor. The commercialization of oil would also represent an important transition for the Middle East. Virtually overnight, as the commercial demand for oil was established, the oil-rich and poverty-stricken nations in the Middle East basked in glory, realizing they sat on a sea of "black gold" needed by the wealthy nations of the world.

President Franklin Delano Roosevelt entered office on March 4, 1933 in the midst of America's darkest period. In an attempt to calm widespread panic, he immediately declared a banking holiday. But unfortunately thousands of banks would never reopen, taking with them the savings of millions of Americans. A few months later, the 1933 Emergency Banking Act was rushed through Congress without proper review by the House. This law allowed the U.S. Treasury Department to acquire possession of all gold in the United States. This would be the first step leading to the eventual detachment of the U.S. dollar from the gold standard. There would be several additional laws (The Gold Reserve Act of 1934) and Executive Orders passed by FDR that would further relieve the government's obligation to settle U.S. currency in gold and silver. Despite these monetary changes, foreign central banks still retained their original dollar-gold exchange privileges.

Thereafter, FDR created several government agencies and laws collectively known as the New Deal, in order to preserve and assist the financial stability and future security of Americans. Of the two installments of the New Deal, (1933 and 1937) the second was more drastic. And although many of these changes enacted were later repealed during the next decade, what stands out most today from this radical and effective policy change is the Social Security Administration, the Federal Depository Insurance Corporation (FDIC), the Securities and Exchange Commission (SEC), and the Tennessee Valley Authority (TVA). Perhaps unlike any other policy changes before and since then, these have continued to serve Americans well for the most part.

Overall, this decade-long crisis was needed in order to encourage the passage of drastic new regulatory laws that would begin to favor the American individual more rather than big industry. Only from the impact of this crisis were politicians able to muster the courage and wisdom needed to implement change. It was a correction period that was required to remove the inequities of wealth and power, greed and excess, exploitation and corruption; all of which had formed for over two decades.

World War II

In the mid-1930s, during the apex of America's depression, Germany began a series of hostile military campaigns in Eastern Europe. Soon, more nations became involved, signaling what would be later known as World War II. Meanwhile, in the early stages of this war, America chose to remain neutral and felt that isolationism was the best way to solve its own problems.

By 1940, America's economy and morale appeared to be stabilizing. But before it would begin to utilize the modernization fueled by the oil industry, America would become a primary player in the war. Yet even during this global conflict, the impact of oil was clearly demonstrated, and America quickly became the world leader in production due to the availability of investment capital required for exploration.

As a silent advocate for its British allies, America showed resentment against the Nazi allies when it refused to sell Japan badly needed oil. As a retaliatory gesture, Japan staged a surprise attack on Pearl Harbor on December 15, 1941. Only a few days later, FDR asked for a declaration of war for which the people of America were too anxious to enter.

Table 1-1. Programs of the New Deal

Program	Description	Outcome
Emergency Banking Act/Federal Deposit Insurance Corporation (FDIC)	Permitted the government to inspect the all banks and created the FDIC to insure deposits up to $5000.	Reestablished American confidence in banks. Most banks were determined to be healthy, and two-thirds were allowed to open soon after.
Federal Emergency Relief Administration (FERA)	Provided funds to local relief agencies and funded public work programs.	Revitalized many deteriorating relief programs.
Civil Works Administration (CWA)	Provided construction jobs for the unemployed.	The CWA provided a psychological and physical boost to its 4 million workers.
Civilian Conservation Corps (CCC)	Provided 2.5 million jobs to single men in forests, beaches, and parks, and similar programs for 8,500 women from 1934 to 1937.	The CCC taught the men and women of America how to live independently, thus, increasing their self esteem.
Indian Reorganization Act of 1934	Banned the sale of tribal lands and restored ownership of unallocated lands to Native American groups.	Positive outcome for the Native Americans.
National Industrial Recovery Act (NIRA) of June 1933	Helped boost declining prices; let trade associations to regulate wages, working conditions, production, and prices and it set a minimum wage.	Temporarily stopped declining prices, but inflation reduced consumer spending. Overproduction and weak consumption caused business activity to decline. Later declared unconstitutional.
Public Works Association (PWA)	Launched projects such as the Grand Coulee Dam on the Columbia River.	One of the best parts of the NIRA.
Federal Securities Act of May 1933/ Securities and Exchange Commission (SEC)	Required companies to provide full disclosure and gave the Fed power to regulate the purchase of stock on margin.	Helped restore a healthy balance between publicly traded companies and the investment public.
Home Owners Loan Corporation (HOLC) / Agriculture Adjustment Administration (AAA)	Refinanced mortgages of middle-income home owners to help prevent foreclosures. The AAA tried to raise farm prices by paying farmers not to raise specific crops and animals.	The AAA ordered farmers to kill off certain animals and crops, resulting in widespread confusion, as many Americans were starving. Declared unconstitutional later on.
Tennessee Valley Authority (TVA) (May 1993)	Helped farmers and created jobs.	Provided cheap electric power, flood control, and recreation to the Tennessee River valley.
Works Progress Administration (WPA) 1935-1943	Provided construction work for 8 million Americans.	Decreased unemployment.
Farm Security Administration (FSA)	Loaned over $1 billion to farmers and set up camps for migrant workers	

Just as war proved to be the defining event in its previous two centuries, World War II was the defining period for twentieth century America, as urgency brought new innovations, strong patriotism, and personal sacrifices that led to an intense unified war effort at home and abroad.   Notably, America's war contributions were significantly aided by its immigrant population.   Despite the intense racism and discrimination in America against Italian-Americans, it was this ethnicity that provided the majority of soldiers for the American military.

Also noteworthy was the participation of several African-American soldiers as segregated units within the military.   In a nation that offered them little freedom, opportunity, or justice at that time, their courageous war efforts and surprising sense of patriotism served as a symbolic message to all that they no longer considered themselves as descendants of slaves, but as Americans.

As well, America became the recipient of many brilliant minds who escaped the repression of Nazi occupation in Europe.   Specifically, the immigration of Albert Einstein in 1940 was a result of German laws which caused all Jewish professors to lose their university jobs.   Although Einstein did not work directly on America's secret nuclear program (the Manhattan Project), it was he who encouraged FDR to start this nuclear fission program for fear that Germany would be the first to develop an atomic bomb.   It was this unique combination of freedom, patriotism, and innovation that, together with British forces, helped liberate the world from the repression and brutality of Nazi Germany and its allies.

President Roosevelt did well to guide Americans through the devastating challenges of the Great Depression and WWII.   His leadership and vision won the hearts of the American people, earning him an unprecedented total of three consecutive presidential terms.   Indeed, FDR remains as one of America's most celebrated political legends, responsible for having led the nation through two of the most difficult periods in its history.   But as we all know, history eventually repeats.   And at some point another depression will occur to correct another long period of excess and inequity that inevitably forms in a cyclical manner within all nations.

Post-war Recovery and the Baby Boom

Due to the devastating effects of WWII on much of the developed world, America emerged as the global leader in manufacturing and production.   Post-war America now served as the world's factory for consumer goods and agricultural products.   This period was really America's second industrial revolution, providing Americans with modern machinery and automobiles fueled by the abundance of oil.

As television sets flooded into millions of homes, this revolutionary innovation soon became the focal point of family gatherings, instilling creativity and social unity in millions of households across America.   For the first time, people from all over the nation could tune in to see how Hollywood thought Americans lived.   And when Hollywood was wrong, Americans altered their behavior to mirror the descriptions portrayed on television. Today, we still see the power of the media and how it can change or create societal norms.

It was during the early post-war period that free trade policies would be enacted to help European nations rebuild what they had lost. The General Agreement on Tariffs and Trade (GATT) was established in 1947 as a part of a United Nations campaign to promote rebuilding operations in Europe and Asia. Similar to many of the free trade agreements today, GATT eliminated tariffs and enacted other laws that were meant to open trade. However, unlike today, America did not suffer any adverse consequences of GATT during the post-war period since most of the economic infrastructure of the developed world had been demolished, and therefore offered very little competition.

Consequently, America's newly found prosperity, patriotism, and overall "good feelings" during the post-war period fueled a large rise in birth rates from 1946 to 1964. And the 85 million Americans born during that period were labeled baby boomers.

The Power of Oil is Seen

It was during this post-war period that oil production surged and soon surpassed coal use in America. At that time, America had vast oil reserves with no end in sight. But there was one geologist who felt otherwise. According to a presentation given at a national oil conference in 1956, King Hubbert made a shocking prediction that America would begin to experience a decline in daily oil production within the next two decades. He referred to this theory as Peak Oil.

Hubbert's theory was so novel that he was written off as a fool. However, when his prediction proved to be correct less than two decades later, (just one year short from his forecast) the world stood up and took notice. And ever since that time, there has been a cover-up by OPEC, the U.S. government and large oil companies regarding the amount of conventional oil remaining in the world as a means to secure their own interests.

The War on Communism

With its unprecedented economic expansion well under way, America abandoned its isolationist policies and began to "protect" other nations from communist takeover, namely South Korea in the 1950s and Vietnam in the 1960s and '70s. Simultaneously, during the '60s America also entered a "space race" with the Soviet Union.

In the late '70s, shortly after an OPEC oil embargo, inflation rose to double digits. Even after the Iranian embargo was lifted, OPEC raised prices. This resulted in another oil crisis with further inflation. And throughout this period, gold and silver prices soared to unimaginable levels with the help of market manipulation.

In the early 1980s, double-digit inflation sparked by the oil crisis led to several economic difficulties. Fortunately, Fed Chairman Paul Volcker was able to restore the buying power of the dollar using a series of bold interest-rate hikes that resulted in double-digit interest rates which ultimately reached 19 percent. On the heels of the inflation crisis and through the use of unfair trade practices, Japan gained significant traction in U.S. markets, resulting in the destruction of millions of manufacturing jobs.

Simultaneously, America entered a Cold War standoff with the former Soviet Union. These difficulties were remedied by President Reagan but at the expense of mounting national debt. However, low oil prices and continued foreign and domestic investment catalyzed another impressive bull market that began just as Reagan departed from office.

The Collapse of Communism

By 1991, the Soviet Union had dissolved due to several years of a corrupt political, economic, and social system which left little for its citizens. A few years later, the Communist government of East Germany also collapsed and the Berlin Wall was torn down by Germans on both sides. The world was beginning to look much more peaceful, and it appeared as if the 1990s would usher America into the next millennium with further prosperity, as thousands of upper middle-class Americans secured financial stability for their children by creating trust funds linked to the stock market.

The accomplishments of President Reagan might only be surpassed by his appeal from the American people. By the time Reagan finished his second term in office, he had extinguished the Cold War, demonstrated America's dominance in space exploration, strengthened intellectual property laws, and positioned the economy for the greatest bull market in American history. However, all of these triumphs came at the expense of huge levels of debt. But still, things seemed a lot better now that inflation was normalized and fears of a Soviet nuclear attack had been extinguished. After a 22 percent stock market crash in October 1987 ("Black Monday"), the U.S. economy would rebound stronger than ever, ushering in the "Great Bull Market."

The Roaring '90s

The Clinton years were marked by a celebration of world freedom coupled with America's tremendous economic expansion, fueled in large part by the baby boomers who entered their peak income years. As President Clinton approached the end of his first term, America's economy seemed unstoppable as many industries swelled to meet the needs of the boomer generation. Meanwhile the Internet had just been launched.

Overall, the U.S. economy was very strong by virtually every measurable traditional indicator. And many Americans became much wealthier during this period primarily due to the gains in the stock market which was fueled by the spending power of the boomers. However, economic data now indicates that the vast majority of Americans did not extract much benefit from this period as we shall later see.

With freedom and democracy spreading throughout the world like a contagious virus, Americans experienced a shift in priorities with the thought that world peace was a reality. This perception, as well as the prosperity of many helped ignite the liberal movement that still exists today. It has been much of this movement that has served to disrupt and destroy American values that have led to recent disunity and social decay.

Despite the perception of world peace, a new enemy had been gradually organizing. This enemy was even more complex and dangerous than Communist forces because it involved religion, culture, and an unimaginable dedication towards the pursuit of its missions. Extremist Islamic groups had been organizing for several decades. Random plane hijackings, kidnappings of Olympic hostages, bombings of U.S. Marine barracks in Lebanon and hundreds of other acts of violence served to fuel their sense of conviction and mounting strength. The two recent attacks on the World Trade Center served to highlight their strength. Now, America and the rest of the free world continue to face the threat of terrorist activities by these groups, with which many OPEC nations have direct ties.

Oil and the U.S. Economy

Perhaps more so than any other single factor, the formation and rapid expansion of the commercial oil industry gave rise to the economic stability of America's middle-class, enabling most to achieve the "American Dream." Abundant oil for combustion engines and electrical power for devices and machinery fueled the expansion of modern American industries, leading to well-paying and secure manufacturing jobs for those seeking work. As well, many companies began to offer pension plans for their employees, hoping to encourage more workers to spend their careers with the same company. This was the beginning of a new route towards financial stability for American workers.

After the oil crisis of the mid-1970s and early '80s, America enjoyed two decades of tremendous economic expansion leading to the greatest bull market in its history. And to a large extent, it was the availability of inexpensive oil that was responsible for this epic rise in prosperity. As evidence of this hypothesis, consider the direct correlation between GDP growth and oil demand (figure 1-1) that has held for every decade other than the 1970s and early '80s, (due to the oil crisis and the subsequent development of nuclear energy facilities). (1)

One cannot dispute that oil fuels the global economy. It is used by every person in all developed nations everyday. Meanwhile, transportation, manufacturing and communications industries are particularly dependent on adequate supplies of oil at reasonable prices. Thus, when oil prices soar or when supplies become limited, these industries are immediately hurt. And if oil prices remain high over an extended period, all industries eventually suffer, causing widespread inflation that is unresponsive to interest-rate hikes. Over time, high oil prices can obviously lead to a large decline in consumer spending—the worst consequence for America's supply-side economic policies.

Figure 1-1. Relationship between Oil Demand and GDP Growth

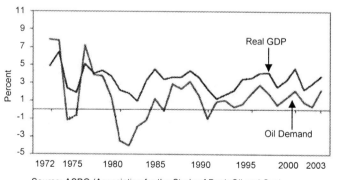

Source: ASPO (Association for the Study of Peak Oil and Gas)

(1) As the U.S. will at best experience only modest growth over the next several years, China and India will make up for any declines in America for oil demand growth. In fact, I predict that China will surpass America's demand for oil within two decades. Already in 2005, China consumed nearly 8 million barrels per day (mbpd), second to only U.S. consumption of about 22 mbpd. Meanwhile, new oil discoveries are diminishing each year throughout the world, but this trend has been masked by higher exploration and refining expenses since a larger share of unconventional oil is now being mined.

Oil Shows its Power

As previously mentioned, in the 1970s, OPEC raised oil prices after the Iranian oil embargo, causing oil to spike to previously unseen levels. Coincidentally, this period would later be determined as peak oil production in America—the period whereby future oil production per day would begin to gradually decline (predicted by Hubbert in 1956). Yet, even before America was aware of its declining output trends, price controls by OPEC made it realize how dependent its economy had become on oil.

Fortunately, President Nixon secured agreements with Saudi Arabia only a few years earlier that would serve to secure America's strength in the global economy. Consequently, ever since the Saudi Royal Family began demanding payment for oil with the dollar, OPEC has followed suit and now *the dollar, once backed by gold, is now backed by oil.* And this agreement has accounted for the mysterious "good relations" between America and Saudi Arabia. As long as America protects the Royal Family from uprisings, the dollar will remain the only legal tender for the world's most valuable economic resource, ensuring the dollar's position as the global currency standard.

From Manufacturing to Technology

When America's second industrial revolution began, the world was soon convinced of its position as the new leader in manufacturing. Shortly after WWII, American industries dominated the world churning out autos, televisions sets, vacuum cleaners, telephones, toasters and other consumer electronics. America's massive manufacturing base enabled it to supply its citizens with automobiles and telephones, helping to mobilize commerce and facilitate a booming economy. After WWII, 27 American television companies led the world in technology and production. America's manufacturing dominance was similar for autos, airplanes, electronics, and many other products.

Of course, during that period patent laws were not highly recognized by the U.S. government since they were thought to promote monopolies. Therefore, it was often difficult to defend the proprietary rights of intellectual property, so infringement was the norm. However, this was not much of an issue at this juncture since much of the war-torn developed world lacked the manufacturing infrastructure to compete with America. Back then, seeing "Made in America" was as common as seeing "Made in China" today. Sadly, America has changed a lot since the post-war boom, and the future does not look particularly encouraging to say the least.

A Radical Change in Economic Policy

As with any form of intellectual property, patents are only as good as their enforcement against infringement. And prior to the mid-1980s, patents had a universally low perceived value due to their lack of acceptance, as well as the difficulty companies had proving infringement. During the 1970s, the chances of a patent being deemed valid by U.S. courts, infringed, and enforceable by litigation were about one in three, as the prevailing opinion of the U.S. Department of Justice held that patents damage the economy by establishing anticompetitive monopolies. Therefore, rather than paying royalties to patent holders in exchange for production rights, many companies chose to risk infringement knowing that their chances of being found guilty were slim.

However, between 1982 and 1985 several government agencies enacted a variety of laws signaling a paradigm shift in U.S. economic policy. In 1982, a federal court of appeals (the USPTO) was established for the sole purpose of hearing intellectual property cases. During that same period, President Reagan's Commission on Industrial Competitiveness issued a report concluding that the enforcement of intellectual property was one of the keys for the United States to maintain its global economic dominance.

Finally, the Department of Justice reversed its earlier ruling, stating that patents promote competition by providing incentive-based rewards to innovators. This abrupt reversal in economic policy signaled a drastic shift in the enforcement and interpretation of patents and other intellectual property. Today, the chances of being found guilty of infringement are quite high. As a result, most companies prefer to pay royalties rather than risk infringement litigation. However, global enforcement of U.S. intellectual property laws remains challenging. Specifically, many Asian nations still refuse to adhere to intellectual property laws, resulting in the annual loss of hundreds of billions of dollars from American corporations. Now that Asia has seized America's manufacturing markets, it continues to benefit from America's innovative engine. The issue is certainly one of much diplomatic sensitivity. Yet, despite growing pressures from Washington, global infringement remains a big problem, threatening to destroy the primary component of America's new economic engine.

The End of "Made in America"

If one examines global economics, it should be apparent that Southeast Asian nations have replaced much of America's manufacturing and production output relative to its two-decade long post-war economic boom. It turns out that U.S. courts began to protect intellectual property just as Asia began to threaten America's manufacturing dominance. Ever since that period, more emphasis has been placed on innovation than production in America. And this shift in economics has accentuated the decline of its manufacturing industries.

In the '80s, as millions of manufacturing jobs were lost and replaced by lower wage service sector jobs, U.S. tax revenues declined. Meanwhile, the national debt continued to soar due to the Cold War. Although patent law was now recognized in America, double-digit inflation was inhibiting the kinds of risk-taking activities needed to fuel new innovations. As a desperate move, Washington loosened credit to encourage more startup ventures. Unfortunately, this led to a disaster with numerous frauds, notably in the junk bond market and the Savings and Loan scandal in the late '80s. Since that period, innovation has led to tremendous economic growth, and has become America's new economic engine. But America's lead in technology innovation is now being challenged from abroad. As we shall see, much of the problem is due to the transfer of intellectual property as a result of free trade dynamics.

Clinton's Free Trade Disaster

When President Clinton urged Congress to pass the North American Free Trade Agreement (NAFTA) in 1994, this would signal the final disappearance of America's manufacturing industries. NAFTA was a critical piece of legislature because it removed all barriers of trade between America and its neighbors in North America, swinging the door open for further sabotage of its manufacturing industry.

The purpose of NAFTA was to encourage exports out of America and raise the standard of living in all member nations. However, since inception over a decade ago, this goal remains only a dream. As a matter of fact, not only has the standard of living remained the same in both Canada and Mexico, but Mexico's minimum wage has remained unchanged at $0.50 since 1994. According to the U.S. Bureau of Labor Statistics, in 2005 Mexican labor wages were second to the lowest in the world with only Sri Lanka having lower wages. Finally, sixteen years after NAFTA, Mexico's wealth is primarily controlled by about 100 corporations. And for America, NAFTA and other free trade policies continue to hurt low- and middle-income Americans, while providing absolute benefit to corporate America and the wealthy.

Even before NAFTA had a chance to demonstrate its damaging effects to middle-class Americans, President Clinton added fuel to the fire by entering America into the World Trade Organization in 1995. With a current membership of 149 nations, the WTO has been criticized for its ties to corporate committees that often advise politicians of member nations involved in its regulation. The most dangerous consequence of WTO membership is that it disallows the U.S. government and any other member-nation's government the ability to legislate industrial policies, such as tariff protection for industries vital to each nation's well-being.

Finally, as his final act in promoting the free trade "machine of destruction," President Clinton provided Permanent Normalized Trade Relations (PNTR) status to China in the year 2000. The consequences of these decisions have effectively removed all protection from unfair trade and labor practices from foreign nations. Interestingly, after China was granted favorable trading status, it strengthened its currency peg to the U.S. dollar in order to ensure that it would become a top exporter of goods. Consequently, the collapse of American manufacturing has been particularly brisk since 2000.

Since the passage of NAFTA, nearly 5 million manufacturing jobs have been lost, over $4 trillion in trade deficits have registered, and over $3.5 trillion in core U.S. assets have been purchased by foreign nations. Perhaps the most disturbing fact underlying this trend is that most of the money used to purchase U.S. companies has come directly from the U.S. government. You see, because an increasingly larger percentage of America's annual deficits have been financed by foreign nations (for instance, 70 percent of the deficit was financed by foreign nations in 2003 and 99 percent in 2004), *America has essentially traded core assets to satisfy its greed and addiction for non-essential consumer goods.* In the process of transferring its job and wealth base to other nations, Americans have been financing the buildup of China and India, while middle-class America continues to face extinction.

Thus far, China has received virtually all of the benefits from trade relations with the

U.S. First, it used price manipulation to drive many of America's core manufacturing industries into bankruptcy. Next, China manipulated its currency to ensure that its products would be purchased by Americans despite a weak dollar. And finally, American corporations have expanded into China, transferring American jobs and wealth.

Toxic Effects of Free Trade

An additional impact of Washington's "free trade" policies has resulted in the gradual loss of America's most prized possessions—its research, innovation and commercialization skills and resources. You see, outsourcing and free trade do not end with a loss of American jobs. In many cases, critical innovative secrets and R&D labs have been sent overseas because they are required for manufacturing.

In addition to the inevitable transfer of innovative technologies, America is now sharing with much of the world some of its most advanced military technologies and production secrets. This alone poses a significant threat to its national security. Already the F-16 is being produced in several nations, one of which is India. And America's most highly prized fighter, the new F-35 is being produced in a team effort along with 17 other nations. As well, many other critical military weapons are being produced in full or in part by various nations throughout the world.

In conclusion, it should be clear that Washington in no way entered into these one-way trade agreements for the purpose of improving the living standards of working-class Americans and impoverished foreign laborers, but to provide more wealth to corporations and their wealthy shareholders. Over the long-term, more industries will be lost to these nations, taking jobs along with them. And NAFTA, CAFTA (President Bush's free trade agreement for Central America) and WTO-member nations will benefit from the inevitable transfer of intellectual property that will occur as more American facilities are relocated overseas.

Figure 1-2. NAFTA-Related Job Losses Since 1993

766,030 Jobs Lost

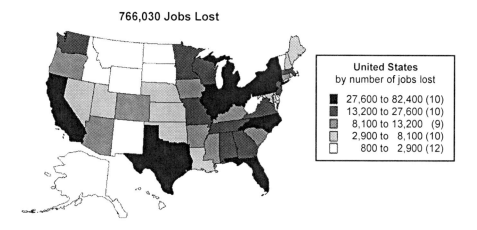

United States
by number of jobs lost

- 27,600 to 82,400 (10)
- 13,200 to 27,600 (10)
- 8,100 to 13,200 (9)
- 2,900 to 8,100 (10)
- 800 to 2,900 (12)

Source: Economic Policy Institute

Finally, permitting these nations to have open access to America's consumer marketplace is of equal priority to Washington as helping corporate America gain open access to the inexpensive foreign labor markets. And this is certain to strengthen America's dependence on imports while exporting jobs abroad.

The bipartisan support for these agreements confirms Washington's long-standing commitment to strengthen corporate America at the expense of American workers. But at some point, providing inexpensive commodities no longer compensates for the loss of American jobs. After all, even at a low price of $6000, you still need money to by a car. Even with medical savings plans and tax deductions for health insurance, you still need money to pay for these essential programs.

As it stands today, the labor market of the average American worker is not particularly encouraging, despite the misleading unemployment numbers reported by the Department of Labor, especially when the minimum wage has not been raised in over a decade. Even if the minimum wage is raised to the proposed $7.25 per hour, this will still do very little to keep millions of Americans out of poverty.

By linking America into a global trade system, Washington has ensured its continued decline in living standards, since in such an interdependent system of commerce, a fixed amount of wealth will be shared between participant nations. Understand that the intense unfair trade competition within this system operates with the dynamics of a "zero-sum" game, as in the stock market, whereby for every winning dollar, a losing dollar stands on the other side of the trade. And until a radical restructuring of free trade policies occurs and America implements a national healthcare program, the majority of Americans will continue to encounter the adverse effects of the losing side of free trade.

2

PAST STOCK MARKET PERFORMANCE

Performance During Major Events

American Wars

In this brief survey of American history, we should examine the effects of war on the performance of the stock market since the emergence of America's commercial oil industry because military conflicts and access to oil have been the most influential components of America's productive capacity.

Shortly after WWI, the U.S. stock market registered gains resulting from the economic boom of the "Roaring '20s." This was America's first major bull market. As we know, the bubble burst in the late '20s, triggered the events leading to the Great Depression. During WWII, the S&P 500 Index delivered very nice annualized average returns of 12.1 percent. And given the threat of Nazi Germany, the attack on Pearl Harbor, and global uncertainty of that period, these returns were very impressive. Yet, the stock market suffered the eighth worst crash in its history in 1940, just over a year prior to the attack on Pearl Harbor. Thus, even this event, as well as America's subsequent entry into this devastating war did not register market losses anywhere near that seen in 1940.

The stock market provided even better returns during the four-year period of America's involvement in the Korean War, averaging 18.8 percent annually. This would be the best performance during any war period to date. Rather than a reflection of war, this bull market period was a consequence of the effects of America's tremendous economic boom after WWII, (otherwise referred to the post-war period from here on).

In the mid-1960s, shortly after America's entry into the Vietnam War, President John F. Kennedy was assassinated, causing a fairly large sell-off in the market. Over the next several years, OPEC would impose an oil embargo as a symbol of discontent against Israel. This led to the largest market sell-offs during this period. However, the last part of 1974 and the first part of 1975 resulted in very large gains in the market, which no doubt helped the overall returns during this twelve-year stretch, yielding average annual returns of 3.9 percent, unadjusted for the high inflation during this period.

Global Events

The performance of the U.S. stock market has shown to be fairly predictable under certain events, days of the week and months of the year, as evidenced by the data compiled in the *Stock Market Almanac* and other resources. However, during periods of crisis, predictive power is much less reliable. Table 2-1 shows stock market returns over different periods after various global events. Note that, regardless of the crisis, the market rebounded within 6 months in most cases.

Table 2-1. Market Reaction and Recovery After Major Global Events

Event	Reaction Dates	DJIA % Gain/Loss During Reaction	DJIA Percentage Gain Days After Reaction		
			22	63	126
Fall of France	**5/9/1940-6/22-1940**	(17.1)	(-0.5)	8.4	7.0
Pearl Harbor	12/6/1941-12/10/1941	(6.5)	3.8	(2.9)	(9.6)
Truman Upset Victory	11/2/1948-11/10/1948	(4.9)	1.6	3.5	1.9
Korean War	**6/23/1950-7/13/1950**	(12.0)	9.1	15.3	19.2
Eisenhower Heart Attack	9/23/1955-9/26/1955	(6.5)	0.0	6.6	11.7
Sputnik	10/3/1957-10/22/1957	(9.9)	5.5	6.7	7.2
Cuban Missile Crisis	8/23/1962-10/23/1962	(9.4)	15.1	21.3	28.7
JFK Assassination	11/21/1963-11/22/1963	(2.9)	7.2	12.4	15.1
U.S. Bombs Cambodia	**4/29/1970-5/26/1970**	(14.4)	9.9	20.3	20.7
Kent State Shootings	5/4/1970-5/14/1970	(4.2)	0.4	3.8	13.5
Arab Oil Embargo	**10/18/1973-12/5/1973**	(17.9)	9.3	10.2	7.2
Nixon Resigns	**8/9/1974-8/29/1974**	(15.5)	(7.9)	5.7	12.5
U.S.S.R. in Afghanistan	12/24/1979-1/3/1980	(2.2)	6.7	4.0	6.8
Hunt Silver Crisis	**2/13/1980-3/27/1980**	(15.9)	6.7	16.2	15.8
Falkland Islands War	4/1/1982-8/7/1982	4.3	(8.5)	(9.8)	20.8
U.S. Invades Grenada	10/24/1983-11/7/1983	(2.7)	3.9	(2.8)	(3.2)
U.S. Bombs Libya	4/15/1986-4/21/1986	2.6	(4.3)	(4.1)	(1.0)
Financial Panic '87	**10/2/1987-10/19/1987**	(34.2)	11.5	11.4	15.0
Invasion of Panama	12/15/1989-12/20/1989	(1.9)	(2.7)	0.3	8.0
Gulf War Ultimatum	12/24/1990-1/16/1991	(4.3)	17.0	19.8	18.7
Gorbachev Coup	8/16/1991-8/19/1991	(2.4)	4.4	1.6	11.3
ERM U.K. Currency Crisis	9/14/1992-10/16/1992	(6.0)	0.6	3.2	9.2
World Trade Center Bombing	2/26/1993-2/27/1993	(0.5)	2.4	5.1	8.5
Russia Mexico Orange County	10/11/1994-12/20/1994	(2.8)	2.7	8.4	20.7
Oklahoma City Bombing	4/19/1995-4/20/1995	0.6	3.9	9.7	12.9
Asian Stock Market Crisis	**10/7/1997-10/27/1997**	(12.4)	8.8	10.5	25.0
Russian LTMC Crisis	**08/18/1998-10/8/1998**	(11.3)	15.1	24.7	33.7
Mean		(8.1)	4.5	6.9	12.9
Median		(6.2)	4.2	6.7	12.1
Days= Market Days					

BOX 2-1: Historical Market Data Should Be Scrutinized

It is important to remember that a given decline in the stock market requires a larger increase in order to regain previous levels; the larger the decline, the larger percentage increase needed to restore previous asset levels. For instance, a decline in the market by 10 percent requires a gain of 11 percent, while a decline of 20 percent requires a gain of 25 percent in order to reach previous levels. A decline of 50 percent would take a 100 percent gain to reclaim previous levels.

In addition, in order to accurately interpret stock and bond market performance, one must always calculate the real performance, which factors inflation into the returns. Otherwise, misleading results could result as they did for stock market performance during the 1970s and 1980s.

Recent History of the Stock Market

The Great Bull

During the early 1990s, a massive stock market bubble began due to Alan Greenspan's lax credit policies, combined with a revolutionary innovation that would forever change the world. After the U.S. military released Internet technology to the public, this led to the beginning stages of the Information Age.

Suddenly, previously unknown gurus, (many of which had no real business experience) were coming up with new dotcom companies to harness the potential economic power of the Internet, and investment capital poured in from investors all over the world. With the early successes of Yahoo!, eBay, Amazon.com and others, even more venture capital flooded into dotcom companies as well as any other company associated with the Internet. Incidentally, much of this investment capital ultimately came from public and private pension plans and individual retirement funds.

Perhaps you remember Grocery.com, Purchase Pro, Pets.com, Exodus Communications, Infospace.com and WebMD. They were just a few of the hundreds of dotcom companies that promised to revolutionize every business under the sun. Often, all one needed was a slick idea jotted on a napkin and they got funded by venture capital firms. Although creative ideas and new ventures seemed endless, too much money was chasing too many bad business ideas.

Even the Asian Financial Crisis in 1997 could only cause a temporary stall of this bull market. Some believe that it was Greenspan's interest rate reaction to this global panic that made the bubble swell even further. Regardless, the loose monetary policies of Greenspan facilitated a climate of speculation fueled by greed—the primary elements of any asset bubble.

But things seemed to be going well for America. Most high-tech companies had more money than they knew what to do with, and business prospects seemed endless. Entry-level employees were granted lucrative stock options packages that promised to make them millionaires within a few years. Many investors were getting wealthy, often effortlessly, while the idea of risk never seemed to enter the picture. Soon things were so good that some became focused on protecting wildlife from human consumption, as if America had reached Utopia with no other things to worry about.

Wall Street helped swell the Internet bubble to unimaginable levels by proclaiming that all brick-and-mortar businesses would soon be replaced by online companies due to the "new business paradigm" created by the Internet. And many of America's greatest companies were being labeled "dinosaurs" if they did not quickly create an e-commerce website and Internet strategy.

But this was only the beginning, as the telecom and computer networking revolutions would also be seen as key players in this "new paradigm." By late 1999, Amazon.com had a price target of over $400, Qualcomm $800, while many Internet, telecom and other high-tech IPOs were closing their first day of trading at over $100 per share. Investors simply could not get enough of these high-tech stocks. Meanwhile, aggressive advertising campaigns by online brokers helped spread these delusions of grandeur, leading to speculative behaviors by investors looking to claim their piece of this "pie in the sky."

Yet, the SEC did nothing to stop these misleading and irresponsible activities that promised to open the floodgates of endless investment returns with the click of a mouse. Ultimately, SEC negligence helped transform the world's largest and most reputable stock market into an online casino. But this unprecedented open access to the stock market mainly favored Wall Street and corporate America, both who now had increased access to the money of greed-stricken, unsophisticated and unwary investors. Sadly, despite the scandals surrounding this recent period, the stock market continues to be used as an online casino, less than 4 years after these catastrophes appeared.

The NASDAQ was seen as the superstar exchange for high-tech companies, promising to provide the expansion capital needed to catapult America into the Information Age. Most believed that companies listed on this exchange would serve as the engines of commerce for the "new economy." And for many of the early investors, profits made from investing in these companies delivered astounding new wealth, often overnight.

By 1999, Wall Street's propaganda campaign worked, and almost everyone thought the rules of business and investing had changed. The Internet-driven technology revolution was envisioned as the sole tool that would create drastic and immediate improvements in living standards. However, it was the loose monetary policies of Alan Greenspan and the effects of the bubble he created that were responsible for this illusion.

Looking back, prior to the first market correction of the NASDAQ in March 2000, Greenspan saw the bubble swelling, but did nothing to stop it. He merely watched in comfort after delivering his "irrational exuberance" speech a few years earlier. Rather than raise interest rates to decrease the money supply and hence put a hold on credit lines, he let asset values swell like never before. Meanwhile, the smart money gradually and quietly made its exit at the top, shifting assets into real estate, basic materials, cash, bonds, and other asset classes that had been beaten down throughout the bubble frenzy.

The Internet bubble of the late 1990s was arguably the largest asset bubble in American history. At its peak, the NASDAQ was trading at over 240 times earnings while the S&P was over 35 times earnings. Yet, this surge in valuations seemed reasonable at the time. After all, "hot-shot" Wall Street analysts and economists were claiming the Internet had created a new business paradigm. And most investors believed this fantasy, as they always do when caught up by the greed surrounding a bubble. Unfortunately, greed is a powerful emotion that often masks rational thinking. But in the end, the majority of people get hurt, while the small number of insiders profit. This bubble was no exception.

The Bubble Bursts

As with all asset bubbles, this one eventually came to a halt, resulting in financial and emotional devastation for millions. By mid-March 2000, the NASDAQ began a series of sell-offs that spread to the Dow over a three-year period, leaving household investors and institutions holding the bag when it emptied by over $7 trillion. Yet, even when the bubble was well into its deflation, most investors were still unaware of the disasters ahead. Wall Street refused to tell the truth about the economy, but the warning signs were clear for those who bothered to pay attention. Inventories were high and rising, Internet ad revenues were dropping off, and soon virtually every business connected with this revolutionary business innovation began a painful downward spiral.

From March 2000, the NASDAQ slowly deflated from its high of over 5000 eventually down to a low of about 1200 over the next two years. And unfortunately, many investors rode the market down, not knowing what to do; waiting and hoping for a rebound. It was only in late 2002, when many stocks were at multi-year lows did Wall Street start issuing sell signals. But by then it was too late, and many of the former "darlings of Wall Street" became penny stocks, were bought out buy financial firms causing tremendous dilution to shareholders, or went bankrupt. Perhaps you recall the scandals surrounding JDS Uniphase, Ariba, Redback Networks, Qwest, Adelphia, Global Crossing, Nortel Networks, Doubleclick, Nextlink, and America Online. The list goes on.

It wasn't all bad in 2000, as the Dow and S&P 500 continued to remain strong. But soon, the uncertainty of the controversial presidential elections caused these markets to drift further downward. Yet most investors were still in a state of denial and felt the markets would recover once a clear winner was named. However, experienced investors could smell the stench that promised to only get worse. Consequently, the markets continued their weakness in 2001. And when the tragic events of September 11, 2001 occurred, all the markets crashed. But the worst had not yet occurred. The markets would not make their lows for another two years, as the economy slipped into a deep sleep.

Despite a reasonable rebound a few weeks after September 11, 2001, the economic data continued to get worse. Then came an avalanche of corporate accounting scandals— Enron, WorldCom, Tyco, Halliburton, Global Crossing, America Online, and a host of other Internet and telecommunication companies once highly esteemed by Wall Street's top analysts. Wall Street was now filled with the blood from the Internet bubble.

All of these events caused the Fed to issue a series of rate cuts beginning in late 2001 sinking short-term rates to 43-year lows over the next two years. And soon, long-term rates followed. But even Greenspan's currency printing presses couldn't prevent the largest bankruptcies in corporate America's history, as well as the biggest earnings restatements, write-downs and write-offs for many companies that survived. By October 2003, investors finally had it, and the markets plunged to new lows, as economic numbers continued to weaken.

Within two years of the stock market correction, much of the wealth Americans had gained over the past decade had vaporized. In total, approximately $7 trillion of paper wealth was lost due to the pernicious events that would cause investors to lose all confidence in the stock market. But not everyone lost money. It is safe to say that the $7 trillion of paper wealth lost during this correction was transferred from the hands of individual investors and pension plans into those of corporate executives, Wall Street bankers, venture capitalists, and big time Wall Street traders.

Greenspan's Illusion

After the market lows in October 2003, the economy appeared to show signs of improvement, with strong consumer spending and robust GDP growth in 2004—all according to Washington officials. In reality, these "economic improvements" were fueled by record levels of federal and consumer debt. Essentially, the Fed was working its printing presses in overdrive in a desperate attempt to stimulate the economy. And ever since that period, low mortgage rates have been feeding a real estate boom that has been enhanced by loose restrictions on credit. Meanwhile, home equity loans continue to be as much in vogue as the iPod.

Throughout this time, Washington and the Fed have applauded the economic "recovery," as if they were blind to what was really going on. All throughout the post-bubble period, consumers have been "growing" the economy by increasing their debt—using their credit cards and houses as ATMs and speculating in the real estate market. As well, much of this consumer activity that was financed on borrowed money was used to purchase non-essential goods from Asia, resulting in further job losses and business failures in America, while increasing its dependence on foreign debt.

Since then, America's auto, steel and other manufacturing industries have all but died due to the inability to compete with the cheap labor, currency pegs, and unfair pricing practices from Asian nations. Meanwhile, America's thirst for consumption has escalated its debt to record levels. As more nations have continued to finance its spending habits, America has strengthened its position as the world's largest debtor nation, owned in large part by Europe and Asia. Despite this transfer of wealth from America to nations abroad, this dangerous pattern of overconsumption continues to delay a much needed correction.

Greenspan dampened the impact of a much-needed economic correction by decimating short-term interest rates. As a consequence, the asset bubble has been transferred into real estate and consumer credit, both which are poised to collapse. The only way out of this mess is for a significantly improved economy, with real wage and net job growth, leading to improved living standards, healthy savings rates, and elevated job and retirement benefits. But as you shall see throughout the remainder of this book, these changes are not going to materialize for several years at best, and not without a difficult period of correction. Payback time is coming for America's long period of overconsumption, and the effects are going to be devastating for most.

The Great Bubble Maestro

At some point in the future, if history books document an accurate portrayal of Greenspan's leadership of the Federal Reserve banking system, historians may nickname him the "Great Bubble Maestro" as I have. Thus far, the media has latched onto praise for Greenspan, calling him a genius and crediting him for the great bull market period of the 1990s. They bask in envy how America "only experienced three small recessions" during his tenure of nearly two decades.   What they do not state is that he avoided recessions and escaped the inevitable economic meltdown by flooding the central banking system with dollars, while adding to the elimination of America's waning middle-class.   Where is he now that America needs a way out of this mess?   Alas, Alan Greenspan has made a timely exit and has since passed the reigns of monetary leadership onto a new Federal Reserve chairman, who will assume the responsibility of the disaster that lies ahead.

While Greenspan single-handedly created the economic bubble, he did his best to mitigate its deflation via instructions from the White House, driving interest rates down and printing money as fast as possible, debasing the dollar—all in order to delay the effects of a massive economic correction that is well overdue.   As a consequence, America now faces an economic adjustment of even greater magnitude, with a real estate bubble ready to deflate and a stock market that still needs a large downward correction, or at best, stagnant growth for several years.   Accordingly, I find the timing of his resignation interesting.

As hard as he tries, Federal Reserve Chairman Bernanke won't be able to fix the problems created by his predecessor.   And if America slips into a depression while Bernanke is in office, he alone will be blamed.   But it will be Alan Greenspan and several years of mismanagement by Washington who will share the dual responsibility.   Until another Fed Chairman matches Greenspan's performance of forming three asset bubbles (arguably four, if you include the commodities bubble) in just under two decades, Alan Greenspan will continue to be known as the "Great Bubble Maestro," at least in my mind.

Figure 2-1. Examples of the Devastation Caused by the Internet Bubble and its Correction

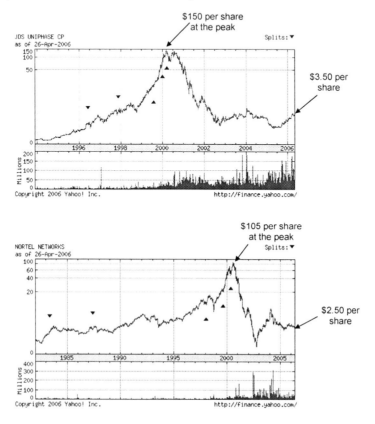

3

Social Change

Virtually everything in America is very different from fifty years ago; its demographics, societal norms, political environment, governing laws, socioeconomic distribution, standard of living, trade and diplomatic policies, and much more. Just when most thought the end of the Cold War would bring America more prosperity, the opposite has occurred. Today, many of the principles that have previously served as the foundation for America's unique greatness are no longer in place or are in jeopardy of being dissolved.

Americans do not have many of the freedoms they once had. Freedom of speech continues to be more restricted each year. Already, the NSA is listening in on potentially all phone calls, opening postal mail as desired, emails are monitored, cameras are installed in many cities to monitor activity, and GPS technologies are being used to monitor certain individuals. Even now, the technology is available to look within a dwelling by a device that has been externally placed. It's only a matter of time before the U.S. government begins spying on all of its citizens.

Finally, it seems as if today the freedoms that are protected most fervently in America are those that frequently result in homicide—abortion and the right to bare arms. But we cannot despair, as social and political change is inevitable in all societies. As demographics change, so do economic and social behavioral patterns. And these two variables always alter the political and economic landscape. As progress advances, societies experience inevitable change.

Whether or not social behavior has advanced over the past three decades is up for debate. But consider this; when I was a teen I had never heard of one single case of a youth anywhere in America bringing a gun to school. Today, many schools have metal detectors. Nor did I hear of children suing their parents (and winning) because they didn't get the gifts they wanted for Christmas. Clear evidence of societal decline is all around us.

On the other extreme, freedom of speech has led to the growing wave of violent and dysfunctional social change in today's youth. The most destructive effects have been registered within America's pop culture by endorsing low moral values reflected by many entertainment personalities. Such can be said about the negative messages spread by "hip-hop" music, which promotes violence, drug abuse, hate, and low-self esteem. And the mainstream media has magnified the influence of the dangerous messages delivered by this music by portraying criminals and drug users as "cool."

Corporate America has also done its part by sponsoring ads by "artists" who praise this hateful, violent "music." If there was no demand for these demonic performers, they wouldn't be floating on a pile of money. But demand if huge for these role models because America is facing a social crisis stemming in part from the breakdown in the family, which has created millions of troubled teens.

I suppose as one ages, embracing societal change becomes challenging, and in some respects represents one of the difficulties of the aging process itself. Regardless, even the most cynical viewpoints cannot state that these changes have been all bad. Social change has decreased racial and gender discrimination. It has changed the perceptions of the disabled, who have progressed from stigmatic to productive. And this has led to more adaptive facilities and opportunities for this previously neglected segment of society. But America still has a long way to go towards the permanent improvement of the disadvantaged.

Despite improvements to American society, many of these changes have come at the expense of personal liberties and capitalist policies that have crippled America's freedoms and competitive landscape. The acceptance of socialist policies has created a trend of individual protest against core American principles. And this has been nothing short of destructive to American societal unity and morale.

As politicians have attempted to position America as a nation of moral, religious, ethnic, gender, and racial equality, much of its core foundation has been compromised. Freedom of speech becomes more restricted each year, prayer in public schools has been banned, and religious symbols have been removed from government buildings—in many cases all because one person feels offended. In just over a decade, the defining values of America's forefathers have been abandoned, causing this nation to have lose its identity.

In the Sacramento Public School System, students are no longer permitted to say the "Pledge of Allegiance to America" because of the phrase, "One Nation under God." And if history is any predictor of the future, this law will eventually reach all fifty states. There is even talk of removing the phrase "In God We Trust" from U.S. currency notes because it offends atheists. In the past, America has always protected the interests of the majority. But today, *the liberal movement has opened the door to protect the interests of anyone who is unhappy with the system or who feels offended due to religious or ethnic beliefs.* And that has destroyed the foundation of traditional beliefs and values that the majority embrace, while catering to a handful of individuals who claim to be Americans.

American Unity in Decline

The Immigrant Factor

How did we get into this mess? How is it that more social and political change has occurred in America over the past two decades than in its entire history? To understand this we need to go back in time and take a look at America during its infancy. As reviewed in the first chapter, America won its independence from British rule in 1776. Thereafter, word spread of this nation formed on a foundation of democracy and capitalism, promising to protect freedom of individual choice; a nation where hard work was rewarded; a nation open to all possibilities.

Consequently, over the next 150 years, several waves of immigration would empower America's greatness. Clearly, without immigrants, America would never be. The first major immigrant movement was from England, followed by the Irish and Germans in the early 19th century. Next, a large number of Chinese came to California during the gold rush. In the early part of the 20th century, many other Europeans immigrated to the U.S. Along with their efforts, the uniqueness of each ethnic and racial group added to the ill-defined, yet resilient American culture. Each immigrant wave brought with it several barriers and sacrifices for every ethnic group, but somehow they endured and added to America's greatness. Today, each racial and ethnic group should stand proud of its unique accomplishments and resilience. As a symbol of America's open arms for immigrants, France gifted this new nation the Statue of Liberty, which was erected on Ellis Island to greet the new arrivals as they entered New York City.

But today, complex factors have positioned America's most recent immigrants to destroy the nation that has always been so dependent upon the power of diversity. America's early immigrants were in many ways like the immigrants of the present day. Many of them were not fluent in English, had little money or education, and all had a dream of freedom and a better life. However, America's early immigrants responded to challenges in a different manner than most of the immigrants from the past three decades.

Up until the Reagan administration, most American immigrants worked hard to rise above the hurdles. And in the process, they embraced the American spirit as they integrated within society. But a strange thing happened that caused the immigrant pool to shift. Fueled by the demands placed upon the economy by the boomer generation, America's growth during the 1980s and 1990s was tremendous despite the Cold War with the Soviet Union. The problem was that in order to sustain this acceleration of growth, America needed workers to do work that the middle class was too busy for or unwilling to do. And this was the beginning of the rise of America's service economy.

As more open trade with foreign nations was encouraged, the global marketplace wanted a piece of America's credit-spending consumers. The only problem was that much of this trade was one-sided, especially in Asia. And when NAFTA was enacted, this all but assured America would now be transformed into a service economy since American companies would no longer be able to compete with the cheap labor of other nations. Border patrol was a mere illusion, and Washington looked the other way when illegal aliens entered because they would serve a vital role in providing inexpensive labor to compensate for America's declining net productivity and standard of living.

The Immigrant Threat

The problem is that, over the past three decades, too many illegal aliens and immigrants were allowed in too fast and most have been unprepared or unwilling to assimilate fully into American society. In addition, because many of these newer immigrants and illegal workers were exploited for short-term benefit by contractors and companies, much of this population has been unable to make up for gaps in language and education. What was once a small minority, the Hispanic population in America now stands as the largest non-white race and is expected to become the most populous racial group in America within the next fifty years. And their continued inability or unwillingness to integrate fully within American society is going to be very problematic.

Is America losing its nation to these groups? Only if they are not integrated fully within American society so that they can begin to feel the strong sense of patriotism that Americans have become so famous for. Unfortunately, it appears as if they are not being integrated, much to their own preference. And corporate America has facilitated this polarity by integrating the Spanish language into its business commerce.

Not only have many Hispanics isolated themselves from mainstream America, but many Asian-Americans have as well. Even second generation Hispanic- and Asian-Americans refer to Americans as "white people," reflecting their perception of who Americans represent. But as we know, this is a drastic departure from reality. *Unfortunately, when a large group of individuals believes something that is in reality untrue, it becomes true for all practical purposes.*

Figure 3-1. Immigration to the United States (1900-2000)

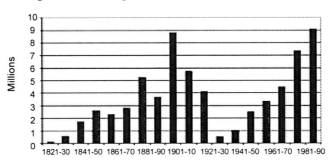

Source: Department of Homeland Security (2002). Created by: Munnell, Alicia H. "Population Aging: It's Not Just the Baby Boom" Issue in Brief 16, Figure 3, CRR April 2004

Because many recent immigrants do not see themselves as truly American, this has had an adverse affect on the unity and patriotism of the United States. It appears as if many of these immigrants treat America as a nation with no central theme or culture and chose to retain their own culture without realizing the importance of America's multicultural theme.

While America is a land of many ethnicities, races, and cultures, there are certain things that distinguish Americans from other nations. The American culture is about embracing all others from different backgrounds, races, ideas, religions, and other differences. An implicit tenant of American culture is the acceptance of one's own cultural roots as a secondary identity, while embracing the American spirit as the top priority.

Indeed, American culture is complex and lacks the definition found in most other nations due to both its inherent flexibility and recent formation. But it is the concept of diversity that lies at the core of American culture and it determines the strength and unity of American society. This concept remains undiscovered by many groups in America, as they view themselves as Mexican or Asian first, and only American when they need something from the system. This behavioral trend is in stark contrast to the immigrants prior to the Vietnam War. In conclusion, *unless America corrects this trend, it will continue to suffer the effects of declining unity, which could also lead to increased vulnerability to national security. And at some point it could result in another civil war.*

Social Disarray and Economic Decline

Over the past two decades, America has largely reverted to what I would identify as *socialist leadership to govern a capitalist nation.* And I do not see how this can work. America has employment quotas for businesses based on race, gender, disability, and sexual orientation. At America's universities, these quotas have caused many of the most qualified individuals to take a back seat in the name of "equal representation." In many cases, these social policy quotas are rewarded by tax and grant awards from state and federal funds. *And while they may do well to promote fairness and help to distribute wealth and opportunity, they are destructive forces for a capitalistic economy.*

Capitalism or Socialism?

America was intended to be a nation built on democratic and capitalistic principles; you work, you achieve, you earn. You do not waste your time and energy complaining about barriers; you just do what is expected and you will be rewarded. While the rewards are not always equitable, life is never fair. Regardless, in a true capitalist economy, greater dividends are to be paid to those who focus on self-improvement and productivity rather than moaning and making excuses.

When a society begins to place individuals who are deemed to come from some type of disadvantageous background in educational and employment positions at the expense of more talented Americans, you have declared war on capitalism and have begun to embrace the economic values of socialism. You have also converted one type of discrimination into another. *The solution lies in creating permanent change for future generations of underprivileged Americans rather than the temporary illusion of improvement through quotas. America cannot punish its best achievers in the name of the underprivileged. It must address these problems at their core. This is how permanent change is created.*

Capitalism is built upon rewarding the best, regardless of race, gender, religious values or any other factors. And today more than ever, a strict adherence to these principals must be followed if America expects to remain globally competitive. Now that modern advances in transportation and telecommunications have facilitated the free trade marketplace, only those nations that can provide the best goods and services at the best price will succeed. *But without a strong system of reward based on merit, American goods and services will continue to fall in quality resulting in diminished global competitiveness.* This is a trend that has already begun. *As well, without a system that creates permanent change for the disadvantaged, a two-class society is inevitable.*

One of the tenants of the "American Dream" is that everyone in America has a chance to do anything and be anyone if they work hard enough. The three key words here are "if" and "work hard." In a sense, the "American Dream" overlaps with a democratic capitalistic society. Every race and ethnicity has had challenges in America. Challenges have been a central theme for all people throughout the world since the beginning of time. That's what you call part of life. It's how you deal with these challenges that matters.

In contrast, bailing out those groups who face barriers will never lead to permanent change. *America should focus on helping those who help themselves rather than helping those who are in need of help. Otherwise, blanket assistance will only create a temporary illusion of equity, while masking the disparities and increasing individual dependency on the government. Yet, America's welfare system has been designed to imprison future generations rather than provide them with financial liberation and equal opportunities.*

The Illusion of a Helping Hand

How can you impose socialist economic policies on a capitalist nation and expect to remain competitive? You simply cannot. America's greatness was created by rewarding the best prepared, rather than socializing opportunities. The disadvantaged must be lifted up by their own hand rather than the hands of sociopolitical welfare system. *Disadvantaged groups that are elevated by social policies are not able to form a core level of independence and responsibility required to ensure the sustenance of future generations.*

Affirmative action policies have been one of the most damaging silent weapons of America's socioeconomic destruction. And although many will claim that this disastrous policy is no longer practiced, that is a myth. Affirmative action was intended to create a more representative population in the workplace when the white majority (white male) is as equally qualified as the targeted minorities. However, this policy has been poorly executed and has created discrimination against white heterosexual males.

Data from numerous sources clearly indicates that affirmative action has provided educational and labor opportunities for underqualified individuals in order to fill quotas for a variety of reasons. For some employees, having a certain minority representation in the workforce qualifies them to receive federal aid. For others, the lack of representative numbers of employees raises the chance of litigation due to "discriminatory hiring practices," despite any validity. In many cases, these rewards and fears have resulted in the hiring of underqualified individuals even from non-minority groups. Rather than assessing applicants by interviews in order to determine their full capabilities, human resource departments have been instructed to view resumes as legal documents that could be used in discrimination litigations. And these behaviors have helped strengthen the trend of underutilization and underemployment of American workers.

While these policies have certainly opened doors for some minorities and females that would have otherwise been very difficult to pass through, they have done little to improve the overall living standards of these groups. In short, the way in which affirmative action is now executed has created an illusion of improvement when in fact, the living standards of America's disadvantaged have actually worsened due to the inability of welfare benefits to keep pace with the inflation of basic living costs.

Finally, disadvantaged Americans need access to resources more than money. Government assistance only lets them live to see the next day. In contrast, adequate resources will provide them with the hope of economic independence, as well as a means to make positive contributions to society. This should be the goal of all politicians. The government must restructure assistance programs for those disadvantaged Americans who truly have the will and determination to excel, rather than issuing blanket assistance to many who only see such assistance as a way to beat the system.

Clear evidence of mismanagement of these challenges is already apparent. The failure of current sociopolitical policies has resulted in little change in America's transfer of intergenerational wealth. Accordingly, 42 percent of children born into the poorest 20 percent of American families stay poor when they become adults. In contrast, only about 6 percent of children from the wealthiest 20 percent end up in the bottom fifth of wage earners as adults. *Consequently, children born into the top quintile are five times more likely to end up at the top quintile of wage earners as the bottom 20 percent.* Hence, the ability of Americans to climb the socioeconomic ladder now appears to be quite small.

When we look at other comparable nations, we see that in fact, America does not exhibit a particularly high level of earnings mobility from poverty to wealth (see appendix Chapter 4 Supplement, figures 4.1 and 4.2 and table 4.1). Are these inequities primarily a reflection of America's educational system or are they the direct result of the collapse of the family unit? I think the answer is heavily weight towards the later. And clearly, government policies have not created positive permanent change for these disadvantaged groups.

If Americans want to continue to enjoy the advantages of a capitalistic and free society, they need to realize that you cannot impose reckless socialist policies and expect to preserve its dominant economic status. There is a much better way. *People must learn to look the other way when these improprieties occur rather than complain and use them as an excuse for underachievement. They must use their energy in a positive manner to cause change for their own well-being instead of looking to the government for assistance.* That is precisely what Americans did prior to the Reagan Era.

And finally, Americans must devote more effort towards building a strong family unit so the children of tomorrow's generation are provided with adequate nurturing, sufficient for the normal childhood development needed to facilitate the progression towards their dreams. But this is a difficult task to achieve when many two-income households continue to struggle to make ends meet. And for single parents, many of which work more than one job, it is almost impossible to provide the type of parenting required for adequate development of their children.

Americans should not forget the values, policies, challenges, and events which made its nation so strong. *America must approach social problems with social rather than economic solutions if it wants to preserve the spirit of capitalism that fuels the "American Dream."* Otherwise, it will accelerate the current trend towards a two-class society and declining living standards. Creating willing change within a free society is always more effective and permanent than forcing it.

Societal Destruction by "Political Correctness"

Today, America is a nation where the white male is discriminated against for being a heterosexual white male. Government tax breaks and the threat of lawsuits have repositioned corporations, which must now answer to socialist policies and the threat of class-action lawsuits rather than address their needs as they see fit.

Meanwhile, the defeminization of American females has contributed to the diminished responsibility of marriage and parenthood. Everyday in America, women are being told that they need to act, think, and behave like males by women who disguise themselves as advocates for women's rights, but who are in fact anti-male with different agendas. They seem determined to convince men that they are just like them and they can do anything men can do. Meanwhile, it is unacceptable for males to be aggressive, while female aggressiveness is seen as a positive characteristic. And in this childish process, *many American females have abandoned their core responsibilities as parents and females, undermining the uniqueness and value of being a female and the messenger of human life.* Only in America do we see these trends and it is causing social disarray that no one dares mention because it is not "politically correct."

The legal and societal acceptance of homosexuality has led to the feminization of many heterosexual males. And all of this has caused gender role confusion that is spread to younger generations. Homosexual couples that cannot be legally married can adopt children, yet heterosexual dating couples cannot. In both cases, a marriage is not present, yet there seems to be discrimination against the heterosexual couple. Does that seem fair to you? Some might say that "fairness" in such a case fails to address more fundamental issue of how a healthy family unit should be defined.

In today's politically correct world, you cannot say anything that might offend anyone, apparently because Americans have lost their spines. Everyday, people are being criticized for things they say because others are looking to interpret different meanings than were intended. Today in America, it is very difficult to voice one's opinion in an intelligent manner without the fear of being labeled a racist, chauvinist, or homophobic. This "social intimidation" in itself is contributing to freedom of speech.

All one has to do is examine the trends in family disunity, teenage homicide and suicide, crime, and so forth to realize that American society is confused and lacks spiritual and moral leadership. And unfortunately, most people do not address these issues because they are seen as politically incorrect. Yet, this *political correctness is a form of socialism in disguise, which acts to restrict the freedoms once enjoyed by all Americans.*

Economic Decline and Recent Immigrants

Throughout its brief history, most immigrants entered America with some type of disadvantage or hardship. Most did not have money and were not educated, while others did not know English. Some had all three deficiencies. But they did not complain, nor did they demand help because they knew it would not get them anywhere. Instead they helped themselves. And this was the philosophy that instilled a strong work ethic for their children to live by.

In contrast, many of today's immigrants are not at all like those of the past. Unfortunately, a large percentage of immigrants from the past three decades have been transformed into slave labor by the economic policies of the U.S. government. Consequently, the effects of NAFTA caused a massive illegal migration of Mexican corn farmers into America. And of course, many were legalized by the "birth law," which has encouraged illegal entry of pregnant women across both Mexican and Canadian borders to have their children. Can you blame them? The rewards are very large. They receive free healthcare and guaranteed citizenship since their newborns would be U.S. citizens. This ridiculous law must be modified.

Unlike the immigrants of several decades ago, many of America's most recent immigrants have lived by the day-to-day mentality, in part due to their own choice but also due to government actions. As a result, *they have not made good use of the resources America has to offer, and have therefore missed out on many of its best opportunities.* Of course this has been the plight for the majority of these new immigrants but not for all of them. Yet when the president appoints an African- or Hispanic-American to his cabinet, many view this as progress, when in fact it is only done to gain voter support from representative groups. This is the illusion of progress that the herd sees.

Liabilities of Two-Income Households

For over three decades, Washington has turned its back on border patrol and has allowed illegal aliens to enter America to work in hard-labor jobs that no Americans wanted to do. Washington has allowed these activities as a way to hide the trend of declining living standards. America's long period of declining living standards has also made it a necessity for two-income households. All one has to do to see the effects of these changes is look to America's youth, who often suffer the societal consequences of inadequate parenting and emotional support that was once a top priority.

Today, most Americans measure living standards in terms of material possessions while failing to recognize the potential adverse consequences of two-income households. In short, two-income households can create gender identity issues, inadequate parenting, and many other effects which can weaken the family unit. But for many Americans, there is no alternative because most workers are getting beaten up by the effects of free trade.

NAFTA and Illegal Aliens

Why have so many Mexican citizens illegally crossed U.S. borders? Of course there are many reasons. America is the world's role model for opportunity and freedom and claims to provide the highest living standard in the world. But as I have already discussed, this is no true. Regardless, living standards in America are certainly much higher than in Mexico. Given this obvious assumption, it follows that the major reason for the explosion of Hispanic illegals over the past decade is due to the effects of NAFTA. While NAFTA has certainly created tremendous opportunities for the industrialization of Mexico due to one of the lowest labor costs in the world, it has also destroyed the livelihood of many Mexican farmers.

Subsidies for America's corn farmers enabled an influx of American corn into Mexico at much lower prices, forcing most Mexican corn farmers into bankruptcy. Faced with no other alternatives, millions of Mexicans relocated to America along with their families. And this wave of illegal migration has been welcomed by Washington as a way to create short-term economic gains to mask America's declining living standards. Ironically, with most of Mexico's corn farmers now out of business, the recent use of ethanol in the U.S. has caused corn prices to soar in Mexico. It's a shame there are no Mexican farmers to take advantage of this trend.

By facilitating the entry of both legal and illegal Hispanic workers into America, Washington has created a source of cheap labor for companies, enabling goods and services to be delivered at a lower cost to consumers. Unfortunately, these exploited individuals are rapidly forming a large percentage of the American population.

The Real Cost of Cheap Labor

Over time, the costs of education, healthcare, welfare assistance programs, and incarceration of illegal aliens will strain federal, state and local budgets. And because America has become dependent upon this cheap labor, it would be very difficult if not impossible to replace their economic value. But now that the economy is in trouble, America cannot afford this added liability on its social system, yet it cannot afford to lose the economic benefits of cheap labor because Americans have become accustomed to these benefits for over two decades.

Today, America has over 40 million Hispanics, many living in poverty, and over 12 million who are illegal, despite previous amnesties. The cost of short-term gains in economic productivity has already taken its toll on local, state and federal programs that provide for educational and healthcare services. And all taxpayers will continue to pay dearly for the short-term benefits provided by these laborers for many decades.

Virtually every government assistance program is backlogged with non-English speaking Hispanics which has created a bottleneck in all welfare programs. It is a very big problem that has been a leading cause of state budget shortfalls due to education and healthcare costs. California provides a good example of this. What has Southern California done to try and recover these costs? It sends school buses to Mexico daily to transport illegal students into the school system so each district can beef up its total enrollment figures for a larger chunk of tax revenue appropriations. These activities represent taxpayer fraud and are in direct violation of federal law.

Washington's open border policies are a direct reflection of its inability to reverse the economic effects of a nation in economic decline. Allowing illegal aliens to enter America adds productivity at inexpensive rates. That is precisely why the minimum wage has not been raised in over ten years and has not kept up with inflation for a much longer period. Washington does not want to raise the minimum wage because it would neutralize the positive economic effects of allowing illegal aliens to work in America. The only problem is that there are many American citizens who work for minimum wage, and this has led to the impoverished conditions of millions.

Table 3-1. Changes in Cost-of-living and the Minimum Wage Since September 1997*

Overall inflation	26%
Food	23%
Housing	29%
Medical care	43%
Child care and nursery school	52%
Educational books and supplies	61%
Gasoline, unleaded regular	134%
Minimum wage	0%

Source: CBPP
*Adjusted for inflation, the buying power of minimum wage is lower than it has been since 1955.

4

ECONOMICS & EDUCATION

The Beginning of a Disaster?

Present-day America is certainly much different than the great post-war period. As we have seen, shortly after the war, America's manufacturing industries were growing rapidly to accommodate the demands of both American and foreign consumers. Meanwhile, the growth of the commercial oil industry helped expand the availability of the combustion engine automobile (despite an electric alternative), leading to the rapid modernization of America's transportation infrastructure, which strengthened its economic machine. Soon, middle-class America represented the majority due to the rapid growth of pension plans, which for the first time provided the security of financial stability after retirement. This was all possible due to America's oil-fueled economic machine.

This period of epic prosperity was marked by greatly elevated living standards, causing more Americans to feel they could provide for more children. Consequently, this resulted in the surge in birthrates, otherwise known as the "baby boom," creating a generation that would later contribute to what most have considered another great economic expansion four decades later.

However, in contrast to the tremendous post-war expansion six decades ago, that during the 1990s was fueled by inexpensive oil, overconsumption masked by increasing consumer and federal debt, and the comfort of national security. The shear number of middle-class consumers during this period entered their peak earning years, as the baby boomer generation continued to live what they thought was the "American Dream" of having a better standard of living than their parents. But this was only an illusion fueled by massive credit spending and foreign investment. This led to the stock market bubble which further magnified this illusion of economic growth due to the "wealth effect."

Since 2001, the economy has been kept on life-support by the loose monetary policies of Greenspan. As real estate prices continued to surge, Americans have used their homes as ATM machines while piling up record debt, buying gas-guzzling autos and plasma TVs. But all is well for Washington, as long as consumers spend; even if they spend what they don't have. And corporate America is also happy in generating its most profitable four-and-one-half year period since 1947, despite the absence of net wage growth. But over the next several years, corporate America will do more than take advantage of the cheap labor overseas. Many of America's largest companies will begin a more aggressive marketing campaign directed at foreign consumers since Americans will not have much money to spend.

Greenspan's Phantom Recovery

As the only way to stimulate consumer spending during the devastating aftermath of the stock market collapse, the World Trade Center attacks, and hundreds of corporate accounting scandals, the Federal Reserve, then under Alan Greenspan smashed short-term rates to a 43-year low of 1 percent in 2003. As well, Bush's tax cuts were also aimed at stimulating the economy. And indeed, spending was boosted. The problem was that this spending has been supplied by record levels of federal and consumer credit spending, while job and wage growth have been absent.

While consumers took advantage of Greenspan's massive release of credit, corporations have downsized, conserved cash, and bought down debt. We all know what we did with access to that low interest credit; we bought things we didn't need because they were "bargains." And during the process, America's household savings rate turned negative as the credit bubble swelled further. Americans love a good buy. After all, they are the world's best consumers. In fact, Americans are such great consumers that, for three decades now, they have produced more than they have consumed. The problem is that much of this overconsumption has been for products supplied by Asia, and has resulted in consecutive record trade deficits, adding to record debt.

Throughout his leadership, President Bush has continued to report job growth, when in fact jobs have continued to be lost on most fronts. No one can deny that economic recoveries are fueled by job and wage growth rather than the current stagnation that has been propped up by massive credit spending by consumers and the government alike. During the first three years of Bush's first term about 5.3 million American workers were laid off. Three years later, by January 2004, only about 65 percent of these workers found employment and many of them were forced to work in jobs that paid less, adding an underemployed element to the grossly misreported unemployment situation.

Even the Bureau of Labor Statistics has made it clear that the economy continues to suffer from the effects of weak job growth and a decline in job quality. According to the BLS, nearly 60 percent of these re-employed 3.5 million workers, or about 2 million were forced to take jobs for which they experienced pay cuts of 20 percent or more. And the IRS reports that, since 2000, Americans reported declining real incomes for two consecutive years—the first time this has ever happened. Because real income accounts for the effects of inflation, you should note that the economy was in a deflationary mode from 2001 to 2004. Therefore, these declines were in no way a result of high inflation.

As a consequence of China's widespread industry underpricing and currency manipulation, millions of manufacturing jobs have been lost. But a huge wave of job loses have also hit white-collar workers due to outsourcing. This is a trend that America has never witnessed. During the past two years, Japan and China have become two of the top three foreign holders of U.S. treasuries as a way to keep their currencies on par with the dollar so goods from Asia would continue to represent a good bargain for American consumers.

By purchasing more U.S. treasuries, China helped finance the federal deficit, (created primarily by the trade imbalance and Bush's tax cuts) which enabled Americans to continue buying imports. However, interest rates began to rise in June 2004 and have risen 17 times consecutively—not because the economy had recovered as Greenspan stated. Short-term rates rose because there was so much money in the economy that inflation was becoming a problem. Yet, Washington has continued to deny the existence of inflation. As well, *higher rates were needed to encourage continued foreign investment into U.S. Treasury securities, especially since the dollar has remained weak.*

While short-term rates are still below their historical mean (around 5.5 percent), the two big problems with the recent increases are that long-term rates have only moved north by a small amount causing the yield curve to remain relatively flat, which usually signals a future recession. Finally, higher short-term rates have hit U.S. consumers hard by causing higher interest payments on credit card debt and have caused millions of home buyers with adjustable-rate mortgages (ARMs) to struggle with monthly payments.

Greenspan's Real Recovery

Throughout this post-recovery period, only corporate America has benefited, recording the highest cash positions, profit margins and profit growth since the post-war period. The fact is that *the only recovery has been with American corporations at the expense of American jobs.* Yet despite these record earnings, the stock market has lingered in a relative sense, perhaps because many institutional investors realize that the gains made by corporations have only repositioned them for short-term improvements. Such gains have only registered due to intense outsourcing and overseas expansion trends, while the longer-term prognosis is a much different situation.

Aided by the cost advantages of outsourcing, relocation to foreign soil, corporate refinancings, hoarding cash, no domestic expansions, and record stock buybacks, corporate America is a leading player in Greenspan's illusion of an economic recovery. But the big money sees well what is going on, as skyrocketing oil and utility prices, global tensions, the war in Iraq, and the lack of net job and wage growth have alerted them to the fact that, soon the American consumer will falter now that short-term interest rates have risen. Finally, although the Washington has refused to acknowledge inflation as a problem, it is clear that this is not the case, and soon inflation will grow to a magnitude for which the government will no longer be able to deny.

Already, nearly $1 trillion of consumer credit card debt has repriced upward as a result of the 400 basis point increase in short-term rates since 2004. And by the end of 2006, an additional $3 trillion will be repriced in the adjustable-rate mortgage market, leading to devastation for millions. Indeed, the smart money sees these risks and that is precisely why the stock market is not much higher than it was 6 years ago. Regardless what Wall Street would have you believe, the stock market continues to demonstrate clear evidence of a secular bear market.

The effects of this massive credit spending-spree have been masked thus far due to low interest rates and the wealth effect created by the real estate bubble. However, the reality is that the net worth of both America and its consumers has declined as a result of this record credit spending. When the real estate bubble corrects, reality will set in and it is not going to be a pretty sight.

Already, the effects of America's diminished competitiveness can be seen by noting the record deficits created by the credit bubble and exacerbated by Bush's ineffective tax cuts for the wealthy. *In less than six years since entering office, Bush's record-setting deficits have resulted in a 50 percent increase in the national debt.* Meanwhile, the 2005 deficit alone was nearly 6 percent of the GDP, which poses significant challenges for the already problematic dollar.

Always Remember....

You cannot have an economic expansion when the dollar is weak, oil prices are high, interest rates are high, inflation is high, or when commodity prices are high.

All you need is just <u>one</u> of these to have an economic contraction and we currently have three, with interest rates and inflation soon to follow.

America's Service Economy

Out of Balance

Contrary to what some may believe, most of America's high-technology companies can be considered a part of the huge service industry that has replaced its once dominant manufacturing infrastructure. However, just a few decades ago when American companies had a healthy balance of innovation and manufacturing, it was innovation that led to better products and more jobs for Americans.

Today we see a much different picture. *Instead of innovation creating manufacturing jobs as it once did, the emphasis on intellectual property (in the form of patents, trade secrets, and licensing royalties) has generated a large chunk of revenues for corporate America.* And this has been a growing source of foreign revenues at the expense of exported products from America. The problem with this type of business structure is that, when extreme as it is today, it relies on a heavy R&D infrastructure that does not necessarily result in direct employment-per-dollar of revenue, as you might imagine.

For instance, in an automobile assembly plant you can correlate the number of workers needed for a certain output of cars produced. In contrast, for a high-technology development enterprise, you cannot make these same correlations due to the reliance of technology on a variable number of services, individuals, and institutions external to the company. Many of these services are rented or paid for by other companies, university research centers, and even foreign companies. *Therefore, there is a lower level of direct job creation in America as a result of such an infrastructure since there are no set requirements to employ American workers to assist with the development of these services.*

As a matter of fact, free trade policies almost guarantee that American companies will outsource much of the R&D work if possible. And once one company begins to outsource, the others must follow in order to remain competitive. Therefore, *companies that focus on innovation and royalty payments or that are free to expand overseas to utilize cheaper labor force will ultimately end up creating very few jobs in America. And because manufacturing outsourcing ultimately leads to technology transfer, nations that focus on innovation without domestic manufacturing (as America now does) are not only exporting wages overseas, but they are vulnerable to losing their innovative edge to partnering nations through the inevitable transfer of technology that occurs.*

Now let's take a look at how this can hurt America's global competitiveness. There are hundreds of examples we can use but let's consider the computer manufacturing industry. Because about 90 percent of all computer parts are made overseas (primarily in China), it's easy to see that for every computer bought in America from an American manufacturer like Dell, Americans are really buying imported goods.

Does America export anything that leads to direct job growth? While the United States still serves as much of the world's food supply, advances in farming technology have not led to growth in this industry. As a matter of fact, the number of American farmers continues to decline each year and many farm crops are now supported by government subsidies in order to keep farmers in business.

So what about the jobs resulting from these innovations that have led to declining agricultural labor growth? As mentioned previously, this can come from any foreign nation. And even if this equipment came exclusively from America (and it does not by any stretch of reality), the source of its development could arise from anywhere in the world.

The Illusion of Value, the Reality of Scavengers

Certainly, the service industry in America extends well beyond technology innovation. Over the past two decades, the non-technology segment of the services industry has grown tremendously. However, *many of these service sectors focus on scavenging revenues from hard-working Americans by offering services to companies and individuals within the United States.* Essentially, for every consumer dollar of earned wages, America has a multitude of companies or independently employed individuals looking to get a piece of the pie.

For instance, let's consider the consumer activity of buying a car. Ideally, this would involve a buyer and a seller. However, today this simple transaction can be quite complex and involve several service industries. If you want to buy a car, you will need financing (unless you pay cash, which is very rare today), so the financial industry becomes involved. As well, you might want to purchase an extended warranty; again, this involves a different sector of the financial industry. Of course you will need insurance as well. But we aren't finished. The loan you take out on the car will most likely be resold to another financial institution, and this loan will be sold to large investors (usually representing the wealthy). If you default on your loan, it might be sold to a collection agency that also stands to benefit from the original consumer transaction.

So as you can see, something as common as an auto purchase can easily involve several corporations, all grabbing for a piece of that transaction. The process is similar for consumer electronics, real estate, and many other transactions. What begins as a simple consumer transaction for a basic necessity turns into financial gains for corporate America and its wealthy investors. *The take-home lesson is that when you have many companies taking a bite out of every consumer transaction, that requires a large volume of units sold in order to generate revenues for each company. Thus far, America has been successful in operating this "scavenger economy" through credit spending, which can't last much longer.*

While some may argue that this division of labor system has helped create more jobs and has lowered the prices of goods and services, the problem is that *it has trivialized the value that the overall workforce in America produces, and serves to widen the income and wealth gap.* Does such an economic system represent real productivity? In my opinion, it often resembles a pack of vultures looking to share the same carcass, and results in a redistribution of income from the middle class and poor to the America's wealthy elite and foreign investors, who provide the financing for goods purchased by consumer credit.

Productivity of the Service Economy

As America has shifted from a manufacturing to a service economy, one must question who will be its customers in the future. Let's look at another extreme of the service industry—non-essential services such as landscaping, valet parking, pet care, (grooming, pet sitting, retail) massage therapy, and housekeeping services.

If you think these are small industries you would be wrong. Many represent multi-billion dollar, high-growth markets. But how much do they add to productivity growth? What is the need in having valet attendants for restaurants, malls, bars, and even hospitals and how does this service add to productivity? How can the pet sitting business be one of the most lucrative and fastest growing industries in the service economy? Have Americans become so disillusioned that they need pet sitters to watch their dogs while at work? The growth in these industries implies one of two things; *either more Americans are becoming wealthier and can afford these services or they are purchasing them through credit spending even though they cannot afford them.* Of course, Americans rarely consider any item to be unaffordable because they have open access to credit. And rather than acting financially responsible, most Americans have become impulse-buying credit-junkies, rarely stopping to consider the ramifications of debt.

While many of these services can be valuable for those who are very busy, we must ask whether these services have not hit mainstream America. The fact is that many of these businesses have sprung up to fill the needs of the wealthy, at the expense of those who perform the labor; the poor and uneducated. However, many Americans pay for these services with credit. Does it make sense to finance pet sitting with a credit card? Perhaps these individuals use cash for valet parking but need to use their credit cards to pay for groceries and utilities. Either way, these examples illustrate only a small portion of the overconsumption trends in America. How can Americans continue to consume non-essential services if their incomes are not strong, if their jobs are not secure and if employee benefits are in decline? It's easy to see how if you consider the 80 percent growth of consumer credit spending over the past decade.

Will the vast majority of Americans be providing service labor to the small but rapidly growing wealthy elite? Or will America gradually shift to the service economy for the world?   Unfortunately, *the low-education, low-wage segment of the service industry is not transportable overseas.   The problem is that this is the most rapidly growing portion of America's service industry (see figure 4-9).*   As it stands today, unless you are at the top of the financial hierarchy, America's future doesn't look good.   America has become a nation of imports and credit spending financed by large corporations (who represent the wealthy) and foreign nations.   *No nation can remain strong if it imports non-essential products, while exporting valuable limited natural resources and intellectual property.*   The effects of these behaviors are further heightened when consumers use credit to buy these goods.   *One can only consume more than they produce for a finite period before a crisis results.*   For now, America is only buying time until its credit bubble pops.

NAFTA's Role in the Service Economy

NAFTA was a failure from the start due to the structural differences between America's economic system and that of foreign nations.   *How can America expect to receive free and fair trade with nations that subsidize their industries, depress wages, do not provide for employee retirement benefits or healthcare, limit foreign investment and foreign competition, and engage in uncontrollable counterfeiting of U.S. products?*   Yet, these practices were not viewed as problems when NAFTA and CAFTA were passed or when America joined the WTO.

However, it is quite clear that these inequities have created an economic environment that makes it impossible for American companies to fairly compete with foreign nations.   As a result, since NAFTA was passed there have been hundreds of corporate bankruptcies and the disappearance of entire industries in America due to the effects of outsourcing, insourcing, and acquisitions of core companies by foreign interests. And this has resulted in an accelerated decrease in America's standard of living, a heightened dependency on foreign-backed credit spending, and an increased threat to its national security due to the transfer of critical technologies abroad.

President Bush continued the anti-American policies of free trade when he signed the Central American Free Trade Agreement (CAFTA) in 2004.   This law extends the free trade policies of NAFTA to the Central American nations of El Salvador, Honduras, Nicaragua, Guatemala, Costa Rica, and the Dominican Republic.   Similar to its NAFTA counterpart, CAFTA facilitates the relocation of American manufacturing facilities to Central America, thereby decreasing the cost structure of American goods at the expense of the American labor market.

Similar to NAFTA, the officially stated goal of CAFTA is to increase the living standards of all member nations.   However, even before the passage of CAFTA, member nations were already afforded duty-free exemptions for about 80 percent of their exports. Therefore, it would appear as if corporate America stands to gain much more than Central America.   And while American consumers might benefit from short-term gains, low-income and middle-class Americans will suffer from the longer-term effects of overseas expansions, which all but guarantee the continued exportation of American jobs.

Finally, *along with the NAFTA nations Mexico and Canada, CAFTA participants are serving as back-door portals for products from China, Japan, and Europe.*   What this means is that these nations are able to indirectly utilize the economic benefits of NAFTA and CAFTA to import goods into America duty-free. As well, *these nations can build production facilities in NAFTA and CAFTA member-nations where they can more directly supply American consumers with duty-free goods, thereby circumventing WTO regulations.* And they have been doing just that. Clearly, such abuse of these trade policies ensures a continued trade deficit with China, although this avenue will allow these effects to remain hidden from official data.

Already, with an estimated 1 out of every 4 dollars spent directly on imported manufactured goods, America is exporting its wealth overseas in exchange for non-essential consumer goods, or what I like to call "stuff." In addition, this amount does not count the dollars spent on insourced products (e.g. buying Japanese cars, many of which are now manufactured in the U.S., but whose profits are funneled back to Japan), nor does it count the money spent by Americans on goods and services supplied by American companies owned by foreign interests, such as Japan's ownership of Universal Studios.

Perhaps the most obvious impact of these "free trade" policies is that they have eliminated the ability of the U.S. government to invoke tariffs, which have historically been effective in safeguarding the financial viability of corporations and entire industries in America. Without the ability to impose tariffs, America is trying to compete on a level playing field with nations that play by their own rules by offering industry subsides, low wages, and no employee retirement or healthcare plans. How can American companies be expected to compete against foreign competitors that do not share these labor costs? The only way to compete is to outsource American jobs overseas. Obviously, the long-term impact of free trade will continue to exert downward pressure on employee benefits for American workers, further widening the gap between the wealthy and the middle class until a two-class system is all that remains.

Wealth and Poverty

A Close Look at Poverty

In August 2004, the U.S. Census Bureau reported a poverty rate of 12.7 percent. This was the rate used by government economists and politicians to determine expenditures for numerous government programs. However, the Census Bureau added that this rate could be as high as 19.4 percent or as low as 8.3 percent depending on how income and basic living expenses were treated.

I for one feel that the real poverty rate in America is much closer to the 19.4 percent figure (and most likely even higher) due to the unwillingness of Washington to update its criteria for poverty levels. And over the next two decades, as the majority of America's estimated 76 million baby boomers are expected to retire in poverty, (as defined by the U.S. government's conservative criteria) the real poverty numbers could easily surpass 30 percent (more on this in Chapters Eight and Nine). According to the U.S. Census' conservative formula for poverty, in 2004 there were:

- 37.0 million Americans in poverty (12.7%), up from 35.9 million (12.5%) in 2003.

- 7.9 million American families in poverty (10.2%), up from 7.6 million in 2003.

As defined by the Office of Management and Budget and updated for inflation using the Consumer Price Index, the average poverty threshold for a family of four in 2004 was an income of $19,307; for a family of three, $15,067; for a family of two, $12,334; and for unrelated individuals, $9,645. How is it that record oil prices have not allowed for upward adjustments in these levels? *Keep in mind that inflation of basic necessities such as food, energy, and healthcare affects the poor by a much larger factor than wealthier Americans because they have less to spend on other items.*

Consider that it's almost impossible for a single individual to survive today in America with an annual income of $10,000. And if they are surviving, they do not have the money needed to advance their employment options. For instance, with only $10,000 per year, it would be very difficult to afford housing and utilities, food, a computer, a mobile phone, and a car—all required for today's modern society. Car insurance alone would be at least $1000 annually and Internet/land phone would be another $1000, while a cell phone might run you $1000. Even using public transportation would cost at least $500 per year. Add another $4000 for government-assisted housing, $1500 for utilities and $2000 for food, and you have a very conservative estimate of basic survival expenses.

And in many regions of America such as California, New York, and New Jersey, $10,000 per year won't even cover your government-assisted housing, food and utilities. And you certainly won't have anything left over for incidentals, such as laundry, clothes, transportation, etc. Of course, you can forget about any savings, retirement plan or out-of-pocket healthcare expenses.

> "Inequality, rather than want, is the cause of trouble."
>
> A Chinese Saying

It seems odd that the poverty level is not adjusted for the living expenses of each city or state since this would account for large metropolitan areas with higher costs. As it stands today, the government's formula for poverty is only applicable to states with the lowest cost of living such as West Virginia, Mississippi, Arkansas, and Alabama. Yet, even in these states, poverty levels are quite high according to Washington's conservative criteria. *How many Americans living in larger, more costly metropolitan areas are making more than the government's poverty level, yet are not counted in its official numbers?*

BOX 4-1: Poverty in America*

The Poor Are Becoming Poorer
The average poor person's income was farther below the poverty line in 2002 than in any other year since 1979, when the data first became available, according to the CBPP.

The Poverty Line is too Low
In most areas of the United States, it takes roughly double the federal poverty level to provide a family with basic necessities such as food and housing, according to the National Center for Children in Poverty.

The Income Gap is Increasing
The real average after-tax income of the top one percent of the population rose 201% in the 1980s and 1990s, while that of the middle fifth of the population rose a mere 15%, according to CBO data released in September of 2003.

If the appropriate adjustments for basic living costs were made, the poverty level in America could easy be 80 percent higher than current levels. *Even with all the tricks government agencies use to hide the truth, they cannot dispute that poverty in America is on the rise. Even based on the government's conservative data, nearly 40 million Americans are literally on the verge of being homeless.* And although the majority of baby boomers are expected to retire in poverty over the next decade, even more will sink into impoverished conditions due to uncontrolled healthcare costs and inadequate retirement assets. Consider that up to 90 percent of a person's total lifetime healthcare costs occur over the age of 60. Both of these factors will surely increase the poverty rate to levels unseen in decades, even when using the government's outdated definition of poverty.

Poverty and Bankruptcy Reform

The passage of President Bush's new bankruptcy bill is a message by Washington to the people of America that financially irresponsible consumers will have no second chances. Arguably, bankruptcy reform was needed due to nearly two decades of abuse. In many cases, it became common practice for individuals to file for bankruptcy just to eliminate credit card debt since there were no real consequences attached, other than a bad credit rating. But the consumer credit industry has been permitted to exploit consumers and make them addicted to credit spending. Therefore, much of the blame must rest with this industry. Yet, *this new law provides consumer finance institutions with a way to deliver a higher earnings predictability since, with rare exception, all debts must be paid.*

Until other major problems are solved such as astronomical healthcare costs and the high rate of uninsured, it seems as if *the timing of this new bankruptcy law was extremely poor unless Washington's main priority was to empower the financial industry.* During a period when American consumers are struggling more than in the previous six decades, one would expect more emphasis to be placed upon them rather than the companies that work hard to make them become dependent on credit, while engaging in unfair and misleading business practices (see Chapter Thirteen for more on the credit card industry).

Why would Washington permit a law that punishes consumers for their inability to pay for a ridiculously priced healthcare system while favoring a credit card industry that addicts Americans to credit and engages in deceit? *It simply makes no sense to pass such a bill after Greenspan handed out money like it was free and after so many jobs have been destroyed.* Of course, the financial industry lobbyists in Washington are quite influential.

America's Wealthy

Washington likes to remind its critics that Americans enjoy the highest living standard in the world. As evidence of this, government "experts" discuss statistics such as GDP growth, wealth, income and wage growth, and other economic indicators without defining exactly what they are referring to (see Chapter Eleven for a detailed discussion).

In fact, when one examines the data, it is clear that *only America's wealthiest 5 percent have benefited from the credit-driven economic expansion that began over two decades ago.* As you can see from figure 4-1, shortly after 1980, real incomes of the top 5 percent of Americans soared over the next two decades from about 3.5 times to 5.5 times the median income (in 2001 dollars). In contrast, real incomes for the bottom 80 percent of Americans barely moved during this period, while inflation for critical necessities such as healthcare, energy, and higher education have soared, which has further reduced the disposable income of the majority of Americans. In contrast, during the post-war period, America's economic expansion was much more evenly distributed across all wage earners and this continued until the high inflation period of the early 1980s (figure 4-2).

Figure 4-1. Income in Various Parts of the Distribution, 1979-2001 (2001 dollars)

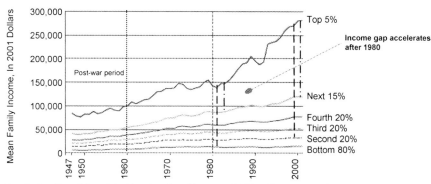

Source: The Century Foundation. "Life and Debt: Why American Families Are Borrowing to the Hilt" 2004. Historical Income Tables—Households, *Current Population Survey* of the Census, U.S. Department of Commerce, Table H-3.

Figure 4-2. Income Distribution, 1947-2001 (2001 dollars)

Source: The Century Foundation. "The New American Economy: A Rising Tide that Lifts Only Yachts." Figure 1.

Even more disturbing is that *America's wealth disparity is much greater*, with the top 5 percent having accounted for a much larger percentage of wealth growth from the decade since 1979 than the bottom 95 percent (figure 4-3). Ten years later, the results are even worse, with the wealthiest 5 percent of Americans having on average 23 times the wealth of the remaining 95 percent (figure 4-4). The problem this creates is that *households with low net worth have very few assets and will therefore be affected more by price increases in basic necessities such as energy, utilities and healthcare. In addition, they will be less able to weather unexpected difficulties, such as medical emergencies or a job loss.* Accordingly, Edward Wolff of New York University has estimated that for households headed by individuals aged 25 to 54, the poorest 40 percent could exhaust all of their financial assets (excluding their home) within one week if they lost their income.

46

Figure 4-3. Mean Wealth at Various Points in the Distribution (1979 and 2001)

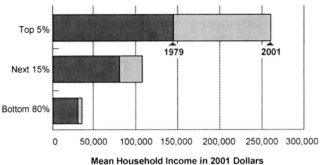

Source: Ibid, The Century Foundation. Figure 2.

Figure 4-4. Mean Wealth at Various Points in the Distribution (1989 and 2001)

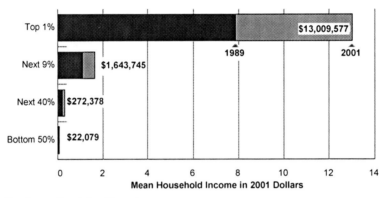

Source: Ibid, The Century Foundation. Figure 3.

How America Stacks Up

The reality is that while America's wealthiest 5 percent have enjoyed a greater percentage of the nation's wealth for over two decades, the remaining 95 percent of the nation's people have benefited very little. *And when one examines America's poorest 10 percent, they have less purchasing power than almost every other developed nation. Meanwhile, America's wealthiest 20 percent own almost 80 percent of all household wealth (figure 4-5). And compared to other developed nations, America has the largest income gap between the top 10 percent of income earners and the median income, as well as the largest gap between the median income and the lowest 10 percent of income earners* (see Chapter Four Supplement in the appendix figures 4.1 and 4.2).

Finally, when comparing America's impoverished to other developed nations, *the U.S. government does much less to help raise the living standards of its citizens than other nations* (figure 4-7 and appendix table 4.1). What was once a nation of fairness, opportunity and moderation has become a nation of favoritism and extremes. Some view America's economic strength to be confirmed by the annual growth of new millionaires. However, this has come at the expense of shifting more Americans into poverty or near poverty.

Figure 4-5. Share of Total Wealth Owned by Wealthiest 20 Percent (Early 1990s)

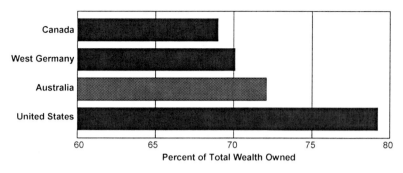

Note: these data are for various years in the early 1990s and are for households with heads ages twenty-five to sixty-four.
Source: Ibid, The Century Foundation. Figure 4.

Figure 4-6. Average Income for Bottom 40 Percent of Population, GDP per Capita (1999)

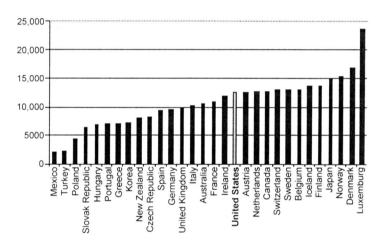

Source: World Bank (2003). Created by Munnell, Alicia H. Hatch, Robert E. Lee, James G. "Why
is Life Expectancy So Low in the United States?" Figure 5, CRR Number 21. August 2004.

Figure 4-7. Percent of Population in Poverty Before and After Government Programs

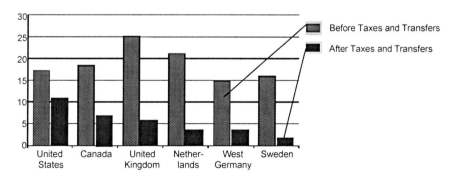

Note: Households headed by persons 25 to 64 years old that are in poverty, both before and after the effects of public policies.
Source: Ibid, The Century Foundation. Figure 7.

Consumption by Credit

Two decades ago, most Americans began to use credit to purchase goods and services that they could not afford. And during the 1990s, this greed became more intense. Today we see the effects of three decades of economic decline in America, as many are now using their credit cards to pay for basic necessities. To illustrate America's consumption trends, consider the American staple; the house. Three decades ago, the average American family consisted of about 4.5 individuals with an average home size of about 2200 square feet. Today, with about 3.6 members in the average family, the average home has increased to about 3500 square feet. That represents an increase (per individual) of 100 percent.

Instead of having fewer bedrooms, the average home now has more. As well, today's average new home has many additional rooms that did not exist in the past such as a study, an entertainment room, Jacuzzi room, and others. But that is not the end. This consumption trend has extended to the number of autos, televisions, and other goods purchased by the average American family. Americans must begin to ask themselves if they really need to consume so much, and if so, whether they are producing enough to justify such consumption. The trends in consumer debt spending indicate the reality.

While the increase in home size has extended to all segments of wealth and income distribution, the rich are much wealthier and more numerous today. In contrast, much of the middle class has been demoted to the lower middle class. In a similar manner, much of the lower middle class has encroached upon poverty, creating a gap where the middle class once stood as the majority.

Similar to many third-world nations that have an inadequate manufacturing infrastructure, America has reverted into a service economy, and much of the service industry is providing services for the rich. As well, many of America's dwindling middle-class consumers have been utilizing these services when they really cannot afford them. However, since they have access to abundant credit, they are living an economic fantasy as they pay for pet sitters, valets, and landscaping with credit cards. Clearly, America is becoming a nation of the "haves and have nots," similar to third-world societies. *The "have-nots" continue to reach for what they cannot afford through credit spending. But in some cases, we already see a change in the way Americans are using credit; from greed to need*—paying for necessities with their credit cards.

Begging China for Jobs

This is not the future. It is a current reality. Already, city councils from some of America's largest cities have traveled to China hoping to convince government officials and business owners to make their city one of its distribution centers. Of course, local governments do not care about America's trends of self-destruction fueled by overconsumption and declining productivity. Most likely, they are not even aware of these trends. All they really care about is generating badly needed jobs in their metropolitan areas. *I find this particularly humiliating, especially when American consumers have been responsible for empowering China's economic expansion at the expense of American jobs.*

Educating America

Problems Begin Early

At the root of America's declining competitiveness is the ineffectiveness of its public K-12 educational system, which continues to fail in preparing America's youth for the modern economy. When comparing the educational skills and achievement scores of America's K-12 students to their foreign counterparts, America consistently scores in the lower quintile. However, money is not the real problem as many seem to believe. When one compares students from China, Korea and other developing nations to their Chinese- and Korean-American counterparts, similar disparities exist. Therefore, it must be the family unit and value system within these nations that are responsible for their high achievement relative to that in America.

K-12 Education

Less than one-third of American 4th grade and 8th grade students performed at or above a "proficient" level in mathematics; "proficiency" was defined as the ability to exhibit competence with challenging subject matter. About one-third of America's 4th graders and one-fifth of the 8th graders lacked the competence to perform even basic mathematical computations.

In 1999, 68% of American 8th grade students received instruction from a mathematics teacher who did not hold a degree of certification in mathematics.

In 2000, 93% of students in grades 5-9 were taught physical science by a teacher lacking a major or certification in the physical sciences.

American youth spend more time watching television than in school.

While America still retains a significant edge in higher education, this gap is narrowing. Despite the vast research and technological advantages afforded to American college students, the U.S. continues to produce fewer scientists and engineers than in the past, while Asia and Europe continue to produce more. The early results of these trends have already materialized, as the economies of Asia and Europe are expanding daily, narrowing the gap between what was once without question the greatest nation on earth.

Higher education

In South Korea, 38% of all undergraduates receive degrees in natural science or engineering; France (47%), China (50%), Sinapore (67%). In the United States only 15% receive such degrees. But in the U.S., most of these students continue on in the bloated healthcare field because even low-level jobs in this industry pay more than science and engineering careers.

About 34% of doctoral degrees in natural sciences and 56% engineering in the United States are awarded to foreign-born students.

In the U.S. science and technology workforce in 2000, 38% of PhDs were foreign-born.

For many of these changes, there is a cause-effect relationship with economics. Declining living standards in America have caused many couples to work, leaving less time to spend with the family, weakening the family unit that was so strong just a few decades ago. And this has indirectly contributed to the widespread and complex social problems faced by America's youth. One must wonder how America's youngest and most troubled generation will contribute to the nation's productivity when they finally enter the global workforce ill-prepared to compete with foreign counterparts.

America's Socialist Educational System

Today in America's public school system the most talented secondary school students no longer have the resources they once enjoyed. In contrast, a larger portion of resources are being spent on special education programs due in large part to the American's with Disabilities Act passed during the Clinton administration. While it has provided a great service to those with disabilities, it has opened the door for frivolous lawsuits and limited the authoritative powers of teachers, resulting in more harm than good.

When the global marketplace opens up for daily business, consumers do not care whether you have transformed special education students into overachievers; they only care about where they can obtain the best goods and services at the best price. Certainly, everyone deserves a chance at a good education, but in order to preserve its global leadership, American schools should not overweigh special education programs at the expense of traditional or accelerated programs. It's just plain bad business for a capitalistic economy.

Washington must encourage more philanthropists to provide the funds needed to finance programs for the disadvantaged rather than government programs aimed at slashing the funding of America's core educational programs. *More of America's philanthropists need to keep more of their charitable dollars in America to help their own citizens rather than trying to win a Nobel Peace Prize.* America has its own problems to deal with.

Teaching in America

One problem with America's declining educational performance has been the inability of American K-12 schools to attract qualified science and math teachers. And even when qualified teachers are found, bureaucracy, waste and corruption by school administrators has overshadowed the efforts of the finest teachers to deliver their best resources to America's youth. In many cases, it has even become difficult to find qualified non-science teachers for inner city schools due to the violence and lack of respect exhibited by many American teens, as well as the lack of disciplinary authority schools must cope with. *The inability of teachers and principals to discipline students in an effective manner has accounted for part of the breakdown in the American public education system.* But how can you expect teachers to have the power to discipline students when parents are even limited in the ways they can legally discipline their own children?

No doubt, the increase in behavioral issues seen in American teens has been an adverse consequence of two-income households, which provide badly needed income in a period of declining living standards. No longer do parents have the time to become involved with their child's education or social development because they are working all of the time. In short, *many American parents have sacrificed parenting responsibilities for better wages thinking that two incomes will lead to a better life for them and their children, when in fact it has led to a breakdown of the family unit.*

That is not to say that there are no students exiting secondary schools with a solid foundation. But for those who have attained a strong educational background, most prepare for high-paying, higher "status" careers, such as medicine, business and law, rarely choosing science or engineering. As well, one can obtain any undergraduate degree and follow it up with an MBA or law degree and be rewarded with many times the salary of a Ph.D. scientist, which requires several more years of rigorous study.

Who Wants to Be a Scientist?

America's population has one of the highest percentages of high school graduates in the world, at around 96 percent, as well as a literacy rate of 97 percent. In addition, it has the world's best university system equipped with the finest research institutions. However, when it comes to continuing their education in what are considered the "rough" fields of academics like the physical sciences, engineering and math, America's youth no longer makes the grade. For over two decades, America has been producing a declining number of scientists and engineers relative to its economic growth.

Because Washington has embraced free trade policies that have led to the destruction of America's core manufacturing base, *one would expect an emphasis on intellectual property to have positioned it with an abundant supply of future scientists and engineers.* However, with declining rates of new American-born scientists and engineers, one can only fantasize how America will be able to hold on to its last remaining economic leg.

With such a high dependency on innovation, one might reasonably assume that the average American would have math and science skills comparable to Asian and European counterparts. However, this is hardly the case. As you might suspect, the problem for American students begins in grade school, where Asian counterparts perform decisively better in science and math. Yet, when you examine literacy and high school graduation rates of India and China, the numbers are quite low. But this is to be expected since most of these populations are located in remote areas with poor access to educational resources.

However this is changing, as China continues to expand its modern transportation infrastructure that will link urban and rural regions. Already, China has built the world's fastest superconducting train that ascends to an elevation of up to 2 miles and easily reaches over its mountainous regions. As China completes its national highway and railway expansion projects, soon all will have mobility and better education. With 50 percent of Chinese college degrees in either science or engineering, China is already producing a much higher percentage of scientists and engineers even with these barriers.

In contrast, America's youth continues to show a declining interest to pursue science as a career. The academic rigor is too difficult and the pay is too little. And while enrollment in B.S. science programs has increased over the past few years, most use this preparation as a stepping stone for higher-paying healthcare fields.

Figure 4-8. Percentage of 24-year Olds with First University Degrees in the Natural Sciences or Engineering Relative to All First University Degree Recipients
(in 2000 or most recent year available)

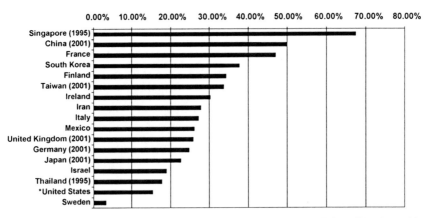

Source: Analysis conducted by the Association of American Universities. 2006. *National Defense Education and Innovation Initiative* based on data from Appendix Table 2-35 National Science Board. 2004. *Science and Engineering Indicators 2004* (NSB 04-01).

But compensation is not the only problem. The career of a scientist is not viewed with the same level of prestige in America as it is in other nations. And it is never portrayed in an attractive or sexy manner by the media, unlike careers in business, law and medicine. The most popular television shows continue to be based on physicians, businessmen and attorneys, with exciting portrayals of sexual escapades and drama, despite the fact that they are all fictitious. However, *Hollywood's portrayal of these occupations, whether fact or fiction, affects the perception of both young and old.*

So who can blame America's youth for not wanting to study science and math only to be underpaid and underappreciated by society? Many other career choices offer better wages, less time in school, less effort, and more respect.

Figure 4-9. Occupations with the Largest Projected Growth (1996-2006)

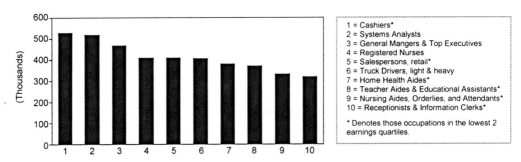

Note: According to the Bureau of Labor and Statistics' occupational projections, more than half (54%) of the new jobs created between 1996 and 2006 will be in occupations that pay below the median earning rate. In addition, 40% of these new jobs are projected to be in occupations with earnings in the lowest quartile.
Source: Economic Policy Institute

As American corporations continue to outsource high-technology jobs, how can parents justify encouraging their children to pursue the cost and rigor of a science or engineering degree? Given demand forecasts for American jobs and outsourcing trends, it is difficult to argue that the cost of higher education in America will be worth the high price (figure 4-9). *In the past two decades, the average annual cost of a four-year university has increased by over 240 percent, or more than three times the rate of inflation.* Today, the average annual cost of a four-year public university in America is over $23,000.

Government Waste and Corruption

America's failures in public education are well-known even to the least informed, and the results have caused a wave of home-schooled students which barely existed two decades ago. The bureaucracy in school systems has become ridiculous. School administrators are too numerous and serve as a destructive force by denying educators the flexibility to allocate funds as they see fit. As well, most administrators are overpaid, often under-qualified and corrupt. In California, there is an average of 132 administrators for every 100 teachers in public schools, while only 18 per 100 teachers in parochial schools.

Across America, the average cost per high school student in the public school system is roughly $5200, while only about $2200 for private schooling. Yet we see clear differences in both the quality of education and maturation level of teens graduating from these two systems. The abuse of public tax dollars earmarked for educational costs has been a problem for decades. Even with the tremendous funding provided to the public school system, billions of tax dollars are wasted annually, and thus unavailable for creating productive private businesses and jobs. Many city- and state-financed infrastructure projects are negotiated with generous fees for contractors. Local projects are awarded to the friends of administrators or through the use of bribes.

The lack of money is not the problem. School districts have so much money that some employees are using taxpayer funds to buy personal items. But over the next decade state budgets are going to be squeezed to the core due to massive Medicaid and government pension liabilities. Perhaps cutting school budgets would increase the scrutiny of expenditures and might provide a more efficient and less corrupt educational system.

Government-Subsidized Fraud

The epidemic of America's declining K-12 public school system has not gone unnoticed by businesses. Over the past two decades there have been hundreds of colleges that have sprung up to fill the gap in education for many who could not get accepted into a four-year university or those already working but wanting to advance or change careers.

Every year, hundreds of thousands of Americans enroll in one of the many non-traditional, for-profit, two- and sometimes four-year degree programs offered throughout the United States. In the past, these colleges focused on traditional blue-collar skills such as carpentry, plumbing, welding, machinery, and so forth. However, as the high-tech field has been seen as the most lucrative career choice for modern America, these colleges now focus on providing relatively low-grade, "dead-end" technical skills disguised as high-quality degrees that promise to open the door to a lucrative professional career.

Many of these colleges have inappropriately used success stories of high-tech careers in order to position themselves as institutions that provide an entry into lucrative jobs, when in fact this is often not the case. They make use of television airtime during programs targeted towards specific socioeconomic groups, offering a "better life," higher wages, and job stability by enrollment into their programs. While many of these schools teach valuable skills and offer certification degrees that have market demand, they often exaggerate job placement rates and the abilities of their graduates.

Often, these schools are very expensive, but financial aid is a virtual certainty due to student loan programs offered by the government. When post-secondary schools begin operating as for-profit entities and make exaggerated claims of a better lifestyle and secure future resulting from completion of their degree programs, this creates a major problem that should be investigated by the FTC. However, when federal-backed funds are made available to these institutions, you are talking about taxpayer fraud. It's a great business to be in if you run these schools. You make exaggerated promises to Americans wanting to improve their situation and you are able to provide them with loans from the government which are guaranteed by taxpayer dollars. As a matter of fact, many of these companies are now publicly traded.

Some of the problems reflecting the low quality of these schools are outdated curriculums, inadequate or outdated equipment, incompetent teaching staff, and false claims about graduate placement rates. If it were that easy to change one's life from two years of moderate study, the laws of supply and demand would kick in and nullify these opportunities. However, many of the jobs these schools claim to prepare one for never materialize, leaving many with broken dreams and a pile of inescapable debt.

There have already been hundreds of accounts of former students forced into bankruptcy due to their inability to obtain employment after graduation. However, as these unfortunate victims have discovered, student loans are exempt from bankruptcy relief under all circumstances.

Who's to Blame?

When one examines this short list of change in America, it is difficult to understand how things could have spiraled out of control in such a short period of time. It appears as if America's leadership has been inconsistent, misdirected, and confused for over three decades. In part, the strong polarization between the two major political parties is a partial cause of this confusion and poor leadership. I place blame for over three decades of financial mismanagement on both political parties. Republicans have caused more harm to the middle class by promoting legislature favoring exploitation of consumers by corporate America. These policies have ultimately benefited the nation's wealthiest 5 percent. Meanwhile, democrats have wasted taxpayer money on ineffective social programs that have destroyed American values and have done little to create permanent change. Finally, both parties have continued to allow corruption and fraud by corporate America, as well as the continued destruction of the middle class.

5

THE FUTURE IS NOW

Everything is a Cycle

Where will America be in twenty, fifty or one hundred years? In order to predict the future, we know that an examination of historical events often serves as a useful tool. In part, this may be explained by the dynamics of cycling patterns. The cyclical nature of the universe dictates that everything must obey some type of cycle. It provides the equilibrium of the universe; what goes up must come down; the higher you rise, the harder you fall.

Everything on earth goes through a growth and decline phase. Life has this as its universal cycle. The sun rises and sets each day. The seasons of the year come and go. Most likely, these patterns are based upon the astronomical cycles related to the force of gravity, both of which are poorly understood. On earth, amidst the broader cycles of the universe, people have periods of highs and lows based on biological rhythms that are controlled by the cycles within the human body, such as circadian rhythms influenced by physiological and sensory stimuli, which act together to alter our emotions and behavior.

In addition, these smaller biological cycles are in fact tied into the more complex and larger cycling events of the universe such as the oscillation of night and day. And these events repeat, as do all events within cycles. Yet with every movement through the oscillation of each of these cycles, we see changes in other cycles due to the dependency of each cycle upon the next. *It is likely that all cycling patterns within the universe are mutually dependent upon one another, each with a different force and hierarchy.*

The same may also be said for the events controlled by human interaction and behavior. Economics serves as an excellent example of this since it is largely a behavioral science. Business cycles rise and fall, as do the broader economic cycles of contraction and expansion. And this cycling directly affects the stock and bond markets, although the timing is variably delayed. Real estate markets also rise and fall like the tides of the ocean. And this cycle too is affected by the economic cycle which also affects the stock and bond markets. What was once a poorly developed, run-down area now serves as the site of a wealthy neighborhood or upscale commercial development. And surely, what are now viewed as wealthy neighborhoods will eventually be forgotten areas, only to be inhabited by the poor. And the cycle will repeat, given enough time.

Directly attached to economic cycles are economic and societal variables such as demographic trends, interest rates, inflation, productivity, and virtually every other variable that involves human affect. We see the impact of economic cycles in the stock and bond markets, which are directly controlled by the interpretation, motives, and the behavioral responses of investors. Of course, each individual investor is affected by variable oscillations of their own biological rhythms, which influence the interpretation of their surroundings, alters their mood and therefore impacts their decisions. What might be viewed as pleasant by one person on a given day might be interpreted by the same individual as unattractive on a different day based upon the progression of their own biological cycles, which are controlled by larger cycling patterns within the universe.

Diamonds Aren't Forever

The fact that diamonds are the hardest known substance on earth has led to the expression that they "last forever." However, because everything in the universe is dictated by cycling dynamics, even a diamond—as hard as it is and as long as it takes to form—will not last for eternity. Eventually, perhaps over a one million-year period, the diamond you see today will have reverted back to some allotrope of carbon from which it originally came, completing a full turn through its lifecycle.

There have been many great empires in the world—the Greek Empire, the Roman Empire and many others. But none have lasted forever. Each has risen to greatness and fallen to decline. And no doubt these nations will rise again at some point. But until that time, they will have to recon with the down period of their socioeconomic cycle. When the decline of these empires has occurred it has never been pretty, nor has it been expected. Yet, in every case, there has been a variable period of warning signs unrecognized by most until the cycle reverses its trend towards the path of devastation.

Is America in the declining phase of its socioeconomic cycle? The same question might have been posed by critics in the 1970s during the oil crisis along with double-digit inflation in the early '80s. During that turbulent period, Japan purchased vast amounts of U.S. real estate while entering American markets with imports. That was the period when American debt held by foreign nations began to escalate due to the massive expenditures from the Cold War arms buildup. Yet today, America has only engaged in minor conflicts since that period. And while economic growth was tremendous during the '90s, America has accumulated massive amounts of consumer and national debt causing some to question the real magnitude of this "tremendous" economic expansion.

For over two centuries, the "American Dream" has brought millions of migrants to America from around the globe, by both legal and illegal means. Many who have entered illegally have risked their lives for the economic mobility, freedom and prosperity America offers. Yet, today it appears as if America is now approaching the nadir of its socioeconomic cycle much like it did eighty years ago before the Great Depression.

The perception by most is that America is still the greatest nation on earth, as many die each year trying to cross its borders for the chance to live the "American Dream." And they are right. America is the greatest nation in the world. However, soon it will face some very difficult adjustments through its transition towards the new modern economy. This is merely a normal event of the ubiquitous cycle of ascent and decline.

Who Really Owns America?

Currently, U.S. national debt held by foreign nations is just over 50 percent of total outstanding, prompting the question of who really owns America. While these debt levels have occurred in the past with no severe long-term consequences, this time things are much different. *U.S. national debt as a percentage of GDP is above 80 percent, and if one counts the total debt, (consumer debt, mortgage debt and government debt) this number is nearly 320 percent, as America's total credit bubble has surpassed $42 trillion.*

Still, massive debt in itself will not be sufficient to cause a depression, but merely an escalation of the downward trend of its economic cycle. But once extremes in this cycle have been reached, it won't take much to push things over the edge. *Debt of this magnitude has never been amassed in America and has even surpassed that due to the Great Depression and the massive spending during WWII.* However, rather than definitive evidence of a future depression, America's current record debt is but only one economic manifestation of its difficulties that have been growing for three decades.

Surely the day will come when the "American Dream" is but a distant memory of the past. When that happens America will no longer be the place sought out by millions each year. The only question is whether that day will occur over the next two decades. Already, we see dangerous signs of decline in America that have continued to worsen for over two decades—its education, healthcare, and pension systems, both public and private. And all of this has caused the standard of living to gradually decline without notice by most due to habitual credit spending.

Similar to a company burdened with huge amounts of outstanding debt, Americans have traded their nation's claim to assets for credit issued by foreigners. But instead of receiving a healthy return from the use of this debt, many have squandered it on cheap consumer goods imported from abroad, filling their addiction to acquire "stuff" they really don't need.

Of course there have been some items made in America that have been purchased by Americans—gas-guzzling cars and SUVs. But these items merely highlight America's disregard for the world oil crisis that is about to take center stage. In any other nation where oil reserves are approaching depletion, autos with low gas mileage would have extra taxes. But in America, the political process has encouraged the purchase of these vehicles by offering a business tax credit of up to $100,000 for a large SUV.

The "Big 3:" A Lesson in Business

Rather than try to compete with Japanese and German auto manufacturers by matching their style and fuel efficiency, the "Big 3" chose to continue making big cars with outdated styling. And rather than compete head-to-head with foreign automakers at a time when it was still financially feasible, they chose to retreat from direct competition and focus on making big trucks while convincing Americans that this was a symbol of power on the road. But brainwashing marketing ads can only work for so long.

As American automakers continued to lose market share to foreign competitors, they realized the need to diversify into finance as a way to improve auto sales. And for nearly two decades now, the sales pitch from the "Big 3" has focused on affordable financing. In contrast, Japanese and German automakers did not need to take this route since their vehicles were clearly superior. In short, foreign automakers met consumer demand by offering features and styling at a superior value to that provided by the "Big 3."

What was once the driving engine of the American economy has been transformed into the driving force of consumer debt. Today, Ford and General Motors barely make any profits from auto sales, but rather from their massive consumer finance divisions. But as we know, the lack of vision by the "Big 3" was only a small part of their downfall. *The primary enemy of these companies, as with all companies in America has been the skyrocketing cost of healthcare.*

Yet, we must give the "Big 3" credit for their early realization of American consumers' Achilles' Heal; credit spending. You see, when your living standards are declining, it is only human nature to continue to maintain them even if you use credit to make up the gap. And that is precisely what most Americans have been doing for over two decades, using borrowed money to purchase everything from the latest gadgets to groceries. With interest rates on the rise, the housing market is beginning to cool, as is the home equity business. But don't think the vultures will stop luring consumers into more financial irresponsibility. Soon, I predict a wave of reverse mortgages to occur especially with baby boomers, as they continue to struggle to make ends meet amongst climbing healthcare costs. And when they depart from this world they will have nothing to pass on to their relatives. This will certainly impact the future generations.

Technology: America's Declining Edge

As previously discussed, when the U.S. government decided to take a different position on intellectual property in the early '80s, this sparked a rapid increase in R&D spending by corporations. Consequently, this led to the rapid growth of venture capital investment funds that fueled the development of numerous entrepreneurial innovations, many of which led to some of America's greatest high-tech companies. The timing of this policy reversal was fortunate, as many foreign nations were beginning to give American manufacturing stiff competition.

Ever since these changes, the focus in America has been on innovation fueled by its superior higher education, creative scientists, and various sources of private investment capital and government aid. It was this change in economic strategy that allowed America to pull far ahead of all other nations. But as we have seen, this reemphasis was due to the realization that America would no longer be able to maintain its manufacturing dominance.

Despite its realignment since that period, there has also been a gradual and steady decline in the infrastructure needed to maintain America's edge in innovation. As discussed in the previous chapter, for over two decades now, America's K-12 public education system has been in decline due to many factors—lack of qualified science and math teachers, declining interest in studying science and engineering, declining performance scores on world exams, and a decline in college science and engineering graduates. However, other forces are at work that could be even more detrimental.

Core Research Derailed?

After the devastating effects of the '80s, America's investment environment facilitated a surge in both corporate R&D and venture finance that helped create the illusion of an economic boom during the '90s. Subsequently, private funding for research has replaced much of the declining funding growth from the government. And this has shifted the emphasis on shorter-term projects which has hurt core research efforts.

Even the U.S. government has shifted its research priorities to shorter-term goals. When the American government declared war on AIDS in the early 1990s, something very wrong happened with federal research funding. As massive amounts of funds were being added to the NIH annual budget, the growth in funds for physical science research programs, such as the National Science Foundation (NSF) declined. As a result, funding for America's most highly valued basic research programs have not kept up with inflation (figure 5-1).

Yet, despite the billions of dollars per annum devoted towards AIDS research, America has made no real advances in AIDS therapy, and no one has even isolated the full virus in-vivo to this day, nor has there been a single scientific paper that has proved that HIV causes AIDS. Instead, the pharmaceutical industry has profited handsomely from largely ineffective and toxic drugs and has delivered a message to the public that significant progress has been made towards AIDS.

There is even strong evidence by several prestigious researchers that HIV does not cause AIDS (see the reference section). And the failure of the scientific community to acknowledge this reasonable possibility stems from their focus on obtaining grant money, or in essence playing the "grant game." Unfortunately, as corporate R&D and private investment capital continues to flood into research institutions, many scientists now focus on landing large research grants as a means of survival, even if that means a departure from the principals of the scientific method. This is a disturbing trend that may result in dire consequences if not corrected soon.

Figure 5-1. Growth of Science Research funds (1970-2004)

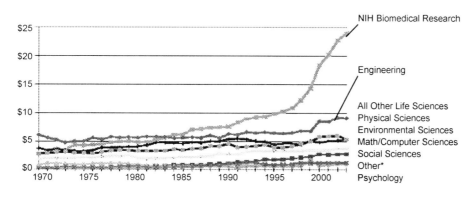

Life sciences-split into NIH support for biomedical research and all other agencies' support for life sciences.
*Other includes research not classified (includes basic research and applied research; excludes development and R&D facilities)
Source: National Science Foundation

The extent of the problem is already epidemic. Universities are pressuring professors to land research grants or else they will be asked to leave. Meanwhile, virtually every university now has a technology transfer department whose goal is to capitalize on discoveries made by research professors. *What this has done is connect corporate America, along with its focus on short-term solutions and quarterly earnings statements, with academia.* And this has damaged the strength of America's core scientific research. As one example of the damaging effects of this shift from government to corporate funding, safety and efficacy studies for drugs are financed primarily by the same pharmaceutical companies that stand to benefit from their approval and acceptance.

Early Signs of Trouble

Already, some of the damaging effects of America's declining innovation growth are apparent. Since 1988, U.S. patent growth has remained fairly constant. In contrast, patent applications from Western Europe and Asia have steadily increased. As of 1996, *the number of patent applications from Western Europe surpassed those from America for the first time ever.* Since then, the gap has continued to widen.

Meanwhile, as the rate of R&D spending has remained fairly constant in the U.S., Asian nations have been accelerating these expenditures. If current patent growth rates remain, Asia will surpass America within the next 20 years (figure 5-2). *Since 1980, America's world share of new patents has declined by 15 percent while Japan's share has risen by almost 200 percent. Already, Japan has bumped the U.S. down to the number two spot in the amount of capital spent on R&D as a percentage of GDP (figure 5-3).* Consider that, with the exception of Japan, most of the nations in figure 5-3 have experienced tremendous GDP growth over the past decade, while America's growth rate has been more contained. Therefore, this data is somewhat misleading in that it does not account for the huge increases in funding other nations have made (relative to GDP) over the past several years as their GDP has soared.

Most impressive is China, which has increased both its overall R&D spending as a percentage of GDP while continuing to deliver double-digit GDP growth over the past decade. Of course, *China would not have been able to post these amazing gains without the help of American consumers and the consumer credit industry.*

Figure 5-2. U.S. Patent Applications (1988-2001)

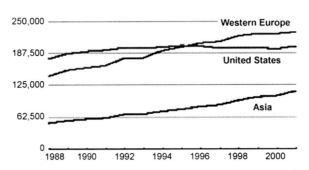

Source: Task Force on the Future of American Innovation based on data from the National Science Foundation. Science and Engineering Indicators 2004. Appendix Table 6-11. Arlington: APS Office and Public Affairs.

Figure 5-3. R&D Expenditures as a Percentage of GDP are Rising Worldwide

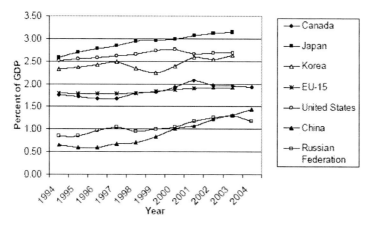

Source: Organization for Economic Co-Operation and Development. Main Science and Engineering Indicators. Paris: Organization of Economic Co-operation and Development (OCED), 2005.

Despite the shift of R&D funding from government to corporate, America is still not keeping up with many nations. According to a study by MIT, *overall foreign corporate R&D spending is almost twice that of American corporate R&D*, with spending 12 times higher in electronics, 3 times higher in automotive research, 3 times higher in chemicals, 2 times higher in energy, and 1.5 times higher in aerospace.

Already, the effects of America's declining technological edge have been registered, as can be seen from figure 5-4. From 1990 to 2003, the United States has reversed its position from a $33 billion net exporter to a $30 billion net importer of high-technology products. *Given the declining production of U.S. scientists and engineers and the lack of patent growth, America will loose its technology edge within the next 15 years. And without its leadership in innovation, America will have very little to fall back on now that most of its manufacturing industry has been exported overseas.*

Figure 5-4. United States Trade Balance for High-technology Products (1990-2003)

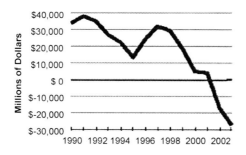

Source: Force on the Future of American Innovation based on data from the U.S. Census Bureau Foreign Trade Statistics, U.S. International Trade on Goods and Services. Compiled by the APS Office of Public Affairs.

America's Future Scientists

At this point, there should be little question that America has been suffering a gradual decline in both the quality of core scientific research and the number of Americans choosing science as a career. *Unlike the previous decade when America ranked third in the world, the number of new American scientists now ranks a pathetic seventeenth.*

However, consider that the effects of these statistics have not yet registered within America's R&D base because of the lag time required to transform the next generation of young Americans into scientists. For instance, the average time it takes to train a Ph.D. chemistry researcher, including an almost mandatory post-doc stint is 12 to 15 years from the beginning of college. In addition, consider that *the consequences of a declining population of newly-trained American scientists on the quality of core research has an even longer delay since the direct benefits of quality research usually take decades to be seen.*

If current trends remain in place, it won't be long before America will have to import the majority of its best minds for scientific research. While importation of research talent has been occurring for decades, it has only accounted for small gaps. But the number of foreign scientists needed may not be sufficient even if America opens its borders amidst new national security laws. Already, the number of TOEFL exam applicants from China has been decreasing dramatically for the past few years, as most Chinese want to take part in their nation's promising future. And with sluggish economic conditions in America, this has further discouraged foreign migration. Yet, *many foreign students still use America's university system to obtain their high-tech education only to return back to their homeland to take advantage of the huge economic growth and opportunities that corporate America and American dollars have created there.*

So why does America still continue to provide foreign students admission to its best schools only to see many of them return home? This denies advanced training for American citizens while empowering foreign nations. *Hopefully at some point, permitting foreign students into American universities will be recognized as both an economic and national security issue, not only for science disciplines but for all disciplines.* Those spots need to be reserved for Americans or foreigners who are legally obligated to remain in America for an extended period after graduation. American universities represent a large portion of the nation's intellectual capital. And by allowing foreign students admission, America needs to see a return on this investment. When foreign students return home after graduation, the only investment returns are registered by the economies of foreign nations.

Research

In 2001, U.S. industry spent more on tort litigation than on research and development.

Beginning in 2007, the most capable high-energy particle accelerator on Earth will reside outside the United States for the first time.

Federal research funding in the physical sciences, as a percentage of GDP was 45% less in FY 2004 than in FY 1996.

The amount invested annually by the U.S. federal government in research in the physical sciences, mathematics, and engineering combined equals the annual increase in U.S. healthcare costs incurred every 20 days.

World Supply and Demand for Oil

Approximately 1000 billion (1 trillion) barrels of conventional crude oil have been extracted from the globe, representing about half of the original supply since commercial oil exploration began in the 1930s. And most of the oil consumption has occurred within the past three decades. Yet, the world continues to thirst for more fossil fuels each year. Global demand has recently intensified by the rapid development of China, India, and other Asian nations.

Many industry experts believe that about 90 percent of the total oil available on earth has already been discovered. In other words, we can only count on about another 100 billion barrels of conventional crude to be discovered in the future. What does this mean? Either more discoveries of conventional crude must be made at a faster pace or the world will rely more on lower quality, higher-priced non-conventional crude. Either way, this guarantees that *oil prices will continue to remain high for a long time since much of the current exploration is off-shore or extracted from mining non-conventional crude, both which are very expensive.*

When experts discuss crude reserves, they often distinguish between conventional and non-conventional oil. This is a very important distinction since our current ability to mine and refine non-conventional crude is very limited due to technology and cost constraints. While the volume of conventional crude reserves were originally equally dispersed throughout the world, each region now differs in the amount remaining, the quality, the cost of production and refinement, the size of the oil wells, and the estimated time until a decline in production will be reached.

North America has exhausted nearly all of its conventional crude reserves, with Alaska as its only remaining large source. This has led to a shift by U.S. oil companies towards expensive off-shore exploration projects in the Gulf of Mexico and recent massive capital infusion into the Canadian oil sands, with the hope of providing a large supply of unconventional crude over the next three decades. However, *the Canadian oil sands reserves are not only very difficult to mine, but the oil is of low quality and requires a large expenditure of both mining facilities and natural gas to harness and refine this crude.* Finally, the intense refining process emits significant pollutants into the atmosphere. It has only been the recent surge in oil prices which has made many of these off-shore exploration and non-conventional mining projects economically feasible.

In contrast to America's bleak oil outlook, the largest remaining conventional oil reserves are in the Middle Eastern nations of Saudi Arabia, Iran, and Iraq, whose reserves are also associated with the lowest production costs in the world. As the world's top consumer of oil, the U.S. is looking for alternative sources of inexpensive oil to fuel its economic engine. It should be apparent that the Middle East is the primary focus of America's interest due to its vast supplies of high-quality crude.

Peak Oil

As discussed in the first chapter, oil is the lifeblood of the U.S. economy. And although oil is vital to all modern economies, in no other nation does access to abundant supplies of inexpensive oil impact economic growth than in America. It has built its entire economic infrastructure on the use of fossil fuels, and without its extensive transportation network, the consumer marketplace and labor force would be very restricted.

While America is one of the top three oil producers in the world, it only provides for about 33 percent of its annual needs (about 8 million barrels per day), relying on the rest of the world (over 14 million barrels per day imported) to supply its lifeblood. This dependence on foreign oil has grown every year since America reached its peak production in 1970. Since then, America has spent more money to find less oil each year, shifting most of its efforts to costly off-shore exploration projects. And *because oil is vital to the U.S. economy, those nations that have the largest reserves could create a financial crisis by using oil as a tool for economic and political extortion.* America has indicated many times in the past that it will go to war for oil, and Iraq and Afghanistan are just the latest in a long series of oil-crusade activities by the U.S. military.

If you ask the major oil companies about any future global oil shortage, they will insist that the world has enough reserves to supply future demand for several decades to come. However, inaccurate and inconsistent reporting of reserves, misleading data, and a lack of understanding of the full impact of the continued economic expansion of Asia paint a very different picture. Regardless, *it is not the total oil reserves potentially available that are important as much as the maximum mining output per unit time, otherwise known as the peak oil production capacity* (Peak Oil Theory).

Because oil becomes more difficult to extract from each well when less than half of the oil in a reservoir remains, the peak production occurs when half of the oil within a specific reserve has been extracted. Upon entry into its peak oil production, crude is extracted at a maximum rate but drops off at a variable rate permanently until the well finally dries up or it is no longer economically or technologically feasible to continue extracting oil from the "peaked out" reservoir.

This peak production behaviour has been described by a bell-shaped curve and was first introduced by geophysicist King Hubbert in a 1956 report presented at an oil conference in San Antonio, Texas. (1) According to the Peak Oil Theory, the time period of peak production is highly variable and unpredictable and it can last a few months or several years. Thus, the peak oil production period can demonstrate a long time plateau or a rapid spike of maximal output, followed by a variable rate of declining production.

Most critical is the variable and uncertain nature of the decline period after peak oil production has been reached. In other words, once peak oil production has expired and production begins decreasing, there is no way to determine how long the well will last before running dry. Unfortunately, there is really no definitive way to determine the rate of this decline other than through observation. In other words, the peak oil period is difficult if not impossible to spot and can only be verified many years after it has occurred.

---

(1) Hubbert predicted that America would reach peak oil production in 1971; just one year late from reality.

Figure 5-5. Oil Production Dynamics and Peak Oil

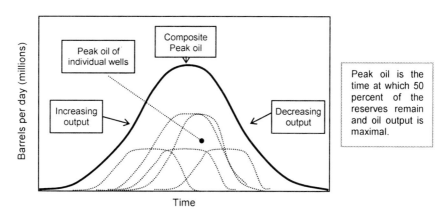

Consequently, most U.S. officials and oil optimists usually refer to oil reserves rather than peak oil and this undermines the problem of expected oil shortages over the next decade. Once again, the amount of oil reserves is not important but rather the estimation of peak oil production since Peak Oil Theory tells us about the rates of production decline. *You can have 10 trillion barrels of oil in the ground, but if you have no way to extract it rapidly or economically, it is equivalent to not having abundant reserves.* And the supply-demand curve will necessarily increase the price of crude.

While Hubbert's Peak Oil Theory is largely accepted, the problem lies in disagreements as to when peak production will occur due to the assumptions used by various groups. However, several highly respected geological experts and organizations without ties to the oil industry (French Petroleum Institute, Colorado School of Mines, Uppsala University and Petroconsultants in Geneva) feel that the peak oil will be reached by 2010. However, some think it will occur even sooner. Finally, the ASPO has estimated the global oil peak at around 2008 (figure 5-6).

Regardless of one's support of Peak Oil Theory, what must be scrutinized are the assumptions which underlie the application of this theory. Consequently, oil companies have advocated overly generous estimations in order to protect their own interests. *If Americans are alerted that the world will soon begin to experience a decline in the amount of oil produced per day, (i.e. the post-peak oil period) this would prompt more investment into alternative energy technologies, which the oil companies have no interest in since this would threaten their monopoly.*

Rather than address the peak oil question, Exxon is just one of many oil companies that has chosen to approach the coming global oil shortage in terms of required capital investment for continued exploration to meet global demand. *For Exxon and other large oil companies, peak oil only means that more capital will be required to extract the same or even less oil through riskier projects. What that means for consumers is higher prices at the pump.* We have already witnessed the unhindered ability of oil companies to raise prices as they see fit in order to ensure their profitability (see Chapter Five Supplement of the appendix for expanded coverage). This unchecked extortion by the oil industry will continue as long as corrupt politicians remain in power.

Figure 5-6. World Oil and Gas Liquids Production Curve

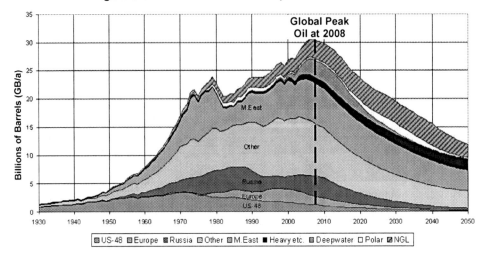

In the USGS study, recoverable oil includes cumulative production, proved resources, undiscovered resources, and reserves growth in discovered fields. The USGS group assumes a higher recoverable oil figure (3 trillion barrels) versus the data by Campbell and Laherrere (1.8 trillion barrels). This results in a higher recovery factor for the USGS group. What that means is that the USGS has assumed a higher percentage of oil can be recovered, resulting in a more distant peak oil production horizon. These differences imply a significantly different degree of economic and technological resource capability and application, which may or may not be feasible.

Source: Association for the Study of Peak Oil & Gas (ASPO)

America's Health and Retirement

Where are the Pensions?

Imagine what would happen if the retirement benefits promised to employees were cut or even eliminated? This has already happened to millions of Americans, and no doubt it is only going to get worse. As a result of the economic disasters of the past few years, most Americans over fifty do not imagine ever retiring due to the poor performance of the stock market, higher healthcare costs, and the failure of Social Security to keep pace with inflation.

Add pension shortfalls to this mix and it's easy to see how retirement isn't going to be an alternative for many. Already, it has been estimated that over 50 percent of Fortune 1000 companies' pension funds are underfunded. What that means is that there is not enough income from these funds to pay benefits to retirees. The Pension Benefit Guarantee Corporation (PBGC) is the government agency responsible for insuring the pension assets of over 44 million Americans. Of the participants of the PBGC, it has been estimated that over $450 billion in pension assets are unavailable to retirees, and the PBGC would not be able to pay these claims if all current underfunded pensions defaulted. Currently, the PBGC is in deficit by nearly $23 billion due to insufficient funds needed to pay benefits to the recipients of pension plans that have already defaulted.

If the PBGC were a privately held insurance company, it would be forced into bankruptcy protection. But because it is a government insurance agency, it has access to tax revenues to fund its deficits. And of course this is going to divert funds from other government programs. However, over the next decade, a $23 billion deficit might be welcomed compared to estimates by government agencies that have predicted this deficit to climb to almost $150 billion.

As well, state and municipal pensions have also been affected. *Every major city and state has a deficit and this has resulted in cutting education and Medicaid funding and other important programs,* thereby weakening the future competitiveness of America further. And with state and local property tax revenues at all-time highs due to the real estate bubble, imagine what is going to happen to their budgets once this bubble deflates.

Social Security: America's New Pension

Currently, up to 50 percent (or about 38 million) baby boomers have no savings or retirement assets and will therefore rely on Social Security as their only source of income. Already one-third of Americans over 65, or 7.7 million, rely exclusively on Social Security benefits as their sole source of income. Plan benefits are about enough to pay for utilities and food because the buying power of program benefits has dwindled over the years due to its indexing to wages instead of inflation. As a consequence, it appears that impoverished Americans are the fastest growing population in the United States.

The Healthcare Crisis

Estimates are that around 19 percent of all Americans have no health insurance, and in Texas that number is above 26 percent. If you slip and break a leg, without health insurance the bill could run as high as $50,000. Thus, something as relatively benign as a broken leg could send millions into bankruptcy; or can it?

Prior to 2005, uninsured Americans did have a way to bail out of enormous medical bills, but that is no longer an option with the passage of the bankruptcy reform bill in October 2005. Over the past several years, it has been estimated that up to 50 percent of all Americans declaring bankruptcy stated medical bills as their main reason for insolvency. And now that personal bankruptcy laws have been changed, uninsured and underinsured Americans will no longer be able to get a bail out after a medical disaster.

Stock Market

The "Good Ole Days" Are Gone

America's standard of living has been in decline for three decades while middle-class America continues to become extinct. When you consider the extortion by energy companies, it is not difficult to see why. Who ever thought they would have a total monthly energy bill (fuel plus gas and electric) that was as much as their monthly mortgage payment? How can you maintain a healthy economy when consumers are paying $500 for gasoline and $600 for utilities each month?

In some states such as Texas, ridiculous electricity bills are causing some to lose their home in foreclosure. The travesty in this is that Texas Utilities (the states largest electric company) has been reporting record profits while investigations have shown that it manipulated prices and electricity inventories. As well, the state's natural gas company has been found to have spent millions on expensive lunches and artwork, while overcharging its customers. Meanwhile, the big oil companies refuse to invest in alternative energy and continue to report record profits at the expense of consumers who struggle to pay for gas and utilities.

More jobs are continuing to be exported overseas, as outsourcing to foreign nations remains at an all-time high and expected to get worse. And the average American worker does not have the educational skills to transition into lucrative careers to replace these lost jobs. During economic expansions, outsourcing is good for consumers because it provides less expensive goods. But outsourcing is bad during severe economic contractions because consumers need jobs more than they need inexpensive goods. They also need affordable energy, utilities and healthcare. Yet the cost of these basic necessities has risen by more than twice the rate of inflation over the past decade. The only beneficiaries of the current outsourcing trend are U.S. corporations and foreign workers.

What to Expect Before the Depression

So how does this all relate to the stock and bond markets? First of all, investors need to realize that the U.S. economy is in a post-bubble correction period. Historically, such periods have lasted from 12 to 15 years and market returns have averaged 1 to 3 percent annually (unadjusted for inflation). And while there will be good performance years for the market, there will be equally bad or perhaps much worse years. And if you are still waiting for the NASDAQ to cross 5000 again, it's going to be at least another 8 years. And during this period you can forget about index funds, unless you want to settle for 2 percent average annual returns (over the course of the secular bear market, from 2001 to 2012) before inflation and fees.

Unfortunately, many investors are still clinging onto the "darlings of Wall Street" from the 1990s—the Ciscos, Oracles and other large cap, high-tech stocks. If you fall into this category you really need to wake up. First of all, large caps have not performed well throughout the post-bubble period, and most will continue to perform poorly over the next few years as long as interest rates remain below their historical mean. This is especially true for the large cap high-tech stocks.

One cannot equate record profits with the metrics used by growth investors to valuate stocks because there is a big difference between earnings due to cutting expenses and share buy backs versus pure growth and investment expansion. And since 2001, most American companies have achieved growth through the former strategy.

Even the gains made by outsourcing cannot last forever since profits are being generated at the expense of American jobs. And when the American consumer falls on its face things could turn ugly real fast.

Major Problems America Faces
• Trade Deficit & Federal Debt
• Foreign Debt
• Weak Dollar
• Real Estate Bubble
• Healthcare Crisis
• Pension Crisis
• Social Security Crisis
• Consumer Debt
• Global Oil Shortage
• Global Tensions
• Iraq Post-War Period

The Next Great Depression?

What all this comes down to is my belief that America is setting itself up for a major economic disaster, unlike anything seen since the Great Depression of the 1930s. I do not know precisely when it will happen, but my guess is that it will occur sometime over the next 10 to 20 years, perhaps coinciding with the global peak oil period amidst the retirement of America's baby boomers, or around 2018. But until then, you can be assured that the secular bear market will continue for several more years.

A depression might be triggered by a major terrorist attack or some other overwhelming event. Major crises are often triggered by unrelated events, which serve to make consumers more cautious about the realities that have built up but have been masked by, in this case, credit spending and the wealth effect from the real estate bubble.

This phenomenon occurred during the Great Depression, as well as after 9-11. The real market lows were not reached until two years after 9-11, once consumers realized the economy was in trouble. But it was 9-11 that really triggered the wake up call that the economy was in bad shape.

I cannot tell you whether the market will continue to trade sideways for the next 6 to 8 years or whether it will experience several crashes sending the Dow to devastating levels. But what I can tell you with very high certainty is that the secular bear market will remain for the next several years. *And at some point, the day of reckoning will occur that could be independent of the current bearish conditions. Such a payback period must occur to correct for the years of overconsumption by America.*

> **Munger**
>
> *"The present era has no comparable referent in the past history of capitalism. A lot of what I see now reminds me of Sodom and Gomorrah. You get activity feeding on itself, envy and imitation. It has happened in the past that there came out bad consequences."*

> **Buffett asking Munger**
> *"What do you think the end will be?"*
>
> **Munger:**
> *"Bad."*

Figure 5-7 shows the historical returns of the S&P 500 under different price-to-average (P/E) ratios. As you can see, when the P/E has been high, market returns were low. Right now the P/E ratio is just under 19, placing it somewhere between the 5 percent and 0 percent return level for the next ten years total.

America the Bankrupt

If drastic policy changes are not made immediately, astronomical sums of money will have to be generated over the next three to four decades in order to fund the current liabilities in Social Security, Medicare, and Medicaid. *Today, these liabilities have a total present value of anywhere from $51 to $72 trillion, or $473,456 to $602,914 per U.S. household.* These numbers do not include the total U.S. debt figures which add another

$8.5 trillion, the $8 trillion borrowed from the Social Security and other trust funds by Washington over the years, or consumer debt and mortgages, which could add another $14 to $15 trillion. *In total, these liabilities range from $757,530 to $964,665 per U.S. household.*

Figure 5-7. Quintiles of Market Average P/E to Predict 10-Year Returns: 20% of the Time, Stocks Return 0% Real Over 10 years

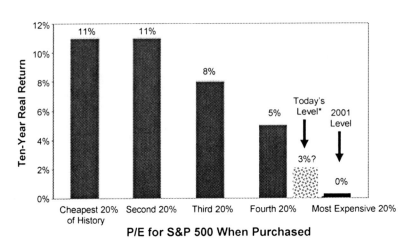

Source: GMO, Standard & Poor's Data: 1925-2001.
* Modified to reflect author's estimates of "today's level."

Each day Washington delays funding these core programs, these future liabilities increase. Consider for instance, that according to many well-respected think tanks, in order to provide complete solvency of these three programs through the period of baby boomer life spans, America has one of three viable options:

1. All federal taxes would have to double immediately and permanently, and all state taxes would have to increase by 20 percent immediately and permanently.

2. Benefits for Social Security, Medicare, and government pensions would have to be reduced by 50 percent immediately and permanently. At a current average monthly Social Security benefit payment of $1500, retired Americans would only receive $750; military pensions would be slashed from $1782 per month to $891, and Medicare spending would be cut from an average of $7500 to $3740 per recipient. Finally, the Medicare Part D (the prescription drug subsidy) enacted by President Bush in 2005 would be completely cancelled.

3. Or some combination of tax increases and benefit cuts would have to be made in addition to raising the retirement age, price controls on prescription drugs, and limiting or eliminating tax benefits to the wealthy.

A Nation of Lost Dreams

What happens when the people of a great nation no longer have affordable access to the essentials of modern life—healthcare, utilities, and retirement funds? That nation, or in America's case, the empire reverses towards a devastating decline. Why can't America provide healthcare for all of its citizens or reasonable prices for gasoline and utilities, yet can spend trillions of dollars as the "world's peace keeper"? How long can America remain the world superpower if it cannot provide these basic needs for its citizens?

Why is corporate America unable to follow through with its legally-binding guarantees to provide full pension benefits to its employees? How can Washington stand by and watch American jobs disappear as corporations earn record profits?

> "It's just a matter of time before we have some kind of economic event that I think is just going to change the political situation 180 degrees and make deficit reduction the order of the day. I don't know what it will be. I just know that when you've got gasoline spilling onto the floor of your house, it doesn't really matter where the spark comes from."

The "American Dream" can only exist if America maintains a competitive edge with foreign nations. However, due to the passage of free trade laws, competitive forces are acting from several regions throughout the world that do not play by fair rules. And this has forced American corporations to relocate or outsource overseas as the only way to remain competitive.

But for many of America's industries, it's too late. Unfair trade and pricing practices of China and Japan have already caused the collapse of critical industries such as steel, chemicals, rubber, furniture, and textiles, causing the permanent exportation of jobs and wealth out of America.

End of the Rainbow?

Déjà vu might well be on the minds of many who remember the early 1980s. Burdened with record inflation and unthinkable gasoline prices, Americans became even more nervous about their future, as Japan began flooding its products and cash into this nation, while millions of American jobs were exported, never to be seen again. Things were looking pretty bad for America at the time, causing many to rush into gold and silver. And of course, this led to record prices for these metals.

While America has not yet reached double-digit inflation, we already see record oil prices and rising prices in precious metals. But during the Reagan years, the government recognized what was happening and took a completely different stance on safeguarding intellectual property, igniting an explosion of venture capital investments to fuel the innovations of America's entrepreneurs. Consequently, the following decade gave rise to new industries that replaced those lost from the past.

Will Washington create opportunities that lead to a recovery from the most recent loss of millions of jobs overseas? Will they implement economic policies that will create a competitive landscape for free trade? If so, when and how will it occur? Or perhaps America will be stuck in this period for a decade or longer and only adjust to change once an economic meltdown occurs.

Similar to most other nations, America has experienced its fair share of crises. However, what has separated America from many other nations is that it has come out of each crisis even stronger, but only due to its empire status. But once America's decline forms a stronger trend, its ability to rebound from a large-scale disaster will be much more difficult, similar to all previous empires that inevitably entered their decline phase. Regardless, I am confident that America will survive the devastating corrections that lie ahead. However, there is going to be a huge price to pay for decades of overconsumption and financial mismanagement.

In the chapters that follow, I detail the destructive forces that are positioned to create economic devastation in America and serve as a stimulus for a greatly needed correction period. After I have exhausted this theory, I will discuss some ways investors can save their investment portfolios and perhaps profit both during the current secular bear market and during the potential apocalypse that appears inevitable.

Only by immediate and radical change can America avoid a major depression. And such change will only occur if enough Americans demand it from Washington.

PART II

WEAPONS OF
DESTRUCTION

6

FINANCIAL MISMANAGEMENT

Prior to the first phase in the abolishment of the gold standard in the early 1930s, the U.S. Treasury was limited by the Constitution in issuing only that amount of currency that could be backed by its gold reserves. But when the government began to exhaust its gold supply, it decided to remove the currency system from the gold standard, as discussed in Chapter One. However, foreign central banks still had gold-dollar exchange rights until 1971, when President Nixon severed the final link to the gold standard by removing all claims to gold by foreign nations. That action would mark a critical event for U.S. economic policy.

Ever since that time, the Federal Reserve has been able to distribute as much money as it wanted from the U.S. Treasury, which has enabled it to navigate the inflation-deflation cycle. And now, because holders of the dollar have no claims to gold or silver, the dollar only has meaning if America remains the world's economic engine. You might also recall the dollar's universal acceptance is strongly linked to mandatory payments for oil, as established originally by negotiations between Nixon and Saudi Arabia.

Judging by the performance of the dollar on the foreign currency exchange markets, the perception of the dollar's strength is in the decline. Despite unlimited control over the printing of currency notes by the Federal Reserve, one must wonder why major banks still use the gold standard and actually transfer gold bullion to settle intra-bank debts.

Federal and Trade Deficits

It should be no news to anyone with a pulse over the past three years that the federal deficit has gotten out of hand, in large part due to the trade deficit, which has been magnified by the trade imbalance with China. This imbalance has been fueled by Americans' addiction to spend credit combined with the disappearance of numerous manufacturing industries. Consequently, this reckless behavior has amassed record levels of consumer debt. Finally, combined with Bush's ineffective tax cuts and irresponsible spending, Americans have watched the national debt rise by nearly 50 percent in just 6 years. Yet, throughout his tenure there have been no real improvements in the economy.

Misconceptions of GDP

Washington likes the fact that Americans are spending, even if it has been for imported goods, and even though these purchases are made using credit because strong consumer activity keeps GDP numbers high, pointing to the illusion of economic growth. Since the stock market fallout that began in early 2000, Washington has been desperate to keep consumers spending at any cost, and this is creating damaging consequences in exchange for superficial, short-term gains.

Washington likes to extinguish any criticisms of large federal and trade deficits by pointing to GDP numbers, since "experts" claim that GDP is a direct measure of growth and thus living standards, while supporting the contention that deficits are a factor of many variables that have no real meaning. However, the overuse of GDP data as an indicator of economic strength has been one of the biggest errors made in the field of economics today.

The gross domestic product is a measure of the value of all goods and services produced in the national economy that are available for consumption. But GDP numbers say nothing about the source of consumption, whether it's from cash on hand or mounting debt. As well, GDP numbers include government spending, such as that for Katrina and the wars in Iraq and Afghanistan. It does not take a genius to realize that such expenditures have not resulted in improved living standards for Americans.

Finally, GDP can be calculated using constant or current dollars; the former does not consider the effects of inflation while the later does. Therefore, when making comparisons of GDP data over time, investors should only use constant dollar GDP data. Unfortunately, when GDP data is plastered throughout the media, rarely has the source of this calculation been mentioned, leaving investors to assume that in fact constant dollar GDP data has been reported. I will revisit this topic in more detail in Chapter Eleven.

As a result of its record trade imbalance and dependency on foreign debt, America is losing control and ownership of its wealth and most highly-prized assets. Already in the past decade, America has generated nearly $4 trillion in deficits that has not only added to the national debt, but has resulted in the exchange of over $1.3 trillion of U.S. assets due to direct foreign buyouts and acquisitions. In total, about 8,600 American companies have been bought by foreign interests during the past decade. And since foreign nations have been the primary financing arm of these deficits, America has essentially traded cheap consumer trinkets from Asia for a tremendous source of investment capital (see Chapter Fourteen Supplement in the appendix for a partial list of these companies).

What to Expect

All throughout this attempted economic recovery, the Greenspan-driven consumer spending credit spree has delivered misleading economic growth figures, while Americans face a healthcare crisis that has already forced hundreds of companies into bankruptcy, with the remaining survivors being forced to outsource, relocate overseas, or slash employee benefits. This growing trend in corporate America has left millions without health insurance and has created doubt about retirement assets for those not only relying on Social Security, but also for recipients of pension plans, public and private. Add another $9 trillion over the next decade for President Bush's Part D Medicare program and I cannot see the deficit shrinking anytime soon. Adding insult to injury is the fact that this drug subsidy plan is filled with coverage gaps (i.e. the "doughnut hole") and will really only benefit big pharma, while providing a false sense of security to seniors. Washington continues allows big pharma to charge what it wishes, thus avoiding the real problems.

Beginning in 2011, the first wave of baby boomers will reach full retirement age. And government benefits for these social programs will quickly mushroom to unthinkable levels, pushing the deficit and debt much higher due to higher mandatory expenditures. And because military spending and homeland security comprise a significant portion of discretionary spending, this is going to put an additional squeeze on mandatory spending, resulting in further pressure to cut Medicare, Medicaid, and Social Security benefits. Therefore, some combination of significant tax hikes and benefit cuts is likely after 2008.

Since deficits add to the total debt, we must view the federal debt as the real problem. Currently, *the national debt stands at 80 percent of the GDP*; a high number by any comparison in history. Accordingly, the national debt is certain to continue its ramped growth over the next several years even in the midst of expected tax hikes and benefit cuts. As the deficit continues to increase, it will be added to the nation's debt which could easily surpass 100 percent of GDP over the next 5 years (see Chapter Six Supplement for government estimates).

There is no way the dollar can mount any type of recovery at these debt levels. As a result, the dollar will continue to weaken along with the economy. Either way, America's record debt will continue to be surpassed in the coming years. Even massive benefit cuts will not reverse this trend, but would further harm the economy.

Adding to the demise of the dollar is the effect of America's record trade deficit. During the economic boom of the '90s, the trade deficit averaged about 1.1 percent of GDP. Today we see a different picture, with a *trade deficit at around 6 percent of GDP*. It is commonly accepted that when the trade deficit extends above 5 percent of GDP, the chances of major adverse economic consequences become very high, with a revaluation of the dollar being one.

Deficit Spending

It should be no mystery why America's trade imbalance has continued to increase at record rates during most of President Bush's leadership. America has become a nation of credit consumers, unlike generations before that were more balanced in consumption and production. This financial mismanagement is equally prominent within the U.S. government. *Prior to 1969, America was actually the world's largest creditor.* But since that time, America has held the title of the world's largest debtor, with Europe and Asia as its bankers. Deficit spending has become routine policy in Washington, enabling the government to spend more than it makes, shifting its debt burden to future generations. This has created a lack of financial accountability for many of Washington's costly and wasteful programs.

To finance this debt, the U.S. Treasury sells bonds, much of which are bought by foreign central banks. You see, it's in the best interest for China, Japan, and other manufacturing powerhouses to finance America's debt because these nations benefit two-fold.   First, they are purchasing what are considered the safest investments in the world—U.S. Treasury bonds, for which they receive interest payments.   Next, they are financing America's trade imbalance, thereby diminishing political pressure for trade restrictions from Washington.   Therefore, foreign nations have been loaning the American government money to minimize the effects of the trade imbalance, while American consumers continue to buy more imports, whose profits go towards building the infrastructure of developing nations like China and India.   This has to stop.

How and Why a Deficit is Formed

Each year the government proposes spending for the future fiscal year by creating its annual budget.   And when the expected expenditures exceed the estimated income, this is referred to as a *proposed budget deficit*, which would require the U.S. Treasury to borrow money in order to finance the shortage of income.   Generally, this is done by having the U.S. Treasury sell bonds and other forms of government debt to the American public and foreign central banks.   If all federal bonds and other debt obligations are added up, we obtain a measure of the federal debt, which increases whenever the government sells more bonds to finance deficit spending in a given year.

As long as the government spends more than it collects, it will create an annual deficit, which is added to the total national debt.   If Washington has a zero budget deficit one year, that doesn't mean the debt will go away; it just means the debt has not gotten any larger for that year.   Many Americans have seen the same effects with their credit cards. The amount they charge for the month and fail to pay (i.e. their monthly deficit) gets added to their total credit card debt or balance.   And of course, as the debt becomes larger, so do the interest payments.

Sometimes a deficit is planned by the government; other times it occurs because factors in the economy have reduced the amount of revenues or increased the amount of expenditures.   When President Bush passed his ineffective tax cuts aimed at the wealthy and corporate America, this assured Washington that government tax revenues would decline.   And due to the massive spending in Iraq, for Katrina, and Medicare Part D, record deficits were a certainty even without the effects of the huge trade deficit.   Finally, because these expenditures are not one-time items, they have created future liabilities which will continue to fuel future deficits for many years.

Figure 6-1. Balance on Current Account or Deficit (1925 to 2006)

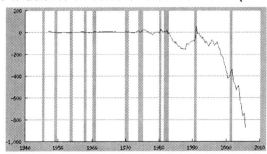

Source: U.S. Department of Commerce: Bureau of Economic Analysis
Prepared by: 2006 Federal Reserve Bank of St. Louis: research: stlouisfed.org
Shaded areas indicate recessions as determined by the NBER

As figure 6-1 clearly shows, each year since 1969, the federal government has spent more that it received causing a deficit. Even the four single-year surpluses that have been claimed since 1969 were created by accounting tricks (off-balance financing) and borrowing money from the Social Security, U.S. Postal Office, and American Indian trust funds.

Consequences of Deficits

Imagine if you were able to get secured loans anytime you needed. You could basically borrow as much money as you wanted even when your collateral was not enough to cover these loans. Because you borrowed so much money, there would be no way you could repay the debt so your co-signers would be responsible for repaying the loans. Unfortunately, the co-signers of Washington's debt are the American people. And *because much of the creditors of the national debt are foreign nations, foreign creditors have claims on assets held by the U.S. government—essentially taxes.* Ultimately, foreign nations can be thought of as the creditors of the American people. Due to the lack of taxpayer protest, the financial mismanagement by Washington has gone unchecked. As a result, future generations of Americans will be stuck with these enormous debt liabilities.

We have recently witnessed a drastic shift of the current account balance (see figure 6-4) from a surplus during Clinton's last years, to increasing deficit levels during each year of President Bush's two terms. The swing has been very drastic because these record deficit levels are expected to continue to soar throughout his term. The last time America experienced a similar turnaround was during the '80s, when President Reagan was battling the Cold War with the former Soviet Union. During that period there was great concern for the economy because Reagan reversed what was a surplus of $8 billion into a $147 billion deficit in 1987. As well, inflation was high, oil was at record prices, and many jobs were being lost overseas. *But President Bush's deficit trend will continue even after he leaves office because of the future liabilities he has created.*

During Reagan's tenure, the inflow of foreign capital was seen as a threat by many Americans. However, there was job growth during that period, although modest. And the investment capital from foreign nations actually helped America's productivity. Rather than corporate assets being bought from America as is occurring presently, money was invested into a variety of projects.

Thus far, the recent record deficits have not reached the levels (measured as a percentage of GDP) incurred during WWII, and throughout the '80s with the implementation of "Reaganomics." However, mounting liabilities for Iraq, the war against terrorism, and social insurance benefits for America's baby boomers could cause these records to be surpassed within the next decade. And this would crush the dollar even further, which would have drastic ramifications for America's already declining economy and standard of living.

One thing seems obvious about deficits. While they may not matter over any given year, *large annual deficits over an extended period will increase the total debt burden of the government, which will cause interest rates to rise and the dollar to fall.* This will lead to a restriction in credit available for consumers and business expansion. It is entirely possible that America's deficit and debt trends will lead to a series of financial crises that will push the dollar and the stock market lower over the next decade, with anemic consumer spending followed possibly by an increase in savings. Finally, you should not forget that *a weak dollar also serves as a strong force to keep oil prices high since oil can only be bought and sold with the dollar on the major global exchanges.*

What's Different this Time?

Will the current deficit trends surpass those during the Reagan years? There are many similarities between both periods for sure. As in the early '80s, America is currently struggling with record oil prices, while precious metals are soaring. Although we are not yet experiencing the type of inflation seen during Reagan's first term, I believe there is very good chance inflation will soon become the major problem stemming from America's consequential consumption-production disparity, continued high oil prices, and declining competitiveness. As well, similar to the Cold War, America is currently engaged in an unconventional war (although very different than the Cold War arms buildup). Finally, both periods share the trend of exportation of millions of jobs due to the development of Asian economies.

During the Reagan years, America had a good answer for job exportation—new laws that emphasized intellectual property protection. This policy reversal served to replace some of the economic benefits of its ailing manufacturing industries. However, what is the solution for job exportation today? Already, America is losing its innovation edge to Europe and Asia. Meanwhile, Asia still retains the top spot in manufacturing.

Consider the indisputable assertion that record inflation and high gas prices during Reagan's first term were the main reasons for the economic slowdown. However, the exportation of millions of jobs to Japan, while damaging to American industries and workers, was beneficial to the American consumer as a means of providing less expensive consumer goods.

During both of President Bush's terms, workers have been in pain as well, with the loss of over 5.5 million jobs between 2001 and 2003. And consumers have benefited from the effects of outsourcing and low interest rates. However, oil prices only began to soar after the recession of 2001. As well, inflation is nothing like that seen during the Reagan years. For the most part, during the 2001 to 2004 period, America experienced deflation (according to the manner in which the government calculates inflation numbers). However, this time things are different because both foreign and domestic investment is absent. America is also dealing with the aftermath of a stock market bubble. Record low interest rates have now shifted assets from this partially corrected bubble into the real estate market.

If in fact foreign investment is being pumped into the U.S. economy it certainly has not been responsible for any appreciable net job growth thus far. It appears that much of the foreign investment entering America is in the form of U.S. treasuries, which is doing nothing to help the economy, other than financing the mismanagement of America's record debt. In the past, foreign nations invested in America. But today they are interested in buying American businesses. That is not investing, that is owning; a big difference.

The Federal Budget

For each term in office, the president is responsible for four fiscal year budgets starting October 1ˢᵗ of the first year in office, and ending September 30ᵗʰ eight months after leaving office. Each year, the president creates an annual budget with the help of hundreds of financial experts. As a matter of fact, up to ten years of future annual budgets are created and refined yearly by a huge staff of officials, adding a new year as each one passes, while making revisions to previous budget forecasts. The general process is shown in figure 6.2 of the appendix.

From figure 6-2 (below), notice how spending for Medicaid, Medicare, Social Security, and interest payments—all mandatory spending items—are increasing. These expected increases are going to reduce the amount of income available for discretionary spending (the rest of the programs funded by the government). And as the baby boomers retire, this trend will continue to accelerate over the next several decades. I will explore these trends as well as their implications in further detail at a later time.

Figure 6-2. Total Federal Outlays for Fiscal Years 2005 to 2007

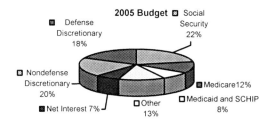

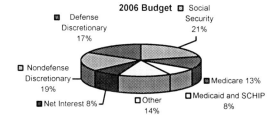

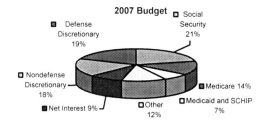

Source: OMB, FY 2005 Budget, February 2004

China's Role

For 2005, the federal deficit swelled to an all-time high of $726 billion, with $202 billion due to trade imbalances with China. Think about that number for a moment. That's about 9 percent of America's federal debt and almost 6 percent of the GDP. No doubt the deficit will move higher during Bush's remaining term before any chance of trailing off, and this alone will cause further devaluation of the dollar.

Over the past five years, America should have actually recorded a net trade surplus with China because of the dollar's low value relative to other currencies. But since China kept its currency tied to the dollar, the effect of a weak dollar did not manifest with China's trade imbalance. Although China officially unpegged its currency from the dollar in the late summer of 2005, it has since only allowed a minor appreciation (about 3 percent). Consequently, it is thought that China's currency is still anywhere from 40 to 50 percent undervalued.

Whether Washington can change this trend of record deficits or not will depend upon how much it pressures China to properly value its currency and how much it is willing to cut spending. However, I do not see either of these alternatives as a feasible means to lower the trade deficit over the next few years without further damaging the economy because American consumers are not strong enough to stand on their own without credit spending and inexpensive goods from abroad.

Between a Rock and a Hard Place

The U.S. government wants to strengthen the dollar but doesn't want consumer spending to drop. If America is successful in pressuring China to properly value its currency by say mid-2007 to at least 30 percent above present levels, this will increase the price of Chinese imports which will slow consumer spending. If on the other hand China does not value its currency appropriately and in a timely manner, the U.S. might impose tariffs on its goods, which would also diminish consumer spending. But in order to impose tariffs, Washington will have to answer to the WTO. So, there is really no way out of this mess other than for the U.S. economy to pick up significant steam, which simply isn't going to happen for at least the next several years at best.

On the other hand, China is not anxious to decouple its currency from the dollar since it owns over $1 trillion in U.S. treasuries and would therefore stand to lose up to 50 percent of this if the Yuan was fully valued. Of course, if Washington does nothing the deficit will continue to increase rapidly, causing a higher federal debt, higher interest rates (long and short), and a continued weak dollar. This will ultimately lead to a recession but could serve to correct the deficit due to decreased consumer spending.

> "The federal budget is on an unsustainable path, in which large deficits result in rising interest rates and ever-growing interest payments that augment deficits in future years."
>
> Alan Greenspan, former Federal Reserve Chairman

Washington already knows all of this but President Bush wanted to hold off on another recession until he secured his second term. Greenspan helped in this matter by keeping short-term rates so low for an extended period. But low rates cannot rescue

America from the other financial problems that have been in the making for over two decades. As a matter of fact, Greenspan's monetary policy has all but assured the economic correction will be even more severe. Quite possibly, a recession could worsen into a depression if other factors come into play which I will discuss in the coming chapters. *Regardless what happens with the dollar, the deficit and the Yuan, both short- and long-term rates are going higher and that alone will stifle consumer spending.*

Fueling China's Economy with American Debt

Even a proper valuation of the Yuan will not resurrect the estimated 3 million manufacturing jobs lost in America since 2000 as a result of China's unfair trade practices. *For every $1 of American goods sold to China in 2005, China sold $6 in goods to America.* More important, virtually none of the goods bought by American consumers was absolutely needed, but only provided a lower price alternative, which stimulated consumer "bargain" spending. What this spending did however, was make it appear as if America's GDP growth was reasonable. But in order to buy these inexpensive goods, many Americans maxed out their credit cards or took out home equity loans in the midst of the biggest real estate bubble in history. But GDP numbers don't correct for credit spending.

In contrast, *most of China's imports from America were in the form of food and natural resources; all vital ingredients for their economic revolution.* Americans continue to consume more than they produce while China keeps producing goods to feed the appetite of credit-addicted Americans. And China is reinvesting these profits into its infrastructure, getting stronger each day as America's competitiveness and standard of living weakens. Meanwhile, the free trade policies embraced by Washington continue to allow China and other foreign nations to destroy American manufacturing and many other jobs from virtually every other industry.

Finally, Bush's massive spending for Iraq and Katrina also helped GDP figures. And *as much as 40 percent of the recent GDP growth during 2004 to 2005 has been attributable to the cash supplied by home equity loans.* Is GDP data valid if it occurred primarily by consumer credit and government spending for programs that have not resulted in a net improvement of American lifestyles? Definitely not. As figure 6.3 (appendix) shows, America's deficit has grown over the past several years while Asia and oil-exporting nations have registered surpluses.

When Deficits Turn Into Troubles

Most politicians (including President Bush) claim that deficits don't really matter and are just "numbers on paper." And to some extent they are right since the government has the flexibility to determine what constitutes a tax, receipt, payment, liability, or credit, and can therefore raise taxes as needed and record liabilities in any way it deems fit.

While there are two different schools of thought behind the methods to create economic expansions, you can decide for yourself which seems more reasonable. On the one hand, some believe that deficits do not matter and are unrelated to economic growth due to the reasons mentioned above. On the other hand, others subscribe to the Austrian economic thought which states that economic expansions can only arise from savings and investment, whereby increased production and sales drive the economy.

If you agree with the later viewpoint, you should consider the premise that America has created a phantom boom over the past two decades and a post-bubble recovery illusion through the use of credit (deficit) spending. This illusion of economic growth has masked the diminished domestic productivity needed to establish a true balance of trade.

How can Washington continue to spend at twice the growth rate of the economy? Where are the jobs and increased living standards that were supposed to come from this reckless government spending and series of tax cuts? *If foreign nations continue to finance these deficits as they have to the tune of more than 80 percent since Bush entered office, and without clear economic progress as a result of these loans, how can one not agree that America is slowly selling itself off to foreigners?*

> *"The scary part is that there doesn't seem to be any prospects for getting the deficit under control.....raising the debt ceiling is a sort of red flag that says, 'You've got a real problem here.' "*
>
> **Alice M. Rivlin**
> Senior Fellow and Director, Greater Washington Research Program, Brookings Institution

Figure 6-3 shows the dollar's slide since President Bush entered office. As you can see, it has broken a critical support trend line and appears as if it will continue this downward trend for several years to come due to mismanagement of debt.

Figure 6-3. U.S. Dollar Exchange Rate versus 26 Currencies (Y/Y%)

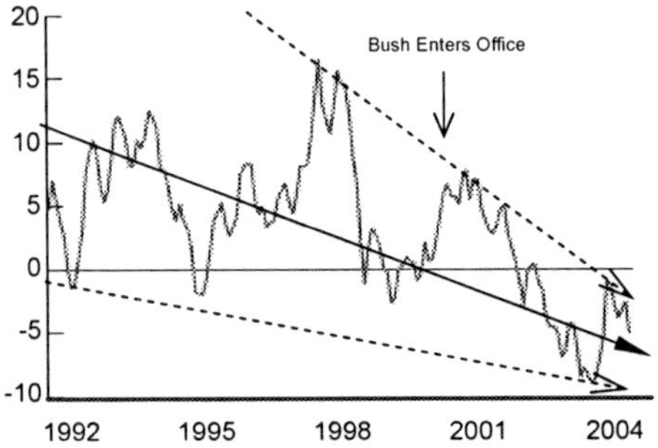

Source: Federal Reserve Board of Governors

Box 6-1: How Deficits Can Hurt Consumers

All major currencies of the world are bought and sold the on the foreign exchange market known as the forex. This market determines the price of each currency relative to others and is a critical factor controlling imports and exports. One of the major factors that influence a currency's value is the financial stability of the government. As well, a nation's trade balance, national debt, productivity growth, inflation and interest rate trends also determine relative currency rates. When a nation is under heavy deficit spending, the federal debt accumulates and this tends to weaken that nation's currency. The result is that in order to keep foreign investment in U.S. treasuries attractive to foreigners, the Fed must raise interest rates to compensate for the weak dollar.

If investors are no longer interested in owning U.S. treasuries, the U.S. government will not be able to pay its bills and will become insolvent. And because the percentage of U.S. debt held by foreign investors now stands at over 50 percent, it is critical to keep raising interest rates so new auctions for U.S. Treasury securities will draw sufficient interest from investors. Finally, since U.S. Treasury coupon rates are tied to interest rates, this is a dynamic that affects all Americans, causing credit card, auto and home loans to increase. The consequence is that when the government is mismanaging its books, Americans pay the price in many ways. This illustrates one way Americans are paying foreign nations for the price of overconsumption relative to productivity.

Off-Balance Financing

Within the next few years there is a very good chance that the deficit could surpass record levels reached during the Cold War Era and perhaps even WWII relative to GDP. However, in order to fully assess the extent of Washington's financial mismanagement, we must also consider the amount of funds that are classified as "off-budget" (off-balance) because this accounting trick is often used to minimize deficit numbers. For instance, in early 2005 you may recall President Bush approved another $82 billion off-budget for defense spending, primarily earmarked for Iraq and Afghanistan. These off-balance items do not show up when the Congressional Budget Office (CBO) releases budget data.

By allocating a large amount of expenditures to the off-budget category, the deficit will appear smaller to Americans who might otherwise express concern and criticism regarding the financial mismanagement by the president. Social Security and U.S. Postal Service trust funds are considered off-balance items as a standard treatment. But there are many other programs in this category, all referred to as "special items."

> "We can borrow and borrow, but eventually there will be a day of reckoning."
>
> Joseph Stiglitz, President Clinton's chief economic adviser from 1995 to 1997

Furthermore, unlike America's public companies that are required to report liabilities in a financially responsible manner, *the U.S. government is not legally obligated to report the future value of annual liabilities generated by the annual budget deficit.* The CBO merely records the amount overspent each year without accounting for the expected appreciation on the debt that will occur over the life of the loan due to interest expense.

For instance, over the course of 10 years, a budget deficit of say $800 billion (which is funded by selling 10-year treasury notes paying around 4.5 percent) will incur a total cost of borrowing of around $650 billion. And when this deficit is funded over a thirty year period at 6 percent, the cost of borrowing goes to over $2 trillion (not including principal). But these future liabilities are not reported. Incidentally, *this is similar to the manner in which Enron cooked its books.* Washington feels that it does not need to account for future liabilities because it can always raise taxes or cut funding from any government program. And although Social Security and Medicare benefits are thought to be guaranteed, (mandatory expenditures) Washington can reduce benefits at any time.

As you can see from figure 6-4, while the Clinton years were mainly on-budget, the Reagan and Bush years showed large off-budget expenditures. But remember that the deficit disappears each year and becomes a part of the growing national debt. Hence, it is the transient nature of the deficit which might explain why more Americans fail to recognize it as a problem since the national debt is typically not mentioned by Washington.

Current trends show increasing levels of off-budget financing and increasing annual deficits. What this means is that the deficit is worse than it appears and it is going to get much worse before it gets better. Consequently, the national debt will continue to surpass record levels for many years to come, causing further financial risk to the U.S. economy. Of course any improvements in the annual deficit and total debt outstanding will be a matter of subjective debate, since they will most likely involve cuts in critical domestic programs for Americans.

Figure 6-4. Historical Budget Surplus/Deficit as a Share of GDP (1962-2004)

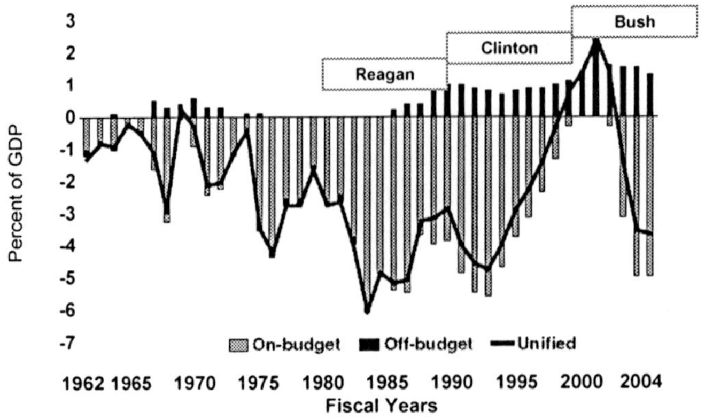

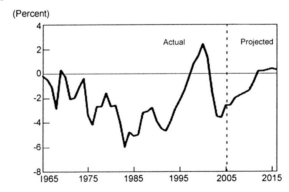

Source: Office of Management and Budget and Congressional Budget Office

According to the CBO's estimates, the deficit is expected to decline beginning in 2006 until it reverses into a surplus starting in 2011 and continuing through 2016 (refer to figure 6.4 of the appendix for a chart of outlays and revenues). It is difficult for me to see how Washington will be able to produce these expected changes even with the use of off-balance financing, unless it raises taxes and slashes spending across the board.

Figure 6-5. Federal Surplus or Deficit (as a percentage of GDP)

Source: Congressional Budget Office
See figure 6.5 (appendix) for the CBO's error measurements associated with this forecast

Mandatory Spending on the Rise

Over the past few decades, the percentage of mandatory spending for the annual budget has increased dramatically. Mandatory spending encompasses all programs that the government has promised, such as Social Security, Medicaid, and Medicare, as well as debt service payments on U.S. Treasury securities. *These spending hikes reflect the growing income gap between the poor and wealthy in America.*

As America's baby boomers reach retirement age, mandatory expenditures are going to balloon, leaving less for discretionary spending. Keep in mind that military spending is considered discretionary. However, one could argue that global hostilities have made a certain level of military spending mandatory for the foreseeable future. Therefore, as mandatory payments continue to increase, you can decide for yourself which programs will be cut. Alternatively, taxes will be raised. Otherwise, critical programs such as education and scientific research could be targets of budget cuts.

Comparison of World Deficits

Each year since 1969, when you count off-balance items, Congress has spent more money than it has received and has therefore generated a budget deficit. And in order to keep government operations going, the U.S. Treasury Department has borrowed money (by selling U.S. treasuries) to cover the deficit in order to meet Congress' budgetary appropriations. The total borrowed thus far is over $8.5 trillion and continues to grow daily. And when you count the money borrowed from Social Security and other trust funds, the total federal debt has been estimated at over $16 trillion.

You see, Washington can "borrow" money from these trust funds to cover other expenses because any shortfalls will not be reported on the deficit statement. As discussed, they will be included as off-balance items. Therefore, *even when Washington claims to have a surplus, it can still spend more than it takes in due to expenses categorized as off-balance.* Of course debt is a burden for which interest payments must be made. *The interest expense on the National Debt was $352,350,252,507.90 at the end of 2005, representing the third largest expense in the federal budget.* Only Defense and social programs such as The Departments of Health and Human Services (Social Security and Medicare), HUD, and Agriculture (food stamps) were higher.

The fact is that *no other member of the G-7, as well as any other first-tier world economy has a current account deficit.* On the other hand, as figure 6-6 demonstrates, America's current account deficit is sixth from the highest among all developed nations. Such a statistic should cause one to question whether the U.S. is really the world's economic superpower it claims to be. I too could claim to be an economic superpower if I spent more than I had and was able to run up endless debt.

Figure 6-6. Current Account Balance of Payments, as a percentage of GDP (2001-2003)

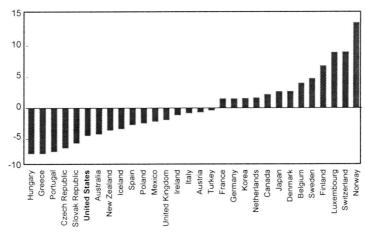

Source: OCED

How Did We Get in This Mess?

One cannot place the full blame of the current deficit problem on President Bush. He happened to enter office with a big mess that has continued to get worse mainly due to the consequences of the Internet bubble, for which Alan Greenspan is to blame. Even before Bush entered office, President Clinton rode the coattails of Greenspan's loose monetary policies which helped the stock market soar to new heights, and this created a global excess of cash. But things were different then. Companies had tremendous investment capital supplied by a booming stock market, and money was spilling out from the foundations of most American companies; mainly from the high-tech industry.

During the late '90s, many companies were reporting earnings gains from pension plan returns and awarding ridiculous amounts of stock options to even entry-level workers as a way to minimize cash payouts. Of course during that time, stock options were not expensed on income statements. But after the fallout in early 2001, it was clear that most high-tech companies would have to scramble to survive.

As consumers stopped spending, inventories continued to rise, causing what was thought up until recently as a recession (March 2001 to November 2001). And when 9/11 occurred, the economy would continue its downward spiral. As earnings melted, hundreds of companies faced record write-downs and write-offs, many leading to accounting scandals, forcing dozens of bankruptcies in the high-tech sector. And many companies that escaped these perils faced another problem that would only get worse in the coming years—underfunded pension plans.

Attempts to realign America's economy began on two fronts; one by Washington and the other by corporate America. As a way to stimulate consumer spending, Greenspan lowered interest rates 15 consecutive times, finally reaching a 43-year low of 1 percent in 2003. Meanwhile, President Bush continued his series of tax cuts while starting a war in Iraq.

For corporate America, everything was different. Faced with the consequences of a struggling economy, most companies utilized the low rates to refinance or pay off debt, issued stock repurchase plans to raise earnings per share, and focused on downsizing and raising cash flows for the purpose of holding it rather than for domestic investments.

> "The US dollar is facing an imminent collapse and the global economy will suffer a catastrophe when it is rejected as the currency for trade. But the catastrophe will come one day because even the most powerful country in the world cannot repay loans amounting to seven trillion dollars."
>
> Former Malaysian Prime Minister Mahathir Mohamad

After no signs of improvement, corporate America increased overseas expansions and outsourcing as a way to reduce expenses. The component of the trade deficits due to the collapse of domestic manufacturing has continued to increase nearly every year since the inception of NAFTA (figure 6-7). And when China entered the WTO in 2001, things got even worse for American trade. But U.S. companies have had little choice but to outsource, with skyrocketing healthcare costs, underfunded pensions, and the lure of Indian and Chinese workers willing to do the same work as Americans for one-fifth the price.

Even in the early stages of the fallout, most officials were still in the dark. Just as

President Clinton left office in 2001, the Congressional Budget Office was still predicting trillions of dollars in surpluses for Bush's first term. But we all know what has happened. A sluggish economy finally swung the free trade door wide open, causing the redistribution of income and wealth from American consumers into the hands of foreign nations.

Figure 6-7. Components of U.S. Trade Deficit, Manufacturing vs. Everything Else

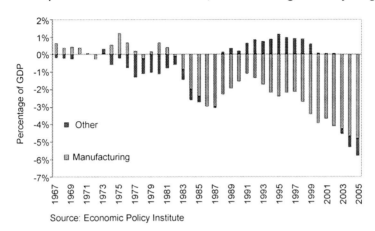

Source: Economic Policy Institute

Where Do We Go From Here?

The most recent annual deficits have served to highlight America's long period of declining competitiveness. Thus far, interest rates have remained low due to the willingness of foreign nations to finance America's financial gluttony. But this may change soon, as a weak dollar represents the longer-term consequence of America's declining competitiveness and record debt.

Goldman Sachs estimates the deficit will grow by $5 trillion over the next decade while the bipartisan Concord Coalition expects it to grow to $5.7 trillion. These forecasts account for reasonable assumptions for President Bush's war initiatives in Iraq and Afghanistan, and the extension of his tax cuts. Yet the estimates still neglect to factor in the $9 trillion expected over the next decade due to Medicare Part D.

Several organizations including the OECD and CBO have concluded that the deficits generated by President Bush "will neutralize or even reverse any economic benefits of his tax cuts." *Furthermore, they concluded that these tax cuts will raise the deficits and hinder economic growth.* Even the Federal Reserve has concluded that Bush's dividend tax elimination has not positively affected the stock market, but that is obvious to everyone.

President Bush's deficit spending has not boosted the economy because the largest expenditures of federal funds have gone towards the war in Iraq, Katrina disaster relief, and to pay the interest on the national debt—none of which have improved living standards in America. Meanwhile, foreign nations have financed most of the President's deficits. *Since March 2001 through September 2005, foreign creditors purchased 81 percent of all new U.S. Treasury securities (i.e. they financed 81 percent of the deficits).* This has led to an increase in the total share of the national debt by foreigners to about 50 percent.

Federal Debt

Thus far in America, the new millennium has been marked by record spending in defense and special situations, such as hurricane Katrina relief, three ineffective tax cuts (2001, 2002 and 2003), Part D Medicare, and the wars in Iraq and Afghanistan. Funding for these programs has come from borrowed money which has resulted in an increase in the interest paid (at 1.7 percent of GDP) on the national debt (at nearly 70 percent of the GDP).

As we have seen, the national debt grows each year there is a deficit. And in order to continue financial operations, Washington must issue treasury securities to finance its spending activities. Debt held by the Federal Reserve System is purchased by printing money; the purpose of these "open market operations" is to put more currency into circulation. But debt also grows when the nation's budget is over-expensed, which can occur if tax revenues do not meet expectations. And as we shall see later, tax revenues as a percentage of GDP have been at record lows despite record corporate profits (figure 15-1).

The problem with holding debt is familiar to most Americans who have run up large credit card bills. While access to credit can provide an improvement in living conditions and more business opportunities, debt is poorly managed by most consumers, sometimes leading to bankruptcy. Likewise, we have seen strong evidence of government mismanagement of debt for over three decades.

Benefits and Dangers of Leverage

When you borrow funds you do not have in order to pay for items, this creates financial leverage. And because leverage is a double-edged sword, it can work either in your favor or against you. Many large corporations make use of both operational and financial leverage in order to increase earnings. When operational leverage is used, this may or may not require debt income, but could be a result of using existing cash flows or changes to the business that result in economies of scale (savings due to volume). Some examples of operational leverage are increasing production, marketing, and new business expansion projects.

When companies utilize financial leverage, they take on debt that can be used for a variety of purposes, most often for operational leverage. Well-run companies manage their debt load by refinancing (when interest rates decline) or debt retirement (when cash flows from operations are sufficient to finance future operations). The point is that *companies alter debt levels to reflect internal business conditions as well as external economic conditions.* It is through the prudent use of debt and interest-rate management that many corporations are able to survive difficult economic environments and changes in their business cycle.

However, Washington has not managed debt in this way. All it has managed to do is increase debt exponentially for two decades (figure 6-8). That alone implies a decline in living standards because eventually someone has to pay for this debt. And in the meantime, escalating debt has increased debt service payments, reducing funds available for critical programs such as scientific research.

Figure 6-8. Growth of the National Debt (corrected for inflation in 2000 dollars)

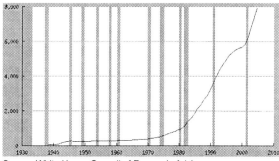

Source: White House Council of Economic Advisors
Prepared by: 2006 Federal Reserve Bank of St. Louis: research: stlouisfed.org
Shaded areas indicate recessions as determined by the NBER

The premise is that if you can produce a return on investment of all outstanding debt that is greater than the return of investing the money in low-risk funds (after a risk element has been factored in), then you have made good use of the debt. However, no leverage is good when it has become too high since it can hinder the ability of the company (or in this case the government) to make payments of interest and principal. Consequently, after being held to these mandatory payments, very little is left for investment and savings.

When we consider the amount of debt held by the government (and consumers), we should try to measure the return on investment resulting from the use of this debt. However, because many government programs have long-term benefits, it can be extremely difficult to calculate an accurate figure. If we examine long-term trends that address this bottom line, it can be a useful exercise. The trends I would consider to be the most relevant are real wage growth, standard of living, poverty levels, and inexpensive access to basic goods and services such as energy and healthcare.

"Under existing tax rates and reasonable assumptions about other spending, the federal budget is on an unsustainable path, in which large deficits result in rising interest rates and ever-growing interest payments that augment deficits in future years…Unless that trend is reversed, at some point these deficits would cause the economy to stagnate or worse."

Alan Greenspan, April 2005
Federal Reserve Chairman (1987-2005)

Figure 6-9. Deficits With and Without Tax Cuts (billions of dollars, 2000-2014)

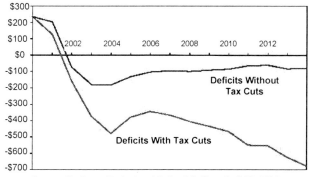

Source: Center on Budget and Policy Priorities, April 23, 2004.

History of U.S. Debt Policy

America was not always owned by the world. For the first few decades of the last century, America had no real debt problems. Notable levels of debt only began to appear in 1929 at $16.9 billion, just prior to the Great Depression. But after FDR created the New Deal, America's debt began to rise significantly. However, this enormous debt spending was justified since it gradually extinguished America's greatest financial crisis and provided stability to millions of devastated and hopeless Americans.

Just a few years later when World War II commenced, the United States, still under the leadership of FDR began true deficit spending, which resulted in an enormous debt burden. By 1940, the national debt had grown to $42.9 billion, but quickly soared to $258 billion due to America's participation in the war. From 1945 through 1961 the debt grew minimally, increasing to only $296 billion by 1961. When adjusted for inflation, the debt actually declined significantly.

Over the next twenty years, America would fight in Korea and next in Vietnam. It was also during this period that America became involved in a "space race" with the former Soviet Union. Yet, despite these costly undertakings, the debt only grew modestly increasing to $789 billion by 1979. Regardless, the economy could easily handle this level of debt due to low inflation and solid GNP growth up through that period.

> "The budget should be balanced; the treasury should be refilled; public debt should be reduced; and the arrogance of public officials should be controlled."
>
> Cicero. 106-43 B.C.

America's real debt problems began during President Reagan's administration in 1981 with the passage of the *Emergency Recovery Tax Act* which lowered taxes but increased spending, notably for the military due to the Cold War. In addition, America was faced with double-digit inflation. These forces combined to create a huge debt, rising from $930 billion in 1980 to $2.6 trillion in 1988. *In only eight years, Reagan managed to triple the debt despite no real war, while the previous thirty years saw a 150 percent increase in debt amidst the Vietnam War.*

During the Clinton administration, debt spending slowed as America's economy was experiencing tremendous growth. By 1997, the national debt reached $5.4 trillion and rose only to $5.6 trillion by the end of 2000. However, since the election of George W. Bush the debt has begun to rise dramatically. In only six years, the debt has risen from 5.8 trillion in 2001 to its current high of over 8.5 trillion dollars, or by nearly 50 percent, due to ineffective tax cuts (figure 6-9), spending in Iraq, and the trade imbalance.

In early 2006, the U.S. government had to raise the debt ceiling once again in order to continue to finance another deficit; an event that's occurred more than 70 times over the past 50 years. As a consumer, imagine asking your bank to give you more secured loans each year. In order to be approved, the bank would do a credit analysis to determine if you had sufficient increases in income and net worth to support the additional debt. I have performed a credit analysis on the financial position of the U.S. government, and in order to justify lending it further money, the coupon rate of U.S. Treasury bonds would have to be in excess of 8 percent. And as the economy continues to wind down, an 11 percent coupon might not be unreasonable. Higher inflation would raise this value further.

Box 6-2: Attempts to Control Federal Spending

Balanced Budget and Emergency Deficit Control Act of 1985 (Gramm-Rudman-Hollings)
This law tried to mandate a balanced budget in the midst of the massive defense spending for the Cold War by creating a set of federal deficit targets for Congress and the President to meet over a six-year period. The federal deficit was to be decreased each year until it reached zero by 1991. If Congress and the President could not agree on a budget that met the target in any given year, automatic and equal reductions would occur in defense and non-defense expenditures.

Politicians liked this law because it reduced spending without forcing them to vote against popular programs, enabling them to face voters without the threat of blame for voting for programs cuts. Unfortunately, the GRH ultimately failed, leaving the government with a $269.5 billion deficit by 1991. Congress discovered that there was a loophole in the law that allowed it to pass spending bills that took effect two or three years later. And because the GRH only set the deficit estimate for one year at a time these bills passed through. Furthermore, in July of 1990, a special exception in the law took effect and suspended automatic cuts due to recessionary conditions. The combination of spending bills, the suspension of automatic budget cuts, and the lower federal revenues caused by the declining economy all added to the enormous budget deficit.

Budget Enforcement Act (BEA) of 1990
This law combined spending caps with a "pay-as-you-go" provision to limit discretionary spending. Budget reductions elsewhere had to counteract any new program that required additional spending. If offsetting cost reductions could not be found, then across-the-board spending cuts would be made to offset the extra costs. Although the BEA was harder to get around than the GRH, it only applied to discretionary spending. Therefore Social Security, Medicare, and Medicaid were exempt from the provisions. As well, the BEA was to be suspended if the economy entered a "low-growth phase," or if the President declared an emergency.

Omnibus Budget Reconciliation Act of 1993
The third attempt by Washington to curtail the deficit was the President Clinton's *Omnibus Budget Reconciliation Act of 1993*, which aimed to cut approximately $500 billion from the deficit over a five-year period. The major provisions of this package were tax increases and spending reductions. Specifically, this act made the personal income tax even more progressive, and targeted the richest percentage of Americans for a tax increase. While this law was somewhat effective in controlling the deficit, it has had no predecessor since President Bush entered office.

Deficit Reduction Act of 2005
Signed into law by President Bush in February 2005, it was designed to cut the budget deficit by $39 billion. Thus far, it has been ineffective.

GDP-Adjusted Debt

Let's take a look at debt as a percentage of GDP since that seems to be the most reasonable gauge of historical debt liability. In business analysis, the most common measure of relative debt load is the debt-to-equity ratio. However, I also like to look at debt-to-revenue and debt-to-free cash flow ratios to determine a company's ability to service debt with future expected and current cash flows, respectively. In the case of the government, the GDP would be similar to revenues (in the form of tax revenues from commerce transactions), which can be thought of as cash flows. Similar to a bank that looks at net income or wages when assessing credit worthiness for a loan, the nation's GDP represents a fraction of available the revenues that can justify a certain debt load.

Figure 6-10 traces the course of America's debt as a percentage of GDP. The nation's debt peaked at 121.7 percent of GDP in 1946 because of World War II spending. By 1980, debt-to-GDP ratio was about 33 percent. Thereafter, the national debt soared, nearly doubling to the 60 percent range during the administrations of President Reagan and the first President George Bush.

During the Clinton years, the debt reached 67.3 percent of GDP in 1996. But budget surpluses (due to off-balance financings) drove the national debt back down to about 57 percent in 2001. *As of mid-2006, the debt stood at an estimated 68.7 percent of GDP.* While the 2006 budget forecast has predicted a 70 percent debt/GDP ratio by 2010, financial estimates of government expenditures are almost always on the low end.

> *"We're seeing the future. The decisions that have been made over the last five years have resulted in the chickens coming home to roost."*
>
> Bruce Bartlett,
> Former Treasury official, George H.W. Bush Administration

Figure 6-10. Federal Debt as a Percentage of GDP

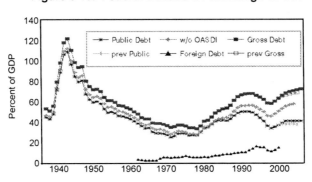

> Note that while the deficit as a percentage of GDP has not yet surpassed that during President Reagan's tenure or during WWII, (as discussed in the previous section), the debt as a percentage of GDP has already surpassed the Reagan years.

Source: Federal Reserve and Bureau of Economic Analysis

By 2010, the percentage of American workers versus retirees will still be relatively high. But by 2020, this ratio will have declined significantly due to the retirement of up to half of the 76 million baby boomers. *Not only will the lowered tax revenues drive the debt-to-GDP ratio higher, but added costs of Medicare, Medicaid, and Social Security benefits will add further strain to the system.*

According to some estimates by the budget administration, assuming all Social Security benefits are paid and Medicaid and Medicare expenses grow by rates that are lower than current (which is remarkably conservative), *by 2050 the debt will be nearly 450 percent of the GDP without any tax increases. This debt ratio would place the U.S. in the same financial position as Venezuela, with over 21 percent of GDP going just to pay the interest on the debt.* Currently, that figure stands at around 1.7 percent of GDP for interest-only payments.

Dependence on Foreign Debt

America's growing dependence on foreign debt has perhaps been no more significant than during today's world, filled with complex and conflicting social and political agendas, tensions in the Middle East, and China's commitment to become a world power. Today, the percentage of national debt held by foreign interests (from U.S. treasuries) is around 50 percent and expected to go higher in the next few years (figures 6-

11 and 6-12).

As China moves towards a more diverse economy, it will gradually wean itself off dependence of the U.S. consumer and will therefore have no further need to finance the poor spending practices of the U.S. government. *As well, with the weakness of the dollar expected to continue, foreign governments may soon lose interest in buying more treasuries, especially if interest rates do not rise and remain high enough to compensate for the dollar's weakness.* Finally, it is entirely possible that we could witness a global shift from a dollar-denominated world economy to a more widespread global acceptance of the Euro, or in the very least a flight to gold bullion by Asian nations as a way to hedge against the fall of the dollar.

Figure 6-11. Foreign Holdings of Federal Debt

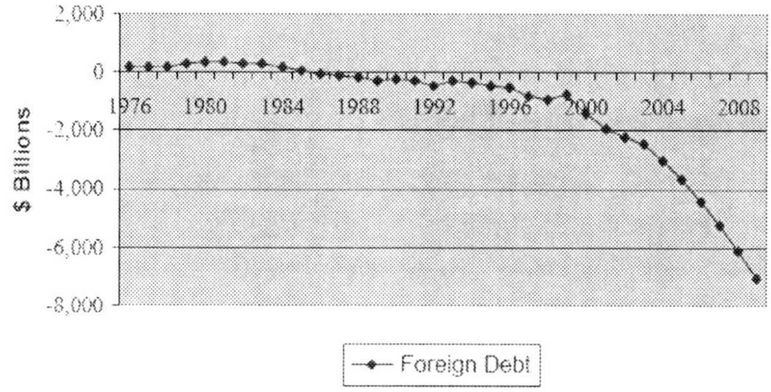

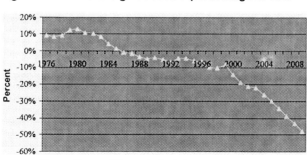

Source: Bureau of Economic Analysis

But for the present, the world is still highly dependent upon the American economic engine, fueled by the reckless spending habits of Washington and American consumers. Presently, it's still in the best interests of nations to continue loaning the U.S. government money to finance its debt. However, at some point, there will be diminishing returns for foreign holders of U.S. treasuries, as American consumers taper off their spending and the dollar fails to rebound. This could trigger the beginning stages of a major economic disaster.

Figure 6-12. Net foreign debt as a percentage of GDP

Source: Bureau of Economic Analysis

Financial Terrorism

A high debt burden financed by foreign nations destroys U.S. sovereignty because the American economy becomes more dependent on the actions and political motives of foreign governments, much like its foreign dependency on oil. *How can America claim to be the world superpower when it is the world's largest debtor?* No person or nation can ever be truly "free" if they are a debtor since creditors by definition have a claim on assets of the debtor.

China and other foreign creditors could wage an economic war against America by threatening to dump their huge holdings of U.S. treasuries or even by threatening to not purchase anymore, driving the value of the dollar sharply downward and interest rates to double digits. This thought has been reinforced by former Treasury Secretary Lawrence Summers, who has warned about "A kind of global balance of financial terror," noting America's dependency on "the discretionary acts of what are inevitably political entities in other countries."

Interest Expense on the Debt

The monthly Interest Expense represents the interest expense on the U.S. Government's Debt Outstanding at the end of each month. The interest expense on the Debt includes interest for Treasury notes and bonds; foreign and domestic series certificates of indebtedness, notes and bonds; Savings Bonds; as well as Government Account Series (GAS), State and Local Government series (SLGs), and other special purpose ("special interest") securities, such as those issued to the Social Security trust funds when Congress has used the surpluses. The amortized discount or premium on bills, notes and bonds is also included in Interest Expense data. The fiscal year Interest Expense represents the total interest expense on the Debt Outstanding for a given fiscal year.

For 2005 alone, $352 billion of American taxpayer money was spent by the government just to make interest payments to holders of U.S. Treasury bonds (see appendix tables 6.3 and 6.4). Meanwhile, during that same year, NASA only received $15 billion, the NIH $28 billion, Department of Education $61 billion, and the Department of Transportation received $133 billion.

Clearly, the interest expense is already damaging federal funding for critical programs. For 2006, federal funding of many of America's most vital programs will fail to keep up with inflation. Notably, for the first time in over two decades, NIH funding failed to keep up with inflation, rising by only 0.5 percent. What this means is that, as the interest payments on the national debt are increased, several critical programs will continue face budget cuts.

The 30-Year is Returning: A Coincidence?

Back in 2001, the U.S. Treasury Department announced that it would stop holding auctions for new 30-year U.S. Treasury bonds by early 2002. Subsequently, in less than two years after these auctions stopped, short and long-term rates were at 40-year lows. Looking ahead, one could reasonably assume that, with interest rates at these levels the demand for the 30-year would surely be low. Therefore, if you think the timing of this announcement and the subsequent lowing of rates were unrelated events, then you missed the message sent by Washington.

In my opinion, Washington realized the economy was in such bad shape that Greenspan would have to collapse short-term rates in order to stimulate consumer spending. If the U.S. Treasury continued to auction off new bonds while rates dropped, this could have created a problem with the yield curve due to decreased demand in the secondary markets. And this would have jeopardized the reckless deficit spending by President Bush. However, as I had anticipated, in 2005, *the Treasury Department announced that it would bring back auctions for the 30-year bonds, expected to commence by early 2007. What does that imply about the future direction of long-term rates?*

Consumer Debt

Similar to the U.S. government, consumers have embraced the "buy now, pay later" mentality. Since the onset of the most recent recession in March 2001, consumers have been utilizing inexpensive credit provided by the Fed; it's been a boom in credit spending unlike anything ever seen by anyone in America. Unfortunately, over the same period, improvements in employment, job quality and wage growth have been difficult to spot unless you live in India or China. But *this credit bubble has been forming for over two decades as a way for the bottom 80 percent of Americans to maintain their living standards amidst sparse real wage gains and skyrocketing costs of healthcare and higher education.*

American Consumers

The problem with most consumers is that open access to credit has made them focus on consumption more than production and saving because they do not realize the full ramifications of credit spending. Americans want and think they deserve someone to look after their pets each day, take care of their lawns, and park their cars, when in fact, most people who pay for these services cannot afford them and are using this time for leisure or inefficient production. As a result, Americans now have dangerous levels of consumer and mortgage debt (see tables 6.5 and 6.6 of the appendix). Sadly, many *Americans are running in overdrive, pushing forward each day with two-hour commutes to jobs that are no longer secure, just to pay the bills for the vices they really do not need.*

There have been numerous studies at retail shopping centers, fast food restaurants, bars, etc in America. And the *overwhelming evidence points to overspending by the use of credit cards for things consumers would not normally purchase at all or in higher amounts than if they had used cash.* McDonalds finally realized this and its recent introduction of credit card payments has led to record profits, despite lack of product innovation and noted adverse health effects of many of its menu items.

Finally, the misuse of credit by the typical American household has resulted in a boom in the debt collection industry, with over 500 companies (2005 data) up from just 12 in 1996. What have many done to pay their debt? They have refinanced their homes and even their credit cards through low-interest promotional transfers. *While greedy consumer spending behaviors created the boom in credit spending in the '90s, today we see evidence of necessary credit spending to pay for basic necessities* such as groceries, utilities, and prescription medications by millions of Americans.

Figure 6-13. Total Consumer Debt Outstanding

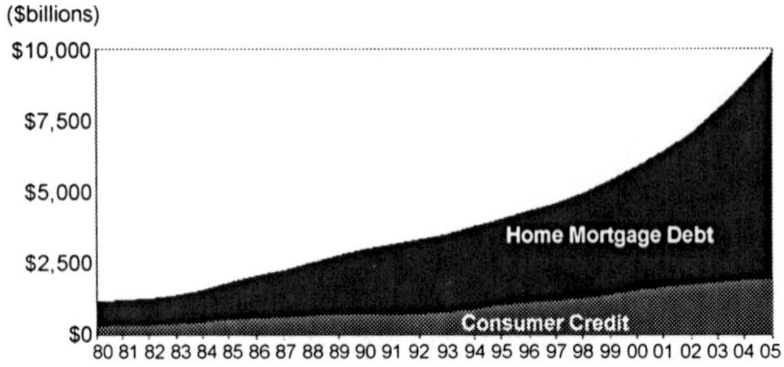

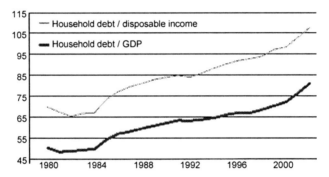

Source: Federal Reserve Z-1

Figure 6-14. Outstanding Debt as a Percentage of Disposable Personal Income and GDP

Source: "Flow of Funds Accounts of the United States," statistical release, Z.1 release, Federal Reserve Board, June 10, 2004. Created by The Century Foundation. "Life and Debt: Why American Families Are Borrowing to the Hilt" 2004.

Figure 6-15. Household Debt as a Percentage of Assets

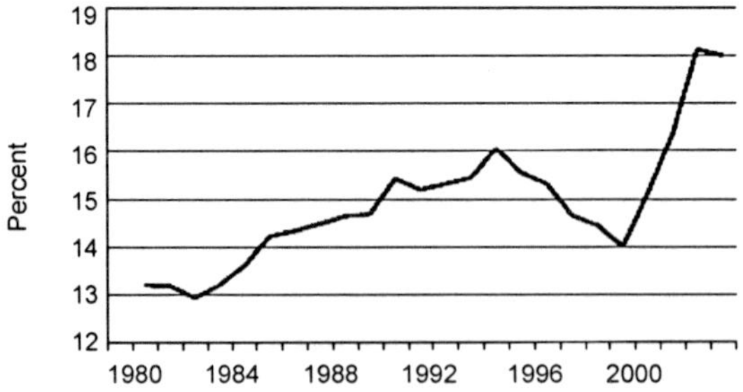

Source: Ibid, The Century Foundation

Sooner or later, overconsumption will catch up with America. It's basic arithmetic; you cannot maintain consumption that exceeds production over an extended period. Eventually the interest payments alone will lead to insolvency.

7

HEALTHCARE IN AMERICA: PROGNOSIS NEGATIVE

Reality in Middle-Class America

The pleasant melody of children playing in the hallway goes unnoticed by a man sitting on his bed, staring into the window, wondering how bad things will get. He has lived in that house for nearly twenty-one years now, and Pittsburg has been the only home he knows. He was recently laid off due to a plant closing and relocation overseas. Now he has no job and no health insurance for himself or his children. He can't afford the $1500 private health insurance premiums per month.

So far, he has barely kept up with mortgage payments thanks to loans from friends and family. His unemployment benefits have run out, and with very little saved, he sees no way out of this mess. Fortunately, he still has a few credit cards he can use.

He has very good expertise in what he does, but his skills are not readily transferable to other industries. And while he has sought work in low-skill trades, he now realizes that employers want younger workers. Even his occasional handyman jobs are difficult to find due to the underpricing from illegal aliens.

But even more so than the immediacy of work, he worries about his children who have no healthcare insurance. The rates quoted to him are simply too high due to the preexisting conditions of one of his children. As well, he is a smoker and unlike health insurance through work, individual insurance has exclusions and higher premiums for smokers. But this was not a factor when he had coverage at work since employer-sponsored HMO plans don't inquire about health status or know whether you are a smoker.

For the first time, he is beginning to realize that having a job opens the door to affordable healthcare. Already, he fears his fate will be like that of his brother, who filed for bankruptcy last year due to $100,000 in medical bills. But right now, all he can focus on is the security and well-being of his children.

He is trying to enroll in various special needs assistance programs offered by the state, but they're filled with unbelievable bureaucracy and are in such huge demand that he is on a long waiting list. For other relief, such as help with utilities bills and emergency assistance from Social Security, he has been unable to schedule an appointment due to the continuous busy signals on the one day per week that appointments can be made. He has been told that he needs to call at 8 am on Friday in order to schedule an appointment, but the office receives over 3000 calls that day.

Throughout his futile struggles for government aid, he now realizes that all of the state and federal social services programs are beyond capacity due to claims by others under severe hardship including illegal aliens. Getting through this backlog of claimants will consume valuable time. He cannot afford to waste anymore days trying to get through these backed up phone lines just to schedule an appointment to see whether he can get assistance with utilities. He needs to find a job with healthcare coverage, and soon.

This desperate man hopes he will be able to hold on until the government begins making partial payments on his pension plan which was turned over to the Pension Benefit Guaranty Corporation a few months ago. He feels young at only 53, but even with twenty years of service under his belt, his monthly pension checks won't amount to much due to penalties for early retirement. But he wasn't the one who chose early retirement. The effects of free trade did. This man is like many average Americans who are now suffering the devastating consequences of the beginnings of America's economic correction.

Not so far away, a neighbor has just finalized the divorce from her husband of nearly thirty-seven years after continuous episodes of infidelity and refusal to get treated for alcoholism, which led to random periods of domestic abuse over the years. The woman could take no more and only lasted this long for the benefit of the couple's children. But now, both of her daughters have graduated college and she can finally detach herself from the years of torture she has endured.

The woman does not expect to receive much from alimony, as her husband only earns $55,000 per year as a union employee of a large retail grocery chain. Finally, she knows that she cannot rely on her daughters for assistance, as they have been unable to find work since graduating six months ago. Even when they do find work, they will be burdened with thousands of dollars in school loans, which have already come due. They have already begun to work in low-skill jobs while trying to pay off their enormous student loans.

Yet, what is most troubling for this distraught woman is how she will pay for health insurance. At the age of 55, she is too young to qualify for Medicare. And her expected $15,000 per year alimony settlement will make it difficult to qualify for Medicaid. Still, she feels fortunate, as she never worked and will soon move into a small condo that will be paid for with the settlement from the house the family once shared. Of course, back when she got married, it was rare for women to work. As well, medical costs were reasonable and were not causing millions of bankruptcies as they are today.

Finally, the neighborhood general store is preparing to close down after twenty-five years in business. The owner can no longer afford to compete with larger corporations such as Home Depot and Wal-Mart, which have priced him out of business. The last straw came when he had to drop healthcare coverage for his long-time employees a year earlier due to rising costs. Shortly thereafter, he was faced with the difficult task of finding competent replacements willing to work without employee benefits. As a small business owner, he simply could not afford these added costs. America must find a way to control healthcare costs and make access to this vital basic necessity available to all. Life is too short to fear medical bills more than a life-threatening illness.

Overview

The opening passage sums up the current reality for millions of Americans, as corporate America has taken control of this nation. The healthcare industry is now competing with the oil and financial industries for the top spot on Washington's most favored list. As long as America goes without a national healthcare system, the vast majority of Americans will continue to experience declining living standards and inadequate access to healthcare, while workers from developing nations benefit from being added to the payrolls of America's biggest and best companies.

For several years now, corrupt politicians and corporate greed have reaped financial rewards from America's bubble economy at the expense of impoverished and middle-class Americans, many of which are now jobless and without hope. Underlying the complexity of America's economic decline is the weakness of its free-market healthcare system, which is forcing jobs overseas and denying affordable access to millions.

Healthcare is absolutely the single biggest problem facing America today. In short, the high cost of healthcare is destroying the finances of both consumers and employers alike, while compromising the health of millions. While employers struggle to contain employee benefits as a way to remain globally competitive, healthcare costs continue to grow at three times the inflation rate and twice the rate of the economy, forcing many companies to drop coverage, shift more out-of-pocket expenses to employers, or outsource work to contractors both domestically and overseas. Meanwhile, lobbyist groups in Washington have ensured that the healthcare system remains unchanged, showing no regard for some 50 million uninsured Americans.

Ridiculous healthcare costs and inadequate coverage for millions continues to add to America's problematic economy, while HMOs and drug companies rake in huge profits. In 2004, the largest HMOs brought in over $100 billion in revenues, up by over 33 percent from the previous year. This might lead one to think that there was an increase in illnesses by 33 percent. But of course that was not the case. The pharmaceutical industry has an even longer and more robust string of profits.

As money continues to be pumped into this industry, tens of thousands of distraught workers are switching careers in mid-life, opting for many of the high-paying, low-skill healthcare jobs. Who can blame them? Pharmacy technician salaries began at $30,000 to $35,000 per year; not a bad investment for a two-year degree. However, all one has to do is pass the national certification exam, which does not even require this degree. There are many similar jobs in healthcare today. In total, the healthcare industry is expected to lead the nation in employment growth through at least 2014. When this type of situation exists, you know there is too much money flowing into an industry. And Americans are paying the price.

The uncontrollable increases in healthcare costs have created a downward spiral for the U.S. economy, responsible for millions of personal bankruptcies and forcing many companies to drop coverage or relocate overseas. Yet, despite these costs, the quality of America's healthcare is relatively low even though it spends more on this vital service than any nation in the world on a per-capita, GDP and total dollar basis.

Destroying America's Competitiveness

In contrast to American companies that have continued to increase out-of-pocket healthcare costs to employees or drop coverage altogether, all nations in Europe and Asia (as well as most of the world) have a system of universal healthcare paid for by the government. And this has registered positive economic advantages for both consumers and companies of these nations.

Unlike their American counterparts, foreign consumers have complete access to healthcare, regardless of age, income or employment status. And within these universal programs, one finds evidence of less waste due to the absence of middlemen such as insurance companies, pharmacy benefit managers, and for-profit hospital management organizations—all prime players in America's healthcare system. And of course, all other nations of the world have price limits on prescription drugs.

Consider that for companies in America opting to provide healthcare for employees and their families, these expenses create enormous and uncertain potential liabilities, leading to future earnings uncertainty and potential solvency issues. As a result, foreign corporations are more competitive than their American counterparts since foreign governments provide these costs. This disparity in socioeconomic policy, combined with the abandonment of government responsibility has resulted in the ability of foreign nations to induce downward pricing pressures that have significantly disrupted, and in many cases have destroyed America's manufacturing and service industries.

It appears as if *the free trade agreements enacted by Washington are in direct opposition to the current free-market healthcare system.* And America's declining competitiveness is a direct result of this oversight. As a consequence, the lack of a universal healthcare system has indirectly accounted for the growing trade imbalance and exportation of several industries overseas, all of which have combined to heighten America's economic and job instability even further. Instead of providing for the healthcare of its citizens, Washington has decided to let the free-market healthcare system prevent millions of Americans from having access to healthcare. Meanwhile, corporate America continues to report record profits while they abandon this obligation.

Employers Have an Option, Employees Don't

After two decades of skyrocketing healthcare costs, many employers have recently shifted much of the out-of-pocket expenses to their employees. And because healthcare in America is now linked with employment, the overall uninsured rate stands at nearly 18 percent. But since most elderly Americans over 65 qualify for Medicare, the percentage of uninsured Americans under age 65 stands at nearly 19 percent. Astonishingly, the *uninsured rate of seniors 65 and older is 17 percent, despite the estimated 80.2 million (2005) Americans who are considered insured by Medicare and Medicaid.* Most likely, America's total real uninsured rates are over 20 percent.

Yet, even for those covered by the government's public healthcare system, millions face the threat of financial ruin due to their inability to provide much needed supplemental insurance, such a Medigap. And as the outsourcing trend continues to gain momentum, the number of uninsured Americans will grow each day with no end in sight.

When one considers *the number of Americans who are without health insurance for a portion of the year due to job loss or change, the number of uninsured nearly triples, adding an additional 82 million to the already 47 million* who have no insurance whatsoever. Yet, due to the powerful lobbying efforts by the insurance, pharmaceutical, and healthcare industries, Washington is reluctant to nationalize America's broken healthcare system, forcing many companies to relocate, outsource overseas, or face potential bankruptcy.

> *"The paradox is that the costliest health system in the world performs so poorly. We waste one-third of every health care dollar on insurance bureaucracy and profits while two million people go bankrupt annually and we leave 45 million uninsured"*
>
> Dr. Quentin Young,
> national coordinator of Physicians
> for a National Health Program

When one company outsources, its competitors must follow suit or else they too may eventually face bankruptcy. And every time an American company outsources work overseas, Americans lose jobs and health insurance. Mention of healthcare by Washington has become taboo. No politician wants to acknowledge that the healthcare crisis is destroying jobs and decreasing net wages because they fear backlash from powerful industry lobbyists, as well as millions of voters linked to this industry. In 2004, the Department of Labor estimates that 13.5 million Americans were employed in healthcare, not including drug makers and insurance agents.

Placing the burden of healthcare on the public has not allowed the U.S. government to escape the pitfalls of what is the most inefficient and costly healthcare system in the world. The soaring cost of healthcare services and insurance has forced millions into bankruptcy due to their inability to pay for medical bills that have been inflated by hospital bureaucracies and pharmaceutical companies. When will this charade end? *Until America restructures free trade policies and enacts a system of universal healthcare, its living standards will continue to decline as it faces the humiliation of being the only developed nation in the world that does not provide for the healthcare needs of its people.*

Public Healthcare is Ineffective and Inadequate

Despite the enormous amount of taxpayer money earmarked for Medicare and Medicaid each year (estimated at a total of $533 billion for 2006, see figures 7.8 and 7.9b, appendix), most Americans lacking private healthcare coverage have not been rescued by these ailing programs. Benefits continue to be cut on an annual basis. Meanwhile, fraud is ramped throughout both the public and private healthcare system with drug companies, physicians, dentists, pharmacists, hospitals, and consumers extorting taxpayer money from this poorly policed system.

Even for the elderly, who are covered by government healthcare programs, supplemental insurance is an unaffordable necessity for most, since exclusions and spending caps are reached early on for this aged group. Therefore, everyone in America regardless of age cannot escape the manipulation of healthcare expenses by the insurance and pharmaceutical industries.

Over the past decade, Washington has slashed major benefits and coverage criteria for millions of Americans on Medicare who have no other options. And states have done the same with Medicaid. This has resulted in loss of coverage for many suffering from otherwise easily treatable and preventable diseases. This situation alone has accounted for the unnecessary morbidity and mortality of millions. Some states have even eliminated childhood dental care from their Medicaid program. Texas has gone one step further by eliminating its vital CHIPS healthcare program for children from low-income families. Remarkably, Texas leads the nation in the percentage of uninsured residents, at over 26 percent. Indeed, it appears as if the momentum in public healthcare benefit cuts now mirrors that of escalating healthcare costs.

Perhaps the most alarming trend for public healthcare programs is that the inefficiency and bureaucracy of Medicare (the federally sponsored plan) and Medicaid (sponsored mainly by the state) have actually created the biggest financial liabilities for the U.S. government, somewhere in the neighborhood of $40 to $60 trillion in present-day dollars. And these liabilities have been accentuated by the demographic trends of the baby boomer phenomenon, which is not expected to reverse anytime soon.

Healthcare Myths in America

Best in the World?

Longer life spans and the high costs of healthcare cannot be explained by better quality. The United States has one of the most technologically sophisticated healthcare systems in the world, but in terms of quality it is only *ranked 17th globally among developed nations*. The root causes of America's inefficient healthcare are like so many of its other problems, with big money and political corruption as the key elements.

For the most part, increasing life spans have not been due to the majority of pharmaceutical agents, as most believe. *All developed nations are experiencing increased life spans primarily due to better sanitary conditions, better infant mortality rates, and the wider availability of core medications such as antibiotics and flu vaccines, which in the past have caused many to die at early ages.* Yet these critical medications make up only a very small part of annual drug sales. Today, the focus with drug companies is on copy-cat and lifestyle-enhancing drugs rather than breakthrough drugs developed in the past.

For those who have access to healthcare, many are receiving more than they need, less than they need, or the wrong kind of care. In addition, preventable and harmful errors are a regular occurrence. Millions of Americans are injured and tens of thousands die unnecessarily each year because of treatment errors, as well as the overuse, underuse, or misuse of services. Moreover, these problems are not being recognized or addressed adequately (see Section 7.7 of the Chapter Seven Supplement, appendix).

Much of the reason for medical errors is due to poor management by HMOs. The division of labor approach to healthcare created by HMOs was an attempt to make healthcare delivery more efficient, but has been short of a disaster. Instead of a physician and nurse, patients can be treated by ten or more different healthcare providers including a nurse's assistant, physician's assistant, surgical assistant, radiology tech, pharmacy tech, etc. *This fragmented approach has contributed to the explosion of medical errors that have led to unnecessary mortality and morbidity.* Yet, these troubling issues remain unaddressed by the healthcare industry because it is still very profitable, so lobbyists have not been pressuring politicians for change.

Healthcare should not be treated like a manufacturing assembly line designed as a profit center. It is critical for the primary physician to be intimately involved with the patient from start to finish. Yet HMOs will not allow this. Instead of proper exams and referrals to specialists, HMOs have pressured physicians to cut costs by encouraging them to practice a pill-pushing approach and limiting them to 15 minutes per patient visit.

The United States spends far more on healthcare per person than any other nation in the world, or nearly 50 percent more than the number two spender, Switzerland. Yet, the quality is relatively low, as are the average life spans of Americans (see Section 7.7, appendix). *In 2005 alone, America spent over $2 trillion on healthcare, or about 16 percent of the GDP, yet over 47 million or about 16 percent were uninsured* (other sources state this figure to now be near 18 percent). In addition, *over 82 million Americans went without health insurance for at least part of 2003 and another 70 million Americans were underinsured.* That amounts to nearly 200 million Americans with some form of inadequate or absent coverage. In 2003, guess what country had 11.4 percent or 8.4 million children without access to healthcare. That's right—the great, rich, powerful nation of America. All other developed nations have universal healthcare, with lower costs and still rank higher than America in total quality and accessibility of care.

Can a nation with nearly one-fifth of its population without access to healthcare and two-thirds without adequate coverage claim to be the world's greatest and wealthiest superpower? I suppose it all depends on how you define "great" and "wealth." Why can't the "strongest, most powerful nation in the world" provide a healthcare system that is available to all of its citizens? Of course it can, but Washington won't allow it because there are too many large industries profiting from this free-market healthcare system. And these industries have the largest, strongest, wealthiest and most intense lobbyist groups sitting at the steps of Capitol Hill with millions of dollars to hand out, ensure things stay the way they are.

BOX 7-1: High Quality or Highly Costly?

The National Patient Safety Foundation of the American Medical Association (AMA) recently estimated that the number of injuries caused by medical accidents in in-patient hospital settings nationwide could be as high as 3 million and cost as much $200 billion each year. Conservative estimates indicate that 300,000 Americans die annually as a result of medically induced injury or negligence, or 9 times the number of Americans who die on highways, and 3000 times the annual airline fatality rate.

According to a 2004 study published in JAMA, physicians are the third leading cause of death in America only behind cardiovascular disease and cancer. These unnecessary deaths are the result of iatrogenic activities (results induced in a patient as a result of a physician's activity, manner, or therapy).

As a way to justify the relatively poor health of Americans, politicians, managed care organizations, insurance providers and others who stand to benefit from the America's poorly run and inefficient healthcare system have created the perception that the American public brings poor health upon themselves. However the data does not support this assertion (see section 7.7 in the appendix).

The Exercise Myth and Big Money

Americans are spending astronomical amounts of money on disease management focused largely on toxic drugs and unnecessary surgeries. But when one factors in the cost-benefit ratio of these procedures, their return on this investment is very low. Meanwhile, the absence of proper nutrition in the typical American diet has added to the problem. And corporations have added to the obesity epidemic by infiltrating processed food products with toxic additives and making food containers larger, such as those seen as discount warehouses. *This repackaging trend has been shown to cause one to consume much more than they normally would—an effect that is similar to credit spending when individuals have been provided with larger credit lines.*

America's huge fitness industry has led many to believe that a healthy lifestyle can be attained by strenuous exercise, when in fact this is not true and actually may lead to a diminished life span. Yet, as a desperate measure to improve their overall health, Americans spend billions of dollars annually on diet pills and books, workout videos, and fitness club memberships. Despite these conscious efforts, Americans have an unimpressive relative life span, and are amongst the most obese humans on earth (see sections 7.1 and figures 7.7b-e of section 7.7 in the appendix).

Over the past two decades, as America's obesity problem became classified as an "epidemic" several industries blossomed to help Americans stay fit. Bally's, 24-hour Fitness, Nike, GNC, and hundreds of others have become huge businesses, providing Americans with a buffet of goods and services thought to promote better health. Ironically, more Americans have swelled in size since that time, along with the profits of sports gear and health and fitness companies (see Sections 7.1 and 7.2 in appendix).

Just ask European and Asian nationals how often they exercise and you will begin to understand that the multi-billion dollar fitness industry has brainwashed Americans into thinking that strenuous exercise is the solution to good health. All it really takes in most cases for a healthy life style is to remain moderately active, avoid the toxic additives from the food industry and to abandon many of the unnecessary pill-pushing recommendations issued by physicians who have been brainwashed and manipulated by pharmaceutical drug reps (see Sections 7.4 & 12.1).

The Great American Drug Myth

The confidence Americans have placed in the healthcare system has caused many to abandon common sense and accept the pill-pushing recommendations of physicians without question. However, the fact is that anytime you ingest a chemical, whether it is from Merck, Pfizer, or any other drug maker, your body is being flooded by toxins. *Drug makers prefer to label these toxicities as "side effects." A side effect is one or two minor unintended consequences—not dozens of potentially harmful effects, some of which are worse than the original condition!*

When these adverse effects are apparent they often lead to drug recalls. But many other times the effects do not register until a point in the future, when it can be impossible to correlate the drug as the source of the injurious agent. Despite the ubiquitous toxicity of all man-made prescription drugs, the pharmaceutical-controlled FDA has erected huge barriers for more natural therapies to enter the marketplace since it is the pharmaceutical companies that fund the FDA. Clearly, the FDA is protecting big pharma's drug monopoly. Why bite the hand that feeds you, right? (see Sections 7.3 and 7.4, appendix)

The Healthcare-Employment Link

When America entered World War II, many employers faced a shortage of qualified workers. Therefore, as an incentive to secure the best talent available, employers began offering pension plans and employer-sponsored health coverage. By providing these attractive perks, employers could offer benefits beyond the War Labor Board's ceiling on wages that was enacted to prevent war-induced inflation. Finally, offering healthcare benefits became more advantageous to employers when the IRS ruled that health insurance premiums could be treated as tax-deductible business expenses.

The growth of employer-sponsored health plans continued during the post-war period, as America enjoyed a tremendous economic boom. Unlike the 1990s, this was a real boom that wasn't fueled by credit spending, but by net productivity, savings and investment. Soon, most Americans had access to healthcare through their employers. Even those without employer-sponsored insurance could afford medical expenses since costs were reasonable.

> "If you want total security, go to prison. There you're fed, clothed, given medical care and so on.
>
> The only thing lacking... is freedom."
>
> Dwight D. Eisenhower

However, over the past two decades the dependency on employment for healthcare has created huge problems for Americans. Of more recent impact, sluggish economic conditions have resulted in millions of unemployed workers who no longer have access to healthcare for themselves or their families. And the outrageous cost of individual health insurance makes it unaffordable for most. Added to increased energy costs, lack of real wage growth, and record consumer debt, it should be easy to appreciate how millions of Americans are struggling just to get by.

The full impact of unemployment numbers and uninsured rates have been difficult to monitor since the government excludes "discouraged workers"; the silent millions in America today with no employment. As well, Washington does not distinguish between employment in jobs with healthcare benefits and those without.

Despite America's strong link between healthcare and employment, loss of coverage can occur by many other ways besides losing one's job. In addition, life events such as divorce, chronic illness, pre-existing medical conditions, and even a felony conviction (due to the inability to find reasonable employment) can leave one without healthcare insurance. Yet, prison inmates have full access to healthcare services. *Employment is also linked to one's credit history, so if you have bad credit you could be denied access to the most affordable healthcare conduit—full-time employment.*

How can America justify government policies that provide full healthcare benefits and reasonable living conditions to incarcerated individuals using taxpayer funds, yet not to struggling, law-abiding citizens, most of which are from working families? This is clearly an embarrassing situation for a nation that claims to be the greatest on earth.

Free Trade Has Decreased Coverage

What may have served in the past to boost America's economy by assisting with the growth of the healthcare-related industries has now caused most other American industries to eliminate jobs and outsource. But ultimately, corporate America will not suffer because it can continue to transfer jobs overseas. Only American workers will suffer the lasting effects of America's misaligned healthcare system. Clearly, *Washington is placing the interests of corporate America and the wealthy in front of the vast majority of Americans.*

In today's modern economy, the average American will change jobs over 10 to 12 times during the process of four to five career changes. During these transitions, there are usually three to six-month gaps, whereby coverage must be paid for by the employee. But the government's solution to provide for this gap (COBRA) is a joke because the premiums are simply too high for most. In addition, if workers have pre-existing conditions they may not be covered upon changing jobs.

Over the past decade alone, millions of Americans have seen blue chip industries disappear to Asia and other regions of the globe. Many industries have fallen victim to the economic transition America now struggles with, which has sent mining, forestry, textiles, steel, and other manufacturing industries abroad. *Some industries even focus on employing part-time, temporary, or contractual workers so they will not be responsible for providing the fastest growing business expense in America today.*

Healthcare Costs in America

Most experts agree that America's healthcare system is riddled with inefficiencies, excessive administrative expenses, inflated prices, poor management, inappropriate care, massive waste and inexcusable fraud. These problems significantly increase the cost of medical care and insurance premiums for employers and workers. And while some politicians and industry leaders have complained, no one has taken action.

Rising healthcare costs make it difficult for small businesses to provide basic coverage, forcing many to eliminate insurance altogether or hire more part-time workers. Meanwhile, larger corporations are shifting an increasing burden of healthcare costs directly to their employees, leaving many without affordable coverage or serving to decrease net wage compensation.

> *"We are an enormously rich country. Providing health care and a modest living for our elderly is certainly something we can afford."*
>
> Economist James Galbraith of the University of Texas in Austin

Over the past few years, health insurance costs have increased by several hundred percent over wages, resulting in a hidden source of inflation that no one in Washington mentions. Even more troubling is the fact that insurance premiums are now growing faster than healthcare expenses. In 2004, employer health insurance premiums increased by 11.2

percent, representing a growth of 400 percent over inflation. Yet, *while government and employer-sponsored plans pay for more than 75 percent of all healthcare costs, nearly one-fifth of all Americans have no health insurance.*

A recent study by USA Today reports that the average hospital profit margin was 5.2 percent in 2004, but the average hospital expense increase was 6.9 percent in that same year. Consequently, about 25 percent of all U.S. hospitals were losing money as of the 2004 data. Therefore, it appears as if only a few managed-care organizations are making all of the profits, while the others are poorly managed.

> *Healthcare expenditures were nearly $1.9 trillion in 2004, up by 265% since 1990 ($717 billion) and nearly 750% since 1980 ($255 billion). These expenditures comprised 16% of the GDP--three times larger than the industry's share in 1960. About half of this rise occurred from 1980 to 1993, when healthcare expenditures rose from 9.1% to 13.8% of the GDP.*

Healthcare costs are rising at double-digit rates and increasing their share of the economy without commensurate increases in quality of life. Across the board, *while the quality is increasing at a rate of 2.8 percent annually, the costs are increasing at an annual rate of 8 percent.* In *1960 America only spent 5.1 percent of GDP on healthcare.* Government estimates indicate that by 2014, total healthcare costs will reach 19 percent of GDP. I expect this number to be reached by 2010.

For several years now, *Europe has been spending only about one-half as much as America relative to GDP, but has delivered more effective healthcare with fewer medical errors, virtually no fraud and very little waste.* And of course, Europeans also have longer life spans and everyone is guaranteed coverage.

Figure 7-1. Public and Private Healthcare Spending

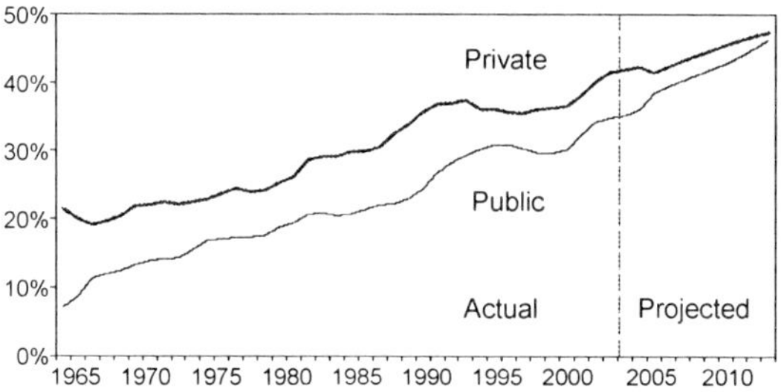

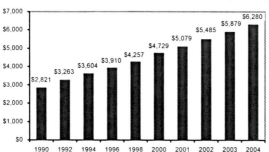

Source: Center for Medicare and Medicaid Services

Figure 7-2. Healthcare Expenditures per Capita

Source: Social Security Administration, Health and Human
Services Centers for Medicare and Medicaid Services

The Boomer Liability

With about 85 million Americans born between 1946 and 1964, an estimated 76 million remaining from this so-called baby boomer generation will begin to turn 65 in 2011. Currently, with approximately 35 million aged 65 or older, America's elderly comprise 13 percent of the U.S. population. However, by 2018, the U.S. Census predicts this age group will represent 18.5 percent of the population and therefore place huge demands upon the healthcare system.

Estimates indicate that America's elderly consumes 4 times as much healthcare per capita as those under age 65. And combined with the effect of increasing life spans upon future healthcare expenditures, there appears to be no end in sight for rising Medicare and Medicaid liabilities. Add to that the other mandatory liabilities such as Social Security and debt service payments for U.S. debt, and it's easy to see that this generation of Americans poses a huge problem for a nation that has been mismanaged for over three decades. Increased mandatory spending means less money available for research funding, education, transportation and many other critical programs (figures 7-3 and 7-4).

Figure 7-3. Mandatory Spending Increases While Discretionary Spending Falls
(As a percentage of GDP, FY 1962-2013)

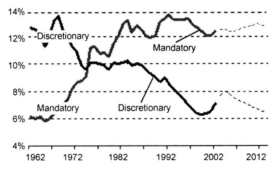

Sources: Congressional Budget Office (Baseline Forecast), Office of Management and Budget

Figure 7-4. Mandatory Expenses as a Percentage of GDP

(Interest Payments on the national debt are not shown but are currently about 1.7% and expected to balloon)

Percent of GDP

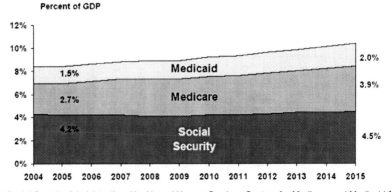

Sources: Social Security Administration, Health and Human Services Centers for Medicare and Medicaid Services

How is it possible that America spends far more money than any other nation in the world on healthcare, yet the number of uninsured Americans is so high while the quality and access is relatively poor? Even the government's contribution to the system of around 25 percent of total healthcare expenditures is more than most nations. Clearly, *Washington has decided to allow the free-market system dictate who will get access to healthcare as a way to promote the growth of the pharmaceutical and insurance industries—two of the most profitable industries in America.* As costs continue to escalate, more and more working Americans are finding they have to choose between paying rent, utilities, or insurance premiums—that's a choice working Americans and seniors trying to enjoy their "Golden Years" should never have to make.

Health Insurance Costs

Many experts agree that the high cost of employer-sponsored health insurance is undermining the competitiveness of the U.S. economy and eliminating good jobs. According to a recent study by economists Sarah Reber and Laura Tyson, the rise in healthcare costs will "depress wages, affect hiring and ultimately lead to further outsourcing." The Kaiser Family Foundation and the Health Research and Educational Trust report that premiums for employer-sponsored health insurance in the United States have been rising an average of five times higher than workers' earnings since 2000. As a consequence, the employee portion of health insurance premiums has increased by 126 percent between 2000 and 2004.

For nearly two decades, employers have been decreasing healthcare benefits to employees due to escalating costs. Overall, the percentage of employees covered by insurance at work has declined from 75.5 percent in 1987 to 68.6 percent in 2003. And *30 to 40 percent of employers offer no insurance to employees at all. In 2004, as many as one in three small businesses in America did not offer health benefits to employees.* As figure 7-5 shows, *the number of companies with 200 or more employees offering healthcare coverage has decreased by 50 percent since 1988.* The Kaiser Foundation estimates that in 2004 there were at least five million fewer jobs providing health insurance than in 2001 (see Section 7.5, appendix).

Figure 7-5. Percentage of Large Firms (200 or more employees) Offering Retiree Healthcare Benefits

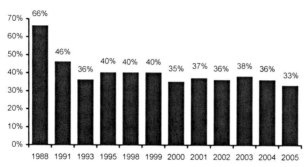

Source: **"Trends and Indicators in the Changing Health Care Marketplace,"** (#7031), The Henry J. Kaiser Family Foundation, February 2005. *This information was reprinted with permission from the Henry J. Kaiser Family Foundation. The Kaiser Family Foundation, based in Menlo Park, California, is a nonprofit, private operating foundation focusing on the major health care issues facing the nation and is not associated with Kaiser Permanente or Kaiser Industries.*

Meanwhile, *from 2001 to 2005, employees' share of health insurance costs soared 63 percent for single coverage and 58 percent for family coverage.* In 2004, the annual premium charged to employers for a plan covering a family of four averaged $9,950, or $829 per month; workers contributed $2,661, or 10 percent more than they spent in 2003. For single coverage, workers contributed an average of $558 towards the $3,695 annual premium. Health insurance premiums are expected to rise to an average of more than $14,500 for family coverage in 2006 (see Section 7.5, appendix).

Estimates indicate that the average benefits package for the average full-time worker in America can amount to about 42 percent of the total compensation package, with as much as 75 percent of this being due to healthcare benefits. Therefore, it is not difficult to see how American corporations are having major problems competing with foreign peers who do not bear the burden of healthcare costs.

More than 25 million Americans own a small business. But since small businesses and the self-employed aren't able to purchase insurance as cheaply as large corporations, rising healthcare costs are making it increasingly difficult for them to afford basic coverage for their employees and families. Today, *less than half of small businesses offer health insurance* (see figure 7.5b, appendix). As a result, workers in small companies are three times as likely to be uninsured as workers in large companies.

America's Fastest Growing Industry

It's no wonder why so many Americans are headed for the healthcare industry. With no price controls and record spending, a career in healthcare can provide a nice life, often with minimal training. *Wage and salary employment in the healthcare industry is projected to increase 27 percent through 2014, compared with 14 percent for all industries combined* (table 7-1). *Employment growth is expected to account for about 3.6 million new wage and salary jobs—19 percent of all wage and salary jobs added to the economy over the 2004 to 2014 period.* Projected rates of employment growth for the various segments of the industry range from 13 percent in hospitals, the largest and slowest growing industry segment, to 69 percent in home health care services. Nursing aides, orderlies and attendants, and home health aides are among the occupations expected to add the most new jobs between 2004 and 2014, about 675,000 combined (table 7-2).

Table 7-1. Employment Growth in Healthcare, United States (2004-2014)

Industry segment	2004 Employment	2004-14 Percent change
All industries	145,612	14.0
Health Services	13,062	27.3
Hospitals, public and private	5,301	13.1
Nursing and residential care facilities	2,815	27.8
Offices of physicians	2,054	37.0
Home health care services	773	69.5
Offices of dentists	760	31.7
Offices of other health practitioners	524	42.7
Outpatient care centers	446	44.2
Other ambulatory health care services	201	37.7
Medical and diagnostic laboratories	189	27.1

Source: Department of Labor

Table 7-2. America's Hidden Employment Boom (2004-2014)

Occupation	Employment, 2004		Percent change, 2004-2014
	Number	Percent	
Total, all occupations	13,062	100.0	27.3
Management, business, and financial occupations	574	4.4	28.3
Top executives	101	0.8	33.3
Medical and health services managers	175	1.3	26.1
Professional and related occupations	5,657	43.3	27.8
Psychologists	33	0.3	28.1
Counselors	152	1.2	31.8
Social workers	169	1.3	29.3
Health educators	17	0.1	27.0
Social and human service assistants	99	0.8	38.6
Chiropractors	21	0.2	47.8
Dentists	95	0.7	18.5
Dietitians and nutritionists	32	0.2	20.1
Optometrists	18	0.1	29.6
Pharmacists	63	0.5	17.3
Physicians and surgeons	417	3.2	28.7
Physician assistants	53	0.4	54.8
Podiatrists	7	0.1	22.2
Registered nurses	1,988	15.2	30.5
Therapists	358	2.7	32.8
Clinical laboratory technologists and technicians	257	2.0	22.7
Dental hygienists	153	1.2	43.7
Diagnostic related technologists and technicians	269	2.1	26.4
Emergency medical technicians and paramedics	122	0.9	27.8
Health diagnosing and treating practitioner support technicians	226	1.7	18.0
Licensed practical and licensed vocational nurses	586	4.5	14.2
Medical records and health information technicians	134	1.0	30.0
Service occupations	4,152	31.8	33.2
Home health aides	458	3.5	66.4
Nursing aides, orderlies, and attendants	1,230	9.4	22.2
Physical therapist assistants and aides	95	0.7	41.0
Dental assistants	257	2.0	43.6
Medical assistants	361	2.8	53.7
Medical transcriptionists	81	0.6	22.1
Food preparation and serving related occupations	462	3.5	12.6
Building cleaning workers	365	2.8	20.6
Personal and home care aides	312	2.4	60.5
Office and administrative support occupations	2,379	18.2	16.2
Billing and posting clerks and machine operators	179	1.4	10.9
Receptionists and information clerks	353	2.7	31.3
Medical secretaries	347	2.7	17.3
Note: May not add to totals due to omission of occupations with small employment			

Source: Department of Labor

Behavioral Modification and Inadequate Solutions

In some cases, the unbearable cost of health insurance has been a catalyst for employers to impose behavioral standards upon employees. In some companies, employees are required to stop smoking or be fired. In others, on-site exercise facilities have been provided and often mandatory participation is required to reduce insurance premiums. For these employers, it is the only way they can keep insurance coverage.

As a way to help American workers cope with more out-of-pocket expenses, Washington created a medical savings plan that provides a tax deduction from wages allocated into a special fund to be used by the employee during the year. However, this savings plan does not directly address the rising costs of healthcare or declining net wage growth as a result of these costs. As well, employees must use these funds by the tax-filing date. Incidentally, many health expenses are not planned and therefore cannot utilize these tax savings. This plan only provides more affordable access to non-critical care expenses. But you still have to be making adequate income in order to contribute money to this plan.

Rather than address America's healthcare problem appropriately, President Bush has delivered a strong message to Americans, similar to that implied by his recent increases in contribution maximums to IRA and 401(k) retirement plans, as well as proposed privatization of Social Security—*Fellow Americans, you are going to be on your own for retirement savings and healthcare coverage, so I am passing this great tax-deduction for planned medical expenses to save you money! (Cheers).*

Of course most Americans do not see the real implications. These policy changes offer a look into the future when *the two most important and largest concerns of Americans will be up to each to plan and pay for—healthcare coverage and retirement income.* And this is going to continue to erode the net wages of all and add to the trend of America's declining living standards.

How Does America Stack Up With the World?

As figure 7-6 points out, America spends a much higher percentage of GDP (2006 data is expected to surpass 17 percent GDP) on healthcare than every OECD nation, yet is sixth from the bottom in life expectancy. As well, America is the only nation in the OECD that does not have a national healthcare program. In contrast, *Japanese citizens have the highest life expectancy with total healthcare expenditures of only 8 percent of GDP.*

Finally, South Korean nationals have the same life expectancy as Americans but the Korean government only spends about one-third (5.6 percent of GDP) of the amount spent in America on healthcare. As a matter of fact, *the U.S. government spends about the same amount on its public healthcare (5.0 percent of GDP) as S. Korea, but only provides partial health insurance for about 80 million people (27 percent of the population), while S. Korea provides full healthcare for all of its citizens* (as do all of the other nations in figure 7-6).

Figure 7-6. Healthcare Expenditures as a Percentage of GDP and Life Expectancy (2003)

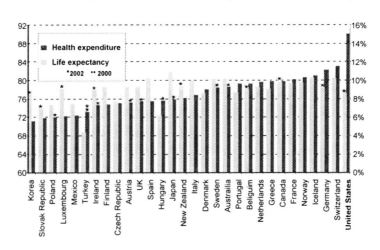

Source: OECD in Figures 2005; or see StatLink: http://dx.doi.org/10.1787/132836124886

Why Are the Costs So High?

So far, I have discussed the poor quality and high expense of healthcare. As well, I have highlighted the direct link between employment and health insurance, and the consequence of skyrocketing healthcare costs on employers and workers. Now I will discuss why healthcare costs are so high in order to understand what potential remedies might be offered (short of a national healthcare program) so that more Americans can be provided with access to this vital necessity.

Depending upon whom you ask, you will get vastly different reasons for the high and rising healthcare costs in America. Hospital administrators will insist that these costs are due to treatment of the uninsured, lawsuits, advances in care, and unpaid medical bills. Drug companies will tell you that rate hikes are needed to ensure that research and development is funded so they can continue to "deliver effective drug therapies." As well, they will point to the enormous costs of the FDA drug approval process. Insurance companies will tell you that premiums have to increase with overall healthcare costs. And finally, many Washington politicians will claim that high costs are needed to ensure delivery of the world's best healthcare system.

Of course none of these reasons can explain the hyperinflation of healthcare costs. The real reason for America's costly healthcare stems from the free-market system, which allows waste, encourages fraud, and is focused on profits.

Price normally serves to maintain equilibrium between the supply and demand for goods and services. However, since individuals will seek the best possible treatment when they are ill, without any price ceilings the demand will be relatively independent of the price—partially explaining the double-digit annual inflation in healthcare costs. Essentially, the healthcare industry is raising prices unhindered, knowing that desperate people with medical problems have no choice but to pay for the costs of treatment.

Figure 7-7. Factors Driving Rising Costs in Healthcare (2001-2002, in $ billions)

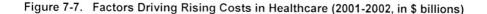

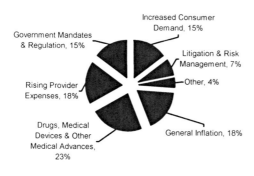

Increased Consumer Demand, 15%

Government Mandates & Regulation, 15%

Litigation & Risk Management, 7%

Rising Provider Expenses, 18%

Other, 4%

Drugs, Medical Devices & Other Medical Advances, 23%

General Inflation, 18%

Someone explain to me the economics of increased consumer demand leading to a 15% increase in healthcare costs in one year. Does that imply that our healthcare system is understaffed?

How is it possible for "general inflation" to account for an 18% increase in healthcare within one year?

"Rising provider expenses" at 18% over a one-year period? Someone please explain.

A figure of 18% for "general inflation" seems obscure given that the average annual inflation rate is around 3%

Source: PricewaterhouseCoopers

Figure 7-8. Healthcare Expenditures (1994-2004)

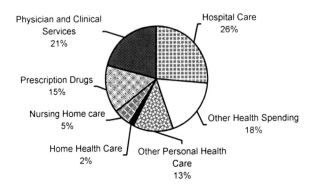

Hospital care contributed 26.4% and physician services contributed 20.8% of the total growth in healthcare expenditures between 1994 and 2004. Meanwhile, prescription drugs contributed 14.7% of the total spending during this period.

Source: Ibid, The Henry J. Kaiser Family Foundation

Costs of Prescription Medications

Without question, the fastest growing component of healthcare costs in America is due to increases in prescription drugs. It doesn't take an analyst to see that pharmaceutical companies have intensified marketing campaigns for drugs over the past 10 years, helping to make prescription drug use mainstream for many conditions that should not be treated with these relatively toxic agents.

As a way to deliver earnings growth, pharmaceutical companies have marketed many of their products as lifestyle-enhancing drugs. First there was Rogaine (now an OTC), then Prozac, Viagra, and a host of others. The marketing of these drugs has been highly manipulative, yet unregulated by the FDA. The enormous success of lifestyle-enhancing drugs has grown due to societal pressures induced by manipulative marketing campaigns from drug producers.

> "It was really kind of a mystery why people at the FDA would be pushing so hard for a drug that had so little benefit and risks on top of that, especially when it was being targeted at otherwise healthy people."
>
> Michael Elashoff, biostatistician and former drug reviewer for the FDA

Amongst the biggest players in this wave of deceitful marketing campaigns have been makers of anti-psychiatric drugs. Rather than promote anti-psychotics for severe debilitating disorders, drug companies have marketed their use for typical "down" periods that are normal in one's life. According to drug companies, no one should ever feel down (depressed) because they have great treatments for you. However, the fact is that transient depression is normal. And until it becomes chronically debilitating, it cannot be diagnosed as real depression. *But most physicians do not take the time to perform an adequate diagnosis of depression due to time constraints by HMOs.* Drug companies have even been able to convince the FDA that anti-depressants are also effective for pets, headaches, smoking cessation, PMS, sleep disorders, and many other "medical conditions."

Today, most patients come to physicians convinced of a depression diagnosis based upon television ads by drug makers. They even request the name of the drug they want (or feel they need), and physicians are ever so happy to provide them with their drug of choice. It makes their job a lot easier and provides a more cost-effective healthcare delivery system for HMOs. Drug companies are aware of these trends; that is why they spend billions to make their products household names.

> "[At the FDA] there is no room for bad news, particularly when large pharmaceutical companies are involved..I mean, it's called the drug approval process. It's not called the drug review process. So that really sets the mindset on what the job is."
>
> Michael Elashoff, biostatistician and former drug reviewer for the FDA

Large drug companies now focus their efforts on developing "me-too" drugs rather than emphasizing R&D on breakthrough drugs. The fact is that many of these copycat drugs have been approved despite evidence showing adverse effects. Big pharma has chosen the less costly route of producing these "me-too" drugs because it yields higher profits with less risk (see Sections 7.3 to 7.4).

> "If it looked like it was going to be turned down, then Glaxo would go to the highest levels at the FDA and really make a big complaint and start trying to make life miserable for all the reviewers of Relenza."
>
> Michael Elashoff, biostatistician and former drug reviewer for the FDA

Americans consume about 3 billion prescriptions annually. *And in 2004 alone, they spent over $200 billion on prescriptions drugs* (see appendix table 7.4d). Spending for prescription drugs in the Unites States rose 11 percent in 2003 to $180 billion, with similar increases in each of the previous two years. Retail prescription prices have increased an average of 7.4 percent annually from 1993 to 2003, almost three times the average inflation rate of 2.5 percent. Between 1995 and 2002, the average increase for drug expenditures was 15 percent higher than for any other type of health expenditure.

America's Only Legal Monopoly

America is the world's best market for drug makers because the patent protection is so good and it's the only developed nation without drug price controls. In 1990, the average retail prescription price was $22.06. In 2000 it was $45.79. According to the Wall Street Journal, prescription drug spending increased by 17 percent in 2001. Today, estimates are that the average prescription is close to $65. Keep in mind these averages include generics too, and many of the patent-protected drugs cost over $150 per month. Finally, the average retail prescription price increased more then 3 times the rate of general inflation (CPI-all items) and more than twice the CPI for medical care from 1998 to 2000.

Americans pay more for prescription drugs than any other nation even when the drugs are produced by American companies because its free-market healthcare system permits it. In contrast, because other nations have government-sponsored healthcare, they have set limits to what drug companies can charge. As a result, Americans are paying twice as much as Canadians for the same drugs that were made in America. The bottom line is that *Americans are actually subsidizing the cost of prescription drugs for other nations since it is the only nation with no price controls.* It's no wonder why so many Americans are buying prescription drugs from Canada and Mexico. However, the FDA has banned the importation of prescription drugs from abroad, where prices are up to 70 percent lower, stating a "safety" concern. It is clear that the FDA is more concerned with protecting its financing arm (big pharma) than Americans.

Even though the pharmaceutical industry has been hit with several product recalls and other issues over the past few years, it was still *300 percent more profitable than the median for all Fortune 500 companies* at 15.8 percent compared to the 5.2 percent (figure 7.9). In the early 1990s, drug spending kept pace with increases in other healthcare spending items. However, ever since the mid-1990s (when the FDA started receiving all of its funding from big pharma), increases in drug spending were 200 to 500 percent greater than expenditures for hospital care and physician services. Only since 2003 have spending increases for prescription drugs fallen in line with normal increases in healthcare expenditures, which are very high already (figure 7-10).

Figure 7-9. Profitability Among Pharmaceutical Manufacturers Compared to Other Industries

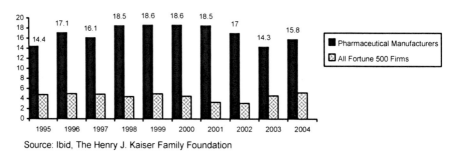

Source: Ibid, The Henry J. Kaiser Family Foundation

From 1995 to 2002, the pharmaceutical industry was the most profitable in America. Since 2002 the profitability has been in a modest decline, ranking as the third most profitable industry in 2004 at 15.8 percent, after mining and crude oil industries which registered 22.1 percent. But this recent setback should only be temporary, especially after the passage of Part D Medicare.

Why Are Healthcare Costs So High?
- Pharmaceutical Monopoly and Manipulation
- Fraud
- Waste
- Lack of Price Controls
- Misdirected Healthcare System

Figure 7-10. Annual Rise in Health Care Expenditures by Service

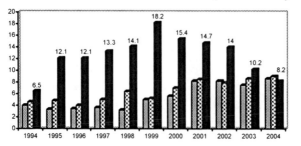

Source: Ibid, The Henry J. Kaiser Family Foundation

What President Bush has essentially said to the pharmaceutical industry by passage of Part D Medicare is, *go ahead and charge any price you want and I will spread the expense to all Americans in order to provide discounts to those on Medicare because I favor the wealthy and the drug company monopoly.*

Money is Not the Solution

Contrary to popular American belief, throwing money at a problem is not the best way to solve it. We have seen this approach fail with K-12 education and we see it now with healthcare. Throwing more money at a problem just increases fraud and waste. Western Europe's healthcare delivery is considered the world's best, holding the top nine spots, yet each of these nations have healthcare expenses per capital that are much less than in America (table 7-3).

When you examine the three primary gauges of healthcare—quality, access and cost, America scores poorly in each. From this alarming data, America should feel worried and humiliated. With over 3 billion annual prescriptions written in America and total healthcare expenditures estimated at over $2 trillion in 2006, Americans must ask why their healthcare is not at least in the top five.

Table 7-3. World Health Care Rankings

Country	Rank
Belguim	1
Iceland	2
Netherlands	3
France	4
Switzerland	5
Austria	6
Sweden	7
Italy	8
Norway	9
Australia, Germany, Denmark	10
United States of America	**17**
United Kingdom	23

The World Markets Research Center survey of the health status of people in 175 countries and the index measured the health status of individuals by looking at the amount each country spent on health and at health indicators including life expectancy, infant immunization rates and death rates of mothers and babies.

The Uninsured in America

According to the U.S. Census Bureau, nearly 50 million Americans did not have health insurance in 2005. As well, estimates show that an additional 150 million Americans lost their insurance for part of the year or are underinsured. According to reports released by the federal government in early 2006, "the quality and opportunity of healthcare access is not equal across all economic and social population groups."

For nearly two decades, the percentage of Americans without any insurance has held constant at around 16 percent annually; not exactly something to be proud of. However, this percentage has already increased by over 2 percentage points over the past three years. Surprisingly, eighty percent of the uninsured are working or in families with current workers. When you factor in public healthcare, these numbers are magnified, given that Medicare covers disabled Americans and the elderly, while Medicaid covers many of the indigent. For the most costly healthcare expenses such as those incurred during chronic illnesses, many are uninsured as well. For instance, about 11 percent of cancer patients under the age of 65 are uninsured, as are up to 20 percent of minority cancer patients. In conclusion, it's the working poor and middle class who are left out of these social health programs.

Most of America's uninsured do not have the ability to pay for medical treatment, yet they do not qualify for Medicare or Medicaid. These people are refused treatment by hospitals unless they are in the critical stages of illness. As it turns out, these are often the most costly of all healthcare expenses. Therefore, *by not providing Americans with basic healthcare needs and preventative treatments, those without any form of health insurance are actually placing a larger financial strain upon the system.*

Figure 7-11. Uninsured in America

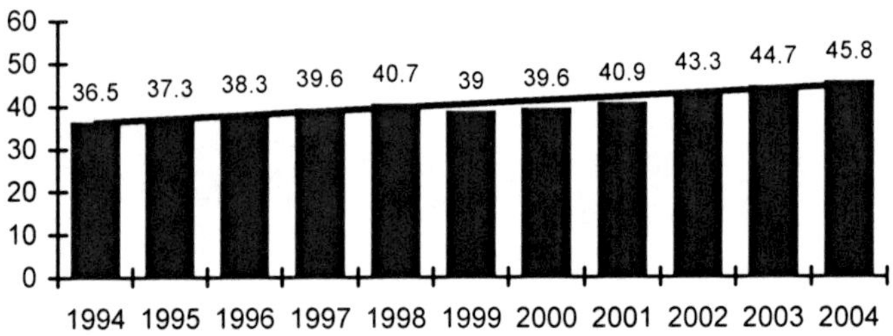

Source: Employee Benefit Research Institute, "Sources of Health Insurance and Characteristics of the Uninsured: Analysis of the March 2004 Current Population Survey." Issue Brief No. 276, December 2004.

Lack of Insurance is Affecting Everyone

As the state of America's healthcare crisis continues to surpass epic proportions, it has shown no particular preference, touching the lives of Americans from all backgrounds, regardless of race, ethnicity, income, education, employment, and age. For instance, in 2004, the number of Americans earning more than $75,000 per year who lost their insurance increased by 28 percent. And the number of Americans with college degrees who lost their insurance increased by 29 percent. In 2006, estimates are that more than 2 million of those who will lose their health insurance will still have a full-time job.

While more than 80 percent of America's uninsured belong to working families, 66 percent come from low-income families. However, about *30 percent of the uninsured come from households with incomes exceeding $50,000, and 50 percent work at small businesses or are self-employed. Additionally, 52 percent of the uninsured are minorities, 10 percent are college students, and 59 percent have been without coverage for two years or more.*

The widespread lack of health insurance is affecting the productivity of America, as well as the health and morale of millions. Nearly one-quarter (23 percent) of the uninsured reported "changing their way of life significantly in order to pay medical bills." And nearly 50 percent of the American public says they are "very worried about having to pay more for their healthcare or health insurance," while 42 percent report they are very worried about not having the money to pay medical bills. If one member of a family is uninsured and has an accident or a health problem, this can affect the economic stability of the entire family.

Each year, the United States spends nearly $100 billion per year to provide uninsured residents with health services, another $533 billion for Medicare and Medicaid, while hospitals provide about $34 billion worth of uncompensated care. Another $37 billion is paid by private and public payers for health services for the uninsured, and $26 billion is paid out-of-pocket by those who lack coverage. In total that amounts to about $730 billion or 35 percent of total 2005 healthcare expenditures (5.6 percent of 2005 GDP). But still, affordable access to healthcare remains an unreachable dream for many Americans.

> More than 3,500 working families lose healthcare coverage every day. The number one concern for people is the rising cost of health care, even exceeding any concerns they have over losing their job or terrorism. Sadly, 80 percent of those without insurance are from working families, who just can't afford insurance.

In any other nation with a national healthcare system, $730 billion would be sufficient to provide for total healthcare expenditures. However, due to the waste, fraud, and lack of drug price controls, Americans spend more than all other nations but get less in return, while lining the pockets of millions linked to the healthcare industry.

Table 7-4. Health Insurance Coverage (2001-2005)*

	Uninsured		Medicaid/ SCHIP	Employer-sponsored Insurance	Individually-purchased Insurance	Medicare	Military Healthcare
	Number (millions)	Percent	Percent	Percent	Percent	Percent	Percent
2005	46.6	15.9	13.0	59.5	9.1	13.7	3.8
2004	45.3	15.6	13.0	59.8	9.3	13.6	3.7
2003	45.0	15.6	12.4	60.4	9.2	13.7	3.5
2002	43.6	15.2	11.6	61.3	9.3	13.4	3.5
2001	41.2	14.6	11.2	62.6	9.2	13.5	3.4

*Based on Current Population Surveys. Percentages do not sum to 100% because some have more than one type of coverage.
Source: Center on Budget Policy and Priorities. August 29, 2006.

Why Are the Uninsured Increasing?

Due to escalating costs, many employers no longer offer a healthcare plan to their employees. Rapidly rising health insurance premiums is the main reason cited by all small firms for not offering coverage. *In 2003, one-third of American companies did not offer coverage. And in 2001, this percentage was twice as high.* Nearly two-fifths (38 percent) of all workers are employed in smaller businesses, where less than two-thirds of these firms now offer health benefits to their employees.

Meanwhile, the problem is only getting worse as insurance premiums continue to rise at unthinkable rates. *Over the past five years, the average annual increase in inflation has been about 2.5 percent while health insurance premiums have escalated an average of 11.4 percent annually*—over 450 percent higher than the average annual inflation rate.

Even when employers offer insurance coverage, workers can't always afford their portion of the premium. *Employee spending for health insurance coverage (employee's share of family coverage and deductibles) has increased 126 percent between 2000 and 2004.* Finally, only seven percent of the unemployed can afford to pay for COBRA health insurance (see Section 7.6 for expanded coverage of America's uninsured).

Figure 7-12.   Percentage Uninsured, by Age, People Under Age 65 (First Half of 2004)

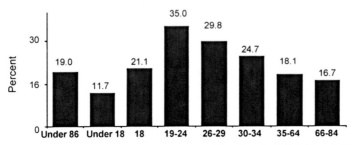

Source: Center for Financing, Access, and Cost Trends, AHRQ, Household Component of the Medical Expenditure Panel Survey 2004 Point-in-Time File.

Medical Bankruptcy

In 1997, 28 percent of all personal bankruptcy filings were related to medical bills. In 1999, when the economy was supposedly "booming," 40 percent of America's 1 million-plus bankruptcies were related to medical bills. Two years later, in 2001 about 50 percent of the 2 million personal bankruptcies in the United States were due to medical bills. Latest estimates are that in 2004 and 2005, as bankruptcies reached all-time highs in excess of 2 million, 50 percent were attributed to medical bills. As it stands today, *the rising costs of healthcare and job instability have made medical bankruptcy the leading cause of personal bankruptcies in the United States.*

A recent study by Harvard University researchers found that the average out-of-pocket medical debt for those who filed for bankruptcy was $12,000. In addition, the study found that 50 percent of all bankruptcy filings were partly the result of medical expenses. *Every 30 seconds in the United States someone files for bankruptcy in the aftermath of a serious health problem.* Yet, Washington refuses to acknowledge America's obvious healthcare crisis. Why would any "superpower" permit even one citizen to declare bankruptcy due to their inability to pay for healthcare?

But the problem doesn't end there. Even individuals with health insurance can find their way into bankruptcy court, or at the very least, with a major financial hardship. The study by Harvard also found that *68 percent of those who filed for bankruptcy had health insurance.* Keep in mind that most insurers have a lifetime cap on the amount of benefits that can be paid to a policy holder, and if you get a major illness, the expenses needed may well exceed this cap.

> *"Unless you're Bill Gates you're just one serious illness away from bankruptcy. Most of the medically bankrupt were average Americans who happened to get sick."*
>
> Dr. David Himmelstein, Associate Professor of Medicine at Harvard

Alternatively, several illnesses over one's lifetime may cause this cap to be reached, leaving the policyholder with little insurance to provide for a major illness. And if you get a chronic disease such as cancer, without supplementary insurance, you will most likely depart from this world with nothing left in your estate except medical bills. Why does one need insurance companies if they aren't willing to spread risk? How can they claim to be spreading risk among policy holders if they have benefit caps, refuse coverage to individuals with preexisting conditions, and other fine print limitations that ensure high annual profits?

Peter Cunningham, a researcher at the Center for Studying Health System Change published a study that reported about 13.5 million families with health insurance had trouble paying medical bills. One-half of workers in the lowest-compensation jobs and one-half of workers in mid-range-compensation jobs either had problems with medical bills in a 12-month period or were paying off accrued medical debt. One-quarter of workers in higher-compensated positions also reported problems with medical bills or were paying off accrued debt.

Finally, even seniors who typically have fewer expenses, and who qualify for public healthcare are not immune to medical bankruptcies. In fact, many bankruptcy attorneys have seen a recent surge in filings for seniors who have run up huge debt on their credit cards to pay for prescription drugs. Perhaps the only factor that will serve to decrease the rising trend in medical bankruptcies is the fact it is extremely difficult to erase insurmountable medical or any other debt due to the passage of President Bush's bankruptcy reform bill in 2005.

> "I'm filing a lot of bankruptcies for senior citizens on fixed incomes and I can tell you that a substantial amount of the unsecured credit card debts…are for prescriptions."
>
> Dennis Spyra, bankruptcy attorney

Those Without Are Charged the Most

To make matters worse, those without insurance are charged the most by hospitals. Does it make sense that those with the least ability to pay for a basic necessity like healthcare are the ones who are charged the highest prices? According to a state agency in Pennsylvania, *health insurers only pay only $0.38 for each dollar of healthcare used by its policy holders due to the large discounts offered by HMOs and PPOs to insurers.*

Insurance and hospital spokespersons claim that volume discounts are "the norm in any industry." But this raises some interesting issues about a service that most would consider a basic necessity. Should healthcare providers be forbidden from issuing discounts to insurers while refusing the same discounts to individuals paying out of their pockets? Absolutely. As a matter of fact, those without insurance should be provided with bigger discounts. To compound matters, the uninsured can't exactly shop around for the best rates during emergencies, since they are taken to the nearest hospital. Even for less immediate life-threatening procedures, the lack of price transparency often inhibits shopping around for non-emergency healthcare.

Medicaid

In 1965, Congress created Medicaid for low-income and disabled Americans who were not able to afford health insurance. Over the past 40 years, Medicaid has provided healthcare for about one in six Americans. Medicaid pays for the delivery of one-third of the nation's babies, provides healthcare for one in four children, reimburses healthcare costs of 50 percent of HIV and AIDS patients, and covers two-thirds the cost of nursing home patients.

Enrollment in Medicaid continues to increase and is approaching a double-digit annual growth rate not seen since 1992 when it was 11.9 percent. Yet in 2003, just over half of all Americans scraping by (or an income of less than 200 percent of the poverty level for a family of four, or $36,800) received Medicaid. Note that, by the admission of the Department of Health and Human Services, "Medicaid does not provide medical assistance for all poor persons. Even under the broadest provisions of the Federal statute (except for emergency services for certain persons), the Medicaid program does not provide health care services, even for very poor persons, unless they are in one of the designated eligibility groups."

Medicaid accounts for over 20 percent of state government spending and currently commands the number two spot after education. However, this may change soon, as it has easily become the fastest growing expense for most states. And it is only going to get worse as 76 million Baby Boomers get older. Even though most states are cutting both education and Medicaid expenses, by 2009 Medicaid will most likely take over the top spot as the number one expenditure of most state budgets (Section 7.8, appendix).

Medicare

In 1965, Medicare was approved by Congress to provide medical insurance for the elderly but was expanded in 1973 to cover some disabled Americans under age 65. Today, Medicare provides medical expenses for over 35 million elderly and 6 million disabled Americans. Similar to Medicaid, America's aging population combined with its declining birth rates have put Medicare on a collision course with financial reality.

In the 1930s, when Washington defined the retirement age at 65, most Americans didn't live that long. Since then, life expectancies for women have increased from 66 to 79, and for men from 61 to 77. Meanwhile, the birth rate has dropped from 25 per 1,000 residents in the 1950s to just 15 today. The lower birth rate means fewer workers are paying taxes to finance Social Security and Medicare benefits for the rapidly growing population aged 65 and over.

To fund Medicare, each American worker pays 1.45 percent of wages (withheld from pay checks). However, unlike the case with Social Security taxes, there is no cap on wage taxes for Medicare, so each worker is taxed 1.45 percent on every dollar of earned income. In addition, employers also pay 1.45 percent of workers' wages towards the

Medicare tax. Thus, a combined tax of 2.9 percent on employee wages is paid to the Medicare program to provide funds for its eligible participants. But even the money earmarked for Medicare is poorly spent. The U.S. Department of Health and Human Services (HHS) spends 80 percent of its budget on administrative overhead (see Section 7.9, appendix).

America's Medicare Landfall

Medicare has had about 3.3 workers paying taxes for every recipient for the past 30 years. However, baby boomer retirements will reduce that to just two workers for each recipient by 2040. Immigration has helped offset some of the decline in birth rates, but immigration (legal and illegal) would have to increase annually by up to ten times the 1.2 million figures reported in 2001 to provide sufficient payroll taxes to fund Medicare.

As Medicare recipients are growing older their healthcare costs are rising as well. Annual medical costs for an 85-year-old are double those of a 65-year-old. And the costs for Americans 65 and older are four times more than that of a younger adult, and as much as seven times more than a child.

In 2006, federal spending per Medicare recipient will average about $7,500. And by 2050, Medicare will be responsible for paying $26,683 per recipient (in 2004 dollars). In the largest increase in its history, Medicare premiums paid by elderly and disabled enrollees for routine care rose 17 percent in 2005, boosting the monthly fees from $66.60 to $78.20 and affecting nearly all of the 41.8 million beneficiaries.

Figure 7-13. Projected Medicare Spending Per Person

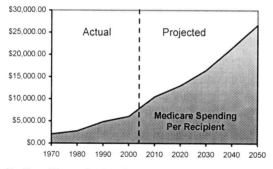

Sources: Health and Human Services Centers for Medicare and Medicaid Services

Overall, the costs for Medicare and Medicaid are increasing by up to 6 times faster than even Social Security. This trend will continue to accelerate as the boomers get older and live longer. According to Gokhale, Medicare alone has a present value shortfall of about $30 trillion over the next few decades. However, this liability only accounts for ten years of Part D.

> *"the long-term picture is pretty bad"*
>
> Gokhale commenting on the Medicaid and Social Security crises

Figure 7-14. Medicare Trust Fund Annual Cash Deficits or Surpluses (1967-2020)

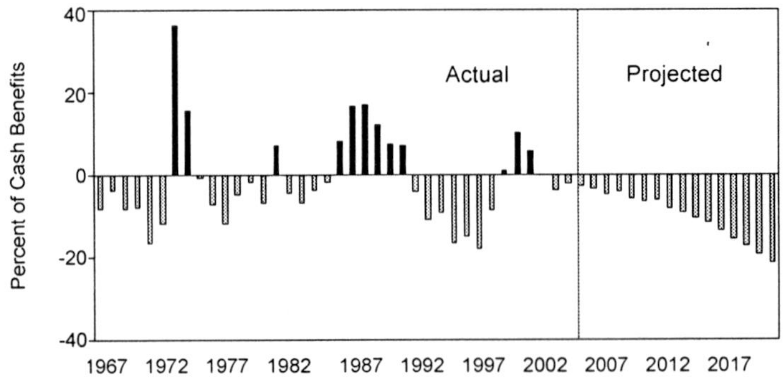

Sources: Social Security Administration, Health and Human Services Centers for Medicare and Medicaid Services

Bills for Your Grandchildren

According to the Urban Institute, a married couple entering their final year of work earning the median income of $46,400 will retire the following year with a joint Medicare benefit valued at $283,500 on a present value basis. Over this couple's life expectancy, this amount will of course be much higher. Regardless, over the years in which this same couple had worked, they only contributed a total of $43,300 in Medicare taxes (calculated in present day value), or a deficit in Medicare of $240,200. With this example alone, it is easy to see how America's youth will be faced will an enormous financial burden of funding the Medicare benefits for the boomer generation.

However, this couple also qualifies for $22,900 in annual Social Security benefits, which are adjusted annually for inflation (COLA). The present value of $22,900 is estimated at a lump-sum amount of about $326,000. But the total amount of Social Security taxes paid over the couple's lifetime was only $198,000, resulting in a deficit of $128,000 for Social Security. Therefore, the total loss for taxpayers for this couple's Medicare and Social Security benefits is $368,200.

> "As a nation, we may have already made promises to coming generations of retirees that we will be unable to fulfill."
>
> Federal Reserve Chairman Alan Greenspan told the House Budget Committee

But the children of today will be entitled to receive even higher benefits due to general inflation as well as the out-of-control healthcare inflation that affects Medicare benefits. According to estimates by the Urban Institute, when the children of this couple retire they will receive total benefits that are 45 percent higher than their parents, or $884,000 versus $609,500 (present value).

Universal Healthcare

Washington could easily provide for universal healthcare coverage. Combined with the $730 billion already paid for by public healthcare and hospitals, Washington could structure a plan of national coverage for every American without any additional payroll tax increases. America should be able to create such a plan with an additional $400 to $500 billion. These extra funds would come from the loss of employer-sponsored plan tax deductions (adding $200 to $300 billion) and elimination of middle-men (an estimated savings of $200 billion), which have acted as a force to drive costs up.

Finally, a nominal fee-for service for those who can pay will provide the last remaining source of funds needed for a national healthcare program in America. These fees would provide perpetual solvency to the program and discourage wasteful use. Drug price controls would discourage drug over- and misuse. Within this program, the healthcare industry would be required to focus on efficiency without insurance premiums to fall back on. Physicians would finally focus on preventative medicine, and Americans would adapt healthier lifestyles, forcing the food industry to provide healthier alternatives. Ultimately, such a system would furnish all Americans with better overall coverage.

At the very least, Washington could provide for the uninsured. According to the Institute of Medicine, providing insurance for America's uninsured population would add only $34 to $69 billion in costs, equivalent to less than 0.5 percent of total healthcare costs. The benefits would be dramatic—a gain $65 to $130 billion in terms of lives saved, better health, reduced Medicare and disability costs, and gains in workplace productivity. The amount to cover America's uninsured is small compared to the cost of tax breaks for employer-based insurance, estimated at $125 billion in 1988 and probably higher than $300 billion today.

So why does America remain the only developed nation without universal health coverage? No politician wants to be the one who votes for universal coverage because it will ensure a very difficult re-election. While universal healthcare would create less waste and lower salaries, it would make America's labor force more competitive with the rest of the world.

Unfortunately the majority of healthcare providers in America are more concerned with lining their pockets than saving lives. With the help of hundreds of insurance and drug lobbyists in Washington, America probably won't get a universal health system anytime soon. Imagine how much money these industries stand to lose if universal healthcare replaced the current free-market system. The health insurance industry would be wiped out completely and drug companies would be held to strict price controls.

During the Clinton administration, there was some momentum over a national system that would provide coverage for all Americans. However, Congress never approved Clinton's proposal, perhaps due to the influence of big pharma, the large pool of healthcare voters, and industry lobbyists. Since that time there have been so many problems that President Bush has been able to avoid the topic of how to fix healthcare. Rather, as a way to appease the large number of senior voters, he passed Part D Medicare, which is going to increase healthcare fraud. Already, millions of seniors realize that this program provides a false sense of security due to the "doughnut hole," while serving to line the pockets of big pharma (see Section 7.9, appendix).

Parallels with Wall Street

The parallels between America's healthcare industry and Wall Street are quite apparent. While the healthcare industry has the FDA as its regulator, Wall Street has the SEC. Drug reps serve as the salesmen to push drugs and manipulate physicians, similar to stockbrokers who push analyst recommendations onto their clients. Pharmaceutical and medical device companies have "hired guns" to conduct their research that always shows positive effects of their drugs. And Wall Street has analysts who are paid to issue favorable recommendations as a reward to those companies who deliver investment banking business to their firm. Finally, physicians control the health of their patients by providing diagnosis and treatment regimens much in the same way as fund managers analyze the stock market and prepare investment management approaches based upon their skills and "diagnostics" of the market.

Figure 7-15. How Wall Street and Healthcare in America Are Similar

Category	Healthcare		Wall Street
Government Regulator	FDA	←→	SEC
Primary Provider	Physicians	←→	Fund Managers
Secondary Providers	Drug Company Reps	←→	Stockbrokers
Information Providers	Clinical research	←→	Analysts
Issuers	Drug Companies	←→	Investment Banks

Conclusions

The economic system that created the strong link between healthcare coverage and employment in America is much different today. Expansion of free trade has made job security a vision of the past. The unfortunate reality is that until America's healthcare system is fixed, the majority of Americans will remain without affordable, continuous and complete access to healthcare. And job benefits will suffer and continue to decrease net wage growth. More American companies will relocate overseas, and the financial security of Americans, especially in their "Golden Years" will remain questionable.

The only reasonable solution is to create a national healthcare system. Only then will America be prepared to compete globally. Removing the healthcare middlemen alone would save billions due to elimination of fees. And the disintegration of unrestricted price hikes by pharmaceutical companies would make healthcare costs even more affordable. Finally, the huge administrative fees that currently serve to keep costs high would be reduced even through a government-sponsored national healthcare program.

Already, many have gone overseas to have costly procedures performed at a fraction of the cost that America's overpriced healthcare system charges. Places like India, Singapore, and Europe are amongst the hottest spots for healthcare outsourcing, saving Americans up to 80 percent of the costs charged at home. Many of these facilities have been specifically built to profit from the effects of America's healthcare crisis.

But don't think these overseas facilities are shabby. In fact, many of them resemble 5-star hotels. For many Americans with a need for surgery, a trip to an Indian hospital provides a two-week vacation overseas while saving thousands of dollars in medical bills. What is left for America when its citizens have to travel abroad for affordable healthcare?

Healthcare outsourcing for non-emergency treatments will only grow in popularity until Washington decides to provide a healthcare system that is accessible and affordable for all.

No nation can claim to be "great" when one-fifth of its population is without healthcare. Yet, this is only one of many of America's problems. With a badly damaged economic scaffold, America must construct a new foundation if it intends to remain the world superpower. And healthcare will be the primary component of this foundation. This transition will consume many years and require numerous hardships, but if initiated now, it will be less painful to current and future generations. Most likely, only a huge disaster will provide the incentive for Washington to enact policy changes required to once again position America as the most powerful and greatest nation on earth. Until that period, things are only going to get worse for America.

8

THE SOCIAL SECURITY DEBACLE

Overview

One of the greatest developments in American domestic policy has been the evolution of a social insurance system that provides a core income and healthcare benefit base to those who may not be as fortunate as others. This social insurance system consists of *Social Security*, which pays benefits to retired Americans, widows, the disabled and their families; *Medicare*, which pays for medical benefits for Americans aged 65 and over and disabled of all ages; *Medicaid*, a state and federal program that pays for the medical services of low-income Americans; *Workers' Compensation*, which pays for wage replacement and medical costs for Americans who have been injured while at the workplace; and *Unemployment Insurance*, which provides a temporary and partial wage replacement for those who have lost their jobs through lay-offs or closed operations.

Among these social insurance plans, Social Security has been the most successful. But in addition to providing a needs-based subsidy, it is a true entitlement program since people earn the right to participate by working and contributing to the trust fund from payroll taxes. Thus, Social Security is America's only social insurance program providing a basic level of income to prevent poverty, while allocating benefits, although reduced, to higher-income retirees who have paid into the system. Because of its uniqueness, Social Security is America's only social program that has provided for the well-being of millions of Americans during both good times and bad.

Also due to its uniqueness, the full value of Social Security is difficult to measure since it has no private market counterpart. While a dollar value can be assessed to one's life benefits based upon their earned benefit level, it is difficult if not impossible to measure the value of the total assurance that Social Security provides. What is the value of having a guaranteed insurance policy that insures workers against failed careers and prevents them from slipping into poverty? Indeed, for decades, many Americans took for granted the assurances afforded by Social Security. In fact, in the past, many viewed it as "bonus income" during retirement because they had sufficient savings.

Today however, Social Security is no longer considered "bonus income" but as the main source of income by most elderly Americans. Despite its current use in America, Social Security was never intended to provide the sole or even primary source of retirement income, but rather to serve as a supplement to pension plans and savings. Yet today, *2 out of 3 elderly Americans rely on Social Security as their main source of income*, and for 1 out of 5, it is their only means of income. Therefore, without Social Security most elderly Americans would live in poverty. These disturbing facts highlight the gradual decline of the American living standard and reemphasize the importance of strengthening Social Security for current and future generations. However, it is the definition of "strengthen" that is most critical to consider.

Historical Background

On August 14, 1935, FDR signed the Social Security Act (SSA). At that time, millions were unemployed, had no savings and risked losing their homes, as America was suffering the affects of the Great Depression. And while Social Security taxes began in January 1937, it was only on January 31, 1940 that the first recipient of this program received a benefit check (Ida May Fuller from Ludlow, Vermont for $22.54).

The Social Security Act consists of two main programs, Old Age Assistance (OAA) and Old Age Insurance (OAI). The OAA provides matching funds to states to subsidize state pension plans and covers retired workers, disabled, and their eligible dependents. Monthly benefits are based on a formula that favors lower income workers' earnings adjusted for wage inflation. OAI is the portion of Social Security that is responsible for paying monthly retirement benefits.

At the time of inception, payroll taxes that financed Social Security were only 1.0 percent each from employers and workers, capped on the first $3000 of annual earnings. By 1938, payroll taxes were doubled to 2.0 percent where they remained constant over the next decade. Over the next 30 years, they began a gradual ascent as did the cap on wages.

By 1989, payroll taxes had increased to 12.4 percent where they have held constant to this day. That poses the question whether Washington may feel it's time for another increase. Unlike most federal taxes, Social Security (payroll) taxes have never been decreased so we should not expect any changes in fiscal policy that would cause them to decline (figures 8-1 and 15-22).

Figure 8-1. History of Payroll Tax Increases (combined employer/employee OASDI tax rate)

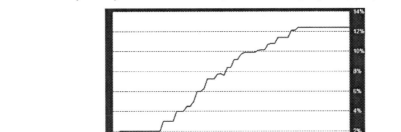

Sources: Social Security Administration
Prepared by: Joint Economic Committee (JEC) 2/2/2005

Changes to Benefits

Up until 1956, retirement benefits could only be collected after workers turned 65, which was quite old at the time. However, recognizing the need to provide income security for household wives, the SSA was amended to provide an early retirement benefit from Social Security that began when females reached age 62. Six years later, this option was extended to males. Meanwhile, benefits to divorced wives were not covered until 1965 after divorce rates began to increase, creating a gap in income for many women who were still greatly underrepresented in the workplace. Only in 1977 did the SSA extend the same option to divorced husbands. Disability benefits were added in 1956 but were only made available to those between the ages of 50 to 64. While benefits have been reduced for the optional early retirement election, they allow low-income individuals to enter the benefit stage at an earlier time period.

Cost-of-Living Adjustments

In 1972, President Nixon signed into law a 20 percent cost-of-living adjustment (COLA) to combat the effects of inflation. However, since the late '70s, Social Security benefits have failed to keep pace with inflation. During the inflation crisis of the late '70s and early '80s, Social Security benefit growth was decreased due to economic conditions and the fear that there would not be enough funds to cover future beneficiaries. Consequently, in 1983 a cost-of-living adjustment (COLA) was delayed, up to half of the benefits became taxable, and payroll taxes increased.

During the same year of his delay of the COLA, President Reagan added a gradual increase in retirement age to be phased in at 67 for those born in 1960 and thereafter. The original early retirement benefits remained at age 62 but were reduced from 80 to 70 percent, while those opting for the new early retirement age of 65 would receive 86.7 percent of full benefits.

While the Reagan administration was successful in curbing the double-digit inflation that crippled much of the American economy, appropriate adjustments for Social Security were never made, perhaps due to the massive expenditures and debt resulting from the Cold War arms buildup. Today we see the effects of benefits that have much less buying power, combined with a heightened dependency on Social Security by millions due to the massive losses in retirement assets during the Internet bubble correction, poor savings trends, and declining living standards. (1)

As a result of these trends, today most Americans opt for early Social Security retirement, decreasing their annual benefit amount, despite the fact that life expectancies continue to increase. This trend further highlights America's growing dependence on Social Security income. In 2004, about 76 percent of Americans (74 percent men and 78 percent women) covered by Social Security received reduced benefits by opting for the early retirement designation.

---

(1) In 2000, President Clinton eliminated the retirement earnings test for beneficiaries above the full-benefit retirement age. This test previously required to retirees at or above the full-benefits age to forfeit a portion of their benefits if they earned an amount in excess of a threshold. However, the earnings test still exists today for beneficiaries below the full-benefit age.

Shortly after Reagan left office in 1988, a new bull market period began. Fueled by the tremendous economic growth in America, the Social Security program was elevated into a much healthier position, resulting in annual surpluses in the Social Security Trust Fund. As we shall see in the next chapter, a similar trend occurred with both public and private pension plans. However, the reversal in pension surplus trends will soon be mirrored by forthcoming annual deficits in the Social Security Trust Fund due to the retirement of America's largest generation.

Unlike a declining stock market which has led to a record number of underfunded pension plans, Social Security will be facing a solvency issue beginning in 2040 mainly due to demographics. Yet, many seem to think a crisis begins in the first year of deficits, expected by 2017. Regardless, one could argue that weaknesses in America's pension system and Social Security are indirect consequences free trade, which has exposed America's declining global competitiveness.

Historical COLAs (1975-2006)

July 1975—8.0%	Jan 1992—3.7%
July 1976—6.4%	Jan 1993—3.0%
July 1977—5.9%	Jan 1994—2.6%
July 1978—6.5%	Jan 1995—2.8%
July 1979—9.9%	Jan 1996—2.6%
July1980—14.3%	Jan 1997—2.9%
July 1981—11.2%	Jan 1998—2.1%
July 1992—7.4%	Jan 1999—1.3%
Jan 1984—3.5%	Jan 2000—2.5%
Jan 1985—3.5%	Jan 2001—3.5%
Jan 1986—3.1%	Jan 2002—2.6%
Jan 1987—1.3%	Jan 2003—1.4%
Jan 1988—4.2%	Jan 2004—2.1%
Jan 1989—4.0%	Jan 2005—2.7%
Jan 1990—4.7%	Jan 2006—4.1%
Jan 1991—5.4%	

The first automatic COLA, for June 1975, was based on the increase in the CPI for Urban Wage Earners and Clerical Workers (CPI-W) from the second quarter of 1974 to the first quarter of 1975. The 1976-82 COLAs were based on increases in the CPI-W from the first quarter of the prior year to the corresponding quarter of the current year in which the COLA became effective. After 1982, COLAs have been based on increases in the CPI-W from the third quarter of the prior year to the corresponding quarter of the current year in which the COLA became effective.

Source: Social Security Administration

How it Works

In keeping with the tenants of a social insurance program, Social Security funnels more money to lower wage earners because they are the ones who need it the most. Benefits provide wage income replacement during retirement relative to wages earned during working years. Retirees who earned lower wages throughout their career have paid less money into the system, yet receive a greater percentage of replacement income (known as the *replacement rate,* or the ratio of benefits relative to pre-retirement earnings).

A Board of Trustees for the Social Security Trust Fund was established by the Social Security Act for advising Congress on the financial status of the trust fund. (2) The Trustees' annual report estimates benefit costs, revenues, and benefit amounts and provides forecasts for the short- (10 years) and long-range (75 years) actuarial and financial status of the trust fund. These estimates are based on certain assumptions regarding mortality, fertility and immigration rates, and economic forecasting.

---

(2) This board also reports to Congress on the financial status of Medicare and has six members from Washington—the Secretaries of Treasury, Labor, Health and Human Services, the Commissioner of Social Security, and two trustees representing the public from different political parties, appointed by the president.

Because trust fund surpluses are borrowed by the government, the funds are credited with U.S. Treasury ("special interest") securities, adding to the national debt. At the end of fiscal year 2005, 23 percent of the national debt was owed to the Social Security Trust Fund while an additional 19 percent was held by other federal trust funds.

Payroll Taxes and Eligibility

To fund the Social Security Trust Fund, American workers pay 6.2 percent of their annual earnings up to a maximum of $94,200 (up from 90,000 or 4.7 percent in 2005). This is part of the payroll tax known as FICA (Federal Insurance Contribution Act). The other half of this tax is paid by the employer, resulting in a total tax of 12.4 percent.

Currently, elderly Americans qualify for full Social Security retirement benefits at age 65 or partial benefits at age 62 for early retirement (with changes for those born on or after 1960 as stated previously). In order to qualify for Social Security retirement income, a typical worker must have earned 40 Social Security credits, meaning they must have worked 40 quarters (10 years) in a job that was covered by Social Security (i.e. one where payroll taxes were paid). As well, some disabled Americans or minors who have lost a parent may also qualify for benefits with no age requirements. The maximum Social Security benefit at age 65 is currently about $23,000 ($22,500 in 2005) representing an approximate 25 percent replacement of average wages.

Social Security is a pay-as-you-go social insurance program, whereby beneficiaries are compensated according to specific formulas. However, due to changing demographics and changing economic conditions, it is only natural to expect periods of trust fund surpluses and deficits. Yet, Social Security was never meant to be a system that financed future benefits, unlike pension plans. Therefore, when surpluses have occurred, Washington has borrowed these funds.

> "We have instructed our politicians not to tell us about this problem. If they even mention cuts to Social Security, we vote them out of office."
>
> Lawrence Kotlikoff, Boston University economist

As of January 2006, the Social Security program covered 48.5 million Americans (30.6 million retired workers, 4.7 million widows and widowers, 6.5 million due to disability or loss of a working spouse, and 769,000 severely disabled adult children of deceased, retired, or disabled workers)—about 1 in 6 Americans or 1 in every 4 households. In 2006, the average benefit paid to retired workers increased by only $43 to $1002 from 2005 for cost-of-living adjustments. While this 4.1 percent COLA appears to be generous relative to a lower inflation figure, consider the large financial impact that record oil and utilities prices have had on the majority of Social Security recipients.

Excluding the initial period of crisis during the Great Depression (when no taxes were paid for Social Security), the OASDI taxes have risen by 625 percent from their initial rate of 2.0 percent in 1936, to 12.4 percent in 1988, where they remain today. However, benefits simply do not provide the same level of buying power as they once did. During this fifty-year period of continuous Social Security tax hikes, corporate taxes have declined, highlighting the rising power and influence of corporate America over this nation amidst a declining middle class (figure 15-22).

Disability Insurance

Social Security Disability Insurance (DI) pays monthly benefits to workers who are no longer able to "engage in any substantial gainful activity by reason of any medically determinable physical or mental impairment work due to illness, physical or mental impairment which is expected to last at least 12 months or which is expected to result in mortality within 12 months. Furthermore, the impairment or combination of impairments must be of such severity that the applicant is not only unable to do his or her previous work but cannot, considering his or her age, education, and work experience, engage in any other kind of substantial gainful work which exists in the national economy (Social Security Act, section 223 (d))." Medical records, work history, and the applicant's age and education are considered in making the determination of eligibility.

As previously mentioned, an additional criterion of eligibility is that the worker must have been employed for a sufficient time period (10 years) in jobs that were covered by Social Security. The formula for compensation is determined by earnings the employee made prior to the disability. An example of this schedule has been listed in table 8-1. As of January 2006, approximately 6.5 million Americans received DI from Social Security. Of the current 12.4 percent payroll taxes paid into the Social Security Trust Fund by workers and employers, 1.8 percent of this amount (0.9 percent for workers and 0.9 percent for employers) is allocated to the DI benefits trust fund.

Table 8-1. Social Security Disability Insurance Payout Schedule [1]

Earnings Before Disability (Lifetime Average*)	Annual DI Benefit	Percent of Earnings Replaced by Benefit
$15,000	$9,160	61%
$30,000	$13,960	46%
$55,000	$20,320	37%
$90,000	$25,570	28%

*Average indexed earnings
(1) The average DI benefit paid to workers in January 2005 was $894 a month/$10,730 per year.

Supplemental Security Income (SSI) is a program run by the SSA which pays monthly benefits to low-income aged, blind and disabled Americans. However, the benefits are not financed from the Social Security Trust Funds, but rather from the general tax revenues of the U.S. government. The SSI test of disability is identical to the one for DI. For applicants who are not disabled, only those with low incomes and limited financial assets are eligible for SSI. For individuals with no other "countable income" the monthly SSI benefit for 2005 was $579. However, benefits are reduced when other countable income is generated. As of June 2005, approximately 6.1 million low-income American adults received SSI benefits; 4.1 million were under the age of 65 and received eligibility due to disability or blindness while 2.0 million Americans over 65 received benefits.

While individuals receiving SSI are immediately eligible for Medicare, those only receiving DI are eligible for Medicare after two years of DI benefits have been earned. However, this presents a great problem for many disabled Americans because many who receive disability benefits are uninsurable, and when they are their premiums are absolutely unaffordable.

Current Status

For several years, American workers have been paying more into the Social Security Trust Fund than has being paid out in benefits, resulting in annual surpluses. Because Social Security was designed as a pay-as-you-go plan, annual deficits and surpluses were to be expected due to changing demographics. Regardless, it is the deficit expected in

2017 which has caused many to be alarmed. However, it's really not a reason for concern since the annual surpluses throughout the years have accumulated into a large fund of several trillion dollars that has been invested in interest-bearing U.S. Treasury securities ("special interest") and can be used to fund annual deficits for several years.

Because of this pay-as-you-go plan, Congress has borrowed Social Security's annual surpluses and spent the funds on programs such as the war in Iraq, Katrina, and many others, much the same as it has done with the U.S. Postal Service and American Indian trust funds. However, Congress is only acting in accordance with the SSA of 1935 (see Box 8-1).

By law, each year there is a surplus, Social Security funds are invested in U.S. treasuries, designated as "special interest" securities to distinguish them from other debts, where they are guaranteed principal and interest payments.(3) To date, these special interest securities have yielded an average annual return of 6.0 percent which has been added to this special account. *The interest income alone from this multi-trillion dollar surplus trust fund will be sufficient to pay for benefits for several years. After that, the fund will slowly be liquidated to pay benefits. Consequently, it is the 2040 time period that these total surplus funds will have been exhausted, leaving current payroll tax revenues as the only source of funds for beneficiaries.*

Figure 8-2. Social Security Trust Fund Annual Cash Deficits and Surpluses (1957-2020)

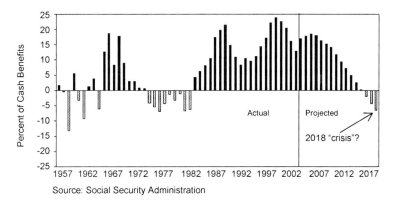

Source: Social Security Administration

As of 2003, the "special interest" surplus fund stood at about $1.5 trillion. Estimates indicate that the Social Security Trust Fund will have a surplus of $177 billion for the 2006 fiscal year after all benefits have been paid. Therefore, this $177 billion will be added to the "special interest" surplus fund that will be used after 2017 to make up for annual shortfalls in payroll taxes. *At the end of 2006, estimates by the Trustees report show that trust fund reserves ("special interest" surplus fund) should be around $2.035 trillion. But this amount is expected to grow even larger since annual surpluses will continue over the next ten years, (although declining each year) and together with accruing interest, will generate a total reserve base of $4.186 trillion by 2015.*

---

(3) Recall from Chapter Six that these special items are treated as off-balance items.

136

Beginning in 2017, the tax revenues flowing into the fund will be less than the total benefits flowing out, creating an annual deficit, which will continue for many years. Therefore, this $4.186 trillion surplus fund will begin a long period of depletion that will result in its complete consumption by 2040.

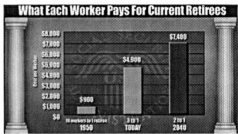

All dollars are current 2005 dollars. Assumes 2005 annual benefits of $14,000 for an average-wage retiree
Source: Social Security Administration

After that period, the incoming revenues from payroll taxes will only fund about 73 percent of the benefits needed. However the Congressional Budget Office has estimated that the trust funds would be able to pay full benefits until 2052, and about 80 of benefits thereafter.

Currently, Social Security benefits account for about 4.3 percent of the GDP, or a little more than 4 cents per dollar of economic output. In contrast, Social Security tax revenues are 4.9 percent of GDP, meaning that a surplus is being generated. However, by 2030, all of America's 76 million baby boomers will have entered retirement, causing an increase in benefits estimated to reach 6.3 percent of GDP (figure 8-3).

Estimates from the 2006 Trustees Report indicate that 84 percent of Social Security benefits for 2006 will come from 2006 payroll taxes, 14 percent of benefits will come from interest on the trust fund reserves (or "special interest" surplus trust), and 2 percent will come from taxes paid by Social Security beneficiaries (figure 8-4). Table 8-2 illustrates just one of the many factors contributing to the approaching trend of annual Social Security deficits. As life spans have increased, fewer workers remain in the labor force after 65, and are therefore extracting benefits.

Table 8-2. Labor Force Participation Rates of Men Age 65 and Over

Year	Labor Force Participation Rate (percent)
1850	76.6
1860	76.0
1870	-----
1880	78.0
1890	73.8
1900	65.4
1910	58.1
1920	60.1
1930	58.0
1940	43.5
1950	47.0
1960	40.8
1970	35.2
1980	24.7
1990	18.4
2000	17.5

Sources: Moen (1987), Costa (1998), Bureau of Labor Statistics

Figure 8-3. Social Security Costs as a Percentage of GDP and Taxable Payroll (1900-2080)

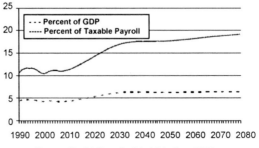

Source: Social Security Administration, 2006

Box 8-1: Social Security Act of 1935

"It shall be the duty of the Secretary of the Treasury to invest such portion of the amounts credited to the Account as is not, in his judgment, required to meet current withdrawals. Such investment may be made only in interest-bearing obligations of the United States or in obligations guaranteed as to both principal and interest by the United States."

Figure 8-4. Income Received by Social Security Trust Funds (estimates for 2006)

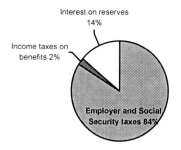

Source: Social Security Finances: Finds of the 2006 Trustees Report, National Academy of Social Insurance. May 2006, No 21.

Estimates show that *by 2031, there will be over 71 million Americans over the age 65, or nearly twice that of today.* While there are currently about 3.3 workers for every American receiving Social Security, by 2031 the number of workers will have declined to 2.1. What this means is that less tax revenues will be going into the trust fund and more benefits will be paid from it. Therefore, the trust surpluses generated

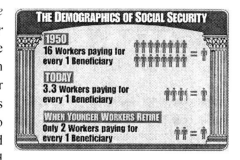

throughout the years (and continuing until 2015) will be responsible for providing for annual deficit gaps until this fund runs out in 2040. After that time, only current payroll taxes will be available for benefit payments.

Table 8-3. Summary of Social Security Finances

	2005 Report	2006 Report
Year when outgo exceeds current revenue	2017	2017
Year when trust fund revenues become fully drawn-down	2041	2040
Long-range actuarial deficit (expressed as a percent of taxable payroll)	1.92	2.02
Annual deficit in 2080 (expressed as a percent of taxable payroll)	5.75	5.38

Source: Social Security Finances: Finds of the 2006 Trustees Report, National Academy of Social Insurance. May 2006, No 21.

Let's look at the situation another way. Figure 8-5 illustrates the best estimate of the Social Security trustees' beneficiary-to-covered worker ratio. As you can see, by 2050, there will be 50 beneficiaries for every 100 workers paying into the system. By 2030, the number of workers paying into Social Security will have increased to 181.1 million from the 158.7 million number reported in 2005. However, the increase in beneficiaries during that period will have grown at a much faster pace from 48 million in 2005 to 83.5 million by 2030. Recall that this increased burden is due to the boomer phenomenon, and it will be compounded by vastly higher Medicare costs, as previously discussed.

Figure 8-5. Beneficiary-to-Covered-Worker Ratio: Beneficiaries per 100 Workers
(data represents the "best estimate" of the Social Security trustees)

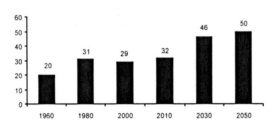

Source: Social Security Finances: Finds of the 2006 Trustees Report, Chart 1. National Academy of Social Insurance. May 2006, No 21.

What Went Wrong?

In order to trace the roots of the challenges facing Social Security, we must first identify the real problem. As previously mentioned, while annual deficits due to demographics will ultimately result in solvency problems, this will not occur for over three decades. Thus, there is adequate time to make the needed adjustments to prevent insolvency. *The real problem is the inability of Social Security to keep up with the high inflation of basic necessities, combined with America's increased reliance on this program as a primary source of retirement income.* Here, I discuss the smaller problem of insolvency that receives all of the media and political attention.

Insolvency Problem?

Similar to Medicare, the aging of America, increased life spans, and declining birth rates have put Social Security on a collision course with what some politicians consider a financial disaster. However, as we have seen, the picture is not so bad. In 1983, the Greenspan Commission enacted a law that increased Social Security taxes to account for the baby boomer phenomenon that is now only a few years away. This extra money added by the boomers is enough to account for the expected shortfalls in Social Security up until 2040, when the youngest of boomers would be 78 years old.

The bottom-line is that, without any changes to the program, Social Security will begin to incur annual deficits within the next decade mainly because the number of

Americans aged 65 and older will grow much faster than the number of workers who pay into the system over the next several decades. And this demographic trend is not expected to change even after the boomers die (more on this in Chapter Thirteen).

Hence, while Social Security has some challenges over the longer-term period, the insolvency issue can be remedied with modest changes, since reserves in the surplus trust will be sufficient to pay benefits until 2040. The insolvency problem is primarily a reflection of increased life spans over the past few decades but has also been compounded by declining birthrates and the more recent trend of declining retirement age (table 8-2).

Let's review the course of Social Security since early inception. As discussed, the first benefits did not begin until 1940. By 1942, there were about 42 American workers paying for the Social Security benefits of each retired American. Shortly thereafter, the number of workers paying into the system began declining rapidly. By 1950, there was an average of 16 American workers paying into the trust for each retired American. Since that time, the ratio of workers-to-retired Americans has fallen drastically due to increased life spans, declining birth rates, and earlier retirement ages (figures 8-6 to 8-8).

Since the 1950s, the birth rate has dropped from 25 births per 1,000 residents to just 15 today. Due to declining living standards over the past two decades, American couples are having fewer children. Instead of having four or five children as was common a few decades ago, many Americans now opt for one or two.

Think about it. How can the average American afford to have more than two children these days with the rising costs of everything? Just consider the costs of a college education at an average four-year state university of over $23,000 per year, and you can see that many couples having two children are stretching their limits. One consequence of America's lower birthrates is that fewer workers will be available, so total payroll taxes will be insufficient to provide the full benefit amount for retirees over the next 3 decades and beyond.

Currently, for every retired American, there are only about 3.3 workers paying into the system. In a few years, there will only be about 2 workers for each retiree. And this ratio could go even lower when all baby boomers are in retirement, especially since life expectancies will most likely continue to improve. *In 2030, the youngest baby boomers will turn 66 while the oldest boomers will turn 84, as the percent of Americans age 65 and older is expected to increase from 13 to 20 percent.*

Figure 8-6. Fewer Workers More Retirees

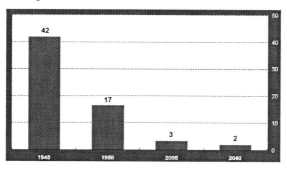

Sources: Social Security Administration
Prepared by: Joint Economic Committee (JEC) 2/2/2005

140

Figure 8-7. Seniors Are Living Longer
(Additional life expectancy for those who
reach 65, by year in which person turns 65)

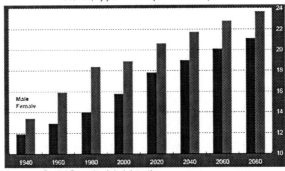

Sources: Social Security Administration
Prepared by: Joint Economic Committee (JEC) 2/2/2005

Figure 8-8. Average Retirement Age of American Men (1910-2001)

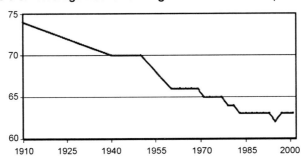

Source: Ransom et al. (1991), Munnell (1977), and authors' tabulations of March CPS files. Created by Burtless, Gary Quinn, Joseph F. "Is Working Longer the Answer for an Aging Workforce?" Figure 2, CRR Number 11. December 2002

Fortunately, we are living longer due to a host of factors. Improved healthcare, better sanitation, and other factors have contributed to the increased American life span from about 50 in 1900, to around 78 (77 for men, 79 for women) currently. In addition, birthrates are expected to remain at their historical lows for a variety of reasons, such as declining fertility rates, women delaying pregnancy due to career choices, and the declining economic feasibility of having more than 2 children due to costs.

Lower birth rates and earlier retirement ages ultimately mean fewer workers paying taxes to finance Social Security and Medicare benefits for the rapidly growing population of Americans 65 and over. Immigration has helped offset some of the decline in birth rates. However, population estimates by the SSA indicate that *between 2003 and 2030, the number of working-age Americans (ages 20-64) will increase by 13.3 percent, while the number of retired individuals will increase by 93.1 percent.* During the previous 30 years, these increases were 51.6 percent and 71.1 percent respectively. By 2030, the percentage of Americans 65 and over will comprise nearly 18 percent (Munnell estimates 20 percent) and by 2050 will reach 21 percent (figure 8-9).

To reiterate, by 2018, using the current tax rates and adjusting benefits for inflation, there will less going into Social Security than will be paid out creating a deficit for that year. From this point forward, the annual deficit of the fund will skyrocket (figure 8-10). But as previously discussed, the Social Security Trust Funds have generated a large surplus over the years, which continue to grow up until 2017. This "special interest" surplus fund will be sufficient to provide full annual benefits without endangering the solvency of Social Security until after 2040 (figure 8-11).

Figure 8-9. U.S. Population Will Age Rapidly as Baby Boomers Retire (1950-2050)

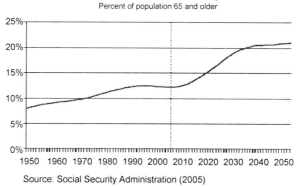

Percent of population 65 and older

Source: Social Security Administration (2005)

Figure 8-10. Social Security Costs to Soon Exceed Revenues

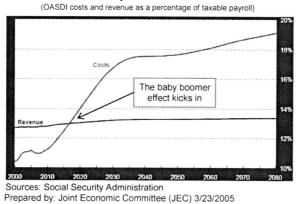

(OASDI costs and revenue as a percentage of taxable payroll)

Sources: Social Security Administration
Prepared by: Joint Economic Committee (JEC) 3/23/2005

Figure 8-11. Annual Deficits in Social Security Benefits Can be Paid by the Surplus Trust Until 2040

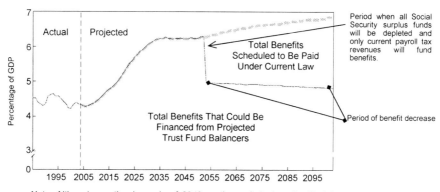

Note: Although mention is made of 2040 as the period when the Social Security surplus funds will have been exhausted, this chart shows a time period that uses the mean value of other estimates, including the CBO.

In fact, figure 8-12 shows that the insolvency problem is really not much of an issue compared to the loss of future government tax revenues if President Bush's recent tax cuts are made permanent.

Figure 8-12. Effects of Bush's Tax Cuts (if made permanent) on the Future Deficit in Social Security

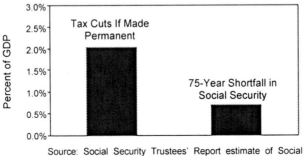

Source: Social Security Trustees' Report estimate of Social Security shortfall, CBPP calculations of tax cuts costs based on Joint Committee on Taxation and CBO estimates.

The Real Problem

The establishment of Social Security was one of the programs that helped strengthen the faith and financial stability of Americans, knowing that they would never be completely broke. Since inception, it has helped millions avoid poverty as defined by the U.S. government. But as we have seen, *the government's definition of poverty is in need of updating, as current criteria are simply too low and have not kept up with inflation of critical basic necessities* such as energy and healthcare. When we compare the percentage of GDP spent on Social Security benefits to other nations with similar programs, America clearly has not made proper adjustments for cost-of-living expenses, or does not pay as much as it should (figure 8-13).

Figure 8-13. The U.S. Social Security Program as a Share of GDP
Public Old-Age Benefits as a Percentage of GDP, 1999

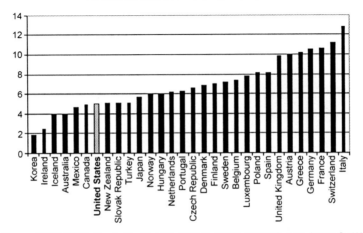

Source: OECD (2003). Created by Munnell, Alicia H. Hatch, Robert E. Lee, James G. "Why is Life Expectancy So Low in the United States?" Figure 8, CRR Number 21. August 2004.

Annual Social Security benefits have not kept up with inflation for many years. Therefore, *it is the buying power of Social Security that is of most concern.* The U.S. government does not use the proper variables to calculate critical cost-of-living expenses needed by seniors. Otherwise, it would overweigh inflation due to healthcare and would count food and energy, rather than merely indexing annual adjustments to wage inflation.

The increased reliance on Social Security for retirement income highlights the weakening financial position of the average American, who has fallen victim to the effects of a nation in decline, as reflected by low savings rates, high debt, low retirement savings, and an overpriced and inadequate healthcare system. As it stands today, even without entry of America's 76 million baby boomers into the system, *Social Security already accounts for nearly three-quarters of the income of middle-income Americans aged 65 and older* (figure 8-14). As well, Social Security accounts for nearly one-half of the wealth of the middle 10 percent of Americans aged 55 to 64 (table 8-4).

Figure 8-14. Non-Earned Retirement Income of Those 65 and Older by Source, Middle Income Quintile (2004)

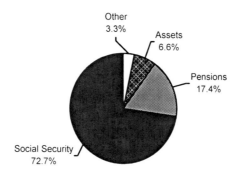

Source: Munnell, Alicia and Sunden, Annika "401(k) Plans are Still Coming Up Short. Figure 2. CRR Number 43 March 2006. Calculations based on *Current Population Survey.*

Table 8-4. Wealth Holdings of a Typical Household Prior to Retirement, SCF (2004)

SOURCE OF WEALTH	AMOUNT	% OF TOTAL
Primary House	$125,208	21
Business Assets	$10,370	2
Financial Assets	$42,014	7
Defined Contribution	$45,244	8
Defined Benefit	$96,705	16
Social Security	$251,983	42
Other Nonfinancial Assets	$26,402	4

Note: The "typical household approaching retirement" refers to the mean of the middle 10 percent of the sample of households headed by an individual aged 55-64.

Source: Munnell, Alicia and Sunden, Annika "401(k) Plans are Still Coming Up Short. Table 1. CRR Number 43 March 2006. Calculations based on *Survey of Consumer Finances.*

Sadly, most Americans over age 65 do not have a pension (figure 8-15). As a result, almost 66 percent of Americans over age 65 receive half or more of their income and 20 percent of the elderly receive all of their income from Social Security. And as we shall see in the next chapter, the shift towards 401(k) plans promises to strengthen this trend. Thus, when the baby boomers retire, reliance on Social Security will only increase. People from all around the world view America as the wealthiest nation. I'd say they'd be shocked to learn that most of its elderly rely on Social Security as their primary source of income.

Figure 8-15. Most Americans Over Age 65 Do not Have Pensions

Demographic	Percent Elderly with Employer-sponsored Plans
All age 65+	41%
Couples	51%
Unmarried Men	39%
Unmarried Women	32%

While Social Security benefits are expected to grow faster than prices due to their indexing to the CPI-W (wage inflation), benefits will not grow as fast as wages due to the gradual phasing-in of the 1983 law which increased the full benefit age from 65 to 67. This increased age lowers the benefits from 100 to 87 percent for full-benefit retirement compensation. In contrast, early retirement benefits (age 62) will shrink from 80 to 70 percent due to these changes. According to the CBPP, the replacement rate for median wage-earners will be reduced from a current 42 percent of earnings to 36 percent over the next two decades, as the increased retirement age takes effect.

Under current law, part of the Social Security income is taxable for single persons with annual income over $25,000, and for couples with countable income over $32,000 (these taxes account for 2 percent of the funding of Social Security for 2006, as seen in figure 8-4). Munnell has estimated that after the phase-in of the full-benefit stage (full benefits at age 67 for those born after 1960), increases in Medicare premiums, and favorable tax treatment of Social Security income for low income wage earners, the net replacement rate for a 65 year old will diminish from 42 percent to 29 percent in 2030.

Figure 8-16. Replacement Rate for Different Wage Earners at Age 65
(Benefits as a Percentage of Earner Average Earnings for Hypothetical Workers)

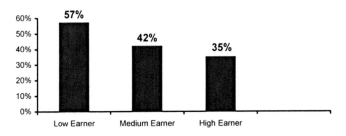

Source: Social Security Administration (2005)

Currently, the percentage of Americans 65 and older as a ratio of Americans between 24 and 64 (typical working age range) is around 18 percent. However, over the next two decades, this percentage is expected to reach over 34 percent and peak at around 38 percent by 2050 (figure 8-17). While this data pertains to Social Security's future solvency issues, *the real problem of decreasing wage replacement rates cannot be addressed until fund solvency is remedied since raising the annual COLAs will necessarily increase insolvency.*

Figure 8-17. The Population Age 65 or Older as a Percentage of Ages 20 to 64.

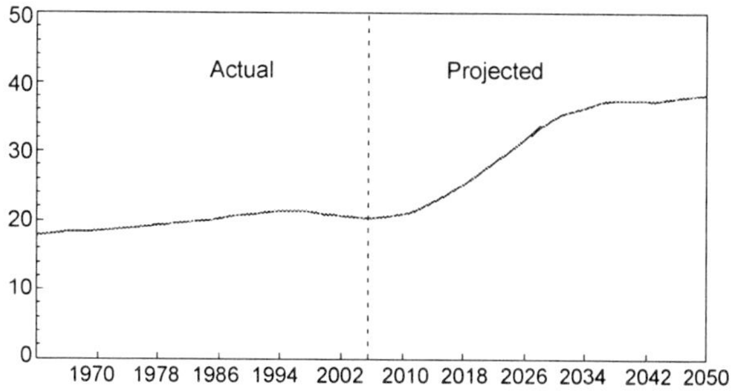

Source: Social Security Administration

During a period when energy and healthcare costs are at record highs and expected to continue their ascent, Social Security will increase its importance as a security blanket against poverty. But *unless adequate COLA adjustments are made, the only thing that will prevent the majority of baby boomers from slipping into impoverished conditions will be the government's outdated definition of poverty.*

Summary of the Real Problem

(1) Approximately 76 million baby boomers will enter retirement age beginning in 2011 and extending through the next two decades. And they will live longer than past generations and will therefore consume Social Security benefits for a longer period.

(2) The number of American workers paying Social Security payroll taxes relative to those receiving Social Security benefits is small, but this ratio will get smaller as more baby boomers reach retirement age.

(3) Even without addressing the future expected annual deficits, the surplus Social Security Trust Fund will be able to pay full benefits until 2040. However, Social Security benefits continue to retain less buying power due to inadequate measures of inflation used for the COLA. Therefore, wage replacement rates will continue to decline. This is not a problem of insolvency but of declining buying power due to inflation.

(4) America's growing dependency on Social Security as the primary source of retirement income highlights its declining living standards and global competitiveness.

Bush's Solution: Private Accounts

Throughout his warnings expressing the "critical" need to fix the Social Security solvency problem for future generations, President Bush has assured Americans that he will not change the system in any way for those born before 1950. However, he has proposed a radical and potentially dangerous plan known as *privatization*, which represents a drastic departure from the current system of social insurance that Social Security provides.

In 2001, President Bush appointed a group of individuals to conduct a study to determine options for a voluntary program by which *individuals under the age of 55 would have the option of investing 2 to 4 of the 6.2 percentage points of their Social Security payroll taxes into personal accounts. These funds would be invested in the stock market and would be thought to have a higher long-term appreciation potential.* Most of the proposals for privatization would allow participants to invest the assets from individual accounts into a very limited and conservative group of investment products, such as stock and bond index funds. This is the basis of the privatization plan that would transform Social Security into an investment account rather than the security blanket it was intended to serve.

He was not the first to propose such a plan however, as it has been talked about for several years in Congress. President Bush's outcries about a "pending crisis," mirrored by exaggerated media coverage has caused many Americans to think that Social Security is facing a huge insolvency crisis, when in fact as I have explained, it is in excellent shape for the near-term and decent shape in the long-term as far as solvency. Ironically, *the various privatization proposals from Washington do nothing to address the future insolvency issues, but actually worsen them* (see Chapter Eight Supplement for various privatization proposals).

Finally, *nowhere in Washington will you hear mention of the real problem of Social Security—its declining buying power and the reasons behind its unintended use as a primary source of retirement income by millions of Americans.* Social Security has been America's most successful social and financial program, and has prevented millions from slipping into poverty, while delivering income to wealthy retirees. However, if benefits are not indexed to more accurate measures of inflation, it will fail to keep beneficiaries out of poverty. Meanwhile, *privatization will transform Social Security from a safety net into a risky investment program that will be at the mercy of the stock and bond markets.* It is clear that something must be done to increase the declining replacement rate of benefits, but privatization is definitely not the answer.

The financial industry has contributed to the propaganda of this "eminent insolvency crisis" as a way to encourage Americans to support Bush's privatization proposal, which is essentially a market-based individual investment program. And if successful, this industry stands to gain big from privatization while Americans will lose. *With an estimated $950 billion in fees and management costs for privatization, the financial industry is already drooling.*

Astonishingly, the privatization plan proposed by the president does nothing to address the solvency issue, but rather serves to transform Social Security into a 401(k) type plan, whereby no benefits are guaranteed from private accounts. Ironically, *in order to fund such a plan, it would require shifting assets immediately out of the Social Security Trust Fund, causing the deficit phase to occur even sooner (by 2015) than the 2018 period.* As well, there are dozens of administrative and legal issues that would need to be resolved such as the extent of access to the funds, the types of investment products that could be purchased, survivorship regulations, and many other uncertainties.

But perhaps the most radical consequence of privatization plans proposed by the President and other politicians is that *each would sever the relationship between the amount of benefits received and total lifetime earnings for each recipient under the current Social Security system.* Specifically, privatization would depend upon the size of investments in each private account, which would obviously depend upon the returns of the capital markets. In other words, much of the benefits would be dependent upon the performance of the stock and bond markets, as well as the investment decisions made by each participant. And the volatility of these markets could cause these accounts to suffer major declines in individual account balances when these funds are needed the most.

You see, the establishment of private accounts would protect individuals' future benefits, but only to the extent that FICA taxes are paid into the system. Certainly, Washington will have a more difficult time taking funds out of your retirement account to use on other things. But *it still does not account for future expected shortfalls and actually makes the surplus trust (or the special interest treasuries fund) run out of money within twenty years.* Finally, the funds allocated to these private accounts do not necessarily become part of the legal estate of the beneficiary since certain expenses will be deducted to determine the payout.

BOX 8-2: Examples of Privatization Benefits

Consider an individual who earns only $15,600 per year for twenty years and decides to allocate two percentage points of his portion of the Social Security tax revenues into a private account. This would amount to a total of $9,400 assuming an annual rate of return at 4 percent above the inflation rate (known as the real rate of return), which when converted into an annuity would only yield $55 per month.

Consider an individual who earns the average annual wage, $34,700 (2005) and allocates two percentage points of Social Security tax revenues into his private account. This would amount to an annual contribution of $694. After 20 years of work, this participant would be expected to have an individual account balance of about $21,000 assuming an annual rate of return at 4 percent above the inflation rate. Upon turning 65, this individual decided to start taking retirement benefits so he was required to purchase an annuity with these funds. The annuity from this amount would yield $125 per month.

In contrast, another individual earning $55,500 and allocates two percentage points of Social Security tax revenues into his private account. This would amount to a balance of $33,300 in his individual account after 20 years assuming an annual rate of return at 4 percent above the inflation rate, yielding an annuity that would pay $536 per month.

These annuities would not be adjusted for inflation each year so the buying power would continue to diminish. Of course, these returns would not be guaranteed. In addition, the replacement rate from the private accounts would be equal regardless of income, thereby removing the social insurance structure of Social Security, which was meant to favor lower wage earners.

Consequences of Privatization

One of the main flaws with privatization is that is does nothing to address the solvency problem since it does not call for any contributions to be made into the trust. As a matter of fact, it actually makes the trust funds less solvent at an early period since the money needed to fund these private accounts will come from the trust reserves.

Among the many adverse consequences of privatization are an increase in the insolvency of the trust fund, an increase in the national debt, a decrease in the amount of guaranteed benefits, and a decrease in benefits for certain groups. Finally, privatization would transform America's only system of social income insurance into a retirement account that is neither guaranteed nor safe, unlike the present Social Security program.

More Rapid Insolvency

We must not lose sight of the fact that the formation of private accounts would not change the amount of revenue entering the Social Security Trust Fund, and would therefore *not solve the insolvency issue* that President Bush has claimed is of most concern. Rather, *privatization would actually increase government spending* since the federal government would need to immediately begin funding these private accounts and continue funding them annually (figure 8-20).

Decreased Guaranteed Benefits

The president's plan is *expected to decrease guaranteed benefits by as much as 60 percent.* But *even those who do not choose to participate in private accounts will still see a major benefit reduction.* Privatization transforms the social insurance system of Social Security into an investment account which *rewards high-wage earners with uninterrupted work histories.* We already have several retirement-based investment accounts available to workers that work in this manner. We do not need to create another and destroy the only safety net available to Americans. *Privatization will transform the nation's only social insurance program into a risky investment program that will have a major cut in guaranteed benefits for all Americans.*

Figure 8-18. Bush's Price Indexing Would Decrease Social Security Benefits Over Time
(Benefit Reduction for an Average Wage Earner Retiring in 3 Different Years)

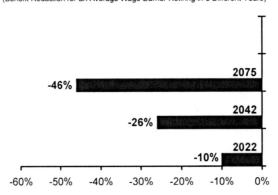

Source: Social Security Administration, CBPP, the President's Commission to Strengthen Social Security

**Figure 8-19. Future Benefits Would be Lower Under Privatization
Than If No Actions Were Taken**

(Average Annual Benefit for Median Wage-Earner Born in the 1990s and Retiring at 65)

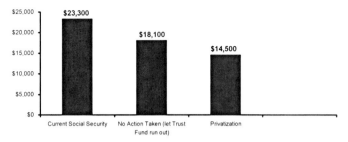

Source: CBO, CBPP, Long-term Analysis of Plan2 of the President's
Commission to Strengthen Social Security, July 21, 2004.

Increased Federal Debt

Funding private accounts would increase federal spending, which would widen annual deficits. In order to transition Americans who are currently in the Social Security System, think of privatization as paying a portion of earned benefits to all Americans immediately, rather than waiting for each individual to retire. The increased borrowing needed to fund these accounts *would increase both the national debt and the cost of interest payments on the debt.* Therefore, America will rely on the rest of the world to finance a significant portion of its retirement. While privatization is expected to result in benefit reductions that would lessen the effect of the massive borrowing required to fund private accounts, it would still increase the federal debt and interest payments significantly. *Bush's plan would create $17.7 trillion in additional debt by 2050, representing a 19.3 percent increase relative to GDP in year 2050* (see table 8.3, appendix).

Higher Risk

Younger Americans are excited at the possibility that they will have investment control over their Social Security benefits. Ads and television commercials by online brokers have led many to believe that they can "do it themselves" and "investing is fun." However, investing is extremely difficult even for seasoned professionals. It's only "fun" when you're doing well. And unless you have several years of real investment experience, you'll most likely end up having regrets after trying to invest on your own.

I find it amazing that anyone in Washington would consider privatization of what was intended to provide the last layer of protection for Americans. Think what would have happened if privatization had passed a few years ago before the Internet bubble collapse. The fact is that the stock and bond markets are no place for Social Security funds. And over the next 10 to 20 years, these capital markets are going to be extremely risky as America has its day of financial reckoning.

It's easy for those with high-paying jobs and stable careers to conclude that privatization would be the best solution. However, life is full of uncertainties and we can never know what might happen. Having a social insurance system as a safety net against poverty is critical towards preventing a devastating poverty trend.

150

Figure 8-20. Balance of the Social Security Trust Given Three Scenarios

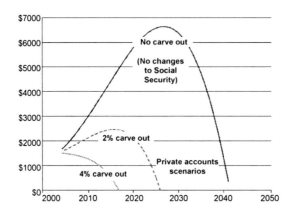

Social Security will still be funded by FICA taxes after the trust runs out of money, but benefits will have to drop by 20 to 30% if no changes are made. With Private Accounts, shortfalls will occur sooner and rely on stock market gains, which may not occur.

Therefore, privatization introduces a large amount of benefit risk which is transferred to individuals. This alone creates a fundamental deficiency in the Social Security program and thereby presents a tremendous risk for a program that was meant to be a guaranteed insurance policy against poverty.

Source: Based on analysis in Peter A. Diamond and Peter R. Orszag, "An Assessment of the Proposals of the President's Commission to Strengthen Social Security," The Brookings Institution, Washington D.C., June 2002. Created by Greg Anrig and Bernard Wasow. Twelve Reasons Why Privatizing Social Security is a Bad Idea. Figure 1. The Century Foundation. February 14, 2005.

Finally, most elderly Americans are drastically opposed to privatization. Most of the elderly have gained wisdom throughout their years and understand the risks of the stock market. As well, they realize that life is filled with uncertainty and challenges grow with age. Not only do the elderly oppose privatization of their own accounts, but they also oppose it for their children and grandchildren because they understand the importance of having a safety net that is guaranteed and not subject to the volatile performance of the capital markets or the effects of Wall Street and corporate fraud.

Increased Administrative Costs

Currently, the administrative fees for Social Security are about $0.01 for every dollar of benefit received. Because privatization would create millions of individualized accounts to be administered through retail (for-profit) entities, *expenses are expected to increase by up to $0.15 per dollar of benefit* in commissions, management fees, and other expenses.

Severe Damage to Specific Groups

Under the President's privatization proposal, Americans receiving disability benefits would be subject to the same regulations for private accounts as everyone else. Consequently, *disabled Americans would be severely disadvantaged in cases where their disablement occurred early in their work career* since they would not have contributed much income to their private accounts. Therefore, they would potentially face much lower returns from not only their private accounts, but also due to the reduced guaranteed benefits that have been traded for these private accounts.

Bush has assumed that reductions in guaranteed benefits would be made up by the potentially higher returns generated from private accounts. However, in the case of disabled individuals who may not have been able to contribute as much, these presumed higher returns would never materialize.

Similar to all who would have private accounts, *the disabled would not be able to access their private accounts until reaching retirement.* And as you might appreciate, the importance of Social Security in the everyday lives of disabled Americans is a critical portion of their entire pre-retirement income. Consequently, the President's Commission to Strengthen Social Security has stated that the cost of financing private accounts would be heightened if disability and survivor's insurance are to be preserved. Why would he deliver this negative message when trying to pitch privatization? What is he really trying to say?

Finally, *women and minorities would stand to lose through privatization.* These groups are particularly dependent on Social Security. And because they tend to have lower incomes and larger gaps in unemployment, they would receive a small percentage of benefits under privatization.

BOX 8-3: 10 Reasons Why Privatizing Social Security is a Bad Idea

#1 The insurance afforded by Social Security to protect workers and their families against death and disability would be compromised

#2 The solvency problem would actually worsen

#3 Might weaken long-term economic growth which would further threaten solvency

#4 Privatization has failed elsewhere

#5 Individuals do not have an adequate level of investment sophistication

#6 Privatization benefits will be influenced largely by the timing of your retirement

#7 Expensive fees and administrative costs, while Wall Street receives huge fees

#8 Young workers, women, African Americans, and Hispanics would be worse off

#9 Retirees would not be protected against inflation

#10 It is bad for people who are close to retirement

Alternatives to Privatization

As previously discussed, if Washington does nothing at all, the Social Security Trust Fund should be sufficient to pay all benefits including all COLAs up until 2040. Thereafter, for several years it will be able to pay at least 73 to 80 percent of benefits even if no changes are made. Therefore, *it should be relatively easy to make minor adjustments now that will enable Social Security to pay full benefits indefinitely.*

As we have seen, privatization is not the solution to providing solvency, stability or extending the longevity of Social Security. It will in part relieve the government's commitment to provide a base level of assistance for otherwise impoverished Americans and will primarily benefit Wall Street at the expense of millions of Americans who rely exclusively on Social Security. Yet, while Social Security is certainly in no desperate shape as many in Washington would have you believe, it does need some fine tuning to ensure its strength and solvency throughout the second half of the twenty-first century and beyond. But these changes must be made now or else the problem will grow exponentially.

As of the Trustees 2005 Report, Social Security had a long-term deficit of 1.89 percent of payroll taxes. That is, over the course of the next few decades, the amount of payroll taxes would need to be increased (as of 2005) from 12.4 to 14.29 percent in order to completely fund all benefits throughout the expected shortfalls for the next 75 years. However, since this increase was not made, the Trustees Report for 2006 has calculated the new long-term actuarial deficit at 2.02 percent (1.01 percent for the employer and 1.01 percent for the employee), or an increase in the payroll tax to 14.42 percent (table 8-3).

Currently the maximum tax rate amounts to $5,840.40 annually for those making $94,200 and higher. Therefore, raising the payroll tax to 14.42 percent would increase the maximum rate to $6,791.82, or an increase of $951.20 for each employee and the employer. This measure alone would provide for approximately one-half of the expected shortfall after 2040. However, each year changes are not made to fund Social Security, the solutions will need to be larger.

BOX 8-4: Myths of Social Security Privatization

Myth 1: Privatization will Rescue Social Security

Privatization would actually cause insolvency of Social Security as early as 2015. Bush's privatization plan would divert up to two-thirds of the current employee-paid Social Security tax into private accounts, causing a major cash-flow problem and threaten benefits.

Myth 2: Returns from Private Accounts will Make up for the Cuts in Benefits.

Estimates of over $19 trillion will be needed to privatize Social Security. Bush's price-indexing plan for privatization would reduce the guaranteed Social Security benefits by nearly 50 percent even for those who decide not to choose a private account. Those who opt for private accounts would face an even larger decrease in guaranteed payments.

Myth 3: Private Account Assets Are Transferable to One's Heirs

Upon retirement, the assets in the private accounts would be converted into an annuity sufficient to raise their total Social Security benefits to a poverty income level. The remaining assets will be used to compensate for the benefit cuts and costs of the plan. Only the excess after these costs and conversions have been made could be passed onto heirs, but any excesses are unlikely.

Myth 4: Private Accounts are Voluntary

While the decision to have part of the contributions put into a private account is an option, everyone will suffer at least a 50 percent cut in guaranteed benefits.

Myth 5: Retirees and Near Retirees Will Be Exempt from the Effects of Privatization

Because privatization will require use of two-thirds of the employee-paid Social Security tax base from the trust funds into private accounts, the solvency of Social Security will occur very soon, forcing increased federal debt.

Myth 6: Privatization Will Provide Younger Workers with Higher Rates of Return

Younger workers will receive lower rates of return since they will have to pay twice into the system. They will have to pay to fund the benefits of the current retirees under the current Social Security system and they will have to pay to fund their private accounts. Even the Congressional Budget Office concluded that the costs incurred to transition into a privatization system would reduce the rate of return on today's young generation to a lower level than the rate of return on Social Security.

Myth 7: Private Accounts Would Only Cost About $750 Billion in the First 10 Years

According to the CBPP, privatization will increase the national debt by $5 trillion over the first twenty years and thereafter costs will continue to grow to nearly $20 trillion over the ensuing four decades. The President's plan is misleading since the accounts are not fully phased in until 2011.

Some have proposed raising the retirement age to 70 or beyond. Already, the retirement age for Social Security has been raised to 67 for those born on or after 1960. Alternatively, the solvency problem could be corrected by increasing the FICA tax. However, raising FICA would hurt low-wage earners the most. The most reasonable solution is to raise the limit by which Social Security is taxed on wages, currently at $94,200.

If Social Security is indeed a social insurance program, it does not make sense that wage earners making $2,000,000 are only taxed on the first $94,200 of salary. While a tax up to the full amount of one's salary is a bit extreme, I do feel that the limit could be raised from $94,200 to $160,000. With only 6 percent of the American workforce earning more than this wage cap, it would not affect the disposable income of many Americans.

One of the problems with this is that it would cause higher income wage earners to get double-taxed on Social Security. That is, because Social Security income is taxable, those who make above the poverty level must pay taxes on benefits. For instance, consider John Doe who has a total retirement income of $16,000 annually, mainly from Social Security. Due to the standard deductions, John would owe little if any taxes on these benefits, which were provided from the payroll taxes to begin with. Now let's consider Sarah, who has a total retirement income is $50,000. Although John and Sarah receive roughly the same amount of Social Security benefits annually at around $13,000, Sarah's benefit is reduced by her tax rate on this amount. Therefore, if the salary payroll cap is raised, the tax rate for Social Security benefits should also be adjusted so double-taxation is curtailed.

There are many other viable options to improve the solvency of Social Security. For instance, newly hired state and local workers could be entered into the system. Another solution would be to earmark other taxes for Social Security. Finally, while addressing the solvency issue may be achieved by one of many modest changes, this still will not alter the trend of diminishing buying power and increased reliance on Social Security benefits. Therefore, in order to account for the real problem, Washington should consider phasing in additional changes that have been proposed in table 8-5.

Why is Privatization Being Considered?

After demonstrating that privatization is a no-win scenario for most Americans, why would President Bush and other members of Congress propose these changes? There are several possible reasons why Social Security has been one of the biggest topics for President Bush's political agenda—as a decoy to healthcare, as a way to help the stock market, or in keeping with the Republican Party's commitment to minimize "big government" such as that required by the Social Security program.

First, privatization of *Social Security would help minimize the effects of a potential stock market decline when baby boomers retire.* Remember, most baby boomers will retire broke and will need Social Security to keep them out of poverty. Therefore, many who do have retirement assets in the stock market will need to sell these securities at some point in order to survive. However, *privatization would add trillions to the stock market over several years and would continue to on an annual basis.*

In addition, consider that republicans have always been against social government programs. Rather than big government controlling Social Security, republicans might prefer to release the liability and risks of this program to individuals, and privatization is the first step towards achieving this goal.

Finally, Bush's focus on Social Security privatization serves to deliver the perception that he is providing value for Americans. But similar Medicare Part D, privatization creates the illusion of improvement when in fact it only benefits corporate America, and allows him to avoid talking about America's biggest problem—its healthcare crisis.

Conclusions

Rather than address the real problems inherent within Social Security, President Bush has chosen to use America's growing reliance on this program as a way to promote an ineffective and very risky privatization plan, which will destroy America's dwindling but only safety net against poverty. We must remember that Social Security is an insurance program and not an investment account. As such, it was never intended to serve as the primary source of retirement income. Yet, due to three decades of declining living standards, many Americans have become desperate and now look to Social Security as their only guaranteed retirement income.

This emphasis on Social Security benefits as a primary source of retirement income has been further compounded by America's underfunded public and private pension plans, as well as increasing costs of all basic necessities without adequate COLA adjustments. Even worse is the fact that dependency on Social Security is expected to increase over the next two decades since most boomers will retire in poverty.

Privatization not only worsens solvency, but removes much of the guaranteed benefits that Social Security currently offers, in exchange for the hope that stock market performance will compensate. Without privatization, insolvency of the trust will not even be a problem until after 2040; with privatization, insolvency will occur as early as the next 10 years.

There are many options that can provide a solution to future insolvency. Many of the solutions would only result in minor changes, as long as these changes are made now. But privatization is not a solution. It's a potential disaster. It would totally change the entire structure and finances of Social Security and create a much higher level of risk for retired Americans. And it would cause the federal debt to soar. The recent and current stock market woes should serve as an example of the fragility of these markets, for which Social Security has no place.

In conclusion, the real threat to Social Security is privatization from current funds, rather than privatization in addition to current funds. However, even if one of Washington's proposed privatization plans is not passed, Americans will continue to rely more heavily on Social Security for their primary retirement income as a result of declining economic conditions. The only way to decrease America's dependence on Social Security is to improve its global competitiveness and ensure that basic goods and services are affordable to all. Otherwise, middle-class Americans will continue to disappear, making the chances of the "American Dream" all but an unachievable fantasy.

Table 8-5. Summary of Alternative Methods to Restore Social Security to Solvency

Solvency Option	Percent of 75-year Shortfall met
Raise the Tax Cap	
1. Make all earnings subject to Social Security taxes, but retain the cap for benefit calculations beginning in 2005	116
2. Make all earnings subject to Social Security taxes and Credit them for benefit purposes, beginning in 2005	93
3. Make 90 percent of earnings subject to Social Security taxes and credit them for benefit purposes, phase in 2005-2014	40
Extend Coverage	
4. Cover newly hired state and local employees with a 5-year phase-in	10
Raise the Age for Full Retirement Benefits	
5. Speed up the increase to age 67 and index the age to 68 by raising it one month every two years	28
6. Same as #5, but index the age to 70 by raising it one month every two years	36
Cut Benefits for New Beneficiaries	
7. Cut Benefits by 3 percent for those starting to get benefits in 2005	20
8. Cut benefits by 5 percent for those starting to get benefits in 2005	32
9. Price index the benefit formula	111
Change Cost of Living Adjustment (COLA)	
10. Lower the COLA by 1 percentage point each year	79
11. Lower the COLA by ½ percentage point each year	41
12. Shift to the new "chained" CPI	18
Raise Social Security Taxes	
13. Raise tax rate for workers and employers from 6.2 to 7.2 in 2005	104
14. Schedule tax rate for workers and employers, each of 7.25 percent in 2020-2049 and 8.3 percent in 2050 and beyond	104
Use Other Taxes	
15. Earmark for Social Security the remaining tax on estates over $3.5 million in 2010 and beyond	27
16. Instead of making 2001 and 2003 tax cuts permanent, earmark part of federal income taxes or capital gains taxes for Social Security after 2009	/a
Invest Trust Fund in Equities	
17. Invest 40 percent of trust funds in equities, phased in 2005-2014, assuming a 6.5 percent real return (over 3.0 percent inflation)	48
18. Same as #17, assuming 5.5 percent real return (over 3.0 percent inflation)	35

9

RETIREMENT BLUES

In the recent past, all Americans looked forward to retirement as the period in life to be spent in leisure, with few financial worries. However, American attitudes about retirement were not always so upbeat. Several decades ago, retirement was almost synonymous with death, as the average life span was very close to the normal retirement age. Thus, retirement was seen as the declining period of one's life, the end not expected to be far off.

Over the past two decades, many Americans began to retire in their fifties and some even earlier, as average life spans gradually increased beyond age 77. As America's wealth and dominance increased through the decades, so has the duration of retirement. And this signaled a shift in mentality that indeed retirement was not the end, but a new beginning of a long period of enjoyment, known as one's "Golden Years." This period signified a more cheerful conclusion to the human life cycle, when the elderly could look back on their life while enjoying their role as grandparents. This was to be a period when retired Americans earned the free time to enjoy life without the worry of so many expenses that burdened their once growing families.

While these attitudes have not changed, many are starting to doubt their financial security, worried that their "Golden Years" may not end up so golden. Questions surrounding the certainty of Social Security, skyrocketing healthcare costs, the recent downturn in the stock market, and inadequate savings threatens to make the retirement phase a dark period for most Americans.

As it stands today for the majority of baby boomers, retirement will not commence at 65, but will most likely be delayed until 70, or may not ever occur due to their lack of retirement assets and the rising cost of basic expenses. Consequently, many will never get to experience that rewarding retirement period they hoped for because they will continue to work by necessity, until the day they depart from this world. This is the new reality of twenty-first century America, and is partly the result of the "New Economy."

The retirement problem in America is complex because numerous forces are converging from different areas within the nation's economic system. In order to understand the basic problems with retirement, we must separate the dominant forces and address each individually, and then as a contribution to the entire retirement picture. The main issues are America's baby boomer phenomenon, Social Security, public versus private pensions, savings and pension contribution rates, increased life spans, declining birth rates, and the declining competitiveness of America.

There are several reasons why the retirement assets of most baby boomers will be inadequate for a normal-age retirement. First, longer life spans means retired Americans will spend more years consuming without producing (working) which will require a larger retirement asset base. Obviously, this pertains to the savings rates of Americans which has been in decline since the 1970s. It's also related to the baby boomer phenomenon, or the discrepancy between the number of retired workers versus current and future workers funding Social Security, Medicare, and defined benefit pension plans. This phenomenon has also been accentuated by declining birth rates and declining age at retirement. Next, massive investment losses due to the recent Internet bubble deflation alone have forced many to delay retirement. And the continued weakness of the stock market only adds to the uncertainty of retirement for most.

Of course there are many other reasons why retirement assets are experiencing a relative diminishment of benefits versus income needs. Social Security benefit taxes are not indexed to inflation so that as one ages, retirees share an increasingly higher proportion of taxes on real income from Social Security. As well, I have previously discussed the uncertain direction of Social Security, its diminished buying power, and the surging costs of healthcare and energy, which can amount to huge expenses for the elderly. Combined, these forces threaten to prevent many Americans from enjoying a long period of retirement, free from financial worries.

The two remaining reasons for retirement income shortfalls are due to characteristics inherent within America's pension system that are in part related to the poor stock market returns since 2000. As well, America's declining competitiveness has been accelerated by free trade policies embraced by Washington, which have led to the elimination of millions of jobs, declining retirement benefits, and declining healthcare coverage—all at the benefit of corporate America and at the expense of working-class Americans.

Even with the meager benefits of Social Security, the paucity of retirement assets of most Americans will not be adequate to sustain a long period of retirement, as most will struggle to pay for basic living expenses such as out-of-pocket healthcare, utilities, and food. Even those who choose to continue working past age 65 will most likely be provided with low-paying jobs that will not exploit their decades of experience and wisdom, adding further insult to this skilled and important generation of Americans.

If President Bush's Social Security privatization program is passed, this would surely help the stock market, as well as line the pockets of Wall Street. But as we have seen, privatization is a risky plan that would not only worsen the future solvency of the program, but would also significantly add to the national debt and reduce guaranteed benefits for all Americans, compounding the uncertainty of their retirement income.

America's retirement problems are complex and also dependent upon variables outside the control of those affected. Obviously, pension plan and other retirement assets are controlled by stock market performance. However, retirement savings are still adversely affected by declining living standards, reflecting America's weakening position among its competitors. And if basic living expenses continue to increase without a commensurate increase in net wages, most Americans won't have much to save for retirement.

The Four Pillars of Retirement

All American seniors rely on a solid foundation of resources to provide a graceful transition into retirement and ensure the longevity of their "Golden Years." There are four resource categories thought to function as structural "retirement pillars," providing the foundation upon which a quality retirement depends. When one of these pillars is compromised, a certain amount of instability appears, similar to a three-legged chair. And when two of the pillars are dislodged, similar to a large building that can come tumbling down, a retired person can lose all or part of the stability needed to sustain their livelihood.

Health Insurance

The first pillar of a stable retirement plan is health insurance. It would seem reasonable that every developed nation should be able to provide a system of affordable healthcare to all its citizens. Yet, the United States is the only developed nation in the world without a national healthcare program. We have already seen how America's free-market healthcare system has diminished the global competitiveness of the nation's workforce and positioned millions without medical services, leaving them vulnerable to financial ruin if they become hospitalized.

Even with the help of Medicare and Medicaid, the sad truth is that nearly 17 percent of all Americans aged 65 and older are not covered by any type of health insurance at all. It takes a long time to sort through the bureaucracy of these government plans. And many uninsured either cannot qualify for these programs or they simply do not know how to apply for them. For the low-income elderly who qualify for Medicare and Medicaid (a complex and variable eligibility requirement depending on the state), this is often not enough since these programs have many exclusions and limitations. Therefore, in order to provide full healthcare coverage, even the poor need to enter the private free-market healthcare system to obtain supplemental insurance.

But of course, supplemental insurance is not affordable for most elderly Americans since two-thirds of this group rely on Social Security as their main source of income. And Bush's Part D Medicare plan is not expected to help seniors much with drug costs due to the "doughnut hole" or coverage gap that most are expected to face each year.

Accordingly, 17 percent of retired Americans will not have any presence of this pillar. And for as much as 50 percent of the elderly, this pillar will be weakly constructed due to underinsurance. When the boomers retire, the percentage of uninsured over age 65 could easily reach 25 percent, while underinsured rates could exceed 70 percent. At the very least, public healthcare benefits will be slashed upon the entry of 76 million boomers into the system, resulting in a weak pillar for millions of seniors.

Employment Income

The second retirement pillar consists of continued earnings from work. This is a fairly recent addition to America's retirement pillars, and itself highlights the current problem with retirement in America. A few decades ago, retirement actually had a meaning. And as recently as the late 1990s, many Americans were continuing the trend of earlier retirement. But today, declining living standards have prevented many from saving the needed income that would guarantee a permanent retirement from work.

Mandatory employment income almost excludes one from enjoying their "Golden Years." Unfortunately, most Americans will have to delay retirement and continue to work because they never imagined they would face the current high costs of basic goods and services. Finally, many will continue to work in order to obtain healthcare coverage. Only a small minority will continue to work merely to stay busy.

Social Security

America's third retirement pillar is Social Security. Unlike decades in the past, Social Security has become nearly as important as it was when first utilized towards the end of the Great Depression. Since the post-war period, many middle-class Americans with pension plans thought of Social Security as a source of "bonus income" they could count on to use for anything they wanted. But even now, most of America's 35 million elderly rely on Social Security as their primary source of retirement income.

As discussed in the previous chapter, Social Security will need to be restructured, and soon, in order to provide full benefits for future generations. And while the boomers have no direct threat of loss of benefits, the buying power of Social Security has been in decline for three decades. Combined with the increased dependency on this program for retirement income, this pillar has several vulnerabilities. And if the President's privatization plan is passed, this pillar will surely be compromised.

Retirement Savings and Pensions

The fourth and final pillar of retirement consists of personal savings and pension plans. Unlike the post-war period when Americans were amongst the world's best savers, they have since mirrored the government's debt patterns, having been transformed into the world's worst savers and largest debtors. The household savings rate in America has been in sharp decline over the past two decades and was recently -0.5 percent (March 2006). During late 2005, it actually reached an astonishing -2.8 percent. Prior to this period, the last time the savings rate was negative was during the Great Depression.

Figure 9-1. Personal Savings Rate (1958 to 2005) As a Percentage of Disposable Income

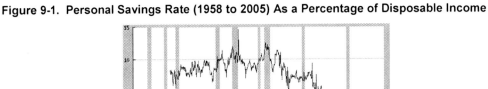

Source: U.S. Department of Commerce: Bureau of Economic Analysis
Prepared by: Federal Reserve Bank of St. Louis: research: stlouisfed.org
Shaded areas indicate recessions as determined by the NBER

The problem of America's dwindling savings trends are further magnified by staggering levels of consumer debt. It's very difficult to save if you have a large debt burden, especially during a rising interest-rate environment, since this causes interest payments on variable-rate loans to rise. This poor savings rate has a direct consequence for the newer 401(k)-type retirement savings plans since contributions are voluntary.

Today in America, *only about one-half of the private workforce is covered by some type of retirement savings plan.* Therefore, *up to one-half of America's 76 million baby boomers will rely on Social Security as their only source of retirement income, adding further stress to this pillar.* For the other 50 percent, two-thirds are covered by a 401(k)-type plan while the remaining one-third are covered by a defined benefit plan.

For companies that do offer a 401(k)-type retirement plan, most workers do not even participate or only participate to a small extent since it's a voluntary plan. More alarming is that *only one-third of all individuals over 65 have any type of pension income at all.* And even those with 401(k)-type or defined contribution plans are at the mercy of the stock and bond markets, unlike the predetermined and guaranteed benefits of defined benefit plans. Of course, recent bankruptcies in several industries have reminded many Americans that even defined benefit plans are never absolutely guaranteed.

The future trends promise to get worse. As *of 2005, only half of Americans aged 55 had an average balance of only $50,000 in their 401(k)-type plan.* In addition, over 18,000 private pension plans are underfunded. Already, many widows have lost all pension benefits after their husbands have died, pushing them into poverty. During 2004, according to the Department of Agriculture, 1 in 5 American households had difficulty affording food. Surely, the elderly comprised a large percentage of this group. Why should 20 percent of the people living in the world's agricultural powerhouse go hungry?

As a result of these trends, most baby boomers will face a greatly diminished lifestyle, adding further stress to the employment pillar. But we have already seen the difficulties that free trade has caused in the workplace. In conclusion, the combined effects of healthcare costs, Social Security dependency, pension plan uncertainties and risky 401(k) assets of millions will most likely prevent many from ever enjoying their "Golden Years." And these consequences alone will result in a major economic slowdown that will last many years. In this chapter, I will focus on the fourth retirement pillar that involves retirement assets. I have included the savings component of this pillar in Chapter Thirteen.

Overview of the Pension Crisis

Over the past two decades there has been a dramatic change in both the funding structure and stability of retirement assets in America, the consequences which could result in a financial crisis for the majority of baby boomers. In order to fully understand these separate yet dependent issues, we need to distinguish between the current underfunded pension plan crisis and the growing reliance on 401 (k) plans. The endpoint of each of these issues is identical—declining and less certain retirement income. Only the timing of their impact is different as we shall see.

Problem #1: Defined Benefit Plans Are Underfunded

Unlike the 1990s and several decades earlier, America's huge pension system is currently in a state of disarray. On the one hand, most pensions, private and public, are financially unstable and have become underfunded due to increasing life spans, rising healthcare costs, and the recent correction in the stock market. As a result, most companies and government entities do not have sufficient funds to pay full pension plan benefits over the expected life span of retired employees, as originally promised decades earlier.

But for some employers, deficit funding issues are not a problem since they offer a defined contribution or 401(k) retirement plan, which immediately becomes the property and responsibility of each worker. However, these plans are riddled with their own unique problems. Yet, over the past two decades, 401(k) plans have exploded in growth and popularity, adding to the vulnerability of America's retirement income.

Unfortunately, as the stock market continues its bearish conditions over the next several years, it is apparent that the underfunded pension problem is only going to get worse, as more companies terminate their pensions and transfer the burden of pension liabilities to the government insurance agency responsible for protecting these plans, the PBGC. However, the PBGC is also facing its own insolvency problems due to a record number of pension terminations for which they have assumed financial obligations. To a large extent, it's a snowball effect—pensions become underfunded due to poor performance in the stock and bond markets resulting in smaller pension returns, leading to insufficient funds to pay current benefits, which decreases consumer spending, which trickles back down to the stock market, causing further declines in pension assets.

Problem #2: The Shift to 401 (k) Plans

A different problem is that America's retirement plan structure has been experiencing a rapid shift away from the more traditional defined benefit plans towards the newer defined contribution or 401(k) retirement savings plans. This trend is not a consequence of the underfunded pension problem but is more of a function of the high costs incurred by companies that offer defined benefit plans.

Over the past two decades, many companies began eliminating these all-in-one defined benefit plans (known as "pension plans") and replacing them with less costly defined contribution plans, commonly referred to as 401(k)-type plans. This trend has recently accelerated due to the underfunded defined benefit pension problem.

Because 401(k) plans are the responsibility of employees, employers can free themselves from the risks of underfundedness that can occur with defined benefit plans when stock and bond market returns or interest rates are low. However, extensive data has shown that compared to defined benefit plans, *defined contribution or 401(k) plans have inferior performance and higher fees. As well, unlike many pension plans, 401(k) plans do not provide healthcare since they are merely retirement accounts. In contrast, pension plans are usually more comprehensive and include several benefits in addition to retirement income, such as healthcare, disability insurance, and other perks.* Finally, unlike the mandatory participation requirements of defined benefit pension plans, *401(k) plan participation is voluntary.* Therefore, *many employees either do not participate at all or do not contribute enough to amass the recommended 10 to 12 times annual salary needed to ensure sufficient retirement funds.*

Wage growth and disposable income have not grown at rates seen prior to the 1980s, causing many to save less (figure 9-2). As a consequence, many have been short-changing their retirement because they do not understand the importance of planning ahead and/or they do not have the discipline to save (also refer to figures 8-14, 8-15 and table 8-4). However, this reckless behavior is going to cause a collapse in the life styles of many boomers during their "Golden Years."

Therefore, any way you look at it, the transition to retirement for the majority of America's boomers will never materialize, as most will have to continue work just to survive. And for some, their "Golden Years" might be best remembered for the time they spent under the golden arches of McDonalds trying to make ends meet.

Figure 9-2. U.S. Median Family Income Growth has Slowed Dramatically Since 1980[a]

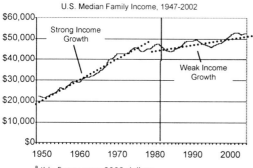

The best-fit straight (dotted) lines have been drawn through each period before and after 1980. The slope or rate of growth for the post-war period up to 1980 is 62%, while that after 1980 is 16%. Therefore, the rate of growth in the median family income has declined by nearly 400% since 1980. Note these are rough estimates.

[a] this figure uses 2002 dollars

Source: U.S. Bureau of Census. Created by Munnell, Alicia H. Hatch, Robert E. Lee, James G. "Why is Life Expectancy So Low in the United States?" Figure 11, CRR Number 21. August 2004.

Historical Background

Growth of Defined Benefit Plans

The first pension plans in America were provided by the colonial militias prior to finalizing its independence from Great Britain. However, the first private defined benefit plans in began about 125 years ago, when American Express (then a railroad freight company) introduced its plan in 1875 to help attract career-oriented employees. These plans were the perfect solution for attracting high-quality, dedicated workers since they rewarded employees based upon their number of years of service. Soon after, many other companies began offering these plans, such as AT&T in 1906.

After the Great Depression, defined benefit plans surged in popularity due to their appeal of providing retirement security during the uncertain wartime period. The Wage and Salary Act of 1942 caused wages to freeze in an attempt to control inflation. And as an incentive to attract and retain employees in a very tight labor market, many businesses began offering employee benefits, including pensions. Furthermore, since company contributions were tax-deductible, this shielded them from high wartime tax rates.

Over time, defined benefit plans began to include healthcare benefits during a worker's employment years. And in exchange for several years of dedicated service to their company, many employers provided workers with full healthcare benefits for themselves and their spouse after they retired. Upon entering retirement, workers had no worries about healthcare costs and knew exactly how much income they would receive for as long as they lived.

The stability and financial security of defined benefit plans provided much of the financial strength that helped the middle class emerge as the main force driving the American economy. From 1940 to 1960, the number of Americans covered by private pension plans increased from 3.7 million to 23 million, or about 30 percent of the labor market. By 1970, participation in private pension plans increased to 45 percent and peaked just over 50 percent shortly thereafter.

That Was Then, This is Now

In the early part of the twentieth century, when a person retired he could expect a retirement period of five years on average before death. But today, the average life span is higher, causing the need to plan for life without work. Unfortunately, most Americans have failed to plan adequately for a retirement period that can last twenty years or more.

As well, healthcare costs were not out of control as they are today. Just a few decades ago, healthcare was affordable by most, so Americans were able to cope financially with the pay-as-you-go system. In part, the reason why healthcare costs were manageable was because management of chronic end-stage disease was immature, so most patients did not live long after receiving a diagnosis of diseases such as cardiovascular, kidney, and various forms of cancer. Now people are kept alive longer when diagnosed with chronic disease and that costs a lot of money.

In a previous chapter, I discussed the profit-driven, corruption- and fraud-ridden healthcare industry that continues to increase costs at will. It turns out that much of the rising costs since 1990 are most likely due to the paradigm shift in the 1980s when the U.S. government decided to protect against patent infringement. This allowed drug monopolies to form.

Ironically, as much of the healthcare industry has risen to its highest profits over the past two decades, defined benefit plans have been shrinking due to their replacement with 401(k) plans, as employers continue to slash or eliminate healthcare coverage and shift more of the cost and risk of retirement benefits to employees. These measures have been inspired by the intense global competition created by free trade. But, as you may appreciate, *slashing employee benefits and shifting to 401(k) plans has decreased overall employee compensation* since pension plans are structured with a larger built-in financial commitment from employers. This alone is direct evidence of a decline in living standards.

Today, the majority of American workers covered by employer-sponsored retirement plans have some type of 401(k) plan lacking many of the benefits once provided by employers. In addition, retail financial institutions (middleman) have been added and are extracting a bigger chunk of expenses from these plans. Therefore, *similar to the healthcare industry, the retirement industry in America has given rise to the growth of huge financial institutions that serve to siphon money from working-class Americans.*

The Rise of 401(k)s and Decline of Pensions

In 1981, Johnson Companies introduced the first 401(k) plan that afforded employees the opportunity to defer a portion of their pre-tax salary to be taxed only when the employee reached retirement age and began mandatory withdrawals (a deferred tax retirement contribution). Shortly thereafter, the IRS allowed this tax-deferred retirement savings plan, encouraging many companies to begin offering a 401(k) in addition to other defined contribution and defined benefit plans. In that same year, ERISA offered those who were not working for companies the opportunity to open a tax-deferred individual retirement account or IRA. *But ERISA never intended 401(k) plans to serve as a substitute for pension plans. They were created primarily as a means for self-employed and small companies to provide a retirement plan for workers.* And for large companies, *401(k) plans were intended to serve only as supplemental retirement assets to defined benefit plans and personal savings.*

But now, due to rising healthcare costs and corporate failures, 401(k)-type plans are being offered as the exclusive retirement plan by most small companies and many larger ones; that is if they even offer retirement plans. While defined benefit plans do still exist, the number of companies offering them to new employees has been declining rapidly over the past decade. Consequently, as a result of this trend, many American workers are now faced with a pool of less stable and uncertain retirement assets that are directly affected by the performance of the capital markets.

The initial surge in popularity of 401(k)-type plans was sparked by the competitive effects of Japanese products entering into American borders about three decades ago. Employers realized they needed to cut costs in order to remain competitive, and since defined benefit plans were a costly luxury, many employers began to shift to 401(k) plans. Since that period, the remaining defined benefit plans have come under further expense strains due to the skyrocketing cost of health insurance. But there are other contributing factors, such as increased life expectancies that were not adequately accounted for by benefits specialists.

The institutionalization of private pensions during this period was also mirrored by many large failures that inspired federal regulatory statutes. These changes in reform ultimately led to adoption of the Employee Retirement Income Security Act (ERISA) in 1974. ERISA was enacted to ensure certain fiduciary standards were met by employer-sponsored retirement plans, as well as the investment advisory firms that were responsible for management of these plan assets.

By the time the Great Bull market was under way in the '90s, the popularity of 401(k) plans grew enormously by employees wishing to gain direct benefit from a surging stock market. As well, smaller businesses seeking skilled workers but wishing to reduce the expense and future liabilities of defined benefit plans began to offer 401(k) plans as a cost-effective way of attracting qualified employees.

BOX 9-1: Reality in America

Prior to the death of her retired husband, Thelma Long, an 86 year old widow received pension plan income but now struggles to pay for food costs. When Mr. Long died in 1994, Mrs. Long faced the devastating reality of losing her husband's pension benefits, which included a nice annual income and healthcare coverage. With a total income of only $588 in monthly Social Security benefits, $125 of that amount goes to pay for federally subsidized housing. And without her food stamps, she literally would have no money to eat.

Mr. Long never chose to add pension benefits for his wife in the event of his death because this would have decreased his monthly pension income by up to 33 percent, a reduction that he could not afford. Now his wife barely makes ends meet due to her exclusive dependency on the social insurance system.

Today, nearly 3 million Americans are in a similar situation and must look to food banks to help them pay other expenses. But the problem is sure to get worse over the next decade due to the increasing fragility of the public and private pension systems. No elderly American should have to face these living conditions, especially when they are approaching the end of their life. Americans deserve to depart from this world gracefully and with dignity. And no financial hardship should further complicate their inevitable health-related problems, especially when it leads to hunger.

Soon, it became easier for employers to convince workers that 401(k) plans were a "great deal." Most companies would match contributions up to a certain limit, so it was "free money." As well, these contributions would be tax-deductible for both the employees and employers. And companies that replaced pensions with 401(k) plans freed themselves from future decades of pension liabilities due to benefit payouts, rising healthcare costs and increasing life spans.

Early on during this shift, many companies continued to offer a defined benefit plan in addition to the newer 401(k) plan. But slowly, employers began dropping their defined benefit plans or freezing benefits to new employees. *As a consequence, the shift from defined benefit plans towards 401(k)-type plans has resulted in diminished overall employee compensation since 401(k) plans have more investment expenses, lower investment returns, and lower employer contributions.*

In addition, 401(k) plans do not provide other forms of employee benefits such as healthcare and disability insurance. According to the NCPSSM, three out of every ten 20-year olds will become disabled prior to reaching age 67. However, *75 percent of the private workforce has no long-term disability insurance.* Much of this is due to the decline of defined benefit plans in America.

From 1985 to 2002, the total retirement assets in the United States rose from an estimated $2.4 trillion to $10 trillion, or as a percentage of GDP, from 67 to 95 percent. This rapid increase highlighted the entry of baby boomers into their retirement savings years, christened by America's seemingly strong economic growth. However, the main source of retirement asset growth over this period has been through 401(k) plans. But since the Internet fallout during 2000-2003, an estimated $7 trillion of retirement assets have been lost, and now those with 401(k) plans are faced with large shortfalls of retirement income. Likewise, millions of workers with defined benefit plans are uncertain if they will receive the benefits promised years earlier when they joined the company due to over 18,000 of these plans which are now underfunded.

From table 9-1, you can see the growth of each type of retirement savings plan over the past two decades. Notice that, while defined benefit total assets have increased 2-fold from 1985 to 2002, IRA and Keogh assets (401(k)-type plans) have increased by over 11-fold, and 401(k) plan assets (labelled as defined contribution plans) have increased by nearly 5-fold. From 1980 to 1999, (the most current and reliable data available) the number of defined benefit plans in America decreased by over 70 percent, while the number of 401(k) plans has increased by 100 percent (table 9.2, appendix). Note however that most state, local, and federal government retirement plans (which are considered defined benefit plans) have shown a 5-fold increase over this same period, similar to defined contribution plan growth. What this implies is that *while government employers have in large part kept their defined benefit plans, the private labor force has shifted from defined benefit to defined contribution or 401(k) plans* (table 9-2).

But this trend may change soon, as the underfundedness problem with public pensions is thought to be worse than that of private pensions. Already, many state governments are pushing to replace defined benefit plans with 401(k)-type plans as a way to save money and eliminate future liabilities. Michigan no longer offers a defined benefit plan and California will be closing its plan to new hires after January 1. 2007.

Table 9-1. The Growth of Pension Plans in the U.S. by Type (1985 to 2002)

	1985 (trillions $)	1994 (trillions $)	2002 (trillions $)	Total Change
IRA and Keogh	0.2	1.1	2.3	1150%
State and local Governments	0.4	1.1	2.0	500%
Federal government	0.2	0.5	0.9	450%
Private defined Contribution plans	0.4	1.1	1.9	475%
Private defined Benefit plans	0.8	1.2	1.6	200%
Total	$2.4 trillion	$5.7 trillion	$10 trillion	417%

Source: Reproduced with permission from the *Benefits & Compensation Digest* Volume 43, No. 2, February 2006 published by the International Foundation of Employee Benefit Plans (www.ifebp.org), Brookfield, WI. Statements or opinions expressed in this article are those of the author and do not necessarily represent the views or positions of the International Foundation, its officers, directors or staff. All rights reserved.

Table 9-2. Growth of Participants by Plan Type (1975 to 1999)

Types of Plans	1975	1985	1995	1999
Private defined benefit	103,000	170,000	69,000	50,000
Private defined contribution	208,000	462,000	624,000	683,000
State and local	NA	2,589	2,284	2,209
Federal	NA	8,591	8,630	8,615

Notice that the number of public DB plans has decreased by 70% from 1985 to 1999 (row 1). During this same period, DC plans have increased by 50% (row 2).

In contrast, private pension plans (all are DB or similar) have not grown in numbers (expected since government agencies were formed long ago).

Source: Ibid, International Foundation of Employee Benefit Plans.

According to the Employee Benefit Research Institute, *as of year 2000, only 20 percent of Americans were covered exclusively by defined pension plans.* Given the stock market scandals, corporate bankruptcies, and pension problems since that time, it is fair to assume that this number is now below 20 percent, although Munnell reports that this percentage has not changed as of 2004 (figure 9-3). And at least for the next several years, this number is expected to decline further, due in large part to the competitive effects of free trade.

The declining growth trends of defined benefit plans should be viewed as very disturbing for a variety of reasons. First, *a change from defined benefit to defined contribution plans should be interpreted as the expected inability or unwillingness of corporations to provide full benefits for retirees. Second, more of a future retirees' income will be directly dependent upon the stock and bond markets,* which can show periods as long as 12 to 15 years of little or no growth.

In contrast, because defined benefit plans are designed to provide for perpetual benefits (since new employees are constantly being added to the plan as new workers replace retirees), fund managers can take a longer-term approach and can better weather a secular bear market, while providing promised benefits to retirees.

Figure 9-3. Participation in Workplace Retirement Plans: Defined Benefit vs. Defined Contribution (1983-2004)

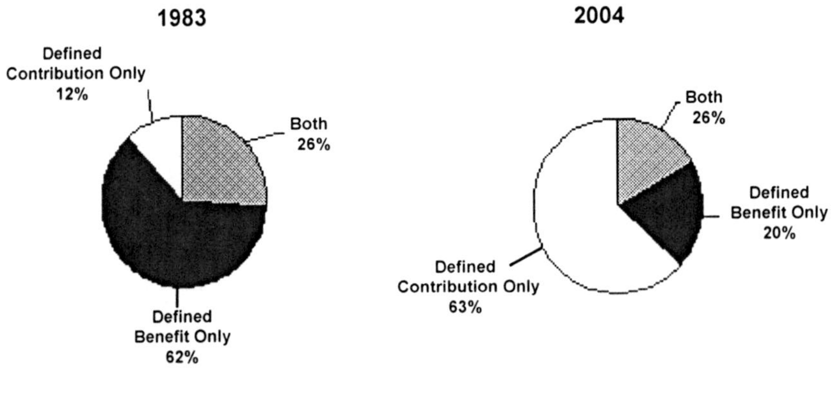

Source: Munnell and Sunden (2006)

What are the Differences?

While both defined benefit and contribution plans are thought to increase employee tenure, these affects are minimal for employers offering defined contribution or 401(k)-type plans since employer contributions are paid in full and deposited into the 401(k) account of the employee with no further future financial commitments. In contrast, employers offering a defined benefit plan do not transfer any benefits into the employee's legal possession until they retire. The contributions are merely documented as company liabilities in the name of the employee. Therefore, if the employee changes jobs before some set period, he could lose most or even all of the employer contributions that have been set aside for his pension. In addition, if the company files for bankruptcy, pension assets are in jeopardy of forfeiture. That is why the government provides insurance to pensions via the PBGC.

As a consequence, workers who change jobs can take their 401(k) plans with them, including all employer contributions (except for funds that have not satisfied vesting criteria). This portability feature of 401(k) plans has been viewed as a huge advantage by employees. However, it favors employers much more since they are showing an unwillingness to commit to a long-term career for their employees. Hence, *the rise of 401(k) plans in America signifies the growing trend of job insecurity that has accelerated since the acceptance of free trade policies by Washington.*

No longer is corporate America concerned with employee retention as a means of securing profitability. Today, the world is an open marketplace, and the rapid development of China and India offers companies inexpensive labor force alternatives at the cost of American jobs. Therefore, employee retention is no longer seen as a valuable attribute by most American companies. And this is just one of several reasons why companies are losing the incentive to continue these more costly defined benefit plans.

Similar to Social Security, defined benefit plans specify the benefit amounts workers will receive in advance, thereby providing strong assurances of retirement income—as long as these promises are kept. This is not the case with 401(k) plans. If workers happen to retire during a secular bear market, they could face major financial difficulties.

BOX 9-2: Types of Defined Contribution Plans

Examples of defined contribution plans are money purchase, target benefit, profit sharing, SIMPLE IRAs, traditional IRAs, Roth IRAs, Simplified Employee Pension plans (SEPs), 457, 401b3, Keoghs, and 401(k) plans. The different names are due to the type of work one is employed, such as government, teaching, self-employed, etc., with each having subtle differences. But they are all structured the same general way. Of course there are other supplementary portions of defined contribution plans such as ESOPs, but the majority of employees will have a 401(k)-type plan as their primary means of retirement savings.

401(k) Plans Eliminate Employer Risk

Employers favor 401(k) over defined benefit plans because 401(k)s shift the risks of returns onto employees, unlike the case with defined benefit plans, which promise guaranteed retirement benefits that must be delivered regardless how poorly the capital markets have performed. In short, employers who sponsor defined benefit plans provide guarantees of retirement benefits in advance and must keep these promises unless they file for bankruptcy. With 401(k) plans, employers leave the returns up to the worker, who has the freedom (and responsibility) of selecting the funds offered by the financial company administering the plan.

As well, employers offering 401(k)s no longer have to worry about increasing life spans of workers that could add unexpected future liabilities under a defined benefit plan sponsorship. In addition, 401(k)s allow employers the flexibility (but not obligation) of paying matching funds (at any amount they want) annually with no further obligations into the future. Therefore, 401(k) plans have a wider variability of payout that will depend on employee contributions and the performance of these investments, which are the responsibility of employees. (1)

Flexibility & Control of 401(k)s

For the employee, 401(k)s provide better transparency and more direct control of where and how their retirement funds are invested, since they can select and change the types of funds within their plan. Thus, the shift to 401(k) plans provides a way for employees to become more involved with their retirement investments.

As previously mentioned, 401(k)s provide portability of assets since the funds are legally owned by the employee (except for unvested matching contributions). And when employees leave for another job, they can roll their 401(k) into an IRA, which will enable them to buy and sell stocks in the market as they chose. Thus, IRAs provide the ultimate in individual control of one's retirement investments. However, *such responsibility requires a sophisticated and disciplined investment approach, which most people lack.*

In contrast, most defined benefit plans are not transportable or at least require a certain minimum number of work years in order to qualify for pre-retirement age benefits. This ensures that employees will be committed to the company for several years or face losing much if not all of their pension benefits.

A unique characteristic of 401(k) plans is that they can be used as a source of funds for certain expenses such as a first-time home purchase or medical bills, as long as these funds are paid back by a specified period.

And although most employees view this as advantageous, it actually introduces an added layer of risk due to fees and penalties associated with non-compliance of timely repayment. *When Americans have to use their retirement savings to purchase a home, it paints a troubling picture of their living standards.*

Advantages of Defined Contribution Plans
• Employees have control over investments (a disadvantage since investors lack sufficient experience and sophistication in finance and the stock market)
• Employees can borrow against the assets in certain instances (a disadvantage since it creates more risk for preservation of retirement income)
• Larger variety of investment choices
• Plans are transportable
• Most employers provide matching funds
• No business risk (if company goes bankrupt the plan is not affected; only the unvested amount would be in jeopardy)

---

(1) Each year, employers provide matching funds based on the amount of contributions by each employee with no further commitments. In contrast, most defined benefit plans promise to provide retirement income and (usually) healthcare benefits to employees (based upon their salary and years of service) for the rest of their lives. Thus, employers offering defined benefit plans have unknown future plan liabilities because they are responsible for lifetime retirement and healthcare benefits.

Why 401(k) Plans are a Bad Idea

Because participation in 401(k)-type plans is purely on a voluntary basis, most Americans do not contribute the maximum. Several studies have shown that *the average participation rate for companies that offer 401(k)-type plans is 75 to 80 percent.* In other words, between 20 and 25 percent of workers who have a 401(k)-type plan available to them do not participate (figure 9-5).

Therefore, while 20 to 25 percent of employees are jeopardizing their retirement security, they are costing the employer zero expenses since no matching can occur if employee contributions are not made. As a matter of fact, estimates are that only about half of all American workers even have a 401(k)-type plan (including 403b and 457 plans, which are for teachers and government workers respectively).

And only about 11 percent of all employees who have a 401(k) contribute the maximum. It turns out that higher paid employees tend to contribute more to their 401(k). Figure 9-6 shows that nearly 60 percent of all employees earning over $100,000 contributed the maximum amount to their plan. In contrast, only 0.90 percent of those earning $40,000 to $60,000 contributed the maximum.

Part of the problem of participation rates is that American workers are already being squeezed with slower wage growth, fewer benefits, and more out-of-pocket healthcare costs. According to McKinsey and Co., *as of 2005, only half of Americans aged 55 had an average balance of only $50,000 in their 401(k)-type plan.*

Figure 9-4. Percent of Workers With Pension Coverage By Type of Plan from SCF (1983-2004)

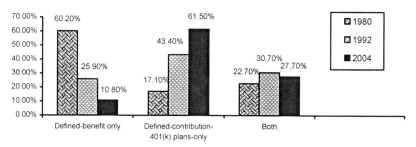

Source: Munnell, Alicia and Sunden, Annika "401(k) Plans are Still Coming Up Short. Figure 3. CRR Number 43 March 2006. Calculations based on *Surveys of Consumer Finances*.

Figure 9-5. Percent of Workers Not Participating in a 401(k) plan

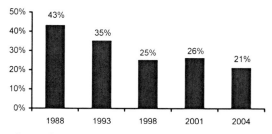

Source: Bureau of Labor Statistics (2003) and authors' calculations based on *Surveys of Consumer Finances*. Created by Munnell and Sunden, "401(k) Plans are Still Coming Up Short. Figure 4, CRR Number 43 March 2006.

Defined benefit plans have a "defined benefit" for employees so they know ahead of time what their lifetime benefits will be based upon their wages and years of service. **Defined contribution or 401(k)-type plan benefits** are variable and depend upon both the amounts contributed by the employee (as well as employer matching if applicable) and the investment returns.

172

Figure 9-6. Percent of Participants Making Maximum Contributions, By Earnings*

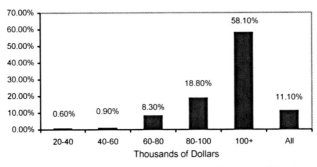

Source: Created by Munnell, Alicia and Sunden, Annika "401(k) Plans are Still Coming Up Short. Figure 5, CRR Number 43 March 2006. Authors' calculations based on *Surveys of Consumer Finances*.
Note: Since the legal maximum of $15,000 is virtually out of reach for low-wage earners, this table assumes that the maximum is either $15,000 or 25 percent of wages—whichever is lower.

The shift by employers to 401(k) plans also distorts the wage growth and living standards of American workers since no portion of wages are counted as mandatory retirement contributions. As wages fail to keep pace with inflation, more Americans contribute less to these plans because they are fighting the effects of America's declining standard of living. But when they retire with inadequate funds, they will have to face severely diminished living conditions.

It is clear that American workers need more incentives to save for retirement because they do not have the discipline or financial understanding that will cause them to save sufficiently on their own. Regardless, for many future retirees who have contributed a reasonable amount annually to their 401(k), the biggest factor determining their retirement plan balance could very well be the health of the stock and bond markets during the time period they will need this income.

Disadvantages of Defined Contribution Plans

- Employees bare the risk of benefits
- Contributions are voluntary
- Participation rates are low
- Investment fees are more expensive
- Investment returns are lower and uncertain
- Employer contributions have vesting periods
- Only provides a source of retirement income
- Not good for older workers
- Workers must take an active role
- Market risk

BOX 9-3: Defined Benefit Plans Have No Market Risk

Regardless how the stock and bond markets perform, employees covered by a defined benefit plan are guaranteed a specific amount of income based upon their length of service and wages, but the formula more heavily weighs the last few years before retirement. Due to these predetermined payouts, these plans have no market risk. However, they do have business risk (see BOX 9-7). In contrast, 401(k) plans expose employees to market risk since in this case, the employer is no longer responsible and serves merely as the plan administrator.

Defined Benefit Plans Perform Better and Cost Less

The majority of studies have shown that on average, the investment returns of defined benefit plans are superior to those of 401(k)-type plans. Alicia Munnell of the Center for Retirement Research at Boston College has estimated that *the average defined benefit plan outperformed the average defined contribution plan by 0.8 percent per year from 1981 to 2001.* When compounded, this difference yields a total in excess of 20 percent.

Finally, the Investment Company Institute determined that *the expenses of defined benefit plans are lower than defined contribution plans.* This study found that the expense ratio of defined benefit plans was on average 40 basis points (0.4 percent) lower than that for defined contribution plans.

Advantages of Defined Benefit Plans
• Employees only bare a small risk of benefits
• Employees know what their benefits will be when they retire
• Contributions are mandatory
• Investment fees are less expensive
• Investment returns are higher
• Provides income and healthcare benefits for life
• No market risk

And when 12(b)-1 fees are added from mutual funds within 401(k) plans, the cost can add an additional 25 to 50 basis points (or 0.25 to 0.50 percent). Estimates from Brooks Hamilton have shown that *while defined benefit plans costs about 1 to 3 percent of payroll to administer, 401(k) plans cost from 6 to 8 percent.* (2)

Over time, these costs add up to large expenses due to compounding. For an employee who has had a 401(k) plan for three or four decades, estimates are that up to 80 percent of the plan balance has gone to fees, leaving them with only 20 percent of the gross investment returns; a total fleecing of retirement assets by the financial industry.

Disadvantages of Defined Benefit Plans
• Not transportable (typically)
• Could lose some benefits due to company bankruptcy
• Business risk

This difference in fees stems from the fact the 401(k) plans are managed by the retail financial industry, while defined benefit plans are not, so there is no middle man. Table 9-3 summarizes the main differences between defined benefit and defined contribution or 401(k)-type plans.

---

(2) In part, these discrepancies might be explained by ERISA regulations that require oversight by trustees who then hire outside advisors to manage these pools of assets. While 401(k) plans do have similar regulations, the controls do not appear to be as rigid because the two plan types are completely different. Defined benefit plans are structured for the benefit of all employees so extra attention must be taken. In contrast, for 401(k) plans each employee has a separate account and can make investment decisions within the fund choices of the plan. Therefore, companies sponsoring defined benefits plans have a larger fiduciary responsibility. Basically what this means is that these plans have higher accountability standards. And therefore, management fees are among the many things that are closely monitored by plan advisors.

Table 9-3. Comparison of Defined Benefit and Defined Contribution Plans

Strategic Considerations	Defined Benefit Plans	Defined Contribution Plans
Employee retention	Attracts longer tenured employees (stronger effect)	Attracts shorter tenured employees
Financial liabilities	Placed on the corporate sponsor	Placed on the participant
Responsibility placed on employee	Very little	Significant-voluntary contributions, Necessary investment decisions
Responsibility placed on employer	Significant-investment decisions, financial liability	Less significant
Employer fiduciary responsibility	Significant	Significant
Investment results	Average returns are higher, narrower distribution of returns	Average returns are lower, broader distribution of returns
Personal retirement savings	Maximizes savings for retirement	Allows withdrawals and loans before retirement, depleting retirement savings
Fees	Lower overall	Higher overall
Administrative complexity	High	High
Portability	Usually not, sometimes partial	Yes
Loans	No	Yes for certain situations

Source: Ibid, International Foundation of Employee Benefit Plans.
Note: table has been modified to include additional comparison categories.

The Pension Problem

So far in this chapter, I have discussed the disturbing trend of increasing defined contribution or 401(k) plan growth rates at the expense of defined benefit plan growth. In order to understand the consequences of this trend, I have also explained the fundamental differences between these two plan types. At this point, it should be clear that having a comprehensive retirement plan with predetermined guaranteed benefits and lifetime healthcare coverage is critical for the boomer generation due to skyrocketing healthcare and energy costs, and the uncertain future stability of Social Security.

Ever since the correction of the Internet bubble, many employers began to "freeze" their defined benefit plans, (i.e. no longer allowing new employees entry and ceasing new benefit accruals by current members into the plan) and instead began using 401(k)s as their primary form of employer-sponsored retirement plans. Quite possibly, within the next two decades, defined benefit plans may be a thing of the past, as companies continue to freeze current plans and shift to 401(k)s as a way to transfer the expense and risk of retirement benefits to employees.

Yet, even though defined benefit plans are in decline, they still make up a large percentage of retirement assets of Americans as we have seen (figures 9-3 and 9-4). However, it has been estimated that *over 50 percent of Fortune 1000 companies' defined benefit plans are underfunded.* A defined benefits plan is considered underfunded when pension assets fall below 80 percent of that required to provide full benefits. In other words, there's not enough income from pension assets to pay benefits to retirees. Notably, this definition was recently changed to 100 percent by Congress as a concession to increase the time available to get plans funded.

Here I address the more immediate problems with defined benefit plans, namely the underfundedness and pension-freezing trends, which threaten to force even more Americans to depend primarily on Social Security income throughout their retirement years.

BOX 9-4: The Myth of the 401k Greatness

During the late 1990s, when the great bull market was in full swing, having a 401(k) was viewed as a sign of career success, because employees could monitor and control their retirement plans in the midst of an amazing bull market. And today, this myth is being further strengthened by the bad press about defined benefit plans due to the freezing of plan assets, the underfunded pension problem and the cancellation of pension promises when companies have entered bankruptcy.

However, what many Americans do not realize is that employers are getting off easy at the expense of employees by substituting defined benefit pension plans with 401(k)s. The overall result is that employers are decreasing the total compensation of their employees by shifting to the less comprehensive and more uncertain 401(k) plans.

One of the big sales pitches for 401(k)s is that they provide matching funds. But employers are not required to contribute any matching funds of the 401(k) plan. And when they do provide matching, these contributions (referred to as matching assets) are usually very low.

Matching funds are measured by two variables—the ratio of the match, as in dollar-for-dollar, or say a generous $2 matched for every employee dollar matched—and the amount of employee contributions matched which is usually around 5 percent. Consider for example that an employer matching of around 5 percent on a dollar-for-dollar basis is considered high. With a current annual maximum 401(k) contribution by each employee of around $15,000, you can see that even a generous match of 5 percent only amounts to about $750. And the fact is that most employees do not contribute the maximum amounts.

In addition, there are vesting requirements which do not allow these matching funds to enter the 401(k) until after a certain number of years have elapsed (depending on the type of vesting). Therefore, when employees change jobs, employers will not have to provide matching funds for the last three to five years of the departing employees' tenure.

Finally, 401(k) plans do not provide for any healthcare benefits, and even when employers do provide healthcare as a separate benefit, many will not provide healthcare insurance when employees retire. This further lowers future financial liabilities of these companies.

The Big Freeze

Before I discuss the underfunded pension problem, I'll discuss what the media has inappropriately determined to be a more benign trend; that of pension freezes. While it does not immediately impact future retires unlike pension underfundedness and terminations, the freezing of pension plans signals the continuing trend of replacing defined benefit with 401(k) plans. Ironically, the growing trend of freezing defined benefit pension plans comes on the heels of competitive forces from abroad, as well as the already large and growing underfunded pension problem in America.

Freeze versus Termination

At any time and for any reason they choose, companies can freeze their defined benefit plans unless they are under some type of collective bargaining agreement such as a labor union contract. In so, companies must first obtain approval from the union prior to making any changes to the plan.

Companies can freeze their plans to new employees and recently hired employees (called a *partial or soft freeze*). Alternatively, they can freeze their plans to all employees (called a *full or hard freeze*). A partial freeze means that new employees will not be entered into the plan at all, but current employees will continue to accrue future benefits from the plan. In contrast, when a hard freeze is declared, not only are new employees restricted from inclusion into the plan, but current employees will no longer accrue benefits. However, current employees will retain their right to payment of previously earned benefits upon retirement. They just will not be able to accrue new benefits.

The main differences between a pension plan freeze and termination are that in the former, companies cannot take away any of the future benefits that employees have earned prior to the announcement of the freeze and the plan remains in operation. While frozen plans can at a later time become unfrozen and resume previous activities, this is not thought to represent current trends with frozen plans in America.

In contrast, *plan terminations* essentially remove the company from the responsibility of paying benefits and plan operations are shut down. If the company can demonstrate to the PBGC that is has sufficient funds to pay all benefits to plan participants, it can end the plan using a *standard termination*. In this case, the company either purchases an annuity for all employees or issues each eligible employee a lump-sum distribution if the plan allows it.

If the company is financially unstable, it can apply for a *distress termination*. This would be granted by the PBGC only if it is shown in a bankruptcy court that the employer cannot remain in business unless the plan is terminated. In this case, the PBGC will assume the responsibility of providing for retiree benefits, often at reduced rates.

For 2006, the maximum benefit guarantee was set at $3,971.59 per month ($47,659.08 annually) for workers who retire at age 65. (3) This sum will be lower if workers begin receiving payments from the PBGC before age 65 or if workers had previously designated benefits for a survivor or other beneficiary prior to plan termination, and greater if they begin receiving payments after age 65. (4) However, *the PBGC does not provide healthcare coverage.* At most, employees may only quality for the Health Coverage Tax Credit administered by the IRS.

Finally, in some circumstances, the PBGC will end a pension plan if it decides that plan termination is necessary to protect the interests of plan participants or of the PBGC insurance program. Either way, whether companies freeze their plans as a prelude to eventual transition into a 401(k) or whether they terminate their plans, the days of having a defined benefit plan for American workers seem to be numbered.

---

(3) When the PBGC assumes the plan they will not provide a lump-sum distribution.
(4) ERISA determines the provisions of PBGC annual benefit guarantees.

The Affects of a Freeze for Employees

While a full pension freeze is not thought to result in large adverse consequences for younger employees, it shortchanges the retirement benefits of workers who have been with the company for a longer period. The reason for this is because defined benefit plans are typically structured with an accelerated compensation towards the last few years prior to retirement. Therefore, *when a company places a hard freeze on its plan, employees who may have worked there for 20 years, yet may only be age 55, will be missing the majority of future benefits.*

And due to their older age, it is much more difficult for them to make up these shortfalls with 401(k)s since these plans are self-funded and self-directed, and require many years of participation in order to build up a sizable asset base. In addition, if the stock market happens to perform poorly over the remaining period or just prior to retirement, the investment returns can be small.

Why Are Companies Freezing?

Rather than terminate their pension and be hit with financial penalties by the PBGC, companies facing severe financial difficulties usually put a freeze on their defined benefit plan so that no new benefits accrue. In the past, plan freezes have been a part of the normal process of bankruptcy protection. However, a newer, growing trend is that of freezing pensions by healthy companies as a way to decrease future liabilities of healthcare costs and other benefits that could be affected by increases in life spans and continued inflation in healthcare.

Table 9-4. Percentage of PBGC-Insured Single-Employer Plans That Had a Hard Freeze in Place in 2003, by Industry

Industry	Percent Hard-Frozen	Industry's Percentage of All Plans
Agriculture, Mining, and Construction	9.1	8.4
Manufacturing	10.1	26.9
Apparel and textile Products	15.9	1.0
Chemicals and Allied Products	7.6	2.3
Fabricated Metal Products	16.1	4.6
Food and Tobacco Products	8.5	2.4
Machinery and Computer Equipment	12.0	3.3
Motor Vehicles	4.6	1.1
Primary Metals	12.3	1.6
Rubber and Plastics	12.4	1.4
Other Manufacturing	10.2	9.2
Transportation and Public Utilities	7.2	3.6
Air Transportation	12.1	0.2
Other Transportation	9.5	2.0
Public Utilities	2.7	1.3
Wholesale Trade	11.8	7.2
Retail Trade	12.3	5.1
Finance, Insurance, and Real Estate	5.6	17.4
Services	8.9	31.4
Total	9.4	100

Source: PBGC 2004 Databook, taken from "An Analysis of Frozen Defined Benefit Plans" Table 7. December 21, 2005.

Since 1970, American companies that provide for healthcare under their pension plans have seen healthcare costs rise by more than 350 percent; much more than any other expense (table 9-6). And as figure 9-7 clearly demonstrates, *the underfunded liabilities of defined benefit plans have been dwarfed by their healthcare liabilities.* While good performance in the stock market can correct the underfunded or pension deficit problems, employer healthcare liabilities will only get larger regardless how well the stock market performs.

Table 9-6. Private Sector Retirement and Healthcare benefit as a Percentage of Total Compensation (1970-2004)

Item	1970	1980	1990	2000	2004
Total Compensation	100.0%	100.0%	100.0%	100.0%	100.0%
Wages and Salaries	89.4	83.4	82.5	83.5	80.6
Retirement Benefits	**6.5**	**9.7**	**8.8**	**7.9**	**9.1**
Social Security	2.6	3.4	4.1	4.0	4.0
Private employer pensions	2.1	3.3	1.9	2.0	3.0
Public employer pensions	1.7	3.0	2.8	2.0	2.2
Health Benefits	**2.4**	**4.4**	**6.3**	**6.9**	**8.4**
Medicare	0.4	0.7	1.0	1.2	1.2
Group health	2.0	3.7	5.3	5.7	7.2
Other benefits	1.8	2.5	2.4	1.6	1.9

Source: A. Munnell, F. Golub-Sass, M. Soto, F. Vitagliano. "Why Are Healthy Employers Freezing their Pensions?" March 2006, Vol 44. CRR. Author's calculations from the U.S. Dept. of Commerce (2006).

Figure 9-7. S&P 500 Retiree Healthcare Funding and Defined Benefit Funding Shortfall (2000-2004)

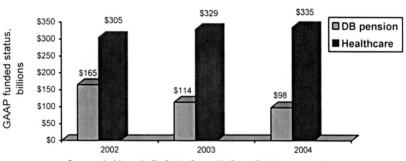

Source: A. Munnell, F. Golub-Sass, M. Soto, F. Vitagliano. "Why Are Healthy Employers Freezing their Pensions?" March 2006, Vol 44. CRR.

Some companies have frozen their plans as a way to help them become more funded since liabilities do not accumulate (during a full freeze) or only add based upon workers already in the plan (during a partial freeze) while the plan is frozen. However, frozen plans are still subject to market performance, which can affect the funding status. Alternatively, many believe that the recent record low interest rates have caused some otherwise healthy corporations to freeze plan assets since low rates inherently causes plan liabilities to increase. For otherwise financially healthy companies, putting a freeze on pension plans may signal the eventual shift out of a defined benefit plan system, but in the very least it will spare the company from these retirement costs while the plan remains frozen. IBM's announcement in 2006 of a full freeze in its defined benefit plan is expected to result in $3 billion in savings over a five-year period, affecting 117,000 workers; that's money that will be added to its bottom-line. As well, Hewlett-Packard's partial freeze is expected to save about the same amount over a ten-year period.

Table 9-5. Companies in Good Financial Standing that Froze Pension Benefits (2004-2006)

Company	U.S. Employees	Participants Affected	Type of Freeze	Funding Status
-2006-				
Coca-Cola Bottling Co. 6,100	4,500	Total	89.1%	
Nissan NA, Inc.	15,200		New Employees	85.2%
IBM Corp.	125,000	117,000	Total	104.6
ALCOA	48,000		New Employees	85.0
-2005-				
Verizon Communications	240,000	50,000	Partial	104.6
Sprint Nextel Corp.	82,900	39,000	Partial	82.2
Milliken and Co.	10,200	9,300	Total	97.8
Lockheed-Martin Corp.	118,800		New Employees	70.3
Hewlett-Packard Co.	71,000	32,200	Partial	90.6
Ferro Corp.	2,500	1,000	Total	67.2
Russell Corp.	8,800	5,700	Total	66.5
-2004-				
Circuit City Stores, Inc.	42,400	19,900	Total	102.6
Motorola, Inc.	30,600		New Employees	74.5
Hospira, Inc.	9,800	8,250	Total	87.7
NCR Corp.	11,400	9,200	Partial	93.8
Aon Corp.	21,000		New Employees	89.6

Source: A. Munnell, Golub-Sass, Soto, Vitagliano. "Why Are Healthy Employers Freezing their Pensions?" March 2006, Vol 44. CRR.

In addition to saving costs, employers freeze plans as a way to lower overall compensation as an alternative to lowering salaries. Many companies also state that defined benefit plans make them less competitive with smaller companies that never offered such plans, or due to foreign competitors whose pensions are funded by their government. Another reason for the freezing trend is due to the inability of plans to provide adequate compensation for top executives. Because ERISA sets certain limits on the amount employees can receive, defined benefit plans no longer provide the amount of compensation CEOs are demanding (figure 9-8). Accordingly, most companies have established non-qualified (non-tax-exempt) plans for executives known as Supplemental Executive Retirement Plans (SERPS) which allow them to provide the type of ridiculous compensation we see today in America's largest corporations. Therefore, the need for a general pension plan has been diminished since it only provides for the mass workers. (5)

(5) The main distinguishing features of defined benefit plans relate to whether they are qualified or unqualified. Qualified plans receive more favorable tax treatment to the employee and are typically the type of plans provided to most employees. In contrast, the executive management is usually covered by unqualified plans, which do not receive favorable tax treatment. The basic differences between qualified and unqualified are related to certain maximums, percentage of employees required to be covered, tax treatment, and regulation by government bodies.

Finally, new laws passed by Congress and expected changes from the FASB will make the growing trend of frozen pensions all but certain. While Congress has recently provided extensions for pensions to gain funded status within seven years (airlines get up to twenty years and some companies get up to 30 years), they have raised the definition of fully funded which is now at 100 percent, up from 80 percent. This will add to the financial pressure many companies may face when trying to fund these plans, especially if the stock market does not recover soon.

Figure 9-8. Total Compensation Relative to Average Wages (1936-2003)

Period	CEO	Next 2 Officers
1936-1939	82	56
1940-1945	66	44
1946-1949	49	37
1950-1959	47	34
1960-1969	39	30
1970-1979	40	31
1980-1989	69	45
1990-1999	187	95
2000-2003	367	164

Source: A. Munnell, F. Golub-Sass, M. Soto, F. Vitagliano. "Why Are Healthy Employers Freezing their Pensions?" March 2006, Vol 44. CRR. Authors's calculations from the IRS (2005 and 2006) and the Department of Commerce (2006).

As well, companies that have underfunded pensions are limited in the amount of executive compensation they can provide to top executives. Finally, the fees paid by each company for insurance coverage by the PBGC have recently been raised by a rather large percent, adding to the already growing costs of administering these plans; one more reason why to eliminate them altogether.

In conclusion, the growing trend of defined benefit plan freezes should be interpreted as a clear sign that eventually, all American companies will gradually eliminate these plans in favor of 401(k)-type plans. And this is going to hurt the total compensation and retirement security of American workers, adding to the three decade-long decline in American living standards.

Box 9-5: Suspect Determinants of a Possible Pension Freeze

According to a survey conducted by Towers-Perrin HR Services in March 2006, corporate executives stated that any of the following negative developments might be a reason for the company to freeze its pension:

Company cash flow (60%), company earnings (48%), lower credit rating (43%), company share price, shareholder's equity, or administrative costs of managing the plan (21%).

Underfunded Pensions

When ERISA created legislature for pension (defined benefit) plans, it provided companies with too much flexibility on how to fund them. As a result, companies are not required to fully fund their pension plans. It might be helpful to think of a funded plan similar to a balanced budget. In extreme cases, some companies use current cash inflows from incoming employee contributions to pay benefits to retirees; a very risky practice. Of course, when the stock market experiences a period of poor returns, a huge problem can arise, namely, a pension that is underfunded.

This is precisely what happened to thousands of companies after 2000. And it has resulted in a potential $450 billion shortfall in private pension benefits. But this doesn't even count the huge healthcare benefits promised to employees of these plans, which have always been funded from current cash flows (and are not counted on the pension liabilities section of the balance sheet) as a matter of standard pension accounting practice.

As of mid-2006, more than 18,000 corporate pensions (i.e. defined benefit pension plans) were underfunded by over $450 billion. And public (government) pensions are underfunded by an additional $460 to $700 billion; a total of around $1 trillion in liabilities for current and future retirees that is not available. You don't hear about the massive shortfalls in government pension plans because they aren't required to file financial statements with the SEC. But as you can see, the government pension system could potentially be a much bigger problem. Needless to say, government pensions are not insured by the PBGC because they are backed directly by tax dollars.

According to ERISA regulations, when pension plans remain underfunded for a certain period, companies are required to use their earnings to fill the gap. That could hammer the corporate earnings from hundreds and potentially thousands of public companies if plan funding status is not corrected over the next few years.

The amount and timing of required funding needed to establish plan solvency depends upon both the amount and duration by which the plan has been underfunded. When a plan becomes underfunded, benefit payments to retirees are halted. In the past, an underfunded plan had three years to become funded, but as mentioned, this limitation has recently been extended. However, because Washington has also redefined a fully funded plan from 80 to 100 percent, it's going to be very difficult for these 18,000 underfunded plans to gain solvency without contributions from corporate cash flows or a sustained surge in the stock market. Perhaps this is another incentive for President Bush's Social Security privatization plan.

Box 9-6: Interest Rates Affect Plans

The reason interest rates affect defined benefit plan assets is because each plan is set up to provide a certain payout (i.e. defined benefit) based upon actuarial tables and estimates for wages throughout each employees' tenure. Because plan assets are invested in stocks and bonds, they are designed to provide a certain rate of return annually so that future benefits can be paid to retirees. However, when interest rates are low, this limits the ability of plan managers to provide the needed income for retiree benefits. The extended period of record low rates has therefore added to the underfundedness of pension plans. And this affect has been compounded by the weak performance of the stock market.

Figure 9-9. Total DB System Underfunding, PBGC Single-Employer Program

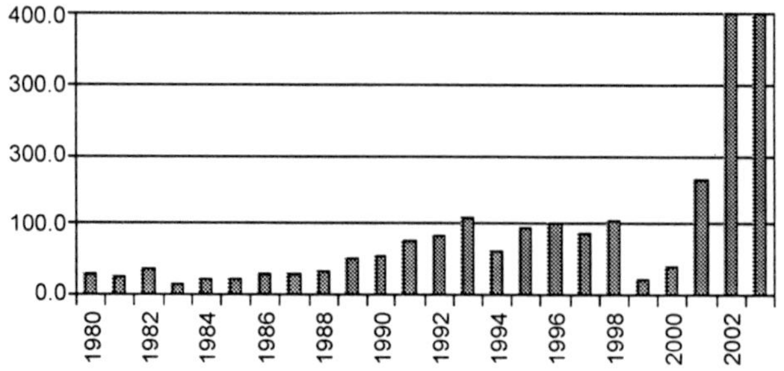

Source: PBGC. Mark Glickman and Charles Jeszeck, U.S. Government Accountability Office. April 4, 2005.

In June 2005, Delta and Northwest Airlines told Congress their plans would default unless legislators extended the funding deadline. Since then, Delta has received a 20-year extension to fund its pension plan, meaning retired employees may not begin to receive benefits for up to twenty years. And the "Big 3" automakers, with pension deficits of $55 to $60 billion are also requesting an extension of funding deadlines. Of course, these companies have not escaped bankruptcy, which if occurred, would most likely cause a significant loss of pension benefits for many workers, sending shockwaves throughout the economy.

With over 18,000 pension plans in the red, millions of workers are not able to receive full retirement benefits. But they're the lucky ones. Millions of others have had their pensions completely eliminated or trimmed down due to corporate restructurings and bankruptcies. In the last three years, almost 600 companies have weaseled out on pension obligations, with 21 plans each totaling $100 million or more, topped by United Airline's pension fund failure of $9.8 billion; the biggest since the government began guaranteeing pensions in 1974. These failures add to the already large pool of retired Americans who are counting on Social Security to provide up to 100 percent of their income.

BOX 9-7: Defined Benefit Plans Have Business Risk

Business risk is the largest risk faced by employees with defined benefit plans. This is the risk that the sponsoring company becomes financially insolvent forcing it into bankruptcy. In such a case, the pension is often reduced or terminated completely, and the liability passes onto the PBGC. However, the PBGC often does not pay full benefits to employees, especially for those making large wages or for those who begin receiving PBGC payouts prior to age 65.

In the case whereby a company does not become insolvent but is financially troubled, the pension plan may become severely underfunded and could result in the company filing to terminate the plan and pass the liabilities onto the PBGC. Regardless whether the plan remains underfunded beyond the deadline or files for bankruptcy, the company will usually terminate the plan and request a bailout by the PBGC.

However, the PBGC will not automatically assume the financial responsibility of the plan. First, the it reviews the request intense scrutiny, with no guarantee it will accept the termination. If it rejects the termination request, it will sue the company in court to remove the pension liabilities. Finally, keep in mind that not all companies are insured by the PBGC, as it is a voluntary insurance plan.

Table 9-7. Top Five PBGC Benefit Payments by State (2004)

State	Amount
1. Pennsylvania	$514,931,866
2. Ohio	$325,001,140
3. Florida	$221,521,125
4. Illinois	$206,436,290
5. Indiana	$200,423,088

What Happens After Termination?

When a company terminates its pension, this usually occurs as a last resort to avoid bankruptcy. And if this can be proven to the PBGC, then it will step in to provide retirement benefits replacement to qualified workers. However, many workers will not receive what they were supposed to depending on their salary and years of service. For instance, for 2006, terminated plans insured by the PBGC provided a maximum benefit of $47,659.08 per year for 65 year old retirees.

Fees

Other than setup fees, the PBGC charges annual premiums of $19 per employee from each plan. But due to the huge deficit problems of the PBGC, Washington raised these premiums to $30 or by nearly 40 percent, effective on January 1, 2006. Still, with about 44 million employees covered, this still only amounts to just over $1.3 billion for its annual budget. However, the *Deficit Reduction Act (DRA) of 2005* allowed the PBGC to also charge fees to companies that terminate their plans.

As a result of the DRA, when under bankruptcy, companies that terminate their plans are now required to pay the PBGC a fee of $1250 per employee annually for three years. This $3750 per employee termination fee helps fund the added liabilities the PBGC will face. However, if every underfunded plan (60 percent of the plans insured by the PBGC and assuming an equal distribution of plan participants of the 44 million workers covered, or 26.4 million) was terminated over the next 15 years, the total fees (annual premiums plus termination) would only amount to about $118 billion; way short of the $450 billion potential liability.

You might assume that termination of all plans is unlikely. But termination is not the only route that can result in non-payment of plan benefits. At the very least, even if plans are eventually funded, retirees could go many years without receiving benefits since benefit payments are halted when the plan is underfunded.

Corporate Restructuring

Over the past two decades, the stigma associated with bankruptcy has evolved into a respectable corporate strategy when a company is faced with financial difficulties. This transformation has partly been due to corporate bankruptcy laws passed in 1974, which gave companies a tremendous amount of flexibility in how they restructure their assets and liabilities, including those of their pension plans.

According to these laws, when a company files for bankruptcy protection, the creditors (bondholders) have first claims to firm assets. However, in order to convince creditors to continue to finance these risky ventures, the law states that financing companies involved in bankruptcy restructurings are to receive "super priority" of firm assets. Therefore, financiers are given the final say in virtually every aspect of the company's management, which often leads to concessions in the pension plan, or in some cases its termination.

Over the past decade, corporate restructuring has become a very lucrative portion of the specialty banking business, with huge fees and high rates of return. But the banks aren't the only ones who make out at the expense of employees. Attorney fees have been so large that this area of law has experienced a boom over the past several years.

Unfortunately, while the banks and attorneys are charging massive fees to help the company try to emerge from bankruptcy, the employees are often left with very little. Therefore, underperforming companies or those with cash flow problems can file for bankruptcy and release themselves from the financial liability of their pension plans. And it has been the growth of this trend that has added to the insolvency of the PBGC.

The PBGC

The PBGC is the government agency responsible for insuring the pension assets of over 44 million Americans (about 34 million employees covered under single-employer plans and about 10 million workers covered under multi-employer plans). This agency can be thought to provide a role similar as the FDIC in the commercial banking industry that insures bank deposits up to $100,000 per account holder in the event of a bank failure.

Ever since the Internet bubble correction, hundreds of companies have turned to the PBGC to assume the financial obligation of paying retirement benefits from terminated plans, causing the PBGC to incur increasing record deficits. However, the full extent of these deficits has not yet manifest, as its total liabilities could swell to higher levels if any of the 18,000-plus underfunded companies in America terminate their pensions. Because these companies have a combined deficit (underfunded amount) of $450 billion, this is considered the total of the PBGC's contingent liabilities.

While it is unlikely that the majority of these plans will be terminated, even Washington has estimated that a significant amount of terminations will occur. This would obviously result in further devastation to the PBGC, which is already near bankruptcy. Since 2003, the PBGC has been in deficit, ending its 2005 fiscal year with a shortfall of $22.8 billion. For Q3 of the 2006 fiscal year, the PBGC had a deficit of $18.1 billion, (assets of $60 billion against liabilities of $78.1 billion). This deficit represents the amount the PBGC is unable to pay to retirees of companies that have terminated their pension plans (figure 9-10).

The Congressional Budget Office (CBO) has predicted PBGC liabilities to increase to $87 billion over the next decade and up to $142 billion in 20 years. According to some pension experts, the PBGC is expected to deplete all of its cash by 2022. These estimates assume normal investment returns from the stock and bond markets. Therefore, if the market underperforms, the PBGC could exhaust its cash much earlier.

Figure 9-10. Net Position of PBGC's Single-Employer Program

Billions

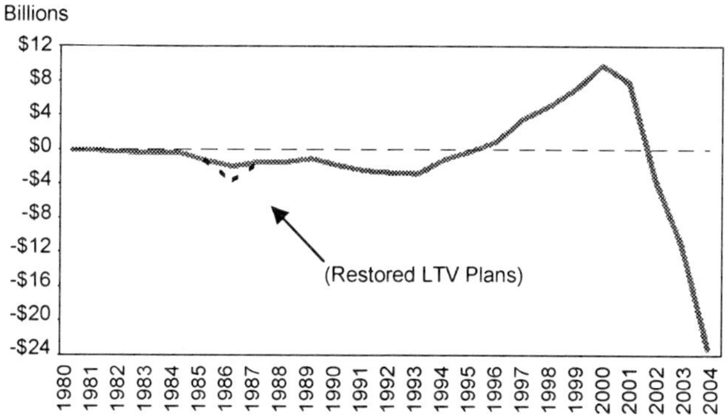

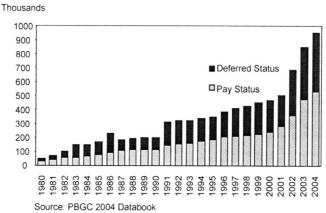

Source: PBGC's Annual Reports (1980-2004). Reference Table S-1 of the PBGC Pension Insurance Data Book 2004.

PBGC's Net Position is the difference (with some adjustments) between the insurance program's total assets and total liabilities. The originally reported $3.8 billion deficit in 1986 decreased after a Supreme Court ruling restored pension plans and returned their pension obligations of $1.8 billion to LTV Corporation.

Figure 9-11. Participants and Beneficiaries Receiving PBGC Payments
(Single-Employer Program)

Thousands

Source: PBGC 2004 Databook

Based upon my forecasts for the economy and stock market, the insolvency of the PBGC is going to get much worse over the next several years. Most likely, the PBGC will run out of cash prior to the 2022 period unless Washington raises fees even more. And this is going to encourage even more companies to shift from defined benefit to 401(k) plans. Regardless of the final solutions and outcome, you can bet it's going to hurt consumer spending. And we all know what happens when the consumer is weak—the stock market does poorly.

It Gets Worse

Pension assumptions may suffer from the same misconceptions about market returns that the majority of investors do; namely that it's reasonable to expect an 8 percent average annual return with a 60-40 mix of stocks and bonds. Such returns are only reliable if the

186

investment horizon is say 80 years because this period accounts for a sufficient number of bear market periods. But over a 10 or 20-year period during a secular bear market, the annual returns can vary anywhere from 1 to 3 percent for stocks and about 5 percent for bonds, both unadjusted for inflation.

And finally, the 401(k)-type retiree plans represent a major problem for the markets. Because these individuals are able to receive a lump sum distribution by age $59_{1/2}$, many Americans might opt for this if they need money. However at the very least, over the next several years, many retirees will most likely pull the maximum amount from their plans on an annual basis, causing a more gradual exit from the stock market. And this will add to the other forces that will work to keep pensions underfunded.

Figure 9-12. Total PBGC Benefit Payments Single-Employer Program

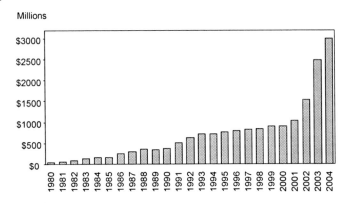

Sources: PBGC Participation System (PRISM), fisal year calculations, PBGC Management Reports. Reference Table S-20 of the PBGC Pension Insurance Data Book 2004. Note: Payment figures include periodic payments and lump sum payments in each year.

Figure 9-13. Concentration of PBGC Claims, Single-Employer Program

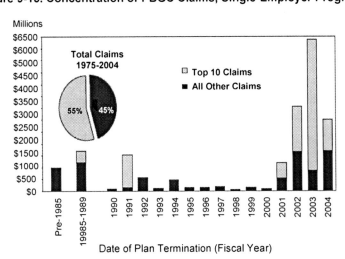

Sources: PBGC Fiscal Year Closing File (9/30/2004) and PBGC Case Administration System. Reference Table S-4 of the PBGC Pension Insurance Data Book 2004. Note: Claims are termination liabilities minus plan assets. They do not include recoveries.

Figure 9-14. PBGC Claims by Industry Single-Employer Program (1975-2004)

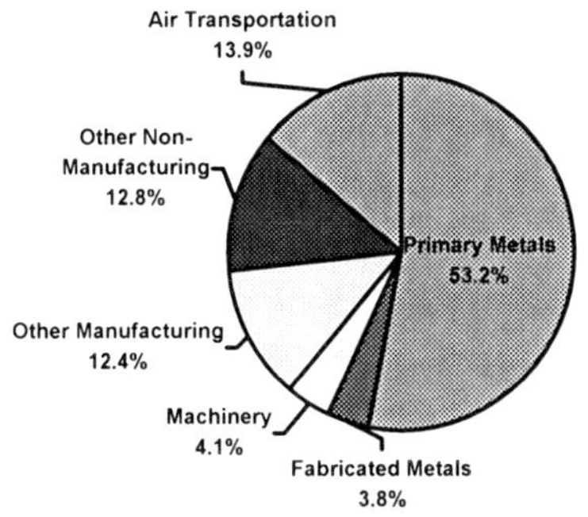

Sources: PBGC Fiscal Year Closing File (9/30/2004) and PBGC Case Administration System.
Reference Table S-19 of the PBGC Pension Insurance Data Book 2004.

Conclusions

The stock market is the nation's depot for risk capital, serving as the primary fuel for business investment and economic growth. And when compared to other nations since inception, the U.S. stock market has provided best investment returns in the world. Not only are foreign nations invested in the market, but also $11 trillion of retirement assets. However, this market is in a transition period that is likely to last for several more years despite any catastrophic devastation.

Already, America's pension system is facing huge challenges that will not be easily solved. Studies have shown that the average worker aged 60 to 65 has only about three times his current salary in retirement funds. In order to achieve the recommended 10 to 12 times annual salary by retirement, workers need to save anywhere from 15 to 18 percent of their annual salary. But as we have seen, this is rarely done due to the trend of diminishing net employee compensation. Therefore, as more Americans enter retirement, the question of Social Security will become an even greater concern.

The affects of declining defined benefit plan growth is serving as another force to diminish total employee compensation, thereby adding to the long-standing trend of declining living standards in America. And free trade promises to make this trend a permanent fixture of American society if significant changes in debt management, healthcare, Social Security and the pension system are not made.

As boomers enter retirement, many will be forced back into work, mainly in low-paying jobs. This will not only serve to destroy the morale of the largest group of Americans, but it will also have a chilling effect on working generations, who will begin to wonder if their "Golden Years" will be a filled with a period of living concessions.

The government is ultimately to blame for millions of Americans expected to face a retirement with inadequate funds. Washington permitted the corporate raid on employee benefits, and Washington alone has allowed America to enter into free trade arrangements that force companies to outsource in order to remain competitive. Washington tells us that Social Security was never meant to serve as the primary source of retirement income. However, it has been these same politicians who have permitted corporations to eliminate pension plans in favor of 401(k)s, which were never intended to serve as the primary source of retirement income.

As it stands today, we are witnessing the gradual disappearance of America's most stable and secure retirement compensation programs—Social Security and defined benefit pension plans, as Washington and corporate America act as partners while shifting the responsibility of a secure retirement to each American. And if you have a 401(k), you're basically on your own, with no guarantees of retirement benefits. You and your 401(k) will have to face the stock and bond markets, along with the professional traders on Wall Street. And as we know, the stock market is a zero-sum game, whereby each side of the trade has only one winner and one loser.

10

THE REAL ESTATE BUBBLE

The Big Recovery Myth

The big myth being told by Washington, Wall Street and the media is that the recession of the post-Internet bubble ended in November 2001 and the economy has since gained "significant ground." However, the fact is that the economy actually got worse since 2002. That's right, worse. And when these economic trends finally surfaced, they were reflected by the stock market lows established in October of 2003.

Since 2003, the economy has staged a *phantom recovery* fueled primarily by massive consumer debt, heightened by record low interest rates and out of control federal spending, all of which have led to record national and consumer debt and trade imbalances. Since 2002, companies have conserved cash, moved jobs and facilities overseas, bought down debt, and issued share repurchase plans as a way to increase earnings per share. And this has been enough to please Wall Street.

As a part of its strategy to enhance consumer confidence, Washington has hidden the true state of the economy using various means, hoping to buy more time until conditions improve. To stimulate spending, the Federal Reserve loosened credit to unthinkable levels and consumers responded. First, Greenspan ordered the U.S. Treasury to run its printing presses in overdrive, sinking short-term interest rates 15 times consecutively to a 43-year low with long-term rates not far behind.

Next, the mortgage industry all but eliminated responsible criteria for mortgage applications, allowing millions of financially unfit Americans to take out loans on overpriced homes. This historic release of money spurred what will be documented in history books as the largest real estate bubble in the past 80 years, if not ever. Consequently, low rates and relaxed credit standards have allowed an unprecedented number of mortgages, most notably in the booming sub-prime market, resulting in record home ownership rates.

Washington continues the charade of proclaiming a strong economic recovery using deceptive tricks to distort the gross domestic product (GDP), unemployment numbers, consumer price index (CPI), producer price index (PPI) and many other statistics (a detailed analysis of this deception will be presented in the next chapter). These critical economic indicators have been misrepresented in order to make consumers "feel good" about the economy so they'll continue to spend more money than they have.

Washington's "dog and pony" tactics have proven to be very effective, as most consumers think it is only they who are struggling to make ends meet amidst this "robust" economy. However, Americans now have the lowest household savings rate since the Great Depression. Short-term interest rates are now much higher than in 2003, as is total consumer debt, while net job and real wage growth continue to linger. And there is no more credit to spend. Without the aid of David Copperfield, Washington will no longer be able to continue its illusion, and the consumer will soon fall flat on its face.

Because virtually every type of payment benefit from Social Security, pensions and Medicare are tied to the CPI, Washington has had further incentives to under-report inflation data. These fuzzy calculations have been especially prominent over the past 15 years. The consequences of this deception are now pushing many Americans towards financial suicide through excessive credit card spending and extraction of home equity during a swollen real estate bubble.

Consequently, I find the timing of the recently passed bankruptcy reform bill quite unfortunate for consumers, while very favorable to the consumer finance industry. Now that short-term rates are on the rise, credit card companies are putting "the squeeze" on consumers with higher interest rates, knowing that it will be much more difficult to file for bankruptcy.

The Real Estate Investment Myth

A few decades ago, the real estate and mortgage industries devised a marketing campaign to increase business. They began preaching a myth to Americans that home ownership is always a great investment with no risk, because "home prices always go up." As a matter of fact, these industries have even made claims that real estate is a better investment than the stock market and has led to more millionaires. These statements are simply not true as historical data indicates.

As a result of this propaganda, most Americans have the misconception that they can buy a home and it will always go up in price. But this is not necessarily true, especially when buying during the peak of a real estate bubble. Even without the effects of a bubble, in many cases the annual expenses associated with home ownership wipe out most of the gains in appreciation, yielding relatively modest annualized returns.

For the average American, the fact is that residential real estate typically provides about the same rate of return over a twenty- to thirty-year period as a money market mutual fund after you deduct the total costs of property ownership. However, unlike a money market fund, owners of real estate have significant liquidity risk and other risks specific to this asset class.

Of course, there are several variables that can deviate from these results such as obtaining a low-interest rate-fixed mortgage, buying a home in an area that becomes rejuvenated with extensive development, and so forth. But these are not typical conditions and therefore cannot be relied upon with much certainty. Regardless, widespread speculation continues to fuel perhaps the biggest real estate bubble ever seen in America.

Costs of Home Ownership

Although a mortgage interest tax deduction provides financial benefit to home owners, they rarely consider property taxes, insurance, PMI, HOA dues, and maintenance expenses when factoring in their decision to buy a home. Yet, no other asset appreciates in value like real estate; right? *But this is an illusion created by the time-value-of-money effect on mortgages; not due to a real appreciation.* Think for a moment; how is it that all other tangible, non-collectible assets depreciate in value, yet real estate appreciates? As we all know, depreciation of real estate is logical, since over time "wear and tear" diminishes its inherent value and thus buyer appeal. In fact, *what appreciates is not the actual physical property, but the cost effects of assuming a mortgage with compounding interest.*

The Cost of a Mortgage

For example, if your mortgage rate is 6.0 percent, your home has to provide an annualized rate of return of around 6.5 percent (to account for the annual percentage rate, or the actual rate you pay due to fees such as closing costs) just to keep up with the cost you are paying for this loan. Now, because you get a mortgage interest tax deduction, the savings effect would amount to about 2.0 to 2.5 percentage points (depending on your tax bracket). Therefore, factoring in the expenses paid for the loan, the home would have to appreciate by at least 4.0 percent annually, or else you would lose money each year.

Property Taxes

As well, if we assume the average property tax is around 2 percent (a valid assumption, unless you live in AL, KY, MS, AR, TN, OK or a few other southern states with low rates, or in some parts of CA, which assesses property taxes based on the original purchase price), you will also have to add the expense of 2 percent of the annual appraised value of the home in property taxes, which can end up averaging 3 to 4 percent of the original purchase price over the life of the loan (depending on the rate of appreciation).

Let me explain. Most property taxes are based on the annual appraisal value which is determined by the city government. Of course these appraisals are highly inflated in order to extort higher tax dollars from unsuspecting home owners. Regardless, what appears to be a 2 percent annual property tax ends up averaging out to 3.5 percent relative to the original purchase price if your home doubles in value by 15 years (a reasonable assumption). So, in order to factor in these annual tax expenses, you have to keep track of the annual assessed value of your home, as appraised by the city government. As your home appreciates, annual property tax expenses will grow. Therefore, your home would have to appreciate annually by an average of 7.5 percent (the tax-adjusted 4 percent mortgage expense plus 3.5 percent average property tax) over a 15-year period just to break even. These annual tax costs essentially suck equity out of your home.

Other Expenses

Now if we assume an annual 0.50 percent cost for home owner's insurance, as the home value increases so will the amount needed to maintain full insurance coverage. This amount will average around 1.0 percent of the annual cost relative to the original purchase price when the home value doubles.

Maintenance costs could be anything from a new roof, carpet, AC unit, kitchen appliances, etc., and can be estimated at a conservative 0.5 percent per annum, based upon the original purchase price. Consider that in most cases, home owners will need to spend anywhere from $4000 to $20,000 to make a home older than 5 years competitive on the new homes market. Of course, this would be the most variable of all expenses listed thus far. Regardless, we can estimate the average annual costs for home ownership over a 15-year period to be 9.0 percent or about three times the original sales price. Alternatively, you can assume an 8.5 percent figure and subtract the total dollar amount spent for maintenance from the expected sales price.

Adjustments

In order to determine a real rate of return on your real estate "investment" you must factor in the effects of inflation, which averages around 2.5 percent annually. When comparing the investment attributes of real estate with a safe investment such as a money market account, the effects of inflation would cancel. Therefore, any amount beyond this 9.0 percent annualized return will be profit (after you deduct the real estate sales fees). *The real benefit is the tax treatment of mortgage interest and exemption from capital gains tax after the sale.* Because the sales proceeds are tax-free (as long as IRS criteria are met), the 9.0 percent breakeven figure is reduced to about 7.0 percent. (1)

Therefore, generally speaking, if your home does not yield at least a 9.0 percent average annual appreciation through year 15, your investment yield will be similar to a money market mutual fund (after-tax) but with much greater risk and much less liquidity. Achieving a 9.0 percent annual appreciation under non-bubble conditions is not easy, but if accomplished it would lead to over three times the original purchase price. Good luck.

Shorter periods of home ownership will tend to reduce some of these costs, such as maintenance, insurance and property taxes. As well, the mortgage interest tax deduction provides more savings in the early years of a mortgage since most of the mortgage payment is due to interest. In the later years, as the mortgage deduction declines, the property tax deduction will increase due to home appreciation. The point is that home ownership entails many other costs that buyers rarely consider, and by no means represents a "slam-dunk" investment as the real estate industry would have you believe.

(1)   Estimates are based on a home originally valued at $200,000 to $500,000, with several assumptions, as stated, regarding tax brackets, appreciation, and other expenses. The mortgage interest savings will depend on the holding period and the financing terms, since interest payments are determined by the financing. The costs of PMI and HOA dues were not factored in, which can amount to large sums of money over an extended period, especially when adjusted for inflation. Real estate transaction costs (usually 6 percent of the sales price) were also not factored in. Savings due to the property tax deduction were not factored in. For simplicity, consider these opposing items a wash. In the best of scenarios, assuming there is no PMI or HOA fees, assuming a 2 percent property tax, and assuming you are in a high tax bracket, the annual savings due to the property tax deduction would still cause this tax expense to be at least 2.5 percent, annualized over 15 years. Thus, the breakeven rate would be reduced by one point to 6.0 percent—the average annual appreciation required to breakeven on a home purchase.

Exceptions Are Not the Rule

There are exceptions to my argument. In certain areas of California, the relatively low and fixed property tax treatment favors those who hold a home over a long period. Therefore, they benefit from the appreciation in property values while being taxed only on the original purchase price. As well, some get lucky and buy a home in an area that experiences a surge in development.

Investors should understand that, *over a long period real estate has shown an appreciation rate in line with the average annual inflation rate which is around 2.5 percent.* Only during bubble periods does this trend deviate upward, causing many to think that real estate is a great investment. However, after the bubble corrects, home prices are suppressed for long periods or by excessive amounts for shorter periods. And some home owners may be forced to move during a collapse in home values, due to a job change, divorce, unexpected death or other event, adding further insult to injury.

Similar to the stock market, investment returns in real estate generally increase as the holding period increases, but only if one assumes a minimal holding period such as 5 years (under normal conditions) and 10 years (under bubble conditions). Such a period is required to account for price volatility. However, there are no annual fees when you hold stocks. Therefore, expenses do not accumulate, unlike with real estate. The effect of these annual expenses (insurance and property taxes) increases the total cost basis. But unlike the situation with stocks, there is no tax benefit from the sales transaction (unless it is an investment property) since proceeds are free from capital gains taxation. However, home owners do receive annual tax deductions for mortgage and property taxes, as mentioned.

Rather than an investment, in most cases, home ownership provides an expensive method to obtain security of shelter, and over long holding period, a rate of return comparable to a money market mutual fund. But with property taxes so high and eminent domain so common, one should question whether they really own their property.

Flipping and Rentals Do Better

While real estate can provide generous investment returns, they generally occur over short holding periods; specifically for property "flippers" since the mortgage interest deduction is at its maximum, while property tax fees are at their minimum. Yet, short-term strategies such as flipping can be extremely risky. Owning rental units is a safer way to invest in real estate. But it usually takes many years before any profits are registered. If one wants to invest in real estate using a short-term strategy, they must allow for a cushion to absorb downward pricing pressures that occur in real estate, much the same as in the stock market.

The Housing Bubble

Today, virtually everyone believes that home ownership will provide the solution to their financial woes if they can hold on. And even if they fail to profit within a few years, they have no doubt that a longer holding period will generate handsome returns. Obviously, they have not thought about home ownership expenses, the weak economy, job insecurity, and trending demographics.

Unfortunately, many Americans have bought homes during the last stage of the current real estate bubble, which began over a decade ago. And when this bubble deflates, many of these recent buyers will get caught holding properties they won't be able to sell for a long time. Even worse, many won't be able to continue their mortgage payments due to millions of variable-interest rate loans that have repriced upwards.

Over the next two decades, most of the estimated 76 million baby boomers will retire and many will scale down to condos or retirement communities. This will create a buildup of existing home inventories, causing prices to decline independent of any other factors. Most likely, the deflation of this bubble will take many years and occur at different time periods around the nation.

In many parts of America, home prices have risen as high as 150 percent in just a few years. Amongst cities with the biggest housing bubbles are Phoenix, Las Vegas, Portland, Los Angeles, Boston, San Diego, San Francisco, Miami, and Washington D.C. As well, much of California and Florida have experienced a huge appreciation in home prices. While Boston and San Diego represent the highest median home prices in America, these trends have been in place for many years due to their strong local economies, boosted in large part by the growth of their biotechnology industries. However other cities are not so fortunate, and the rise in home prices has caused many to relocate to one of the few regions that have not been hit by this bubble.

Where is the Middle-Class Living?

Despite its strong economy, unless you are in the top 10 percent of income earners in America, you won't be able to afford the average home in San Diego unless you use alternative financing. And that is precisely what many have done, placing them in danger of foreclosure. But San Diego is not an isolated case, as millions of Americans have been forced to use interest rate-sensitive financing as their only way to afford home ownership.

As of December 8, 2005, Los Angeles was the least affordable American city to live in when comparing its median home price with median income. With an average home price of $495,000 and a median income of $54,500, (2005 data) calculating this ratio yields a 9.09 value for the "City of Angels." The next highest was Honolulu at 6.77, Boston at 4.97, and Washington D.C. at 4.72.

These figures illustrate the harsh effects of a housing bubble that's caused the average American to be priced out of the market. Therefore, *many have borrowed using loans that are not compatible with their financial means, in part because they do not understand the risks.* These unconventional loans allow buyers to purchase a home for a lower monthly mortgage payment. However, these loans are not suitable for long-term home purchases and introduce many layers of risk as we shall see.

Yet, remarkably, home ownership rates are the highest in U.S. history, at 70 percent. If this is not a warning sign of what's ahead, I don't know what is. Is the economy so much better now than in the 1990s? You might recall that household ownership in equities approached the highest point ever during the peak of the stock market bubble. And of course we all know what happened shortly thereafter.

Tourists Spots Are in Big Trouble

What about Las Vegas? How can property values remain high there? After all, it has no major industries other than gaming. Las Vegas is basically fueled by a service industry with low- to mid-paying jobs stemming from its huge tourism and gaming business. The same can be said of Florida, with its huge tourism and service economy catering to retirees and seasonal tourists. As a caveat, recent increases in hurricane incidence in the "Sunshine State" over the past few years, as well as expectations for more over the next several years could be enough to cause an exodus from beachfront properties, adding to the effects of the real estate bubble deflation.

Even California Will Get Hit

Relatively low property taxes have always been at least partly responsible for the high appreciation of property values in California. Fueled by the nation's largest high-tech output and the world's fifth largest GDP, it's easy to appreciate why California is a state where successful techies have money to burn. But these individuals are only a tiny minority. In reality, the majority of residents are struggling with living expenses. Consequently, with major state deficit problems, I have little doubt that more taxes and fees are on the way.

Not everyone in California is a biotech or Internet millionaire. Every region needs workers at all levels to provide the right balance of labor and consumer demand required to sustain the health of its economic engine. However, some parts of California are experiencing a shortage of lower income service workers due to the state's high living expenses.

This has been the situation in San Jose for well over a decade, where it's difficult to find restaurant workers due to the high cost of housing. Perhaps that's why San Jose has the highest average number of inhabitants per room at nearly 4. Of course California has its own minimum wage, which is higher than the federal rate, and in the Bay Area it is nearly $9 per hour. But still this is no where near enough for its working-class to match the high costs of living in the Bay Area.

> **Warren Buffett**
>
> *"I recently sold a house in Laguna for $3.5 million. It was on about 2000 square feet of land, maybe a twentieth of an acre, and the house might cost about $500,000, if you wanted to replace it. So the land sold for something like $60 million an acre"*

Can You See the Bubble?

Over the past decade, the price of the average home in America has increased by over 62 percent (from 1995 to 2004) unadjusted for inflation. At the time of publication of this book, *the average home price in America since 1995 has increased by over 75 percent (unadjusted for inflation).* Meanwhile, real income growth has declined due to decreased employer benefits, while costs for basic necessities such as energy and healthcare continue to increase at alarming rates. *The gimmick for the real estate and mortgage industries was to convince Americans that record low rates had created the best home-buying opportunity in over 40 years, regardless of swelling home prices; and it worked.* However, most home buyers have not thought about the consequences of buying a home that is on average 35 to 40 percent overvalued.

According to a 2004 report by the Economic Policy Institute, *the median household income for all American households had declined by $1669 (3.6 percent) since 2000.* Yet, many Americans feel wealthier due to the rise in their home values on paper. This "wealth effect" has been the result of a transfer of assets from the stock market bubble into the housing market, sparked by a partial, yet devastating stock market correction and Greenspan's record rate-lowering campaign enacted to delay the inevitable financial apocalypse.

For nearly two decades, the loose credit policies of Greenspan encouraged Americans to spend beyond their means, while piling up massive debt. And that is part of the reason why Americans do not realize their standard of living has been in decline for three decades. When the real estate bubble finally corrects, there will be no other way to extend the wealth effect because the stock market will not recover for several years. And this period might very well represent the beginning stages of America's economic correction.

The main stimulus for the housing bubble has been extremely low interest rates, along with the proliferation of alternative financing products such as interest-only and adjustable-rate mortgages (ARMs). Whether you live in one of the real estate hotspots or not, the fact is that most *Americans have chosen to use their homes as ATM machines, extracting cash based upon property values that are in most cases ridiculously overvalued.* And rather than use this money for home improvements, the vast majority of home equity dollars and cash-back financings have been applied towards paying off credit card debt, for vacations and auto purchases. Even when Americans have paid down their credit cards, they have found it irresistible to ignore the generous offers of "0% financing for one year." Soon after, their credit card debt reappeared, similar to a junkie relapsing after a drug rehab treatment program.

In large part, Washington is to blame for this irresponsible behavior, by allowing finance companies to flood the market with tempting credit offers and low barriers for under-qualified home buyers. Washington knows well what it did. It wanted these home equity loans and sub-prime mortgages to propagate as a way to stimulate consumer spending. But all it means is that a large correction of the real estate bubble is a more certain outcome.

Although most Americans view their home as an investment, approximately 25 percent of home purchases over the past 2 years were made by real estate investors. At the best of situations, when the bubble does correct, many will be stuck holding properties that they will have to sell for much lower than they bought.

But don't expect this shakeout to occur overnight. Most likely, it will take several years for the full effects of this deflation to be seen. And during the decline, many will rush in thinking they are getting bargains, when in fact they will end up losing as well.

According to the Center for Housing Policy, *from 2000 to 2004 the number of working families paying more than 50 percent of their income for housing soared by 76 percent.* And because home prices have been rising much faster than the average median income, this has actually caused many Americans to purchase homes they can't afford for the fear (or greed) that home prices will go even higher. *Since 1980, household debt has increased by 623 percent (figure 6-13) while personal savings has declined by 75 percent* (figure 9-1). As a result, interest-only and option ARM mortgages have become very popular for many Americans who could not normally afford a home during this bubble.

Figure 10-1. New and Existing Home Sales (thousands)

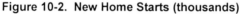

Sources: U.S. Census Bureau, National Association of Realtors

Figure 10-2. New Home Starts (thousands)

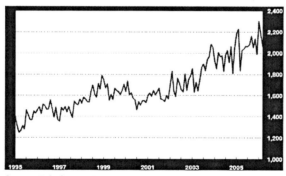

Source: U.S. Census Bureau

Figure 10-3. Housing Prices (Year-over-year percentage change)

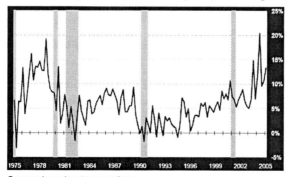

Grey regions denote recessions
Source: Office of Federal Housing Oversight, U.S. Census Bureau

Figure 10-4. One-Year Change in House Prices (First Quarter 2005 to First Quarter 2006)

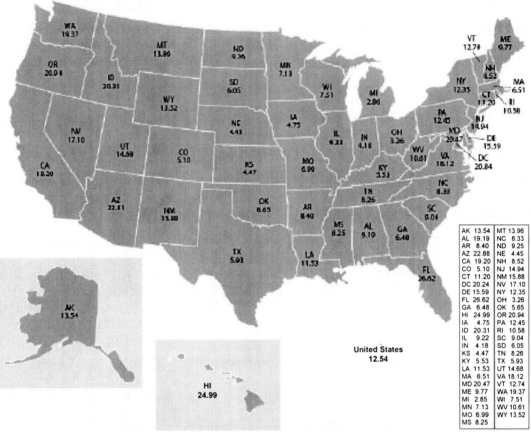

AK	13.54	MT	13.96
AL	19.19	NC	8.33
AR	8.40	ND	9.25
AZ	22.88	NE	4.45
CA	19.20	NH	8.52
CO	5.10	NJ	14.94
CT	11.20	NM	15.88
DC	20.24	NV	17.10
DE	15.59	NY	12.35
FL	26.62	OH	3.26
GA	6.48	OK	5.65
HI	24.99	OR	20.94
IA	4.75	PA	12.45
ID	20.31	RI	10.58
IL	9.22	SC	9.04
IN	4.18	SD	6.05
KS	4.47	TN	8.26
KY	5.53	TX	5.93
LA	11.53	UT	14.68
MA	6.51	VA	18.12
MD	20.47	VT	12.74
ME	9.77	WA	19.37
MI	2.85	WI	7.51
MN	7.13	WV	10.61
MO	6.99	WY	13.52
MS	8.25		

United States
12.54

Source: Office of Federal Housing Enterprise Oversight, June 1, 2006

Figure 10-5. Increase in Home Prices 1995-2004

	Nominal	Real*
U.S.	62.6%	33.4%
Northeast	94.3%	59.4%
Mid-Atlantic	65.1%	35.4%
East South Central	39.9%	14.7%
West South Central	41.5%	16.1%
South Atlantic	60.7%	31.8%
East North Central	50.5%	23.5%
West North Central	60.8%	31.9%
Mountain States	87.0%	53.4%
Pacific	86.9%	53.3%

*Real indicates adjustments for inflation.
Source: Office of Federal Housing Enterprise Oversight 2004

Further Evidence of a Bubble

One would assume a housing bubble is present if buyers were purchasing homes primarily for investment purposes rather than for housing needs. Accordingly, if we examine the cost of home prices versus renting, there should be a similar rise in both if consumers have been driven by housing needs. However, if the cost of renting falls well below that of home price increases, this would indicate that consumers are willing to absorb higher home prices hoping ownership will lead to investment gains.

Figure 10-6 shows the rent index from the CPI and the OFHEO Home Price Index from the first quarter of 1975 to the first quarter of 2002 (data is reported for each consecutive quarter and the indexes are deflated by the CPI-non-shelter index). As you can see, shortly after 1995 home prices began an upward divergence relative to rental units. As it stands today, monthly rental prices have been suppressed significantly relative to total housing demand. However, the dynamics of supply-demand have not trickled down to rental units since rental occupancy has not picked up and has failed to drive prices higher.

One of the primary reasons for the depression in the rental market has been the relative ease of mortgage financing. Why rent when you can buy for smaller monthly payments? Of course these payments do not include total costs such as insurance and property taxes. Regardless, monthly payments will balloon as interest rates increase for variable-interest and interest-only loans. Consequently, *as the real estate bubble continues to deflate, we should see rental unit pricing pick up strongly.*

Prior to 1995, since the end of World War II home prices have moved in line with inflation. However, as figure 10-7 illustrates, home prices began to diverge from the inflation rate in 1995 and skyrocketed towards the end of the Internet bubble. Ever since the Internet bubble correction, we have seen a surge in mortgages (table 10-1). As of 2005, there was over $9 trillion in residential mortgages outstanding in America, which is close to the entire capitalization of the stock market ($13 trillion). As of mid-2006, the $10 trillion mark was passed. It is thought that *at least $3 trillion of this mortgage debt is due to overvaluation.*

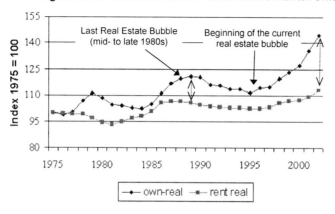

Figure 10-6. Costs of Home Prices versus Rental Units

Sources: BLS and OFHEO

As a contribution of its efforts to swell the housing bubble further, the Federal Reserve Bank of New York published a report attributing the recent appreciation in real estate to home improvements. However, their own data suggest this is not the case at all. As table 10-2 shows, the rise in home prices is in no way due to the rapid increases in spending for home improvements. As the data indicates, the percentage of spending for improvements has remained relatively constant. Obviously, this not only helps to confirm the presence of a real estate bubble, but it also has implications for home improvement companies once the bubble deflates.

Figure 10-7. Existing Median Home Prices and Consumer Prices (Jan. 1990 = 100)

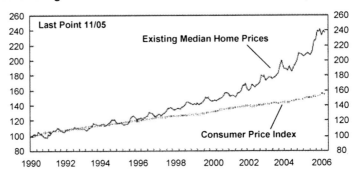

Source: National Association of Realtors and Bureau of Labor Statistics

Table 10-1. Total Mortgages Outstanding 2001-2005 ($ billions, end of year)

	2001	2002	2003	2004	2005
Total mortgages	$7,422.6	$8,244.4	$9,234.4	$10,472.4	$11,942.2
Home	5,571.3	6,244.2	7,024.1	8,016.2	9,149.0
Multifamily residential	447.8	486.7	557.3	612.2	674.5
Commercial	1,285.6	1,388.1	1,519.6	1,702.1	1,967.9
Farm	117.8	125.5	133.5	141.9	150.9

Source: Board of Governors of the Federal Reserve System, Insurance Information Institute.

Table 10.2. Value of Housing stock and Spending on Improvements (billions of 2002 dollars)

Year	Value of Residential Of Housing Stock	Spending on Improvements	Spending on Improvements as a Value of Housing Stock
1991	$6709.2	$62.6	0.9%
1992	7018.8	72.9	1.0%
1993	7248.3	77.6	1.1%
1994	7405.7	85.9	1.2%
1995	7870.3	79.0	1.0%
1996	8194.0	84.5	1.0%
1997	8652.2	90.7	1.0%
1998	9406.8	96.2	1.0%
1999	10250.1	95.8	0.9%
2000	11268.3	100.2	0.9%
2001	12362.3	106.0	0.9%
2002	13573.0	116.2	0.9%

Source: Federal Reserve Board and Bureau of Census

Effects of the Bubble

As of estimates during 2002 by the Center for Economic Policy Research (CEPR), the housing bubble correction would imply a drop in value from the average home of 11 to 22 percent, evaporating between $1.3 and $2.6 trillion of paper wealth. Since that time, there has been an 18 to 25 percent increase in median home prices, which would imply an even larger decline when the bubble deflates.

At its bottom, I would estimate a 30 to 35 percent correction for the average home. And in "hot spots" such as Las Vegas, selected areas of Northern and Southern California and Florida, home prices could plummet by 55 to 60 percent from peak values. Keep in mind that I expect the fallout in home prices to affect different regions at different time periods. This will be one of the confusing dynamics that will cause some to think the correction is over, when in fact it is likely to move in waves, from region to region as a repeating cycle.

Diminished Morale and Disposable Income

At this point, you might be thinking "a correction won't really destroy wealth for those who plan to live in the same home for many years," but you'd be wrong. Once you agree to a price for a home and take out the mortgage, you are stuck with that final sales price (the total cost of the mortgage over the period financed), unless of course you refinance at a lower rate. But even if you were able to refinance at a lower rate, it's not going to lower the price you paid for your home. It would only lower the interest portion of the loan. Most likely, there will be no more refinancing opportunities for current home owners for many years since we are just coming out of the lowest mortgage rates in decades. *In fact, I expect long-term rates to move higher over the next few years due to the weak dollar and mounting national debt.*

When home values plunge, Americans will be stuck with monthly payments that are inflated relative to the value of their home, causing further erosion of disposable income. Of course, these are just the consequences for those who have purchased homes using a fixed-rate mortgage. For those who have used interest-only or adjustable-rate mortgages, the effects of a correction in the housing bubble will be much more pronounced.

The "Poor Effect"

Considerable research has shown that Americans view their homes as a significant portion of their future wealth. Therefore, when home prices increase rapidly, they save less. Instead, they consume excessively because they feel richer than before. A similar situation occurs during stock bull markets, as previously discussed. But can not the opposite be true as well?

The average ratio of homeowners' equity-to-value as of early 2002 was 55.2 percent, which is near its low for the post-war period (figure 10-8). With a large drop in house prices expected from the bubble deflation, this ratio would fall much lower (table 10-3). Across the nation, even if we assume a very conservative 20 percent correction, there will be several major regions that would experience declines of 35 to 40 percent. The consequences of these declines will wipe out the wealth effect, as many will see the equity in their homes evaporate into thin air. This will not only halt consumer spending, but it will also force millions of foreclosures across America, causing housing inventories to rise, which could cause a further collapse in home prices. The aftermath of the record foreclosures will send shockwaves to the stock and bond markets.

Figure 10-8. Ratio of Homeowner's Equity to Market Value

Period	Equity/Market Value
1950-59	77.1%
1960-69	66.7%
1970-79	67.5%
1980-89	67.7%
1990-99	56.8%
2001-2002	55.2%

The ratio of household debt to disposable income reached a record 108.3 percent at the end of 2003, mainly due to rising mortgage debt. In addition, the ratio of consumer debt (mainly credit card and car loans) to disposable income was at near record levels. The cost of servicing this debt will increase due to the continued trend of debt spending, as well as increasing interest rates. This will cause a record number of foreclosures, as over 10 million are possible within the next 6 to 8 years.

Will the deflation of the housing bubble cause Americans to start saving again? Perhaps Americans will once again recognize the importance of saving rather than amassing debt. But many won't be in a position to save. They'll be overburdened with interest payments on debt and higher monthly payments for a good portion of the 10 million homes that have been financed using ARMs.

Table 10-3. Declines in Housing Values have Significant Effects on Home Equity
(Changes in Home Equity Resulting from Declining Housing Values for Households Aged 50-62, 2001)

Change in Housing Value	Produces a Multiplied Change In Housing Equity
-10%	-14%
-25%	-35%
-50%	-71%
-75%	-106%

Source: Soto, Mauricio "Just the Facts: On Retirement Issues" CRR Number 15. March 2005. Calculations from the author.

The Next Boom: Reverse Mortgages

Over the next decade, as America's boomers reach retirement age, the effects of the Internet bubble correction will be compounded with a deflation in the housing bubble. This could cause existing home inventories to rise, as many boomers downscale to smaller homes. Alternatively, as more boomers feel the credit squeeze amidst higher inflation, we could see a massive increase in reverse mortgages. This type of financial arrangement allows home owners 62 and older to sell their homes to a bank or mortgage company in exchange for monthly payments. It's a way to sell your home gradually and generate income, while continuing to live in it.

The Home Equity Conversion Mortgage (HECM) is a federally insured reverse mortgage product that accounts for over 90 percent of all reverse mortgages in the United States. Already, we see a rise in reverse mortgages, representing the harvesting of Americans' last tier of wealth (figure 10-9). This is going to be a great business to be in over the next two decades.

Figure 10-9. Reverse Mortgages (HECMs), Fiscal Year 2000-2004

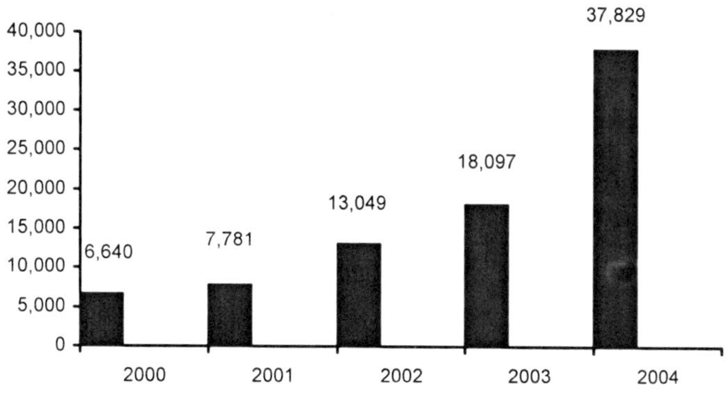

Source: National Reverse Mortgage Lenders Association.

Real Estate Cycles

The real estate market is similar to the stock market in that both oscillate through cycles of boom and bust. According to the FDIC, a real estate boom is considered to have occurred when prices rise by 30 percent or more, while a bust is a decline of 15 percent or more (over a 5-year period in inflation-adjusted prices). Using these definitions, since 1978 there have been 50 booms and only 21 busts.

America's last major real estate crisis occurred in 1988, but the current one is of much greater magnitude, comparable only to that in the 1920s. Back in 1988, much of the cause of the real estate bubble was due to international issues, such as Cold War spending, yet it only affected California for the most part. In contrast, the current real estate bubble has effected more regions of America than any in the past, having reached approximately

65 metropolitan regions throughout the United States. However, over 200 additional cities have seen above average appreciation in the 2005 to 2006 period alone.

While the boom in the 1920s is comparable to the current housing bubble, it was of much smaller scope. Unlike the devastating effects of the more localized real estate bubble of the '20s, today's housing boom has been fueled by record low mortgage rates and loose lending practices such as heavy use of interest-only loans, adjustable-rate mortgages (ARMs), and other creative financings. Therefore, it has affected a larger percentage of Americans throughout the nation and in all socioeconomic categories.

As with all bubbles, the current one can be thought of as a sequential stage of the longer-term dynamic oscillation of the economic cycle, and is therefore not an unordinary event. What are less ordinary are the broader economic effects of America's declining global competitiveness, which have resulted in diminishing living standards for three decades. This trend has been masked by misleading government reporting standards, exploitation of illegal aliens, two-income households, heavy use of credit, and a disproportionate share of wealth from the upper class.

Figure 10-10. Number of Areas affected by Previous Real Estate Booms (1978 to 2004)

Year	Number of Metro Areas		Year	Number of Metro Areas
1978	3		1992	1
1979	9		1993	0
1980	1		1994	3
1981	0		1995	4
1982	0		1996	3
1983	0		1997	0
1984	0		1998	0
1985	5		1999	1
1986	13		2000	9
1987	16		2001	14
1988	24		2002	22
1989	14		2003	32
1990	15		**2004**	**55**
1991	5		**2005**	**65**

Source: FDIC

While the deflation of this bubble will definitely impact the economy and stock market, it is difficult to say by how much or when. If it deflates independent of other economic woes, its affects will be minimal but still very large. If the deflation occurs in phases over a long period, it could coincide with or magnify other problems, such as rising fuel prices, terrorist attacks, peak oil, or any other broad-reaching event. Alone, this bubble could very well signal the beginning of a major economic crisis that could send the markets plummeting.

Who Stands to Gain?

Most real estate investors and home owners believe they will be the beneficiaries of the housing boom. However, the only definitive winners have been builders, mortgage brokers, appraisers, and local governments (due to higher property tax income). For those investors who have profited thus far, the game isn't over until you leave the table. And many will no doubt get caught holding properties they planned to flip or sell only after a few years when the bubble deflates. Regardless, even those investors who have profited are the small winners. The big winners are the Government-Sponsored Enterprises (GSEs), investment and mortgage bankers, and everyone else who creates or sells mortgage-backed securities (MBS).

When house prices go up, larger mortgages are needed. Therefore, the loans required are bigger. This results in more interest dollars over the life of each loan for banks, even though the house value may go down by 30 percent thereafter. Banks have been in stiff competition with each other, opening up the sub-prime market in order to lock in these huge-dollar interest payments while the bubble has not yet deflated. But they have only been able to provide this endless inventory of loans due to the liquidity created by GSEs and their repackaging of these mortgages onto the MBS market. Throughout this credit frenzy, someone has been assuming these risky loans, and you might be surprised to find out who it has been.

Mortgage Mania

According to the U.S. Department of Housing, the total monthly "home cost" should not exceed 28 percent of a household's gross income. The "home cost" consists of the mortgage, interest and principal payments, home insurance costs, property taxes, property mortgage insurance (PMI) and home-owners' association (HOA) dues. But due to skyrocketing home prices, most Americans don't make the income needed to meet these minimum criteria and have therefore opted for non-traditional mortgages, allowing millions to buy a home, many which will end in foreclosures.

But if so many Americans are in no financial position to purchase a home, why have they done so? The wealth effect has caused many to think of home ownership as an investment. And given such low mortgage rates, the real estate industry has delivered a sense of urgency for Americans to take advantage of these rates. But many fail to realize the almost invariable equilibrium that exists between mortgage rates and home prices.

There is almost always an inverse relationship between mortgage rates and home prices that serves to balance the supply-demand relationship between home buyers and sellers. In other words, when mortgage rates are high, home prices drop to counter the effects of the mortgage expense. In contrast, when mortgage rates are low, home prices capture this savings in financing costs and increase in value. Under normal circumstances, a balance in overall cost of the home (the home sales price and the mortgage cost) results in an annual appreciation right in line with inflation. *In other words, there is never really a "great" time to buy a home because the market balances the total price point by adjusting the home price versus the mortgage rates.*

However, several forces have caused an imbalance in this normally steady relationship which cannot be explained even if one were to assume the economy were healthy. As mentioned, the real estate and mortgage industries have convinced Americans that it is the best time to buy a home in the past 40 years due to low mortgage rates. They did such a great job of convincing them of this myth that supply could not keep up with demand. As well, many were already looking for another place to invest their money due to the stock market scandals that continue to this day.

It was this imbalance in home supply that led to the bubble-type acceleration in home prices early on. As prices continued to rise, many prospective home buyers were being priced out of the market. So the mortgage industry began offering a larger number of sub-prime and alternative mortgages by around 2002 in order to convince people they could afford a house or even a more expensive house, when in fact, these ARM and interest-only loans are financially irresponsible for most.

The large increase in short-term rates since 2004 has already created hardships for those who have used ARMs, causing many to cut back on necessities. It's safe to say that most home owners who financed with variable-rate loans have very little disposable income remaining to fuel consumer spending. If long-term rates can remain relatively low over the next 2 years, many home buyers who purchased ARMs with 3- or 5-year durations might be able to refinance with a reasonable fixed rate.

Figure 10-11. Mortgage Rates Have Bottomed and are on Their Way up

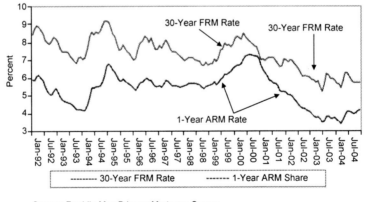

Source: Freddie Mac Primary Mortgage Survey

According to David Rosenberg at Merrill Lynch, approximately $2.5 trillion of household debt, or 21 percent of outstanding household debt will reprice upwards in 2006. Unless there is a surge in disposable personal income, the already record high debt-service ratio will move higher in 2006 and beyond. And I will state with confidence that disposable income will not surge for at least a few years. As a matter of fact, it will only continue to decrease since much of consumer debt is tied to short-term rates, employers continue to cut benefits, and healthcare costs are going nowhere but up. Already in the first half of 2006, new home sales have begun to cool off, forcing prices south. But it's still too soon to determine if a trend reversal has occurred.

One cannot know for certain how the correction in the real estate market will play out because it depends primarily upon how developers decide to handle it. If they are concerned they may scale back on new developments which will prevent an excess inventory buildup. However, if they ignore soft new home sales and the trend continues, the inventory buildup could extend to existing home values, magnifying the problem.

Figure 10-12. The Large Number of ARMs Makes Many Vulnerable to Rising Rates

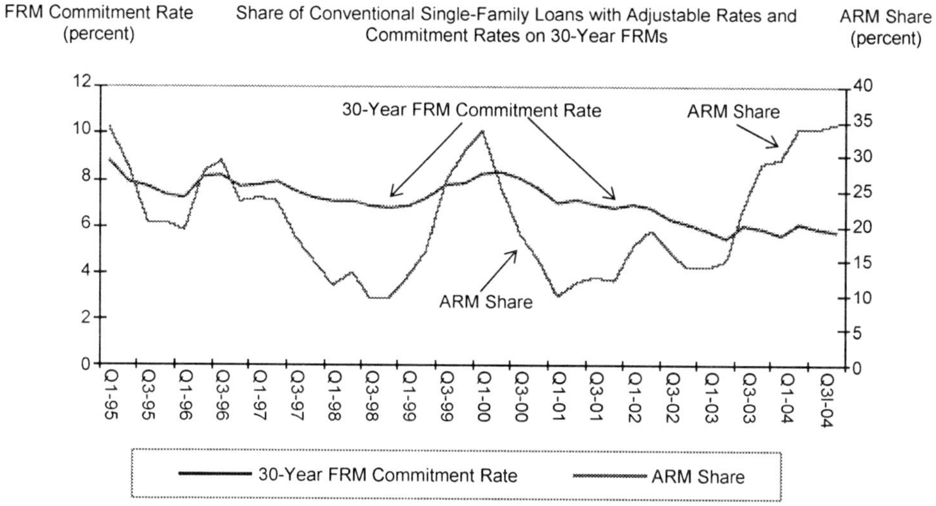

FRM Commitment Rate
(percent)
Share of Conventional Single-Family Loans with Adjustable Rates and
Commitment Rates on 30-Year FRMs
ARM Share
(percent)
30-Year FRM Commitment Rate
ARM Share
ARM Share
0
2
4
6
8
10
12
0
5
10
15
20
25
30
35
40
Q1-95
Q3-95
Q1-96
Q3-96
Q1-97
Q3-97
Q1-98
Q3-98
Q1-99
Q3-99
Q1-00
Q3-00
Q1-01
Q3-01
Q1-02
Q3-02
Q1-03
Q3-03
Q1-04
Q3I-04
30-Year FRM Commitment Rate
ARM Share

Source: Freddie Mac Primary Mortgage Market Survey

Finally, if a correction in home prices occurs in conjunction with higher long-term rates, real estate values will be depressed even further. I do not think we will see appreciable increases in 30-year mortgage rates until at least late 2007. But thereafter, I am expecting rates to reach their historical mean of around 8.5 percent within 2 to 3 years, and head north of that by 2012. If things continue to play out as I have proposed, I expect long-term rates to reach the low double-digits within the next 10 to fifteen years.

Figure 10-13. Mortgage Rates at a Historic Low (Average 30-year fixed rate mortgage)

20%
15%
10%
5%
0%
1972
1982
1992
2002

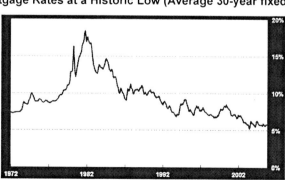

Source: Federal Home Loan Mortgage

Choices, Choices, Choices

The past few decades have witnessed an explosion of creative financing options available to home buyers. Just over three decades ago, an ARM was rare. But when interest rates soared during the '80s, the use of ARMs exploded. By 1984, ARMs peaked at 60 percent of loan originations. Most recently, ARMs have begun to take off again as a way to decrease the total home purchase price since short-term rates were so low (figure 10-14 and tables 10-4 and 10-5). *ARMs were less than 2 percent of all mortgages in 2001, and peaked at 34 percent in 2004 when short-term rates were at their lows. But just in the first three months of 2005 they reached 19 percent.*

Record low rates have also caused a boom in interest-only loans, which are the only way many can afford housing in places like San Diego, Los Angeles, Boston, San Francisco and dozens of other cities. But *the use of interest-only loans during record-low rates is like burning money since you are not paying off any principal. And when interest rates rise, these mortgages can actually create negative amortization.*

Finally, there are even riskier mortgages that even allow one to pay less than the current short-term interest rate. These are referred to as option-ARMs. Also referred to as cash-back financings, these mortgages create the illusion of home ownership while accelerating a negative amortization schedule. In other words, each month you are paying the mortgage, the total amount owed on your home actually increases.

Option-ARMs are truly the epitome of desperation utilized to take advantage of what many feel will be a great investment in real estate, while lacking sufficient income for a fixed-rate mortgage (FRM) or conventional ARM. And although most statistics do not count option-ARMs as home equity loans, they have a much worse affect since home equity is depleted, allowing the buyer to have more disposable income. Finally, these loans expose buyers to interest-rate risk since they're usually 3- to 5-year loans.

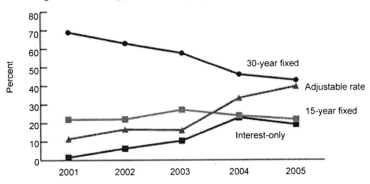

Figure 10-14. Types of Mortgages Issued, 2001-2005[1]

(1) Represents outstanding credit on all 1-4 unit residential mortgages. Percentages will add to more than 100 percent because some loans fit into multiple categories.

Source: LoanPerformance, a Unit of First American Corporation, Insurance Information Institute.

As rates continue to climb, many who expected to sell their homes in 3 to 5 years may be out of luck. Increased rates have already pushed monthly payments as high as 40 percent from just two years ago. And millions of Americans with interest-only and ARM loans have had to cut back on all expenses. Some have even had to cancel health insurance or face foreclosure. For others, high gas and electric bills have caused foreclosures. Many expect to cash out with big profits if they can just sit tight for a couple of more years. It's a shame so many will be disappointed.

ARMs

According to the California Association of Realtors Affordability Index, San Diego has an affordability index of 9 percent, meaning that only the top 9 percent of income earners in America can afford to purchase the median-priced home using a 20 percent down fixed rate mortgage. This explains the massive increase in interest-only and ARM mortgages in this area.

In 2004 alone, 80 percent of all new mortgages in San Diego were ARMs, 47 percent were interest only, and 27 percent required no down payment. Other regions of Southern California had similar statistics.

For over two decades now, Americans have embraced the "buy now, pay later" mentality. In part, this has led to America's "tremendous economic expansion" over this period. However, during the same period, income growth has not kept up with inflation, forcing many to borrow in excess. Payback is inevitable and it is going hurt most Americans really bad.

ARMs are linked to some type of economic index, typically short-term interest rates, so they adjust up and down along with this rate. Because borrowers assume the risk of rising rates, they are offered lower interest rates than FRMs. Given the extremely low rates provided by FRMs, one would expect them to dominate the mortgage markets. Despite this, in 2004 alone according to Freddie Mac's Primary Mortgage Market Survey, ARMs accounted for 34 percent of single-family mortgages.

ARMs are attractive because they allow buyers to make lower monthly payments so they can buy a home that they would otherwise not be able to afford. More important is the fact that ARMs are much easier to qualify for since the debt holder has a shorter duration of repayment, thereby lowering the risk to the lender.

Because of the way they work, *ARMs are usually popular when the yield curve is steep* (short-term rates are much lower than long-term rates). And although the yield curve remained steep for much of 2004, even when the curve flattened thereafter, the share of ARM loan originations remained fairly constant.

How can we explain this? Basically, due to the huge appreciation in homes over the past several years, many first-time home buyers could only afford to buy a home if they used ARMs and variants of ARMs. Interest-only ARM applications were high for the same reason. As a result of the increase in sub-prime lending, ARMs accounted for almost 20 percent of sub-prime loans in 2004.

As of mid-2006, nearly 25 percent of American home owners had an adjustable-rate mortgage (ARM) of some kind. It's no wonder why home ownership hit a record 70 percent. But what will that number will be once the bubble deflates? Misperceptions of America's economic status have led most home buyers to engage in these risky behaviors. As well, most consumers don't even understand the concept of compounding interest. Therefore, it's safe to assume that most home owners with ARMs and other sub-prime loans do not fully understand how they work, and thus have no idea how risky they are.

Table 10-4: Interest-Only Loans	
Metro Area Loans	Interest-Only (as a share of total, 2004)
San Diego	47.6%
Atlanta	45.5%
San Francisco	45.3%
Denver	43.4%
Oakland	43.1%
San Jose	41.1%
Phoenix-Mesa	38.8%
Seattle-Bellevue-Everett	37.2%
Orange County, CA	37.0%
Ventura, CA	35.3%
Sacramento	34.9%
Las Vegas	33.7%
Stockton, CA	32.0%
Washington, DC	31.4%
Charlotte, NC	29.1%
W. Palm Beach-Boca Raton	28.0%
Portland, OR	27.8%
Los Angeles	26.7%
Salt Lake City	25.6%
Nation-wide	**22.9%**

The most disturbing trend in mortgage data is that *the majority of the 10 million ARMs issued have occurred towards the end stages of the housing boom, and after short-term interest rates were already on the rise (i.e. between 2004 and 2005).* Americans have become greedy and the credit economy has trained them to always overextend themselves and make up the difference with credit. Subsequently, excessive use of ARMs and interest-only loans has also been a reflection of consumer greed and financial irresponsibility that has reached dangerous levels in America.

According to First American Real Estate Solutions, of the *7.7 million Americans who took out an ARM from 2004 to 2005*, up to 1 million could lose their home through foreclosure over the next 5 years due to rising mortgage payments. However, I feel that these estimates are way too conservative. *I expect anywhere between 25 to 30 percent of these mortgages (or around 2 million) to face foreclosure during the next six years.* And that does not include the other types of non-FRM mortgages, nor does it include foreclosures from the sub-prime market, or the average foreclosures expected even without a real estate bubble, *all of which could result in over 10 to 12 million foreclosures over the next 8 to 10 years.* Of course, the ultimate outcome will depend on how Bernanke handles inflation. The higher rates go over the next 3 to 4 years, the more foreclosures we will see.

But there is a strong force acting to keep rates high and push them even higher—the need to create an incentive for foreign investors to buy more U.S. treasuries to support Bush's deficit spending. And this upward force on rates is further accentuated by the weakness of the dollar (diminished value on the foreign currency exchange). Therefore, Bernanke has a difficult decision to make.

Even for those who are able to hold on, many will owe more than their home is worth for several years. Imagine making payments on a mortgage you took out for

$600,000 and having your home worth only $450,000 ten years later. That scenario is very possible and it doesn't exactly do much to help consumer sentiment or disposable income. If you don't think this scenario is possible, ask the Japanese about it.

Table 10-5. Family Home Mortgage Originations, 1995-2004 ($billions)

Year	Total Volume	Refinance Share	ARM Share [1]
1995	$639	21%	33%
2000	1,047	19	25
2001	2,080	59	12
2002	2,745	59	17
2003	3,711	65	19
2004 [2]	2,227	40	38

(1) ARM share is percent of total volume of conventional purchase loans.
(2) Projected by Freddie Mac.

Source: HUD Survey of Mortgage Lending Activity; Mortgage Bankers Association; Federal Housing Finance Board; Freddie Mac, Insurance Information Institute.

First American also expects the pressure on borrowers to peak in 2007 and 2008, as the largest number of mortgages reset to higher rates. After 90 days of no payments, the foreclosure process begins. And many with ARMs wishing to refinance to a FRM do not seem to have many options. In order to prevent some from refinancing their ARMs early in order to lock in low FRMs, some companies have $20,000 penalties if they refinance within 3 years. These restrictions are due to the structure of mortgage-backed securities markets, which seek to lock investment gains for their investors. As a disturbing side note, minorities and low-income home owners have been the subject of these predatory practices by the mortgage industry. And it will be these groups who suffer the most from the fallout of the sub-prime market.

Figure 10-15. Home Loan Delinquency Rates by % Past Due (1972 to 2005)

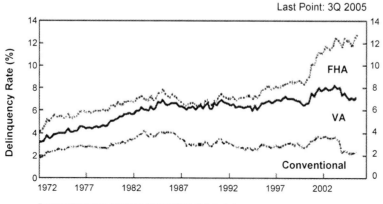

Source: Mortgage Bankers Association of America

Short-term interest rates have already climbed significantly over the past two years and home owners who financed using ARMs are starting to feel the heat, with monthly payments rising up to 40 percent in less than a year. For the first 9 months of 2005, delinquencies for new sub-prime ARMs were 6.2 percent compared to 3.7 percent in the same period in 2004. And credit default swaps on sub-prime ARM pools have almost doubled in price from mid-Sept to December 2005. What this means is that the insurance policies against defaults has almost doubled in price, indicating that the industry itself sees a much higher risk of mortgage defaults.

Mortgage Debt

Despite the huge run-up in real estate prices, the debt-to-value ratio of real estate holdings in America is at dangerous levels due to the enormous cash-out financings and home equity loans. By the beginning of 2006, the total household mortgage debt relative to the market value of residential real estate (the debt-to-value ratio) stood at just under 45 percent. In contrast, in 1955 when the economy was vibrant, this ratio was 25 percent and climbed to a peak of about 37 percent in 1965, only to fall to about 32 percent over the next twenty years. Double-digit inflation during the Reagan years pushed this ratio above post-war levels, where it has gradually climbed since then (figure 10-16). With real estate values extremely high, there seems to be no upper limit for this ratio once market values correct downward.

While mortgage rates are fixed for many home owners, consider that on average *about 9 percent of existing homes are sold every year, which means that after five years close to 40 percent of homes will have been sold* (assuming homes are sold twice). What this implies is that there is a fairly high turnover of homes under normal circumstances. Accordingly, even many who refinanced or bought a home when FRMs were at 40-year lows will not be so lucky when long-term rates begin to rise in 2008. And this will put an additional downward pressure on home prices.

Figure 10-16. Mortgage Debt Use for Home Purchases Has Been Rising

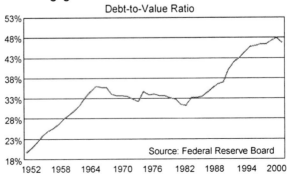

According to estimates by the Federal Reserve Board, by the end of 2013 residential mortgage debt is expected to top $17.2 trillion, assuming a mid-range estimate of 8.25 percent annual growth rates. The Fed's higher growth rate assumption of 9.5 percent per year would place this debt at $19.2 trillion (see appendix figures 10.1 and 10.2). Either outcome will result in a huge debt burden for Americans.

In 2003, the total residential mortgage debt outstanding (MDO) grew by 13.2 percent to $7.8 trillion, which at that time was the fastest rate since the last major real estate bubble in 1986. Therefore, in 2003, the MDO was nearly as large as the national debt. In 2005, the MDO grew by a record 13.8 percent to $9.8 trillion. As of mid-2006, the MDO was approximately $10 trillion, or about $1.5 trillion larger than the official national debt. Overall, *since the early stages of the bear market, the MDO has risen by 50 percent between 2002 and mid-2006.*

Over the next decade, expected increases in mortgage debt will surely put a strain on disposable income. Figure 10-17 estimates the current debt-to-value ratio (mid-2006) at around 48 percent (versus the 45 percent data in Jan. '06, figure 10-16). As mortgage debt will continue to increase according to these projected growth rates, notice that the debt-to-value ratio will experience a disproportionate increase as the bubble deflates. Finally, forecasts show that by 2010, the debt-to-value ratio will range between 53 and 55 percent. But when the housing bubble deflates, this ratio will most likely surge to previously unseen levels and could easily surpass 70 percent within the next decade.

The Real Estate ATM

According to the Federal Reserve Board, American home owners extracted $600 billion in equity from their homes in 2004 (up by $39 billion from 2003) and spent half of this money on goods and services. *This $300 billion accounted for 40 percent of the GDP growth in 2004.*

Figure 10-18 illustrates the effects of mortgage equity withdrawal on GDP growth from data reported by the Federal Reserve. Between 2003 and 2004 alone, the Federal Reserve estimates that Americans tapped into over $1 trillion of equity from their homes using home equity loans, refinancings, and cash-out purchases at closing (figure 10-19).

Figure 10-17. Debt-value Ratio is Expected to Surpass 50 Percent Soon

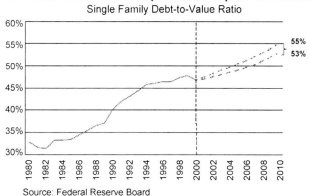

Single Family Debt-to-Value Ratio

Source: Federal Reserve Board

Figure 10-18. The Effects of Mortgage Equity Withdrawal on GDP Growth

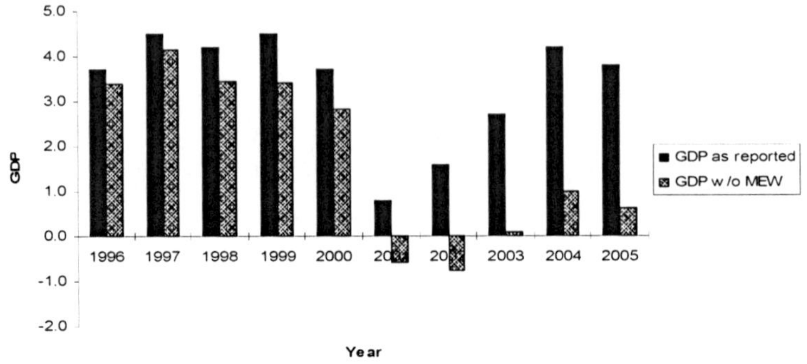

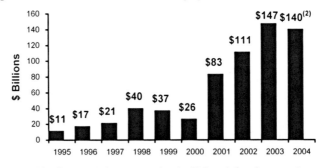

Source: Mortgage Bankers Association of America and Federal Reserve Flow of Funds

Alone, these cash-out financings have been estimated to account for a significant portion of inflated values during the more recent stages of the bubble. It has been this source of credit that has fueled the primary portion of GDP growth since 2003.

Ironically, it has been the flight from the scandals of the recent stock market bubble that have caused many to seek real estate as a "safe" investment alternative. And while the stock market is by no means finished correcting from the bull market period of the 1990s, we now have a real estate bubble that must also correct.

Figure 10-19. Cash-Out Home Mortgage Refinancing, 1995-2004 [1]

(1) Represents home owners' cash withdrawals from home mortgage refinance transactions. Includes prime conventional loans only and are net of retirement of outstanding second mortgages.

(2) Estimated.

Source: Freddie Mac

The Mortgage Money Machine

How is it possible that the mortgage industry has been able to lend so much money to so many under-qualified consumers? Even back in the late 1990s when the economy was at its peak, it was more difficult to obtain mortgages than today. With few options remaining, *Washington has permitted this industry to engage in irresponsible lending practices to increase access to credit for the purpose of fueling the phantom recovery.* This has served to enhance consumer spending that has boosted many industry wages; fees and commissions of brokers in the financial industry, real estate agent commissions, items bought at home improvement stores, refinancings with lower monthly payments to increase disposable income, and home equity loans to spend on anything.

Hence, without this real estate bubble, there would be very few signs of improvement in the economy since 2003. As well, remember that the majority of government discretionary spending since that time has been for Iraq, Afghanistan, Katrina, and homeland security—none of which contributed to a direct improvement in living standards, as normally implied by GDP numbers. Therefore, *if we adjust for the effects of spending due to credit released from the real estate bubble and due to government expenditures that have not resulted in an improved economic benefit, America has actually registered negative GDP growth since 2003.* Yet, aided by the loose monetary policies of Greenspan, the financial industry has helped create the illusion of a recovery.

Securitization of the Credit Bubble

Over the past two decades, the consumer finance industry has become so specialized that most loans now pass through several hands after they are originated. Today, all consumer and mortgage loans are packaged into special types of securities sold to institutional investors in transactions outside of the stock market. In the process, thousands of loans are combined into a single debt product and then sliced into smaller securities, each with different credit scores. This allows financial institutions to mask very risky sub-prime loans within a package of higher quality loans. It's been the strength of this large market for hybrid debt products that has provided massive liquidity to banks. In large part, the strong demand for investment products from this market has led to the swelling of the real estate and credit bubbles.

The process of converting these loans into investment-grade products of variable risk is called securitization. It's the process used by banks to package otherwise unmarketable credit card debt, mortgages, auto loans, business lease payments, tax liens, and many other debt payments into what are categorized as investment-grade securities, purchased by large financial institutions such as pension plans; most likely, yours.

> "The old wisdom that you had to be of mid- to high-investment grade quality to compete in the finance business was turned on its head by securitization."
>
> Scott J. Ulm, managing director of Credit Suisse First Boston.

Virtually all consumer and business loans in America are analyzed and packaged into a pool along with hundreds or even thousands of other loans. This is the basic process of *securitization*, and once it has occurred, these securities are considered *collateralized*, since they are backed by cash flow payments of the borrowers.

When this debt has been securitized from auto loans, collection notes, business credit, royalties, TV syndication deals, or virtually anything else with a revenue stream (except mortgages) they are known as *asset-backed securities*. They are then resold to institutional investors outside of the stock and bond markets in what is known as the asset-backed securities (ABS) market. Mortgage loans securitized in a similar manner are known as *mortgage-backed securities* (MBS) and are bought and sold by the same institutional investors on the mortgage-backed securities market.

The complexity of the MBS market has evolved to match that of the ABS market, due to the various levels of securitization and multitude of mortgage derivative products now sold in this market. The vast majority of MBS exist due to the upstream liquidity provided by Fannie Mae, Freddie Mac, and Ginnie Mae (the GSEs). Together, these three government agencies are responsible for securitizing and marketing the majority of the $11 trillion of outstanding residential mortgage debt in America.

Once packaged and rated for credit risk, institutional investors supply the downstream liquidity needed to keep the cycle running, through their purchase of these securitized mortgage products from these GSEs. Meanwhile, loan origination companies get cash to issue more loans. In short, *the asset- and mortgage-backed securities markets (collectively known as the collateralized securities market) serve to create a perpetual money machine that has fueled the massive credit and real estate bubbles seen today in America.*

Secondary Mortgage Market

The same financial institutions that originate mortgage loans are not required to service the loans. In fact, over the past two decades the rapid growth of America's financial system has led to a changing trend in which most banks that originate loans sell them to other companies in exchange for cash flows to originate more loans. This has given rise to the *mortgage servicing industry*, which is now larger than the *loan origination industry*. Together, both industries comprise the *primary mortgage market*.

Closely associated with the primary market is the *secondary mortgage market*, which specializes in buying and selling mortgages packaged in bulk and sold to institutional investors on the MBS market. The mortgage servicing industry works closely with the providers of MBS to ensure these investment products meet certain standards, as well as a timely collection of payments.

Incidentally, government-sponsored student loans are the least risky of all collateralized securities and possibly the safest and best investment one can make in a financial company due to the guaranteed repayment requirement set forth by Congress a few years ago. Unlike other collateralized securities, debtors who owe money to Sallie Mae or other similar agencies cannot get out of their debt under any circumstances, including bankruptcy.

These companies even have the power to garnish Social Security benefits until the loans have been paid off (if you are looking for a safe financial stock, look no further; Sallie Mae is your answer). This is in contrast to the remaining types of collateralized securities, which can be eliminated through bankruptcy, although now more difficult. In contrast, it's still very easy for home owners to walk away from their mortgage commitment with no major ramifications other than the loss of their home.

The MBS Money Machine

The first mortgage-backed securities were created during the 1970s by the former Salomon Brothers, when housing demand was greater than the availability of credit. Basically, the mortgage cash-flow cycle works like this: homebuyers go through a mortgage broker who advertises the loan applicant to larger financial institutions, who then place competitive bids for the loan. This broker collects origination and other fees. Next, a finance company buys the loan and places it among thousands of similar loans to create the mortgage-backed security (MBS). The company gets some agency to oversee the process and receives a rating on the loan based upon the individual credit records of the borrowers.

Typically, financial institutions will use a cooker-cutter formula to determine loan suitability while the homebuyer's interest rate is based upon the perceived risk of default. Then an investment banker underwrites the security and markets the deal to institutional investors, slicing each security into different levels, each with a different risk level. Institutional investors purchase the debt slice of their choice based upon the amount of risk exposure they want. In return, these investors receive principal and interest payments from the homeowner's monthly mortgage payments. When home owners obtain home equity loans, a similar process occurs. However, home equity loans are often (but not always) placed into the ABS category, secured by the equity from the home.

Bigger than the Stock and Bond Markets

The MBS and ABS markets have exploded over the past two decades and now are considered amongst the biggest investment markets worldwide. Most consumers aren't aware of them since these securities aren't publicly traded like the stock and bond markets. Rather, ABS and MBS are typically bought by pensions, insurance funds, mutual funds, and other large institutions. But since the primary companies involved in securitization of ABS and MBS are publicly traded, (Freddie Mac, Fannie Mae, and Ginnie Mae for MBS; Sallie Mae, Citigroup, Chase, and Bank of America for ABS and some MBS) a significant portion of mortgage and consumer debt is indirectly linked to the stock and bond markets.

Figure 10-20 shows a breakdown of the $12 trillion collateralized securities markets, mainly made up of MBS and ABS. The entire pie excluding the ABS slice makes up the $9 trillion MBS market (note that 2006 data has increased to nearly $11 and $4 trillion for MBS and ABS respectively). As you can see, the MBS market has become so large that it now dwarfs the $2 trillion ABS market. The extra $1 trillion comes from collateralized derivative securities. Note that the ABS market includes not only credit card and auto loan securitization debt, but also student and home equity loans.

Figure 10-21 illustrates the size of the ABS and MBS markets relative to the overall publicly traded bond markets. As you can see, the $10 trillion MBS market alone (Agency MBS and Agency debt, private MBS, and ABCP) is larger than the corporate and U.S. government bond markets individually, and nearly as large as both of these markets combined. And when you add the $1.9 trillion ABS market to the MBS market, the entire $12 trillion ($14 trillion 2006 data) collateralized market is larger than the U.S. government and corporate bond markets combined. In comparison, as of June 30th, 2006, the estimated value of the collateralized securities markets stood at over $14 trillion while the total value of the U.S. stock market stood at around $13 trillion. Combined with the fragility of the economy, it should be easy to appreciate the enormous credit risk the collateralized markets have generated.

Figure 10-20. Breakdown of Debt Type in the Collateralized Markets by Asset Class

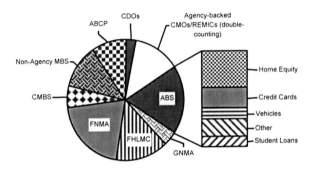

Based on a total $9.02 trillion total as of September 30, 2005
Source: Bond Market Association, 2005

Depending on how, when and to what extent the real estate and credit bubbles correct, large aftershocks could ripple throughout America's financial system, triggering a massive stock and bond market sell-off, as well as huge problems for Fannie Mae, Freddie Mac, and all other banks involved with ABS and MBS, depending upon their exposure.

Imagine for a moment how the stock and bond markets would react to a large number of bond defaults by corporations. Now think about how vulnerable the MBS and ABS markets are, given the potential effects of the real estate and credit bubbles. Remember, *it's very easy to walk away from a mortgage with no real consequences.* Thus, it should be clear that America could face a devastating financial crisis from a misstep in the MBS market alone.

Figure 10-21. U.S. Capital Debt Markets (selected components as of September 30, 2005)

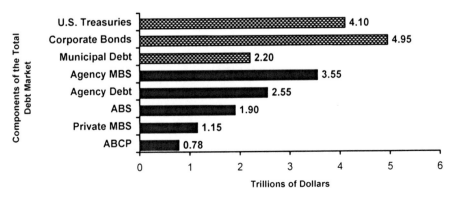

Source: Bond Market Association, 2005

MBS & ABS Markets Created the Bubble

While many think record low interest rates led to the housing boom, it was actually the enormous amount of liquidity generated by the ABS and MBS markets that allowed the lax credit standards resulting in ridiculous financing terms such as interest-only, high-loan-to-value loans (HLTV, where the borrower borrows up to 125 percent of the value) and ARM mortgages. Augmented by low rates and consumer greed, it has been these irresponsible mortgage products that have fueled the housing boom.

However, if financial institutions did not provide demand for these securities, many of the irresponsible lending practices would not have occurred. In fact, the overwhelming demand for these securities spurred the growth of the sub-prime market as a way to feed this demand.

Similarly, it was the securitization of credit card and auto debt that enabled financial companies to offer great rates. After all, many of the originating banks simply sold off the debt notes to institutional investors who provided them even more cash for new loan originations. Yet, with so much importance to the U.S. economy, *neither MBS or ABS are sold on any exchanges, so they are not subject to the strict reporting and disclosure requirements of the SEC.*

Risks of Collateralized Securities

The great thing about securitization is that it creates liquidity and makes credit widely available to consumers and businesses at competitive rates, all of which helps drive the economy. While securitization is often an invaluable resource for generating abundant credit for economic expansions, it can also lead to busts if a sufficient number of consumers default on payments.

Noteworthy of mention are some of the shortfalls of the securitization process. For instance, securitization does not eliminate the risk of collateralized loans and assumes their liquidity and marketability will remain in tact. As well, there is an enormous amount of guesswork that goes into structuring the risk of these loans. In short, GSEs and other financial institutions have to estimate how much revenue they can expect at any given time, how much of that money they will need to back their bonds safely, and how much cash will remain as a profit—a lot of uncertainties.

Even the riskiest of these loans can be manipulated into AAA-rated debt and sold to pensions and other large funds because the same standards that apply to corporate debt are not applied to collateralized debt products. In addition, these ratings do not account for whether the investors will receive a return on principal. And since companies that securitize these loans are not regulated like banks, they do not have a capital requirement that would ensure adequate reserves to fund payments to investors.

Ever since the birth of the collateralized securities market three decades ago, we have yet to see a blowup. However, that scenario may not be so far off, as credit risk continues to increase. Consequently, recent concerns emphasizing the vulnerability of this huge market might be the major reason for the new bankruptcy law passed in October

2005, since it provides some security to the ABS markets, knowing that it is much more difficult to walk away from consumer debt. However, it's still relatively easy to walk away from a mortgage. Therefore, the vast majority of this market remains very vulnerable.

Government-Sponsored Enterprises

GSEs are corporations created by Congress to increase Americans' access to mortgage loans. There are three GSEs and several related agencies: the Federal National Mortgage Association (Fannie Mae), the Federal Home Loan Mortgage Corporation (Freddie Mac), and the Federal Home Loan Bank (FHLB) system.

Fannie Mae was created in 1938 during the Great Depression to help Americans afford housing. It sells conventional mortgages as well as those insured by the Federal Housing Administration (FHA). Freddie Mac was established in 1970 for the purpose of providing more funds to lenders. It is Freddie Mac that buys mortgages from lenders and repackages them into mortgage-backed securities and sells them to investors. In addition to these GSEs, there is also the Farm Credit System (established in 1916) and the Federal Agriculture Mortgage Corporation (Farmer Mac).

As far as the real estate and mortgage industries are concerned, the primary function of GSEs is to sustain a liquid mortgage market. As we have seen, the primary mortgage market is created by banks and other lenders providing financing for mortgages. But without a place to go, these creditors would soon run out of funds to loan customers. So in order to keep mortgage cash flows robust, Fannie Mae, Freddie Mac, and Ginnie Mae buy these origination loans, providing banks with cash to approve more loans. From these agencies, loans are packaged into a variety of securities including derivatives, all of which are typically purchased by pension funds, mutual funds and banks. Therefore, *the secondary mortgage market (the GSEs) generates money for lenders (the primary mortgage market) to continue supplying mortgages to consumers.*

The original intended purpose of the GSEs was to focus on affordable housing for the private sector. Yet, dozens of studies have shown that Freddie and Fannie have not been dedicating their resources towards this mission, but have been supplying funds to the overall market. Therefore, *the GSEs have been a significant stimulus for the rapid growth of sub-prime loan market that has contributed to the enormous risks we see within the real estate bubble, as reflected by the MBS market.*

Why GSEs are Dangerous

As confirmed by the Office of Federal Housing Enterprise Oversight (OFHEO), an arm of the government that regulates Fannie Mae and Freddie Mac,

"The housing market contributed significantly to the Nation's economic recovery. Falling mortgage rates stimulated housing starts and sales, and many refinancing borrowers took out loans that were larger than those they paid off, providing additional funds for consumption expenditures."

Because Fannie and Freddie lack sufficient government oversight, they have not maintained adequate capital reserves needed to safeguard the security of payments to their investors. And due to their exemption from the SEC Act of 1933, they are not required to reveal their financial position. In fact, *they are the only publicly traded companies in the Fortune 500 exempt from routine SEC disclosures required for adequate transparency and investor accountability.* As well, due to their exemption from the Act of 1933, they are not required to adhere to the rules governing tender offers and public reporting of insider stock transactions. And they are not required to register their MBS and debt offerings with the SEC, which diminishes transparency further. As a result, there is question as to whether they are exposing themselves to excessive risk. Oddly enough, while Washington subsidizes Fannie Mae and Freddie Mac each year by over $10.6 billion (2002), they do not require complete disclosure or insist on standard capital requirements.

Fannie and Freddie hold between 20 to 50 percent of the capital required by bank regulators for depository institutions holding mortgages. As of 2003, the GSEs had $1.6 trillion in combined assets, $1.4 trillion in retained mortgages in their portfolios, $1.5 trillion in outstanding debt, and $1.5 trillion in derivatives. In addition, outstanding MBS generated by the GSEs but held by third parties totaled $1.7 trillion.

What would happen if one or more GSE got into financial trouble? Not only would investors get crushed, but taxpayers would have to bail them out since the GSEs are backed by the government. Everyone would feel the effects. With close to $2 trillion in debt between Freddie Mac and Fannie Mae alone, as well as several trillion held by commercial banks, *failure of just one GSE or related entity could create a huge disaster that would easily eclipse the Savings & Loan Crisis of the late 1980s.*

Furthermore, the GSEs have created very risky derivatives exposures for themselves and many financial institutions. Fannie Mae has taken about half of its MBS and pooled them into another security called a Real Estate Mortgage Investment Conduit (REMIC), otherwise known as a restructured MBS or Collateralized Mortgage Obligation (CMO). These securities are complex derivatives and considered to be very speculative. As these debt instruments evolve into different products, less transparency and more uncertainty is created.

According to recent data, the total derivative exposure for all securities stands at nearly $300 trillion. However, it's not known for certain what the net exposure is. In other words, how much of these derivatives are used as hedging securities versus leverage. As a simple example, if $1 million in derivatives are in call options for Microsoft stock with the same strike price and expiration as another $1 million in put options, the net derivatives exposure is 0. It's also not known with certainty how much of these derivatives are in mortgage-related securities, since only a small portion are listed in the collateralized securities markets. But even a 5 percent net exposure would be huge.

Now I want you to stop and think for a minute about all of the fraudulent practices that have occurred within the housing industry, from known problems of poor workmanship and cheap materials by some builders, to inflated appraisals performed to generate ease of lending and to support cash-out deals. I am not going to go into these problems but if you do some research, you will see that they are large issues that have not hit the mainstream media.

From inflated appraisals alone, 10 to 15 percent of MBS securities or up to $1.5 trillion have been overvalued by conservative estimates. Combine that with the lack of transparency, questionable risk exposure and fraudulent practices by executives at Fannie and Freddie, and you have a disaster ready to strike. Now combine that with over 10 million Americans holding interest-only and ARM mortgages, throw in a million or two job losses due to say the failure of Delta, Ford, General Motors, or some other large vulnerable company, and you could end up with a blowup in the MBS market. This scenario would devastate the stock, bond and real estate markets. Most likely, there would also be an even bigger mess in the swaps and derivatives markets.

In conclusion, the collateralized securities market is a very tall and fragile house of cards poised to collapse, and all it might take is one card to be dislodged. A breakdown in just one of the GSEs is very possible and could result in a financial collapse of far greater magnitude and scope than Enron, triggering massive losses.

Troubles Already Showing

The lack of congressional oversight combined with the reluctance of the GSEs to provide transparency has already resulted in mismanagement, fraud, and abuse of power. Already, significant fraud and deceit has been partially uncovered at both Fannie Mae, and its smaller peer Freddie Mac. Recently, Freddie Mac had to restate several years of earnings. And only in 2003 did Fannie Mae finally agree to register under the SEC Act of 1934 to provide annual and quarterly financial reporting due to mounting pressure from outside critics. As a result of this, Fannie has had to restate earnings to the tune of nearly $11 billion from 1998 to mid-2004. The SEC has fined them $400 million and the management is now being investigated by the Department of Justice. The SEC has a long track record of acting too little too late, and this could prove to be another example.

Thus far, Fannie Mae was found to have misrepresented its risk position, acted irresponsibly, and manipulated earnings so company executives would receive huge bonuses. Figure 10.3 (appendix) shows that Fannie Mae was able to meet earnings goals for all bonuses from 1996 to 2003. No doubt, these bogus numbers would have continued if they were not caught. Box 10-1 (appendix) shows a partial summary of the 311-page special report of the OFHEO's special investigation of Fannie Mae.

Lack of Government Controls

Given the lack of standards for traditional FRMs and interest-only ARMs, it seems odd that America's home ownership is not closer to 90 percent. Think about a person who pays $600 per month for an apartment; he can get a loan for $200,000 and have lower monthly payments using an option-ARM. There is virtually no limit to the different types of mortgage products that have been issued. If you want you can get a 1 percent interest payment loan (a negative amortization loan) reducing the monthly payment even further.

The problem with this explosion of mortgage options in the midst of America's biggest housing bubble is that there is no one to provide financial advice to homebuyers regarding the suitability and financial risk of these loans. With the complexity of mortgage products thrown out in the market to entice buyers there is a big need for such an industry.

We have the NASD and SEC for the stock and bond markets. Why isn't there a similar regulatory agency to prevent consumers from making potentially disastrous mortgage decisions? As well, one might ask the question why the government has not created an agency to protect consumers against unfair business practices by credit card companies. Of course, having the NASD and SEC did not prevent the Internet bubble, devastating accounting scandals, and hundreds of other episodes of large-scale fraud.

By now you should realize the answer. Washington supports any industry that encourages consumers to spend. Creating an agency to help consumers make wise consumer financing decisions would destroy all the efforts the government has made to pump credit into the banking system.

If the economy was truly healthy, Washington wouldn't need to rely on these cheap tactics. While producing deceptive gains in productivity via credit-driven consumer spending, the longer-term consequences are just one more straw (and a very large one at that) added to the camel's back. And eventually the camel's back will break.

What to Look For

As the real estate and credit bubbles begin to lose steam, cautious investors may be able to spot early warning signs and avoid loses or even make profits. For the real estate bubble, investors should keep an eye on rising inventories of new homes and the length of time homes are on the market, coupled with price declines. Although large one-month drops would be a reason for focused attention, investors should look for a change in trends over a several month period.

For the credit bubble, any major problem in the real estate market would naturally lead to difficulties in outstanding mortgages, affecting all of the GSEs and many large financial institutions such as Citigroup, Bank of America, Chase, General Motors (GMAC), General Electric (GE Finance), and Washington Mutual, depending upon the extent of their exposure. As well, if things get really nasty the credit problems could extend to the ABS market which would cause further devastation.

What Can We Expect?

America has become a nation of credit spending, and most believe that home ownership is the biggest and safest investment they will ever make. These perceptions have been further magnified since the deflation of the Internet bubble. However, as I have discussed, there are tremendous risks for both home owners and real estate investors alike.

Already, outstanding residential mortgage debt has continued to surpass record levels. And even amidst tremendous price appreciation, the debt-to-value ratio is approaching record highs. When home prices correct downward, these effects will be more pronounced and the "poor effect" will kick in.

Housing prices are absolutely critical to the success of companies such as Lowe's, Home Depot, and Sears. As well, most banks are closely tied to the health of the housing market because one way or another you can bet they have exposure to the MBS market. Many of the larger financial institutions have a much larger risk exposure with real estate derivative products. Overall, the biggest threat of this bubble may be the broad-reaching impact of a blow-up in the MBS market that would send shockwaves throughout the capital markets.

Based on today's grossly overvalued housing prices, a 35 percent correction on average seems very likely. And in some areas, a 50 to 60 percent correction is possible. However, don't expect a sudden fallout. Most likely, it will take several years for the washout in real estate prices to be completed. We can only hope that the MBS market doesn't experience its first blow up since inception, but don't bet on it.

Conclusions

There is indisputable evidence that most Americans have been buying homes as an investment for at least the past ten years. And this behavior is the primary indicator of a real estate bubble. Specifically, this evidence arises from the disparity in home prices versus rental costs, lack of real wage growth, and the massive expansion of credit provided by Greenspan's reckless monetary policies. And GSEs have added to the real estate boom by providing endless liquidity, thereby encouraging the growth of the sub-prime market.

Since 1997, the U.S. total home mortgage debt outstanding for has risen by over 160 percent to about $11 trillion. With an estimated *75 million home owners* and over $4 trillion of increased residential real estate value in the past few years, there should be no doubt that the real estate bubble is peaking. At least 30 percent of the $11 trillion residential mortgage debt market will correct downward leading to record foreclosures, which will affect the MBS and ABS markets. If this correction has not ended by 2011, the housing share of consumer expenditures will decline gradually as the boomers reach retirement.

Under normal conditions, anywhere from *25 to 30 percent of the U.S. economy is directly affected by the housing sector.* However, due to exaggerated asset prices from the housing bubble, this share is significantly higher. I have shown the magnified effects of a loss of housing value on home equity, but this also has a magnified affect on the stock market because the wealth effect is reversed, resulting in dampened consumer spending. Accordingly, numerous studies have shown that *housing prices have up to two times the effect on consumer spending as they do on declines in stock prices.* Consequently, if housing prices decline by 25 percent, the economic impact will be as if the stock market declined by 50 percent.

On average, since 2001, U.S. home prices have risen by over 57 percent, (33 percent adjusted for inflation) and in many cities this number is closer to 150 percent. As of June 2006, the median home price in America approached $230,000. Therefore, as it stands today, unless you take out a risky ARM or interest-only mortgage, the average home is not affordable for the average American. Already, with short-term rates above 5 percent, ARMs are no longer an option, forcing those who cannot afford a home (but who believe real estate is a great investment) to take out interest-only loans.

Just as Greenspan denied any existence of an Internet bubble a few years back, he has also denied any trace of a real estate or credit bubble. He even recommended that Americans consider financing their homes with ARMs in January 2004, just a few months before he began raising rates by nearly 400 basis points over the next two years.

PART III

GREED, DESPERATION & DECEIT

11

WHAT THE GOVERNMENT HIDES

Hidden Liabilities

Politicians use several means to hide the real problems from American voters, while using the media to deliver messages they want the public to hear. And when critical issues are discovered within the administration, this often leads to replacement of politicians who tried to serve the best interests of voters. This has often been the price of loyalty to the American people. As we shall see, this was the fate of former Secretary of Treasury Paul O'Neill.

The U.S. government has several ways to hide its liabilities and reduce benefits for many of its programs. In Chapter Six, I discussed the federal deficit problems and noted how Washington hides some of its liabilities through the use of off-balance financing. Regardless how much of the deficit is cloaked by accounting tricks, Washington cannot hide the national debt.

If held to the same standards as corporate America, Washington's off-balance financing tricks would be considered accounting fraud by the SEC. But alas, this is the United States government, leader of the richest, most powerful nation in the world, capable of raising taxes anytime it needs and printing as much money as it chooses. After all, the world must accept the dollar regardless how low it declines. But soon, the dollar may lose much of its international clout. And if that happens there will be a catastrophe on the order of magnitude for which I cannot fathom.

The annual budget and trade deficits are adding to the problem of America's unmanageable debt burden—all direct consequences of its excessive consumption and unwillingness to concede a decline in living standards. Therefore, the mismanagement of the annual budget, deficit, and total national debt reflect America's weakened economic position and declining global competitiveness. This monetary irresponsibility is a direct indicator of Washington's inability to solve the nation's economic problems.

As we have seen, the prognosis for Medicare is bleak due to the enormous liabilities expected over the next three decades. America's entire healthcare system should be viewed as disgraceful due to ridiculous costs, unjustified expense acceleration, lack of affordability, endless fraud, medical errors, control by the pharmaceutical industry, and most notably the large percentage of Americans who remain uninsured.

Finally, healthcare is linked to employment during a period when job security is rare. Much of America's declining competitiveness is a result of the large costs American companies must absorb to provide health insurance and other employee benefits. In contrast, foreign companies do not have these expenses due to nationalized healthcare and government pension plans. Consequently, Washington's unwillingness to provide for these programs is the primary factor that has resulted in the outsourcing trends we see today. Sadly, President Bush refuses to address the healthcare crisis at any scope, preferring to distract Americans with other issues such as homeland security and misconceptions about Social Security.

While Social Security continues to experience diminished wage replacement, political agendas have ignored this trend and have misrepresented its long-term solvency as a crisis, when in fact it is Bush's privatization plan that will create a crisis. Of more concern are the trends of increased dependency and diminished buying power of Social Security in the midst of a pension plan crisis and soaring healthcare and energy costs—two of the most expensive items for seniors. These items should be expensed in proportion to the median costs for seniors when annual COLAs are added to Social Security benefits.

I also discussed the magnitude and scope of the current real estate bubble, which forms a large portion of America's credit bubble. These bubbles are a reflection of America's long period of declining living standards linked to excessive consumption. All of these issues factor into what could result in a huge crisis for America's baby boomers over the next two decades. With very little in retirement savings, the majority of this generation will rely primarily on Social Security as their source of retirement income. And as Medicare and Medicaid benefits continue to be cut, more of America's seniors will have little funds to ensure their health and dignified departure from this world. It's truly a shame.

Already, we see the damaging affects of record oil prices on consumers, yet Washington refuses to respond appropriately, and has even denied that inflation has become an issue. But remember the effects of high oil prices are delayed in the economy by up to one year due to the juggling of inventories. In addition, the longer-term effects may be delayed by up to two years since inflation is a lagging indicator. Surely, when you have a long-term trend of high oil prices, a tipping point cannot be far off.

Bush's Dirty Little Secret

In preparation for his reelection campaign against Democratic Party Nominee Senator John Kerry, President Bush instructed his Secretary of Treasury, Paul O'Neill to commission an economic study to determine how much the U.S. government owed for the fiscal year 2004. As a part of this study, Dr. Jagadeesh Gokhale, senior economic adviser to the Federal Reserve Bank of Cleveland and Dr. Kent Smetters, an economics professor at the University of Pennsylvania, examined Social Security, Medicare, and Medicaid. The results of this study concluded that the total present value of the liabilities needed to pay the baby boomers for Social Security amounts to $22 trillion (note that the recent provision to allow illegal immigrants to collect Social Security will increase these liabilities if final approval occurs). When Medicare and Medicaid were added, this obligation totaled $43 trillion. Finally, adding Part D Medicare brought the total to $51 trillion.

However, other similar studies were done and it turns out that the estimates by Gokhale and Smetters were conservative by comparison, with total liabilities reported as high as $72 trillion. How much is $72 trillion? Well, it is almost twice the total amount of the $42 trillion in total assets held by all Americans, liquid and illiquid (cash, securities, real estate, autos and collectables). As well, it is nearly twice the $42 trillion total debt held by the American government and consumers (i.e. America's total credit bubble). Finally, these liabilities exceed the total GDP of the world.

Based upon all of the studies conducted, the *present value* of these mandatory spending liabilities is somewhere between $51 and $72 trillion (table 11-1). However, the *future value* of Social Security, Medicaid and Medicare liabilities over the next thirty years is probably somewhere around the $120 trillion.

> "It's a number that's so large that people find it implausible, and so they don't think about it."
>
> Alan Auerbach
> UC Berkeley economist speaking of the fiscal imbalance in Medicaid and Social Security

If the government funds these programs as they are needed (instead of now) and without any benefit cuts, the total amount needed over the benefit period (which is about five decades) could be as high as $120 trillion, depending on when these expenditures are funded. Therefore, by delaying the fiscal solutions, the present value will increase accordingly each year, only making matters worse. What all of this means for certain are higher taxes and fewer benefits for Americans.

Of the three liabilities, the greatest challenge is by far with Medicare, especially since these liabilities are rising six times faster than that of Social Security. Medicare costs are directly related to the healthcare crisis that no politicians want to talk about. Rather than address America's healthcare crisis, President Bush has chosen to create distractions by passage of Part D Medicare, which is flawed and does not provide solutions for nearly 50 million Americans who are without healthcare coverage.

> "I am desperately trying to get people to understand the significance of this for our country, our children, our grandchildren. How this is resolved could affect not only our economic security but our national security. We're heading to a future where we'll have to double federal taxes or cut federal spending by 50%."
>
> Comptroller General David Walker, the government's chief accountant

As well, it does not address the overall costs of healthcare, which have even forced many with health insurance into bankruptcy. In addition, Bush has created another decoy by claiming an immediate solvency crisis in Social Security, without addressing its real problems. So what are some of the possible solutions to fix these shortfalls? In the report written by Gokhale and Smetters, several options were identified as the only solutions to provide for these gigantic liabilities. The list is as follows:

1. Increase the payroll tax by over 100 percent *immediately and forever* from a current 15.3 percent of wages to nearly 32 percent

2. Raise income taxes by nearly 70 percent *immediately and forever*

3. Slash Social Security and Medicare benefits by 45 percent *immediately and forever*

4. *Or eliminate forever, all discretionary spending*, which includes the military, homeland security, highways, courts, national parks, and most of what the federal government does outside of the transfer of payments to the elderly

Sound scary? It should since option 4 is absolutely impossible. Likewise, option 3 is not feasible and if followed would sure destroy the economy…"immediately and forever." As well, no president or member of Congress would endorse such an action because it would jeopardize their chances for reelection. Options 1 and 2 are more likely, or some combination thereof. In my opinion, some combination of the following will need to occur:

- Raise payroll, income, and corporate taxes

- Eliminate Bush's capital gains tax cuts

- Increase the retirement age to age 72

- Raise fixed taxes such as the gasoline, telecom, cigarette and alcohol taxes

- Raise less noticeable taxes, as well as consumer and business fees

- Decrease deductions and tax credits

- Create new taxes, such as a sugar and caffeine tax

- Relax immigration standards (especially with Mexico)

Box 11-1: Present Value

What's the relevance of present value figures anyway? The future liabilities of these programs have been adjusted for the amount owed today (known as a present value) in order to account for what is known as the time-value of money, or the effect of compounding in a risk-free investment such as U.S. Treasury securities. Think of it as the inflation affect if you want.

For instance, if you have ever bought a lottery ticket, you may recall that you were asked if you wanted the cash value or the thirty-year payment, otherwise known as an annuity. Of course you are told that the $300 million lottery will only result in about $120 million if you take the cash value. That is because if you take payments over thirty years, that $120 million is expected to turn into $300 million if invested in a low risk or risk-free investment such as a money market or U.S. T-bills.

Therefore, that $300 million lottery figure represents a future amount assuming a guaranteed rate of return. In order to calculate the cash or present value of this $300 million, they do a reverse annuity calculation that discounts (reduces) that amount compounded over each of the thirty years by the expected rate of return of the investment.

Table 11-1. The Results of Various Economic Studies on U.S. Government Social Programs

Study	Estimate of Present Value of Obligations For Social Security, Medicaid and Medicare
Gokhale & Smetters	$51 trillion
International Monetary Fund	$47 trillion
Brookings Institute	$60 trillion
Government Accountability Office	$72 trillion

Already, Medicare and Medicaid are being slashed annually. As well, Medicare compensation to physicians continues to be cut, causing many healthcare providers to discontinue servicing needy recipients. Recently, Washington announced it would further decrease Medicare reimbursement to healthcare providers by another 20 percent. This is going to hurt the public healthcare system even more, as many physicians opt to discontinue servicing these patients. *I find it puzzling that Washington has set price caps for virtually all Medicare and Medicaid reimbursement expenses except prescription drugs.*

Technically speaking, America is already bankrupt, but unfortunately it's not over. Each day Washington allows these liabilities to persist, America's financial problems get worse, and foreign nations gain more control over its sovereignty. And the possible future unwillingness of foreign nations to continue financing America's reckless spending sprees and financial mismanagement could cause a major collapse of the dollar.

For over three decades, the world has continued to support America's irresponsible spending habits through the purchase of U.S. Treasury securities. However, as American consumers become weaker, the world will soon realize that America's economy is in a long-term downward trend. When this happens, more nations will turn to Asian consumers, whose living standards continue to mount dramatic improvements, have robust savings, and represent the future growth of the world's consumer marketplace. Even American companies will soon refocus their efforts to target over two billion Chinese and Indian consumers.

What Happened to the Report?

When the White House read the study commissioned by O'Neill, Bush called for his resignation and removed these findings from the final report. All you will see in the official report are claims that the economy is in full recovery. The official word is that O'Neill's resignation was due to disagreements with Bush's tax cuts. But it's reasonable to assume that these disagreements were related to the study by Gokhale and Smetters, since the tax cuts were contrary to the recommendations made in the report.

Already, Social Security taxes per paycheck are 900 percent higher than those paid by workers in 1951, even on an inflation-adjusted basis. So rather than announce a hike in the payroll tax or raise the wage cap for Social Security, President Bush wanted to come across as an "anti-tax president" and propose a radical and very risky privatization plan that threatens to dissolve America's only safety net against poverty.

Off-Budget Accounting

As discussed in Chapter Six, The White House hides the extent of the deficit by allocating a large amount of expenditures in the off-budget category. However, these expenses don't disappear because they are added to the national debt each year. *Hiding the deficit from Americans is an attempt to hide the growth of America's record-setting national debt, while communicating to consumers that the economy is strong.*

The U.S. government has over 150 trust funds, and the Social Security and Postal Service trust funds are amongst the two largest that are considered off-budget. However, Washington's off-budget financing extends to expenditures other than these funds. For instance, in mid-2005, President Bush spent another $82 billion off-budget for defense, the majority for Iraq and Afghanistan. This amount alone was more than spent for NASA and the Department of Education combined. He added another $70 billion in off-balance financing for the war in Iraq in mid-2006.

For 2006, the off-budget liabilities due to Social Security outlays are estimated to account for about $500 billion. Although revenues for Social Security will continue to be greater than expenditures over the next decade, this is going to reverse beginning in 2017, when annual deficits will begin to grow. And since Social Security is treated as an off-balance item, it will be hidden from the annual deficits.

The evolution of these off-budget financing regulations is quite complex, but basically Social Security was finalized as an off-budget item in 1992. However, because Social Security was running net surpluses over a several year period, for the most part, its off-budget treatment has not yet distorted budget expenditures. But after 2017, increasing annual deficits for Social Security will be hidden by this ridiculous accounting treatment.

Economic Numbers

The problem with deciphering the nation's economic data is that it's so voluminous and appropriate frames of reference are rarely provided, making interpretation problematic. This leads to reporting by the media that mirrors what the "experts" state about the economy. But this deception has a purpose. For Wall Street and off-beat financial institutions, it provides more confidence to investors who shuttle more money in the stock market, leading to increased business. For corporate America, it provides higher profits as consumers spend more credit thinking their future is promising.

For several years now, this financial deceit has kept the economy running. Perhaps if Americans are kept in the dark long enough the economy will rebound; or so Washington figures. But where will future spending come from now that home equity loans and credit cards have been maxed out, interest rates are higher and rising, and there's no evidence of net job or wage growth while outsourcing strengthens each day? How will Washington convince foreign banks to continue financing its record debt against the dollar, while American diplomacy continues to create global discontent?

Discouraged by the Economy

The government and related agencies are responsible for reporting the nation's economic data, and are therefore in the driver's seat to manipulate this data or dump so much of it onto consumers that they can't possibly analyze what's really going on. Each day, "critical" economic numbers are released by one or more of the numerous agencies connected to Washington. And consumers look to Wall Street and the media to make heads or tails of this data. Of course, Wall Street is always going to paint a rosier picture than reality for its own interests. Meanwhile, the media merely serves as a puppet for Wall Street. But the main problem is that by the time this data has been reported by the government it's already been manipulated. And when Wall Street gets a hold of it they make matters worse, tugging and pulling on the meaning of the numbers as a way to create market volatility which generates commissions.

Virtually every economic indicator has been altered by the government and its affiliated economic organizations for over three decades. I argue that this has occurred to distort the realities of America's economic picture. For instance, when the Labor Department measures unemployment rates, it only counts those who have searched for jobs within the past four weeks. Previously under President Lyndon Johnson, this cut off was six weeks but was lowered to make the numbers look better. As well, the government makes no distinctions between part-time workers who want full-time work but cannot find it; they're considered "employed" which is assumed to mean fully employed.

A much better measure of employment status is to look at the *underemployment rate*, which is always much higher. While this data is available, you'll never hear much about it from Washington because it demonstrates America's declining job quality and competitiveness. Consider what would happen to consumer confidence if the real data was reported.

Government employment figures also count workers who are employed in what are known as "non-standard jobs" with no distinctions. Typically, these jobs include temp workers, independent contractors, part-time workers and the self-employed. The main problem with counting these individuals as "employed" is that *non-standard jobs rarely include critical employee benefits such as healthcare or retirement plans.* And because America's labor force depends upon a large percentage of employee benefits as a part of the total compensation package (up to 42 percent of the median wage earners total compensation), a proper analysis of employment trends must consider non-standard employment data. However, this data is not included.

As well, non-standard jobs are much less secure than standard jobs so they don't provide the assurance and benefits of a stable career, making it difficult for these workers to plan for the future. Consequently, the rapid growth of the non-standard employment labor market over the past two decades has added to the growing job insecurity that is increasing within the traditional workplace.

Employment data does not indicate how long workers have been with a particular employer. But this information is also very important in order to understand the financial security of Americans. Because so many consumer costs are now annuitized in the form of financing agreements or contracts (mortgages, auto loan, mobile phone contacts, credit card payments), *American consumers are becoming increasingly dependent upon having a steady and reliable source of wage income* to meet these committed future expenses. Yet, the average American worker has never seen a greater amount of job insecurity as today.

Even before the last recession, estimates show that over 25 percent of America's workforce was engaged in non-standard employment. And there is little doubt that this percentage is significantly higher today due to the competitive effects of the free trade. Therefore, *employment numbers, as reported by the government provide a false picture of employment and do not account for diminishing wages and total compensation.*

As an additional way to make employment numbers look better, Washington economists came up with a new designation a few years ago called the "discouraged worker." Such a person is thought to have "thrown in the towel" after six unsuccessful months searching for work. This designation provides another way for the government to distort the true employment numbers. What happened to these discouraged workers? Why aren't they counted? More important, *what is it about the economy that has caused these "discouraged workers" to be unable to obtain a new job after an extended period?*

Knowing the number of discouraged workers is vital to understanding trends in the overall competitive landscape of the American economy. Yet, these individuals are simply dropped from the list as if they no longer exist. Why was there no such thing as a "discouraged worker" fifty years ago? Back then, Americans who were willing to work found stable jobs so there was no need to hide the truth. The economy was much better back then. However, ever since the 1980s, America has been in decline unless you're in the top 20 percent of wage earners.

Old Definitions Help

There are many other examples of the government's use of outdated definitions and modifications, and even the creation of new terms to suit its needs. These definitions are utilized to assist in a type of accounting trickery that is even more noxious than that used by corporate America.

Among the many government statistics that are inaccurate, twisted or misleading, amazingly those on poverty have come under little scrutiny. In Chapter Four, I discussed the government's outdated definition of poverty and how the unwillingness of Washington to modify its criteria has resulted in a misleading indicator of America's overall financial health.

> *"I know virtually no one who thinks the current poverty rate is an accurate measure of poverty."*
>
> Rebecca Blank
> Co-director of the National Poverty
> Center at the University of Michigan

The problem with inaccurate reporting of poverty data is that this information is critical for determining how much should be spent on programs providing basic necessities and outreach for this large group of Americans—for Social Security, Medicare, Medicaid, and other programs. *The big weakness in the government's definition of poverty is how to define basic living expenses and how to measure financial well-being.* For instance, the government's current poverty calculation includes only cash income before tax deductions, excludes capital gains taxes, and does not factor in accumulated wealth or assets such as securities or property ownership. *How can poverty calculations neglect figures for net worth and capital gains?*

Despite more reasonable definitions used by outside organizations, the Office of Management and Budget determines how poverty is measured for benefits. Currently, the official poverty level for a family of four is $19,307, and $12,334 for a family of two (2006). Therefore, a family of four might have a total income of $20,000 and be considered above the poverty line while another person with a $5 million investment portfolio and a $2 million home who takes a year off of work would be considered impoverished since he earned no income that year. By definition, poverty is the extreme opposite of wealth. And *because wealth is measured in terms of net worth, it's unreasonable that the government's definition of poverty only includes income.*

The GDP Myth

Up until the 1980s, the Gross National Product (GNP) was used as the predominant measure of economic growth in America. The GNP measures the total amount of goods and services that a nation's citizens produce regardless of the location of production. Therefore, GNP includes corporate profits that multinational companies earn overseas. As an example, the profits earned by General Electric's facilities in China are counted towards America's GNP rather than China's.

However, as globalization began to alter America's economy, the GDP (Gross Domestic Productivity) was thought to serve as a more reliable indicator of economic growth. Since the '80s, economists have pointed to the GDP as the single most reliable indicator of the health of the U.S. economy. *This proclivity has led to a kind of "follow the leader" mentality, with few to question its accuracy.* But as we shall see, there are some major problems with the way GDP is calculated and accepted as a measure of economic growth and standard of living.

Released quarterly (at 8:30am EST on the last business day of the next quarter) by the Department of Commerce, the GDP is defined as the total value of goods and services produced within a territory during a specified period, regardless of ownership. GDP differs from the GNP in excluding inter-country income transfers, thereby attributing to a territory the product generated within it rather than the incomes received in it. *In other words, the GDP only counts goods and services produced within a nation's geographic borders.*

GDP = Consumption + Government Expenditures + Investment + Exports − Imports[1]

Going back to earlier example, all profits earned by General Electric's facilities in China would not be counted towards America's GDP but rather China's GDP. However, America's GNP would benefit from these profits as mentioned above. Therefore, unlike GNP, the GDP is thought to provide information on domestic economic growth after adjusting for trade deficits or surpluses.

---

(1) Consumption and investment in this equation are the expenditure on final goods and services. The "exports minus imports" part of the equation adjusts this by subtracting the part of this expenditure not produced domestically (the imports), and adding back in domestic production not consumed at home (the exports).

At first glance, it might appear as if the use of GDP provides an accurate measure of domestic productivity since it does not count the earnings from multinational companies. And during current outsourcing trends, one might imagine that GDP serves to dismiss earnings made overseas. However, this is not necessarily the case for several reasons. In short, *the complexities of global production and commerce make it relatively easy for companies to alter how much of what gets made or serviced where.*

First, consider that multinational corporations and companies using outsourcing can shift earnings and expenses from one business unit to another without detection. Next, companies that outsource services packaged as a part of a total service or product can assign arbitrary earnings and expenses to the portion of the services or products that have been outsourced.

For instance, let's assume that General Electric has operations in China that are responsible for the production of a component used in refrigerators. Not only will the effect of an undervalued Yuan cause these costs (and therefore earnings) to be understated, but the expenses involved with the production of this component can be assigned an artificially high value then shipped to America for final assembly in order to receive more favorable tax treatment. For services such as IT, random assignment of such expenses can be even easier to conceal.

Finally, as we will see in Chapter Fourteen, a significant amount of U.S. assets and companies have been purchased by foreign interests. And when such purchases have not been in full, domestic operations of these assets or companies are considered as components to the U.S. GDP, when in fact, a significant portion of these earnings are leaving American borders and entering the hands of foreign owners.

Problems Measuring Living Standards

The importance of GDP as an economic indicator is in its frequent use as a measure of living standards within an economy or nation. In this regard, GDP affords the advantages of being a broad economic indicator that is measured frequently and consistently, allowing the identification of domestic trends as well as comparisons with other nations. However, there are many weaknesses in the use of GDP as a method to measure a nation's living standard. In short, *GDP only provides an overall measure of economic output of a given nation and speaks nothing of individual living standards or the overall well-being of a population.*

As an example, consider a nation that exports 100 percent of its production (Iraq for instance, which currently has a 95 percent rate of production exportation due to oil) might have a high GDP but not necessarily a high standard of living. Many other factors are involved in determination of living standards, such as employment and wage data, inflation, interest rates, currency exchange rates, debt levels, fiscal and monetary policy, and government benefits. Finally, quality of life is determined by other factors unrelated to finances such as life span, work week, minimum required vacation days, social factors, and many other variables. Incidentally, America is the only developed nation without required vacation days in the workplace.

The counterargument is that while GDP data may not provide an accurate measure of living standards, trends in living conditions tend to move in the direction of changing GDP numbers. While that may be true over a long time frame, in my opinion that cannot be said necessarily for less than a five-year period. Yet, when GDP figures are released each quarter, the stock and bond markets react as if this number provided an accurate picture of the economy, when this is rarely the case.

Shortfalls in Accounting Adequately for Deficits

Because consumer spending accounts for about 66 percent of the U.S. GDP, and since the majority of goods purchased in America are produced overseas in full or in part, *GDP growth indicates the extent of exportation of America's asset base when America is running large annual deficits.* In order to better understand this rationale, recall that each federal deficit is added to the national debt, which is financed by selling U.S. treasuries. And because foreign nations have financed 50 percent of this debt, the end result is that America has been trading ownership rights for imported goods. Therefore, *even if GDP data indicates net productivity, this data does not factor in the deficit incurred as a result of government spending or the trade imbalance, all of which adds to the national debt and decreases America's net worth or wealth.*

As well, consider that the most recent portion of the annual deficits have been financed by foreign nations to the tune of 99 percent in 2004, and by 81 percent between 2003 and 2005. If you were selling your goods and services to a customer who could not afford to pay using cash, wouldn't you extend them credit? Sure you would; you'd benefit two-fold in receiving profits from sales and financing charges.

Many point to America's annual 5.0 percent GDP growth rate over the past decade as a sign of its continued stability and economic dominance. However, during that same time period, *America's trade deficit has grown by over 25 percent per year, household debt as a percentage of disposable income has doubled, and household savings has declined by 75 percent.* What does that tell you? To me it says America's "growth" has been fueled by credit spending that has been grossly disproportionate to this "growth" (figure 13-12). And credit spending is certainly no indicator of wealth, but lack thereof.

Figure 11-1. Gross Domestic Product (percent annualized change), 1987-2006

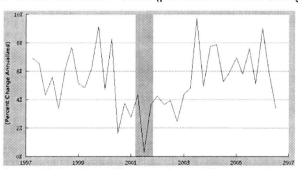

Source: U.S. Department of Commerce: Bureau of Economic Analysis,
St. Louis Fed Reserve 2006

America has been consuming much more than it produces for three decades. Early on, this excess consumption was cushioned by the enormous wealth surplus created after WWII. However, the consumption trends from the past 15 years have surfaced due to the depletion of its post-war wealth. As a result, America is now faced with a huge debt burden that has been financed by foreign central banks and both domestic and foreign financial institutions mainly representing the wealthy.

America's global competitors have been transformed into its bankers and suppliers, providing financing for its undisciplined government and consumer spending practices. This chronic behavior has allowed foreign nations to gain more influence over America, both economically and politically. And when they decide to no longer lend the American government money, interest rates will skyrocket to double digits and the dollar will nose dive. There are several other criticisms using GDP data to compare living standards with those of foreign nations, but for the remainder of this discussion, I will focus on potential distortions of the GDP within a single nation.

Failure to Account for Savings and Debt

Calculation of GDP also neglects to factor in the external effects of saving versus spending. Japan's case is particularly illustrative of this point. The savings rate in Japan has been high since the NIKKEI collapsed nearly decade ago. As well, Japanese companies have been investing large amounts of capital overseas (e.g. auto facilities, insurance and media in the U.S.) resulting in a much lower GDP than one might expect.

In the case of America, decades of declining savings and increased debt burdens are not factored into the GDP numbers. Meanwhile, this borrowed money tends to falsely inflate the GDP, similar to the increase in cash flows that occurs when companies borrow money. Likewise, *economies experiencing asset bubbles (eg. real estate and the stock market) tend to show higher GDP figures than in reality since consumption is higher than can be maintained over an extended period.* And during these asset bubbles the credit bubble grows along with the GDP. This is the current state of America.

Failure to Account for Resource Depletion

Growth sustainability cannot be predicted by looking at the GDP. Upon initial glance, it appears that some nations (eg. in the Middle East) are able to maintain high GDP numbers despite the lack of industrialization. In the case of the Middle East, productivity is solely dependent upon the amount of fossil fuels remaining. And because natural resources are limited, some nations disregard environmental protection laws in favor of increasing production, such as in the United States, China, Europe, and Canada. However, in the long run huge expenses could be incurred for cleaning the environmental mess that was made decades earlier.

Accordingly, short-term gains in GDP are inflated, since the economic activities that have led to GDP data have created future liabilities that have not been reflected in America's financial statements, such as the massive liabilities for mandatory expenditures. Therefore, *GDP data should be adjusted for estimates of contingent liabilities that may be incurred as a result of say, a nation's disregard for maintaining a clean environment* and government benefits, similar to the practice required by all publicly traded corporations.

Failure to Adjust for Net Output

Another shortfall of GDP data is that *it measures output that produces no net change or productivity*, such as that seen for reconstruction of New Orleans after hurricane Katrina. While capital was pumped into the region to help restore the living standard of those affected by this catastrophe, no net improvement was made relative to before the disaster (unless you count the estimated $1.5 billion stolen from FEMA by some). Yet, GDP data assumes that these expenditures resulted in improvements in living standards.

GDP data counts government spending at all levels, from the war in Iraq and hurricane Katrina, to homeland security. And *despite President Bush's enormous spending spree, tax revenues as a percentage of GDP have not been this low in many years* (see figures 15-1 and 15-8). What does that tell you? Basically, the government has been borrowing money to pump up into the economy without registering commensurate returns. *If these investments had been successful, America would have net job and real wage growth, affordable energy, utilities, and healthcare.* But we see a much different picture despite record federal and trade deficits and record consumer and national debt levels. The overall impact of these trends can be seen by the weakness of the dollar.

Thus, it's easy to see that *a nation that is increasing its debt can show healthy GDP numbers* when in fact the picture is not as rosy as reported. This is especially true when government spending is accounting for a large amount of the GDP growth, as in America's case. *Therefore, when examining GDP data, one should investigate where and how the productivity occurred, whether there was a net improvement, and what costs (debt or deficit) were incurred, rather than focusing on the magnitude of the number.*

Failure to Report Year-over-year Changes

When the Commerce Department reports GDP figures each quarter, the data is not reported like a U.S. corporation. When a corporation provides an earnings statement, it makes comparisons of revenue, earnings, etc. from the same quarter in the previous year (called year-over-year reporting). In contrast, the U.S. *government reports changes in GDP relative to the previous quarter.* In addition, each *quarterly GDP figure is annualized or multiplied by a factor of four, which implies that this quarterly figure will continue over the next three quarters.* Why is it that corporations report year-over-year numbers but the government reports a rolling, highly inaccurate, annualized number?

As far as I am aware, all other developed nations report GDP changes as year-over-year. Why does this matter anyway? Consider that year-over-year numbers minimize the effects of business and economic cycles. The fact is that all businesses (and therefore the government) experience changes in business health and earnings due to seasonal or business cycle fluctuations that are inherent to their industry, the dynamics of the company, and the economic cycle. Therefore, in order to minimize the effects of these variables, companies report the year-over-year changes.

For instance, let's take a look at Mattel, a toy manufacturer that is known to generate the majority of its revenues during the month of December. Let's assume that the fourth quarter is responsible for 70 percent of its annual earnings (an accurate assumption), while subsequent quarters contribute 10 percent equally to its earnings. If Mattel reported its fourth quarter earnings like the U.S. government, it would appear as if its growth was exploding during the first quarter of earnings announcements.

Therefore, because each quarterly GDP figure is extrapolated over 12 months, it's virtually impossible to detect accurate GDP trends even if the numbers, when reported were accurate. But as we shall see next, accurate reporting is rare.

GDP Numbers are Inaccurate for Five Years

If all of these considerations were not enough to cause you to reexamine the use of GDP data, you should keep in mind that *the government provides GDP revisions for up to five years* after the data was first reported. That's why you often hear adjustments to GDP numbers long after they were reported. It's also why the government often changes the dates of recessions several months and sometimes years later. While these adjustments might be a valuable exercise for historians, they do nothing to alert consumers and investors of the current and future expected economic environment. Hence, there is no way to consistently and accurately predict future growth trends using GDP data due to these inaccuracies.

The official definition of a recession is two consecutive quarters of negative economic growth, as measured by GDP data. As a recent example of the inaccuracy of GDP numbers, on July 30, 2004, the Bureau of Economic Analysis (BEA) issued its revised GDP data for 2001. *And according to the definition of a recession, we now know that there was none during 2001, since the latest numbers do not show two consecutive quarters of declining GDP growth.* As a matter of fact, the economy was reported to have grown by 0.8 percent in 2001. Looking back to that period, I leave it you to determine if America was in a recession.

In conclusion, the basic rules of reasoning never change. And when one begins to think they can paint an accurate picture of a complex multivariate dynamic such as the health of the economy or living standards by looking at one number, they are fooling themselves and the people they represent. The best way to measure economic growth and changes in living standards is to consider many other macroeconomic indicators in addition to GDP, such as interest rate (yield curve) and inflation trends (the CPI and PPI, core and non-core), trade imbalances, currency exchange rate trends, job loss and recovery, underemployment, real wage and benefit growth, debt and money flow trends. (2)

With thousands of economists and other experts working for the government, it seems strange they're unwilling or unable to provide a comprehensive analysis of the economy based on other data. Then again, the current system of illusion and confusion serves Washington just fine. Yet, most people serve as parrots, mimicking the same lines they hear from the many confused and myopic economists in their ivory towers. With all the forecasts economists make, I know of none who have made a fortune in the stock market as a result of their "timely and valuable" economic analysis and forecasts.

---

(2) Note that indicators such as trade imbalances, exchange rates, debt and money flow provide better real-time estimates of economic strength.

Hedonic Pricing: Washington's Best Friend

How is it possible that inflation has remained low over the past decade while housing, healthcare, energy and higher education costs have skyrocketed? Does that seem reasonable to you? How has the government been able to conclude that inflation doesn't present a problem for the economy? As it stands currently, while government data indicates an average rate of inflation, there has been a 120 percent increase in inflation growth in less than two years. I don't care if inflation was 0.2 percent; when you have a rapid increase such as what has occurred, it's going to take a big toll on the economy (figure 11-2). Furthermore, how can the government report inflation without measuring food and energy costs? Does that seem reasonable?

Washington and its partnering economic organizations take a very rigid approach to economic analysis that often leads to myopic conclusions. Instead of forecasting based on trend analysis and global macroeconomics, many government economists focus on daily and monthly data as reported. And as we have seen, this data is not only inaccurate, but it doesn't reflect other issues of larger magnitude, scope and duration.

Figure 11-2. Consumer Price Index (core-inflation)

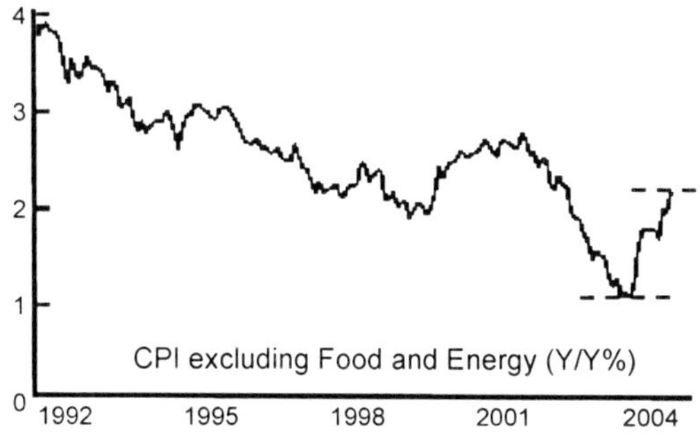

Notice the surge in inflation from the deflationary levels late in 2003 to average levels of 2.5% in late 2004; a 120% change in about 14 months.

CPI excluding Food and Energy (Y/Y%)

Source: Board of Governors, Federal Reserve (2005)

As previously discussed, Washington feels that the best indicator of the nation's economic health is the quarterly GDP, which is extrapolated over the next three quarters and subject to revision for up to five years. But Washington uses another method to distort economic data. Similar to many economic numbers reported by the U.S. government, the GDP is also subject to what is known as *hedonic price indexing, which can at times create investments when there were none or much less than reported, resulting in an understatement of inflation and improved living standards.*

The primary use of the hedonic pricing method is to identify price factors based on the premise that price is determined both by internal and external characteristics of goods and services. The most common example of the hedonic pricing method is in the housing market, whereby the price of a property is determined by the characteristics of the house (size, appearance, features, condition) as well as those of the surrounding neighborhood (accessibility to schools and shopping, crime rate, level of water and air pollution, value of other homes, noise, traffic, etc.).

Application of the hedonic pricing method provides an estimate of the extent to which each factor affects the price. In other words, *price is rated high or low relative to the direct and indirect features of the product (or house, in the example above). When comparisons of price change are measured over time, a determination is made whether these changes represent low or high prices relative to the previous reporting period.* Advocates of hedonic pricing argue that it provides a way for the government to account for improvement in the quality of goods and services by adjusting the price or relative amount of inflation that has occurred.

Altering Inflation Data

Washington's use of hedonic pricing explains why both core (includes healthcare but not food and energy) and non-core CPI (which includes food and energy) numbers have not been that bad considering healthcare and energy costs have skyrocketed. In essence, *Washington uses hedonic pricing as a way to hide the effects of inflation* from consumers not because they are evil, but because it provides a way to manipulate data when needed to boost consumer confidence. And they get away with this with little scrutiny because hedonic pricing is very difficult to calculate, is based upon the assumptions laid forth by the government, and there is little transparency in their methodologies.

Even Bill Gross, the fund manager of the world's largest bond fund has stated that the manner in which the government calculates the CPI is a "con job" due to hedonic pricing. And he is not the only one. Many others also understand that the government distorts economic numbers to give the perception that the economy is much better than it really is. Unfortunately, you're not to going to hear much about these inaccurate reporting methods because the media lacks the intelligence to question anything besides the lifestyles of Hollywood celebrities. *As well, there is no financial incentive for large financial firms to blast the improper reporting of economic numbers since the majority of financial products rely on a bullish economy.*

Let's look at a working example of how hedonic pricing works. According to a price analysis of television sets for calculating the CPI in 2005 by Tim LaFleur, (a commodity specialist for the Bureau of Labor Statistics) while the price remained at $329.99 over several months, significant improvements were made such as a better screen. Using hedonic pricing, LaFleur concluded that these improvements resulted in an increase in valuation of these television sets by more than $135. Therefore, when determining inflation data for this product, he reduced the price value of these television sets by 29 percent (a deflationary effect) due to these improvements, although the sales price remained at $329.99. That sounds like "Enron accounting" to me.

The same method is used by the government for many other goods and services from computers to autos. The problem lies in the fact that consumers are still subject to the same price as far as their wallet is concerned. *It is inaccurate to assume that product improvements will enhance the consumer appeal of goods in the same manner as a price cut, unless we assume that capital is not the limiting factor.* While such an assumption might be moderately reasonable by an optimist during a strong economic expansion, (when money is plentiful) it is severely flawed during weak economic conditions.

What this means is that for goods and services that are provided to consumers with improvements over the previous economic reporting period, *hedonic pricing can effectively result in decreased inflation (or is deflationary)* if the cost is the same, or a smaller amount of inflation if the cost is higher, as long as the goods and services have been improved or additional features have been added.

While the hedonic pricing method has some merit for commodities, I hope you can appreciate the disconnect in equating a real price decline with enhancement of services or features which, according to hedonic pricing, has the effect of lowering the sales price of the item due to perceived enhanced consumer value. This is simply not true and in order to have any validity, *one must factor in the relative demand or need for these items. If this is not done, hedonic pricing could add a deflationary component to the economic data* resulting from improvements to say, 10 billion television sets; an amount that obviously will not be purchased by Americans anytime soon at any price, hedonic or real. Maybe you can begin to understand now why the inflation data over the past few years has been low, while energy, healthcare, higher education, and many other costs have been soaring.

Altering GDP

Prior to 2005, the government used hedonic pricing to calculate the change in productivity resulting from computer purchases by businesses. For instance, if a company bought a computer for $2000, then replaced it two years later at a cost of $1000 for a new one with twice the processing speed, this was considered to represent a four-fold increase in computing productivity, leading to a four-fold increase in economic productivity for that component of the GDP.

The rational was that the company replaced the computer for half the cost and with double the processing speed. Therefore, its productivity increased by four-fold per dollar spent, which added $4000 to the GDP, when in fact only $1000 should have been added. While Washington has since abandoned this exercise for the treatment of "computer productivity," it still uses hedonic pricing for GDP calculations of many other goods and services.

Converting Inflation into Debt

When you consider the trade imbalance with China, it becomes easy to see the effect of hedonic pricing. While Chinese imports have been inexpensive, (due to unfair trade practices and currency manipulation) the U.S. government has subsidized these costs through incurring a record trade deficit, which was financed in large part from the purchase of U.S. treasuries by China. And *Washington has been able to keep consumer spending high during stagnant economic conditions by passing out credit and transferring part of the costs of Chinese imports (using hedonic pricing) into the national debt.* Perhaps this is the "New Economy" that the government and Wall Street were referring to.

Why Distort Inflation Data?

I have detailed how GDP data is inaccurate. As well, I have discussed how the use of hedonic pricing can lead to higher GDP and lower inflation data. It should be obvious why Washington would want to inflate GDP numbers. But why would the government distort inflation numbers? Quite frankly, when you have an economy as vulnerable to a disaster as in America, the worst thing would be for consumers to lose confidence.

But there's also a direct financial incentive to understate inflation. Consider that each year, Social Security (via CPI-W) and Medicare benefit increases are earmarked to the CPI. And with these programs already in trouble, Washington is doing all that it can to divvy up cost of living adjustments. The CPI is also used to adjust for annual changes in lease payments, wages in union contracts, food-stamp benefits, alimony, and to determine tax brackets. Therefore, miscalculation of this one number can have a broad-reaching impact on benefits and wages to millions of Americans, as well as limiting the liabilities of government programs.

Hiding Debt

While the reported figure for U.S. debt stands at around $8.5 trillion, there is an amount that has been hidden in addition to the $8 trillion or so that Washington has borrowed from Social Security and other trust funds.

State Debt

Because states are no longer receiving their fair share of tax revenues from the federal government, most have had to increase their amount of debt by issuing municipal bonds. This has shifted more of the federal debt burden onto each state, causing further financial strains for state-funded programs. When this hidden source of federal debt has been accounted for, it could add up to 50 percent more than has been reported.

Over the next decade, as states continue to struggle with deficits and cuts to programs such as Medicaid, education, transportation and many other vital services, there will be hundreds of new fees placed upon businesses and individuals in order to ease this debt burden. Soon, many states may begin to look like California, which already has hundreds of hidden taxes and fees that have forced thousands of small business owners to relocate.

Already, many cities have imposed enormous taxes for hotels, sales tax hikes to finance sports stadiums, and annual fees for pet ownership. The hidden telephone taxes (local, state and federal) that have gradually appeared over the past two decades are most likely a prelude to the America's future fiscal polices.

Illustration of Hidden Taxes from an Actual Telephone Bill from AT&T	
Total Bill (incl. taxes and surcharges):	$75.78
Total Bill (less taxes):	$52.66
Total Taxes and Fees:	$23.12
Telephone Tax Rate: ⟶	44%
Surcharges and Other Fees	
Federal Subscriber Line Charge	$5.67
911 Service Fee	$0.62
911 Equalization Surcharge	$0.07
TIF Reimbursement $ Recovery	$0.80
State TIF Assessment	$0.27
State Utility Gross Receipts Assessment	$0.02
Federal Universal Service Fee	$1.25
Federal Regulatory Fee	$0.06
State Universal Service	$3.69
Expanded Local Calling Service	$0.04
State Rate Group Reclass Surcharge	$0.93
Municipal Charge	$1.45
Taxes	
Federal (local Charges)	$0.00
Federal (Non-regulated & Toll Charges)	$0.00
State and Local (Local Charges)	$6.57
State & Local (Non-regulated & Toll Charges)	$1.68

Total Debt

Excluding the two bubble periods, during twentieth century-America, the amount of total debt outstanding as a percentage of GDP ranged between 130 and 150 percent. When the stock market reached its pre-crash peak in 1929, the total debt as a percentage of GDP rose to around 200 percent. Thereafter, it soared to about 265 percent within four years, as the effects of the depression set in (figure 11-3). *America's second credit bubble began in the early 1980s and has since swelled to surpass levels seen during the Great Depression. Without irony, the appearance and growth of this bubble coincides with the period of declining median incomes and living standards in America (figure 11-4).*

The total national debt (combined government, business and household borrowing) grew by over $13 trillion from 1990 to 2001, to over $35 trillion, or nearly three times the GDP. As of March 2006, it stood at nearly $42 trillion, (or 319.8 percent of GDP) representing a 20 percent increase in just five years. This type of massive debt growth is extremely risky and economists in Washington have no benign remedies. As a matter of fact, *all of the taxes paid each year by Americans are not even enough to pay the interest (over $350 billion) on the federal debt.* If a company were in this situation, it would be forced into bankruptcy protection (see tables 6.3 and 6.4, appendix).

Figure 11-3. Total Credit Market Debt (All Sectors) as a Percentage of U.S. GDP

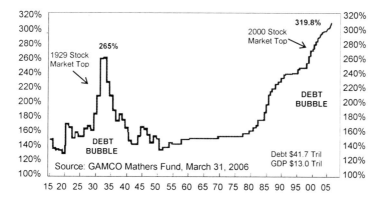

As short-term interest rates move higher, consumers will find it increasingly more difficult to make interest payments on the variable-rate loans, (ARMs and credit cards) forcing millions to file for bankruptcy, or even worse, into debt consolidation. This is already happening. President Bush's Bankruptcy Reform Act could not have come at a worse time, as it will force millions into many years of "debt prison."

The entire economy will be hit hard as millions of Americans will have very little disposable income. In addition, as long-term interest rates climb to their historical mean, consumer and business financing will be much more expensive and could lead to a meltdown in the economy due to America's overall inherent weakness and dependency on debt.

Hiding America's Decline

America's Service Economy

Over the past two decades, quality manufacturing jobs have continued to evaporate from American borders, transforming it into a service-centric economy, fueled by occupations that in many cases provide intangible services, such as consultants—financial, business, strategy, operations, human resources, sales, marketing, security, and technology—to name a few. These are amongst the more "highly-valued" occupations within America's service economy. And although the shift from manufacturing to service labor began during the 1980s, it has accelerated over the past decade due to the free trade policies of Washington that continue to destroy America's most critical job base.

Unlike the overseas job migration that occurred from 1980 through the early 1990s, today white-collar jobs are also being replaced by foreign counterparts for a fraction of the cost. And this remains unchecked by Washington policies. Therefore, *even if Americans were better educated in science and engineering, the effects of free trade on its economic system would do little to provide better wages and job security.*

As a consequence of this shift into a service economy, it seems as if being known as a consultant of some kind, whether you are a sanitation consultant or a retirement consultant is the trend in America today. In contrast to the mandatory service providers (teachers, law enforcement officers, healthcare providers, etc.) that have been in existence for centuries, other occupations providing non-essential services rarely existed prior to the dissolution of America's manufacturing industry—landscapers, event planners, nannies, personal assistants, housekeepers, etc. No doubt, many of these service providers contribute valuable services that would be difficult to duplicate. However, the problem is that in many cases there are simply too many service providers chasing too few dollars, focusing on corporate America or the needs of America's wealthy.

However, one does not have to be a part of America's wealthy elite to feel the need for these services. Two-income households need daycare or nannies to raise their children while they are at work. And rather than taking care of their property, many have hired landscaping companies to do what used to be thought of as a recreational activity because many are too busy working. Some even send their pets to a daycare center. Busy individuals would rather pay for laundry services than do it themselves because they don't have enough time. Others are just too lazy and/or are using credit irresponsibly.

Surely Americans need business services in order to free up more valuable time for their personal and professional lives. As well, some of these services require a certain expertise that is difficult to obtain or takes years of experience to achieve. But we must ask how much net economic value is being provided by America's service economy. Is it generating enhanced productivity growth relative to that seen by America's manufacturing industry during the post-war period? *The fact that the majority of Americans are employed in service industries that are focused on servicing the needs of Americans implies that the U.S. economy is much less productive on a global scale, relative to the post-war period.*

Rather than generating foreign revenues, much of America's service labor depends upon that of other Americans and American corporations. *This lop-sided economy has increased America's dependency on imports and credit spending in the face of diminished productivity, as the primary way to mask declining living standards, accounting for America's long trend of overconsumption.*

Creating industries that serve Americans does little to increase its international productivity and competitiveness. A nation dominated by a service economy will ultimately serve the needs of the upper class, helping to free up their resources. As a result of these dynamics, *America is rapidly becoming a nation of the rich and poor, having lost its most vital asset—the middle class—by transferring stable jobs overseas that were once a predominant feature of the American economy.*

Declining Living Standards

The growth of two-income households in America has seen the rise of nannies, daycare centers, and housekeepers as a necessity for those who can afford these services; and as a luxury for those who cannot but can pay for them with credit. But we must ask why both parents are even working in the first place. Is it because neither parent wants to stay at home or because it's too difficult for most families to survive in with a single income? The answer should be obvious. No one wants to have their children in the hands strangers.

Unfortunately, this trend is partly responsible for the decay of family and social values over the past two decades. In many cases, both parents are busy working to pay expenses due to their greed for consumer goods, expensive gas-guzzlers, and huge homes they have no need for. In other cases, many are working overtime to pay for basic necessities such as energy, utilities, and healthcare—just to get by. Ultimately, America's youth pays the price for a nation that has fallen victim to the effects of declining competitiveness and consumer extortion by corporate America.

If the two-income household decided to shift to one income, declining living standards would be immediately felt by the average American household. Likewise, if illegal aliens were no longer available to subsidize the costs of consumer goods and services through low-wage labor, many Americans would soon feel the effects. *America's declining living standards have also been masked by the wide availability of consumer credit from financial institutions.* Yet, most still have not figured out that their credit card debt is really a variable-interest rate loan tied to the earnings goals of the companies that issue them.

America has become a nation focused on consumption. And its unwillingness to concede a strong trend of declining living standards has created the largest consumer credit debt per capita in the history of the world. Because they are ill-prepared to compete globally, *Americans continue to consume more goods and services than they produce in an attempt to maintain the same lifestyle their parents provided them with.*

For others, the inability to provide basic necessities is becoming a huge problem. Today the combined monthly energy bill (gasoline, gas utilities, and electricity) can easily reach $1000 at current prices; that's $12,000 of after-tax income needed just to keep the lights on, a livable climate indoors, and to get around. When you add other expenses such as food, housing, healthcare and other basic costs needed to raise a family, *it's unimaginable that America will ever again be dominated by one-income households..*

Figure 11-4. U.S. Median Family Income Growth has Slowed Dramatically Since 1980[a]

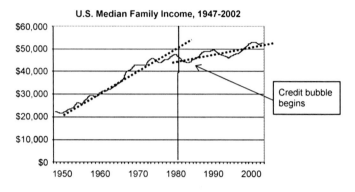

U.S. Median Family Income, 1947-2002

Credit bubble begins

[a] this figure uses 2002 dollars

Source: U.S. Bureau of Census. Created by Munnell, Alicia H. Hatch, Robert E. Lee, James G. "Why is Life Expectancy So Low in the United States?" Figure 11, CRR Number 21. August 2004.

We see a partial reflection of America's living standards when comparing its income discrepancy with other developed nations. While the United States has the second highest GDP per capita in the world (figure 11-5), *the income discrepancy between the top and bottom 10 percent is second highest among all OECD nations other than Mexico* (figure 11-6). In addition, the median income for America's bottom 40 percent wage earners is in the middle of these same nations (figure 11-7). In contrast, Western Europe and Japan have a much better income distribution. Even America's number one trading partner, Canada has a better income distribution. This data alone supports the notion that much of middle-class America has already disappeared.

Figure 11-5. America Ranks Near the Top in GDP per Capita (OECD Nations, 1999)

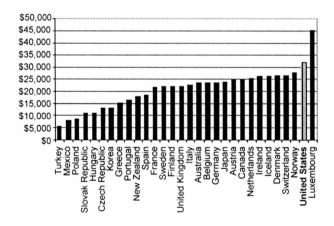

Source: World Bank (2003). Created by Munnell, Alicia H. Hatch, Robert E. Lee, James G. "Why is Life Expectancy So Low in the United States?" Figure 3, CRR Number 21. August 2004.

Figure 11-6. America's Income Distribution is Far Less Equal

Ratio of Income for Top 10 and Bottom 10 Percent of OECD Nations (late 1990s)

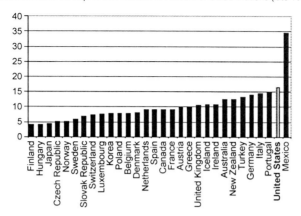

Source: World Bank (2003). Created by Munnell, Alicia H. Hatch, Robert E. Lee, James G. "Why is Life Expectancy So Low in the United States?" Figure 4, CRR Number 21. August 2004.

Figure 11-7. Average Income (As a % of GDP) for Lowest 40% of Each Nation's Population

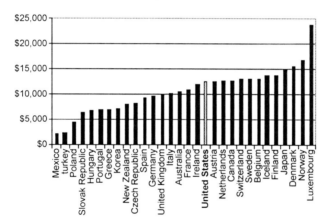

Source: World Bank (2003), based on Authors' calculations. Created by Munnell, Alicia H. Hatch, Robert E. Lee, James G. "Why is Life Expectancy So Low in the United States?" Figure 5, CRR Number 21. August 2004.

Domestic Outsourcing

Due to the complexity of modern economies, the basic necessities required by Americans have never been more numerous and costly. Back in the 1950s, while auto transportation was common, it was mainly reserved for middle-class workers and the wealthy. There were no mobile phones or computers back then either.

Modern America has become dependent on high-tech gadgets, and most Americans need a car, mobile phone, computer, and Internet access to survive the demands of modern workplace dynamics. And unlike in the past, utilities, healthcare, education costs and overall taxes are much higher (if we look at total state, federal, and local taxes). Thus, it takes a lot more money to get by today relative than decades ago. What that means is that a larger share of wages is being used for necessities, representing a hidden tax on the poor.

Therefore, we should address the impact of relatively low minimum wages on America's economy.

You may think that the minimum wage does not affect the stock market but it does; keeping it low is a way to increase productivity while curtailing the money supply. As you might suspect, the stock market does not perform well when the money supply is low because consumers have less access to credit which diminishes spending. However, the Federal Reserve alters the money supply to minimize the severity of economic contractions, while maximizing the intensity of economic expansions.

At $5.15 per hour, the U.S. minimum wage has not been raised since 1997. Meanwhile, Congress has received eight pay raises during this period. Consider that since the 1950s, the minimum wage on an inflation-adjusted basis is down by 50 percent and should be over $9.00 per hour.

The low minimum wage was partly responsible for the cheap labor that fueled the previous economic boom and served as an experiment by the government to show how outsourcing (or its domestic equivalent, insourcing via illegals) can mask the effects of a declining economy. Needless to say, the experiment has been successful, but only for the short-term. Similar to a nation that disregards global pollution standards in order to maximize productivity, there will be high costs in later years to cleanup the mess created by the lure of corruption, deceit and greed.

Raising the minimum wage not only benefits those working at fast food chains and retail outlets but it improves the wages of all Americans by inducing an upward pressure on higher paying jobs. A higher minimum wage can be thought of as a way for corporate America to give back more to working-class Americans as opposed to its wealthy shareholders. As well, *a higher minimum wage would encourage more consumers to both spend and save; a combination not seen in America since the economic boom of the post-war era.* Yet, while the minimum wage continues to be frozen in time, CEO compensation continues to skyrocket (11-8).

Due to the higher basic living costs of most metropolitan regions, several states have enacted their own minimum wage above the federal level in order to provide workers for badly needed entry-level jobs. And although the federal minimum wage needs to be raised above $9.00 per hour, it is unlikely to reach this level anytime soon, at least without major tax concessions for the wealthy.

The reason why politicians have not raised the minimum wage in ten years explains why they've allowed so many illegal aliens into American borders—to make up some of the slack in the declining efficiency of the American economy. But this cannot go on forever without a big price to pay. Already, illegal aliens have exhausted much the nation's social service programs. If you pay a visit to virtually any state, local, or federal social assistance facility in America, from the local IRS office to the county health department, you are likely to see a long line of non-English speaking individuals, many of which are illegal aliens. Even the Social Security Administration is prepared to assist these individuals with signs written in Spanish. Will years of wage suppression for the bottom wage earners, along with years of loosely guarded borders provide more benefits to America than the growth of liabilities of its social insurance programs? It's always easy to spend now and worry about paying later. But payments will need to be made at some point.

Figure 11-8. Ratio of CEO to Minimum Wage (1965-2005)

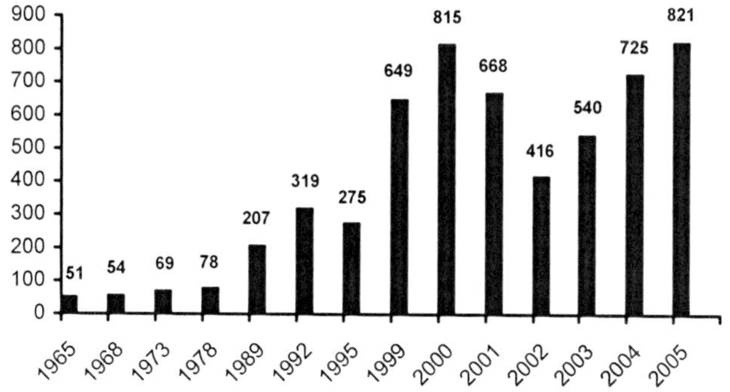

Source: Economic Policy Institute Data of Mercer Survey Analysis

Justifying Extortion

State and Local Government Taxes

As a way to extract more tax revenues, state and local governments have come up with excuses to tax or control certain industries and assets at their convenience. For instance, rather than ban alcohol and tobacco products, the most addictive legalized substances in America, states have chosen to profit at the expense of their unfortunate victims.

Property ownership was once thought of as a part of the "American Dream," but no more because Americans really do not own the property they paid for and live on. For the past two decades, there has been a widespread trend of eminent domain seizures by state and local governments, forcing people out of their homes only to compensate them with settlements that are in many cases unfair. This is done as a desperate attempt to generate higher tax revenues from new development projects. The rational is that older neighborhoods can be "put to better use" by allowing developers to construct luxury high rises and commercial buildings that will generate higher tax revenues for local governments. And although this practice is without question unconstitutional, it continues to gain support by state and local governments facing budget problems.

In some regions property taxes have become so high that they can amount to three times the annual mortgage payment by year thirty. And as you know, if you cannot pay your annual property taxes, the local government will foreclose on your home. *I find it very disturbing that a non-consumption tax based on a very inaccurate and highly subjective valuation method is used to extort taxpayer money from American home owners on an annual basis as a condition of continued property ownership.*

Taxing the Poor, Vegas-Style

Three decades ago, the only gambling permitted by the government was in Las Vegas, Atlantic City, and certain areas reserved for Native Americans. However, as states continued to struggle with annual budgets, they began sponsoring lotteries, stating as their purpose, to provide educational funding rather than raise taxes. Today, virtually every state participates in lotteries. And many have turned their lotto programs into a huge business.

There is no dispute that gambling is a very destructive and addictive behavior, mainly affecting low-income Americans. Lotteries are just another form of gambling but are even more dangerous than casinos due to the availability and low cost of participation. *Yet, states have now added to this addiction by advertising their lotteries on television and radio stations, billboards and buses. They even run television ads during Christmas season to encourage people to buy lotto tickets as gifts for family members!* And each time a big winner is announced, they inspire more Americans to try their luck by holding televised press conferences to show how happy the winners are.

Meanwhile, *state lotteries offer lower odds of winning than any casino game in the United States. While states claim lotteries help fund education, I have previously discussed that America's K-12 problems have nothing to do with the lack of money, but rather how it is spent and managed.* Over the next decade, states will begin to use lotto proceeds to fund Medicaid, as their only way to deal with these rising costs. And many states will pass laws allowing casinos, as they struggle to balance their annual budgets.

How is it that the government can actually justify profiting from addictive and destructive behaviors in exchange for tax revenues? Why is it that only the government can have lotteries but no one else can? Why is it that the government is in control of and places heavy taxes on America's most addictive substances such as alcohol and tobacco rather than banning them? *I call these activities government-justified exploitation and it must stop.*

Death by Taxation

State governments have many ways to raise taxes, but they often impose new taxes in a selective or silent manner so voters are less aware of them. Unfortunately, many of these "silent taxes" are usually targeted towards the poor, causing an even larger income disparity.

First, as a way to exploit the tobacco controversy, state governments realized they could repair their broken budgets by joining forces and suing the big name tobacco makers. They claimed that tobacco use added billions of dollars in extra Medicaid expenses treating the chronically ill. This resulted in the landmark $300 billion tobacco settlement for around eighteen states. Other states chose to attack the tobacco giants individually and won their own damage awards. Oddly enough, for some reason, you never hear of individual smokers suing tobacco companies and winning. It's clear to me that the government struck deals the tobacco companies behind closed doors.

With this settlement money, states have done nothing to help citizens stop smoking, nor have they provided individual awards to smokers affected with tobacco-related disease and death. Instead, politicians have spent much of this money on other projects as needed. Some states have tried to replace declining revenues from tobacco farmers by funding, of all things biotechnology programs. Meanwhile, each day thousands of Americans die directly from tobacco-related illnesses, while each year hundreds of thousands are diagnosed with chronic disease due to the effects of tobacco, including cardiovascular disease, America's number one killer.

One might assume that states would want to help addicted smokers quit the habit of an almost certain premature death, yet this is not at all the case. *Where are the tobacco addiction treatment centers that should be in every neighborhood? With $300 billion, one would think that smokers deserve some effective treatment programs.* I certainly want to quit. Where is the assistance I need? Meanwhile, the various nicotine treatment medications, both over-the-counter and prescription (anti-depressants) are largely ineffective due to the variability and complexity involved with nicotine addiction.

Despite this, these medications do help some quit what is often inaccurately referred to as a "habit." Yet, strangely, insurance plans won't even cover them. I find it puzzling that the government has not pressured insurers to cover these medications even though they are only modestly effective. For some, it could be the difference between dieing at 60 versus living past 80.

The fact is that state governments have no intention of banning tobacco products because they continue to receive significant revenues each year from the cigarette tax. And they raise these taxes as needed to cover budget shortfalls and to fund other programs that the majority will benefit from. As their excuse for raising tobacco taxes, they state that further increases will discourage tobacco use; a completely false statement. Yet, they manage to raise taxes gradually by modest increments so that addicted victims of tobacco products barely notice. *If they truly wanted to use taxation as a weapon to stop tobacco use, each state would raise the tax immediately by $20 per pack.*

It's easy to tax what many experts consider the most addictive drug in America and gain the support of the people since, without cigarette taxes, state governments would have to raise other taxes that would affect everyone, and therefore their chances at re-election. And due to the enigmatic stigma by the public over smokers, any attack on this victimized group is not only welcomed, but often viewed as being "politically correct."

Washington should ban all tobacco products. This would save millions of lives and trillions of dollars in future Medicaid and Medicare expenses. But in America, it's not about saving lives or doing what is right; it's only about big money. The government continues to profit by allowing tobacco companies to profit as they facilitate the premature death of millions. This must stop now.

If you tax a minority based on the premise that they have chosen to pay the financial and health costs of tobacco use by their own free will, it seems like a fair proposition. However, the fact is that *smokers cannot quit this highly addictive activity without a very specialized treatment regimen.* And despite the common misperceptions by the non-smoking public, many drug-addiction specialists have stated that *cigarette smoking is the most addictive form of substance abuse on the planet* due to its rapid delivery to the brain, its widespread availability, and relatively low cost.

Land as Collateral?

During the Johnson administration, when the national debt exceeded the U.S. government's gold reserves, France demanded that America collateralize its loans with gold, causing several other nations to make the same demands in subsequent years. When President Nixon refused to honor these requests, he realized that America needed a way to ensure the world that the U.S. government had sufficient assets to back the dollar. Perhaps coincidentally, he created the Environmental Protection Agency in the early 1970s, which began seizing land rich in minerals from American landowners.

The government continues this practice today by declaring certain areas of land wilderness preservation sites, roadless areas, wetlands, and many other designations—all for the purpose of preventing land owners from tapping into regions of rich mineral deposits, thereby securing the collateral needed to assure continued foreign loans. This theory is reasonable, especially considering the fact that only about 10 percent of America has been developed and therefore does not face any shortage of natural habitats for wildlife. There appears to be no shortage of space in America, other than that due to government-sanctioned areas protected by the EPA.

Figure 11-9. Areas the U.S. Government has Sanctioned as Protected by the EPA (black)

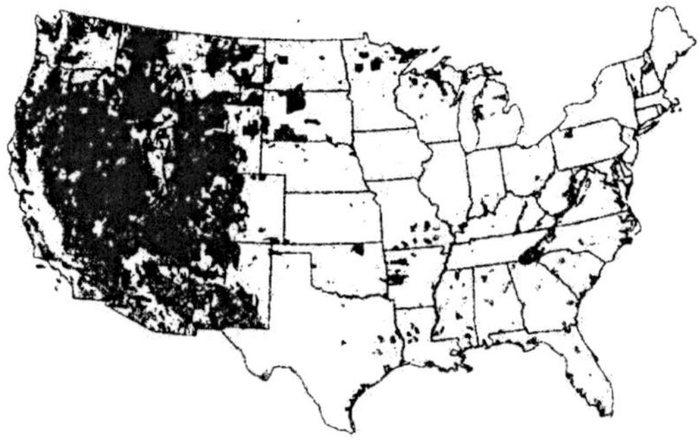

Regions of land sanctioned by the government as environmental protection regions are in black.

Education

Nothing in America is immune from government deceit. Even President Bush's *No Child Left Behind* program is the latest to be exposed as a fraud. According to a study conducted by the staff at the Associated Press, President Bush has allowed many students' national test scores to be "left behind" in the name of cultivating the perception of academic achievement and success of this program.

Under this law, signed by President Bush in 2002, all public schools must be proficient in reading and math by 2014. Students must be tested in grades 3 through 8 and at least once in high school. All schools are required to report scores based on race, poverty, migrant status, English proficiency, and special education. According to the guidelines, when a school fails in one category it has failed in all categories. In addition, *this law requires that all schools receiving federal assistance demonstrate annual improvements for students in all racial categories, or risk penalties such as extension of the school year, changing the curriculum, and firing the administration and/or teachers.*

When this law was passed, it prompted protest from many educators who felt they didn't have the resources or level of disciplinary authority to facilitate the improvements over the time period mandated by the law. As well, *intra-familial instability and parental irresponsibility have been cited by educators as the most common reasons for failure of many children to attain core levels of education.*

But due to a loophole in this law, many teachers may not have to worry about their limitations to improve the educational standards for their students. It has been recently uncovered that *states are helping schools get around the reporting criteria by allowing administrators to ignore scores of racial groups that they consider "too small to be statistically significant."*

As the scores have continued to disappoint, over two dozen states have successfully petitioned the government to allow discarding a larger number of racial groups. Today, *most schools are permitted to ignore the test scores of up to 50 students in any one racial group. The results of a recent study by the Associated Press found that in the 2003 to 2004 school year about 1.9 million scores or 1 in 14 were not counted in the final results.* The vast majority of these uncounted scores were from minorities such as Hispanics, African-Americans, and Asians. As a consequence, *minorities are seven times as likely to have their scores not counted as whites.* And the rate of uncounted scores among minorities is rising each year.

Spread across America in equal distributions, these excluded scores might appear to be reasonable statistical exclusions. However, consider that in California alone, more than 400,000 scores were not counted, and in Texas the total excluded was 257,000. According to Education Secretary Margaret Spellings, excluding the scores of an estimated 1.9 million Americans is "too many."

America's education problem is not something that can be fixed so easily or rapidly. *The solution lies in downsizing the number of administrators, whose salaries make up a large chunk of education expenses, implementing strict accountability standards for monitoring expenditures, ensuring school boards do not have business interests for themselves or their friends, and more involvement of parents.*

Ultimately, it is the parents' responsibility to provide a healthy family environment conducive to learning, ensure their children have the proper level of motivation, and exert the sufficient amount of effort to encourage and assist their children in obtaining a sound education. Unfortunately, the American family unit is in rapid decay due in part to the consequences of two-income households. As discussed in Chapter Three, the demise of the family unit has had broad-reaching effects, and the failure of America's K-12 public school system serves as just one example. You cannot easily solve a problem that is rooted in decades of socioeconomic and institutional decline. It will take much more time and effort than money.

The Global Oil Shortage

I've discussed the impending global oil shortage many times throughout this book. Yet, you'd be hard-pressed to hear the government or oil companies mention a shortage. They merely state that our oil needs continue to grow each day and more efforts (and therefore more money) will be needed for off-shore exploration. Rather than acknowledge the coming of peak oil, oil companies choose to focus on the total known oil reserves as a way to make Americans believe that there will be no oil shortages for several decades. This allows them to charge high prices at the pump to finance these costly and often ineffective exploration programs.

If the government did in fact acknowledge the approaching peak oil production period, it would force oil companies to abandon their oil monopolies and pursue investments in alternative energy. But oil companies like the way things are now, being able to control fuel prices and charge consumers whatever they need to finance these expensive exploration projects—all in the face of record profits. The oil industry has shown its appreciation for continued support from Washington through very generous donations to both parties, especially over the past five years, overlapping its most profitable period in history.

I find it amazingly ridiculous that oil, gas and utilities companies—companies that provide one of the most basic necessities for human life—can be publicly traded or for-profit entities. Every time Exxon reports one of its $10 billion quarterly profit statements, that represents $10 billion that was overcharged to working-class and impoverished Americans who are struggling to keep their home warm, lights on, and a way to get to work.

Oil industry critics will argue that these companies need to be public so they can secure adequate financing for operations and risk-taking ventures. I can tell you that this argument is bologna. First, there is not one single electricity company in America that engages in the kinds of risk-taking activities that cannot be financed by municipal bonds. In fact, these companies often issue corporate bonds for these projects. And because power grid expansion projects can be tied to future revenues, these financings are relatively low risk ventures. We have already seen what happens when an electric company is provided with enormous capital investments from the capital markets—Enron. As well, Texas Utilities also engaged in risky investments in Australia and Europe that failed.

As for oil companies, while higher-risk ventures are certainly required, there is no need for these companies to be structured as for-profit entities. They would be able to secure adequate financing through municipal underwritings and private investments from financial institutions via private equity.

Being a public and/or for-profit company allows these executives to secure their $400 million retirement packages and $50 million annual salaries, like Exxon's CEO has done. Who do you think is paying for that? Think about that the next time you fill up your car with gas. Something must be done to stop this extortion.

CORPORATE
GREED & FRAUD

Over the past three decades, corporate America has become a powerful oligarchy that has seized control of Washington politics. This shift in power, once held by the people, has resulted in the virtual disappearance of America's middle class, while the wealthy have prospered. Yet, some things have not changed, as corporations are still subject to intense pressure by Wall Street to grow earnings. In the best of scenarios, corporations care only about increasing shareholder value, a reasonable aspiration. However, they will achieve it at any cost, even if it leads to the exportation of jobs. In the worst of scenarios, shareholders are overlooked, as management engages in accounting fraud or extorts funds from the company for personal use.

Fraud has always been the invention of human greed. And political corruption has made the extortion of shareholder and taxpayer dollars a huge business in America. Even the recent accounting scandals that rocked Wall Street have not loosened the tight bonds between Washington and America's largest corporations. Fraud continues to reach epic proportions because corporations are rarely caught; when they are, most are faced only with fines. Rarely does anyone go to prison. This is precisely why the fraud continues. Never before has corporate America been so powerful in Washington. The only comparable period was during the "Roaring '20s," and this was one of the contributing factors that led to the "Great Depression."

Corporate Insiders

When Wall Street analysts favor a company, they issue "buy" ratings and raise price targets which causes the stock price to move up. This ultimately generates more cash for the company. You see, all companies own variable amounts of their own stock (known as *treasury stock*) used for stock options compensation and business acquisitions. When companies are on a buying spree, they usually acquire a large percentage of their own stock to be used as stock swap deals for acquisitions. The problem is that once a company owns its own shares, this treasury stock is not considered part of the *float*, or the number of shares readily available for trading in the stock market. Therefore, treasury shares are not used to calculate per-share figures like the price-earnings ratio, often distorting the real picture of a company's business health. And this can mislead unwary investors.

Through buying a large portion of its own stock, a company can create the illusion that earnings per share are growing. Accordingly, while merger and acquisition activity has not been particularly brisk since the fallout of the Internet bubble, stock repurchase plans have hit record-high levels over the past two years, helping corporations report record profits while exporting American jobs overseas.

Because companies know better than anyone what their short-term fate will be, they are truly the ultimate insiders, and can time purchase and sales of their stock as long as they abide by certain minimal restrictions mandated by the SEC. Hence, unknowingly, *shareholders lose when companies purchase treasury stock.* Yet, the SEC has allowed this practice ever since inception in the 1930s. As well, there are very few restrictions for insider purchases of company stock. Don't you think CEOs and CFOs know their company's business prospects over the next few years? Of course they do. Yet, the holding period for stock options execution is remarkably short. *This legalized insider activity by executives has accounted for the bilking of billions of dollars from investors.* Yet, in most cases, the timely liquidation of stock options is transacted legally, although representing an unfair advantage and what I consider *legalized insider trading.*

Executive management cares only about one thing—earnings growth, because that leads to a higher stock price which allows companies to buy more treasury stock. And this makes the company more valuable in a variety of ways, whether through the effects of increased buying power, improved earnings growth, or by providing a source of collateral for loans. And of course, management stands to benefit from short-term performance through the exercise of stock options.

Today, CEOs are much too powerful and overcompensated, in large part due to unchecked stock option programs. Oddly enough, they do not share a proportionate decline in compensation when firm performance lingers. Yet, they stand to profit from overly generous stock option awards when the company performs well. And this provides further incentive to cook the books. It's really not a big deal for them because they know they won't go to jail if they get caught. Enron and WorldCom serve only as rare examples of prosecution due to massive fraud, but only because these scandals received so much media coverage. Executives in hundreds of other companies weren't prosecuted after extorting billions of dollars from shareholders by the timely exercise of stock options. Unfortunately, this will continue as long as corporate America controls Washington.

Figure 12-1. Total Compensation Relative to Average Wages (1936-2003)

Period	CEO	Next 2 Officers
1936-1939	82	56
1940-1945	66	44
1946-1949	49	37
1950-1959	47	34
1960-1969	39	30
1970-1979	40	31
1980-1989	69	45
1990-1999	187	95
2000-2003	367	164

Source: A. Munnell, F. Golub-Sass, M. Soto, F. Vitagliano.

American Jobs

The global marketplace is now a free-for-all that has served to destroy the synergistic relationship that once existed between American workers and companies. No longer are there incentives for corporate America to reinvest profits to create domestic jobs. America's free trade policies encourage companies to find the least expensive workers anywhere in the world. And in order to please Wall Street in a difficult economy, management will do whatever it takes to cut costs. This has led to the exportation of millions of American jobs and huge declines in domestic real productivity.

Corporate America is still in the early stages of helping to destroy the core of America's consumer-driven economy as a trade-off for short-term earnings statements. As overseas expansions and outsourcing trends continue, *American corporations will eventually look to foreign consumers as their primary market when Americans can no longer provide adequate sales figures for strong earnings growth.* As a consequence, corporate America is now in the driver's seat, controlling the fate of America's future prosperity.

In conclusion, it should be clear to all Americans that *job security is a thing of the past, and change, flexibility, and continual learning are trends of the present and distant future.* No longer will you find employees who spent 30 years at the same company. Today, *corporate America is offering jobs not careers.* Therefore, *American workers must develop the capacity to learn new information and technologies as they age,* so they will able to compete with their foreign peers, who ask for a fraction of the wages Americans demand.

From Production to Electronic Transactions

America's Decline

After WWII, America experienced a modern industrial revolution that created an economic boom fueled primarily by its manufacturing dominance. During that period and for two decades thereafter, America supplied exports across all manufacturing industries throughout the globe. In other words, *foreigners paid for American products so net cash flowed into the U.S. resulting in trade surpluses.* As a result, post-war America soon emerged as the world's largest creditor, while Americans had a healthy double-digit savings rate with very little debt.

But during the 1970s, as Asian nations became more organized and competitive, America began to sense a threat to its economy, as many jobs were exported overseas. Foreign investment into America (specifically by Japan) worried many that soon Americans would not own their own country. Ironically, ever since 1970, America has been the world's largest debtor.

As previously discussed, the U.S. government made a drastic change in policy in the '80s, whereby it began to favor the protection of intellectual property rights. This encouraged more entrepreneurial ventures which helped stimulate economic growth through innovation rather than manufacturing. Thereafter, America's manufacturing and production output gradually declined. Aided by the free trade policies that arose in the mid-1990s, domestic manufacturing has now declined to the anemic level we see today.

However, intellectual property laws are still not widely accepted and enforced in other nations—especially in Asia, where piracy is the norm. In part, this has been due to the foreign policy failures of Presidents Bush and Clinton. But leadership in innovation is all that America has left, making global recognition of and adherence to intellectual property laws a vital component of its future economic strength.

Today, virtually nothing of any quality or value is completely made in America, except perhaps the Oreck vacuum cleaner (or so they claim). It's simply too expensive to offer the wages and benefits that Americans have been accustomed to. And when these costs are passed onto consumers, domestically produced goods get priced out of the market by lower priced imports. This is free trade at its best.

Instead of the manufacturing job base seen during the post-war period, American corporations now focus on receiving royalties from foreign companies in exchange for intellectual property rights. This dynamic has been fueling foreign manufacturing industries while exporting millions of American jobs. And while royalty payments have benefited corporate America, middle-class wages have been sent overseas.

While the idea behind the free trade agreement was appealing for enhancing America's competitiveness, the big flaw was that politicians did not consider that *all other developed nations have a national healthcare system, government-sponsored pension programs, industry subsidies, and other policies that reduce the costs of production.* Therefore, foreign companies have lower costs per employee, making them a very attractive alternative for American corporations.

As a result of these inequities, it appears as if corporate America will eventually be located overseas, as will many of the jobs we see in America today. Virtually every type of job offered by corporate America is subject to outsourcing, with the exception of some of the low-level service positions. But many of these jobs are being taken by illegal aliens anyway via *illegal insourcing.*

Outsourcing and Free Trade

Current Trends

Outsourcing is nothing new to America, having occurred for variable periods over the past three decades, as improvements in transportation and telecommunications have permitted a more efficient global economy. Companies outsource their labor force as a way to lower costs, helping them deliver inexpensive products and services to the marketplace. In delivering lower-cost goods and services, companies become positioned as strong competitors, leading to higher profits and increased shareholder value.

Generally speaking, outsourcing has a good effect on the economy, as the delivery of less expensive goods and services encourages consumers to spend more, which leads to business growth and expansion. However, America is now experiencing diminished returns due to excessive outsourcing and free trade policies that favor domestic corporations and foreign nations at the expense of American jobs. By the end of 2003 alone, according to Cynthia Kroll (senior economist at UC Berkeley's Haas School of Business) 40 percent of Fortune 500 firms had already outsourced, while 14 million American jobs were still vulnerable to outsourcing.

But don't think these outsourcing trends are restricted to blue collar workers. The outsourcing trends we see today have no restrictions. Companies can outsource work to a Ph.D. in India for up to 80 percent less than an American employee with a Master's degree. Why? Quite simply, it has to do in part with living expenses and employee benefits, which are influenced by wage growth, inflation, and interest rates. Consider that benefits account for about 42 percent of the total compensation package of the average American worker; something outsourcing does not require. As a result, *free trade essentially redistributes wealth amongst all participant nations so that a balance of living standards is achieved.* And middle-class Americans have been the primary donor of this socialist redistribution of labor-wealth.

Over the past few years, no industry has been more involved in outsourcing than in the high-tech sector. Specifically, many information technology (IT) companies have been replacing employees earning $100,000 to $150,000 per year for Indian counterparts for $20,000 per year. In India, earning $20,000 gives you very high standard of living. In fact, the shear volume of high-paying jobs channelled into India by corporate America has accounted for the economic boom in that nation.

Virtually every American IT and Internet company has outsourced to India and other foreign nations. Even Dell Computers has shifted the majority of its technical support and customer service staff to India, as have Amazon, AOL, EarthLink and hundreds of others. But it doesn't stop there. Software and data services are being sent to India and even tax return services. *American companies need to outsource now because they cannot see the light at the end of the tunnel for the economy.*

Obviously, while corporate America and foreign nations benefit, it is the American worker that loses out during a prolonged period of outsourcing. Only in the short-term do consumers gain superficial benefit through lower-priced goods. Over the longer-term, consumers end up losing due to the exportation of jobs. Consequently, current outsourcing trends make it very difficult to justify the enormous debt many American students accumulate for higher education.

Free Trade: Great for American Companies

When NAFTA was signed into law in 1994, this opened the door for American companies to seek out the best and least expensive workers to supply goods and services to the marketplace. And when America joined the WTO a year later, this all but assured the continued extinction of middle-class America due to the malignant affects of free trade.

One of the biggest problems with traditional theories of free trade is the assumption that all participating nations are at full employment. Accordingly, when all nations do not have full employment rates, the citizens of the wealthiest and highest salaried nations suffer a decline in living standards as a consequence of the redistribution of wealth and income to participant nations. It has been this oversight in free trade theory that has accounted for the most recent declines in America's living standards.

Comparative Advantage for Whom?

The main advocates of outsourcing point to the *Theory of Free International Trade*, published by the economist David Ricardo in 1817. The widespread acceptance of Ricardo's doctrine of comparative costs convinced economic policy makers that free trade with no barriers is beneficial for all. However, this is simply not the case due to changes implicit within the modern economy. Free trade advocates claim that the loss of many American industries and jobs represents beneficial gains in terms of greater productivity through replacement with better jobs. However, these advocates have yet to identify these "better-paying jobs" that were supposed to materialize long ago.

According to Paul Roberts, former Assistant Treasury Secretary under Ronald Reagan, in order for a comparative advantage to persist, a nation's labor, capital, and technology cannot move offshore. This immobility of resources is mandatory so businesses do not evolve into an absolute advantage abroad.

Today, America is in the midst of transferring absolute advantage to its free trade and outsourcing partners. Production and research facilities are being relocated overseas, along with critical intellectual property assets such as trade secrets and patents. It is absolutely ludicrous to think that Ricardo's free trade theory is applicable to a modern society that places its main emphasis on intellectual property. Back in Ricardo's day, intellectual property was barely acknowledged, much less enforced.

Consequently, many economic researchers have concluded that variable levels of benefit are created in a trading exchange between two nations. *When a third-world nation exchanges resources with a first-world nation for the purpose of producing lower cost goods, the third-world nation derives more benefit from the relationship due to the inescapable transfer of intellectual property.* The overall long-term effect of this business relationship is the transfer of income from the nation with higher wages to the nation with lower wages. Essentially, this arrangement levels the playing field for living standards. It has been this phenomenon that has largely accounted for the decline in U.S. living standards over the past decade, while increasing those of developing nations.

In contrast, when two first-world nations engage in a similar relationship, many believe that neither nation receives much benefit beyond that intended; that is, delivery of a less costly end-product. However, considerable research has shown that *even when America engages in exchange with other first-world nations, it has suffered significant loss of relative competitive advantage due to unfair trade practices,* particularly in Japan. Unfortunately, while U.S. corporations certainly engage in transfer of businesses between other first-world nations, the vast majority of outsourcing over the past decade has been with third-world or developing nations, serving to magnify this phenomenon of intellectual property and wage income transfer.

Finally, due to its membership in the WTO, America has little authority in policing unfair trade practices, such as those practiced by China, Japan, and other Asian nations. Essentially, Washington has lost all power to prevent unfair destruction of entire industries that once provided a core job base for millions of middle-class Americans. Apparently, this is the price Washington is willing to pay for the ability to export jobs overseas. It is with little doubt today where the interest of Washington politicians lay. No doubt, corporate America is at the top of that list.

The Foreign Jobs Creation Act

When the American Jobs Creation bill was passed into law back in October 2004, it promised to create more jobs for Americans. It granted multinational companies a one-time tax exemption for overseas expansions, hoping they would send overseas profits back home and create new jobs. But this never happened. As a matter of fact, the largest benefactors of this tax exemption have been corporate America and overseas workers.

What was Congress thinking? If in fact their intent was to create more domestic jobs, why did they not specifically earmark this money for domestic job creation? Why would a large publicly traded company use its profits to employ Americans who can be replaced overseas for a fraction of the cost? As a consequence, this law is just one of many policies that continue to increase the disparity between the rich and poor, leading to the elimination of America's middle-class. *No doubt, as President Bush leaves office in 2009, he will praise this law as having created jobs when in fact it only created jobs overseas at the expense of those lost in America.*

Long-Term Consequences

According to the National Association of Manufacturers, *American producers already face a 22.4 percent cost disadvantage versus their foreign counterparts due to fewer regulations on labor laws, lower wages, subsidies, and the absence of pension and health insurance costs.* In the past decade alone, America has seen nearly 5 million manufacturing jobs disappear due to the collapse of entire industries, relocation overseas, and outsourcing. Meanwhile, since 2002, American corporations have achieved record profits while providing short-term gains for consumers. However, the longer-term effects will be detrimental for most Americans in the coming years.

The surge in international expansion due to irresponsible free trade policies has resulted in a dramatic shift in the way America does business, and this has resulted in the loss of millions of American jobs that cannot be replaced. More important, these workers do not have a retirement nest egg, and they have either lost their healthcare benefits or else won't have any once they retire.

Figure 12-2. China-WTO Deal Will Destroy Jobs in All 50 States

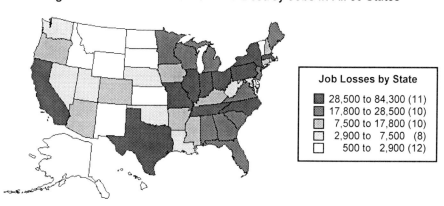

Job Losses by State

- 28,500 to 84,300 (11)
- 17,800 to 28,500 (10)
- 7,500 to 17,800 (10)
- 2,900 to 7,500 (8)
- 500 to 2,900 (12)

Source: Economic Policy Institute

Companies that choose to outsource or set up facilities overseas have the added advantages of tax credits from the U.S. government, no organized labor, no Social Security or Medicare taxes, no federal or state unemployment tax, no OHSA or EPA costs or restrictions, and no employee benefit expenses. These distinctions ensure the continued declining competitiveness of America's labor force, leading to more outsourcing.

America's Most Powerful Industries

Corporate America controls consumer goods but depends on foreign nations to supply and manufacture these goods. That's all well and good if it frees up the American labor force to provide higher or at least equivalent value in other trades. But the problem is that it has not. And that is precisely why real wage growth has been absent in America for several years.

If one examines the twenty most profitable companies in the world for 2005, this elite list is dominated by two industries, mainly American-owned. Anyone care to venture a guess what these two industries are? Oil and finance. Likewise, 42 of America's top 50 most profitable companies are oil and finance-related.

Table 12-1. The World's 20 Most Profitable Companies

Company	Industry	Profits (millions of USD)	Nation
ExxonMobil	Oil & Gas	36,670	US
Royal Dutch/Shell	Oil & Gas	25,311	NE
Citigroup	Banking	24,638	US
BP	Oil & Gas	22,632	US
General Electric	Conglomerates	16,353	US
Bank of America	Banking	16,465	US
Total	Oil & Gas	14,507	FR
Chevron	Oil & Gas	14,099	US
ConocoPhilips	Oil & gas	13,617	US
Microsoft	Software	13, 057	US
PetroChina	Oil & Gas	12,434	CN
HSBC	Banking	12,357	UK
American International Group	Insurance	11,899	US
Wal-Mart	Retailing	11,231	US
Toyota Motor	Consumer Durables	10,928	JA
UBS	Diversified Financials	10,652	SZ
Altria	Food & Beverage	10,435	US
Johnson & Johnson	Drugs and Biotech	10,411	US
Petrobras-Petroleo Brasil	Oil & Gas	10,148	BR
ENI	Oil & Gas	9,870	IT

Source: SEC

Oil companies are holding Americans hostage by manipulating inventories, causing oil prices to soar. Meanwhile, they double-bill consumers for exploration and refining. And Washington stands by, allowing this extortion to continue. Financial firms have set up a great business as well because they have the best possible customer; the American credit-junkie. And Washington has allowed them to disregard responsible lending criteria so they are able to provide limitless credit to those seeking to get their "credit fix."

As you will notice from table 12-1, twelve of the world's largest companies are from the U.S., although many of the non-U.S. companies receive a significant portion of their profits from America such as Royal Dutch Shell, BP, Total, and UBS. Regardless, America's most profitable companies are oil & gas and financial (including insurance). Who is benefiting and who is being victimized here? I contend that both industries are exploiting the U.S. consumer with the help of corrupt politicians in Washington.

Financial Industry

As a result of the change from a manufacturing to a service economy, America has become a nation dominated by consumer finance companies that have addicted consumers to credit spending like a drug dealer does to a junkie. Think about it. *What does a large American company do when it has reached its limits of growth? It forms a consumer finance division!* Why might expansion into consumer finance be seen as a lucrative way to grow earnings? Two reasons: lack of true regulation by Washington and because the American consumer has become addicted to credit spending as a way to compensate for declining living standards.

As Americans have increased their dependence on credit, *corporate America has shifted from making products to making interest.* Name a large company in America and you can be assured that it's involved in consumer finance....General Electric, AT&T, Exxon-Mobil, Dell, eBay, you name it. Consider that the "Big 3" automakers barely make any profits from their auto divisions. The majority of profits have been from their massive consumer finance divisions.

Over the past three decades, America has been transformed into a credit-based society, whereby *the government encourages and rewards consumers for spending, while punishing them for saving.* Even in 2005, President Bush passed a law that allows taxpayers to deduct sales tax from consumer goods—another desperate attempt to stimulate the economy when no other forces are strong enough to resuscitate it.

Everywhere you look, you see teases of the latest gadgets, 0 percent financing for one year or more, and many other lures. "Bad credit? No problem," so as the auto dealers say. Even mortgage companies are speaking the same phrase. But the damaging effects of compounding interest have served to exploit consumer ignorance of basic finance, causing them to accumulate huge amounts of debt. This pattern of irresponsible credit consumption has led to average annual personal bankruptcies exceeding the one million mark, even during the 1990s.

Most Americans have been provided with access to credit levels that are well above their ability to pay. But credit card companies don't want customers to pay off their debt in full. Instead, they have imposed tiny minimum monthly payments so the interest payments will furnish them with a perpetual stream of revenues. Only in late 2005 did Washington finally require that these companies raise the minimum payment to 4 percent of the principal. But this is hardly a financially responsible minimum unless you want to be a slave to debt for the next twenty years. During the same period, President Bush passed a radical law that now makes declaring bankruptcy extremely difficult. The unfortunate consequence is that many Americans will not qualify for bankruptcy created by some hardship such as a job loss or unexpected medical bills. Despite these new laws, the problem remains that *Americans are as addicted to credit spending as they are to oil.*

This disastrous "supply-side" economic model began to spin out of control when the U.S. government realized it could print as much money as it needed knowing that foreign banks would finance its debt. Otherwise, American consumers would be in no position to buy foreign goods. However, what is going to happen when the American consumer falls down and cannot get up? Surely, foreign support for U.S. treasuries will decline and corporations will look to booming economies in Southeast Asia as their new marketplace. Meanwhile, *it's going to be very challenging to convince Japan and China to keep buying U.S. treasuries when consumers run out of credit to buy their goods.*

Oil Industry

Everything on earth of economic value has a finite supply, whether it's natural resources, finished products, services, and even intangible assets such as intellectual property. However, the most obvious limitation is with natural resources, where the laws of supply and demand are quite inelastic. This inelasticity also applies somewhat to the service industry since humans can only create so much productivity in a given workday.

Intellectual property is limited in economic value through patent expiration and obsolescence. Currency too, is theoretically of finite supply even under normal inflationary conditions. And when inflation becomes extreme, too much money chases too few goods, causing demand to diminish. And the inflation-deflation cycle repeats. Therefore, all economic value obeys the laws of supply and demand.

Oil however, is unique in that it is only modestly affected by the laws of supply and demand. While a limited supply will cause an increase in price, demand will only diminish so low because a minimal amount of oil is required for basic living conditions. Thus *oil, more than any other natural resource has the potential to extract wealth from nations and people because it is the lifeblood of all modern economies.*

Therefore, when the price of oil goes up, consumers have no choice but to pay what is asked. And while we might begin to ration, we can only cut down so much before feeling the effects in our lives. Hence oil companies have us in a catch-22. Unfortunately, the oil industry has exploited the volatility and sharp increases in oil prices to extract even more profits than under normal conditions. The result is that, as oil prices have risen, so have the profits of this industry. *In no other industry will you see this odd relationship that appears to be exempt from the laws of supply and demand.* Yet Washington has permitted this extortion ever since the oil industry was commercialized.

It is common knowledge that oil companies manipulate inventory levels in order to raise prices. And when catastrophic events occur, they manipulate inventories more drastically, creating the illusion of scarcity. However, the big oil companies have contracts with suppliers that lock in rates below market prices, ensuring that any unexpected price increase will boost profits. Most large oil companies also refine their own oil and add another markup in price to unsuspecting consumers.

A recent study by Tim Hamilton of the Foundation for Taxpayer and Consumer Rights (FTCR) reported that oil companies have been manipulating inventories in the western U.S. enabling them to charge more for gasoline. But research studies aren't needed to prove common-sense observations. It's obvious that oil companies are manipulating prices and inventories, as are most electric and gas companies. We are talking about extortion for one of the most basic necessities. And this has led to a tax on the poor since they now spend a higher percentage of income for energy resources. Americans need to stand up and protest these criminal activities.

How can the price of gasoline rise by 70 cents in a year (or by 25 percent), yet the cost per barrel increased by only 5 percent? That is precisely what occurred in early 2006. Obviously there are many spreads involved, and the oil industry is creating all of them at the expense of consumers.

Consider these facts about America's oil industry:

❖ In 2001, 2003, and 2005, Exxon-Mobil earned the highest profits in the world. In 2005 it generated over $338 billion in revenues, larger than the annual GDP of every country in the world other than the top six. As well, its $36.6 billion profit in 2005 was the largest by any company in the history of the world. Estimates for 2006 are expected to top previous records with around $40 billion in profits.

❖ The U.S. government offers American oil companies the most favorable tax treatment of any industry. Among the tax breaks they receive are oil depletion allowances and intangible drilling costs, which greatly exceed capital depreciation that occurs with real estate assets. In addition, the National Security Council helped push for a foreign tax credit for oil companies that provided deductions for taxes or royalties paid to foreign governments.

❖ Oil companies do not seem to be held to anti-trust laws that other industries are guarded against.

Figure 12-3. Tax-based Subsidies to the Oil Industry

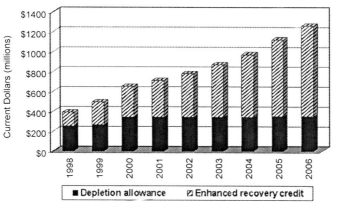

Source: Economic Policy Institute

While oil industry insiders blame much of the oil-gasoline price disparity on state mandates for ethanol additives (to decrease toxic emissions), these costs do not account for the huge price increases seen at the pump. Even in states that do not have this ethanol additive like Washington, you still see large increases. Hence, ethanol use cannot explain the recent surges in gas prices. Even if ethanol was responsible, the equipment needed for implementation is a one-time cost. Therefore, over time, these costs should disappear completely. I am confident the oil industry will continue to use this excuse for several years to come until it creates another reason to raise prices.

Record Profits

Washington has provided corporate America with access to the cheapest labor pool in the world by advocating its "free trade" policies. And while this has served to keep many large American corporations competitive, smaller companies have not been able to survive. As well, these policies have actually caused the death of many American industries due to their inability to take advantage of the tools afforded by "free trade."

You might reasonably assume that America's economic progress has been missing in action since slipping into the post-bubble correction phase of the stock market. Yet, surprisingly, corporate America has done exceptionally well throughout this period. As a matter of fact, *corporate America has delivered its best four and one-half year performance period in nearly six decades.* Since the beginning of what was labeled the last recession (March 2001), production as a share of national income has increased by nearly 60 percent as of June 2006, representing the largest increase since tracking of this data began in 1947. As well, during this same timeframe, production as a percentage of national income has risen from 7 to 12.2 percent at the beginning of 2006.

In addition, according to reports from U.S. News & World Report and the Financial Times, corporate *America has experienced the largest increase in quarterly profits since the post-war period*, soaring from 123 percent ($714 billion to nearly $1.6 trillion) for the first quarter of 2006. And the year-over-year increase represents a gain of 28.5 percent, continuing the fifteenth consecutive quarterly year-over-year double-digit gains. Even during the "tremendous economic expansion" of the 1990s, corporate America only grew profits by 90 percent in its best four and one-half year period.

Finally, even profit margins for America's corporations are at record levels. In the first quarter of 2006, margins represented 8.4 percent of the nation's income for a 65 percent gain over the post-war average of 5.5 percent. Keep in mind these records come at a time when most companies have underfunded pensions and many have terminated or frozen these plans, while others have already filed for bankruptcy protection. Therefore, without these laggards, the recent performance of corporate America is even more amazing. And as you may have guessed, *leading the surge in profits and profit margins were oil companies, followed by the financial industry.*

How were corporations able to deliver record production with fierce competition overseas? The answer is clear: outsourcing and free trade. Since labor costs are thought to comprise about 70 percent of corporate expenses, and given the fact that labor unit costs rose by only 0.3 percent during this record-setting period, the only reasonable conclusion is that companies cut labor costs by outsourcing, lay-offs, and a reduction in benefits.

Corporate Tax Relief

As we have seen from earnings data since 2001, if you define the economy as corporate America, then America is booming. But as we all know, the economy is driven ultimately by American consumers. Certainly, consumers can appear to be strong when provided with endless credit. But this credit bubble has reached its limits. Over the longer-term, the effects of diminished job quality, record household debt and negative savings will expose the true health of consumers.

As corporate America has grown, the average American has become weaker while the wealthy have prospered. The U.S. tax structure has been gradually tweaked over the past two decades to favor wealthy individuals and corporations at the expense of middle-class Americans and the poor. Of recent note, President Bush's tax cuts have been much more gracious to corporations, evidenced by the fact that corporate America has paid fewer taxes than in several prior periods despite record profits. As a result, *corporate taxes as a percentage of GDP have been at their lowest levels since the post-war period (figure 12-4).* And between 2002 and 2003, tax revenues from corporate America were only enough to contribute about 6 percent of total government expenses. While corporate revenues have contributed to the GDP more so than any period in the past five decades, corporate America's share of taxes is at record lows. As we will see in a later chapter, this has led to the overall low tax revenues versus GDP (figure 15-1).

According to a study completed in 2004 by the Citizens for Tax Justice and the Institute on Taxation and Economic Policy, thus far during Bush's leadership, 275 of America's largest companies reported pretax profits from operations exceeding $1.1 trillion (from 2001 to 2003) but were only taxed on approximately half of this amount. In addition, 28 of these companies paid absolutely no taxes on a total profit of almost $45 billion during the 2001 to 2003 period.

One of the most significant factors accounting for the recent decline in corporate taxes is thought to have arisen from President Bush's change in accounting treatment for accelerated depreciation passed in 2002. This change now allows companies to write off their capital investments and file for tax deferrals at a more rapid pace. Finally, we cannot discount the record number of write-offs, write-downs, and earnings restatements that occurred as a consequence of fraud, which have further helped corporate America evade taxes and increase profits.

Figure 12-4. Corporate Profits as a Percentage of GDP Before and After Taxes

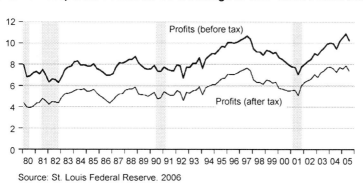

Source: St. Louis Federal Reserve. 2006

Some might argue that low taxes stimulate the economy. However, *when favorable tax treatment occurs at the expense of American jobs and in the face of record profits and corporate scandals, this creates a problem for both consumers and the government because these shortfalls in revenue have to be made up somehow.* Consumers are the driving force of the economy, and with no more credit to spend and the lack of real improvements in the labor market, it is only a matter of time before a meltdown in consumer spending begins its downward spiral.

Taxpayer and Investor Fraud

To devote a discussion on recent fraud in corporate America would require several books. So here, I will briefly summarize the extent of the problem. I have added more detail in the appendix so as not to distract the reader. The real difficulty is where to begin. Overall, it appears that fraud is so ramped within corporate America because Washington does not attach any real penalties for wrongdoings.

Healthcare Fraud

The healthcare industry is flooded with fraud, from the pharmaceutical companies and PBMs ripping off Medicare and Medicaid, HMOs scrapping vital care for patients to save costs, and even individual healthcare providers taking a piece of the Medicare and Medicaid funding pie. But it doesn't end there. The FDA is being controlled by the big pharmaceutical companies, which are usually able to get any drug they want approved for virtually any "disorder," despite safety concerns or lack of efficacy noted by FDA reviewers (see sections 12.1 and 12.2 of the appendix).

Evidence of suppression of adverse drug effects, drugs studies, physician payouts, and many other grievous activities have created a healthcare system as corrupt as Wall Street. And questionable lobbying activities have created a very cozy relationship with Washington politicians. *To date, no healthcare executive has gone to jail for the billions defrauded from taxpayers and shareholders.* As a way to make it look like they are doing their job, the Department of Justice has convicted individual healthcare providers for much smaller crimes.

> *"Safety has definitely been compromised. Efficacy has been compromised, too. I think the whole drug review process, in a lot of cases, is compromised."*
>
> Michael Elashoff, biostatistician and former FDA drug reviewer

Big Pharma Corruption, Fraud, and Manipulation

These are the best words I can think of to describe the activities of the pharmaceutical industry in America. Of course, they are not alone, as the financial, oil, and many other industries could be described by these same adjectives. But the main point of distinction is that fraudulent business practices in the pharmaceutical industry are compromising the safety of millions of Americans.

It has been well-established that the pharmaceutical industry is the single largest source of America's ridiculous healthcare costs, due to its monopolistic control of prescription drugs. In addition to thousands of annual deaths due to adverse effects, there have been millions of unnecessary deaths from prescription drug use that have gone unnoticed. This has largely been a consequence of the corrupt and poorly structured drug safety reporting system, controlled primarily by the pharmaceutical industry. Consider the following activities that occur as commonplace:

- Pharmaceutical companies supply the vast majority of the FDA's budget.

- Drug reps provide compensation and sweeteners to physicians for attending events planned to highlight their drugs.

- Even university medical centers have become involved in this manipulation with reps giving talks and offering free dinners and small gifts.

- The drug rep-physician business relationship is like that on Wall Street, whereby the analysts issue good ratings in exchange for banking business (see appendix sections 12.1 and 12.2).

> "I think Americans need to recognize that every time they put a pill in their mouth, especially a new pill that they've never taken before, it's an experiment. How big an experiment depends on the pill and how well it's been studied. Unfortunately, many of the pills we take have not been studied adequately."
>
> Raymond Woosley, Vice President for Health Services at the University of Arizona and top candidate for FDA Commissioner in 2000.

> "This system has created a very unhealthy relationship between the industry and the FDA, where the FDA says, 'We have to be nice to these people because they are paying our bills.'"
>
> Sidney Wolfe
> Public Citizens Research Group

> "If I'm a stockholder in a company, I don't want my company looking for bad news. I want them to find the good news and invest in finding that. That's what we have (with the pharmaceutical industry)."
>
> Raymond Woosley

Reactive, Not Proactive

And of course we cannot forget the SEC, which focuses most of its efforts on small-time crimes as a way to create the perception that it is policing the securities markets. Meanwhile, widespread fraud continues at the highest levels on Wall Street and corporate America on a daily basis. In almost every major case of Wall Street and corporate fraud, the SEC has acted only as a reactive investigator after someone else discovered the deceit. This has been true in the accounting scandals with Enron and WorldCom, hundreds of other accounting scandals, stock options backdating, mutual fund and market maker trading fraud, and virtually all other scandals that affect millions of shareholders.

Rather than focusing on the major crimes, such as illegal activities of market makers, fund managers and traders, floor traders, Wall Street firms, and corporate insiders, the SEC operates with the mentality of "You might be doing something wrong but don't let us know about it or we will investigate."

In contrast, the SEC should be constantly probing head figures that influence the capital markets because they have been getting away with criminal activity for decades. The passage of the Sarbanes-Oxley Act has had only a minor impact, with much more bark than bite. The fact is that things have not changed and they probably never will. It's still business as usual on Wall Street. As with everything else in America, big money makes and breaks the rules.

Accounting Fraud

We all remember the Enron and WorldCom scandals. In the past five years alone, there have been hundreds of other scandals that have not received much media attention, such as Tyco, Nortel, AOL, JDS Uniphase, Global Crossing, Qwest, Adelphia, dozens of CLECs and Internet companies, Halliburton and many others.

Only recently have corporations had to expense their stock options. But they still have hundreds of other ways to manipulate financial statements. One way to distort financials is to overestimate earnings from pensions. Of course, this is not currently an effective technique since most pensions are underfunded. But prior to the Internet bubble deflation, many of America's largest and most highly prized companies did just that; General Electric, IBM, and so many others. Meanwhile, many Internet and high-tech companies were involved in booking receivables they knew would never arrive (Nortel), reporting revenues that did not exist (AOL), and recording profits that took advantage of accounting tricks (hundreds of others).

Fortunately, new reporting standards have recently been devised to neutralize the effects of pension estimates, such as *core earnings*. The reporting of core earnings specifically addresses the manipulation that was ramped with estimates from pension earnings. Hundreds of companies have had to restate earnings for the misrepresentation of pension surpluses alone.

Corporate Accounting Scandals

Cendant (1998)	Global Crossing (2002)	Nicor Energy, LLC (2002)
Xerox (2000)	Halliburton (2002, and Iraq)	Peregrine Systems (2002)
AOL (2002)	Harken Energy (2002)	Purchase Pro (2002)
Adelphia (2002)	HealthSouth (2002)	Qwest Communications (2002)
Bristol-Myers Squibb (2002)	Homestore.com (2002)	Reliant Energy (2002)
CMS Energy (2002)	ImClone Systems (2002)	Sunbeam (2002)
Computer Associates (2002)	I2 Technologies (2002)	Tyco International (2002)
Duke Energy (2002)	Kmart (2002)	Waste Management, Inc. (2002)
Dynegy (2002)	Lucent Technologies (2002)	WorldCom (2002)
El Paso Corporation (2002)	Merck & Co. (2002)	Royal Ahold (2003)
Enron (2001 and 2002)	Merrill Lynch (2002)	Parmalat (2003)
Freddie Mac (2002)	Mirant (2002)	AIG (2005)

Table 12-2. Worst Corporate Losses Excluding One-Time Losses

Rank	Company	Ticker	Loss ($billions)	Year
1	JDS Uniphase	JDSU	56.12	2001
2	America Online	AOL	54.12	2002
4	Lucent Technologies	LU	16.20	2001
5	Vodafone	VOD	13.85	2000
7	At Home Corp.	ATHMQ	7.44	2000
8	Raytech Corp	RAY	7.06	2000
11	CMGI Inc.	CMGI	5.49	2001
12	Ford Motor Co.	F	5.45	2001
14	Delta Airlines	DAL	5.20	2004
15	PSINet Inc	PSIXQ	4.97	2000
16	Agere Systems Inc	AGRA	4.62	2001
22	American Airlines	AMR	3.50	2002
23	Nortel Networks	NT	3.47	2000
24	PG&E	PCG	3.34	2000
26	LTV Corp	LTVCQ	3.25	2000
27	Verisign	VRSN	3.11	2000

Source: various; modified to include results up to Q1 of 2005.

Along with more insidious reasons for earnings restatements, hundreds of other companies have witnessed a decrease in net worth. With previous earnings reclassified as losses, many companies are not looking as good as before. And when the final effects are reported from earnings restatements and stock options expensing, things could get pretty bad.

A couple of years ago, the SEC finally began requiring all companies to report earnings using GAAP standards as opposed to pro-forma. However, these changes have come slowly and companies still report earnings in pro-forma along with GAAP, allowing Wall Street analysts to basically decide which one to use when determining stock valuations. Therefore, unless investors are experienced accountants with nothing but time on their hands, deciphering Wall Street earnings can still be very misleading.

Stock Options Backdating

This is the latest scandal that's been exposed as an aftermath of the Internet bubble. While investigations are just beginning and are expected to take several years, already several experts have estimated that *as much as 20 percent of all stock options to top executives from 1996 to 2005 were backdated illegally.* In addition, as much as *29.2 percent of stock options were manipulated in some manner* during this period. Options backdating has been linked primarily to high-technology firms since most used stock options as a significant source of compensation during a period when such awards were not expensed on financial statements.

While options backdating is legal, it must be done with proper and timely disclosure according to SEC rules. However, many financial professionals (including myself) had suspected for some time that stock options to executives were being mishandled. Currently, the SEC has identified nearly 80 companies that are under investigation for options backdating (figure 12-5). Already, the CEO of Comverse Technologies cannot be located to cooperate with investigations, and has been reported as a fugitive. Keep in mind that it was not the SEC who discovered these fraudulent activities but rather a business professor.

These brief examples of fraud by corporate America are just scratching the surface of a corrupt system whereby corporate executives have become invincible and many are more powerful than Washington politicians. And you can bet that there will be many more scandals exposed over the next several years. It's a pattern that is consistent with the capital markets and big industry in America. Unfortunately, shareholders will never be properly compensated, but the executives, Wall Street brokers, and litigant attorneys will continue to get rich. Perhaps the most troubling aspect of all of this is that many investors seem to have very short memories and act as if these scandals occurred decades ago, as a large amount of speculation has been noted in the stock market in the past two years.

Figure 12.5. Companies Under Investigation for Stock Options Backdating

Activision	Crown Castle	Molex
Affiliated Computer	International	Monster Worldwide
Services	Cyberonics	msystems
Affymetrix	Delta Petroleum	Newpark Resources
Altera	Engineered Support	Nyfix
American Tower	Systems	Openwave Systems
Analog Devices	Equinix	Power Integrations
Apollo Group	Foundry Networks	Progress Software
Apple Computer	F5 Networks	Quest Software
Applied Micro Circuits	HealthSouth	QuickLogic
Asyst Technologies	Home Depot	Rambus
Barnes & Noble	Intuit	Redback Networks
Blue Coat Systems	Jabil Circuit	Renal Care
Boston Communications	Juniper Networks	RSA Security
Group	KLA-Tencor	SafeNet
Broadcom	Linear Technology	Sanmina-SCI
Brocade	L-3 Communications	Semtech
Communications	Holdings	Sepracor
Systems	Macrovision	Stolt-Nielsen
Brooks Automation	Marvell Technology	Sycamore Networks
CA	Group	Take-Two Interactive
Caremark Rx.	Maxim Integrated	Software
The Cheesecake Factory	Products	Trident Microsystems
Ceradyne	McAfee Inc.	UnitedHealth
Chordiant Software	Meade Instruments	VeriSign
CNET Networks	Medarex	Vitesse Semiconductor
Computer Science	Mercury Interactive	Xilinx
Comverse Technology	Michaels Stores	Zoran
Corinthian Colleges	Microsoft	

13

CONSUMERS & THE CREDIT BUBBLE

Amidst all of the confusing data reported by Wall Street and the government, the single most revealing assessment of the nation's economic health is the financial strength of the consumer. American consumers are the strongest force of the economy, accounting for about 66 percent of all economic activity. When consumers are uncertain about their future economic livelihood, (as gauged by interest rates, job security, wage growth, and inflation) consumer sentiment declines, as does consumer spending. This ultimately affects earnings of businesses, which respond with job cuts and decreased investments. Even when these activities are merely anticipated, they cause the stock market to decline.

The expansion of the consumer credit industry over the past three decades has done well to mask America's loss of wealth and decelerating real wage growth. But credit spending can only go so far. Over the past four years, Americans have enjoyed record low interest rates. Now that rates have risen, there will be no more inexpensive credit, and debt balances will be more difficult to pay off as rates continue to rise. Already, many credit card companies are mailing out "changes to terms and conditions," to feast on the carnage of consumer misfortune.

Aided by the recently passed bankruptcy reform law, credit card companies are now well-positioned to hold indebted consumers hostage, raising rates as high as they want, regardless of credit scores or any other factors. The credit reporting system is another scam that holds consumers hostage to companies that fail to deliver promised services. Many companies have raised rates to 35 percent for over-the-limit accounts or late payments.

Financial institutions were bending over backwards to give you credit when rates were at their lows. Their strategy was to entice you to raise your debt balance to unmanageable levels, knowing that President Bush would pass a law making bankruptcy almost impossible. Now the lions have come to feast. And this alone could be the tipping point that triggers a series of disasters over the next several years.

> **Warren Buffett**
>
> *"We're like an incredibly rich family that owns so much land they can't travel to the ends of their domain and the sit on the front porch and consume a little bit of everything that comes in. They consume 6 percent more than they produce. That scenario couldn't end well."*

The Baby Boomers Are Coming

When baby boomers begin entering the early retirement benefit period in 2008, Social Security claims will start to increase rapidly. And when 2011 arrives, the first group of boomers will begin receiving both Social Security and Medicare benefits. By 2014, Washington will get a taste of reality when trying to fund these programs. Each year thereafter promises to get only worse, as more boomers enter retirement age.

Already, Washington has been slashing Medicare benefits over the past several years resulting in more vulnerability for elderly Americans in need of basic healthcare. Over the next two decades, all 76 million baby boomers will have entered retirement. And shortly thereafter, Medicare and Social Security benefits will consume an enormous percentage of mandatory expenditures. Only a small portion of these expenses will be accounted for by continued tax revenues from the labor force. But even if adequate increases to the payroll tax cap are made as a measure to prevent insolvency, Social Security must be strengthened further so that it keeps up with inflation of critical basic living expenses.

America's Baby Boomer Crisis

Of course there are many possible solutions, but each would come with a hefty price tag. One way to temper the economic effects of America's boomer gap is to legalize millions of illegal aliens. This is currently a hot topic of debate in Washington. But will this pool of 15 to 20 million or so be enough to reverse the diminished productivity expected over the next decade? No way.

Consider that the majority of these workers, even if made citizens, would pay very little taxes due to their relatively small incomes. And while they might prove to be good consumers, their payroll taxes will not make a dent in the future expenditures needed by Social Security, Medicaid, and Medicare. As a matter of fact, legalizing millions will add to the future liabilities of these social programs.

> "It's not unrealistic to think that if we continue to delay -- and the Baby Boomers do start to retire as early as 2008 -- that sooner or later the lenders to this country may decide it's not the best place to park all their savings,"
>
> Maya MacGuineas,
> director of fiscal policy
> New American Foundation

Already, the House has passed a law entitling illegal aliens Social Security benefits (May 2006). What other nation rewards people for illegally entering their country by adding them to their social benefits programs? It appears as if *America's politicians have forgotten who they are supposed to serve.*

Baby Boomer Myths

By now, you should appreciate the potential economic effects of the boomer generation. However, boomer demographics are not confined to America. They actually extend throughout the globe. As a matter of fact, most nations will suffer much harsher effects due to their own boomer demographics. But this global trend is going to cause even more problems for America's economy.

Furthermore, many critics have pointed to this change in demographics as only a short-term trend that will correct within the next few decades. However, current boomer demographics actually represent a future look at more permanent trends. Why is this distinction relevant? Because there are many who try to sell the idea of the boomer generation as a temporary setback that will come and go. However, *the elderly are going to comprise an increasingly larger proportion of the world population for the foreseeable future.* And this has numerous adverse economic implications.

Entry of the world's baby boomers into retirement could result in a global economic meltdown unless radical solutions are devised. Solving the economic problems of America's boomers will not provide a total remedy for America's economic woes because it has become highly dependent on foreign credit. And *as the global baby boomer crisis winds down, the elderly population of the world will begin to harvest their investments overseas and this alone could trigger the collapse of the U.S. economy.*

World Baby Boomer Crisis

As a first issue, let's address America's looming boomer crisis relative to the rest of the world. As you can see from figure 13-1, the United States is actually in pretty good shape relative to the rest of the developed world in terms of the ratio of young workers to an aging workforce. As well, America has higher birth rates than most developed nations, so it is producing for more workers to fill the boomer gap (13-2).

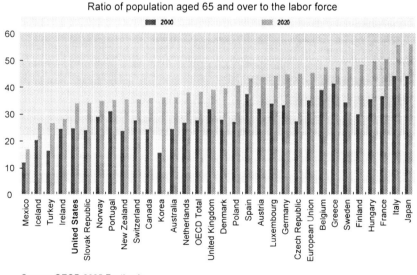

Figure 13-1. The World-wide Baby Boomer Phenomenon (2000 and 2020)

Ratio of population aged 65 and over to the labor force

Source: OECD 2005 Factbook.

What do these global forecasts imply about America's future? Could they perhaps serve to rebalance the cheap labor markets in Asia in twenty years when younger workers become less populous? Will America become the nation of cheap labor used by corporate America? This is certainly a possibility. Could the rest of the developed world also encounter a major crisis due to the overwhelming liabilities each foreign government will face, such as healthcare and pensions? *If the rest of the world is facing a "baby boomer" crisis, who will have the money to buy U.S. treasuries over the next two decades* (see appendix figure 13.1 for global demographic forecasts through 2050)?

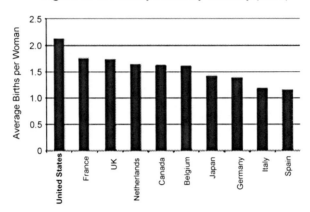

Figure 13-2. Fertility Rates by Country (2000)

Source: U.S. Bureau of the Census (2000). These numbers from the census were obtained from the censuses and surveys from other countries. Created by Munnell, Alicia H. "Population Aging: It's Not Just the Baby Boom." Issue in Brief 16, CRR, 2004.

Boomers Are Here To Stay

Next, let's address the myth that the baby boomer phenomenon is a short-term trend that will disappear within the next few decades. According to proponents of the baby boom theory, the post-war period reunited soldiers with their wives which, along with the post-war economic expansion led to an increase in birth rates. However, consider the fact that much of the remaining world suffered the lasting effects of invasion and military occupation by enemy forces.

In contrast, America emerged as the global leader in manufacturing and production because its infrastructure was unscathed. Yet, even if the increase in births was due to the reunification of soldiers and wives, one might assume this surge in birth rates would have ended after a couple of years. However, it extended for two decades.

The real reason birth rates surged accounts for the reason why the resulting demographic shift will be a permanent rather than temporary change. In 2000, approximately 12 percent of America's population was 65 or older. However, as a result of the baby boomers, by 2025 this percentage will rise to 19 percent, making America a "nation of Floridas" (figure 13-3).

By 2080, when the youngest boomers have reached 116 years of age, the percentage of Americans 65 or older will not have declined by much (figure 13-4). Therefore, *the baby boomer demographics we see today will remain for at least several generations after the last of the current boomers have died.* The reason for the expectations of this continued trend can be accounted for by consequential changes in the economy and the changing societal role of women, which have caused birth rates to decline. And throughout this period, life spans have increased for both sexes.

Figure 13-3. States with at Least 18 Percent of the Population 65 and Over

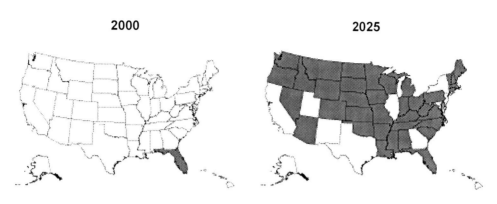

Source: Committee for Economic Development (1999). Updated with numbers from 2000 Census. Created by Munnell, Alicia H. "Population Aging: It's Not Just the Baby Boom." Issue in Brief 16, Figure 1, CRR April 2004

Figure 13-4. Population Distribution by Age and Sex in the United States (1880 and 2080)

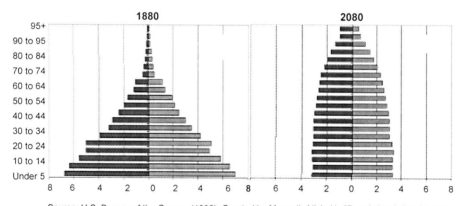

Source: U.S. Bureau of the Census (1998). Created by Munnell, Alicia H. "Population Aging: It's Not Just the Baby Boom." Issue in Brief 16, Figure 2, CRR April 2004

Finally, the higher birth rates generally seen in U.S. immigrant populations have contributed to boomer demographics. This makes sense because immigrants feel better about their future once relocating to the U.S. And this is expressed by their tendency to have more children since they feel better equipped to provide for them with the opportunities provided by America.

As shown in figure 3-1, prior to WWII, immigration was in decline, having bottomed out during the Great Depression as one might expect. Births only began to rise significantly after the end of WWII when the economy was booming. Just as America began entering its birthing boom, the higher birth rates of this new population added to the dynamics of America's baby boom.

Alicia Munnell of the Center for Retirement Research at Boston College has researched this demographic phenomenon extensively. In her analysis, Munnell concludes that birth rates have changed to adjust to the economic opportunity and cost structure of the environment. In order to understand these factors, Munnell examines America's socioeconomic evolution. In 1800, the average American woman bore seven children. Back then, the entire economy was supported by agrarian industries requiring physical labor. And because children could contribute to farm work at early ages, it made economic sense to have several. In support of this theory, data shows that the highest fertility rates were in regions of America where land was the least expensive and labor was scarce.

By early twentieth century, America had entered a new period of economic growth fueled by the industrial revolution. Inventions such as the light bulb, telephone, automobile, airplane and many others ushered in the era of modern industrialization which led to the migration of farm workers into cities in search of higher paying jobs.

Between 1800 and 1900, the population living in urban America grew by over 50 percent, increasing from 26 to 40 percent. And by 1920, over 50 percent of all Americans lived in cities (figure 13-5). As child labor laws were passed it became less financially lucrative for urban dwellers to have a large number of children since they were less capable of earning income for the family. Therefore, birth rates declined significantly during the first half of the twentieth century (figure 13-6).

Figure 13-5. Urban Population as Percent of Total Population (1790-2000)

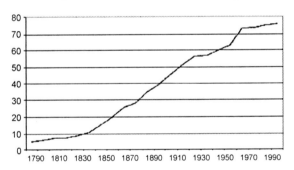

Source: U.S. Bureau of the Census (2000). Created by Munnell, Alicia H. "Population Aging: It's Not Just the Baby Boom." Issue in Brief 16, CRR

Figure 13-6. Fertility Rates in the United States (1800-2080)

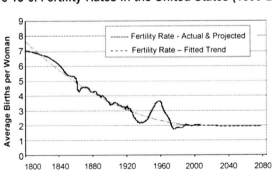

Source: Data prior to 1920: Coale and Zelnick (1963); 1920-1969: Bell (1997); 1970-2080: Social Security Administration (2003). Created by: Munnell, Alicia H. "Population Aging: It's Not Just the Baby Boom." Issue in Brief 16, Figure 4, CRR April 2004

But the effects of the depression also strengthened the declining birth trend. By 1945, America's birth rate had declined to 2.4 children. Obviously, most Americans did not feel good about anything during the depression and wartime period. The low birth rates during these two periods highlight this presumption.

Soon after the war ended, birth rates surged to 3.5 children from 1946 to 1964, peaking at 4.3 million new births in 1957, as Americans celebrated their feelings of economic certainty and high morale. In contrast, the increase in birth rates in Europe after the war was short-lived due to a lower level of economic certainty. *When people feel good about their future ability to provide for themselves and their family, they will have more children.*

Thereafter, there was a drop off in birth rates due to the negative sentiment created by America's involvement in the Vietnam War, as well as the introduction of the birth control pill. Rates continued to decline in the 1970s after the legalization of abortion. By the 1980s, women were emerging as a significant part of America's labor force due to the growing popularity and widespread availability of the birth control pill. As more women pursued higher education and careers, they delayed childbirth until a later time, using the contraception and abortion as needed.

By the late 1990s, women made up the majority of the American labor force. And today, that trend remains in place. Finally, improvements in basic healthcare have gradually decreased the infant mortality rate, helping to push life spans even higher, strengthening current boomer demographics (figures 13-7 through 13-9). However, these societal shifts have come at a large price. Often matched with a professional career that has consumed several years of study, many American women are confronted with a big dilemma. While they have sacrificed their most fertile years to pursue higher education and full-time professional careers, many are having difficulty finding a compatible marriage partner. Other American females seem confused about their role in society, due in large part to societal pressures that have pressured women to eliminate their gender identity.

Figure 13-7. Infant Mortality in the United States (1850-2002)

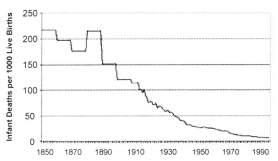

Source: Data prior to 1915: Montgomery and Cohen (1998); 1915-1970: U.S. Bureau of Census (1976); 1970-2002: Centers for Disease Control (2003). Created by Munnell, Alicia H. "Population Aging: It's Not Just the Baby Boom." Issue in Brief 16, CRR

280

Figure 13-8. Life Expectancy at 65 (1900-2000)

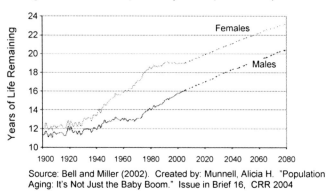

Source: Bell and Miller (2002). Created by: Munnell, Alicia H. "Population Aging: It's Not Just the Baby Boom." Issue in Brief 16, CRR 2004

Figure 13-9. Percent of U.S. Population Aged 65 or Older (1860-2080)

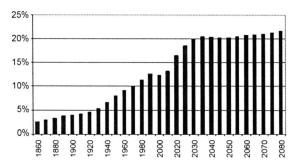

Source: U.S. Bureau of the Census (2000). Created by Munnell, Alicia H. "Population Aging: It's Not Just the Baby Boom." Issue in Brief 16, CRR 2004

The women's liberation movement has certainly produced positive effects. But as of late, we are now seeing many adverse effects. Similar to all societal changes that are initially beneficial, the women's movement has reached the point of diminishing returns and now has a life of its own. As a huge source of jobs, government funding and political clout, this movement has continued to overstep its reach as a way to justify its continued existence. Consequently, as a sacrifice to walk in the footsteps of men, some women have given up their distinct and critical role in childbirth and child-rearing. And the effects of this trend have already registered among the nation's youth.

Indeed, the entry of women into the American labor force has benefited the economy by helping to mask the nation's long trend of declining living standards. However, the unfortunate consequences have been the disintegration of the family unit, social acceptance of divorces (leading to higher rates) and more one-parent households, all of which have contributed to a larger percentage of dysfunctional children. *While the financial independence of women has certainly provided huge economic and societal benefits, we must ask ourselves if the trade-off has been worth it.*

Double-edged Sword

The danger to the U.S. economy and stock market is that its boomer population may in fact turn into a double-edged sword. It was this group that caused the birth of many new industries and spurred amazing growth in older ones. However, the younger generations are not nearly as populous and will be unable to provide the same level of consumer demand as did the boomers. As a result, many U.S. industries will be forced to target foreign consumers as their top priority. Given the potential customer base and healthy savings rates of Chinese and Indian consumers, it would appear as if they will soon represent the bulk of many industry revenues from American companies. And this will further increase current overseas expansion and outsourcing activities.

In addition, due to their smaller numbers, younger American workers will not be able to generate the needed tax base to supply government benefits for the boomers. Finally, because the majority of boomers will retire in poverty even before benefits are slashed, the U.S. economy will experience a gradual meltdown in consumer spending. This will be compounded by the drop off in consumer demand from younger generations, due to their much smaller numbers. Most boomers will be spending the majority of their retirement income on healthcare, food, and energy bills.

It's difficult to know for certain whether the boomers will destroy the economic greatness they built. Much of their fate, as well as that of the entire nation will depend upon how and when Washington addresses the problems. Perhaps Washington is aware that high birth rates tend to follow twenty-year cycles that appear to be tied to post-war conditions. Unfortunately, there is a fairly good possibility that we will be able to retest such post-war dynamics, as WWIII may not be so far off.

Recall the low birth rate during the Great Depression, followed by the baby boom after WWII, and then another downturn in birth rates during the 1970s (figure 13-6). *While demographic forces have not been shown to be the primary factor for bull-bear market periods, we know that technological advances and greater access to consumer markets has been responsible for a good portion of productivity boom periods.* The real question is whether America's capital markets will benefit from future technological innovations and whether this will continue to occur at the expense of the middle class.

> "What bothers me most is the generational aspect. We are leaving an economy with huge debt, huge promises. And it's only going to get worse."
>
> **Alice M. Rivlin**
> Senior Fellow and Director,
> Greater Washington Research
> Program, Brookings Institution

The Credit Bubble

Earlier, I discussed the real estate bubble and mentioned its effect on the swollen credit bubble. Throughout this book, I have been discussing the declining economic position of America by detailing its federal debt, pension woes, declining living standards, and declining global competitiveness. As it turns out, *the growth of the credit bubble is a direct corollary of these economic changes, all of which have been accentuated by the malignant effects of free trade.*

Real Estate-Credit Bubble Connection

As a result of Greenspan's credit bubble, the average American family is highly indebted, and not just for their home. Data from the Federal Reserve shows a total U.S. debt level (consumer and government) of almost $42 trillion—some $540,000 for a typical family of four, or about 320 percent of America's 2005 GDP (see figure 11-3). As you will recall, this massive credit bubble has already surpassed all previous highs.

While average consumer debt for credit cards, autos and other assets are at record highs, credit card companies and U.S. automakers continue to offer credit with numerous incentives, such as "0 percent APR for 12 months" or enticing many consumers to finance their auto purchases for up to seven or eight years so monthly payments will be lower. Due to extended financing terms, most owe more on their car than it's worth. And the same situation could develop in the real estate market due to all of the cash-out financings that have occurred. Regardless, higher interest rates threaten to implode the $11 trillion dollar residential mortgage debt bubble, where home values are estimated to be at least 35 percent overvalued nationally. Any severe shock to the real estate bubble would lead to higher interest rates which would stifle consumer spending.

America is now at a crossroads. While inflation is increasing, the Fed really can't afford to raise rates above 5.75 percent over the next three years without breaking the back of consumers. Already, short-term rates have risen 17 consecutive times since June 2004 and now stand at 5.25 percent. Now the Fed is trying to decide which is worse—inflation or a halt in consumer spending. If the Fed continues to downplay inflation as it has since oil crossed the $50 mark, it might lower rates to stimulate spending or as an attempt to prevent a recession, which appears to be almost certain by late 2007 or early 2008. However, this will only cause the credit bubble to swell further, guaranteeing a more severe correction.

Housing Bubble Affects Everyone

The run-up in real estate prices has created nearly $4 trillion in housing wealth compared to previous decades, whereby housing prices kept up with inflation. This period of real estate increases is unprecedented and accounts for nearly one-half the paper wealth created by the previous stock market bubble.

Unlike the stock market, the recent housing wealth attributed to the real estate bubble is more evenly distributed across America, so it may have larger implications than the bursting of the Internet bubble. In 2005 alone, mortgage debt increased by $885 billion. Since 2001, $3 trillion worth of mortgages have been refinanced. Add to that over $2 trillion in home equity-type loans (including cash-back financings) over the same period and you can see where consumer spending came from. The median home price is up by more than 57 percent (unadjusted for inflation) in the last five years alone, while median income has barely budged. *And when adjusted for inflation and declining employee benefits, wages have actually declined over the past several years.*

Will Asia Keep Buying Treasuries?

When institutional bond investors and foreign central banks lose confidence in Greenspan's inflation commitment, (now inherited by Bernanke) the only other source of support for low rates will be the willingness of Japan and China to pour billions more of their currencies into U.S. bonds. But Japan's economy is not exactly booming and China is trying to wean itself from the dependency of American consumers and the weak dollar.

Soon, no nation will want to increase its amount of U.S. treasury bonds for investment reasons alone, because the dollar will remain weak for the next several years. And America is not exactly the diplomacy champion as of late. The only nation America can count on to keep buying treasuries amidst economic turmoil is the UK. However, England has its own socioeconomic problems. And if America has difficulty financing its irresponsible consumer and government spending habits, long-term rates will soar.

Irresponsible Credit Spending

Ever since the banking industry began deregulation in the late '70s, credit card companies have increasingly preyed on consumers using a variety of deceptive sales and marketing practices. Two Supreme Court Rulings opened the doors for exploitation of American consumers by this industry. Today, *29 states have no limit on credit card interest rates.* They're free to charge any rate they want at any time as long as they comply with consumer disclosure rules, which amount to sending you a letter stating that your rates will increase. (1)

Since 1989, credit card debt in America has risen by nearly 400 percent and is now over $1 trillion. Greenspan's recent loose monetary policies have seen this debt increase by over 32 percent in the past five years alone. With over 1.5 billion credit cards issued in America today, each household has an average of twelve. But that is only part of the picture, as another estimated $2 trillion was extracted from home equity since 2001, much of it to pay off credit card debt. And while this might seem to be a financially savvy move, consider that *those who substitute credit card debt for home equity debt have now transformed unsecured into secured debt,* all but guaranteeing it will take up to 30 years to repay. And these added debt service payments can add up to huge expenses over this period (table 13-1).

For the majority of Americans, the use of credit cards can be considered a destructive rather than productive use of debt. But transferring credit card into home equity debt has only enabled America's credit junkies to spend more. The Center for Responsible Lending (CRL) survey data indicates that the *use of home equity loans to pay off credit card debt did not lead to reduced levels of credit card debt.* This implies households quickly used more credit after paying down their credit card balances.

---

(1) In 1978, the ruling in Marquette National Bank of Minneapolis vs. First Omaha Service Corp allowed national banks to charge their credit card customers the highest interest rate allowed in the bank's home state. This resulted in relocation of credit card headquarters to states that allowed banks to charge high rates. In 1996, Smiley vs. Citibank ruling allowed fees to be defined as interest for the purposes of regulation.

Credit Cards for Lost Wages

While many certainly use credit to buy things they don't need, a growing trend by consumers is the use of credit cards to pay for basic necessities they can't afford. Why are Americans relying on the use of credit card debt so much? Overall, for at least low- and middle-income families, research has shown that the majority of this debt occurs due to unexpected situations such as a job loss, medical injury, and other life events that catch many by surprise. According to a survey by the CRL, *71 percent of low- and middle-income families rely on credit cards to pay for basic necessities such as food, utilities, insurance, or to pay for unexpected expenses such as medical bills and living costs after a job loss.*

The study by CRL also found that *46 percent of households* felt "somewhat" or greatly (16 percent) burdened by their debt, yet *felt that the use of credit cards had resulted in increases in their standard of living.* Already, 7 percent had maxed out their cards, 47 percent had been contacted by bill collectors, just under 50 percent reported a late or missed payment within the past six months, and nearly 25 percent reported paying a late fee at least once over the past year.

Over the past two decades, the bottom quintile of Americans have seen wages grow by only about 5 percent, (adjusted for inflation) while the next quintile has seen a modest increase of 15 to 20 percent in wages. In contrast, the share of family income used for "fixed costs" (taxes, housing, child care, health insurance) has soared by 53 to 75 percent. As the standard of living has declined in America, many consumers have masked this trend by using credit to pay for critical expenses.

Of the 40 percent of home owners (30 million) who refinanced or took out a second mortgage from 2001 to 2004, more than 50 percent of these households used the cash to pay down credit card debt. According to the survey by the CRL, the average amount of credit card debt paid from these financings was $12,000, representing about 12 percent of their existing home equity. The median income in this survey was $48,000, or a bit above the national median income (about $45,000).

Table 13-1. Monthly Payments and Total Interest Paid Under Different Debt Scenarios

	Amount	Annual Interest Rate	Monthly Payment	Number of Years to Repay	Total Interest Paid
Credit Card Debt	$12,000	16%	3% or $20 whichever is greater	18	$9,287
Prime Mortgage Debt	$12,000	6%	$60	30	$13,898
Subprime Mortgage Debt	$12,000	9%	$90	30	$22,752

Source: Demos, "The Plastic Safety Net: The Reality Behind Debt in America."

America's New Safety Net

As a part of the disturbing trend in declining job security shared by most Americans, we see direct evidence of a decline in living standards that has mandated an increased and dangerous use of credit spending (table 13-2). Another recent survey by the CRL also found that 7 out of 10 low- to middle-income families report the use of credit cards as a "safety net." This makes sense when you consider America's negative savings rate. Without savings or even an emergency fund, millions of Americans faced with an unexpected hardship have only their credit cards to rely on for survival. (2)

While the average credit card debt has been estimated at $8,650 ($5000 median with over one-third of families holding a $10,000 credit card debt), when credit spending is examined among race, it appears that White Americans carry higher debt loads. However, this statistic is misleading since on average, African-American and Hispanic families have a much lower net worth. Therefore, credit debt affects these groups much more since they have a diminished ability to repay.

Household Savings and Consumer Debt

Household savings is the main domestic source of funds to finance investment in America, serving to promote its long-term economic growth. Savings can also serve as an emergency fund to provide security for unexpected events such as a job loss. But today, most Americans have neither savings nor an emergency fund.

While America's household savings rate has averaged around 1 percent over the past few years, nations that have obtained net benefit from America's economy have posted much stronger savings rates. Consequently, *as many as one-third of baby boomer households (about 25 million) have absolutely no savings, no investments, and no pensions, and are therefore counting on Social Security as their only source of retirement income.*

As a consequence of poor savings patterns, America's consumption-based economy has turned it into a nation of debt while Europe and Asia have become its creditors. The European Central Bank (ECB) head economist states, "As a result of the high level of savings in Europe we have two different worlds...European households are clear savers and net lenders while U.S. families are net borrowers—this has huge macroeconomic implications."

---

(2) Obtaining accurate data on credit card debt can be difficult since the most reliable data, the *Survey of Consumer Finances*, is released by the Federal Reserve only once every three years. And when numbers are quoted outside of this report, clear explanations are rarely provided for the data.   For instance, depending upon whether you count the average debt per household or the average debt for those who own at least one credit card, you can get very different numbers. From the 2001 Fed report, nearly 24 percent of Americans did not own a credit card. As well, over the duration of the study, another 31 percent had paid off their debt in full. Therefore, approximately 55 percent of Americans had no credit card debt. However, this only magnifies the impact of debt for those who use credit cards.   The Fed's latest survey reports that 46.2 percent of American households hold credit card debt, up from 44.4 percent in its 2001 study.

286

Table 13-2. Why Are Credit Cards America's Most Popular Safety Net?

	Then	Now
Unemployment Benefits Maximum duration	15 months (1975)	6 months (2004)
% Workers Covered by Pensions	40% (1980)	20% (2004)
Federal Budget for Job Training	$27B (1985)	4.4B (2004)
% Workers with Employer-provided Health Insurance	72% (1979)	60% (2004)

Source: Demos, "The Plastic Safety Net: The Reality Behind Debt in America."

According to the ECB, Europeans on average tend to save three times as much as Americans. Most consumers in Asia save even more. For instance, China's savings rate is 25 of annual income. In South Korea the savings rate is about 24 percent; in Japan it's around 12 to 15 percent, while Europe has a savings rate of 10 percent (figure 13-10).

In the 1950s, we saw a drastically different America, with household savings close to 12 percent. That was a time when America's economy was booming with no need for credit, two-income households, or inexpensive labor from illegal aliens. That was the period when America was the world's largest creditor. That was also the period when America led the world in manufacturing. Ever since that period, things have gradually worsened. But even during the high inflation rates of the early '80s, savings as a percentage of income was more than 10 percent annually. Over the past two decades, America's savings rate has steadily declined and is currently oscillating between low single-digit positive and negative numbers (figure 13-11).

Figure 13-12 compares U.S. household debt as a percentage of disposable income with total debt and mortgage debt. The first thing to notice from this chart is that total debt has increased at the same rate as mortgage debt. As well, both are up huge since 2000 and out of line with historical growth rates. That in itself implies counteractive forces that will cause a correction to future economic growth.

Figure 13-10. Comparison of Current Savings Rates As a Percentage of Disposable Income

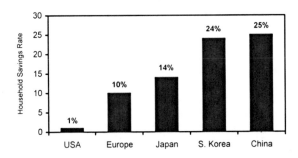

Figure 13-11. U.S. Personal Savings Rate (1958-2005)
As a Percentage of Disposable Income

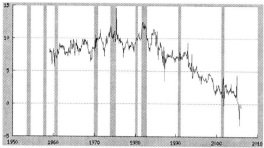

Source: U.S. Department of Commerce: Bureau of Economic Analysis
Prepared by: Federal Reserve Bank of St. Louis: research: stlouisfed.org
Shaded areas indicate recessions as determined by the NBER

The next thing to notice is that consumer debt appears to have remained fairly constant over the past two decades. However, this is misleading because many Americans have actually used home equity loans and cash-out financings to pay down credit card balances over the past several years. *If current trends remain in place, according to the CEPR, household debt as a percent of disposable income will reach 152 percent by 2009.*

Demographic shifts during the past two decades should have resulted in an increase in savings rates when boomers were in their peak earning years and in preparation for retirement. However, *many suspect the absence of improved savings rates was due to the wealth effect created by the stock market bubble of the 1990s.* And this downward trend in savings has continued due to the wealth effect generated by the current real estate bubble. Other factors have led to decreased savings, such as weak real wage growth amidst rapid inflation in healthcare and energy, all which have led to declining real disposable incomes.

Figure 13-12. Household Debt as a Percent of Disposable Income

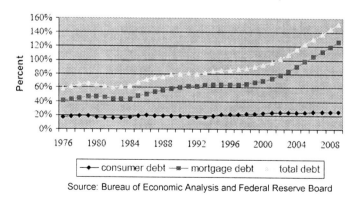

Source: Bureau of Economic Analysis and Federal Reserve Board

Credit Card Death Spiral

According to Travis Plunkett, a legislative director of the Consumer Federation of America, in 2004, the lowest 27 percent of wage earners in America paid more than 40 percent of their income toward mortgage, credit and revolving debt. As I have discussed, although many Americans make use of credit cards to maintain their previous living standards, many more are now using them as a safety net for unforeseen difficulties. However, the nature of unexpected circumstances places these individuals at a much greater risk of making late payments or going over their credit limit. And when this happens, the impact of fees and rate increases can be much more devastating than for individuals with better means to pay. Therefore, what was once thought of as a savior during times of financial difficulty could actually turn out to be the death blow for millions, resulting in an imprisonment of lifetime debt, while the wealthy shareholders of consumer finance companies profit.

Exploitation and Deceit

The credit card industry is unregulated because Washington considers it a powerful resource to assist consumer spending. Unfortunately, the unfair and misleading business practices of this industry are destroying the finances of working-class Americans who have no other way to pay bills during a declining economic period or unexpected emergency.

Credit card companies exploit their customers at every opportunity, charging high penalties for late payments and raising interest rates as much as 300 percent for exceeding the credit limit by even $1. It's obvious they created these ridiculous rules and penalties in order to trap consumers so they can feel justified in raising fees and rates at their will. *These companies use the tactics of psychological warfare on consumers to get them to become their victims,* knowing well that most people who use credit cards do not fully understand the long-term financial ramifications of purchases when made, such as the effects of compounding interest, or the possibility of increasing interest rates.

Most credit card companies bombard consumers with direct mail offers until they submit to temptation, or in some cases, desperation. Capital One has been notorious for this (at least in my personal experience). Yet, there is no way to be put on some "no spam mail" list similar to email. Even if you could prevent their countless solicitations, they have hundreds of other manipulative marketing tactics to get your business.

For instance, many companies now offer cards with images of your college, favorite athletes, or business name, knowing that you will be more willing to use the card as a sign of "school pride," fan loyalty, or business acknowledgement. Other companies, such as American Express offer small business credit cards, but they require your personal tax ID number even if you have incorporated, meaning that it's really not a small business card since you are responsible for repayment; just another misleading business practice.

Most companies "reward" their customers with higher credit limits even when they haven't used their cards in a long time as a way to make them feel they have more access to credit, (a phantom wealth effect) and despite the fact that they do not adequately reassess the consumers' ability to repay. And when you finally start using the card, they send out changes to terms (i.e. higher interest rates) buried along with blank credit card checks and other junk mail they send you, hoping you will discard the notification without looking.

Fees Galore

While credit card interest rates can soar to over 30 percent with just one late payment, the fastest element of revenue growth in the industry is now with fees, such as over the limit, late payment, cash advance, and others. From 1995 to 1998, revenues from late fees grew from $8.3 billion to $17.9 billion while the average late fee more than doubled to an average of $29. Currently, the average late fee has been estimated at around $35 but there are many that charge in excess of $50.

Figure 13-13. Number of Credit Card Solicitations (in Billions)

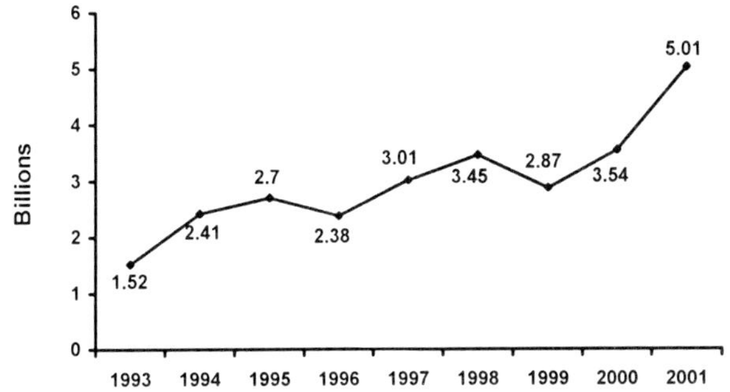

Source: Tamara Draut and Javier Silva. Borrowing to Make Ends Meet:
The Growth of Credit Card Debt in the '90s." Demos. Sept 2003.

Unlike the early 1990s, when the grace period for late payments was on average 14 days, most credit card companies have since eliminated this period, further ensuring more revenues from late fees and interest payments. As well, most companies now consider payments to be late if they arrive after 2:00pm on the due date. To make matters worse, many companies change their terms every few months and send customers written disclosures buried within all the rest of the junk mail they bombard you with each week, causing consumer confusion and neglect. As of 2000, nearly 69 percent of all credit card companies raised interest rates after one late payment.

Throughout all of this, the Federal Reserve has defended credit card companies, stating that they do a good job of assessing customers' ability to repay debt. In fact, *the Fed has stated that there's no correlation between credit card debt and bankruptcy rates since credit card companies assess their customers' ability to repay this debt.* However, it's impossible to provide a full and continuous assessment of one's ability to repay debt by merely checking a credit report since things change; people get laid off and medical emergencies happen.

"We Just Want to Help You"

We've all heard those debt consolidation commercials. And if they seem to be multiplying like rabbits in heat it is because there are now over 500 of these companies, up from just under a dozen ten years ago. One of the sneakiest things these companies do to gain your confidence in their motives is proclaim their non-profit status, when in fact most operate with the intent to earn profits. On May 15, 2006, an IRS audit reported that of the 63 non-profit credit-counseling companies examined, 41 were in the business of earning profits.

Finally, these companies make debt consolidation sound like a painless way to get interest rates reduced, while *neglecting to mention that debt consolidation is a form of bankruptcy, which ruins your credit, leading to higher prices for home, auto, and sometimes health insurance.* Perhaps the only good thing about having bad credit is that high interest rates offered by credit card companies serve as a deterrent towards obtaining credit cards in the future. But that still has not stopped some from reentering the credit trap.

The "Wealth Effect"

Critics who defend the terrible savings rate in America point to the "wealth effect" as the cause. According to proponents of this theory, when Americans experience an increased net worth, savings rates decline because disposable income has gone into investments that have performed well. However, this is simply not the case for the vast majority of Americans.

The net worth of the average American has risen over the past few years due primarily to the effects of real estate bubble. And many Americans have treated this fictitious appreciation in real estate similar to securities in the stock market by taking out home equity loans as if they were selling a portion of their home to lock in the appreciation. But unlike selling stocks at peak prices, when real estate values correct, there will be no profits made. In addition, for the 35 to 50 percent of homebuyers who have financed using ARMs over the past three years, rising interest rates will cause mortgage payments to soar. Although there are a variety of ARM financial arrangements in the marketplace, typically the rate stays fixed for a certain period, such as 2 to 3 years, and thereafter can rise as much as 2 percentage points per year if interest rates increase.

One might tend to assume that the terrible savings rate of Americans only began once Greenspan lowered interest rates to their recent 43-year lows, prompting consumers to spend rather than save. However, this is not at all the case. According to data from researchers at the Federal Reserve Board, the overall savings rate declined in the 1990s from 5.9 percent to 1.3 percent due to the wealth effect generated by the stock market.

During the 1990s, the economy expanded at a rapid pace but the nation's wealth grew even faster at an average annual rate of 6 percent. *By 1998, nearly 50 percent of all American households owned stocks either directly or indirectly* through some type of retirement account, up from 32 percent less than ten years earlier. From 1992 to 2000, while the aggregate net worth of Americans increased from $30 trillion to $41 trillion, the savings rate declined by 4.1 percent. This makes sense if you are a proponent of the "wealth effect." *However, the poorest one-fifth of Americans doubled their savings rate from 3.8 percent to 7.1 percent.* Needless to say, they generally did not benefit from the rise in the stock market.

The Fed also determined America's wealthiest consumers did most of the spending during this period. According to their findings, *the wealthiest Americans went from a savings rate of 8.5 percent in 1992 to -2.1 percent by 2000.* Between 1992 and 2000, the household sector sold $2.3 trillion of directly held stock on a net basis, representing about 50 percent of its net purchases during that period. And an estimated 80 percent of equities were directly owned by the wealthiest 20 percent of Americans in 2000.

Figure 13-14. Personal Savings Rate and Household Financial Wealth

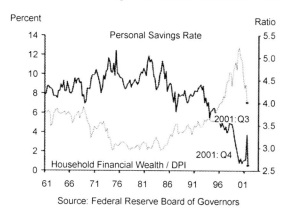

Source: Federal Reserve Board of Governors

The conclusions of this study found that while America's wealthiest quintile shifted $240 billion in savings to consumption in the '90s, American's poorest quintile shifted $40 billion from consumption to savings, accounting for a net contribution of $200 billion to aggregate consumption from changed savings rates. *While the rich got richer during the bull period of the '90s, they helped fuel the expansion by consumption and investment activities rather than saving.* And after the market fell by over 20 percent by 2001, the vast majority of consumers actually did not stop spending. It was only the wealthiest 20 percent who for the most part stopped their spending sprees because much of their wealth was tied to the stock market. When the market declined, so did the wealth effect. And this is why the Fed sensed the need for such drastic measures.

Conclusions

With all of the problems in the U.S. economy and a credit bubble that is swollen at its seams, we must wonder where the cash needed for consumer spending will come from over the next several years. Approximately one-third of the U.S. population will be struggling just to pay for healthcare, food, and utilities. Already, the cost of most consumer goods and services has gone up from 100 to 300 percent in the past two decades. In contrast, real wages have failed to keep pace with inflation. Healthcare costs continue to grow at twice the rate of the economy, while oil prices have surpassed record highs.

Since 1959, real wages (wages adjusted for inflation) across the board have risen by only 1.7 percent, with 1.2 percent of that small increase coming since 1975. So far, America has been able to borrow from other nations to fuel its poor spending habits. But in the near future these funds will no longer be available because America is not the only country facing a "baby boomer crisis." And the weakness of the dollar is not exactly attractive for foreign investors unless interest rates head significantly higher. However, higher rates would devastate American consumers.

Within the next decade, as the global "baby boomer crisis" begins to take effect, government-sponsored pensions in Europe could be in deep trouble. What that means is less investment capital for America; in other words, less buyers for U.S. Treasury securities. As well, with about 10 percent of the U.S. stock market owned by foreigners, it seems likely that much of this foreign investment will be liquidated to provide for the retirement needs of European and Asian boomers.

> *"If you look at financial crises, they occur seemingly overnight. More and more pieces of straw drop on the camel's back, and all of the sudden, the camel collapses ...nobody knew exactly when Argentina was going to go south or exactly what day Russia was going to default. The timing [for the U.S.] is up for grabs."*
>
> Lawrence Kotlikoff, economics chairman Boston University

America's "new economy" is the result of advances in technological innovation, which has enabled a more efficient exchange of information. However, free trade is also part of this new economy, which promised to deliver improved living standards, and it has—for everyone except working-class Americans. Today, the new economy is characterized by outsourcing, insourcing, declining employee benefits, and job insecurity for all categories of wage earners except upper management. And it has weakened the link between workers and employees. Already, declining economic conditions and growth in credit spending have led to huge increases in annual personal bankruptcies, growing from 616,000 to 1.8 million or by nearly 300 percent from 1989 to 2004.

Americans buy today what they plan to pay for tomorrow, but they consume so much of what they cannot afford they end up paying for these items for several years, sometimes passing their debts to the next generation. Such financial irresponsibility has made financial companies amongst the largest and most profitable in America.

14

FOREIGN PLAYERS

America for Sale

During the Reagan years, Americans were troubled by Japanese investment into the United States, prompting many to proclaim that America was "selling out" to foreigners. Since that period, large corporations, many of which are owned by foreign interests, have gained significant clout in Washington. Yet, as large and powerful as corporate America has become, these companies are always for sale to the highest bidder, regardless where they reside.

Over the past decade, ownership of America's most valued assets has been transferred to foreign interests. In fact, foreign interests, in terms of loans, investments and asset acquisitions have totaled four times the foreign investment capital inflows from the '80s. More disturbing, the U.S. Bureau of Economic Analysis states that *as much as 40 percent of foreign investments were funded by channeling U.S. money into the hands of foreigners due to their financing of $4 trillion of trade deficits over the past decade.* (1)

Foreign competitor nations have been anxious to finance America's irresponsible spending sprees because they have benefited from the limitless credit provided to the American consumer, as well job exportation via America's free trade policies. This exported capital has been used to build the infrastructure of developing nations like China and India. And when these nations need vital assets, they have bought them from America's corporate auction block, courtesy of its capital markets.

During the past decade alone, over $3.2 trillion of foreign money has been used to acquire American corporate assets, including 8,600 takeovers in energy ($116 billion), transportation equipment ($146 billion), printing and publishing ($56 billion), insurance ($85 billion), electronics ($61 billion), and pharmaceuticals ($60 billion).

As a few examples, we have seen Mercedes (German) buy Chrysler, CBS Records Group bought by Sony (Japan), and hundreds of other influential American companies change ownership to overseas interests (see Chapter Fourteen Supplement, appendix). And in 2005, an investment group thought to represent the Chinese government made a bid to acquire Exxon-Mobil; an act alone that emphasizes the dangers of America's corporate auction block.

---

(1) These calculations are based upon the total amount of investment versus the amount of the deficit funded by foreign funds.

Today, many of America's most critical industries are largely owned by foreign interests (plastics/rubber: 47 percent, financial services: 36 percent, machinery: 32 percent, chemicals: 30 percent, transportation equipment: 27 percent, publishing: 27 percent, cement: 81 percent, motion pictures: 69 percent, consumer television and electronics: nearly 100 percent).

While the exploitation of consumers continues by corporate America, many foreign interests have been acquiring American-held assets and wealth. Therefore, *if in fact corporate America controls Washington politics, we must question to what extent foreign nations will gain influence over Washington as this trend in foreign acquisitions continues.* Finally, we must pose this question as it relates to America's national security.

Consequences of Foreign Ownership

Most economists agree that foreign investment into America is good for the nation's growth. However, everything has a point of diminishing returns. Already, foreign nations have financed America's national debt by 50 percent, as well as the most recent portion of this debt by as much as 98 percent (in 2004 and 2005). Consequently, this has major ramifications for America's ability to execute foreign political policies.

Control by Foreign Bankers

Unlike in the past, *America is no longer able to tell the world what to do because the world has a significant ownership in its empire,* and could easily cause its collapse by selling or refusing to buy U.S. treasuries. Likewise, with significant ownership of American corporations, foreign nations are not only extracting more of America's intellectual capital and innovative infrastructure, but they now have a say in its economic policies through their corporate influence, which even reaches Washington through industry lobbyists. This threatens to sway the political and regulatory landscape in favor of foreign economic and political agendas.

Foreign Propaganda

There are many other examples of detrimental effects of foreign ownership in America's economic engine. Foreign ownership also means easier access for sabotage by terrorist groups. Equally adverse consequences could result from the silent actions of say, Japan through manipulation of Americans due to its dominance of the U.S. motion picture industry. Due to the powerful control Japan now has over America's media industry, it could do what the U.S. government is not able to—censor, manipulate, and coerce public opinion, as well as social and political attitudes.

During WWII, Germany led a successful propaganda campaign using radio and motion pictures to portray Americans in a bad light and to convince the world that Jewish prisoners were being treated well. During the Korean War, North Korea also used propaganda to convince its citizens how "bad" Americans were. And of course, America has used propaganda many times, especially during the Cold War. The power of propaganda is often underestimated, but its effects can be very destructive during war or war-like conditions. Propaganda is often the most power weapon used by dictatorships and movements that do not have vast amounts of money because it provides a relatively inexpensive means of gaining popular support. We have witnessed this recently with telecasts of inhumane slayings by Al-Qaeda.

Placing America's Strategic Assets with Enemies

The damaging effects of America's foreign-controlled media and other critical industries would not necessarily mandate war-like conditions. Once America sells off its assets, foreign acquirers are free to do with them as they wish, even if this includes selling them to Middle Eastern or Asian nations for oil. With that thought, I will leave you to consider potential ramifications of the following facts:

- Japan imports 99 percent of its oil needs.

- China is starving for oil and continues to strike deals with Russia, Saudi Arabia, Iran and Canada. It has tremendous positive cash flows to devote to its quest for oil, due in large part to its trade surplus with America as well as American and other foreign business investments into this booming nation.

- The Middle East owns the world's largest and highest quality oil reserves and continues to increase hostilities towards America. Price controls by OPEC have occurred in the past and will reappear in the future, representing a major problem for the American economy as long as its dependence on foreign oil remains.

- Russia too has vast oil reserves and Russian-U.S. diplomatic relations are not much better than since the Cold War. Russia has formed an alliance with Iran and China, and this could present major challenges for America's diplomacy efforts.

With much of America's productive and strategic assets already owned in part by foreign nations, and with the remaining ones on the auction block, I will leave it to the reader to play out potential scenarios.

Diminished Ability to Fight a Major War

Arguably, America is no longer prepared to fight in a global war because many of the production facilities for U.S. military equipment and weaponry systems are based overseas; not with its long-standing allies in the UK, but with more questionable nations such as Japan, India and South Korea. Not only does this represent the direct threat of critical technology transfer, but it has already led to indirect transfer to many nations. Already, American contracts for the F-16 have stimulated the birth of India's military aircraft industry. And CIA investigations have shown that hostile nations possessing nuclear capability such as North Korea, gained critical know-how from individuals in Pakistan.

While many believe America's relationships with Japan and South Korea are healthy, one could argue they are merely linked by U.S. military support against hostile communist nations such as North Korea and China. In fact, *despite billions of dollars in financial and military aid provided to South Korea each year, a very large percentage of South Koreans despise Americans due to their desire for reunification with North Korea.*

There are even hundreds of accounts of attacks on U.S. troops in South Korea by Korean citizens who simply want them to leave. And if you understand Korean and happened to watch the World Cup in Seoul a few years ago, you might recall what Korean spectators were shouting in unison. It was very anti-American to say the least, and served as a reminder of South Korean sentiment. *But for some reason, the American media has chosen not to communicate South Korea's attitudes to the American public.*

We have already seen how the sale of arms and U.S. military training of other nations has backfired. Many terrorist groups have benefited from the unchecked distribution of these resources overseas. What appears to be a good relationship with one nation today has many times ended with damaging consequences at a later date. Iraq, under the former leadership of Saddam Hussein is but only one of these examples, as was the Taliban and Al-Qaeda.

The Threat of OPEC

The Organization of the Petroleum Exporting Countries (OPEC) was established in 1960 with the objective to "co-ordinate and unify petroleum policies among Member Countries, in order to secure fair and stable prices for petroleum producers; an efficient economic, and regular supply of petroleum to consuming nations; and a fair return on capital to those investing in the industry." OPEC currently consists of eleven nations, all of which depend heavily on oil exports as their main source of income.

During the 1970's, OPEC began an embargo and subsequently raised oil prices in support of the Palestinian conflict with Israel, leading to worldwide shortages. Sensing an opportunity to gain market share, non-OPEC nations increased their exploration and production efforts. Today, non-OPEC oil accounts for the majority of oil production (figure 14-1).

As an alternative to combat higher prices, many developed nations (U.S., France, Germany, and Japan) increased energy production from nuclear plants. But when the accident occurred on Three Mile Island, followed by the meltdown at Chernobyl a few years later, the U.S. virtually halted all new nuclear energy projects. Consequently, France now produces 99 percent of its energy by nuclear means.

OPEC Members
Algeria
Indonesia
Iran
Iraq
Saudi Arabia
Kuwait
Libya
Nigeria
Qatar
United Arab Emirates
Venezuela

Ever since the post-war economic expansion, the U.S. has exhausted most of its domestic oil reserves from its nearly 600,000 wells, each producing on average, only a few barrels each day. And its ranking as the world's #3 producer is primarily due to the rich reserves in Alaska and its expensive off-shore exploration projects in the Gulf of Mexico.

In contrast, the Middle East contains a handful of oil wells that produce the bulk of their crude. *Approximately two-thirds of the world's reserves are concentrated within five Middle Eastern countries—Saudi Arabia, UAE, Iran, Iraq, and Kuwait. These nations also boost the majority of the world's largest oil fields (table 14-1).* While Saudi Arabia has the largest oil field in the world, Iran has three and Iraq has two of the world's top ten largest oil fields, positioning this region as a key strategic centrepiece for any modern economy.

Figure 14-1. World Crude Oil Production

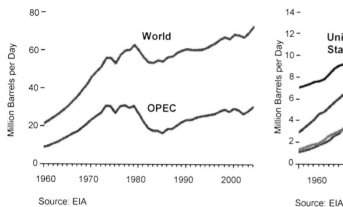

Source: EIA

Figure 14-2. Leading Crude Oil Producers

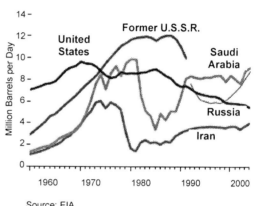

Source: EIA

Table 14-1. The Top Producing Oil Fields by Production

Field, Country	Size estimate
1. Ghawar, Saudi Arabia	75-83 billion barrels
2. Burgan, Kuwait	66-72 billion barrels
3. Bolivar Coastal, Venezuela	30-32 billion barrels
4. Safaniya-Khafji, Saudi Arabia/Neutral Zone	30 billion barrels
5. Rumaila, Iraq	20 billion barrels
6. Tengiz, Kazakstan	15-26 billion barrels
7. Ahwaz, Iran	17 billion barrels
8. Kirkuk, Iraq	16 billion barrels
9. Marun, Iran	16 billion barrels
10. Gachsaran, Iran	15 billion barrels

Source: Energy Information Administration (EIA)

With oil prices at record highs, non-OPEC nations will most likely increase oil production even more since they are less profitable when oil is below $30 per barrel. In contrast, because most OPEC nations have production costs under $5 per barrel, their profit margins are always high regardless of price. Each day, as the reserves of the major non-OPEC producers such as Russia, Canada, and the U.S. are depleted, OPEC is moving one step closer to controlling the world market. Considering the production rates of non-OPEC nations are significantly above that of OPEC, non-OPEC production could reach a maximum over the next 5 to 6 years, plateau, and then begin a permanent decline.

Ever since the oil embargo by OPEC in the '70s, it has been widely accepted that OPEC is a political organization. *If access to oil drives economies, it appears as if OPEC will soon hold the American economy hostage unless it gains access to a huge amount of oil, or rapidly commercializes viable forms of alternative energy.* Already, members of Al-Qaeda have attempted to sabotage facilities at the world's largest oil field located in Saudi Arabia as a means to damage America's economy further. And although this attack was unsuccessful, it highlights the vulnerability of the U.S. economy to oil.

Consider the following scenarios:

1. Middle Eastern nations (Iran, Syria and Saudi Arabia), influenced by individuals tied to Al-Qaeda, strike deals with oil-thirsty China, leaving the U.S. in the cold. As China continues to grow, America will soon no longer represent a dominant oil consumer for OPEC. Therefore, the consequences of upsetting the U.S. will not have as much significance as in the past. To some extent this has already occurred.

2. With about 39 percent of all non-OPEC oil (proven plus undiscovered) within the former Soviet Union, OPEC might negotiate with Russia for a share in the control of the world's oil supply.

3. OPEC could begin demanding non-U.S. currency for its oil, which if successful would cause a major financial catastrophe in America. Iran is already trying this.

Oil Prices and Stock Market Returns

There should be no debate that oil drives the U.S. economy. Access to inexpensive oil shortly after the oil crisis in the '80s created an economic boom that resulted in what many have labelled as the greatest economic expansion in America's history. In contrast, during periods of high oil prices, the economy performs poorly. We saw this during the '80s. Most recently, record oil prices have shown their effects on the stock market. In Chapter One, I briefly examined the correlation between oil demand and GDP growth (figure 1-1). In figure 14-3, a graph of the Dow Jones Industrial Average has been plotted along with U.S. gasoline prices adjusted for inflation over a 45-year period.

There are several key points to note from this figure.

(1) The U.S. experienced a bear market period from about 1967 to 1987. Critical events thought to have caused this bear market or helped sustain it were the assassination of President Kennedy in 1963, U.S. involvement in the Vietnam War from 1965 to 1972, and double-digit inflation of the late '70s and early '80s sparked by high oil prices from OPEC.

(2) Notice the record spike in the price of gasoline (oil) in 1981. In part, this can be attributed to inflation of the dollar. But OPEC was also responsible with an embargo and price increases in the early '70s. This resulted in a global oil crisis.

Figure 14-3. Inflation-Adjusted Gasoline Prices versus the DJIA (1960-2005)

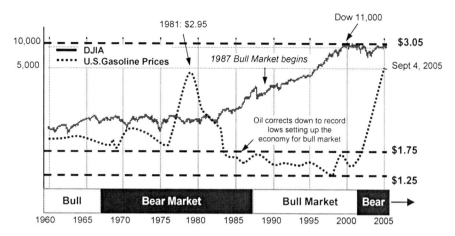

Source: Energy Information Administration (EIA), U.S. Department of Energy, Yahoo Finance

Here it is assumed that oil and gas prices have a 1.0 correlation. And although this is not always true, we can safely assume a 0.90 correlation coefficient (90 percent correlation) which is sufficient for this study.
*Note that by definition, when a bear market ends, a bull market begins and vice-versa.

(3) The period from 1981 to 1987 resulted in a very large correction in oil prices from record highs. This helped fuel the economic expansion and the subsequent bull market of late 1987 to 2001.

(4) The inflation-adjusted price of gasoline in 1981 was recently surpassed in September 2005.

(5) The U.S. stock market is currently in a secular bear market which began in 2001. I predict that this secular bear market or bear period will continue through 2012.

From these observations, one must wonder at what price oil (gasoline) will be selling for over the next several years.

In my opinion, crude prices will continue to remain high over the next decade due to:

(1) Decreasing global capacity and increasing baseline demand due to increasing population.

(2) Decreasing global capacity due to increasing expansion and industrialization of China and India, which represent over one-third of the world population.

(3) Peak oil production, which by some estimates will occur by 2008 to 2012. After an unknown plateau period of peak oil production, global oil production will gradually decline, causing prices to soar.

(4) Elevated tensions in the Middle East due to the reluctance of some Middle Eastern nations to provide full support for Iraq's reconstruction efforts, growing concerns about Iran's plans to build nuclear facilities, and increasing awareness by American citizens of Saudi Arabia's discontent with the U.S. and support of Al-

Qaeda.*

(5) Global economic dynamics dictate that commodity prices will remain high for at least the next few years. And while downward corrections are inevitable, the trend in higher oil prices is very strong and not likely to be broken for several more years. Strictly speaking, *oil is considered a commodity, but its nickname of "black gold" was not a random designation. Hence, oil often does not behave like a commodity because of the control exerted by OPEC.*

(6) Inadequate technology and infrastructure to provide significant amounts of renewable energy will cause a global shortage of oil during the plateau phase of peak oil and for the first few years of the post-peak oil period. Thereafter, oil prices could adjust downward if developed nations have replaced much of their dependency on fossil fuels with alternative energy technologies (possibly by 2020).

All of these factors will most likely result in OPEC using oil as a political bargaining tool as in the past. By 2012, oil will most likely have risen above $100 per barrel. And while oil will correct in price from large spikes during certain periods, I feel that the average price will remain in the mid to high $70s over the next 6 years.

America's Lifeblood

Oil's valuable and varied role in civilization is of great historical significance. Its earliest use was for asphalt materials and lubrication in ancient times. Shortly thereafter, oil was used as "Greek fire" (basically as a firebomb), proving to be the dominant weapon of many ancient battles that led to decisive victories. Oil's importance in battle has extended to modern times, as a critical centrepiece in determining the outcomes of WWI and WWII. In fact, oil can be argued to have been one of the main causes of most modern wars. That certainly was the case for America's involvement in WWII. More recently, America has engaged in military operations in Mexico due to oil interests. Arguably, America has commenced military operations in Columbia, Afghanistan and Iraq, as well as many other nations for the purpose of securing access to oil.

Note that oil provides much more than a combustible fuel supply. In addition to fuel, we use products made from crude oil on a daily basis. Virtually every plastic-based product is made from crude, as well as many chemicals used in manufacturing, special textiles, paints, fertilizers, pharmaceuticals, and hundreds of other products. Thus, *when Washington politicians and economists mention the national security of America, oil must be part of the equation since America is so dependent upon this natural resource.*

---

* As a recent example of these frictions, Saudi Arabia has resisted compliance with Free Religion laws enacted by the U.S., and this has already prompted Congress to threaten trading sanctions. Subsequently, Saudi Arabia and Iran have both expressed their intent to withdrawal oil from the market if the U.S. tries to exert economic sanctions.

Iraq: A "Must Have" for America

Because America is heavily involved with Iraq's reconstruction efforts, we should consider the possibility that Iraq will serve as its access to badly needed oil. Iraq's oil reserves are extremely attractive for investment and development by international companies due to its high quality, huge supply, and low production costs.

This is in contrast to the remaining reserves owned by America, which are of lower quality, much lower supply, and much higher cost to produce. In addition, refinement costs can also be substantial due to the shale and oil sands regions of Texas and Canada respectively. Thus, when oil is around $20 per barrel, these unconventional sources of oil yield virtually no profit for oil companies.

There are many who seem to think that the U.S. went to war with Iraq to secure interests in its large oil reserves, and this premise has been based on a considerable amount of valid support. James Paul, executive director of the Global Policy Forum presented a very compelling argument in which he states that the U.S. and UK entered into a war with Iraq not for national security, but to gain access to its vast oil reserves. It is difficult to deny that securing access to abundant oil reserves serves to strengthen America's national security since the driving force of this nation is its economics.

By some estimates, Iraq could hold the world's largest oil reserves at up to 400 billion barrels since only 10 percent of the nation has been explored. OPEC nations are well aware of this possibility, and they realize that if the U.S. succeeds in gaining a majority control over Iraq's soon-to-be privatized oil fields, OPEC would soon be dealing with a U.S.-influenced OPEC member. Thus, it appears as if Iraq holds the key to America's escape from OPEC oil dependence and subsequent political agendas. That might explain why Washington has already committed $1 trillion to Iraq's recovery efforts over the next decade.

War on Terror

Thus far, the continental United States is the only developed nation that has never experienced a major military attack. However, America is less than 250 years old while most other nations have a much longer history. Conventional wisdom leads us to the conclusion that America will continue to be the primary target of terrorist attacks over the next several decades. And while these attacks may not be classified as military invasions, the fact is that they could cause significant damage.

America's main threat from terrorists will most likely be digitally-based. The rapid proliferation of the Internet has made it possible to simulcast propaganda to all parts of the globe instantaneously and inexpensively. In all likelihood, terrorists will target America's financial infrastructure as a means to devastate its economy. This would provide more "bang for the buck" and could be accomplished overseas using Internet access. In short, digital attacks would create chaos in America's financial system, crippling business transactions, and potentially leading to sabotage of vital databases.

Numerous signs in America point to isolationism as the best remedy for its economic

302

and social problems. Such a policy served America well during the Great Depression. However, today we see just the opposite, with more emphasis on foreign policy rather than its socioeconomic problems. *Unfortunately, by trying to solve its economic problems through foreign policy efforts, it appears as if America will continue to encounter more domestic and international conflict.*

National Security

Despite all of the funding for the Department of Homeland Security, terrorist response units are still ill-prepared to prevent and counter terrorist attacks. Recently, the world witnessed Washington's humiliating display of non-responsiveness after Katrina. It is safe to assume that until America can handle a natural disaster, it will continue to remain unprepared to protect, respond, and mitigate the effects of terrorist attacks.

Significantly more funds are needed to provide disaster response equipment to fire, police, and other emergency personnel. According to recent estimates, only one-tenth of all fire departments have the capacity to respond to a building collapse, only a third of fire fighters are equipped with breathing apparatuses, and only about one-half have radios. Moreover, biochemical and radiation detection systems are not widely available, while urban search and rescue programs are outdated and underfunded.

America's healthcare system is also ill-prepared for managing major biological threats, both incidental and terrorist-induced. Many acute-care hospitals have inadequate decontamination facilities and insufficient bed space. Vaccines for major biological threats continue to be understocked. Finally, the National Guard, military reserve, and most healthcare professionals in the public healthcare system have inadequate training to respond to biological and nuclear emergencies.

Securing America's ports is another concern that has not been recognized as a critical priority by Washington. In early 2006, corporations attempted to sell the majority interest in port-operating companies to Dubai, a Middle Eastern nation thought to have ties with Al-Qaeda. And even though this sparked widespread protest causing the deal to fall through, American ports remain unsecured. *Each day, out of the 20,000 cargo containers arriving in America's 300 shipping ports, only about 2 percent are inspected by federal personnel.* As well, biological and nuclear detection devices at these sites have been shown to be largely ineffective. Rather than money, better organization and oversight is needed to prevent terrorist activities. Thus far, the Department of Homeland Security has been a waste of taxpayer dollars.

The possibility of terrorist attacks by Muslim Americans cannot be overlooked. Shockingly, in 2005 there were nearly 100,000 immigrants from predominantly Muslim countries, representing one of the largest Muslim migrations in any one-year period in American history. Already there have been several Muslims in the U.S. who have been arrested for planning terrorist activities.

Stopping illegal immigration into America will require hundreds of billions of dollars and several years of committed efforts by state and federal governments. Already, America has an estimated 15 to 20 million illegal aliens, and it would be very easy for terrorists to cross Mexican borders and establish satellite bases across America.

But it's an extremely difficult task to fight the war on terrorism when liberals protest the "unfair treatment" of those whom the government feels are high risk. This is war. And the enemies are not playing by fair rules according to the Geneva Convention, despite what liberal judges say. The liberals in and outside of Washington need to stop impeding the efforts of the U.S. military to handle these terrorists in the manner for which they deserve.

Since September 11, 2001, the U.S. military has been planning to invest more money for unconventional threats, such as terrorism and guerrilla warfare. In addition, Washington plans to invest substantial capital to deal with national crises due to terrorist activities such as safeguarding the water supply, stockpiling vaccines of deadly bacterium and viruses, and guarding nuclear facilities. But these efforts have been slowed by the already massive expenditures created by President Bush.

Although Bush incorporates an estimate of these new costs into projections for defense outlays, most budget experts believe that the forecasts have been significantly underestimated. In addition, the administration has decided not to make any projections for future military operations, opting to use funds as needed through emergency appropriations. This means they will be listed as off-budget items.

For the first time in the post-World War II era, the United States will be burdened by major increases in discretionary spending for virtually every federal program under national defense and foreign aid. This is going to add to what should be considered mandatory spending to the budget over the next two decades, and will further strain the finances of the world's leading debtor nation.

Military Commercialization

There is another less often mentioned threat to America's national security. The source of this threat is corporate greed, and has transformed America's defense industry into a global marketplace for weapons. For several years, Washington has permitted publicly traded defense companies to produce weapons for the global marketplace. America is now engaging in joint research, development and production of advanced weaponry systems with many nations around the world. And Washington has created several agencies under the Department of Defense (the Office for Defense Cooperation) to help U.S. defense companies serve as the world's marketplace for deadly weapons.

America has a long history of benefit from war and expansion of military arms. After World War I, the economy boomed due to heightened demand for military production. Likewise, during World War II, America transitioned out of the "Great Depression" due to the economic benefits of supplying the U.S. military and much of its allies with food, weapons, equipment, textiles, and many other products.

During the Cold War, America had built up an enormous inventory of weapons. But, after the war ended business began to slow for America's defense industry. Aided by President Clinton's policies, American defense companies began to partner with the U.S. military to sell weapons as a way to provide financial stability to this industry and to recover some costs of the Cold War arms buildup. Despite the "war on terror," Washington still permits U.S. companies to sell arms to several nations around the world. And although these nations might be allies today, they could become enemies in the future, as has happened so often in the past. Finally, once arms are sold, there is no way to ensure they don't reach the hands of terrorists.

China

Similar to the economic revolution experienced by America after WWII, China is benefiting as the victor from the free trade war which began over a decade ago. Even before China was admitted to the World Trade Organization in 2001, it has benefited at America's expense. For over two decades, China has delivered an estimated 9 percent annual economic growth that has been boosted to double digits since its induction into the WTO and its election of PNTR status with the U.S. in 2000.

The recent easing of credit provided by private financial institutions has created a huge surge in both home and auto ownership. And although China's decade plus double-digit growth has many in disbelief, there appears to be no end in sight. But similar to all excesses, China's economy will eventually correct over the next few years. However, its oscillation through the global economic cycle is on an up-trend, and China will only continue to become more powerful as America weakens.

Today, every major U.S. company is moving at least a portion of its operations to China. Some have moved their entire manufacturing facilities there. Even Mary K Cosmetics has stated that its largest source of future growth is in China. As well, most high-end retailers predict that China will soon be the world's largest market for the wealthy. In fact, China's demand for luxury goods and services is expected to place it amongst the top two markets over the next few years. Already, it commands the world's number three market for luxury goods, generating more than $2 billion annually, according to Ernst & Young China.

Along with this massive growth and improvement in living conditions, China will continue its enormous demand for fossil fuels. Based on estimates from the U.S. Energy Information Administration, by the end of 2006, China will consume 8 million barrels of oil daily, (versus America's 23 million barrels) but that's only the beginning. China is increasing its oil consumption rate at 30 to 40 percent per year.

Figure 14-4. Estimates for Energy Production and Consumption in China

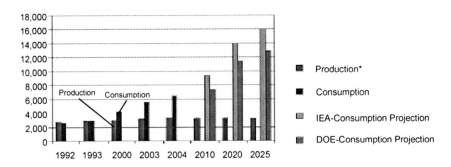

Source: Annual Report to Congress: The Military Power of the People's Republic of China. Department of Defense, Office of the Secretary of Defense. 2005.

Figure 14-5. Current Fossil Fuel Sources for China

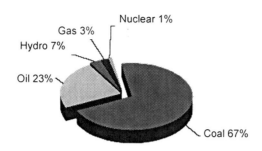

Source: Annual Report to Congress: The Military Power of the People's Republic of China. Department of Defense, Office of the Secretary of Defense. 2005.

China's New Growth Weapon

While many associate Chinese products with inexpensive items found at Wal-Mart and the checkout lanes of smaller stores, China is now becoming a global leader in high-tech goods. However, this should come as no surprise if you consider that up to 90 percent of all components for personal computers made and sold by American companies come from Southeast Asia, mainly China (figure 14-6).

In 2005, China surpassed the U.S. to become the world's leading exporter of technology products, according to data from the OECD (Organization of Economic Co-operation and Development). In 2004 alone, China exported $180 billion in computer equipment, mobile phones and other digital equipment surging past America's $149 billion 2004 IT export figure (figure 14-7). (2)

Figure 14-6. Growth of Chinese Exports of Technology and Telecommunications Goods (in $ billions), 1996-2004

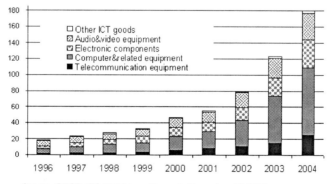

Source: OECD, ITS Database. Figure 3, December 12, 2005.

(2) Information technology (IT) is the key driver of the "Information Age" that began with the rapid dissemination of the Internet in the mid-1990s and includes all forms of technology used to create, store, exchange and use information in its various forms. As you might imagine, IT extends to telecommunications, semiconductors, computer technology and other technologies.

Figure 14-7. Exports of Technology and Telecommunications Goods (in $ billions), 1996-2004

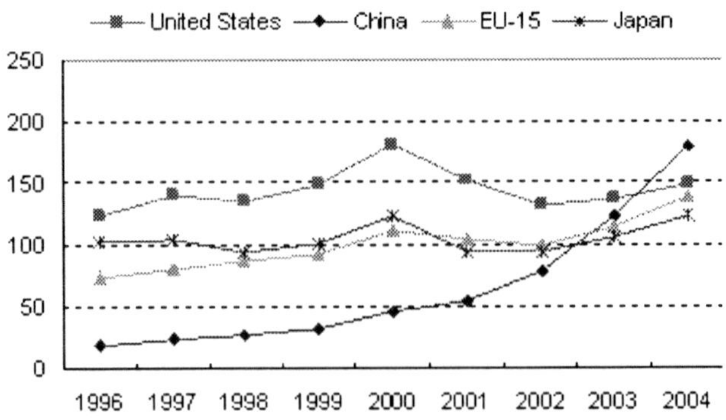

Source: OECD, ITS Database. Figure 1, December 12, 2005.

China Gets Wheels

The Chinese government has stated that it intends to stimulate the economic capacity of its nation by making automobiles affordable to all citizens. Of course, autos will not be the only means of transportation in China. The nation already boasts the world's fastest superconducting train and the government continues to expand railways across its vast mountainous regions, opening access of its large cities to smaller villages. This transportation revolution will help China form an efficient marketplace, all of which will require an enormous supply of fossil fuels.

Even during the early stages of China's expansion, the government has already spent billions on superhighways and has thus far laid down over 34,000 km (21,000 miles) of highways, doubling the 17,000 km it had just five years ago. In total, China's motorway network of 1.8 million km is the world's third largest.

In 2002, demand for autos surged 56 percent, followed by 75 percent in 2003. Only after the government began tightening credit rules for auto purchases did this rate decline to 15 percent in 2004. But China is expected to continue its world-leading GDP growth which should keep auto demand at least in the 10 to 15 percent range for the next several years.

With a per-capita auto ownership of only 7 to 8 per 1000 people, China has a huge potential for further expansion of auto ownership. Yet, *with 5 million autos sold in 2004 alone, China has already risen to become the world's third largest market for automobiles.* And with annual sales in Japan of 5.9 million units (2004), there is no doubt that China will soon take over the number two spot and could even surpass America's 17 million annual unit sales number by 2016.

Typically, a $6000 purchasing power is the level at which car ownership begins to surge. Estimates are that citizens in Eastern China (with an average annual purchasing power of over $7000) will continue to lead the growth of what will eventually become the world's largest auto market. Most notably, *China's demand for autos has also fueled its own auto industry, which has already begun importing low-cost autos into America as of January 2006.*

Even more striking changes have signalled the "Era of the Auto" in China. For instance, in 2004, the local government in Shanghai banned bicycles from the main roads, causing uproar from the some 9 million bicycle users in that city. And China has recently allowed foreign auto makers to invest in its auto plants (as long as the amount is less than 50 percent). Already, Shanghai Automobile Industry Corp has formed a new partnership with Volkswagen.

In 2005, China opened its new National Motor Speedway in Shanghai's Jiading district to showcase the birth of its booming auto industry. By the end of 2006, China plans to erect a $50 million car museum in Jiading. In total, from the beginning in 2002 up until 2008, $6 billion will have been spent to develop China's new auto capital, more than half of which will have come from private investments.

Commodity Bulls Live in China

China can afford to pay high prices for commodities because the only limitations to its continued expansion are natural resources, such as oil, steel, and other construction and industrial use metals and materials. Ironically, America has helped China finance its demand for commodities while impairing its own recovery efforts by contributing to the forces that have kept commodity prices high—serving as China's number one customer for consumer goods.

Make no mistake; the biggest threat to China's rapidly growing economy is expanding its access to an increasingly larger quantity of commodities for its infrastructure build-out. There should be no doubt that *the current bull market in commodities is being led by China's growth demands for raw materials.* And when its economy corrects, the bottom will fall out of commodity prices worldwide. This will be good news for the American economy, which is fueled by inexpensive commodities.

Already China has been very aggressive to secure natural resources around the world—specifically oil—by forming alliances and striking deals with foreign governments. It has even negotiated with Canada, which currently serves as America's number one source of oil imports.

In 2005, investors thought to represent the Chinese government made offers to buy Exxon, silently bought land in the Canadian oil sands, began a new $12 billion pipeline from Canada, and struck key oil and gas deals with Iran and Saudi Arabia. It's obvious that China has become an ally and supporter of Iran, and has used its diplomatic veto powers in the United Nations in exchange for access to lucrative oil deals. At some point, this could create difficulties for the United States, as Iran has gained another ally to use in diplomatic battle while it continues its uranium-enrichment program.

Holding America Hostage

As Wal-Mart's number one business partner, China has benefited over the past decade from the wave of consumer spending stimulated by Greenspan's money machine. In 2004, Wal-Mart purchased around $18 billion in goods from China, which was approximately 10 percent of all Chinese goods sold to America in that year.

All of this business from America has not only led to a huge trade imbalance, but has also resulted in a large ownership in U.S. government bonds. China is now America's number three creditor, behind Japan and the UK with around $1 trillion in U.S. treasuries and other dollar-denominated assets. As American consumers continue to weaken, China will want to diversify its foreign reserves into other currencies such as the Euro and Yen. Currently, over 75 percent of its reserves are in the dwindling dollar. Either way, the question is when China will begin to sell dollars rather than if. And the impact on the stock market could be devastating, causing interest rates to soar and the dollar to plunge. Consider the potential consequences of the mere threat of China selling U.S. treasuries:

- The stock market could drop by 10 percent over a two- or three-day period and could gradually decline by another 10 percent over the next several months from the consequences of this event alone.

- Investors would become more cautious, leading to diminished consumer spending, sending the markets lower over the next several months. Business spending would follow a similar decline, causing unemployment to soar.

- Long-term rates would soar, causing devastation to consumer and corporate credit.

- Investors would sense a drop in wealth, causing even more caution and less spending.

And if China decided to sell a large portion of treasuries over a short time period, the results would be even worse. Of course, China would not be unscathed by such a drastic move. Its interest rates would most likely soar as well. And its central bank would take a big hit on the remaining U.S. bonds held. Finally, declining consumer spending by U.S. consumers and businesses would drastically disrupt the growth of China's economy, collapsing its stock market to lows.

Surely, China would not bite the hand that feeds it. However, it is growing stronger each day, fueled in large part by America's record trade imbalance. And it's using export income to modernize its economic infrastructure while Washington has chosen to address America's economic woes by funding the war in Iraq and Afghanistan. *At some point, China will no longer depend upon American consumers to the same extent it does today. And when that time comes, China will hold the fate of the U.S. economy within its grasp, with very little effects on its own productivity.*

The Best of Both Worlds

Given China's heightened stance in Washington as a top backer of U.S. debt, many American industries have had no way to compete on a level playing field with its unfair business practices and currency manipulation. However, for large corporations, this has created benefit, as outsourcing and relocation to China has lowered costs and increased profits. But this has only benefited shareholders and America's wealthiest citizens at the expense of working-class Americans.

Damage to American companies has not been limited by China's unfair pricing practices and currency manipulation. Many companies without the ability to expand overseas (due to barriers erected by the Chinese government or by geographical restrictions) have gone out of business. Specifically, *anti-subsidy regulations that protect U.S. companies and employees from foreign subsidy programs do not apply to China because it is still considered a non-market economy by the WTO.*

In accordance with the regulations and policies of the WTO, it is considered illegal for the U.S. to protect its industries against Chinese subsides. In addition, further absurd policies of the WTO hold that the U.S. cannot hold China accountable for currency manipulation unless there is evidence that it has also established a large trade surplus with the rest of its trading partners. Of course, this is a ridiculous requirement since China has only pegged its currency to the dollar with good reason; America is the world's biggest consumer marketplace.

India

Not far behind China, India has averaged nearly 7 percent GDP growth over the past several years. Unlike China, India's growth has been sparked by its outsourcing strength, whereas China's growth has been primarily from export revenues. Most notably, India has benefited from the massive outsourcing trends of U.S. corporations, stimulated by the recession in the U.S., as companies have been under pressure from Wall Street to increase profits during sluggish growth. As you might recall, corporate America has responded remarkably well.

Quite simply, India is the world's outsourcing leader, with its IT industry having served as the main catalyst of its growth. Each day, more schools are being built in India to meet the outsourcing demands of corporate America. But it doesn't end with direct call-center outsourcing. U.S. companies have also recently established a large physical presence in India, from GE to Intel, spending billions on new production and research facilities. Microsoft, Oracle and dozens of other software companies are hiring new Indian graduates for their multinational plants as a less expense alternative to American workers. While U.S. companies are saving up to 80 percent in employee costs for outsourcing, Indians are also benefiting by earning salaries up to three times the average wage earner.

Microsoft has recently teamed up with Tata Consultancy Services of India and the Chinese government to develop a global software company in China. As well, Tata has also purchased the world's most advanced and extensive submarine cable system at fire-sale prices. In late 2004, Tyco agreed to sell the Tyco Global Network to the Tata conglomerate for the tiny sum of only $130 million.

With this network, Tata plans to extend to other key nations and expand its already vast outsourcing business model throughout the globe. The sale of this network represents divestiture of the last remaining major intercontinental underwater fiber optic assets by U.S. companies to foreign interests. And this could pose a national security threat as well as further adverse economic consequences for U.S. workers.

The irony of this acquisition is that, since the Internet bubble and scandals in corporate America, U.S. companies, who once owned the vast majority of the world's underwater fiber optics cable networks, have sold what was once valued at $30 billion for only $4 billion. Therefore, *U.S. companies and shareholders have not only financed the transfer of economic power for a small fraction of its value, but they have also helped to transfer the needed telecommunication resources that will further increase offshore outsourcing and the transfer of jobs out of America.* (3)

With all of its growth, India too has experienced a surge in auto ownership. Similar to China, even high-end luxury merchants are anticipating enormous sales, as Asian nations become more familiar with ways to spend their money. Auto sales for small cars have been growing at 17 percent per year, and surprisingly the luxury car market has taken center stage with growth rates of 28 percent. Rather than previous emphasis on fuel efficiency and cost, Indians are now looking at design appeal and brand name, something typical of Western societies.

In 2004, India had over one million new car sales. This number is expected to increase over the next several years, as more Indians continue to benefit from U.S. outsourcing trends. It appears as if corporate America, due to its greed and continued support from Washington, is creating benefit for everyone except American workers.

War on the Dollar

The Dollar: Backed by Oil

Not many will dispute the fact that the United States is the world's economic and military leader. Some might even call America an empire. However, unlike a typical empire which taxes the nations it controls, America uses diplomatic and financial means as a way to exert its power.

Prior to the partial decoupling of gold from the dollar during the Great Depression, America was not really an empire. But in 1971, when President Nixon chose to default on payments of gold for dollars to foreign nations, this began the indirect taxation by America on foreign nations, which positioned America as the global empire.

If America was a corporation, it would have been considered bankrupt when President Nixon defaulted on payments promised in gold. However, since America was so strong, no nation could force it to redeem dollars for gold or stake claim on its assets. Empires usually exert direct control over their captives, but in America's case, control is indirect, and is fueled by the dollar as its weapon of economic and financial control.

Remember that it was during this period that President Nixon also began to sanction many areas of America as government-protected land; regions rich in minerals. Perhaps this was done to assure foreign nations that the U.S. government had sufficient collateral if things got really heated. Shortly after defaulting on its promise to redeem dollars for gold, *Washington negotiated with Saudi Arabia in 1972 to forever support the Royal Saudi Family's reign as long as it demanded dollar payments for oil sales. And soon after, the rest of OPEC followed suit.*

---

(3) As a part of recovery and restructuring from accounting scandals and shareholder lawsuits, Tyco decided to split into three separate companies to focus on its core business. As a result, Tyco wrote down the value of this fiber optic network from $1.2 billion to the $130 million price tag agreed upon by Tata. At the peak of the Internet bubble, these assets were valued at approximately $3 billion.

After OPEC transitioned to dollar-denominated oil transactions, the dollar essentially became backed by oil. This is the primary reason why Washington continues to insist that America has enjoyed a long-standing healthy relationship Saudi Arabia. The fact is that *Washington knows well that Saudi Arabia is not a moral ally, but a financial one, having positioned the dollar as the world currency, in exchange for protection against hostilities that might threaten the royal family's reign.*

Consequently, because the dollar is accepted as the world currency, as more dollars are printed, *foreign nations are forced to accept dollar payments and therefore suffer the effects of diminished buying power. Think of it as an indirect tax on the rest of the world.* Yet, there is little the world can do since holding the dollar is required for international commerce.

But much of the world has changed drastically over the past two decades, and no longer does OPEC depend upon the American economic engine for oil revenues. As well, *free trade is serving to indirectly severe the dollar's clout by forces that have caused America to lose much of its wealth, income and intellectual property.* Herein lays the Achilles heel of America. If the dollar loses its strength as the universal standard, America will be headed for a catastrophe of historic proportions from which it may not recover.

Attacking the Dollar

In late 2000, when Saddam Hussein demanded Euro-denominated payments for Iraq's oil, the U.S. invaded Iraq and overthrew him three years later. Whether, the invasion was due Saddam's attack on the dollar is up for debate, but it was most certainly a factor.

In March 2006, Iran started an international oil exchange (the Iranian Oil Bourse) for buyers and sellers of crude oil to be paid only in Euros. If successful, this could be one of the catalysts that helps destroy the dollar as the universal currency standard. As well, other forces are in motion that may add to an abandonment of the dollar, such as the central banks of Russia and Asia adding more gold reserves.

Payment in Euros for oil would be good for most of the world but disastrous to America. The Middle East and Russia do a significant amount of commerce with Europe, so a shift to the Euro would make exchange rate disparities much smaller. As well, China wants to diversify into other foreign currencies and add gold to its central banks. *Now that Iran is trying to decouple the dollar from oil, it appears as if a military conflict of some sort is inevitable unless Iran ends the Oil Bourse or it fails. Perhaps you now realize why Iran is developing uranium-enrichment facilities.*

Certainly, it will be no easy task for nations to replace the dollar as the universal currency standard, especially since the two largest oil exchanges are owned by America— the New York Mercantile Exchange (NYMEX) and London's International Petroleum Exchange (IPE). However, already there is an alliance between Iran, China, Russia, and India (the Shanghai Cooperative Group) that could present barriers for America in diplomatic negotiations requiring the oversight of the United Nations.

If in fact the dollar begins to be seen as a questionable universal standard of currency, this will wreck havoc in America; interest rates will soar to double-digits, inflation will skyrocket, and any significant sell-off of U.S. treasuries could create a domino effect, as nations rush to exit, causing the price of the dollar to descend further.

Conclusions

Even if America fixes its socioeconomic problems, the risk of an international crisis is huge and could be triggered by a global battle for oil. Alternatively, a large terrorist attack could trigger the economic vulnerabilities hidden within America's economy, sending it into a long downward spiral.

One or more of any potential international episodes—terrorist attacks, continued problems in Iraq, Iran, or a fight for the world's last remaining oil reserves—could lead to future military actions and perhaps WWIII. Many wars have been fought over oil, and even when oil does not appear to be a primary cause, adequate supplies during war is absolutely critical for military power.

The Middle East controls the world's largest and highest quality oil reserves. And given the new era of extreme Islamic activities and their links with OPEC, there could be a worldwide disaster brewing over the next ten to twenty years, with China and Russia as participants.

Part IV

WHAT TO DO

15

LOADED CANNONS

Current State of the Economy

Despite recent reports of outstanding employment numbers and record corporate earnings, the state of the U.S. economy and financial markets are not what they appear. As mentioned previously, much of this data has been due to the "smoke and mirrors" trickery of the government, record low corporate taxes, loose credit policies of the Federal Reserve, and overseas expansions by corporations. However, this illusion of short-term gains has surfaced at the expense of record consumer and national debt, a wave of job losses, stagnant wages, and a healthcare crisis that remains unaddressed by Washington.

With credit tightening and home equity loans depleted, consumers will soon falter due to subdued real job growth, declining job quality and employee benefits, and a negative savings rate. These trends could surface sometime in 2007 or 2008, as up to $4 trillion of outstanding residential mortgage debt is set to reprice upwards by the end of 2007. As well, rising interest payments on up to $2 trillion of revolving consumer debt is sure to take its toll on consumers.

The consequences of these disparities may not be sufficient to cause a devastating depression. But at some point, America will pay the price for over two decades of excess consumer and government consumption that has resulted in a massive credit bubble, free trade policies that have sent millions of jobs overseas, and pension, Social Security, and healthcare crises—all consequences of America's declining living standards. These problems will be further magnified when the baby boomers begin to retire in a few years.

Contrary to popular belief, the U.S. economy is still in a correction phase as a result of the previous bull market period, which was fueled by inexpensive oil, credit spending and massive foreign capital investment. While many feel the U.S. has recovered from the affects of the Internet bubble, Greenspan's rate collapse caused a shift of assets from the stock market into the real estate bubble as a way to delay the inevitable correction needed to restore America's economic balance. In the process of mitigating the stock market fallout, Greenspan's loose monetary policies have swelled America's credit bubble to very dangerous levels. Consequently, the indirect effects of this bubble and the inescapable weakness of the U.S. economy have caused the dollar to remain low.

As well, the expansion of global trade and weakness of the dollar have combined with China's tremendous demand for raw materials to create a commodities bubble that is approaching its end. Accordingly, throughout the duration of the current secular bear market, I am predicting low single-digit average annual returns for the Dow Jones and S&P 500 indices for 2001 to the 2012 period. I will discuss this analysis in detail in the next chapter.

At a time when they are most needed, government benefits programs such as Social Security, Medicaid, and Medicare are not meeting the growing demands of most, due to misaligned economic and monetary policies of Washington. As well, most pension plans (private and public) are underfunded and threaten to force many retirees back into the workforce with low-paying jobs that will not provide healthcare benefits. At the core of America's biggest problems are its poorly designed free trade and its healthcare policies, both serving as a unified and powerful force to assure America's continued decline.

No one knows for certain to what extent the current economic conditions will contribute to the coming economic meltdown. The economy might stage a gradual and superficial rebound in a few years as it has recently, or it could remain sluggish and sink deeper as the problems continue to unfold. Indeed, this is usually how major crises occur. Just when you think things have gotten better, reality sets in and takes everyone by surprise. Regardless, the fact is that the economy has not shown any real improvements since its fallout early in President Bush's tenure.

At the very best of outcomes, America will struggle with these issues, as real economic growth continues to suffer. As a worst-case scenario, America could slide into a deep depression over the next two decades, as the baby boomers reach retirement with very little assets, high debt, and faced with skyrocketing healthcare and energy costs. I have previously detailed numerous alternatives that could trigger America's inevitable period of corrective socioeconomic realignment.

The Economy is Improving?

Hidden from the reports by Washington and the media is the fact is that consumer spending has been fueled with home equity loans, other cash-out financings and record levels of consumer debt. It hasn't been job creation or wage growth that has fueled this phantom recovery, as the masters of propaganda would have you believe. As a matter of fact, net job and real wage growth have been virtually absent, while outsourcing continues to devastate workers, leaving millions without healthcare for themselves and their families. Finally, Bush's tax cuts have registered no improvements in disposable income, but have only provided benefit to wealthy Americans and large corporations.

As has been occurring for many years, America continues to spend money it does not have. Adding insult to injury is that Asia has benefited from unfair trade practices while helping to heightened consumer and national debt. As well, dozens of American industries have had to close their doors due to price fixing and currency manipulation by China. But many of these companies have managed to grow profits through outsourcing and relocation. In contrast, laid off workers have had few options.

Washington remains powerless to stop unfair pricing and currency manipulation by China due to the restrictions set in place by the World trade Organization. But our great leaders knew what they were doing when they entered free trade. The goal was to empower corporate America, with no regard for the working class. And industry lobbyists have rewarded them with large "donations." The recent scandals linking many politicians with bribes are just the tip of a huge iceberg that remains hidden.

In fall 2005, the average American savings rate plunged to -2.8 percent for the first time ever. Meanwhile, consumer debt continued to make new highs. Yet, Washington has allowed mortgage companies to provide credit to virtually anyone with a pulse. As interest rates continue to rise, we will see just how "good" the economy really is.

If the economy is so "good" why has it been driven by credit spending? If the economy is so "good" why are consumers loaded with debt? And why have companies been sitting on over $2 trillion of cash, choosing not to invest in new projects other than those overseas? *During strong economic recoveries tax revenues are high, normally accounting for a large portion of the GDP. But we have seen the opposite* (figure 15-1).

Finally, economic recoveries are the result of net job and real wage growth, as well as an increase in savings rates, none of which have occurred. The inflation-adjusted income of the average American household has declined in every year President Bush has been in office. In contrast, credit-based consumption has mounted steady gains along with federal and consumer debt. These trends have been in place for two decades but have accelerated over the past decade to dangerous levels. Specifically, consumption growth outpaced GDP by 6 percent annually from 1994 through 2005. In other words, *America has been consuming 6 percent more than it has produced for over a decade.* As you might imagine, if you calculate the compounded rate of excess consumption, it is similar to levels of both federal and consumer debt growth over this period at over 80 percent.

Bush's Record-Setting Achievements

President Bush has set many records during his tenure. I have already discussed his annual deficits, which have led to an increase in the national debt by nearly 50 percent in less than two terms in office. As well, a record number of pension plans became underfunded during his first term, and this trend has extended through his second term.

Due to America's consumption-income disparity, debt service payments reached their highs for median income families since 1995, and for all income classes since Bush took office (figure 15-2). *During his first term, America registered a record 5 million personal bankruptcies,* prompting the strict bankruptcy reform bill to be passed in late 2005. In fairness to the President, much of these problems were the consequences of Greenspan's loose monetary policies. But he has only made the problem worse by facilitating the growth of this historic credit-spending spree.

Surely someone has benefited under Bush's watch. Corporate America has recorded its best four and one-half year period of profit growth since the post-WWII period; nearly six decades. Supporters of Bush's tenure might point to the impressive record number of home owners. But you really don't own your home until the mortgage is paid off. And rather than record home ownership, I expect the present housing bubble to be remembered for record foreclosures and possibly a blowup in the MBS market, sending the stock and bond markets plummeting.

> **Paul Volcker**
>
> *"We have a 75% chance of a major crisis over the next five years...I don't know whether change will come with a bang or a whimper, whether sooner or later. But as things stand now, it is more likely than not that it will be a financial crisis rather than a policy foresight that will force change."*

Figure 15-1. Tax Revenue as a Percent of GDP

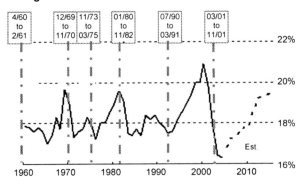

The boxed dates listed indicate recessions
Sources: Office of Management and Budget, Congressional Budget Office

Figure 15-2. Consumer Debt Service Payments to Disposable Income

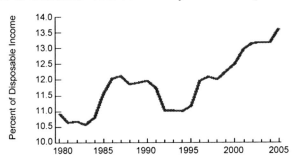

Source: Federal Reserve Board, Debt Service & Financial Obligations Ratios, Survey of Consumer Finances

The real source of GDP growth since its trough in 2003 has been from one source—credit spending by Washington and consumers. In 2005 alone, Washington spent nearly $1 trillion for the relief efforts due to Katrina, the wars in Iraq and Afghanistan, and for interest payments to the national debt—all considered a wash since no improvements were made in living standards. That amounts to 7.5 percent of the 2005 GDP of around $13.4 trillion, accounting for nearly 200 percent of 2005 GDP growth. Over the next decade, the President's Part D Medicare plan alone will add over $600 billion to the GDP (or nearly 4 percent of GDP growth) annually, contributing to the illusion of growth. Yet, millions of seniors will still struggle to pay for prescription drugs.

Expenditures for these programs will continue to soar over the next decade. The GOA has estimated that an additional $6.5 to $7.0 trillion (an additional $700 billion for Iraq, $300 billion for Katrina, and $5.5 to $6.0 trillion for Part D Medicare) will be needed to fund these programs. Other sources such as the CBO quote these future liabilities to be even higher. This ensures the continuation of America's "growth illusion" since GDP will grow from these expenditures alone. But these funds will have to be borrowed.

In exchange for this spending spree, Americans have seen declines in both the quality and number of jobs created, while living standards in Asia continue to improve. Since the end of the recession in 2001 (now in question, Chapter 11), real average weekly and hourly wages have been in decline (as of summer 2006) according to the EPI.

Figure 15-3. Job Growth in the Wake of 2003 Tax Cuts Well Short of Administration Projection

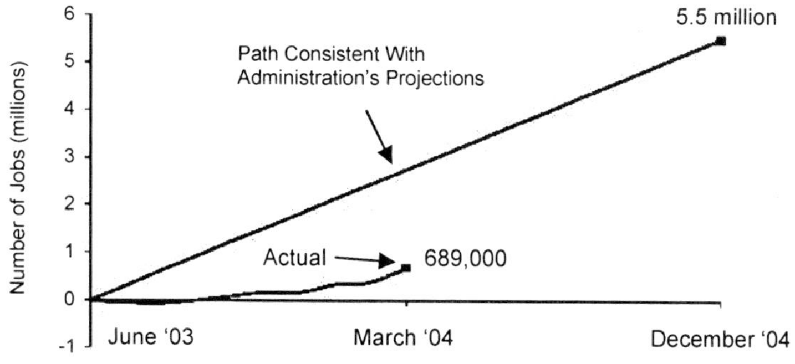

Source: Economic Policy Institute and U.S. Department of Labor

Based upon historical accounts, *President Bush has led the weakest job recovery in the history of America, adding an average of only 34,000 jobs per month for a 0.3 percent annual growth rate.* During all other post-war periods, job growth has averaged 2.2 percent annually. However, it gets worse when you realize that job quality has also declined. Finally, the *recent unemployment numbers that fell below 5 percent in the spring of 2006 were primarily a result of more underemployed and non-traditional positions that offer few if any benefits,* as well as the effect of unemployed (discouraged) workers who are no longer counted in the unemployment statistics.

The President's tax cuts didn't provide any improvement to the economy. They only served to increase spending, while incomes declined. Even the U.S. Census Bureau reports that real median household incomes have declined for every year President Bush has been in office (2001 to 2004), falling from $46,058 to $44,389 (adjusted for inflation). Finally, the poverty rate has increased during this same period from 11.7 to 12.7 percent using the government's ultra-conservative criteria for poverty.

Job growth, quality and wages have been an embarrassment for the President. But the effects on the consumer have been shielded by record credit-spending that has led to record trade deficits with China. We see the first indicators of what the future holds, with household debt soaring by 11.1 percent in 2004 to 121.2 percent of disposable income by the third quarter of 2005. This growth in debt spending has even surpassed the high inflation period of 1986. *And despite the relatively low interest rate environment during the current period, the average American household had a debt service payment of 13.8 percent of disposable income; another record for President Bush* (figure 15-2).

But this massive consumer debt has registered positive effects for Washington. Estimates are that *in 2005, anywhere from 40 to 60 percent of the GDP growth was due to consumer spending fueled by home equity loans.* Similar results were recorded for 2004. Thus, when you combine consumer credit-spending with the $2 to 3 trillion-plus of non-productive government spending, it is easy to see that GDP growth since 2003 has been an illusion. Finally, when one adds the $3 trillion spent from 2003 to 2005 for Social Security benefits Medicaid and Medicare, it's quite easy to appreciate the illusiveness of GDP data. This grand illusion will only magnify, as these expenses balloon when the boomers reach retirement age in a few years. It's clear that Washington has only designed a recovery for corporate America at the expense of American jobs and record levels of debt (figure 15-4).

318

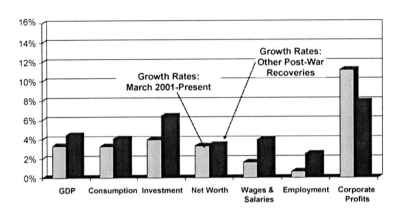

Figure 15-4. Growth Rates of Major Economic Indicators
(measured through business cycle trough)

Source: CBPP calculations based on Commerce Department, Labor Department, and Federal Reserve Board data.

If the Fed Says So, It Must Be True

Since 2004, Wall Street has praised the misleading record earnings of corporate America, and has used this data to spread the propaganda of a strong economic recovery. But the fact is that analysts have been on the conservative side of earnings estimates as a way to boost the perception of a recovery. In reality, most companies have been hoarding cash, cutting costs, buying down debt, failing to invest in new domestic projects, and announcing stock buyback programs—all to increase their earnings per share. Finally, earnings from America's largest companies have benefited from outsourcing and corporate migration overseas. As a result of these activities, total employee compensation in America has been in decline while job security no longer exists.

In the spring of 2006, the official unemployment rate sank to an amazing 4.5 percent for the first time in several years, followed by 4.3 percent in the fall. In general, 5.0 percent unemployment rate is considered "full-employment" and economic theory tells us that when full employment is reached, wages are forced up due to the lack of qualified workers. However, we have only seen real wage declines. This does not make sense unless you consider that employment figures are misleading and do not account for total unemployment, underemployment, or employment in non-traditional jobs that are lower-paying, less stable, and provide little if any employee benefits. *What has actually happened is that the globalization of economies produced by free trade has pushed American wages down (in the form of low raises and cuts in employee benefits) while boosting wages in developing nations, compliments of corporate America and Washington.*

Yet, Wall Street and Washington would have you think otherwise. President Bush continues to report real job growth by cherry-picking misleading statistics. And all throughout 2005, Mr. Greenspan and Wall Street refused to acknowledge inflation as a major problem as oil prices surpassed historical highs. Meanwhile, America's largest oil companies reported record profits (as they have for the past four out of five consecutive years) at the expense of consumers. As a reward for their deceitful manipulation of oil prices, many oil industry CEOs were awarded 9-figure retirement packages.

Even today, Bernanke only mentions inflation as a minor potential difficulty, when in fact it has become a major enemy of the economy. Finally, pension plans continue to struggle, in large part due to a healthcare crisis that has not even been mentioned by Washington. Therefore, *with household savings rates at all-time lows, consumer debt at all-time highs, record Federal debt and trade deficits, no real job or wage growth, a prolonged military conflict in Iraq, a weak dollar, record energy prices, a real estate bubble ready to burst, increasing inflation, a record number of underfunded pensions, increasing dependency on Social Security, and a healthcare crisis that keeps getting worse, how can anyone claim that the U.S. economy is improving? Are you kidding?*

With interest rates on the rise, many home owners and real estate investors with ARMs and other variable rate mortgages are already feeling the heat. In 2004 alone, over 25 percent of all home purchases were made by investors. And in California, estimates are that up to 50 percent of all condo purchases over the past two years have been made by investors. ARMs now account for about 30 percent of all outstanding residential mortgages in America.

> *"This administration and previous administrations have set us up for a major financial crisis on the order of what Argentina experienced a couple of years ago."*
>
> Lawrence Kotlikoff, economics chairman Boston University

Normally, real estate provides a great hedge against inflation, but not when it has been purchased at inflated prices. Regardless, even a soft landing in the real estate market (which is highly unlikely) will not allow America to escape the economic disaster that lies ahead. America continues its record-setting spending spree. Consumers have maxed out their credit cards and have extracted over $2 trillion in equity from their homes in the past five years alone. As the housing bubble continues to swell, residential mortgage debt has already surpassed 80 percent of disposable income, while total household debt is nearly 95 percent of GDP (figure 15-5).

Between 1989 and 2001, the median mortgage debt rose by nearly 300 percent for household incomes in the lowest quintile, while rising by 200 percent for the fourth quintile. Simultaneously, the mortgage industry has posted record profits by handing out loans to many consumers that have no the ability to repay them. Meanwhile, Washington watches, many politicians fooled by their own deceit, while others are praying for a miracle.

Figure 15-5. Household Debt as a Percentage of GDP

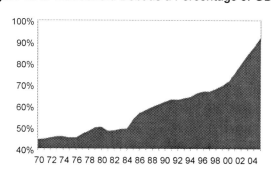

Source: Federal Reserve Z-1, Bureau of Economic Analysis, Q3 2005 data

Since 1989, the rate of foreclosures has increased five-fold to over 550,000 in 2001, reaching an all-time high in the summer of 2003. Currently, the foreclosure rate is not far off these recent highs with an estimated 1.3 million in 2006. In the 2001 to 2002 period alone before interest rates collapsed, the Federal Reserve estimated that up to 45 percent of all refinancing transactions in America resulted in extraction of equity from their home, causing higher monthly payments, while reducing their total home equity. Already as of 2003, despite soaring home prices, home owners' equity as a percentage of real estate value has reached record lows at 55 percent due to cash-back refinancings. Most likely, this ratio is below 50 percent today. When real estate prices collapse, the Center for Economic Policy Research has estimated that this ratio could fall as low as 43 percent; a very dangerous level. When the real estate correction is over, many home owners will be stuck with negative equity due to home values falling below outstanding mortgage balances.

Bankruptcies have already soared since the Internet bubble deflation. Data from 2002 reported 1.5 million personal bankruptcies versus only 289,000 in 1980. Since then, bankruptcies peaked at 1.8 million in 2004. Remarkably, over 90 percent of recent bankruptcies have been from middle-class families.

Figure 15-6. Personal Bankruptcies per 100,000 People

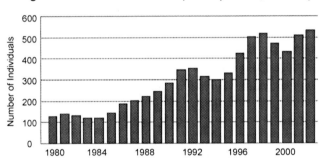

Source: The Century Foundation. "Life and Debt: Why American Families Are Borrowing to the Hilt" 2004. Calculations based on data from the American Bankruptcy Institute and the Bureau of Census, U.S. Department of Commerce. http://www.tcf.org/Publications/EconomicsInequality/baker_debt.pdf

Depending on how the data is amassed, reports range anywhere from $3,800 (spread across all American households) to $8,600 (for each American with credit card debt) as the average balance per consumer credit card. These irresponsible consumption patterns are due to the wealth effect, which will not last much longer, as interest rate increases could reprice over $4 trillion of consumer credit and mortgage debt upwards by the end of 2006 alone, with more to come over the next two years. Washington has served as the role model for Americans, having surpassed record deficit and debt levels, while recording negative savings for each year Bush has been in office (figures 15-7 and 15-8).

Many economists feel that investment is the key for ensuring a strong economy, and I would agree. However, this must be balanced with a responsible level of savings as well as a healthy return on these investments. *Even more important than the activity of spending (investing) is to understand where the money has come from and whether it is truly providing economic benefit resulting in an improved standard of living.*

Figure 15-7. Government Gross Saving (1940 to 2006)

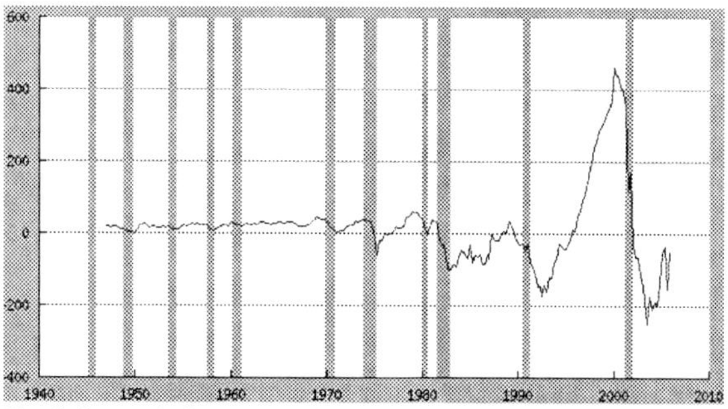

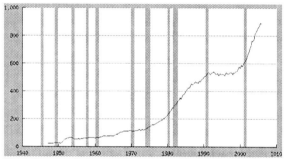

Shaded areas indicate recessions, as determined by the NBER.
Source: U.S. Department of Commerce: Bureau of Economic Analysis
Graph constructed by the St. Louis Federal Reserve Bank, 2006. www.research.stlouisfed.org

Figure 15-8. Federal Government Investment Expenditures (1948 to 2006) in Billions$

Shaded areas indicate recessions, as determined by the NBER.
Source: U.S. Department of Commerce: Bureau of Economic Analysis
Graph constructed by the St. Louis Federal Reserve Bank, 2006. www.research.stlouisfed.org

At some point when debt becomes too high, the risk of default well exceeds any potential benefits. Currently for the United States, interest payments on the national debt are approaching 2 percent of GDP which, along with deficit spending at 6 percent of GDP will cause the further devaluation of the dollar. As well, with about 50 percent of all U.S. treasuries held by foreign nations, America will soon be at the mercy of the developed world, causing it to lose diplomatic momentum, due to the financial leverage held by key nations.

The liberization of the consumer credit industry over the past decade has done well to mask the loss of wealth and productivity experienced by America. But this charade has been going on for over two decades now, and cannot last much longer. Up until mid-2005, Americans enjoyed a two-year period of record low interest rates, providing them with inexpensive access to credit. Now that rates are approaching their historic mean, there remain no other tools by the Fed to prevent an economic meltdown. The deflation of the real estate bubble alone could lead to a recession by late 2007 or early 2008. And this could serve as a prelude to a darker period over the next decade, when the world oil supply reaches peak production, and after nearly half of America's 76 million baby boomers reach retirement age.

The American Worker

Employee benefits comprise about 42 percent of total payroll costs according to the U.S. Chamber of Commerce. What's happening is that the competitive forces of free trade are causing businesses to shift more of the benefits portion of total employee compensation onto workers rather than their lower wages.

As a way to mask their declining living standards, Americans are working longer hours. Many have more than one job or a side business, and while two-income households have become the norm. As the average American struggles just to pay their bills, they enjoy less leisure time, have higher rates of stress and spend much less time with their families than in the past. *Compared to most other developed nations, Americans have shorter life spans, fewer vacation days, work longer hours, and yet America remains the only developed nation that does not provide healthcare to its citizens.*

In early 2006, the unemployment rate gradually declined below 5 percent for the first time since the early stages of the Internet fallout, reinforcing the misconception of a strong economy. However, we must remember that millions of America's unemployed simply gave up looking for work and are no longer counted in unemployment figures (the discouraged worker) after six months. What does a person do when his company goes bankrupt or when production facilities have been moved overseas? It's not exactly an easy task to find a new position in an industry that is on its last leg. And as we all know, when you are unemployed in America you lose your health insurance; not only for yourself, but also for your family.

Finally, we must question not only the number of jobs, but the quality of these jobs. More and more, U.S. companies are hiring contractors, part-time employees, and coming up with other employee arrangements that allow them escape the costs of full employee benefits. This trend has been accentuated by the outsourcing wave that has infected most American companies. Outsourcing is due to the declining competitiveness of the American workforce, exposed by free trade and compounded by employer costs of a ridiculously priced healthcare system. Therefore, these labor trends will continue to persistent until the core problems have been fixed.

Figure 15-9. Real Median Earnings, Full-time Workers (2001Q1-2006Q1)

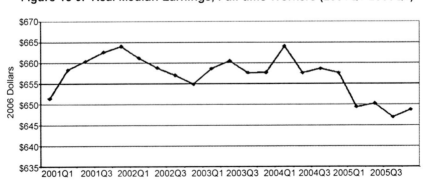

Source: Economic Policy Institute

323

America has exhausted the surplus wealth generated by its post-war manufacturing dominance and has entered the twenty-first century with declining competitiveness, a decreased standard of living, excessive inflation for all basic necessities, and a federal government that relies on foreign capital to pay its bills. And this has led to the desperate efforts of the Fed to lower rates to the point where even the many of America's gainfully employed have maxed out their credit. Meanwhile, *the real value of minimum wage has been in decline for over four decades (15-10). In contrast, CEO compensation continues to reach new highs* (figure 15-11 and 11-8).

Figure 15-10. Real Value of Minimum Wage (1947-2006)*

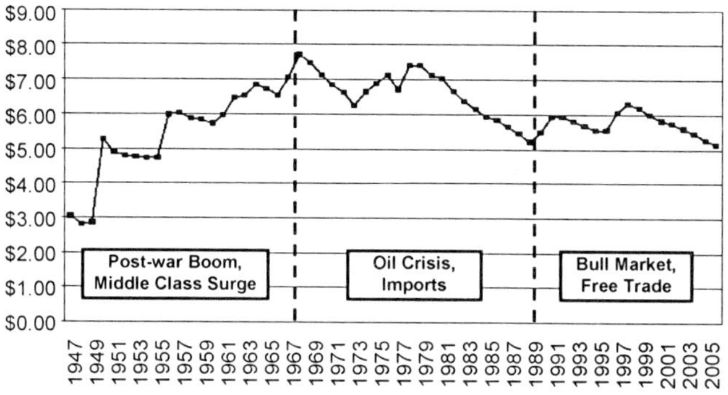

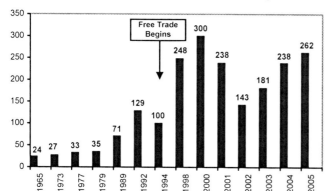

Notice how minimum wage soared during the post-war economic boom, leading to the dominance of America's middle-class.

Notice its decline during the oil crisis and entry of Asian goods during the 1970s and 1980s.

Finally, notice how the "booming economy" of the 1990s caused no increases in minimum wage.

*Through May 2006
Source: Economic Policy Institute; modifications to chart and comments to the right made by Stathis

Figure 15-11. Ratio of CEO to Average Worker Pay (1965-2005)

CEO compensation was held in check during the post-war boom, which gave rise to America's middle-class dominance.

Starting in 1994, America's entry into free trade began a surge in CEO compensation.

Since 1994, CEOs have been rewarded for impoverishing American workers.

Source: Economic Policy Institute; comments to the right made by Stathis

Where Are the Jobs?

President Bush has made many claims about job growth during his tenure. Yet, the fact is that net job growth and quality have been absent. In addition, most of the jobs added during Bush's tenure have been defense and government-related (figure 15-12). However, these jobs might be amongst the better ones created since they provide full healthcare and retirement benefits. In contrast, many of the non-government jobs formed during Bush's tenure have had decreased or no employee benefits.

Figure 15-12. Sources of Change in the Number of Jobs Since Fiscal Year 2001

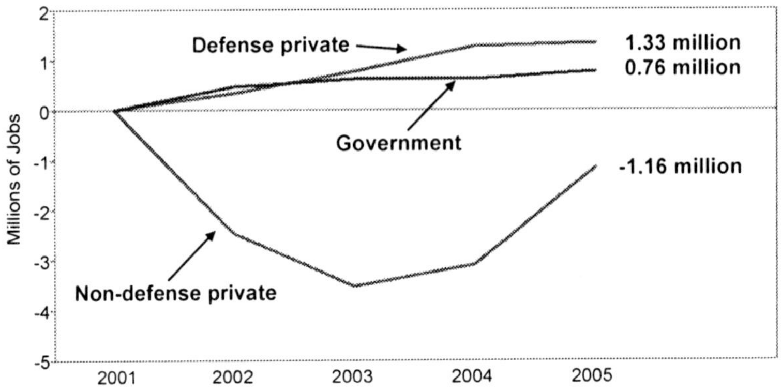

Source: Economic Policy Institute

The Elderly Labor Force

You may have heard the latest buzz phrase regarding age… "the 40 year olds are the new 30 year olds," reflecting the upward mobility of our increasing life spans. Apparently, this mentality has not caught on with corporate America since the common notion is that employees over 40 are considered old. Even worse, employees over 60 are considered mentally slow, less creative, and overall unattractive to the labor force. This is not only ridiculous, but it addresses the widespread problem of age discrimination. While illegal, it's difficult to prove so there really have been no attempts to enforce it.

Barring age-related mental disease that could restrict or impair thought processes, most senior citizens have a wealth of knowledge and experience which cannot be substituted by younger workers. I invite you to visit your local bank or consumer electronics store where you will see poorly-trained kids, often holding managerial positions. Many are only qualified to run a lemonade stand. It's never been more difficult to resolve customer service issues than in present-day America due to the replacement of America's retail workforce with lower-wage, underqualified younger workers.

One thing is for certain—America will never mend its economic crisis until it begins to shed the myths of older individuals being less productive in the workplace. Perhaps this had some merit before 1970, when the economy was based on manufacturing and many occupations required physical strength. But America now has a service economy in the midst of the Information Age, where experience in human interactions and relationship management are as critical as the ability to adapt to new technologies in the workplace.

Economies must shift with demographics, not only to serve consumers, but also to utilize the resources of the local labor force. And if America wants a chance to revitalize its economy, it will utilize those boomers who are able and eager to work instead of throwing them away or putting them in jobs that do not fully harness their experience and wisdom. Of course, with the majority of healthcare expenses occurring after age 50, companies may be reluctant to add the liabilities of healthcare costs for elderly workers. But we already know what must be done to rescue America from a collapse, and a national healthcare system is the first step towards these efforts.

Box 15-1: How to Be a Team-Player in Washington
A Speech from Secretary of Labor Elaine Chao, December 8, 2005

The following speech is a perfect example of how Washington uses inaccurate and misleading data to gain consumer confidence. I wonder if Secretary Chao actually believes what she is saying. Most likely, she's as much in the dark about the economy as Washington. After all, that's one of the required qualifications for serving as a cabinet member. It's unacceptable to be too smart. Otherwise, it would be difficult to serve as the President's cheerleader. What Chao has done is send a message political leaders that she will play the game as needed. And this will most likely land her another political position in the future. And the fact that she is a female from a representative minority group certainly won't hurt her chances either. Read below, as Chao demonstrates how to climb the ladder of political success in Washington. Based upon this speech, in my opinion, Chao is either an idiot or else a complete liar; maybe both. Some might categorize her as a typical politician.

Chao: "Just look at the results for this year (2005). Third quarter GDP growth exceeded expectations at an amazing 4.3 percent."

Clarification: As discussed, GDP figures are highly inaccurate, subject to up to five years of revisions, and do not measure the net benefits created; much of the GDP growth has been due to military and other government spending and credit released from low interest rates and home equity loans.

Chao: "With the exception of the month following the recent hurricanes, job growth has been averaging 200,000 per month. More Americans are on the payroll than ever before—134.3 million people."

Clarification: Net job growth has been negative since Bush entered office, while the job quality has declined. Most of these jobs have been government and military-related, financed by the growing record national debt. Most of the other jobs have been part-time or contractor-based, filled by underemployed Americans.

Chao: "And the unemployment rate is 5 percent—lower than the average of the 1970s, 1980s, and 1990s. And just this last week, the Labor Department released a report showing that productivity rose 4.7 percent over the summer...It means higher wages for American workers. It's one of the reasons American workers have the highest living standards in the world."

Reality Check: Productivity or GDP growth does not necessarily imply higher wages. Apparently, Chao doesn't understand the extent of outsourcing or the illusions of GDP data. How can you measure standard of living when you are living off of borrowed money? If America has the world's highest living standard, why is it the world's largest debtor nation? Why are 50 million Americans without healthcare insurance? Why are more Americans working more than one job and still cannot make ends meet without the use of credit? Why is America the only developed nation without required vacation days or maternity leave?

Chao: "Now education does not have to mean a four year college degree. It could mean an associate degree at a community college, technical school or an apprenticeship program."

Explanation: Yes indeed, America's declining global competitiveness and corporate migration overseas combined with the outrageous costs of higher education no longer makes the expense of a 4-year college a viable alternative. Associate degrees and technical schools in America provide dead-end jobs that make job security and career mobility a virtual impossibility due to outsourcing. What Chao is basically saying is "Don't get your hopes up for that high-paying white-collar job; we can also use low-skill labor because it's cheaper for companies to outsource white collar labor."

Chao: "America's workers have every reason to be confident about the future going into the New Year. By every measure, our nation's economy is strong and growing stronger."

Reality Check: Sounds nice doesn't it? How can Americans feel confident about the future when many cannot afford the cost of oil and electricity, thousands of pension plans are underfunded, millions have no healthcare, job security no longer exists, and over 50 percent of America's 76 million baby boomers will enter retirement in poverty? In reality, the wealthy and corporate America have every reason to feel confident about the future. Over the past two decades, America's richest 5 percent have benefited from huge income and wealth growth, while the bottom 95 percent barely improved.

Meanwhile, corporate America continues to get away with massive shareholder and taxpayer fraud with no threat of penalty. The strong relationship between corporate America and Washington is highlighted by the large number of corporate executives who later enter Washington, and politicians who use their political pull to sit on company board seats. These are the same individuals who approve 8-figure salaries and 9-figure retirement packages of America's CEOs. Fueled by exportation of American jobs, corporate America has registered its largest profit growth over in the past four and one-half year period since in 6 decades. And the employment-healthcare link continues to leave more Americans without health insurance, resulting in up to 50 percent of annual personal bankruptcies.

America's Oil Dependence

The U.S. is by far the world's largest consumer of oil, at over 23 million barrels per day, followed by China (8 million), Japan, and Germany. With only 5 percent of the world's population, America consumes over 45 percent of the gasoline on earth, highlighting its dependency for oil. Prior to 1994, the U.S. was able to produce half of its oil needs. But since then, it has continued to rely more heavily on oil imports. Even prior to the 1990s, the U.S. has been the world's leading importer of oil. Currently, America imports over 14 million barrels per day (million bpd), or about two-thirds of its daily consumption.

As the world's most self-sufficient nation, America has become dangerously dependent on imported oil over the past two decades. Since 1994 the U.S. has steadily increased its percentage imported oil, in part due to rising demand, but also due to diminishing production of existing oil fields and the relative lack of new finds. This trend is expected to continue until Washington makes a strong commitment to alternative energy.

Since reaching peak oil production in 1970, the U.S. has continued to spend more money to produce less oil, driving the cost up. And other than one or two large fields in Alaska and the Gulf of Mexico, America has very few new prospects for oil within its geographical boundaries. Thus, oil has now become America's double-edged sword, been so vital in building the world's most robust economy. But now and in the future, unless the U.S. gains access to substantial reserves or dramatically increases alternative and renewable energy facilities, it will be at the mercy of OPEC and the agendas of the Middle East.

Figure 15-13 shows the source of America's oil imports in 2003 (this data has not changed much since then). Note that the U.S. does not depend on the Middle East for a significant amount of oil imports but this is only a recent trend due to finds in Mexico, Venezuela and Canada. However, the Canadian wells are very expensive to mine and will take more than a decade before the proper infrastructure is in place to tap these resources at full capacity. Regardless, with record oil prices, non-OPEC producers are working at full capacity to squeeze out as much oil as they can. And as they continue to deplete their reserves, OPEC is gaining diplomatic and economic leverage (see Chapter Five Supplement, appendix).

Today, for each new barrel of oil America discovers, it consumes anywhere from 2 to 4 barrels. As of 2005, U.S. imports were around 60 percent of consumption (total consumption was 21.4 million bpd versus 13.21 million bpd imported). As of 2003, Canada was America's #1 source of oil imports at 17 percent, Saudi Arabia #2 (14.5 percent), Mexico #3 (13 percent), and Venezuela at 11 percent. And while Iraq has been a very small source of U.S. imports over the past decade (due to trade sanctions and war) we should expect to see a surge in imports over the next few years as Iraq irons out its problems. Keep in mind that oil was selling for just $12 in 1999. During the 1990s, it was selling in the mid-teens after coming down off its OPEC-induced highs a decade earlier. Over the next decade and beyond, America will have to pay for the inexpensive oil of the 1990's. And I have already discussed the effect of high oil prices on the U.S. economy.

Figure 15-13. U.S. Oil Imports (2003)

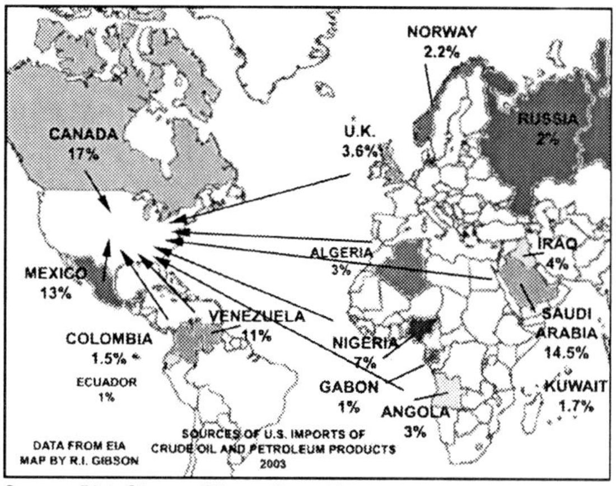

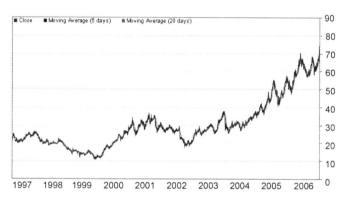

Source: Dick Gibson, Gibson Consulting

Figure 15-14. Recent Oil Prices (2003-2006, NYMEX per barrel)

The NYMEX (New York Mercantile Exchange) trades crude oil, futures and contracts and largely determines the pricing of crude oil in the U.S. via the WTI (West Texas Intermediate)

There are many who claim that oil will not go much higher. But for many reasons, (some of which were discussed in previous chapters) I disagree, and feel that oil will reach the $85 mark by 2009. And there is a good chance it will surpass the $100 mark by 2012 before any chance of reversing its strong upward price trend. At the pump this could translate into $5 per gallon depending upon how much the oil companies decide to line their pockets. The government-biased EIA shows estimates for three scenarios for oil prices through 2030, although many independent experts view even the high-case scenario as conservative (figure 15-15 and section 5.2 of the appendix).

Beyond this difficult period, alternative and renewable sources of energy such as fuel cell technologies, biomass, solar and wind power, and uranium will have matured to replace the drying oil fields of the world. But before the transition to renewable forms of energy, those nations with the largest oil reserves, as well as those companies with access to them stand to gain tremendous economic and diplomatic benefits (figure 15-16).

Figure 15-15. World Oil Prices in Three Cases (1980-2030)

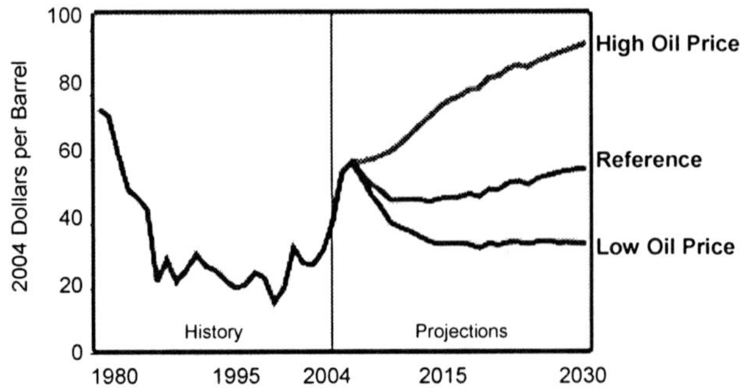

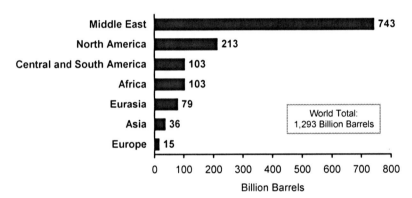

Source: Energy Information Administration, International Energy Outlook 2006, Chapter 3, Figure 32.   June 2006.

Figure 15-16. World Proved Oil Reserves by Geographic Region (as of January 1, 2006)

Source: Energy Information Administration, International Energy Outlook 2006, Chapter 3, Figure 29.   June 2006.
Note: North America's reserves consist mainly of Canada's oil sands, which are nonconventional and have a high cost of mining and refining per barrel.

Higher Prices Hurt Americans the Most

Many Americans are upset over the high price of oil, yet they do not seem to care enough to alter their consumption habits. The "Big 3" continue to make big trucks and SUVs because Americans keep buying them. And Washington politicians refuse to mandate smaller, more fuel-efficient autos using alternative energy because the oil industry has too many lobbyists to keep them in check.

Yet, the reality is that Americans still pay much less for gasoline than people in most nations. In some nations, gasoline prices are three times what Americans pay due to higher gasoline taxes by foreign governments. In contrast, Americans enjoy a relatively low gas tax. As a result, *with each increase in oil prices, America is affected more than many other nations since gasoline taxes are usually fixed.*

Figure 15-17 shows increases in oil dependency for the most oil-dependent industries in America over the past five decades. As you might suspect, if the price of crude goes up over a large amount and sustains these prices for an extended period, the U.S. economy will suffer.

Figure 15-18 shows the factors that make up the price Americans pay at the pump, comparing the changes since the last oil crisis in 1981. As you can see, while gasoline taxes have increased, manufacturing and marketing costs have declined. Regardless, the gasoline tax is still only about 16 percent of the total price per gallon in the U.S. Meanwhile, in Europe the gasoline tax can amount to up to 75 percent of the cost at the pump.

Since these taxes remain fixed, with each increase in oil prices, Americans are affected more so than consumers of foreign nations (since a larger percentage of gasoline costs in America is due to oil prices), even though the overall price for gasoline in America is lower. Therefore, *the prime factor to consider is not the total price paid, but the extent of increases at the pump because rising prices measured against time is the primary indicator of fuel inflation.*

Consumers of other nations are accustomed to higher gasoline prices so they have factored this into their consumer and business spending habits. In contrast, when prices rise over a short period of time, American consumers do not have the opportunity to adjust or budget themselves and this results in a financial squeeze which affects the economy.

U.S. natural gas and coal production has not created as high of a dependency on imports relative to oil. But as demands for fossil fuels continue to approach global production capacity, these energy sources will also begin to dwindle.

Although alternate forms of energy have been available and successfully used in other nations (specifically Western Europe), America has chosen to continue its dependency on fossil fuels, specifically crude oil (see Chapter Fifteen Supplement).

Nation	City	Price in USD Regular/Gallon
Netherlands	Amsterdam	$6.48
Norway	Oslo	$6.27
Italy	Milan	$5.96
Denmark	Copenhagen	$5.93
Belgium	Brussels	$5.91
Sweden	Stockholm	$5.80
UK	London	$5.79
Germany	Frankfurt	$5.57
France	Paris	$5.54
Hungary	Budapest	$4.94
Switzerland	Geneva	$4.74
Spain	Madrid	$4.55
Japan	Tokyo	$4.24
Brazil	Brasilia	$3.12
Taiwan	Taipei	$2.84
South Africa	Johannesburg	$2.62
Nicaragua	Managua	$2.61
Panama	Panama City	$2.19
Russia	Moscow	$2.10
Puerto Rico	San Juan	$1.74
Saudi Arabia	Riyadh	$0.91
Kuwait	Kuwait City	$0.78
Egypt	Cairo	$0.65
Nigeria	Lagos	$0.38
Venezuela	Caracas	$0.12

Prices as of March 2005 when the average price in the U.S. was about $2.20.

Figure 15-17. Energy Consumption by End-Use Sector

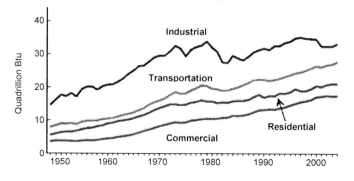

All four major economic sectors have increased their reliance on energy use over the past five decades, most of this coming from the use of oil and gas.

Source: EIA

330

Political and environmental safety concerns in the U.S. have deflected a larger shift towards nuclear power, especially since the Three Mile Island accident and the meltdown at Chernobyl. However, France has successfully transformed almost all of its energy needs through nuclear means without a single problem. No doubt big money and bigger politics have played a large part in America's reluctance to shift to cleaner, more highly available energy sources.

Figure 15-18. Components of Gasoline Price (1981 versus 2005)

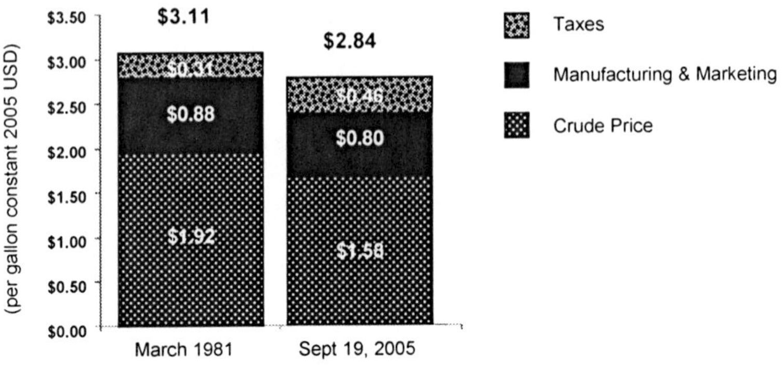

Sources: U.S. Dept of Energy, U.S. Dept of Labor, and API

Nothing Left for America

Oil

As discussed in the previous chapter, China and India are expanding their automotive industries so that they too can begin to enjoy the benefits of a modern economy. With nearly 40 percent of the world's population, these rapidly developing nations are expected to post huge increases in demand for fossil fuels as they continue their aggressive industrial expansion. By 2030, the EIA expects a 47 percent increase in world oil demand relative to 2003. And 43 percent of this increase will come from non-OECD Asia (including China and India).

America's growing thirst for fossil fuels has continued to outpace its productive capacity for over three decades. And this accelerating trend has resulted in a large portion of its imbalance of payments, which has contributed to the recent federal budget deficits. While the U.S. has thus far been able to deliver a higher percentage of its total coal and natural gas needs, it has continued to increase its dependence on foreign sources of crude oil products since coal and gas are limited in their use.

Although the energy usage per dollar of GDP produced by the U.S. has shown a steady decline over this same period, this should not construed as a representation of more efficient energy utilization. Rather, more efficient refinement and production methods have largely resulted in these declines. However, as we approach a global peak production period, these trends may soon reverse, as it becomes more difficult and costly to extract oil from the earth.

Already, many nations appear to be concerned about the approaching global peak oil period, and mounting concerns have stimulated billions of dollars of investment capital into the Canadian oil sands region. Yet, even this huge non-conventional supply will not be sufficient to supply the growing global demand for oil.

Figure 15-19. Crude Oil Well Productivity in America (America's Peak Oil Period)

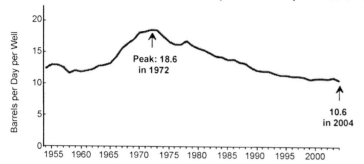

The amount of crude produced daily rose sharply in the mid-1960s and peaked in 1972 at 18.6 barrels per day per well. Since that level, the productivity per well has been gradually declining.

Source: EIA

Government Benefits

In previous chapters, I discussed the trend of increasing mandatory spending by the government and showed that these expenses were due to social programs for low-income, retired and disabled Americans, as well interest expense for U.S. Treasury bonds. The Congressional Budget Office has estimated that these mandatory expenditures will rise to 14 percent of GDP by 2016 (figure 15-20, data excludes interest payments).

These estimates do not incorporate estimates of pension bailout expenses, homeland security, Part D Medicare, or the money earmarked for Iraq. However, I would argue that these items should be treated as mandatory expenses, thereby increasing the number to around 19 percent. But this is only the beginning, as these expenditures are expected to soar by 2030, as the baby boomer generation becomes fully immersed in the benefit stage of Social Security and Medicare.

Even without adding these expenditures, *the CBO estimates by 2050, about 27 percent of the nation's GDP will be used for mandatory expenditures* (figure 15-21). In my opinion, the CBO has severely underestimated the severity of America's finances. Accordingly, *without radical political change or drastic benefit cuts, I would expect this level to be reached by 2030.* Therefore, the question arises; with mandatory spending expected to soar by 2016, and mushroom thereafter, where will the U.S. government obtain funds needed to fuel the economy?

Figure 15-22 shows that income tax revenues are expected to surge over the next 10 years based on estimates of higher income gains from workers. In contrast, excise taxes and corporate tax revenues are expected to continue their long history of gradual declines due to the various loopholes added each year. Finally, *note that the declines in excise and corporate taxes have been made up by increases in payroll taxes. In essence, American taxpayers have been subsidizing the tax breaks provided to corporate America; not exactly the best way to sustain a middle-class society.* It should be evident that Washington has paved the way for America to be controlled by corporations and the wealthy at the expense of the middle class and the poor.

332

Figure 15-20. Spending on Social Security, Medicare, and Medicaid (percentage of GDP)

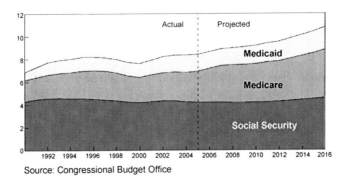

Source: Congressional Budget Office

Figure 15-21. Federal Revenues, Outlays, Deficits % Surpluses (1950-2075) as a % of GDP

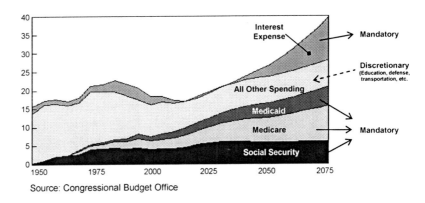

Source: Congressional Budget Office

Figure 15-22. Revenues, by Source, as a Share of Gross Domestic Product

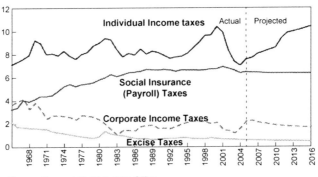

Source: Congressional Budget Office

16

CONSEQUENCES

Healthcare for a Wounded Nation

Sixty years ago, during the post-war population boom, the baby care industry began its explosive growth during a period of amazing economic expansion with virtually no global competition. In the 1970s, when the boomers bought cars the auto industry exploded. A decade later when they purchased homes, the real estate industry grew despite record interest rates.

Ironically, during this time period the consumer finance industry was in its infancy, while Americans had job security, access to affordable healthcare, maintained healthy savings rates, and over 50 percent of the labor force was provided with the stability of pension plans—all the necessary ingredients to ensure the "American Dream." This was also the period when consumer and federal debt were in check.

Over the next three decades, 76 million boomers will file for health insurance claims draining insurance reserves. Currently, with over 35 million Americans over age 65, insurance payments have already contributed to skyrocketing healthcare costs. Yet, 16 percent of America's elderly has no health insurance, public or private because they do not qualify for public assistance nor do they have enough income to afford private insurance. Over the next two decades, the majority of boomers will qualify for Medicare, adding another 40 million into the system, causing further strain on mandatory expenditures.

During America's most recent economic expansion, the stock market soared by over 600 percent from late-1987 to 2000. But the real problems in the economy were masked by growing levels of debt, as America's competitiveness and standard of living continued to decline. Many did not notice however, because they consumed goods and services as before while overall production gradually declined. And as the stock market soared, so did America's debt.

With the approach of peak oil and the entry of millions of boomers into retirement, soon America will be faced with enormous expenses. Already, America has placed a large dependence on foreign nations to finance its record debt. And global tensions emphasize the growing vulnerability of this debt. Regardless how successful Washington may be in reversing its diplomatic decline, no amount of debt will be available to fund the future liabilities of Medicare and Medicaid. Drastic fiscal changes and further benefit cuts will be required to compensate for these shortfalls.

Inflation-Deflation Cycle

During inflation, the money supply increases beyond normal levels, resulting in large increases in credit relative to the amount of available goods and services. As consumers spend more on these items, demand outpaces supply forcing producers to raise prices. Some of the main consequences of inflation are rising commodity prices and changes in currency exchange rates; both huge macroeconomic forces.

Commodities represent the backbone of all economies. And when commodity prices rise, the cost of all goods and services follows. When the price of crude rises, transportation costs increase resulting in higher costs for all goods and services. An increase in fuel prices shrinks disposable income. And many consumers venture to shopping malls and restaurants less often. Higher crude prices also cause the cost of many basic materials to increase—paint, building materials, and plastic goods—since they are made in part by components of crude oil. Finally, high oil prices raise utility bills, shrinking disposable income further.

Modest inflation is a characteristic of a healthy economy because it acts to balance the supply and demand tug-of-war for goods and services. However, when key economic indicators move out of balance, such as interest rates, inventories, etc., this can lead to above average levels of inflation. And when high levels of inflation extend over a long period, it results in a collapse of real wages, savings and investment returns. While inflation has a delayed effect upon the economy, it is a powerful force that is often under-reported due to the prevalent use of core inflation, which excludes food and energy costs. As well, Washington's use of hedonic pricing and Bush's record trade deficits have served well to mask the real inflation that exists today. Essentially, Washington has lowered much of the effects of inflation by borrowing money.

During inflation, bonds perform poorly, while the performance of common stocks is often a mixed bag. When inflation is high, bonds are a bad investment for two reasons. First, bondholders receive a fixed coupon rate which is eroded by the high cost of goods. In other words, the buying power is reduced. Second, because inflation ushers in higher interest rates, those who bought bonds prior to rate hikes will see the market price of their bonds decline, resulting in diminished liquidity. Basically, you have to hold these bonds until rates decline. In the meantime, those coupon payments won't amount to much. *Only when investors are able to time their purchase of bonds at the peak of interest rates and/or when such bonds are indexed to inflation will they come out ahead.* This emphasizes the critical need to for bond investors to really understand the economy.

A sustained and gradual period of inflation allows some companies to raise prices for goods and services, and this can actually result in earnings growth; good for stockholders. However, only certain industries are able to do this, such as alcoholic beverage, tobacco, and gaming companies, for obvious reasons. In contrast, *sharp increases in inflation are bad for nearly all industries. And with rare exceptions, stocks get hammered.*

In general, *the best investments during an inflationary environment are commodities, REITS, and Treasury Inflation-Protected Securities (TIPS), or any other assets tied to floating interest rates.* While commodities are not directly linked to rising interest rates, they tend to perform well during inflation because consumers must pay whatever is charged since these items comprise the basic building blocks of the economy. Typically, commodities won't outperform but they won't get hammered like other assets.

Like everything else, inflation occurs as a part of a cycle which alternates with compensatory periods of deflation. Deflation occurs due to a decrease in money supply causing less credit relative to the amount of goods and services available. This results in a lower demand by consumers which triggers a reduction in prices by businesses. Recently, America was in a deflationary period (2001 to 2004). But prior to that, the last deflationary period occurred some 70 years earlier in the midst of the Great Depression. Therefore, *inflation is the norm and deflation, while still a part of this cycle, is less common and therefore less familiar to most consumers.*

Because inflation is a normal phenomenon, deflation tends to only occur when excesses in inflation have resulted in credit bubbles, such as during the late 1920s and 1990s. During the 1930s, deflation appeared due to the inability of banks to lend money and the lack of credit worthiness of consumers. Those who were good credit did not want to borrow money because they felt prices would continue to decline, making the goods they might have purchased worth less. This deflationary period served to rebalance the supply and demand for goods that was made lop-sided by the actions of the Fed.

Was this recent deflationary period sufficient to restore the economy back to normal? Not at all. In fact, Greenspan heightened the problem by releasing money into the banking system at record levels. Now America is faced with a real estate and credit bubble that have swelled to dangerous levels.

Inflation or Deflation?

There appears to be a debate among those who understand the dangers that lie ahead whether America's economic meltdown will occur by inflation or deflation. America already faces an inflationary environment fueled by record oil prices. And considering I expect these prices to remain high, I am betting on inflation to be the cause and/or the consequence of the fallout. However, if conditions get really bad, deflation could be a later stage consequence.

As previously discussed in Chapter Ten, the capital markets might blow up due to a failure in the mortgage-backed security market, as an aftermath from a correction in the real estate bubble. This could lead to defaults on trillions of dollars in loans, resulting in a deflationary environment. A severe blow to the MBS market would be one of the worst-case scenarios because it would lead to the loss of huge sums of money from pension funds, affecting nearly every American. Needless to say, the stock and bond markets would get hammered. Compensatory alterations in monetary and fiscal policy might later cause extreme inflation.

In contrast, the U.S. might continue its trend towards inflation merely due to continued high oil prices and weakness of the dollar. And only after some disaster such as a Fannie Mae blowup might deflation appear. The reality is that regardless of the magnitude of any economic correction, the next decade or two more will most certainly be characterized by extreme inflation in America. However, a severe catastrophe might usher in a deflationary period as an after-effect. Therefore, the possibility of deflation will most likely be determined by the sequence of events, as well as the extent of the economic correction, while high inflation is a virtual certainty.

Much of the deflationary pressures present during the 2001 to 2004 period were largely due to an inventory buildup. This was one of the forces that triggered the expansion of credit by the Fed. Severe loosening of credit was required to soften the blow of the economic correction. President Bush's tax cuts were also initiated to combat deflation and stimulate consumer spending. However since 2001, the dollar has been in decline which would appear to counteract these deflationary effects. These actions have only served to delay the inevitable full economic correction, which must now occur with more fervor.

> "It's just a matter of time before we have some kind of economic event that I think is just going to change the political situation 180 degrees.........when you've got gasoline spilling onto the floor of your house, it doesn't really matter where the spark comes from."
>
> Bruce Bartlett
> Former Treasury official in the
> George H.W. Bush administration

Thrown into the picture is the unhindered access of inexpensive goods from Asia, which has added to the post-deflationary period. However, much of the effect of inexpensive Asian imports has been due to currency manipulation by China. *Keeping the Yuan pegged to the dollar has helped counter the affects of a weak dollar, thereby adding a deflationary component to the economy.* But at some point, prices on Asian imports will rise as China diversifies into other foreign currencies and gold. Ironically, the weakness of the dollar has actually facilitated the rise in oil prices, due to the diminished buying power of the dollar in the foreign currency exchange. And this dynamic has exacerbated inflation.

A Stock Market Collapse?

Over the next few years the stock market will experience a long period of minor sell-offs, one or more major crashes, and modest compensatory rallies. Alternatively, it will sputter in a trading range with only modest gains. But this may be countered with brief rallies which will create confusion at best, and optimism at worst. No one knows for sure which of these scenarios will occur. It may even stage a false breakout, sending deceptive signals to unwary investors. However, I can tell you with confidence that the stock market will continue to perform poorly (on an averaged annualized basis since the beginning of the bear market in 2001) throughout the 2012 period independent of any depression.

The stock market might gain momentum over the next few years only to crash or gradually melt down after 2012, perhaps beginning in 2017, just when everyone thinks things are going okay. It's really impossible to determine exactly when things will happen or over what duration; much will depend upon the sequence of events that will serve to send economy into a downward spiral. Washington's reaction to these events will also play a key role in determining the timing and severity of the fallout. Regardless of these variables, those who remain alert to the risks and potential consequences will be able to take a defensive posture and react swiftly when opportunity appears.

Higher Taxes

There are several factors pointing to significantly higher taxes in the years ahead, as America tries to salvage its economic engine and standard of living. Unfortunately, when an economy suffers over an extended period, a snowball effect occurs that mandates higher taxes. The question is whether Washington will decide to take a preemptive approach or wait until a crisis to enact radical fiscal and economic change. Most likely, they will have to learn things the hard way.

In any event, taxes will be raised across the board by local, state and federal governments. However, these changes will not result in the restoration of America's greatness. Tax increases and other measures will be needed to pull America through a very challenging period. If the government chooses the correct fiscal policy, much of these taxes will be levied upon the wealthy and corporate America. Only when the power has been balanced between corporate America and the people will middle-class America be reborn. And this will help restore America to its previous greatness.

Over the next few years, I expect continued phantom wage growth masked by increasing debt, increasing inflation and muted retirement savings growth. I estimate the following changes will occur sometime over the next several years:

❖ Eventually something will cause the tide to shift, whereby Americans use less debt and increase savings. It could be before or after the onset of an economic meltdown. Regardless, as total compensation will not markedly improve (wages plus benefits):

1. Federal taxes will increase—from income taxes to gasoline taxes, elimination of tax credits, changes to tax deduction eligibility, and so forth. Spending growth for discretionary items will ultimately trend downward for a long period, causing further cuts to vital programs.

2. State and local taxes will increase. School systems will suffer as local governments struggle with Medicaid costs, resulting in benefit cuts along with tax hikes levied on certain goods and services such as increased fees for auto registration, increased tolls, fees for HOV lanes and driving taxes in some cities, higher cigarette taxes, etc. Property taxes will increase. The ability of local and state governments to create invisible taxes (disguised as fees) is large. Already many cities have annual fees for pets, fire and police fees for security monitoring, and hundreds of fees for businesses. States will also pass specific taxes on select food items such as a "sugar tax" and "caffeine tax." More states will allow casinos, thereby taxing the poor.

Less spending will hurt sales tax revenues, adding to the strain on state and local governments. Perhaps a positive consequence of these events is that Americans might start saving, rather than being held hostage by consumer finance interest payments.

Two Scenarios

The worst-case scenario might be due to a sudden crisis triggered perhaps by some broad-reaching event—a collapse of the MBS market, a sudden oil shortage due to a terrorist attack on a large oil facility, some other terrorist attack, a natural disaster similar to Katrina, or some other unpredictable event. I have already discussed the possibility of a global oil crisis and this could occur through supply-demand forces, or due to the hand of

OPEC for political leverage. If in fact peak oil occurs by the 2012 time frame, it will coincide with the first wave of baby boomers entering retirement, and this could cause a rapid economic decline.

More complicated ramifications could trickle down from these effects, such as growing tensions with China and a battle for the world's last remaining oil reserves. Of course, Middle East tensions will not subside anytime soon. No doubt, U.S.-Iranian tensions will continue to mount, as its link to Al-Qaeda becomes further exposed. At some point, foreign investors may decide to stop buying U.S. treasuries due to the beginnings of an economic slowdown or due to a continued weak dollar. And this will result in the loss of confidence in this currency as the international standard of commercial exchange.

The alternative consequence is a softer landing, although it would still be quite harsh for the U.S. economy. It might be caused by the preemptive actions of Washington, resulting in higher taxes across the board, cuts in Social Security benefits (masked by age increases or low COLAs), controlled healthcare costs or perhaps a national healthcare program. Such a scenario would most likely take a long time to unravel. And most Americans might not sense the shear magnitude of the separate triggering events until they have snowballed. Regardless of the exact course, a soft landing will take several years to complete and is highly unlikely without early political and economic reform.

What Can We Expect From the Market?

It is unlikely that America will escape a disaster similar to the socioeconomic meltdown witnessed during the Great Depression. And although it may look different, the overall effects will be similar, with massive job losses or a wave of underemployment. The end result would be low income for millions, with further societal decay as aftershocks. Only after this devastation has manifest will Washington gain the incentive to make needed policy changes. But these changes will require a long period of adjustment needed to reposition America for the changing world.

Market Performance

Independent of the two possibilities I have described, I have little doubt that the stock market will remain in a bearish period for the next several years. Of more significance, I do not feel America has experienced the kind of post-bubble correction necessary to restore economic balance. The longer it can delay a much-needed market correction, the lower it will recede.

Time is the best weapon for preventing a disastrous crash. However, it would not be shocking to see the Dow Jones Industrial Average (DJIA) fall to the 6500 level if a crash were to occur within the next 3 to 4 years although this scenario appears to be unlikely. Most likely, the DJIA will stay in a trading range for several years, after which a correction might begin around 14,500 and head down to 10,500.

If a series of large market corrections does not occur within this time frame, America will most likely have escaped a post-bubble correction crash. However, there will continue to be tremendous market volatility which could result in a series of rallies followed by sell-offs, resulting in very little market appreciation over the period since 2001. *Note that the DJIA was about 2500 during 1991. Fifteen years later, and 450 percent appreciation (or about 14 percent annually) is still unreasonable.* If making money was only so easy.

What Correction?

In order to better understand my rational, I have listed the major bull and bear market periods since 1900 in figure 16-1. Note that, although there have been several bull and bear markets, I have condensed them into *periods* for illustrative purposes. I have also labeled the two largest stock market bubbles in American history (1920s and 1990s).

I define a *bubble period* as the rapid acceleration of market appreciation during the final stages of a long bull market. The point I want to make is that all major bull market periods are followed by market correction periods that are characteristic of bear markets. However, corrections can either be one or more large market crashes or a long period of sideways market movements (i.e. typical bear markets*). Typically, when bubbles occur within bull markets, they are followed by some combination of crashes and a variable period of sideways trading.* However this would depend upon the severity any crash.

By 2012, at the best of scenarios (and assuming a depression has not occurred) I would expect the market (as measured by the DJIA) to have reached about 14,500. When you annualize the returns since the market highs of just over 12,000 made in 2000, this comes out to about 2 percent unadjusted for inflation. Yet, Wall Street will notify investors of only the most recent market gains to portray the illusion of a bull market.

You should appreciate that *the stock market does not like uncertainty and it tends to overreact to large sudden events due to the ambiguity involved.* Uncertainty is and will remain a continuous corollary of America's fragile economy and vulnerable national security for the next two decades. Thus, a Dow 14,500 by 2012 is quite optimistic given the risks that lie ahead (summarized in table 16-1).

A Look at Market Valuation

Illustrated in figure 16-2 is perhaps the most common metric used to determine the fair value of the stock market (the S&P 500 in this case)—the price-to-earnings (PE) ratio. Basically, this method looks at the PE ratio of the S&P 500 index and compares it to one of several selected historical averages. If the forward PE ratio is above the historical average, the market is considered overvalued; if below the average, it is considered undervalued.

The difficulty with any market valuation method lies in the fact that *the market can endure long periods of over- or undervaluation because investors are never in perfect agreement about the future of the economy.* As well, because investors have different investment horizons and different asset and risk exposures, one cannot readily use historical PE ratios as a market timing tool. However, market valuation techniques can serve as a general gauge to help model a risk management strategy.

Table 16-1. The Problems America Faces and the Expected Consequences

Problem	Short-term Impact	Long-term Impact	Threat to the Economy
Increasing Deficit	Adds to the Debt	Cumulative affects decrease dollar and increase interest rates	Cumulative effects could be large over a number of years; interest payments will increase → less discretionary funds
Increasing Trade Imbalance	Keeps consumer spending up	Keeps dollar weak	Could cause loss of confidence in US Treasuries causing Global sell-off, increasing rate increase, market collapse
Increasing Federal Debt	Can be good if used properly and if total debt is not high	Cumulative effects decrease dollar and increase interest rates	High debt is bad during risky economic conditions; interest payments increase, dollar weakens, rates soar
Increasing Consumer Debt	Can be good for economy but total debt is at dangerous levels	Cumulative effect will result in declining wealth	Already at critical levels, further debt will result in major Bankruptcies and foreclosures, reverse mortgages
Increasing Reliance on Foreign Debt	Investment is normally good but at over 50% → dangerous levels	Eventually you have to pay it off and foreign nations can use it as a lever for bargaining	Foreign investors could decide to sell treasuries or threaten, which would send the markets tumbling
Real Estate Bubble	Record foreclosures, decreased consumer spending	Diminished disposable income for many who bought at highs; could trigger other problems	Should deflate over the next five to six years, but could reappear when baby boomers scale down to smaller units
Healthcare Crisis	Bad and getting worse	If no universal coverage soon, Americans and companies will continue to suffer	The #1 crisis in America; could result in devastating social and economic effects
Medicare & Medicaid Crisis	Minimal; gov hides the problem but they are decreasing benefits	Insurmountable liabilities will cause decrease in coverage and benefits and increased debt	Only long-term impacts, but could be huge over the next two decades, adding to declining discretionary funds
Social Security Debacle	Minimal but affects consumer confidence	Privatization will create financial insecurity; COLA inadequacies will decrease disposable income	Along with Medicare, could destroy consumer spending of approximately 40% of American consumers
War in Iraq	Bad for American morale, Costly to the US economy	Could benefit U.S. in oil, but increase Middle East tensions and threaten national security	Indirect adverse effects with OPEC and oil prices; outcome depends on ability to get access to Iraq's oil
Global Terrorism, International Tensions	Market volatility, decreased consumer confidence	Definite market volatility, decreased consumer confidence	China & Russia forming more alliances with OPEC will strain global relations and could result in global chaos
High Oil Prices	Market Volatility	Market volatility and inflation	Decreased productivity, continued bear market
Education Crisis	Minimal	Major competitive loss globally	America could lose its place to Europe as the economic and technological powerhouse, then to Asia
Overvaluation of Stock Market	Depends on other catalysts	Market will correct to historical mean	Wealth from stock market can evaporate faster than formed. A large market sell-off could be a disaster
Pension Crisis	Could trigger a market sell-off	Will affect all generations of workers	Decreased standard of living increased by other issues

Figure 16-1. Historical Performance of the DJIA

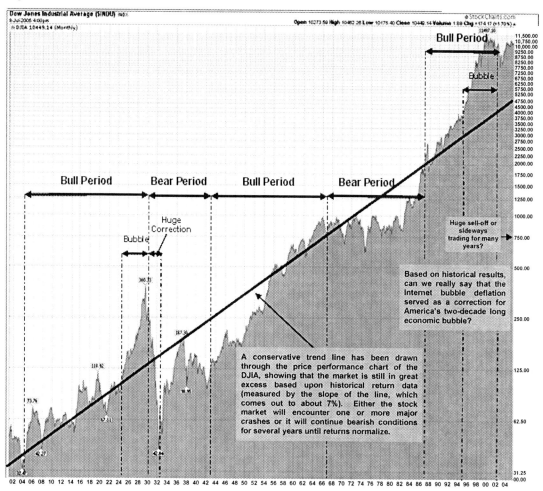

Figure 16-2. Trailing Ten Year Earnings (140 Years)

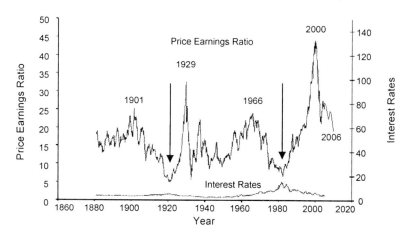

Figure 16-3 shows the PE ratio versus the performance of the S&P 500. The first thing to notice from this chart is that the PE ratio has declined from a value of 35 in 1999 prior to the market collapse. As well, you should notice that the PE ratio actually peaked during the first half of 2002 at around 42, when corporate accounting scandals were being exposed. In contrast to the peak PE ratio made in 1999, the market in 2002 was actually in decline, yet the PE ratio continued to ascend. This was due to the almost sudden collapse of earnings reported by many companies during that period. That gives you an idea how bad analyst and company projections were.

Figure 16-3. Market Valuation Using the Price Earnings Ratio of the S&P 500 Index

Now focus on the period from 2004 to present. As the PE ratio gradually declined, the market has gradually risen. Normally, this is a good sign for the market and might prompt investors to think that the bear market period is over. However, *in no post-bubble period that I have studied has a bull market begun without a drop in the market PE ratio well below undersold levels.* In summary, what you see from this chart is a PE ratio that has remained at high or reasonable levels for a 10-year period. But the fact is that *all bear market washouts have shown PE ratios that reached the low teens or single digits.* Such an overreaction is necessary in order to attract a massive wave of investors who recognize huge discounts in the market. While a capitulation occurred in fall 2003, this only served to confirm a washout of the Internet bubble period and has not addressed America's longer-standing credit bubble.

As you can see from figures 16-1 and 16-2, the two greatest bull market periods began (1920 and 1987) only after the PE ratio went to single digits (any differences in looking at PE ratios from the S&P 500 Index from figure 16-2 and the performance of the DJIA from figure 16-1 are trivial). Based on this, *I would not expect the next bull market period to begin until the market PE ratio (of the S&P 500 Index) descends to 10 or lower.* Until then, the secular bear market will continue. Of course, when you combine this data with the economic woes I have detailed throughout this book, it should be quite clear that we are far off from the end of the current secular bear market.

Similarities to the "Great Depression"

It seems like every nation is experiencing rapid growth at America's expense, from Brazil to South Korea, England to China. Even Germany is mounting a recovery. And after a decade of prolonged recessionary conditions, Japan is finally showing some progress. And in America, the only benefactors of the post-Internet bubble have been the wealthy elite and corporations, which continue to strengthen their financial position at the expense of middle-class America and the poor.

America's poor and middle class continue to loose ground on every front. Jobs are more difficult to find, job quality is declining, wage growth is absent, inflation in energy and utilities is crippling median incomes, consumer credit and mortgage debt are at record highs (on a per-dollar and GDP basis), healthcare coverage is unavailable to millions, and most boomers have insufficient retirement funds. Given the scale of the money-printing frenzy by the U.S. Treasury since 2001, *it is highly likely that a correction of Greenspan's credit bubble will adversely impact global economics.*

Today's global economy depends on cheap U.S. dollar credit. When U.S. interest rates are forced higher, dramatic shocks will hit Europe, Asia and the entire global economy, unlike anything seen since the 1930s. Debts that now appear manageable will suddenly become un-payable, resulting in record bankruptcies and foreclosures. As consumer confidence plunges, Washington will be rushing to create an environment that will restore order and commerce. This could lead to hyperinflation and further devastation.

This leads me to a review of the five main factors that resulted in the "Great Depression." All of these characteristics are already present in modern America, although some differences do exist.

Consumer Credit

Contrary to popular belief, many Americans lived off of credit during the "Roaring '20s." However, back then credit cards did not exist. Instead Americans bought items on layaway or installment plans. The Fed increased the money supply which fueled the boom of the '20s, as Americans continued to spend what they did not have. In place of credit cards, they used huge levels of margin debt to purchase stocks while spending wages on unnecessary items.

Due to the wealth and savings gap created by manufacturing trends and government support for big business, most Americans became reliant on credit. By the late 1920s, 60 percent of all autos and 80 percent of all radios in America were purchased using some type of installment credit. During this "booming" decade, the total amount of outstanding installment credit more than doubled from $1.38 billion to nearly $3 billion. In today's dollars one might think in terms of trillions. This overuse of credit created a false demand for goods, which resulted in overproduction. When monetary tightening began, this triggered the typical sequence of events seen in an economic contraction—diminished spending, less demand for products, layoffs, and increased inventories. Many Americans couldn't afford to pay for items bought on installment, and those who could did not have any money left to buy new items, causing inventories to pile up further.

Today, stock margin debt has more strict controls but consumer credit does not, nor do mortgage loan approvals. And remarkably, stock margin debt is approaching historical highs. Americans have borrowed money to the tune of 6 percent annually for over a decade, and sooner or later rising interest rates are going to crush their budgets.

When one compares the irresponsible lending practices within the current bubble to lending practices of banks and brokerage firms prior to the Crash of 1929, we see many common themes. Similar to the 1920s, much of the today's real estate bubble has swelled due to the lack of controls in the financial system, which has encouraged millions to take excessive risks in a shaky economy.

In both cases, the wealth effect led to the financial irresponsibility and speculation by American consumers. In the 1920s, high loan-to-value margin debt encouraged millions to speculate in the first major stock market bubble in American history. Likewise, the current real estate bubble has swelled due to the excessive availability and use of interest-only, option-ARMs, high loan-to-value mortgages, home equity loans, and massive expansion of the sub-prime loan market.

Overproduction

During WWI, the government took special measures to ensure that farmers would have sufficient agricultural products to feed American troops and their foreign allies. Farm expenses were subsidized with outrageous prices for wheat and other grains. Yet, farmers were unable to keep up with demand, which forced prices higher. In response, the government encouraged farmers to buy more land and modernize their equipment so they could reach full production capacity.

After the war ended, Washington ended these supportive policies leading to an excess of agricultural goods which ultimately depressed pricing. In order to counter these effects, farmers produced even more hoping to "make up the difference in volume." However, this led to major price declines. A bushel of wheat that had sold for $2 fell to $0.67. Meanwhile, Washington did nothing to help stabilize agricultural pricing.

While manufacturing industries such as steel, railroad, and textiles were profitable, agriculture suffered. Farmers became delinquent on loans, many leading to foreclosures. Soon, many rural banks holding these loans failed. While the Agricultural Credits Act of 1923 was an attempt to rescue the agricultural fallout, it was too little too late. American businesses recently experienced a build up of inventories in the early stages of the Internet bubble deflation. This build up has taken 4 years and record low interest rates to deplete. Soon there will be a huge housing inventory when the housing and credit bubbles deflate.

Income and Savings Disparity

As we know, history often repeats. And the booming economy of the 1920s was no exception to other periods of economic growth, whereby the wealthy got richer at the expense of the middle class and the poor. While the unequal distribution of wealth during the '20s probably did not actually cause the depression, it was certainly one of the leading factors that contributed to its severity.

In the 1920s, the income of the wealthiest 1 percent of Americans rose by 75 percent, while that of the nation as a whole rose by only 9 percent. The Brookings Institute reports that the top 0.1 percent of Americans had a total income equal to the bottom 42 percent of all Americans. This ultra-wealthy elite group accounted for 34 percent of all household savings while 80 percent of Americans had no savings at all. While much of the wealth held by the richest Americans was no doubt due to soaring stock prices, it was also due to the control and exploitation of corporations and those who owned them. Of course, the lowest income Americans entered the stock market at the top, as is the usual case with asset bubbles.

The policies of President Coolidge favored big business and all who invested in them. The Revenue Act of 1926 reduced federal income and inheritance taxes so that the wealthy had income taxes as much as 65 percent lower than low-income Americans. In addition, the Supreme Court ruled minimum-wage laws to be unconstitutional in the 1923 case of Adkins vs. Children's Hospital. Already, we have seen that only the wealthiest 10 percent of Americans have benefited over the past two decades, while the real incomes of the remaining 90 percent have barely moved. And of course, minimum wage increases continue to be ignored by Washington, while savings are almost nonexistent.

Economic Dependence on A Few Industries

During the '20s, it was primarily the automotive and construction industries that fueled America's boom. For the most part, only those industries related to auto and construction thrived during that period. The automobile was a revolutionary innovation that was changing the social and business infrastructure of America. It led to the growth of the rubber, glass, and steel industries, as well as motels, gas stations, and roadside restaurants. But when demand for these products fell, the entire economy was devastated.

Today, America is more dependent on a smaller number of industries than in the previous four decades due to the collapse of manufacturing. Oil and finance companies dominate the U.S. economy and exploit consumers while Washington stands by watching. However, America's oil industry could easily collapse due to war with Iran, OPEC price manipulation, or the effects of peak oil. Meanwhile, its financial system could collapse due to the continued weakness of the dollar and the increasing momentum of the Euro as the new global standard.

The "Crash of 1929"

Even during a period without widespread telephone use, no televisions, and no Internet, by the late '20s virtually everyone was in the stock market. Similar to the Internet bubble of the late 1990s, everyone was giving stock tips; a clear sign to get out of the market. Most Americans were speculating but did not realize it, as they felt that making money in the market was a sure thing, so they borrowed on ridiculous margin requirements that were as low as 10 to 25 percent.

After the first sell-off, investors panicked causing many more to sell, resulting in a further decline in stock prices. When margin calls triggered, most could not be filled and this caused a massive sell-off. The bottom fell out on October 29, 1929, known as "Black Tuesday", when a record number of shares were traded, sending the market tumbling.

Shortly after the crash, millions rushed to their banks in a panic to withdraw savings. But many banks had insufficient funds because they too had lost money in the market. By 1933, close to 6000 banks in America, or about 25 percent of the nation's total banking system had failed. Because there was no FDIC at the time, over 9 million savings accounts were lost. Many had massive losses due to margin calls, and since they were unable to pay these loans, they filed for bankruptcy. As most Americans had no disposable income, demand for goods dropped off, causing lay-offs and corporate bankruptcies.

Today, American banks provide $100,000 insurance per person by the FDIC established during FDR's New Deal. However, there is no real insurance for the $14 trillion-plus in collateralized securities, nor is there any insurance for the $13 trillion invested in the stock market. Consequently, the deflation of the real estate and credit bubbles could lead to massive defaults, sending shockwaves throughout America's financial system.

It's only been a few years since the Internet bubble burst, yet many investors act as if nothing happened, as evidenced by massive speculation in the stock market. The SEC allows infomercials from shady companies that claim to teach novices how to trade for a living by "watching red and green lights." In essence, the SEC is permitting the manipulation of millions of desperate Americans who are strapped for cash or worried about inadequate retirement funds.

The stock market has never been more volatile and difficult to navigate due to the massive explosion of hedge funds and programmed trading which now dominates market activity. Yet, now anyone with a computer can short a stock with the click of a mouse, without truly realizing the risk of this manuever. Unfortunately, most people ignore things that are difficult to understand, such as risk, and instead tend to focus on greed, which ultimately leads to their demise.

The Next "New Deal"?

When the depression was in full swing, most Americans were financially and emotionally devastated. But this catastrophe did not appear overnight. It was the product of two decades of neglect and abuse by Washington and corporate America. The solution was a series of drastic laws and government programs that served to provide stability and security to a battered nation.

Back then, the U.S. government did not have the kind of debt and future liabilities it has today so it will be limited in the ways it can restructure itself. Regardless, the next New Deal will arrive, most likely only after a depression has taken full effect. And if Washington decides to create a full solution, part of the package will include a national healthcare system, a truly reformed educational system, and a restructuring of free trade and Social Security.

Radical changes in a nation's social and economic structure usually only occur after a crisis because no politician wants to risk re-election by raising taxes, cutting benefits, or decreasing the power and exploitation of large corporations. Washington prefers to hide the truth, hoping Americans will believe its propaganda. But once the catastrophe occurs, politicians will have no choice but to enact drastic reforms, and Americans will welcome these changes as the only way to regain hope for their future.

17

INVESTMENT SOLUTIONS

In this chapter, I will highlight some of the better investment industries and sectors that, in my opinion will continue to perform well over the next several years, as well as during the devastating economic period of the magnitude I am anticipating. It's important to note that some of these sectors (metals and energy) are very volatile by nature. Therefore, market timing as well as management of investment positions is critical. As well, investors should note that some sectors (base metals) are in the final stages of their bull run, while others such as energy and precious metals will last considerably longer in my opinion. I have divided this chapter into two parts based upon the type of trend-predicting involved. The first potentially lucrative investment category to be discussed is based on predicting lifestyle trends. For this, I focus on demographics. The second category of trend-predicting involves macroeconomic forecasting.

Lifestyle Trends

Baby Boomers

Spotting trends in consumer behavior is vital for identifying the most lucrative industries and companies to invest. And when accurate forecasting has been achieved, it can yield even greater profits. However, the ability to forecast trends in growing or emerging markets must be weighed against the investment horizon, objectives and risk tolerance of each investor. Otherwise, what might be a potentially great investment could turn out bad for some.

As previously discussed, a two decades ago when baby boomers were in the midst of their peak earning years, many new industries arose to serve their needs—housing, automotive, finance and the consumer electronics industries. As this group enters retirement over the next two decades, they will no doubt have a smaller impact in many of the industries they helped build. In contrast, other industries will benefit from their changing needs, despite their greatly diminished buying power.

For instance, looking at current and future estimated birth rates, we should expect an overall decline in industries that obtain a significant percentage of revenues by serving infants and toddlers. However, the effects of an aging, low-income, less technologically savvy boomer generation on the consumer electronics industry should be minimal since these industries are able to control pricing and profit margins by supply and demand. With fewer Americans in the market for electronics, I expect more brick-and-mortar facilities to transition to an online business model. Those companies that are able to achieve this in an efficient manner will continue to benefit from a reduced cost structure despite lower revenue growth. As well, younger generations typically account for most of the demand growth of the latest high-tech electronic gadgets. Therefore, the effect of aging baby boomers in this industry should be minimal.

Healthcare

There are two industries I expect to clearly benefit from the aging boomer population. The first is healthcare. Many boomers will find it difficult to pay out-of-pocket healthcare expenses, regardless of their ability to qualify for government healthcare. Without question, the majority of a person's lifetime healthcare expenses occur over age 60. Treatment regimens for chronic end-stage disease management last longer and cost more, and such treatments create a dependency on pharmacological agents, medical devices, and longer, more expensive hospital stays.

What government or company pensions do not pay for in medical expenses, elderly Americans needing healthcare services will. Boomers on their last leg will pay for critical care and any other goods and services they feel might prolong both the duration and quality of their lives. They will even use their credit cards if necessary. This trend is already present. In short, the pharmaceutical industry will rebound from its current slump, delivering excellent earnings growth despite any economic meltdown. This trend will continue as long as America allows big pharma to operate as individual monopolies. And while I do not anticipate a system of national healthcare anytime soon, I expect the trend of rapid healthcare cost growth to remain even if and when such a system is been created, since it would most likely be implemented gradually, and not without a fight by providers.

The two sectors within healthcare I expect to perform exceptionally well are home-nursing care and retirement community properties. Statistical numbers from the Census Bureau alone provide estimations for this potentially huge market. While there are only a few publicly traded companies serving this lucrative market, I expect many more to spring up over the next few years.

Finally, the most lucrative sector in healthcare that will be resistant to the effects of economic fallout is telemedicine/healthcare IT. This sector is expected to become enormous due to the government mandates for cost reduction in most segments of public healthcare. No doubt, these technologies will spill over into the private healthcare markets as well. The difficulty here lies in identifying the early winners.

Travel and Leisure

The second industry I feel will perform well is travel and tourism. It's no secret that many aging Americans wish to travel and see more of the world before their permanent departure. Depending on where you live, you've probably seen tour buses filled with seniors. Even with most Americans expected to retire in poverty, I still believe that millions will take cruises. Consider that cruises can be very affordable for people on a tight budget when charters are provided. As well, with the high cost of oil, road trips and bus tours are becoming very expensive. However, while potentially lucrative, investment in the travel industry could be very risky due to the vulnerability of terrorist attacks and most likely would not hold up during a depression. Still, this sector is one to watch. Finally, select gaming resorts in Las Vegas will continue their growth and popularity, and should be minimally affected by downturns in the economy. Never underestimate the power of addictive vices, especially when they have been glamorized by a "Hollywood" or "Disney" theme.

Industries Adversely Affected

On the other hand, I would expect the home improvement industry to face declining earnings growth due to the real estate shakeout over the next several years and possibly extending through the next couple of decades, as many baby boomers scale down to smaller homes, condos, or assisted living facilities. I am not saying that Home Depot will shut down. Rather, I am predicting it won't have anywhere near the type of earnings growth produced during the 1990s. The only chance for Home Depot and Lowes would be through business diversification. But management has yet to come up with any clear plans to provide such growth.

As well, I feel that there will be a selective decline in many financial companies. While all will not be affected, those that will be hit particularly hard will have large exposure in mortgages (especially sub-prime), derivatives, and those that have grown earnings primarily through acquisitions, such as Bank of America and Citigroup. Beginning in about 10 to 15 years, I anticipate a wave of divestitures of many of these mega-banks. Derivatives exposure is a particularly critical risk to watch out for.

A Closer Look at Future Healthcare

During the '80s and '90s, the pharmaceutical industry enjoyed the best growth of any industry, but times are changing. A recent wave of drug recalls and lawsuits with Phen-Phen, Vioxx, and many others, as well as whistle-blowers at the FDA and even at the pharmas have caused a small but mounting force of protest among many healthcare providers and recipients. Already, the nutritional supplements and alternative medicine markets are huge and will continue their growth, as more Americans realize that one of the reasons for the escalating costs and ineffectiveness of healthcare is due to their love affair with prescription drugs and medical devices.

Pharmaceuticals and Biotechnology

A record amount of patent-protected drug sales will be ending for many drug companies by 2007. Over the next year, the value of sales revenues disappearing each year due to patent expiration is expected to surpass $23 billion worldwide, the largest decline ever. Previously, the largest decline attributable to patent expiration was $9 billion in 2001. Along with the recent controversy surrounding the FDA process and its ties with the drug industry, the wave of drug liability lawsuits has stimulated a growing shift towards nutritional and other alternative therapies that will continue to present challenges for the drug makers. But this should only be a short-term effect.

Problem #1: Patent Expiration

By the way, with rare exception, the generic drug makers are typically poor investment choices because they are in the drug commodities business, and therefore use a price leadership advantage. Price leadership is nowhere near as strong as the price control strategy utilized by the big drug makers. *The best reason for investing in drug companies is to take advantage of their monopoly status, and generics merely manufacture drugs whose patents have expired.* As well, there can be intense competition from rival generics, as well as parent drug companies, due to billions spent annually to build brand recognition. The following discussion is not inclusive of patent expiration data.

> **Pfizer:** By 2007, Pfizer's patent on the antidepressant Zoloft will expire, opening the door for generics. In 2005, Zoloft had $2.7 billion in U.S. sales, but it is probable that Zoloft will face huge liabilities from future lawsuits due to adverse effects. Overall, Pfizer faces the loss of almost a third of its total revenue during the next three years from the expiration of patents on Zoloft and other drugs, including Norvasc. Pfizer has already announced cutbacks even deeper than Merck and is fighting off competitors from its anti-cholesterol blockbuster Lipitor, an $11 billion drug whose patents start expiring in 2009. Look to pick this one up after a sell-off.

> **Merck:** Amongst many of its other problems, Merck is already suffering declining revenues for Zocor. In June 2006, the generic manufacturers rolled out lower-cost versions of the drug and this is expected to ultimately diminish annual Zocor revenues by $2 billion (revenues were $3.6 billion in 2005). As well, in 2005 Merck's Fosamax patent extension was denied. And of course they lost all future revenues for Vioxx, which yielded over $1.5 billion in the year prior to its removal from the market. Within the next 5 to 6 years, Merck will face a revenue reduction of up to 60 percent due to patent expiration and the loss of Vioxx. And with a very limited pipeline of new drug candidates, their ability to replace a large part of these revenues is unlikely over the next 8 years. Finally, they still have to face a potentially large financial liability due to Vioxx lawsuits, which will continue for several years. Look to pick this one up after it gets hammered again.

> **Bristol-Myers Squibb:** In 2007, Bristol-Meyers will lose patent-protection on its cholesterol drug Pravachol, which brought in $1.4 billion in the 2005. Overall, patent expirations threaten about 31 percent of Bristol-Myers Squibb's total earnings by 2008. But this company has deeper issues within management that will cause it to linger for the next several years. I would stay away from BMY.

> **Wyeth:** By 2007, Wyeth will lose patent-protection for its top-selling drug Effexor, an antidepressant which topped $2.3 billion in sales in 2005. Overall, by 2008, Wyeth faces a loss of approximately 29 percent of sales due to patent expiration. Of course, the company still has a long way to go before paying out over $22 billion in damage awards from previous drug recalls. Similar to Bristol-Meyers, Wyeth is another with too many skeletons in its closet. I would stay away.

Problem #2: Lawsuits and Diminished American Confidence

Drug liability lawsuits have never been larger and more widespread as they are today. Virtually every attorney wants in on the action. And due to major safety issues with many of the me-too drugs, you should expect the wave of lawsuits and drug recalls to grow. This heightened attention has caused more Americans to question its drug-centric healthcare system, leading many to seek alternative therapies and nutritional products. As well, it has partly been responsible for the early growth and success of the organic food industry.

One of the key variables to look out for when analyzing the contingent damages of drug liability cases is where the trials are held. For Enron, holding the trials in Houston was certainly a disadvantage because the scandal cost so many local residents so much. However, for Merck, having trials in New Jersey has proved to be a major advantage due to the support from the local communities. This could be the edge it needs.

Problem #3: Healthcare is Expensive and Poorly Accessible

Solution #1: Drug Price Controls

I do not see drug price controls happening anytime soon in America. Therefore, as long as Washington allows big pharma to control prices, they will continue to produce strong earnings. And with the recent launch of Medicare Part D, I anticipate massive fraud which will help earnings of many drug companies.

In conclusion, look for a modest earnings decline in pharmaceutical industry over the next couple of years, as these companies struggle with pipeline issues and litigations. I expect significant downsizing to occur as a way to cut costs, followed by revitalization in a few years. Even after this brief period, investors should not expect the kind of blockbuster earnings growth witnessed in the '90s due to more effective and safer therapeutic options. Yet, the pharmaceutical industry will never go away and will still continue to make money. It just won't represent the most profitable industry as in the past. Therefore, investors can no longer blindly invest in random drug companies and do well. Selectivity will be the key to excellent investment returns from this industry. Investors should focus on the big names such as Pfizer, Merck, and Eli Lilly, as well as blue-chip biotechs Amgen and Genentech. Relative valuation should be a key consideration, and investors should consider adding positions when valuations have been knocked down.

Finally, I expect biotechnology to overtake big pharma as a better risk-reward investment. Note that biotech stocks tend to be more volatile due to the uncertainty of earnings. And while the larger, more established names provide less volatility, they also have less upside. However it's difficult to determine the potential upside of the entire industry since a merger spree with pharmaceutical companies could change the outcome.

Investing in newer sectors such as stem cells can be dangerous since most of these companies do not have sales revenues. And the political environment currently does not favor an absolute advantage for U.S.-based stem cell companies. However, there is a good chance that this will change after President Bush leaves office. These companies will continue to provide excellent short-term trading (experienced traders only) returns, sparked by announcements of federal funding or changes in the political landscape.

Solution #2: New Alternatives
Nutritional markets and alternative medicine

Nutritional Supplements Market

This industry is multi-tiered. On the one hand, we have already seen the massive growth of the nutritional supplements industry. And while there is more room for growth, these companies are probably not good candidates for conversion into publicly-traded companies due to their emphasis on commodity-based products and high marketing expenses. What these companies have done is increase the availability and awareness of nutritional supplements. And this has created a huge retail market for these products. However, until the FDA begins to regulate nutritional supplements it will be very difficult for this industry to create product distinction and proprietary protection through patents. Therefore, they will remain as commodities, subject to the effects of price wars; never a good situation for profitability.

So where are the potential areas of investment? *Investors should keep on eye out for nutritional/organic franchise restaurant chains which may grow large enough to go public.* This might represent an excellent opportunity to replace your other restaurant stocks. In addition, *organic and specialty grocery stores or markets will continue their surging growth.* Already, in just five years, Whole Foods has experienced phenomenal growth and there is much more on the way.

As well, over time government programs such as Medicaid and Medicare will begin using more nontraditional therapies and advanced technologies as a way to curb the massive cost increases due to an aging population. The only problem is that it is difficult to find any one company that will benefit from these changes since most nutritional therapies are not patentable (the use of advanced technologies in healthcare will be discussed later under Solutions #3). As a result, the current nutritional supplements-based companies should be considered as retail businesses.

Notable exceptions are some of the newer energy-boosting beverage companies and others that sell items such as protein bars, etc. While some of these companies are already public, I would be very cautious because they have not yet demonstrated an ability to extend their business lines and create consistently strong earnings growth. In order to produce staying power, they will have to diversify into newer products.

Most likely, many of these companies will become buyout candidates for beverage names such as Coca-Cola, Pepsi, Anheuser-Bush, Altria, and several others. These blue chips might see this new wave of nutritional products as a way to address declining growth. *Combined with their strong branding power and ubiquitous distribution channels, it is entirely possible that such acquisitions could lead to an enormous market due to the unique ability of these blue chips to alter consumer ideas and buying attitudes.*

When Coca-Cola began experiencing a decline in earnings growth, company executives recognized the huge and growing bottled water market and came out with their own brand, Desani. This move leveraged Coca-Cola's great brand name and extensive distribution channels, resulting in a large market share in a short time period. After all, Desani is only filtered water yet costs $1.50 per 16 ounce bottle. Look for other blue chip beverage makers to enter the high margin nutritional supplements market.

Alternative Medicine

Finally, there is a new and rapidly growing market for healthcare products supported by a small contingency of physicians around the USA. Once each month, an anti-aging society meets to discuss alternative medicine, with healthcare providers from all ends of the spectrum—primary care physicians, specialists, nutritionists, etc. I have listed a few examples of findings presented at these conferences.

(1) Diabetic Wound-Healing Therapies: Amputation due to diabetic wounds is the number one cause of amputations in the U.S. each year. Diabetics have a very poor wound healing system, amongst other things. Often, a small cut (especially in the lower extremities) can develop into a huge lesion, which when infected can turn into a bacterial (Staphylococcus) infection, resulting in amputation. This is a huge problem that is well-known within the medical community. As well, diabetes causes a multi-organ system pathology associated with the number one cause of blindness, one of the leading causes of chronic end-stage renal disease and a top contributor to cardiovascular disease in America.

Revolutionary Metabolic Treatment #1: One physician has been highly successful in the use of table sugar in treating these wounds. Due to the metabolics involved, table sugar is used by bacteria within the wound and creates an anaerobic (no oxygen) environment, killing all of the pathologic bacteria, leading to complete wound healing. Why hasn't the healthcare system embraced this inexpensive and effective treatment? Because big pharma controls physicians like a leashed dog.

(2) Cardiac By-Pass Treatment: Cardiac by-pass procedures have become the norm for both prevention and treatment of severe coronary heart attacks. In large part, they have been successful in preventing morbidity and prolonging mortality. However, there have been many failures and side effects with drastic consequences. Anytime an invasive procedure is used you always run several risks, so the most ideal treatment would be minimally invasive.

Revolutionary Metabolic Treatment #2: One well-respected cardiologist has had amazing results using metabolic treatments as a first line of defense against plaque buildup in coronary arteries. In contrast, there have been recent studies indicating that bypass surgery can actually be worse for patients.

(3) Cardiovascular Disease Treatments: As the number one cause of death in America, cardiovascular disease is often the end-stage result of many diseases. The common thought was that cholesterol excesses lead to the buildup of plaque along arterial walls. This eventually causes hardening of the arteries, resulting in high blood pressure or hypertension, all of which can cause a variety of diseases; ultimately leading to heart failure. This theory led to the explosion of statin drugs by all large drug makers. However, there is now significant evidence that statins are not only ineffective or only modestly effective against preventing heart disease, but may have major side effects, including acting as a carcinogen, or an agent that causes cancer. Statin sales have been one of the drug industry's biggest source of revenues over the past decade. And due to the "follow the leader" mentality so widespread in healthcare, physicians continue to prescribe these agents to anyone with above average levels of cholesterol.

Revolutionary Metabolic Treatment #3: According to several researchers not affiliated with the pharmaceutical industry, the real problem lies not with cholesterol but with the actual damage to arteries by a naturally occurring compound known as homocystein. This is an amino acid, or a building block of proteins which is thought to cause direct damage to the arterial walls. Therefore, lowering homocystein levels should result in a much more effective treatment and prevention of atherosclerosis. This has been demonstrated decisively. But due to the influence of the drug industry, this message has not been communicated to the general public. Fish oil has been proven to reduce blood-homocystein levels, and therefore lower the onset of cardiovascular disease. However, because it takes decades of research to prove the effects, clinical data is unavailable. As well, because drug companies stand to lose billions from reduced statin sales, there is very little funding available for intensive research into alternative approaches. But that hasn't stopped many physicians and others from acting. Already, fish oil is a part of the daily diet of thousands of Americans, including many physicians.

These are just a few examples of revolutionary treatments growing in acceptance by healthcare providers each day. However, one cannot invest in this new area of medicine until companies find a way to make their products proprietary. Eventually, as these treatments become more widespread, big pharma might find a way to make them patentable. Stay alert for potential investment opportunities in this area.

Solution #3: Cost-Effective Alternatives
Federal mandates for healthcare IT and telemedicine

Telemedicine
Telemedicine has been defined as the "Use of electronic signals to transfer medical data from one site to another via the Internet, intranets, PCs, satellites, or videoconferencing telephone equipment in order to improve access to health care" (Telemedicine Information Exchange, 1997). Telemedicine provides access to medical specialists and healthcare services unavailable to many individuals, and does so in a timely and cost-effective manner. As well, it allows expenses to be reduced using advanced wireless and digital technologies so healthcare providers can monitor, diagnose and treat patients located in different geographical regions.

Tremendous time can be saved by the organized storage and fast retrieval of data and the integration of claims forms and medical records. This will cut costs and minimize errors, allowing physicians to spend more time preventing and treating disease, rather than looking for data and doing paperwork. Virtually every discipline of medicine has found benefits in telemedicine, from teleradiology to telepsychiatry. NASA was actually the pioneer of telemedicine a few decades ago, and the military continues to conduct intensive telemedicine research. The first mainstream impact of telemedicine will reach two areas of healthcare delivery:

- **Home-health** and community Medicaid patients. Home healthcare is the fastest growing healthcare delivery sector in America. Demographics dictate this trend will continue its explosive growth over the next few decades. Otoscope and stethoscope attachments can be connected to a home computer or wireless device and monitored elsewhere. Blood pressure and ECG readings can be taken as well.

- **Point-of-Care testing** will improve dramatically. Web-enabled and wireless patient-monitoring solutions include diagnostics and treatment over the Internet enabled by secure archive data centers that can be accessed via standard web browsers or wireless devices. This has applications for monitoring and treating virtually every chronic disease. Already, there are several private companies providing home-health and POC services.

As discussed previously, Medicare and Medicaid are in a huge mess, with insurmountable liabilities and annual decreases in coverage due to lack of adequate funding. Washington cannot possibly fund this $40 trillion public healthcare liability and is betting on telemedicine to cut costs. *Already, Washington has mandated that by 2014, at least 10 percent of all healthcare delivery in America should be through telemedicine.* Based upon the estimates for healthcare expenditures by 2014, that means the market for telemedicine will be over $300 billion within eight years.

Right now the only publicly traded companies investing in telemedicine do not have enough at stake to show a major earnings benefit. But already, many large companies such as IBM, Intel, Siemens, GE, Motorola and several others are investing in telemedicine and bioinformatics. The best way to capture investment opportunities in this space is to keep an eye out for the development of this market and look for IPOs.

Healthcare IT

Of all high-tech industries in America, healthcare IT is by far the most antiquated, least organized, and the most prone to error. Ironically, due to the enormous volume of data and its critical nature, the healthcare industry should have the most advanced and secure IT systems. The lack of efficient IT systems in hospitals costs billions of dollars and thousands of lives each year. It has been estimated that over $25 billion is lost annually in reimbursements due to coding errors, non-inclusion of procedures and other administrative errors. As well, thousands of patients die annually in hospitals due to errors that could have been prevented with proper data management systems.

The plan proposed by the government to modernize healthcare's IT infrastructure is called the Health Insurance Portability and Accountability Act (HIPAA). HIPAA is the first step towards efficiently run healthcare in America. It will revolutionize healthcare delivery, helping to cut costs and minimize errors. In short, HIPAA is expected to protect patient confidentiality, cut provider operational costs, maximize insurance reimbursement, minimize medical errors, and provide more time for physicians and nurses to treat patients.

HIPAA will also provide the backbone needed for telemedicine. All healthcare providers, healthcare clearing houses, or health plans that electronically maintain or transmit health information pertaining to an individual must comply with HIPAA. As well, Employers who provide on-site healthcare for their employees must also comply with HIPAA.

Because HIPAA is a process and not a turn-key solution, there will not be much opportunity for direct public investment. However, *there will be many opportunities for IT service providers, consultants, digital security, and data management companies.* The government will not be able to deliver these radical improvements alone and many companies will be involved. Already, Steve Case (former CEO of AOL) has started a new company to address the digital needs of America's modern healthcare plans.

Leisure and Entertainment Industry

I have already discussed the potential growth of the travel, tourism and gaming industries. Another sector I expect to perform well over the next decade and even hold up during severe economic conditions is the retail golf industry. It's no secret that golf has become America's favorite past time. Golf associations and the media have done well to promote this quasi-sport.

Once a game for upper-class Caucasians, golf now extend across all racial and gender barriers. Golf now celebrates the success of multiracial Tiger Woods, who has become one of the biggest sports celebrities in history. As well, the early success of teenage Korean-American golfer Michelle Wie has helped spark a heightened interest in golf among young females. At age 14, Wie became the highest paid female golfer in history when she turned pro due to huge endorsement deals.

Golf has hit mainstream America and will continue to benefit from increasing interest at all ages. It is an activity that anyone can enjoy at any age and it does not require especially astute physical endurance or agility to play well or to play at all (compared with contact sports). One of the world's greatest (yet inconsistent) golfers, John Daly has been noted for his lack of exercise, poor practicing habits, reckless gambling binges, and his regular diet of sodas, cigarettes, recreational drugs and alcohol. Yet, he is second only to Tiger Woods in popularity because most Americans can relate to his flaws.

In the first three months of 2006 alone, Tiger Woods and Michelle Wie were featured on two separate episodes of 60 Minutes. And just two months later John Daly was featured. In contrast, I can think of no other athletes who have been featured on 60 Minutes over the past few years other than one baseball player, who was interviewed about steroid use.

Teens are now starting to play golf, since for the first time ever they have role models. African-Americans relate to Tiger Woods, as do Asian Americans. And young females (especially Asian) can relate to the 16 year-old Wie. The golf industry will continue its growth over the next two decades, boosted further by the boomer generation. While many boomers may not be able to afford it, the shear volume of this generation will serve to add a larger volume of more frequent golfers, causing general costs to decline. And all of this golfing requires supplies; golf balls, golf clubs, and accessories. As far as investments in the stock market, there won't be much opportunity due to the nature of the business. However, there will continue to be numerous opportunities for entrepreneurs.

Pet Care Industry

Over the past two decades, pets have risen to become a significant member of the American family. Already, we have seen the rise of pet stores and pet care facilities. Some of the most lucrative businesses today are pet grooming and pet care centers. Many of these facilities are owned by huge companies such as the Pet Smart, which receives as much as 20 percent of its profits from this business.

In 2006, Americans are expected to spend nearly $40 billion on their pets, up from $36 billion in 2005. I expect the trends in the pet care industry to continue as more Americans have fewer children and the divorce rate remains high due to the social realignment and complexities of America's modern society. Thus, pets will continue their ascent into the place of American families. Similar to the golf industry, I do not see many public investment opportunities in this growing market. However, it will continue to represent a lucrative investment for small business owners.

Technology

This analysis would be incomplete without mention of high-tech industries. It's very difficult to make specific predictions in technology over the next two decades. The only prediction one can make is that technology will continue to improve business efficiency and provide more access to lower-cost information and communication, while enhancing services in every industry. Whether technological innovations will lead to a higher quality of life is up for debate.

One obvious trend to note is that everything is going wireless. Look for wireless technologies to improve every industry and save costs. As more reliance is placed on wireless digital technologies, the need for digital security hardware and software will be tremendous. The digital and Internet security markets will continue to grow over the next two decades from the continued growth of the Internet alone. However, sophisticated security systems will be needed especially for providers of the healthcare industry, since medical records will soon be floating through cyberspace. In the Chapter Seventeen Supplement of the appendix, I have provided an example showing how investors need to think about industry dynamics and competitive analysis.

Macroeconomic Trends: Metals

Metals have been of immense value to civilizations since prehistoric times due to their utility, beauty and durability. We have come a long way since the use of metals for knives and forks, yet we still use them. But this is not the reason to get excited about metals. The point is that, despite the advancement and use of modern synthetic materials, metals are as valuable to us today as they were in ancient times. And for many of their uses, we have found no substitute.

Of particular significance related to the investment appeal of metals is to note the current status of the economic cycle, which is causing commodities to rise. However, investors must approach the base metals with caution because the commodities bubble has already had an impressive run since 2001. Most likely this bubble will run out of steam when China's economy corrects, which I expect to occur by 2010. In contrast, there are other factors that have and will continue to lead to the appreciation of precious metals for a longer period than the base metals. In short, the *continuing trends of a weak dollar, higher interest rates, trade deficits, and the declining support for the dollar will most likely lead to record prices in most precious metals over the coming decade.*

Base Metals

Unlike gold, the other precious (the non-commodity metals) and base metals (commodity metals) are consumed for industrial means. And due to the tremendous growth of China and India, demand for these metals is outstripping supply. These populous nations must have an ever increasing supply of metals to build their infrastructure and continue to make products for their booming export industries. There simply hasn't been enough nonferrous metals supply to meet the demands of the Chinese industrial machine.

As previously mentioned, I do not expect the base metals to continue their bull run beyond the next 4 years. In contrast, the precious metals bull market should continue for at least the next 7 years. And when a depression hits America, this could send the price of gold and silver to astronomical highs. Such a catastrophe could lead to price levels that exceed historical marks adjusted for inflation, or over $2200 per ounce for gold (based on 2006 dollars) within the next two decades.

Aluminum is a superconductor with high strength, ductility, formability and resistance to corrosion. It's second only to iron in terms of use. It has numerous industrial uses in transportation (autos, aircraft, trucks, railroad cars, marine vessels, and bicycles), packaging (cans and foil), water treatment, construction (windows and doors), consumer durables (cooking utensils), electrical transmission lines, machinery, paint, and components of jewelry.

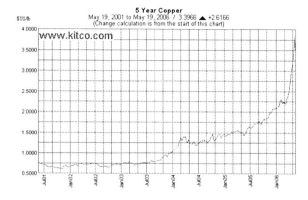

Copper is noteworthy for its malleability and unique ductile qualities, making its widespread use in wiring, plumbing, roofing, (gutters) electrical machines, brass musical instruments, and for cookware—the second most used nonferrous metal.

Zinc is the third most widely used nonferrous metal, primarily utilized as a coating on iron and steel to protect against corrosion (which costs $200 billion annually). Its anti-corrosive effects extend auto body life for several years. Zinc can store six times as much energy per pound as other battery systems—notable since it can serve to increase the range of electric vehicles. In fact, zinc-air batteries have powered cars to speeds of 120 mph. Zinc sheets used in architecture, for roofs or facades, on counters and on bar tops, have a maintenance-free life of over 60 years.

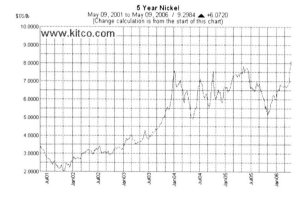

Nickel possesses excellent plating properties, making it widely used for coatings, in both decorative and engineering applications. Nickel can combine with many other metals and is used in a variety of alloys for variable corrosion-resistance.

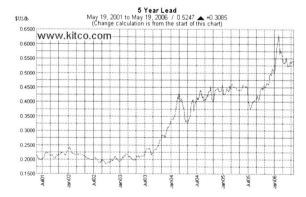

Lead has a controversial past, due to its previous use in paints and as an additive for unleaded fuels—both uses were thought to cause lead-poisoning. However, it is still very important to industry, serving as a component of solder, pewter, and fusible alloys. Lead is the primary element in the lead-acid car battery, and is used for bullets and fishing sinkers due to its high density. It is also used for electrodes. Finally, lead is used as a shield from radiation.

The Gold Rush

The main problem with investing in gold and other precious metals is that these sectors tend to perform poorly relative to the overall stock market over long periods. However, during a post-bubble correction period, (which can last from 12 to 15 years) gold can provide potentially tremendous gains, although investors will be subject to extreme volatility.

Unlike gold, stock prices and company valuations are intangible. And during periods of extreme uncertainty or panic, investors opt for more tangible expressions of wealth like gold and silver. During these conditions, because so many investors rush to buy precious metals, supplies become limited, often leading to magnificent price appreciation. Therefore, if one believes that the stock market is still largely overvalued relative to the economic realities masked by Washington, both now and in the future, you should expect gold to continue its bull run from this consequence alone.

As the dollar has been weak, foreign central banks have been seeking to hedge against further declines by increasing their gold deposits. But the effects on supply have been further accentuated by signs of supply shortages in critical gold-mining hot spots. Even production in the rich mines of South Africa appear to be maturing, after an 80-year record-low production in 2005 amidst soaring prices. Finally, worldwide gold production in 2004 experienced its largest decline in over 39 years, potentially pointing to some significant supply issues. The other possibility to consider is whether producers withheld inventories from the market due to further anticipated price increases. *Regardless of any potential inventory manipulation, worldwide demand for gold is rising from investors and central banks wishing to mitigate the effects of a weak dollar.*

India is the world's largest consumer of gold. In 2004 alone, its demand for gold increased by 47. From Chapter Fourteen, it should be no surprise that many Indians are experiencing significant increases in wealth as a result of outsourcing by American corporations. And most Indians view gold as a stable place to store their newly found wealth. Meanwhile, 2004 also saw China's demand for gold increase by 14 percent—a substantial number, given the 25 percent savings rate by Chinese consumers. Finally, Japanese consumers, worried about the threat of inflation are seeking gold as a save haven.

Gold (London Fix) from 1975 to April 2006

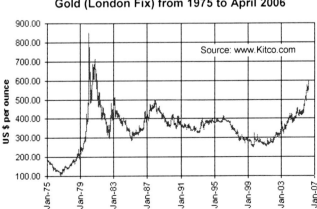

Source: www.Kitco.com

Gold and Inflation?

Gold has been shown to provide a great hedge against deflationary conditions, and in many cases, it has also performed well during inflation. However, to say that gold will always provide a hedge during inflationary periods would probably be unfounded. The most recent evidence of gold's demand during a deflationary environment occurred during the last recession, when the gold bull market commenced. In 2001, at a price of around $230, gold has surged to over $700 in five years.

This leads us to the inverse correlation between gold and stock market performance. Statistical analysis shows that over the past thirty years, *the correlation between gold and the Dow Jones Industrial Average actually declined during the worst-performing 30 months of this index, thereby serving as a hedge against the most severe market declines.* The inverse relationship between gold prices and stock market performance might be explained by the investor-neglect of gold during strong bull market periods, causing severe undervaluation of this precious metal. Likewise, *the retreat of investors from an overvalued stock market during a post-bubble correction could cause the rush into gold as a safer, more attractively valued asset class.*

While gold is variable in its ability to hedge against inflation, it has the added appeal of worldwide acceptance and is not linked to any currencies (which could head south). On Friday, January 18, 1980, gold reached its all-time high of $877 per ounce. The price of gold today in 1980 inflation-adjusted dollars is equivalent to about $2200. Compare that with its current level of $670.

> "the price of gold is still relatively low, with about 20 ounces of gold needed to match the level of the Dow Jones Industrial Average. Gold is considered expensive when the ratio drops below five."
>
> Barron's

Clearly, gold has a long way to go before it reaches its inflation-adjusted high. And although I cannot say for certain whether this will occur over the next decade, I am fairly confident gold will reach the $1200 mark by 2014 for many compelling reasons.

This Time it's Different

While there have been some instances when rising gold has mirrored periods of increasing inflation, much of this behavior has been attributable to factors other than inflation itself. *Rather, rising gold prices usually result from a deflationary economy not an inflationary one. During a prolonged deflationary environment, GDP is reduced, leading to a decline in the purchase power parity of the currency. Therefore, buying gold during a deflationary environment provides a nice hedge against relative changes in foreign currencies.* It so happens that many investors also shift into a gold hedge during inflation, which only reduces the buying power domestically. However, since the dollar is the global unit of currency, inflation also acts to diminish its purchase power parity. And because gold is not linked to any currencies, this might explain why gold is the investment choice for many who are worried about deflation or inflation.

While the 1970s and early '80s showed a correlation between inflation and gold prices, in my opinion there were many other factors that led to this phenomenon. Not only was the price of oil spiking, but there were numerous global issues causing many to flock to gold as a secure investment. Whether gold, inflation, and high oil prices will demonstrate such a correlation again will be dependent upon the overall health of the global economy. *If however, oil continues its surge (a likely possibility), gold in fact may mirror the inflation escalation we are seeing and will continue to see over the next several years.*

You may have noticed back in 2001 to 2004, when deflation was evident, gold made a major upward move (also recall that deflation really did not increase the absolute buying power of the dollar since total wage compensation was contracting). After a correction in prices in early 2004, gold is again on the rise, but this time it's not due to deflation; nor is it due to inflation per say. *Currently, the rise in gold is due to the rise in commodity prices, the weak dollar, and the weakness of the U.S. monetary policy.* Combined, these elements have an inflationary effect.

While significant inflation is certainly present in the economy, it is neither due to nor a direct consequence of the price of gold. Rather, rising energy and healthcare costs, and a decline in total wage compensation are causing inflation. *Although many economic experts claim that rising oil prices cannot in itself create inflation, they are absolutely wrong.*

Finally, consider the possibility that the Fed may eventually create even more inflation in order to pay off much of its debt. This would artificially increase the GDP and earnings growth of corporate America. There are some who contend that the government has caused high inflation in the past to pay down debt, and if true, that would serve as a precedent. As final support for this possibility, consider that the new Fed Chairman Bernanke is considered an expert in the economics of inflation. Perhaps the government thinks it can raise and lower inflation as needed, but I think it's going to have a more difficult time than expected.

Gold ETFs

Gold exchange-traded funds (ETFs) make investing in gold more convenient, less expensive, and less risky for smaller investors. Unlike other ETFs, gold (and silver) ETFs actually buy gold (and silver) bullion and store it in a central bank. Therefore, investors in precious metal ETFs actually own a stake in the metal as opposed to owning shares in the mining companies. In 2005, two new ETFs were launched that track gold—iShares Comex Gold Trust (IAU) and StreetTracks Gold Shares (GLD).

The main advantage of precious metal ETFs are that they protect investors from company-specific and political risks, which can be very high, especially when companies are mining in unpredictable and often volatile nations such as those in South America and Africa. Therefore, the risks are reduced to those affecting trading prices of the metal (i.e. the macroeconomic risks). In contrast, because many of the smaller mining companies use leverage, they can multiply their earnings during a gold bull market. But this can also work against them when gold prices correct.

> *"I don't think we've even scratched the surface of what's possible when these ETFs fall into the portfolios of charities, trusts, institutions, endowments funds, etc. I think these have got a long way to go and they'll help drive the gold price up."*
>
> John Hill of Citigroup Global Markets

Gold ETFs have grown so rapidly over the past year that they now hold over 424.7 tonnes of bullion. Since ETFs actually purchase and store gold, this will help deplete reserves, causing an increase in price. When compared to mutual funds, ETFs:

- Are more tax-efficient
- Have lower costs
- Can be hedged with options
- Have no penalties for liquidation

Other Precious Metals

Perhaps even more impressive than gold has been the appreciation of silver, platinum, and palladium over the past three years. Similar to gold prices, while these precious metals are certain to correct, they are likely to make new highs over the next several of years. But corrections in the precious metals can be brisk and devastating.

Silver

Demand for silver stems from three main areas; industrial and decorative, photography and jewellery, and silverware. Together, these three categories represent more than 95 percent of annual silver consumption. In 2003, 351 million ounces of silver were used for industrial applications, 200 million ounces for the photographic sector, and 266 million ounces were consumed in the jewellery and silverware markets.

Silver has such a high demand for industrial applications because of its unique physical, mechanical, and chemical properties—its strength, malleability and ductility, its electrical and thermal conductivity, its sensitivity to and high reflectance of light, and the ability to endure extreme temperature ranges. In many cases, no substitute materials can mimic silver's physical and chemical characteristics.

The chart below shows the historical price chart of silver since it began trading on an organized official exchange. For the most part, silver prices remained constant for more than 150 years and did not even keep up with inflation. However, silver surged around 1980 to over $22 per ounce. Over the next several years, I expect that previous record to be surpassed and it could easily cross the $25 mark without a depression. Of course, a depression could cause silver to soar over the $50 mark. As the next chart shows, silver has already surpassed a critical technical analysis resistance level which favors its continued uptrend.

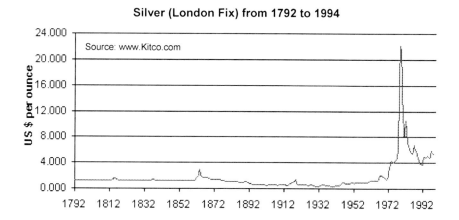

Silver (London Fix) from 1792 to 1994

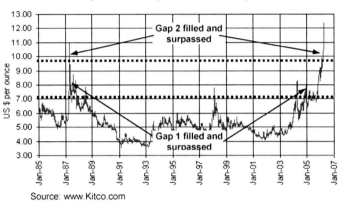

Source: www.Kitco.com

Over the past few years, investment demand for silver has been minimal but has recently picked up due to concerns with the U.S. dollar. The mining of silver has unique dynamics that favor a low-risk, high appreciation potential. Specifically, *about 65 percent of silver mine production is the by-product from copper, zinc, and lead mining. Only 35 percent of silver demand comes from pure silver mines and from gold primary mines where silver is also a by-product.* This unique relationship between silver, gold and the base metals sets up interesting scenarios for enormous silver price appreciation.

Up is the Only Direction for Silver

Silver has been experiencing a huge depletion of inventories over the past decade. Since 1991 alone, the above ground silver supply has declined from about 1.4 billion to over 600 million ounces. Note also that Warren Buffett purchased 130 ounces of silver in 1998. However, it is not known whether he still holds this amount. If so, he would have control over 20 percent of the world silver market. I have read reports that indicate he has since sold this huge amount. But that would be an even more bullish indicator, since a tremendous price appreciation has occurred despite the release of such a large supply.

Annually, silver deficits are around 50 to 100 million ounces. And because reserves are at very low levels, we could face a shock of skyrocketing silver prices well beyond the $20 per ounce level that is most certain to occur by 2012. Of course, now that one silver ETF has entered the market, this will further strain supplies since the precious metal ETFs buy the metals, thereby removing them from the market.

Regardless of the future economic environment, silver is destined to continue its rise along with gold. *Under strong economic conditions, silver's use in industry will no doubt propel its price to new highs. In contrast, under a weak economic scenario, silver prices would soar even more due to the decreases in base metal use and therefore mining.* Once again, zinc, copper, and lead prices are the primary driver of silver production in the form of by-products. And because these metals are used in a variety of industrial applications, base metal mines (65 percent of silver mine supply) will produce more silver when the economy is doing well, and less when the economy is struggling (i.e. when base metal prices are depressed). Therefore, silver demand should remain strong for several years. Given my forecast for overall global economic weakness over the next twenty years, *I expect silver to have more upside than gold.* In fact, I would not be surprised to see silver surpass the $30 mark over this time period even without the affects of a depression. Some might say that this is still a conservative estimate.

World Silver Supply and Demand
(in millions of ounces)

	1995	1996	1997	1998	1999	2000	2001	2002	2003	2004
Supply										
Mine Production	483.0	491.0	520.7	544.0	548.5	587.3	611.8	607.4	611.2	634.4
Net Government Sales	25.3	18.9	--	40.6	93.1	75.2	71.7	54.9	88.2	61.7
Old Silver Scrap	162.9	158.3	169.3	193.9	181.2	180.4	182.4	187.1	183.6	181.1
Producer Hedging	7.5	--	68.1	6.5	--	--	18.9	--	--	2.0
Implied Net Disinvestment	89.9	142.8	85.5	44.0	61.1	88.5	--	14.1	--	--
Total Supply	**768.6**	**811.1**	**843.6**	**829.1**	**883.9**	**931.4**	**884.8**	**863.5**	**883.1**	**879.2**
Demand										
Fabrication										
Industrial Applications	295.7	297.7	320.8	316.4	339.2	375.4	336.3	340.1	350.5	367.1
Photography	209.9	210.1	217.4	225.4	227.9	218.3	213.1	204.3	192.9	181.0
Jewelry & Silverware	236.9	263.7	274.3	259.4	271.7	278.2	287.1	262.7	274.2	247.5
Coins & Medals	26.1	25.2	30.4	27.8	29.2	32.1	30.5	31.6	35.8	41.1
Total Fabrication	**768.6**	**796.8**	**842.9**	**829.1**	**867.9**	**904.0**	**867.0**	**838.7**	**853.4**	**836.7**
Net Government Purchases	--	--	0.7	--	--	--	--	--	--	--
Producer De-Hedging	--	14.3	--	--	16.0	27.4	--	24.8	21.0	--
Implied Net Investment	--	--	--	--	--	--	17.8	--	8.7	42.5
Total Demand	**768.6**	**811.1**	**843.6**	**829.1**	**883.9**	**931.4**	**884.8**	**863.5**	**883.1**	**879.2**
Silver Price										
(London US$/oz)	5.197	5.199	4.897	5.544	5.220	4.951	4.370	4.599	4.879	6.658

Box 17-1: Specific Uses of Silver

Silver's unique optical reflectivity allows it to be virtually 100 percent reflective after polishing. Therefore, it is used in mirrors and in coatings for glass, cellophane or metals. While silver's importance as a bactericide has been documented only since the late 1800s, its use in purification has been known since ancient times. Early records indicate that the Phoenicians used silver vessels to keep water, wine and vinegar pure during their long sea voyages.

In America, pioneers moving west put silver and copper coins in their water barrels to keep the water clean. In fact, "born with a silver spoon" is not a reference to wealth, but to health. In the early 18th century, babies who were fed with silver spoons were healthier than those fed with spoons made from other metals. This led to the widespread use of silver pacifiers in America because of these beneficial, yet unexplained health effects.

Silver also has a variety of uses in pharmaceuticals. For instance, silver sulfadiazine (known as silvadiene) is the most powerful compound for burn treatment. It is used worldwide by every hospital in North America for burn victims to kill bacteria and allow the body to naturally repair the burn area.

Platinum

Platinum plays a critical role in the high-technology industry. For instance, it is used to convert hydrogen and oxygen to heat, water and electricity. However, it has hundreds of other critical industrial uses. Since 2002, platinum is already up by over 250 percent. And while it will most likely continue its bull run, current levels appear to be quite high. Therefore, I would tend to stay away from this metal until it corrects downward by a large amount. In contrast, while other precious metals have also experienced similar surges, on a historical basis they are still quite attractive in price. Once again, *investors opting to invest in the precious metals should only buy after large corrections and trim positions after large rallies.*

Platinum (London Fix) from 1992 to April 2006

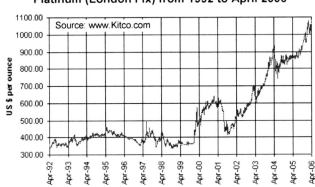

Palladium

Similar to platinum, palladium also plays a key role in the high-tech industry. However, palladium has a wider variety of uses, including medical, dental, chemical, in electronics, as an autocatalyst, in oil refining, water treatment, photography, hydrogen purification, and in small use in certain coins. Palladium will also likely play a role in modern fuel cell technologies but it is unknown yet how large its role will be due to the variety of alternative options. We do know that palladium fuel cells offer some very promising alternative energy technologies since, as a hydride, palladium can absorb 800 to 900 times its own volume of hydrogen. In addition, it can be used to generate, purify, store and detect hydrogen.

Palladium (London Fix) from 1992 to April 2006

Rhodium

Rhodium has a high melting point (resistance to melt by heat), is very reflective to light, and is very hard and durable. It's obtained as a by-product from nickel production and is used

- in alloys to harden platinum and palladium
- in electroplating and coatings to give a hard corrosion resistant surface
- in electrodes for aircraft spark plugs
- as a major component of catalytic systems
- for jewelry

As you can see, Rhodium has skyrocketed in price since 2003, up by over 600 percent. In addition, it has recently surpassed its previous record high of $5000 per ounce made in 1990. No doubt, Rhodium will correct in price soon and that might be a good time to consider an entry point. *Note however, that a clear long-term upward trend in price has not been established as evidenced by analysis of the chart.* So *investors should be extremely cautious with Rhodium and may choose to stay out of it altogether.*

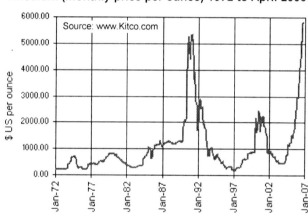

Rhodium (monthly price per ounce) 1972 to April 2006

The Dollar

After a tailspin since the Internet meltdown, the dollar has recently experienced a minor rebound. However, the dollar's longer-term trend remains down. Throughout this book I have detailed the reasons for the weak dollar many times and I cannot see things improving in America anytime soon. Therefore, investors should consider some exposure to other currencies such as the Euro and Yen as a hedge against U.S.-dollar denominated assets.

A couple of years ago, billionaire and legendary hedge fund manager George Soros publicly disclosed that he had built a massive short position against the U.S. dollar. And Warren Buffet announced that he had bought a "massive" basket of foreign currencies to profit from a coming decline in the dollar. According to Buffett, this was the first time he ever bought a single foreign currency. He is now warning of an impending dollar crisis that could last for years. If you doubt my analysis, maybe you will accept his.

368

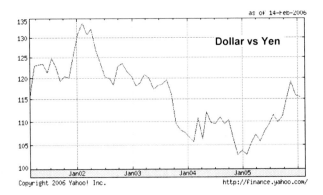

http://finance.yahoo.com/

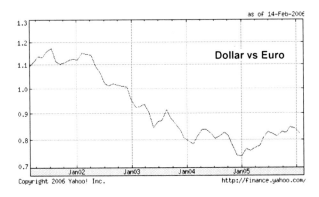

http://finance.yahoo.com/

Special Note: There may be some readers who question or doubt some of the material presented in the alternative health section of this chapter, such as metabolic or nutritional/metabolic cures. As well, some may question some of the statements I have made in the healthcare chapter pertaining to the causes of America's obesity epidemic, or the overemphasis for strenuous exercise as a solution to obesity and overall general good health. However, these findings have been documented and supported by numerous researchers and healthcare professionals. Much of these findings are listed in the reference section at the end of the book. Finally, through an independent analysis of my own and having been trained in science and medicine, I have determined that the findings I have presented are in fact valid.

18

INVESTMENT STRATEGIES

Don't Expect Much Help

As I've mentioned throughout this book, the economic and investment analyses delivered by Wall Street and the Fed is always more optimistic than the real picture; especially when the economy is weak. Wall Street's main objective is to generate business, while it is the job of the Fed to safeguard the economy during turbulent periods. And when the actions of the Federal Reserve chairman can no longer improve the economy, he acts as a "cheerleader," refusing to admit a problem; boosting consumer confidence via deception.

So often in the past we have heard mention of Alan Greenspan as the "Great Maestro." But in reality, Mr. Greenspan has been a disaster for America by having created three bubbles (Internet, credit, and real estate) in less than twenty years. However, when the aftershocks of the financial fallout occur, it is unlikely that Greenspan will be blamed. Yet, I will always think of Alan Greenspan as the "Great Bubble Maestro."

Wall Street Analysts

At some point, America's credit-dependent economy will run out of gas. And somewhere along the way, the markets will be devastated. But don't expect Wall Street or the Fed to alert you until it is too late because of their own agendas. *During my experience working for Wall Street's best firms, I have found that the vast majority of analysts are not only useless, but oftentimes dangerous to investors.* Most analysts really do not understand asset and risk management, and they underemphasize long-term economic forecasting. Finally, they do not consider technical analysis and market psychology as critical components of a comprehensive investment strategy. *They are really salesmen in disguise, generating trading and investment ideas for brokers to pass onto their clients—individual investors, mutual fund companies and pension funds.*

And while the SEC now has laws that forbid analysts from generating investment banking business, you can bet it's still going on. The problem is that it takes huge sums of money to run a research department. And in order to justify the costs, *firms use most of their analysts to cover the larger companies; the ones that have a lot more investment banking business to divvy up.* And with rare exception, Wall Street economists aren't much better. Rather than providing accurate and meaningful forecasts, they try to squeeze out as much optimism as they can.

Analyst Confusion

Have you ever wondered why analysts are always changing their minds about the companies they cover? Think about it. Why does Wall Street preach "long-term investing" as an excuse for bad recommendations, yet they lower a rating for a stock if a company misses an earnings estimate by a penny? What does it matter that a company missed quarterly earnings if the investors are expected to be "long-term" holders of the stock? Answer: they want your business for the long-term, but they also want to generate daily trading activity to boost trading revenues.

The simple fact is that company fundamentals do not change over a three-month period. Fundamentals take a long time to change. Yet, when a company misses earnings or issues a downward revision, some analysts would have you believe that the bottom is falling out. This generates trading activity. *The smart money knows this and uses this investor panic to cash in.* Likewise, what good are analysts' ratings if most stocks are "buy" or "hold" especially in a bear market? When was the last time an analyst helped you "buy low" and "sell high"? Most likely, analysts have caused you to do the opposite.

Have you ever heard an analyst come out and say, "My industry is expected to perform poorly over the current and future expected economic cycle so you should stay out"? Of course not. That would be bad business for the firm because it would decrease trading activity, as well as upset companies in that industry. And you can bet any firm whose analysts made such a call would not receive future banking business from those companies affected.

> *If you think Wall Street is going to guide you through this mess, don't hold you're breath. They're going to drag investors all the way down to the bottom just like they did a few years ago; just like they have.*

Have you ever heard a Wall Street firm state the obvious? *airline, transportation, automotive, and publishing industries are bad investments due to their business and regulatory structure, inherently low profit margins and oil dependency*; of course not. Once again that would be bad business and would surely dismiss the firm from getting secondary stock, bond and preferred stock underwritings from these industries.

But Wall Street has a system they created to insulate analysts from investor retaliation due to their horrendous recommendations. Brokers serve as the pawns who are sued when investors lose money. Oddly enough, analysts are never sued, yet they're the ones who influence the investment public. In conclusion, you should ask yourself the question: does Wall Street REALLY know what's going on? If they do why do they keep changing their minds so often? Why is it that Wall Street rarely delivers analysis and advice that saves investors from the devastating effects of a bear market?

Wall Street Brokers

The handful of truly talented Wall Street brokers serving retail customers is becoming rarer each day due to the emphasis by most firms to sell managed money products, positioning most financial professionals as pure salesmen. Therefore, *the newer brokers (financial consultants, planners, or any other designation you prefer) are not only unskilled and inexperienced in asset management and investment analysis, but many are not even permitted to trade or manage assets, causing them to be out of touch with the pulse of the capital markets.* All they are doing is placing their clients with some money manager who is never seen or heard from. So why not skip the middleman and go direct?

Many Americans have been led to believe that financial professionals who hold themselves out to be financial planners or financial consultants know what is going on in the stock and bond markets, when in fact many of these individuals are amongst the most clueless of all financial professionals, placing them along the same experience and knowledge base as those who transact retail investment business in commercial banks and discount brokerage firms. Note, as with anything, there are always exceptions.

Most financial planners practice traditional asset allocation and diversification, preaching to their customers "take the long-term approach" as an excuse for their inability to navigate difficult markets. In many cases, these advisors should be encouraging their clients to stay out of the stock market during treacherous conditions. But this would impact their wages. *The result is that they charge management fees for very little management. It has become a huge problem in the industry and it is bilking investors of billions of dollars in unnecessary fees, while keeping their portfolios unprotected against major sell-offs in the market.*

Sadly, the small number of brokers who are skilled enough to know what is going on are often restricted from making recommendations that are inconsistent with the analysts of their firm. And when they do decide to solicit a stock for which their analyst has issued a hold or sell recommendation or does not even cover, they face the risk of getting sued if the stock falls. And the firm may not support them in legal proceedings.

> **Analyst Ambiguity**
>
> What does a "Buy" rating mean anyway? Buy it when? The analyst issued the rating 6 months ago and since then the stock has risen by 50%. Is it still a "Buy"? Sure it's above its price target but the analyst may raise this target tomorrow so what are you supposed to do?
>
> What does a "Sell" rating mean? When an analyst issues a "Sell," recommendation it should be effective for only a day. After that, the price should drop sufficiently. After a few months with a "Sell" rating the stock might actually be a great buy due to severe undervaluation.
>
> The fact is analyst ratings and price targets indicate nothing about the investment merits of the stock. They serve two purposes—to generate trading activity and to reward or punish a company for sharing banking business with firms.

Therefore, in most cases, *brokers are restricted to only soliciting those companies that their firm's analysts have issued favorable recommendations, assuring that their clients will be subject to little if any value and often times poor recommendations.*

Because of the recent changes made within the financial industry, most financial professionals are no longer geared to serve the non-ultrawealthy investor. However, as with anything, there are always exceptions. Just don't assume you are dealing with one of the few exceptions until you make a critical assessment of your advisor's skill and experience base. Generally speaking, unless you have $10,000,000 of investable assets, it is unlikely you will be able to get a broker or other financial professional knowledgeable enough to help you navigate this market. The really talented brokers are in short supply and are focused on the big accounts. And if you think the situation is bad for Wall Street brokers, you can imagine how bad it is for the discount firms.

Mutual Funds

There is a very good reason why most money managers and mutual funds cannot match the returns of the indices. The sad reality is that many fund managers do not know what's going on and they really don't care that much. After all, it's not their money and they get paid regardless how they do. Most mutual funds are simply glorified marketing machines that spend billions of dollars each year convincing you that they have some special edge or understand the investment process in a way like no others. All they really understand is dollar-cost averaging and diversification, but so does an eighth grader.

I know this firsthand because I dealt with some of the largest fund companies and I was often amazed at their lack of sophistication and inability to appreciate investment risk. In many cases, recent college grads are put in positions that allow them to make critical investment decisions for the fund. This is especially true for pension funds. Other times, the fund's investment strategy is so generic that it mirrors an index fund with much higher fees. In some cases, they buy stocks that have collapsed, like WCOM or ENE because they "like the fundamentals," and it represents a "great bargain."

Similar to mutual funds, money managers must remain at least 80 to 90 percent invested at all times by law, and this can be very risky, especially during large market swings typically present in secular bear markets. As well, because they can only charge for assets under management, money managers and mutual funds have an incentive (and legal requirement) to always remain invested in the market. This results in the perpetual bull-market mentality preached by these firms.

These two aspects of general fund investment structure explain the lack of fund manager proclivity towards risk management. But even if fund managers could liquidate a large portion of the portfolio's holdings during or prior to a large market sell-off, most funds are so large that they would not be able to dump shares of their largest holdings quickly enough without incurring significant losses. *Therefore, unless a fund has been structured in a way that allows the fund manager to invest in special asset classes that provide hedging strategies, it will have very little means to avoid large market corrections (otherwise known as non-diversifiable risk).*

Fees that Kill

The big secret in the mutual fund industry is that all of the fees charged to customers are not apparent unless one studies the fund prospectus with a microscope and an advanced degree. Even for funds without marketing fees (12b-1 fees, otherwise known as no-load funds), there are other fees that most are not aware of such as ticket charges. You see, those 2 percent annual fees (or in some cases for 4 percent when all fees are added) extract a large sum of money from a fund over a several year period.

If you understand compounding, you can imagine how devastating these fees can be during a prolonged bear market such as the current one. *According to some experts, mutual funds can take away up to 79 percent from the total returns of a fund in fees over the course of several decades.* This is due to the effect of compounding of fees each year and has an especially devastating effect on your holdings when the fund has annual losses.

The historical annual returns of the stock market are around 8 percent. Therefore, assuming a total average annual fee of around 3 percent, (after all expenses) fund managers must outperform the market by around 40 percent (i.e. they must yield gross returns of 11.2 percent) in order to beat the average index fund (after fees). Consider that a near-impossible feat to accomplish especially consistently. Once you factor in all fees, inflation, and taxes you should feel very fortunate if your total net return exceeds that of a CD.

Two-Faced Funds

Due to the intense pressure to perform, there has been a recent trend of many fund managers who have engaged in a questionable practice called *style drift*, whereby they include large holdings of assets that are inconsistent with the fund's stated management style and risk tolerance. Of particular disappointment is the lack of SEC oversight, which has allowed the mutual fund industry get away a host of other deceitful activities.

A certain well-known fund manager has been praised by the financial media for several years as one of the only fund managers that consistently beats the S&P 500 index. However, in 2004 and 2005 he was the number one shareholder of a new high-tech company. And although he manages several funds, this speculative stock was a top 10 holding of his value fund. This raises question of whether the fund has violated the trust provided by shareholders since it has potentially exposed investors to a higher risk than they were led to believe. Since when do value funds have high-technology IPOs? I don't think Benjamin Graham or Warren Buffet would consider any high-tech company a part of value investing, especially when it is new on the market. Most newly traded stocks are very volatile due to earnings inconsistency.

Unfortunately, this example is far from being an isolated case, yet most investors are not aware of these activities. And because the mutual fund industry still remains largely unregulated, this practice is just one of many questionable activities the SEC turns its head away from because the mutual fund industry is now very big and powerful.

Lost in the Crowd?

As previously mentioned, the investment structure of mutual and managed money funds typically does not permit them to use sophisticated asset and risk management strategies. They must remain majority invested at all times and work with these limitations. That is why they are typically not considered skill-based asset managers. Despite these severe limitations, there are still some very skillful fund managers who do an excellent job. The problem is that spotting such fund managers is very difficult and everyone seems to think they have one because they only focus on their returns during bull markets.

Finding a Good Fund

Rather than focus on the most recent returns, investors must look for consistency and the 10- to 15-year performance records because this demonstrates the ability of the manager to navigate different economic and market conditions. Investors must also understand the risks taken by the fund—noting the total percentage of the fund's top ten holdings and looking at the turnover ratio (if the fund is in a non-tax-deferred account). Finally, investors should keep in mind that *a fund that may have had a superior performance during the past decade might actually be poorly positioned for the current secular bear market.* And during such a market, certain mutual funds should be exchanged for money market mutual funds.

Therefore, you should make sure the fund company you invest with has many different well-managed funds, each with different investment strategies so you can shift around as needed without having to pay exit fees. *With over 8000 mutual funds, in my opinion there are probably around 15 fund families with about 100 well-managed funds.* Statistically speaking, it's unlikely that you own one of these funds.

Keep in mind that each investor will have different needs at different points in their life. Many times, the overall assessment process for deciding which fund to invest in will depend on your level of investment experience and skills, the amount of investible assets, risk tolerance, and the time you are willing to spend monitoring the economy, market and the fund. The main problem with evaluating funds and fund managers is that it's very difficult and requires an advanced understanding of finance, economics, risk management, financial planning and practical experience with the stock market. As a matter of fact, if you are one of the rare individuals who have these skills, you're probably better off managing your own investments, assuming you have sufficient time.

In conclusion, mutual funds serve the primary role of providing a way for the small and unsophisticated investor to obtain a diversified portfolio. And in this regard, most funds do a nice job. Mutual funds do indeed have a place in the investment world, as long as investors can identify the best funds and fund managers and understand when and what funds are the best investment choice and when they are not. The problem is that many individuals have too much invested in mutual funds and would be better off by shifting a large portion of these assets with money managers since the fees are lower, tax-loss selling is possible and the performance is similar if not better.

Hedge Funds

Some of the main advantages of hedge funds are that they are permitted to completely liquidate their portfolios, use advanced hedging strategies, and short stocks. This not only accounts in part for the fact that well-managed hedge funds have lower relative risk, but the tremendous growth of hedge funds also explains the increased market volatility over the past decade. However, as you might suspect, the hedge fund industry is not without its problems. Lack of regulation and investment transparency has led to hundreds fraudulent activities that, to this day remain unnoticed by outsiders.

Make no mistake, not all hedge funds are well-managed. Because the structure is wide open and depends on the preferences of the fund, there are many hedge funds that are too risky, poorly run, or charge excessive management fees. This is part of the difficulty in finding a good fund. But there are advisors, otherwise known as gatekeepers who analyze funds and advise accredited investors of fund choices based upon their financial profile.

Because of their lack regulation, and due to the sophisticated nature of these investment vehicles, hedge funds are restricted to accredited investors. In order to qualify as an accredited investor, you must have earned at least $200,000 in the previous year with the expectation to maintain this minimum income. Alternatively, you can qualify as an accredited investor if your net worth is over $1,000,000. Fortunately, these minimums will be raised soon as a way to protect less sophisticated investors from these complex and often risky funds.

Investment Strategy

During the great bull market of the '90s, most investors abandoned economic cycle theory in favor of sector performance driven by technological innovation. As a result, most Wall Street analysts latched onto the *bottom-up* fundamental analysis approach, which stresses business and industry change as a way to spot investment opportunities. Only as an afterthought were economics considered. This is in contrast to the *top-down* approach, which emphasizes the effects of the economy on productivity growth and therefore market and industry performance.

With the emergence of the Internet in the midst of what was already an amazing bull market period, a paradigm shift was heralded all around Wall Street, which provided further support for the bottom-up approach. But that was a period of unrealistic proportions. Now we are back to the realities of asset performance ruled by economics and the cycling of sectors.

In short, we have been in a bull market in precious metals, REITs, and commodities since 2001. And with the exception of certain types of REITs, I expect these trends to continue over most of the duration of this secular bear market. After many of the REITs bottom out, I expect the commodities bubble to begin a downward spiral by 2010. But the bull market in precious metals should last through at least 2014. In part, this bull market has been and will continue to be fueled by the weakness of the dollar. In contrast, *the commodities bull market is both a consequence and catalyst of the dollar's weakness.*

For over a decade now, China has been able to post double-digit growth despite high commodity prices, due to massive investment of foreign capital and trade surpluses—all effects of unfair trade activities. However, even for China, continued high commodity prices will eventually cause a problem. I would expect the full effects to be apparent by 2011; but no one really knows. In contrast, India might be a better insulated from such a bubble since it has not been as dependent on raw materials for its growth.

Declining commodities will be the first of many legs needed to restore the U.S. economy to healthy growth, and I would expect the dollar to gain some strength when commodity prices correct. *But do not mistake the future collapse in commodity prices as a sign of permanent recovery for America.* There are too many major issues to contend with before America can reverse its downward spiral.

Regardless, investors certainly cannot lie down and wait for a possible disaster because they could miss great opportunities in the market. After all, during the '90s, there were many respected individuals who predicted the crash of the raging bull. However, most of them made such predictions several years before it actually occurred and therefore missed out on tremendous investment returns.

It's much easier to predict <u>what</u> will happen rather than <u>when</u>. It might be in ten or twenty years before America's inescapable correction period occurs. Therefore, the first thing investors need to do is to remain cautious, despite any "great news" from Wall Street and other masters of propaganda. As well, they should remain pessimistic when the market rallies. *In this type of market, strong rallies should be considered as selling opportunities, while sell-offs should be approached with great care.*

The Myth of Beta

The use of a security's beta value as an accurate measure of risk is just one of the ridiculous myths preached by Wall Street. In part, the widespread acceptance of beta as a gauge of investment risk has been facilitated by its ease of interpretation. Rather than practice skill-based investment and risk management, the asset management community has permitted academia to determine asset management strategies based on theory. However, *it can be a difficult task to yield effective results when the same people who are creating the industry status quo have never managed money professionally.*

The simple fact is that *beta values do not help investors determine true investment risk. As a matter of fact, if you have a long investment horizon, using a security's beta value to help build a diversified portfolio with lower volatility will actually lower your returns!* If you know your liquidity needs and can be fairly certain about your investment horizon, (i.e. with no need to use any money you have invested over this horizon) using beta as a gauge for risk can lead to diminished relative returns.

You should only consider beta as an asset management tool if your investment horizon is 10 years or less or if you are unsure of your liquidity needs. Otherwise, if you use beta to construct a portfolio that minimizes volatility, you will be lowering your upside if your investment horizon is long. Finally, the reliance on beta values can be dangerous since it gives a false sense of security in assessing overall investment risk.

Risk that Really Matters

High potential rewards mandate high levels of theoretical risk. Traditionally, risk is defined as increased volatility (as measured by a stock's beta value) by academicians, Wall Street and money managers. This definition of risk is only useful for those who manage large funds; not for individual investors. As mentioned, *beta only helps determine liquidity risk, or the probability that a portfolio will decline or rise over a short time period* relative to the overall movement of the market (as defined in this case by the S&P 500 Index).

Fund managers are primarily concerned with total beta portfolio values since they need their funds to have monthly liquidity in order to accommodate investors who might sell their funds. Thus for fund managers, beta helps them manage fund cash flows. *So if you understand your liquidity needs, your focus should be on investment risk rather than beta or liquidity risk.* But this is easier said than done.

Investment risk can be defined as the risk that the investment will fail or perform poorly over an extended period. I determine investment risk by analyzing business risk. In this process, I primary look at qualitative fundamental analysis; that is, the competitive landscape of the industry and company, assessing strategy, and valuation of the overall market relative coupled to economic forecasting. In my view, these are better indicators for long-term investors because they do not change much, unlike earnings statements. Qualitative analysis is supposed to be a significant portion of fundamental analysis, but Wall Street analysts often underemphasize this element in their analysis. I also use quantitative fundamental analysis (to a lesser extent) to check certain key financial ratios so that I can be assured companies have adequate cash flows, liquidity, and for use in relative valuation.

Investors with longer investment horizons seeking growth and with a high tolerance for risk might want to select industries that are either new and have large growth rates or an overall large potential size, or industries where there is very little competition and high barriers of entry for others. The Internet serves as an excellent example of an industry that is new, has an enormous potential market, and a rapid growth rate. However, from the Internet fallout, I hope you can appreciate how risky new industries can be.

In the mid-1990s, just when the Internet was beginning to hit mainstream, the market was seen to be so huge that it really did not matter whether a company had a sound business model. There was so much opportunity and such high expectations that investment capital was thrown at the feet of any company with a dotcom name. But as more companies entered the playing field, competition grew and those companies with weak business models were eventually forced out of the market. *This always occurs with any new, rapidly expanding or large market. Early on, everyone wins and all investors can look like geniuses. But as competition heats up, only the best companies survive.*

Once I spot lucrative industries, I determine the best positioned companies in terms of both potential returns and business risk. Then I match this risk-return ratio with my risk tolerance and investment objectives. For company risk, I look at debt and liquidity ratios and other data such as institutional ownership and short interest ratio. Then I factor in the health, (current and future estimates) of the economy. For instance, I think many alternative energy companies have a relatively low business risk (relative to their small size, since small caps normally have more business risk and liquidity risk) due to the global oil shortage. However, valuations are fairly high. And it's difficult to determine what a fair valuation is since there are only a few of these companies that are public. And even the public companies do not have stable or strong revenues, not to mention the lack of earnings. Therefore, this is a tricky sector to deal with.

Much of the same also applies to small cap biotechs, which one might associate with enormous risk. The basis behind my view that *small cap biotechs have lower relative risk than small caps in other industries is due to the dynamics of the industry, investor expectations and the ability to raise additional capital when needed.* Biotech investors understand the drug approval process is a long haul so they are generally more patient. In contrast, other industries are driven by short-term products and therefore investors are not as patient. They demand results sooner. As a consequence of these dynamics, these industries will have limited ability to raise capital if they become stressed.

Only the largest companies in stressed industries have the ability to weather difficult periods. Investors must also keep in mind that *newer companies will almost always be plagued with earnings inconsistency, which will cause the stock to be very volatile in price* (i.e. high beta values). But as pointed out, a consideration of beta is only important for a shorter time frame or when investors are uncertain about their liquidity needs.

Risk is Relative to the Economy

Also keep in mind that *what may be considered lower risk by conventional wisdom (e.g. bonds, large caps, etc) could in fact represent a relatively high risk depending on the current and future economic environment, as well as your investment horizon.* It is my opinion that on a risk-adjusted basis, some industries traditionally considered lower risk actually represent much higher risk if you are looking at a 5- to 10-year time frame.......based not only on the economic conditions (large caps perform poorly in bear markets and recessions for many reasons), but also due to the overall market risk, which could force most stock prices downward.

During periods of low short-term interest rates, investors should only buy large caps only after market corrections or stock sell-offs and sell them once they become fully valued. Typically, *during low rate environments, small and mid-caps outperform large caps due to enhanced leverage. However, as interest rates rise, this will narrow the edge small and mid-caps have over large caps.* This is exactly what we have seen since 2002, with small and mid-caps leading in performance, and only beginning to trail off relative to large caps by 2006, as rates have approached their historic mean.

Hedging Inflation and Volatility

Inflation is never good for investments. The common consensus has it that it is worse for bonds than equities. However, I do not think this necessarily true. Inflation can be equally destructive for all asset classes except real estate, certain currencies, and securities indexed to inflation. As previously discussed, in many cases gold can provide a good hedge as well. *Investors wishing to hedge against inflation should take positions in TIPS, (Treasury Inflation Protected Securities) REITs and well-managed bond funds. However, they should be especially careful with mortgage-REITs since the MBS market is very vulnerable to a crisis.* While Washington undermines real inflation numbers, TIPS will still provide superior investment returns due to high expected inflation and high long-term rates. After all, Washington distorts most economic data but they don't delete it, and if inflation becomes undeniable they may even exaggerate it in order to provide a more favorable environment to pay off the national debt.

The stock market almost always declines with rising gold (current), rising inflation (current), a weak dollar (current), and high interest rates (coming in a few years). *The need for investors wishing to minimize the volatility of their portfolios in a manner exclusive of frequent trading activity is to hold a small portion of non-mortgage REITS and precious metals stocks.* The reason for this is due to the fact that these are the two asset classes which have the lowest correlation relative to other common stocks (i.e. the overall market). In other words, REITS and precious metals typically cushion large and/or prolonged market declines. In particular, I feel that the bull market in rental unit-based REITS and precious metals will continue for several years.

Hedging Against Deflation

If deflation becomes a problem, investors have little choice for investments. The *emphasis during a deflationary environment should be on capital preservation.* Always remember that minimizing losses is more important than extracting gains since cash is in limited quantities. Cash will be king in such an environment. Alternatively, certificates of deposit in stable banks and Treasury bills will also provide safety along with modest gains. And of course, gold would do well. However, real estate would get crushed along with most stocks.

Asset Classes

Cash

In my opinion, over the next 6 to 8 years, cash will perform in line with the DJIA and S&P 500 on an annualized basis. This is based both upon my expectations for low average annual market returns as well as average to relatively high interest rates.

Bonds and Bond Funds

Investment in bonds is a mixed bag. There is mounting credit risk in not only corporate America, but also for consumer debt. Because much of the consumer debt is repackaged into marketable securities, (i.e. the collateralized securities markets) investors should stay away from certain institutions that engage in these transactions unless you know their exposure to these liabilities for certain. Even still, that will not necessarily absolve them from credit risk, as many finance companies have much larger exposure to derivatives. And they have many ways to hide their real exposures.

In contrast, some financial institutions might profit well from a credit meltdown, but it's too difficult to predict the winners, so I would stay clear altogether. No doubt the *high-yield bond markets will heat up, creating potentially lucrative investment opportunities,* but once again, I would stay clear of this unless you have complete confidence in the company fundamentals and understand how to perform a credit risk analysis of distressed securities and you're willing to monitor changes frequently. As an alternative, experienced traders with high risk tolerance may want to wait for an initial sell signal when mortgage-related companies get into trouble and short these stocks. But always buy protective calls or enter buy-limit orders to limit loses.

Example of Inflation on Investments

As an illustration of the potential damaging effects of inflation, I'll provide a simple example. To calculate the real annual return on bonds, multiply the amount (principle) of the bond by the interest rate. For example, a $10,000 U.S. Treasury Bill with a coupon of 5 percent would be worth $10,500 after one year. Therefore, the gross return would be $500.

In order to obtain the net return from this investment, you must factor in taxes and inflation. To calculate the effect of taxes, subtract the percentage of income tax from the interest, (let's assume a 30 percent tax bracket or $150) leaving you with $350. Finally, the average annual inflation rate in the U.S. over the past five decades has been around 2.5 percent. So, in order to calculate the net return of the T-bill, multiply the after-tax total of $10,350 by 0.975 and subtract this from $10,350. This would give you a real annual return of $91.25, which comes out to less than 1 percent of your original investment amount.

When inflation rises above its mean, you will lose money. Therefore, *investors concerned about high inflation should consider purchasing TIPS since coupon payments are indexed to inflation.* As well, some funds that take short positions in U.S. treasuries, which would also protect against inflation [ProFund Advisors (RRPIX) or Rydex Juno Fund (RYJUX)]. I expect both inflation and long-term interest rates to surge over the next few years. Therefore, investors should time their bond purchases only after rates rise.

Equities

As mentioned, investors should not pull completely out of the market and wait for the disaster to occur because they could miss several years of gains. Rather, a cautious approach emphasizing risk management is advised. As a general rule, equities should constitute no more than 50 percent of the total investment portfolio prior to any clear signs of the manifestation of the meltdown. Conservative investors might wish to allocate no more than 30 percent in equities. Cash will be king and those who have it during the crisis will be positioned to take advantage of large sell-offs. However, every investor has a different financial profile and it's impossible to provide definitive guidelines without knowing specific information. Therefore, *investors should discuss their concerns with a knowledgeable financial advisor and let him or her determine the appropriate allocation based on your financial profile.*

Mutual Funds

In general, most mutual funds perform poorly during prolonged bear markets due to their mandatory exposure to market risk (since they must remain invested) and high fees (even no-load funds can have excessive fees). However, there are some exceptions whereby I would consider investment in funds. Some examples are when investors want a diversified exposure in foreign bonds, emerging markets such as Southeast Asia, foreign currency exposure, and funds that use many investment tools that benefit from bearish conditions, such as shorting strategies and alternative assets such as repos, swaps, etc. I would recommend a diversified exposure—meaning you should invest in funds rather than go at it alone. Also note that there are several closed-end funds that offer diversified exposure in foreign assets with lower fees. However, *you need to understand the differences between these funds, paying particular attention to the amount of leverage used.*

Perhaps the most important consideration prior to determining an investment in a particular mutual fund company is to make sure that the company has many different fund types so you can shift from say a gold sector fund into another fund within the family without penalty fees.

ETFs

Ever since their introduction just a few years ago, ETFs have grown to represent an enormous percentage of assets invested in the stock market. Virtually every type of sector, industry, and index can be found within the ETF universe. Rather than pay for fund fees, investors can get the industry and sector exposure of their choice, with the added flexibility of being able to rotate sectors without the exit penalties charged by some funds. The only transaction costs are those charged by your broker, which can be as low as $2 if you trade online. However, the main drawback of this strategy is that *it requires significant time and expertise in managing your investments.* A more conservative approach is to buy more broad-based ETFs that mimic the DJIA, S&P 500, and bond indices. However, such ETFs would require active management since I do not expect the broad indices to perform well over the next several years. Finally, note that ETFs can be sold short.

Foreign Currencies

There is little doubt that even without a depression-type disaster, the dollar will continue to remain weak until at least 2011, or until the U.S. government gains better control of deficit spending and curtails its total debt growth. As China begins to properly revalue its currency, other Asian nations will follow resulting in higher-priced imports from these regions. Fortunately, most goods needed by Americans can be purchased internally or via its NAFTA and CAFTA trading partners so there is little need to spend the weak dollar against the stronger foreign currencies. However, Americans will most likely continue to suffer the inflationary consequences of high energy and healthcare prices.

Currency investing is very complex and driven by many macroeconomic and political forces, some of which are independent of those that drive the U.S. stock and bond markets. However, when the U.S. economic meltdown occurs, I would expect the Euro to provide healthy returns. Even prior to that period, a German bond fund might be a good investment since Germany is expected to recover soon. But investors would be cautioned against investing in foreign bonds on their own. Such an investment should be assigned to a mutual fund or money manager.

One indirect way to hedge against dollar-depreciated assets due to inflationary effects is to invest in American Depository Receipts (ADRs). Although this is a rather weak hedging strategy, it could provide a more substantial shield against a high inflationary period. As well, investors should look to U.S. companies that have a significant multinational presence such as Microsoft.

Industry Groups

Precious Metals

When dealing with precious metals, it is important to keep in mind that this asset class tends to have periods of extreme volatility and can result in drawdowns of 30 percent or more in just a couple of months. Investors must monitor the longer-term trend, which I expect to remain up for several years. But I could be wrong. Therefore, to manage risk you should only add to positions after large sell-offs and trim positions after long rallies look like they are running out of steam. This will help reduce overall portfolio volatility and lower the overall cost basis your positions. Whatever you do, *don't become too heavily exposed in this asset class* since too much of a good thing can quickly turn into a very bad investment that remains down for a long time. And if your cash gets tied up in the market, you may not have sufficient funds to take advantage of market opportunities. You certainly do not want to use margin under any circumstances.

Gaining exposure in the precious metals is possible by investing in futures, (which I highly advise against unless you have extensive experience) individual stocks, mutual funds, ETFs and of course through buying them directly. Due to the unique company and political risks already mentioned, many investors may prefer to invest in precious metal ETFs. While mutual funds provide diversification, they may not be the best way to play the metals because the fees are not only high, but you are exposing yourself to company, fund manager and other risks. Alternatively, some impulsive investors may wish to directly purchase gold and silver and have it stored in a bank vault. There are some companies that allow you to have it stored in large banks overseas without touching it. This approach would help diminish the impulsivity to trade frequently.

Energy and Utilities

As inflation mounts, energy and utility prices will continue to soar. In addition, continued or further weakness in the dollar could actually serve to increase energy prices further since most fossil fuels are paid for with dollars. Similar to the precious metals, energy stocks can be quite volatile. *A lower risk method to gain exposure in energy is through the oil and gas trusts.* These securities are represented by investment management companies that fund several oil exploration projects and pay investors a high dividend yield. In general, the Canadian oil trusts are paying the highest dividend yields due in part to their tax-exempt status (which will change in a couple of years).

Keep in mind that energy is very cyclical and investors with these securities should expect periods of large declines, similar to the precious metals. But due to their high dividends, oil and gas trusts would be expected to exhibit lower volatility than other oil and gas stocks. *Don't invest blindly based on dividends because these dividends are not required and can be cut or eliminated at anytime.* That would cause the stock price to decline which would lock you in for a potentially long time frame. You need to do some research to understand how these trusts are managed so you are aware of the risks.

Alternative Energy

This might be a place to rest a <u>small</u> amount of assets, but it could be a while before these companies see much market activity. When they do, they should soar. This sector can be extremely volatile, the best way to manage risk is to buy low and sell after surges, rather than buying more. Investors with high risk tolerance and skilled trading abilities may look for short-term trading opportunities based on event-related activity.

Ethanol companies should benefit from Bush's increased financial incentives for development of this fuel source. Already a major component of the fuel industry, ethanol is used by petroleum companies as an alternative additive to substitute for toxic chemicals, thereby creating less water pollution. However, there has been a recent push for ethanol-powered vehicles using an 85 percent blend of ethanol and gasoline (known s E-85) in America and U.S. auto manufacturers are already rolling out new models.

The demand for ethanol combined with limited supplies should result in a surge in these stocks, but this may only last a couple of years, as even the E-85 solution is short-term. Therefore investors must pay close attention to trends in this area in order to maximize gains and minimize risk. *Long-term or conservative investors should avoid ethanol stocks altogether due to their questionable long-term viability.*

Investors with longer investment horizons and a higher risk tolerance might consider a small investment in the fuel cell industry, which should receive continued funding. Finally, investors should be careful with valuations since many of these companies are new, have limited revenues and no earnings.

Healthcare

While the pharmaceutical industry is not expected to deliver the blockbuster earnings growth of the previous decade, the big names like Merck and Pfizer provide more safety and therefore less risk. As well, the blue-chip biotechs like Amgen should do well. And if they are purchased at relatively low valuations, they can provide excellent returns if timely exits are made. Companies involved in the nutritional market, telemedicine and healthcare IT are certain to make a huge impact on healthcare over the next two decades. However, it is very difficult to determine the future winners right now. Those who follow these trends closely could be positioned to do very well.

Global Economies

China & India

It should be obvious that China is benefiting from the poorly managed trade policies of America. Simply on sheer volume alone, several Chinese funds (there are some nice closed-end funds paying high dividends) and stocks should continue to perform well for at least the next 3 years. However, China cannot maintain decade-long, double-digit growth forever. At some point, its rapidly expanding bubble will burst, so I would be more of a 3- to 4-year investor in select Chinese funds and at least trim positions down thereafter. *When China showcases its vibrant economy to the world during the 2008 Summer Olympics, this could result in a further surge in asset prices. Most likely, this will be the time when the smart money begins making its exit.* In general, investors should limit their exposure in foreign securities to a very small portion of total assets since the transparency is limited and the accounting rules are often quite different.

General Asset Allocation Strategy

Below, I have listed a general investment allocation strategy based upon the type of position investors may have. In order to determine whether one is conservative, moderate or aggressive they should speak with a registered financial professional. As well, they should consult these financial professionals to determine their share of suitable securities. This is a very important step to take.

Conservative Position	Moderate Position	Aggressive Position
Cash	Cash	Cash, Dollar Hedge, Euro
	Chinese Funds	Chinese & German Funds
Precious Metals	Precious Metals	Precious Metals
Oil Trusts	Oil Trusts	Energy/Alt. & Traditional
Healthcare	Healthcare/Alt Healthcare	Healthcare/Alt Healthcare
TIPS	TIPS	TIPS

Market Predictions

The stock market will most likely provide maximum annualized returns of 1 to 3 percent during the current secular bear market period (from 2001 to 2012-2014). Thus, *even though the DJIA might reach 14,500 by 2012, this will still only represent about 2 percent annualized returns since the beginning of the bear market period in 2001.*

Beyond the 2014 time period, there may be a short bull market lasting a couple of years, sending the DJIA to the 16,500 range. And then the economic and market disaster might occur during the 2016 to 2020 period. If this scenario occurs, I expect losses ranging from 30 to 50 percent from previous highs. Assuming modest gains in the market during this period, these corrections might send the DJIA to the 9500 to 12,500 range. These ranges will depend upon both the timing and reaction of the economic fallout. The later it occurs, the higher the market will be after the correction. What is most important to consider are the annualized returns over the appropriate time frame.

Risk Management

Managing Risk

Throughout this book, I have discussed the risks to the U.S. economy and their potential effects on the stock and bond markets. However, investors also need to consider the risk characteristics of the asset classes and industries I have highlighted. Because many of these industry groups are considered non-traditional, they have many risks that are independent of more traditional securities. To reiterate, investment risk should always be considered with all securities.

First, investors should consider *company risk*, or the risk of company underperformance or even business failure due to adverse economic conditions. I have detailed many of the economic risk factors throughout this book. Next, we look at company risk due to competitive forces. This analysis can become quite complex if investors are not already familiar with the competitive landscape of the industry for which the company is categorized.

When assessing risk of the less traditional industry groups such as the metals, energy, and foreign equities, the same risks discussed above also apply, but we must also consider risks unique to each group. For instance, *metals, mining and energy companies can have variable levels of political risk depending upon the type of company and its source of production.* Companies like U.S. Steel and Nucor do not have much political risk (other than that in the U.S.) because these industries have their primary production facilities in North America. But they face unique competitive risks due to unfair trade practices imposed by China, as well as restrictions against industry protection by the WTO.

When considering precious metal companies, investors should note the locations of the primary exploration sites and develop a feel for the stability of the government in those regions. For instance, Apex Silver (SIL) has its primary exploration facilities in Bolivia, a South American nation that has been known to have a considerable amount of political instability. If the Bolivian government decides to nationalize mining regions, this could deliver a severe blow to mining companies.

Investors must also understand that *many of the smaller mining companies make extensive use of leverage in the form of derivatives.* While effective use of derivatives can lead to tremendous gains if the price of precious metals goes up, they can also lead to large losses if the price remains steady or declines. This is one of the reasons why the larger mining companies such as Newmont Mining do not benefit as much from a rise in gold prices as some of the small companies. In contrast, the larger mining companies typically use derivatives to stabilize earnings (by locking in metal prices), so they are considered lower-risk. As discussed, *the use of gold and silver ETFs can eliminate political and company-specific risks and provide lower volatility relative to investment in individual precious metal stocks or funds.*

When considering investments in energy companies, you should understand the business structure. Some of the things to consider are the primary sources of exploration and the types of business they do (exploration, refinement, distribution, retail). Larger companies such as Exxon and Chevron have various sources of exploration so political risk is relatively small. However, regardless how high energy prices may go, I do not feel the risk-reward is worth the price of market risk (the risk that the market will decline) because there is not much upside in the large cap oil stocks until prices come down. That is one reason I favor the oil trusts.

Managing Economic and Market Risks

Overall, investors should consider maintaining at least a 50 percent cash position, regardless whether they choose to implement some of the investments noted in this chapter. Conservative investors may elect to hold a larger cash position along with U.S. treasuries/TIPS (only after long-term rates surpass 8.0 percent). Only after clear signs of increasing long-term interest rates and higher inflation should investors substitute some of their cash holdings for TIPS and funds that short treasury bonds during inflationary conditions (Rydex Juno Fund: RYJUX; ProFunds Rs Rt Opportunity Investments: RRPIX; note, these funds are used for illustrative purposes only).

Ultimately, each investor will have a unique financial profile and investment horizon, which will lead to a different level of risk tolerance. Therefore, each investor should consult their financial advisor prior to making any decisions. It is important to make certain that the advisor does not hold any biases and remains open to consider the possibilities mentioned in this book. Otherwise, if advisors are biased or lack adequate sophistication, they may recommend the standard portfolios that perform well only during bull markets.

Overall, cash will be king during this period because much uncertainty remains and this will result in random periods of high volatility. Additional asset protection may be made through the effective use of derivatives and short positions. But these strategies should only be used conservatively and only by very experienced investors. Alternatively, investors may wish to gain exposure in funds that specialize in hedging strategies.

Final Thoughts

Looking back in history, one can argue that present-day America shares many similarities with the early part of the twentieth century that witnessed global unrest, wide swings in monetary policy, emergence of excessive power and influence by corporations, wide disparities in income and wealth, and a heavy reliance on consumer credit. These characteristics helped shape the booming period that ushered in the "Roaring '20s", similar to the economic boom encountered in the 1990s.

Unlike the correction that occurred in the 1930s, Greenspan mitigated the fallout of the Internet bubble, facilitating the shift of investment assets into a real estate bubble. Therefore, America has still not witnessed a correction of sufficient magnitude required to restore a long period of excessive consumption.

Whether the next "Great Depression" will create an unemployment rate of over 25 percent similar to the peak reached in 1933, one cannot tell. However, since the government has created new ways to manipulate economic data, specific figures do not really matter in a comparative sense. *At the end of the day, the only things that will matter to the American people will be their life, liberty, freedom, and hope for their future.*

Does history repeat itself? The clear answer is yes, it most certainly does. What stand out as variables in this cycle are the manner and timing in which the process will unravel. The question is <u>not whether</u> America will encounter economic devastation <u>but when and in what sequence</u>. Regardless whether inflation or deflation will be the culprit, it is clear that America is headed for a major economic collapse that will lead to a depression similar to the 1930s. However, this time it may not be caused by a stock market crash.

It's too late for tax cuts; the debt is too high and the future liabilities are too great. Most likely, the only solution for America is to keep running on empty until its economic engine stalls and a crisis occurs. Devastation of this magnitude will force Washington to enact the needed changes. There can be no avoiding the period of correction for America; there are simply too many problems and no viable solutions. Perhaps the biggest problem facing America is the lack of awareness of its inevitable period of correction. And that in itself is going to heighten the effects of the fallout.

The future of America includes a long period of economic, political and social readjustment. Most likely this period will not represent an end to its reign as an empire, but merely one of the adjustments needed to restore its greatness. And those who are alert to these realities will stand to profit. Politicians will be forced to act on behalf of the American people. And corporate America will relinquish its control back to Washington, which will start serving the American taxpayers. Finally, entrepreneurs will arise from the dust, helping this recovery. Amidst the difficult period, a new America will emerge, perhaps greater than before, and new legislature will help Americans of future generations regain the lifestyles their grandparents enjoyed.

APPENDIX

Chapter 2 Supplement

Table 2.2. Market Reaction and Recovery After Major Global Events

EVENT	DATE	DAY	% CHANGE FOR DAY**	6-MONTHS LATER	1-YEAR LATER
Operation Iraqi Freedom	03/19/03	Wednesday	0.26%	14.59%	23.24%
America Strikes Back	10/07/01	Sunday	-0.57%	12.63	-18.61
Terrorist Attack	09/11/01	Tuesday	-7.12%	10.47	-10.66
Oklahoma Bombing	04/19/95	Wednesday	0.68%	14.92%	32.46%
WTC Bombing	02/26/93	Friday	0.17%	8.41%	14.07%
Somali Crisis	12/04/92	Friday	0.57%	7.80%	12.63%
Operation Desert Storm	01/16/91	Wednesday	4.57%	18.73	30.14
Kuwait Invasion*	08/02/90	Thursday	-6.31%	-5.81%	3.69%
Panama & Noriega	12/15/89	Friday	-1.53%	7.17%	-5.32%
Hostage in Grenada	10/25/83	Tuesday	-0.69%	-7.10%	-3.31%
Reagan Shot	03/30/81	Monday	-0.26%	-14.56%	-17.12%
Iran Crisis	11/04/79	Sunday	-0.77%	-0.32%	14.44%
Watergate					
First Story Published	08/01/72	Tuesday	0.62%	6.60%	-1.36%
Congressional Investigation	02/07/73	Wednesday	-1.15%	-6.91%	-15.43%
Senior WH Aides Indicted	03/01/74	Friday	-1.00%	-21.14%	-14.12%
Articles of Impeachment Passed	07/27/74	Saturday	-1.74%	-10.02%	5.14%
Nixon Resigns	08/08/74	Thursday	-1.59%	-10.74%	2.53%
Vietnam Conflict	02/26/65	Friday	-0.41%	-0.81%	5.48%
Tonkin Gulf Attack	08/04/64	Tuesday	-0.90%	7.58%	5.18%
Kennedy Assassination	11/22/63	Friday	-2.89%	12.04%	21.58%
Cuban Missile Crisis	10/22/62	Monday	-1.85%	25.05%	31.41%
Sputnik Launched	10/04/57	Friday	-2.01%	-4.59%	15.60%
Korean War	06/25/50	Sunday	-4.65%	2.36%	9.34%
Pearl Harbor	12/07/41	Sunday	-3.50%	-9.48%	-1.37%
Lusitania Sinks	05/07/15	Friday	-4.54%	36.01%	32.75%
USS Maine Explodes	02/15/1898	Tuesday	-2.14%	14.91%	24.90%

Chapter 4 Supplement

Figure 4.1. Income at Various Points in the Distribution in the 1990s

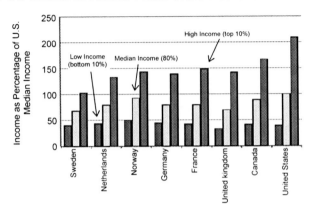

Source: The Century Foundation. "The New American Economy: A Rising Tide that Lifts Only Yachts." Figure 5.

Figure 4.2. The Income Gap Between High- and Low-Income Households in the 1990s.

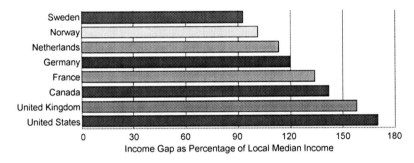

Note: The data for each bar in this figure is calculated by simply taking the difference between the height of the low-income and high income bars in figure 4.1, dividing it by the height of the middle-income bar, and then multiplying by one hundred.

Source: The Century Foundation. "The New American Economy: A Rising Tide that Lifts Only Yachts." Figure 6.

Table 4.1. Annual Percent of Poor People Escaping Poverty (2001 Data)

	Yearly Rate of Exit in %
Denmark	60.4
United Kingdom	58.8
Netherlands	55.7
Ireland	54.6
Spain	49.6
Belgium	48.2
France	46.9
Germany	41.1
Italy	40.6
Canada	36.4
Portugal	37.0
United States	29.5

Source: Organization for Economic Cooperation and Development: *Employment Outlook*, Paris 2001.

Chapter 5 Supplement

Section 5.1: Oil Demand

Table 5.2 lists the six nations I feel will represent the highest demands for fossil fuels over the next several years. Already, the U.S. has led the world in fossil fuel consumption for several decades. With only 5 percent of the world's population, the U.S. consumes approximately 50 to 60 percent of the world's energy production annually and 45 percent of the oil. And now that Europe is under one currency, drastic economic reforms have already begun to reshape European commerce resulting in higher demands for fossil fuels.

For the first time in some European nations, consumers can now obtain loans to purchase homes. This expansion of consumer credit is due to the standardization of the unification of Europe's Euro. No doubt, as Europe continues to enjoy the benefits of a unified open market economy, their needs for abundant energy will continue to grow disproportionate to the growth of its population.

According to Simmons and Hubbert from the University Of Colorado School Of Mines, the world's top 120 oil fields produce about 33 million bpd, representing about 50 percent of the global production. In addition, the fourteen largest producing fields account for about 20 percent of the world's oil production but the average age of each of these fields is 43.5 years. To highlight the significance of this, we look at the effects of peak production on other oil fields. The largest oil well discovered in the Western Hemisphere since the 1970s was the Cruz Beana in Columbia. Since its discovery in 1991, oil production has gone from 500,000 bpd to less than 200,000 bpd in 2002. And the Fourty Field well in the North Sea once produced 500,000 bpd upon discovery in the mid-1980s but as of 2004, it only produces 50,000 bpd.

Table 5.2. Population and GDP by Rank of the Fastest Growing Economies[1]

Country	Rank	Population	Rank	GDP[1]
China	1	1,306,313,812	3	$8,859,000,000,000
India	2	1,080,264,388	5	$3,611,000,000,000
European Union	3	456,953,258	2	$12,180,000,000,000
United States	4	295,734,134	1	$12,360,000,000,000
Japan	11	127,417,244	4	$4,018,000,000,000
Germany	15	82,431,390	6	$2,504,000,000,000
Total		3,349,114,226		$43,532,000,000,000
Total World		6,446,131,400		$60,710,000,000,000

Source: CIA World Factbook 2005.
(1) 2005 estimate of GDP (purchasing power parity)

The Energy Information Administration is one of many government agencies that have continued to preserve the agendas of the big American oil companies. In 2000, the results of a very important study was presented by the USGS. This was the first comprehensive study to look at global reserves and estimate a peak production based on several scenarios (table 5.4). Even if we accept the USGS estimates as given, it is reasonable to assume the 95 percent probability recovery (2248 billion barrels) will best represent the most probable scenario. And if we accept the 2 percent annual demand growth rate, the EIA estimates that the global peak will occur in 2026. However, this estimate has been criticized as very optimistic by many. In addition, if the growth rate increases to 3 percent annually, the peak approaches a level that is more consistent with other estimates (2021). And because we are experiencing a rapid growth of developing nations, a 3 percent long-term growth rate seems reasonable.

Section 5.2: The Effects of Peak Oil

To mask the problem of peak production, many companies in developed nations, specifically in the U.S., have been increasing oil exploration and development costs at an alarming rate just to maintain their current production. For instance, between 1996 and 1999, 145 companies spent a total of $410 billion for exploration efforts which only replaced the oil declines in their older wells. What that means is the older well production is declining. This is especially true in the U.S. since peak oil production occurred in 1970. In addition, the five largest oil companies in the U.S. spent $150 billion between 1999 and 2002, which grew daily oil production only from 16 to 16.6 million bpd. No doubt, these companies are very eager to get their hands on Iraq's oil.

According to a 2003 report in the Oil & Gas Journal, at the onset of 2004, global oil reserves were estimated at 1.27 trillion barrels and natural gas reserves totalled 6,100 cubic feet. These estimates are up by 53 billion barrels of oil and 575 trillion cubic feet of natural gas from the previous year due to additional finds and improved extraction efficiency. According to these estimates and the forecasts for oil development and consumption, the U.S. Energy Information Administration estimates that these oil reserves represent about 44.6 years of supply and 66.2 years of natural gas. But even if these estimates are correct, they do not tell the full picture. When peak production has been reached, it becomes increasingly difficult to extract these fossil fuels at optimal rates of production. Therefore, while we can sill have adequate reserves for 50 years or so, the amount produced per year will begin to drop soon before these wells run dry, causing a global shortage.

Table 5.2. Range of World Oil Forecasts from the USGS Study

World Oil Production Forecast

Probability Estimate	Ultimate Recovery BBbls	Annual Demand Growth, %	Peak Year	Peak Rate MMBbls/yr	Peak Rate MMBbls/day
Low (95%)	2,248	0.0	2045	24,580	67
	2,248	1.0	2033	34,820	95
	2,248	2.0	2026	42,794	117
	2,243	**3.0**	**2021**	**48,511**	**113**
Mean	3,003	0.0	2075	24,580	67
(expected value)	3,003	1.0	2050	41,238	113
	3,003	2.0	2037	53,209	146
	3,003	3.0	2030	63,296	173
High (5%)	3,896	0.0	2112	24,580	67
	3,896	1.0	2067	48,838	134
	3,896	2.0	2047	64,862	178
	3,896	3.0	2037	77,846	213

Source: Energy Information Administration

The only way to delay the onset of peak oil production is to either decrease consumption or increase new oil finds to the level that approximates the amount consumed. And neither of these scenarios is likely. In recent years, global demand for crude oil has been slightly over 2 percent, due to the aggressive expansion of south eastern Asia. And it appears as if this number may increase, since the development of Asia has only begun. To address the question of a potential global oil crisis, the U.S. geological Survey (USGS) released a five-year study of global oil resources, called "The USGS World Petroleum Assessment 2000." This study is thought to be of great significance because it was the first time such a comprehensive study was performed done using modern science to estimate the global oil reserves and demands of the future.

In this study, the USGS designates three types of reserves: proven, or petroleum that can be produced using current technology; undiscovered, pertaining to oil deposits that are highly likely to exist based on oil-producing regions; and reserve growth, which represents potential future oil production from further exploration in existing fields. For peak oil production estimates, only the first two categories are applicable.

There is much disagreement between the USGS findings, which are endorsed by the EIA, as compared to those of many independent research findings such as those by Campbell and Laherrere. In both studies, it is assumed that the oil-in-place, or the total resource base excluding any concerns for recoverability is 6 trillion barrels. Discovered or known oil resources are categorized as proven reserves or unproven (possible or probable). Proven reserves consist of the quantity of oil or gas that can be recovered with current technology and at current economic conditions. In contrast, unproven reserves are those that may be recoverable in the future with advanced technological developments or under different economic conditions.

Section 5.3: The Big Wells Have Been Found

Historically, it has been easier to locate "giant" oil fields with reserves of over 500 million barrels than smaller fields, and most of the world's supply remains in these fields. Given that most of the world has been explored for oil, it is unlikely that we will find many of these giant oil fields in the future. From figure 5.3, you can see that since the peak oil production in America, both the number of oil wells and the total amount of oil discovered per year has been in sharp decline.

In America, most of the growth in new oil exploration has moved to offshore drilling projects such as the Gulf of Mexico, which is one of the more promising regions. And Alaska is really the only large area on land that the U.S. can turn to for large oil reserves. Meanwhile, the continental U.S. has been pillaged for oil over the past five decades and the average well in the U.S. now produces only a very small amount of oil, which drives up the cost per barrel. The biggest oil discoveries of today are nothing like those in the past and the three largest modern finds produce less than 200,000 bpd each. Needless to say, they are not located in the U.S. or surrounding regions, but are in Norway, Columbia, and Brazil.

Figure 5.3. Discoveries in "Giant" Oil Fields per Decade and the Number of Such Fields

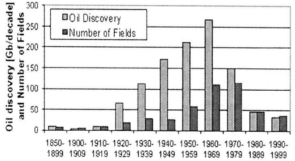

Source: ASPO. Uppsala Hydrocarbon Depletion Study Group, Uppsala University. Work in Progress.

Section 5.4: Can Unconventional Reserves Fill the Gap?

Estimates indicate that there are up to 7 trillion barrels of non-conventional oil that has yet to be mined. However, 80 percent of this estimate consists of unconventional oil lying within the oil sands region of Canada, the shale oil in the United States, and the extra-heavy oil in Venezuela. As well, there is much uncertainty as to the actual amount that will be recoverable, as well as the expense and the time period. But for certain, the costs would run very high due to the advanced machinery needed to extract unconventional oil and the additional refinery methods, which would require large amounts of natural gas. One source estimates that only about 333 billion barrels of this total amount is recoverable, which would represent about 11 years of the world's total production. Regardless, in the best of scenarios, due to the cost structure of extracting and refining these unconventional reserves, this would serve to keep oil prices very high for many years, and therefore increase the incentive by U.S. companies to gain significant access to the low cost, high quality oil in Iraq.

Even now that Canada can argue that it has the world's second largest oil reserves, we must keep in mind that the oil sands are unconventional reserves, meaning the quality of oil is low and the expense and effort to extract this oil are very high. According to the International Energy Agency, by 2030 the global demand for crude oil combined with diminishing conventional reserves will dictate that 37 million bpd be provided by unconventional oil reserves. However, based upon current production and factoring future operations, it has been estimated that Canada will only be able to produce about 5 million bpd. And even if the very optimistic estimations for Venezuela to increase its current production of 0.5 million bpd (by 1200 percent) to 6.0 million bpd, there will still be a shortfall of 26 million bpd. Finally, these calculations do not account for additional requirements that would be needed if the global peak oil occurs prior to 2030.

Chapter 6 Supplement

Section 6.1: Balance of Payments

In theory, a nation's balance of payments is always zero since capital must come from somewhere. When government receipts are less than its expenditures, the shortfall of cash needed is supplied by issuing treasuries to pay off the balance of this current account deficit.

Prior to 1973, balance of payments figures were thought to be very important for determining a nation's economic health since global currencies were converted at fixed exchange rates. However, since that time the removal of fixed exchange rates has created ambiguity in determining the absolute significance of this figure. As a result, many feel that deficits are meaningless.

Today, when we discuss balance of payments, we refer to what is known as the current account, meaning the amount of money on a short-term basis that a nation is in surplus or in deficit due to global trade activities. This account contains trade in goods and services, investment income earned abroad, and unilateral transfers. It excludes the capital account, which includes the acquisition or sale of securities or other property.

Because the current account and the capital account add up to the total account, which is necessarily balanced, a deficit in the current account is always accompanied by an equal surplus in the capital account, and vice versa. Therefore, a deficit or surplus in the current account cannot be evaluated without simultaneous evaluation of a surplus or deficit of equal magnitude in the capital account. Due to this interrelationship, many feel that an account deficit is equated with foreign investment, which is only true if you accept the definition of investment.

Capital account equals:

+ Exports
− Imports
− Increase of owned assets abroad
+ Increase of foreign-owned assets in the country
Money coming in (+), or leaving (−)

Capital Account

1. Foreign Direct Investment (FDI)
2. Portfolio Investment
   • Equity Securities
   • Debt Securities
3. Other Investment (transactions in currency, bank deposits, trade credits etc.)
4. Statistical discrepancies

The relative extent of a nation's deficit or surplus depends on its gross national product (GNP), trade restrictions and tariffs, interest rates, its exchange rate, and the attractiveness of investment opportunities as viewed by foreign nations. High interest and exchange rates, open trade and a high GNP will tend to create a deficit. In contrast, lower interest and exchange rates, restrictive trade and a lower GNP will often create a surplus.

However, a change in one of these factors alone is not predictive of the amount of deficit or surplus a nation will have. Each component must be cumulatively examined for the effects (which are often synergistic) it will have on the net amount of money flowing into the nation since each of these elements are intertwined. A change in any one element alone will not alter the current account balance because compensatory reactions will occur to restore the equilibrium.

A low currency exchange rate will discourage consumers from purchasing imports, since their buying power will be diminished, and this will keep more money in the nation. However, a current account surplus will not be formed unless one or more other changes occur. Likewise, increased tariffs or trade restrictions will have the same effect. The overall effect of a decrease in demand of foreign capital will tend to raise the exchange rate of that nation relative to other currencies. This will then increase the buying power abroad, which will tend to increase imports.

Figure 6.2. The U.S. Budget Bureaucracy

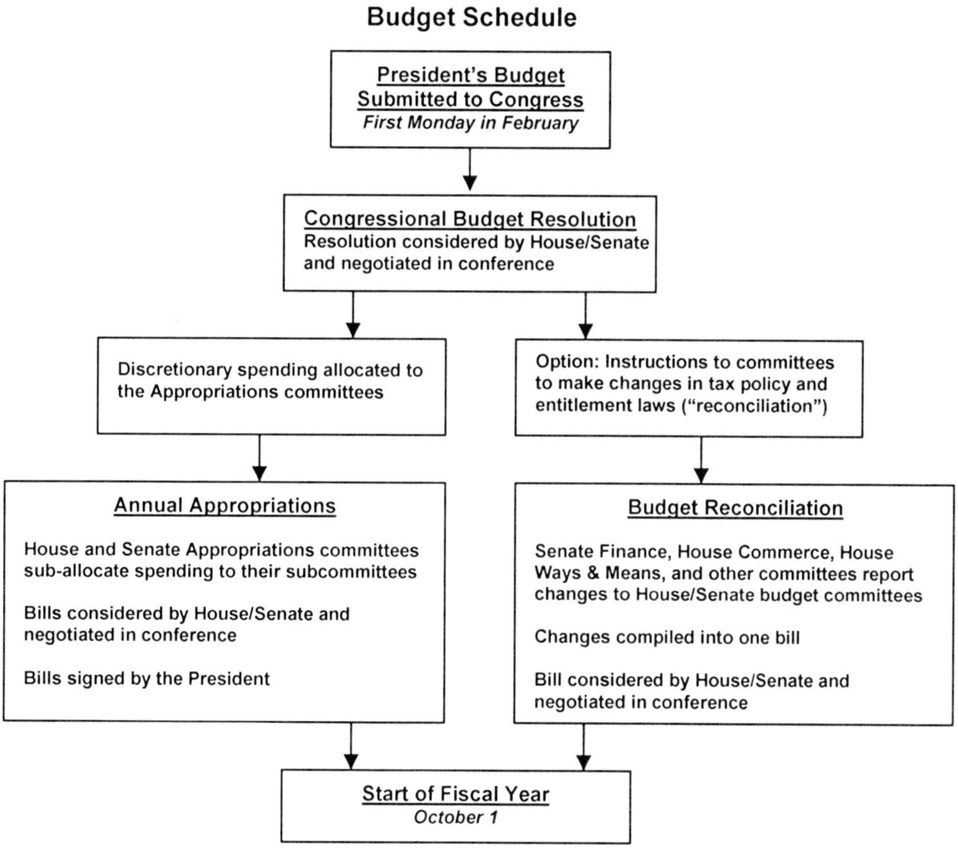

Budget Schedule

President's Budget Submitted to Congress
First Monday in February

Congressional Budget Resolution
Resolution considered by House/Senate and negotiated in conference

Discretionary spending allocated to the Appropriations committees

Option: Instructions to committees to make changes in tax policy and entitlement laws ("reconciliation")

Annual Appropriations

House and Senate Appropriations committees sub-allocate spending to their subcommittees

Bills considered by House/Senate and negotiated in conference

Bills signed by the President

Budget Reconciliation

Senate Finance, House Commerce, House Ways & Means, and other committees report changes to House/Senate budget committees

Changes compiled into one bill

Bill considered by House/Senate and negotiated in conference

Start of Fiscal Year
October 1

Figure 6.3. Current Account Positions of Selected Economies, 1995-2005 (USD Billions)

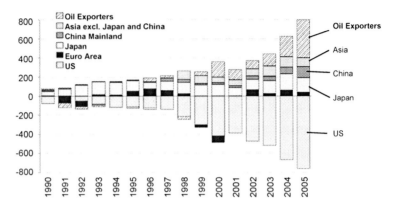

Source: IMF World Economic Outlook and ECB staff calculations, September 2005

As a result, when a current account deficit is present, one cannot necessarily assume this is bad for that nation's economy. It may reflect diminished savings, excessive inflation, global competitiveness, a weak economy, or it may be the result of tremendous investment capital from foreign nations. Therefore, rather than focusing on an annual deficit, we should look at trends of deficit accrual to the federal debt and try to understand its underlying causes. Figure 6.4. Shows the Congressional Budget Office's estimates for federal outlays and receipts through 2015. Over each time period examined, when the outlays (represented by the dark line) are higher than the revenues (light line), a deficit exists for that period.

Figure 6.4. Total Revenues and Outlays (as a percentage of GDP)

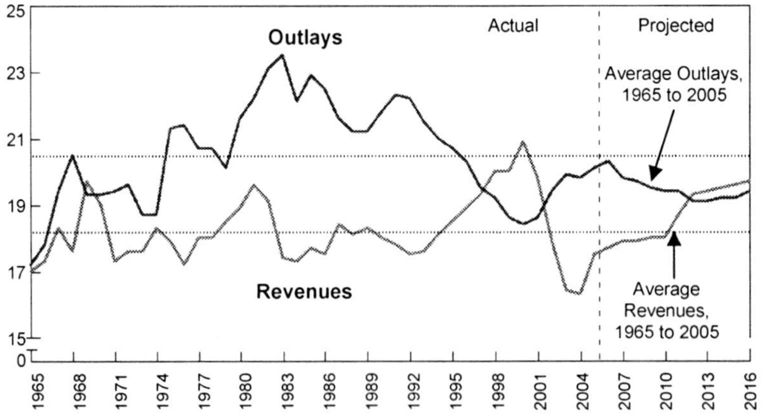

Source: Congressional Budget Office

Figure 6.5. Uncertainties of the CBO's Projections of the Budget Deficit or Surplus Under Current Policies (as a percentage of GDP change)

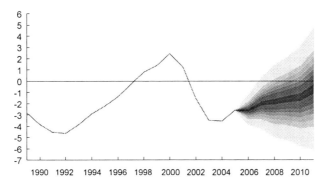

Source: Congressional Budget Office

Figure 6.5 shows the CBO's own uncertainty measurements of their projections. Given the complexity and large number of independent factors that could alter their projections, one should not assume that their uncertainties would be expected to follow a normal Gaussian distribution as they have indicated, but rather to have significant statistical kurtosis. What this means is that the CBO has not adequately shown the probabilities of significant upward deviation from their numbers. Rather, they have chosen to take the generic statistical approach, which is often wrong, especially when numerous complex variables are involved.

Table 6.1. Federal Outlays by Category, 1950 to 2075 (As a percentage of GDP)

Fiscal Year	Social Security	Medicare	Medicaid	Social Security, Medicare, and Medicaid Combined	All Other Spending, Excluding Interest Expense	Interest Expense	Total
1950	0.3	n.a.	n.a.	0.3	13.5	1.8	15.6
1960	2.2	n.a.	n.a.	2.2	14.2	1.3	17.7
1962	2.5	n.a.	*	2.5	15.1	1.2	18.8
1970	2.9	0.7	0.3	3.9	12.8	1.4	19.3
1980	4.3	1.2	0.5	6.0	13.7	1.9	21.6
1990	4.3	1.9	0.7	6.9	11.7	3.2	21.8
2000	4.2	2.2	1.2	7.6	8.5	2.3	18.4
2010	4.4	2.7	1.8	8.8	7.6	0.8	17.2
2020	5.4	3.6	2.3	11.3	7.1	-0.5	17.9
2030	6.2	4.9	2.8	13.9	7.1	-0.2	20.8
2040	6.2	6.0	3.4	15.5	7.1	1.1	23.8
2050	6.0	6.7	3.9	16.7	7.1	3.1	26.9
2060	6.1	7.7	4.3	18.1	7.1	5.8	31.0
2070	6.2	8.9	4.9	20.0	7.1	9.4	36.5
2075	6.2	9.6	5.3	21.1	7.1	11.5	39.7

Source: Dave Koitz, Melissa D. Bobb, and Ben Page. A 125-Year Picture of the Federal Government's Share of the Economy, 1950 to 2075. Congressional Budget Office. No. 1, June 14, 2002; Revised July 3, 2002.

* = less than 0.05 percent.

396

Table 6.2. Federal Revenues, Outlays, Deficits & Surpluses as a Percentage of GDP, 1950-2075

Fiscal Year	Revenues	Total Outlays	Budget Deficit (-) or Surplus
1950	14.4	15.6	-1.1
1960	17.8	17.7	0.1
1970	19.0	19.3	-0.3
1980	18.9	21.6	-2.7
1990	18.0	21.8	-3.9
2000	20.8	18.4	2.4
2010	19.2	17.2	2.0
2020	19.0	17.9	1.1
2030	19.0	20.8	-1.8
2040	19.0	23.8	-4.8
2050	19.0	26.9	-7.9
2060	19.0	31.0	-12.0
2070	19.0	36.5	-17.5
2075	19.0	39.7	-20.7

Source: Ibid, Congressional Budget Office.

Figure 6.6. Federal Revenues, Outlays, Deficits & Surpluses as a Percentage of GDP

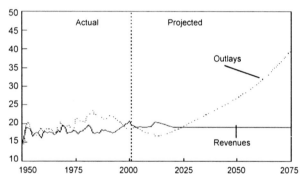

1. The nature of future taxes and spending as well as the aggregate difference between them can affect the growth of the economy. For this analysis, however, no macroeconomic effects that might result from the fiscal policies reflected by the projections are considered.
2. For the purpose of this analysis, the projected shortfall of dedicated taxes to finance Social Security and Medicare is ignored, and spending for those programs reflects the commitments for benefits prescribed by the payment rules currently in place.
Source: Dave Koitz, Melissa D. Bobb, and Ben Page. A 125-Year Picture of the Federal Government's Share of the Economy, 1950 to 2075. Congressional Budget Office. No. 1, June 14, 2002; Revised July 3, 2002.

Table 6.3. The Growth of Annual Interest Payments on the National Debt (1988 to 2005)

Fiscal Year	Interest Paid	Fiscal Year	Interest Paid
2005	$352,350,252,507.90		
2004	$321,566,323,971.29	1996	$343,955,076,695.15
2003	$318,148,529,151.51	1995	$332,413,555,030.62
2002	$332,536,958,599.42	1994	$296,277,764,246.26
2001	$359,507,635,242.41	1993	$292,502,219,484.25
2000	$361,997,734,302.36	1992	$292,361,073,070.74
1999	$353,511,471,722.87	1991	$286,021,921,181.04
1998	$363,823,722,920.26	1990	$264,852,544,615.90
1997	$355,795,834,214.66	1989	$240,863,231,535.71

Table 6.4. Historical Debt Holdings

Current	Debt Held by the Public	Intragovernmental Holdings	Total
02/09/2006	4,745,086,008,273.71	3,460,632,968,774.14	8,205,718,977,047.85

Prior Fiscal Years	Debt Held by the Public	Intragovernmental Holdings	Total
09/30/2005	4,601,238,726,062.04	3,331,470,935,661.46	7,932,709,661,723.50
09/30/2004	4,307,344,596,908.92	3,071,708,099,421.40	7,379,052,696,330.32
09/30/2003	3,924,090,106,880.88	2,859,140,955,862.74	6,783,231,062,743.62
09/30/2002	3,553,180,247,874.74	2,675,055,717,722.42	6,228,235,965,597.16
09/28/2001	3,339,310,176,094.74	2,468,153,236,105.32	5,807,463,412,200.06
09/28/2000	3,405,303,490,221.20	2,268,874,719,665.66	5,674,178,209,886.86
09/30/1999	3,636,104,594,501.81	2,020,166,307,131.62	5,656,270,901,633.43
09/30/1998	3,733,864,472,163.53	1,792,328,536,734.09	5,526,193,008,897.62
09/30/1997	3,789,667,546,849.60	1,623,478,464,547.74	5,413,146,011,397.34

Table 6.5. Median Value of Mortgage Debt by Income Group, 1989 and 2001 (2001 dollars)

	1989	2001	% Change
Lowest 20%	$9,635	$28,000	191
20-39.9%	$17,894	$40,000	124
40-59.9%	$28,906	$56,109	94
60-79.9%	$50,929	$75,589	48
80-89.9%	$57,811	$90,958	57
90-100%	$96,352	$134,000	39

Source: The Century Foundation. "Life and Debt: Why American Families Are Borrowing to the Hilt" 2004. Table 1. Taken from Survey of Consumer Finances, Federal Reserve Board Table 14.

Table 6.6. Outstanding Consumer Debt as Percentage of Disposable Income (in billions of dollars)

Year	Consumer Debt	Consumer Disposable Income	Debt as Percent of Disposable Income
1975	736.3	1187.4	62.0
1980	1397.1	2009.0	69.5
1985	2272.5	3109.3	73.0
1990	3592.9	4285.8	83.8
1995	4858.1	5408.2	89.8
2000	6960.6	7194.0	96.8
2005	11496.6	9039.5	127.2

Source: Federal Reserve, "Flow of Funds Accounts of the United States, Historical Series and Annual Flows and Outstandings, Fourth Quarter 2005. http://www.federalreserve.gov/releases/Z1/current/

Chapter 7 Supplement

Section 7.1: America's Obesity Epidemic

How is it possible that the "world's greatest, richest, most powerful nation" with supposedly one of the best living standards in the world, with abundant access to the latest technologies and widespread awareness promoting healthy lifestyles is the most obese nation in the world? The answer to this question can be found if one examines the power and influence of the food and beverage industry, also controlled by the FDA.

Certainly the fast-paced society of America has led to behaviors that opt for convenience over proper nutrition when selecting determining their dining habits. Look at the selection of foods offered by restaurants in America today. It is dominated by carbohydrates from bread, chips, potato products and beverages to pasta, rice, ketchup, and salsa. Even a well-informed American can find it very difficult, costly and time-consuming to live a healthy lifestyle by consuming a balanced toxin-free diet.

Most of the blame for the low-yield, high-toxin additives consumed by most Americans lies in the food and beverage industries. Even when they try to eat a healthy diet, it is virtually impossible for most Americans to avoid the thousands of toxic food additives used by the food industry. One of the most commonly used artificial sweeteners, NutraSweet is marketed as a natural sweetener. Yet there is extensive evidence that it not only causes significant morbidity, but that it is one of the two primary additives responsible for the obesity epidemic in America.

And the diet industry has capitalized on these disturbing trends, with false advertisements and unproven claims of the hundreds of weight loss agents which have flooded the marketplace. Every six months a new trend that is supposed to be responsible for weight gain is unveiled by someone leading to a new diet, and subsequently billions of dollars in revenues for overpriced products such as a $4 protein bar.

Despite any improvements towards correcting America's obesity problem, the health club and fitness industries and the pharmaceutical industry has profited handsomely. However, the nutritional supplement industry has also seized the opportunity to work around the rules of products not regulated by the FDA by making subtle claims that cannot be refuted. As well, even when these companies do make specific claims, the FDA has acted rather slowly in stopping these actions and some companies have grossed hundreds of millions in sales prior to their challenge by this agency.

The fact is that every single prescription drug, chemical, nutritional product or anything that has been processed in some manner should be regulated by an FDA that is not tied into the pharmaceutical industry. Even nutritional supplements, when processed or taken in large doses can cause toxicity, illness or death. Yet, the FDA does not regulate these substances since they are considered natural when in fact, they are not.

Section 7.2: It All Began With NutraSweet

Three decades ago before NutraSweet was approved for use, health clubs were rare, most Americans did not exercise; yet there were not nearly anywhere the amount of obese Americans as today. Ironically, two decades ago when NutraSweet entered the market, the percentage of obese Americans gradually grew where it stands today at a ridiculous level. Consequently, the perception in developed nations around the world is that America is the land of fat people.

The other food additive that has been a primary cause of America's obesity problem is found in virtually every processed food product including prescription drugs, shampoos, and infant formula is MSG or monosodium glutamate. Together, these two agents have been shown to cause one to eat more food. However, because of the widespread controversy of this agent, the food industry has created minor chemical modifications to this substance so that it is identified by its new chemical name, yet its toxic effects are still present. However, consumers do not recognize it these altered forms of MSG because there are over 250 different names which they have no idea are actually MSG in disguise.

Yet, the effects of additives to food and agriculture by the food industry are not limited to these two substances. How is it that the younger generations of Americans are taller and bigger? No doubt it has been due to the steroids and antibiotics fed to cattle and poultry. Meanwhile, the pesticides used to protect vegetation continue to pose health risks.

For several years, much of Europe has refused to import many of America's food products due to concerns of these agents added to beef products as well as the genetically modified fruit and vegetables that is found in virtually every grocery store in America. The solution to America's embarrassing obesity problem lies not in dieting or strenuous exercise, stomach stapling, or prescription drugs, but moderate consumption, better nutrition, and a lifestyle of normal activity.

Thus the obesity epidemic in America is just another example how the government has allowed corporate America to destroy the safety and well-being of Americans for their own short-term financial benefit. Rather than job losses due to outsourcing, the food industry is a much more insidious enemy of American lifestyle because it is damaging the quality and longevity of American lives in a manner that is not apparent to most.

Section 7.3: Prescription Drug Costs

Figure 7.3. Share of Total spending paid by out-of-pocket healthcare services and other (2003)

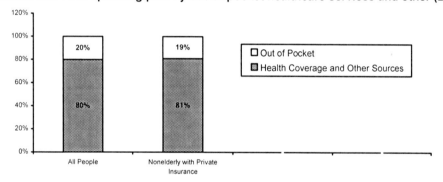

Figure 7.3b. Distribution of out-of-pocket spending for average person, all people (2003)

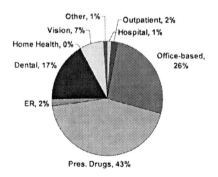

Section 7.4: Me-too drugs

Over the past decade, there has been a growing trend for pharmaceutical companies to produce "me-too" drugs as a way to steal some of the market share from blockbuster drugs. Rather than innovation of new drugs, most companies have decided it is less risky and more cost effective to navigate around the patent of a known blockbuster drug and create their own. Think about it. It's a much better business proposition. For the me-too drug, the company already has a good idea of the market demand. As well, the FDA is more likely to approve me-too drugs since their mechanism of action is usually very similar.   Therefore, they can make more accurate revenue forecasts.

At the same time, the emphasis on these "me-too" drugs has taken away from research that could have been devoted to the discovery of groundbreaking drugs which currently have no therapies. But of course, pharmaceutical companies are more concerned with profits rather than cures. As well, there are no regulations from the FDA that mandate that these "me-too" drugs have to have better efficacy or must be safer than the original drugs. And because many of the me-too drugs are just changes in molecules, it appears as if in many cases these changes are enough to result in more toxic effects. The trend in the focus of me-too drugs by the industry is a recent one, only having taken off about ten years ago. Oddly, this is about the time when drug recalls began to soar.

Figure 7.4. The Dangers of Prescription Drugs

Drug/chemical name (manufacturer)	Approved	Prescribed for	Adverse events	Withdrawn
Pondimin/fenfluramine (Wyeth-Ayerst)	1973	weight loss, obesity	pulmonary hypertension, heart valve disease	sep.97
Redux/dexfenfluramine (Wyeth-Ayerst)	apr.96	weight loss, obesity	pulmonary hypertension, heart valve disease	sep.97
Seldane/terfenadine (Hoescht Marion Roussel)	1985	seasonal allergies	heart problems when taken with other drugs	dec.97
Posicor/mibefradil (Roche Laboratories)	june.97	hypertension and angina	reduced activity of liver enzymes lead to harmful drug build-up, interactions too numerous for risk management	june.98
Duract/bromfenac (Wyeth-Ayerst)	july.97	pain relief	hepatitis, liver failure after treatment exceeded 10 days	june.98
Hismanal/astemizole (Janssen Pharmaceutica)	1988	seasonal allergies	heart arrhythmia caused by interaction with other drugs	june.99
Raxar/grepafloxacin (Glaxo Wellcome)	nov.97	antibiotic (pneumonia, bronchitis, some STDs)	Severe cardovascular problems (torsade de pointes, a ventricular arrhythmia)	oct.99
Rezulin/troglitazone (Parke-Davis/Warner-Lambert)	jan.97	Type 2 diabetes mellitus	liver toxicity	march.00
Propulsid/cisapride (Janssen Pharmaceutica)	july.93	night time heartburn	cardiac arrhythmia	july.00
Lotronex/alosetron (Glaxo Wellcome)	feb.00	irritable bowel syndrome	ischemic colitis, constipation	nov.00
Raplon/rapacuronium bromide (Organon Inc)	aug.99	airway muscle relaxment during surgery	bronchospasm	march.01
Baycol/cerivastatin (Bayer)	sep.97	high cholesterol	rhabdomyolysis (muscle deterioration), possible renal and other organ failure	aug.01
Vioxx (Merck)		Pain		Oct. 05
Bextra (Pfizer)				April. 05

Source: PBS Frontline, Dangerous Prescription, 2005.

Section 7.4a: Manipulatory and Excessive Marketing

Data from various sources indicates that pharmaceutical companies spend more on marketing than for R&D. Each year the industry spends billions on television ads, making certain to target key groups for Viagra advertisements and endorsements (during PGA Golf tournaments). As well, companies have a large sum of money that is earmarked for the drug reps' budgets. When physicians attend a meeting, reps will usually hold them in fine dining restaurants with physicians free to order as much food and drinks as they wish. And when they hold conferences, it's really party time.

Of course there are a variety of kickback programs designed to use the physician as the real salesman— fully-paid trips to Hawaii or Florida, consulting fees for talks given to other physicians, and funding for drug-related research. And if research results do not yield the desired results, this data is either destroyed, hidden, or the physician is informed that he will no longer received funding in the future.

And finally, we cannot forget the power that has been given to big pharma to define what it wants you to think depression is. According to the pharmaceutical industry, if you are depressed you should be on anti-depressants and they voice this opinion in their TV ads. However, the fact is that a certain level of depression is normal, and experiencing periods of depression does not indicate one is medically depressed. Yet, there is really no one who has stepped in to regulate this manipulation; not the AMA or the FDA. And as a result, anti-depressants account for the biggest sales of these companies. And they have not stopped there. They are constantly seeking additional indications for these drugs, from PMS to post-depression after childbirth. However, there have already been several suicides due to the use of these drugs. Meanwhile, big pharma continues to rake in billions each year at the expense of the health safety of Americans. Effectively, the FDA has permitted drug companies to serve as America's TV doctors.

Figure 7.4b. Trends in Promotional Spending for Prescription Drugs (1996-2004)

Promotional spending by pharmaceutical companies involves a variety of activities whose relative contributions to total promotional costs have shifted somewhat over time. Consumers are most aware of direct-to-consumer (DTC) advertising (advertising directly to consumers through television, radio, and popular periodicals and newspapers). Most promotional spending (86%) in 2004, however, was devoted to promoting drugs directly to physicians through sampling (57%), detailing (26%), and professional journals (2%), with the remaining 14% directed at consumers. DTC advertising experienced the highest average annual increase (22%) from 1996 to 2004, compared to 15% for the retail value of sampling, 12% for detailing, and 1% in professional journal advertising.

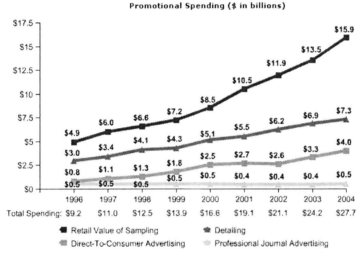

Notes: Numbers may not total due to rounding. *Sampling* is the value of samples left at sales visits to office-based physicians. The samples are valued at the prices at which they would be sold in retail pharmacies. *Detailing* is expenses for the sales activities of pharmaceutical company representatives directed to office-based and hospital-based physicians and hospital directors of pharmacies; approximately 85% of detailing is for office-based sales visits. *Direct-to-Consumer Advertising* is expenses for advertising to consumers through television, magazines and newspapers, radio, and outdoors. *Professional Journal Advertising* is expenses for advertising appearing in medical journals.

Source: Ibid, The Henry J. Kaiser Family Foundation

Figure 7.4c. Health Regulation Costs Outweigh Benefits by $128 billion in (2002 $billions)

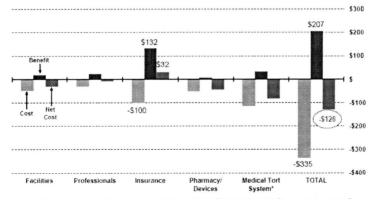

Source: Christopher Conover, Center for Health Policy, Law and Management Duke University. Prepared by: Joint Economic Committee (JEC), Chairman Robert Bennett, May 17, 2004

*Includes costs of medical professional liability insurance, courts and defensive medicine. Claimants' costs not compensated through awards are excluded.

Table 7.4d. Retail Prescriptions Filled at Pharmacies by State: Prescriptions Per Capita and Retail Prescription Sales (2004)

The number of prescriptions (both new and refills) per capita dispensed in retail pharmacies varied by state, from 6.5 prescriptions in Alaska to 15.5 prescriptions in Tennessee, with a U.S. average of 10.6 in 2004. U.S. retail prescription sales totaled $168.0 billion in 2004, with California's total sales the highest at $14.1 billion, and Wyoming's the lowest at $0.3 billion.

State	Prescriptions Per Capita	Retail Prescription Sales (in thousands)
United States	10.6	$168,040,605,058
Alabama	13.6	$3,089,947,095
Alaska	6.5	$298,230,229
Arizona	8.8	$2,420,393,186
Arkansas	14.2	$1,857,154,911
California	7.3	$14,087,494,841
Colorado	8.0	$1,989,562,412
Connecticut	11.4	$2,310,772,560
Delaware	11.6	$562,453,914
District of Columbia	9.4	$383,748,007
Florida	12.0	$10,633,770,622
Georgia	11.0	$4,927,535,131
Hawaii	6.9	$511,508,171
Idaho	8.6	$682,136,675
Illinois	11.5	$7,140,947,721
Indiana	12.1	$3,814,180,545
Iowa	13.0	$1,955,852,687
Kansas	11.9	$1,692,714,334
Kentucky	15.4	$3,104,436,045
Louisiana	13.5	$3,026,741,189
Maine	11.0	$824,544,621
Maryland	10.0	$3,703,467,797
Massachusetts	12.3	$4,309,323,838
Michigan	9.8	$5,719,120,787
Minnesota	10.0	$2,841,125,150
Mississippi	13.6	$2,032,533,755
Missouri	12.5	$3,636,930,760
Montana	9.0	$433,877,348
Nebraska	10.8	$992,775,757
Nevada	8.1	$989,713,910
New Hampshire	10.1	$709,938,758
New Jersey	10.0	$5,801,286,590
New Mexico	9.3	$811,627,244
New York	10.3	$13,131,242,860
North Carolina	13.3	$6,247,096,567
North Dakota	9.4	$333,131,363
Ohio	10.9	$6,468,918,575
Oklahoma	10.9	$2,023,036,488
Oregon	8.8	$1,539,618,122
Pennsylvania	11.0	$7,486,368,998
Rhode Island	10.7	$634,936,670
South Carolina	13.6	$2,820,590,642
South Dakota	10.6	$415,272,003
Tennessee	15.5	$4,506,282,766
Texas	9.8	$11,710,419,016
Utah	8.9	$1,119,281,855
Vermont	10.7	$389,295,827
Virginia	9.8	$4,059,155,173
Washington	8.4	$2,882,205,824
West Virginia	15.0	$1,461,892,338
Wisconsin	11.4	$3,225,792,856
Wyoming	10.1	$283,642,219

Notes: These data are based on Vector One™: National by Verispan, L.L.C., which collects data from a panel of retail pharmacies, third party payers, and data providers. Retail pharmacies include independent pharmacies, chain pharmacies, food stores, and mass merchandisers found in 814 defined regional zones. These data describe the number of prescriptions filled by retail pharmacies only and exclude those filled by mail order. The total sales reflect the amount the pharmacies are paid for all prescriptions filled. Although not included in the Retail Prescription Sales amounts, mail order sales totalled $41.3 billion or 19% of total sales in 2004 according to industry statistics report by the National Association of Chain Drug Stores (http://www.nacds.org/wmspage.cfm?parm1=507).

Source: Ibid, The Henry J. Kaiser Family Foundation

Section 7.5. Employer & Employee Premiums

Table 7.5. Average Annual Employer Health Plan Premiums for Covered Workers, by Plan Type and Region (2005)

Premiums vary by region. The South was the least expensive region for family coverage in 2005, driven by the low cost of HMO coverage in this region. The Northeast had the most expensive family premiums as a result of the high rates for PPOs, which dominate the region.

	Annual	
	Single Coverage	Family Coverage
CONVENTIONAL PLANS		
Northeast	$3,227	$8,544
Midwest	3,250	9,476
South	3,955	10,420
West	NSD	NSD
ALL REGIONS	**$3,782**	**$9,979**
HMO PLANS		
Northeast	$3,932	$10,903
Midwest	3,880	10,592
South	3,950	10,754
West	3,421*	9,809
ALL REGIONS	**$3,767**	**$10,456**
PPO PLANS		
Northeast	$4,313	$11,938*
Midwest	4,235	11,354
South	3,998	10,526
West	4,177	11,012
ALL REGIONS	**$4,150**	**$11,090**
POS PLANS		
Northeast	$4,105	$11,528*
Midwest	3,809	10,806
South	3,726	10,142
West	4,059	10,958
ALL REGIONS	**$3,914**	**$10,801**
ALL PLANS		
Northeast	$4,147	$11,504*
Midwest	4,103	11,115
South	3,950	10,507*
West	3,937	10,638
ALL REGIONS	**$4,024**	**$10,880**

* Estimate is statistically different from All Regions within a plan type at p<.05.

NSD: Not Sufficient Data

Note: Family coverage is defined as health coverage for a family of four.

Source: Ibid, The Henry J. Kaiser Family Foundation

Figure 7.5. Average Increase in Total Retiree Health Costs, by Firm Size (2001-2004)

The total cost of retiree health care (firm and participant contributions) in large firms that offer retiree benefits rose by 13% on average in 2003, a slower growth rate than the 16% cost increase in 2001.

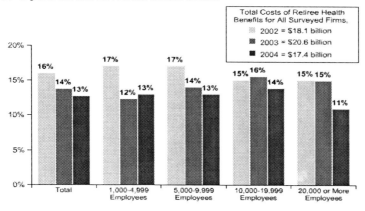

Notes: Based on responses from private-sector firms with 1,000 or more employees that offer retiree health benefits.

Source: Ibid, The Henry J. Kaiser Family Foundation

404

Figure 7.5b. Percentage of Firms Offering Health Benefits, by Firm Size (1996-2005)

Although nearly all large firms (200 or more workers) offer health benefits (98%), firms with fewer than 200 workers are significantly less likely to do so (59%). Since 2000, the percentage of small firms (3-199 workers) offering health benefits has dropped by 9 percentage points. While the year-to-year changes have been relatively small and not statistically significant, the cumulative effect has been a large and statistically significant change over this five-year period. This change is driven largely by a decrease in the percentage of small firms offering coverage, and may reflect several years of high premium growth combined with a sluggish job market.

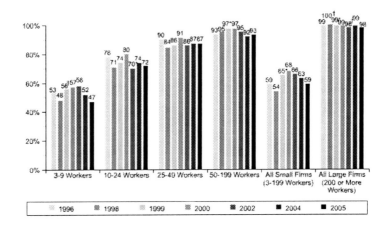

*Estimate is statistically different from the previous year shown at p<.05.
†Estimate is statistically different from the previous year shown at p<.10.

Note: The percentage of all large firms (200 or more workers) offering health benefits in 1999 was 99%, not 100% as reported last year. Data prior to 1999 do not reflect several methodological changes that were made to the survey, including standardizing survey weights to U.S. Census data.

Source: Ibid, The Henry J. Kaiser Family Foundation

Figure 7.5c. Private Health Insurance Administrative Costs per Person Covered (1986-2003)

The cost per enrollee for private health insurance expenses not related to direct care services (such as administrative costs and profits) continued to rise, from $85 in 1986 to $421 in 2003. The most rapid growth occurred in the 4-year period from 1987 to 1990, when these administrative costs rose 125%. For the six-year period from 1998 to 2003, administrative costs per enrollee nearly doubled (+95%).

Notes: These data show the net cost of private health insurance per private enrollee (including Blue Cross/Blue Shield, commercial insurance, HMOs, and self-insured plans), as calculated by the Centers for Medicare and Medicaid Services. Net cost of insurance is the difference between premiums earned and benefits incurred, and includes insurers' costs of paying bills, advertising, sales commissions, and other administrative costs; net additions/subtractions from reserves; rate credits and dividends; premium taxes; and profits or losses. Private enrollment is estimated by CMS using the National Health Insurance Survey and the Current Population Survey.

Source: Ibid, The Henry J. Kaiser Family Foundation

Section 7.6: The Healthcare Insurance Scam

What would America be like if the government allowed all basic necessities to be provided by for-profit companies? Imagine if all public utilities were run by non-government companies. Imagine you're your monthly water bill would be if private, for-profit companies were in control. We already see these effects in the oil industry and in most gas and electric companies. We already see the effects of the free market insurance industry. By law, every driver in America must have collision insurance, and if you have a mortgage, you must have home owner's insurance. Yet, the government has chosen to allow insurance to be provided by for-profit companies. When the most important and most basic necessities are controlled by corporate America you can bet that they will not be available for all or will be expensive because they are only concerned with making profits. As a result, costs for basic services will price many out of the market.

Consider that the government would rather stay away from providing collision or home owner's insurance to Americans because it does not want the liability. Therefore, they allow companies to make a profit for assuming these risks. However, not everyone will file a claim for collision insurance and not everyone will file a claim for damage to their homes. Healthcare insurance is much different because eventually everyone gets sick and everyone dies. Therefore, healthcare insurance has a lower risk to those companies who provide insurance because it is easier to calculate worst case scenarios since we know with certainty that everyone will get sick and everyone will die. And regardless what happens, healthcare insurance companies can never lose. When claims exceed their cash reserves, all they have to do is raise rates. And when regions have a high incidence of a particular claim type, such as floods, tornados, hurricanes, or earthquakes, they will either make these exclusions from coverage or charge a lot more.

Section 7.6a: The Uninsured vs. the Underinsured

In a recent study comparing bankruptcies due to medical bills for insured versus uninsured, Harvard law professor, Elizabeth Warren, found that most medically related bankruptcies were filed by people who had health insurance. It turned out that underinsurance was a much bigger problem due to the limitations, exclusions and waiting periods that result in personal financial liability for large out of pocket expenses. Most of the medical bankruptcy filers were middle class; 56 percent owned a home and the same number had attended college. In 2001, according to a study published by the journal *Health Affairs*, illness and medical bills caused half of the 1,458,000 personal bankruptcies.

Section 7.6b: How Being Uninsured Harms Americans

The uninsured are increasingly paying "up front" before services will be rendered. When they are unable to pay the full medical bill in cash at the time of service, they can be turned away. About 20 percent of the uninsured (vs. 3 percent of those with coverage) say their usual source of care is the emergency room. Studies estimate that the number of excess deaths among uninsured adults age 25-64 is in the range of 18,000 a year. This mortality figure is similar to the 17,500 deaths from diabetes within the same age group. Over a third of the uninsured had problems paying medical bills in the past year. The unpaid bills were substantial enough that many of the uninsured had been turned over to collection agencies - and nearly a quarter of the uninsured adults said they had changed their way of life significantly to pay medical bills. A study has found that insured households paid an average of $26,957 in total medical spending after the diagnosis of a serious new health condition; uninsured households paid $42,166.

Section 7.6c: Do You Really Have Full Coverage?

And for all who escape these tragedies, the threat of inadequate health insurance is a very real possibility due to spending caps, exclusions, and restrictions most insurers place on plan participants. Often, even employees at companies with high-paying jobs may only receive an 80 percent discount on healthcare expenses, which can be similar to having no coverage at all if they or one of their family members gets a costly terminal illness such as cancer. Even when 90 percent or more is paid by the plan, you can bet that there will be lifetime spending caps.

Insurance companies have figured it all out so that they make nice profits while restricting access to the most important basic necessity of any developed nation. Have you ever heard of a health insurance provider that has gone bankrupt? of course not. Washington has passed laws that favor health insurance companies over providing the most essential and deserving necessity of any developed nation---healthcare. But how can you have an insurance company that discriminates based upon pre-existing conditions?

Figure 7.6. The Uninsured is Rising as Employers Drop Coverage

The percent of the nonelderly population without insurance rose from 17.3% in 2002 to 17.7% in 2003 (or 44.7 million uninsured), an increase of 1.4 million over 2002. The proportion of Americans with employer-based insurance declined from 63.3% in 2002 to 61.9% in 2003.

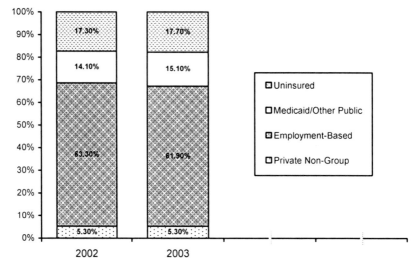

Source: Ibid, The Henry J. Kaiser Family Foundation

The purpose of insurance is to spread risk among a large group of individuals, and therefore, by excluding individuals or charging more, are they really spreading risk? I don't think so. In addition, insurance companies have been given the leisure of basically no government regulation and in many states they aren't even regulated. And this has allowed them to exclude coverage or raise rates for individuals whom they feel represent a higher risk based on absurd things like credit scores, neighborhood, marital status, etc.

Section 7.7: High Quality or Highly Costly?

The following numbers indicate the estimated annual deaths due to improper healthcare management and medical errors:

- 12,000 unnecessary surgery
- 7,000 medication errors in hospitals
- 20,000 other errors in hospitals
- 80,000 infections in hospitals
- 106,000 non-error, negative effects of drugs

Dr. Starfield points out that these numbers only include hospitalized patients and do not include those released from care or outpatient iatrogenic deaths. As well, these numbers do not include any negative effects related to disability or discomfort. And finally, these estimates are lower than a study conducted by the Institute of Medicine in 2003. Another analysis concluded that between 4 percent and 18 percent of consecutive patients experience negative effects in outpatient settings, with:

- 116 million extra physician visits
- 77 million extra prescriptions
- 17 million emergency department visits
- 8 million hospitalizations
- 3 million long-term admissions
- 199,000 additional deaths
- $77 billion in extra costs

Americans have been led to believe that the high expense of healthcare is worth the price in exchange for higher quality. However, evidence from several other studies estimates that 20 percent to 30 percent of patients receive inappropriate care. An estimated 44,000 to 98,000 among them die each year as a result of medical errors. Therefore, if one adds all of the iatrogenic causes of death, American physicians are the third leading causes of death in America.

Of 13 countries in a recent comparison, the United States ranks an average of 12th (second from the bottom) for sixteen critical health indicators. More specifically, the ranking of the U.S. on several indicators was:

- 13th (last) for low-birth-weight percentages
- 13th for neonatal mortality and infant mortality overall
- 11th for post-neonatal mortality
- 13th for years of potential life lost (excluding external causes)
- 11th for life expectancy at 1 year for females, 12th for males
- 10th for life expectancy at 15 years for females, 12th for males
- 10th for life expectancy at 40 years for females, 9th for males
- 7th for life expectancy at 65 years for females, 7th for males
- 3rd for life expectancy at 80 years for females, 3rd for males
- 10th for age-adjusted mortality

I want you to think about these numbers for a minute. If you ask a random person what America's rating would be in each of these indicators what do you think their response would be?

Another study by Drs. Dean, Feldman, Rasio, and Smith has shown that 783,936 Americans die every year from conventional medical mistakes and America spends a minimum of $282 billion annually on deaths due to medical mistakes and iatrogenic deaths. This report mentions that medical mistakes could be up to 20 times higher due to the under reporting involved by doctors who fear legal backlash.

- The proportion of females who smoke ranges from 14 percent in Japan to 41 percent in Denmark; in the United States, it is 24 percent (fifth best). For males, the range is from 26 percent in Sweden to 61 percent in Japan; it is 28 percent in the United States (third best). These nations are amongst the healthiest in the world.

- The U.S. ranks fifth highest for alcoholic beverage consumption.

- The U.S. has relatively low consumption of animal fats (fifth lowest in men aged 55-64 years in 20 industrialized countries) and the third lowest mean cholesterol concentrations among men aged 50 to 70 years among 13 industrialized countries.

Lack of technology is certainly not a contributing factor to the U.S.'s low ranking.

- Among 29 countries, the United States is second only to Japan in the availability of magnetic resonance imaging units and computed tomography scanners per million in population.

408

- However, in studies conducted by the World Health Organization, Japan ranks highest on health, whereas the U.S. ranks among the lowest.

- It is possible that the high use of technology in Japan is limited to diagnostic technology not matched by high rates of treatment, whereas in the U.S., high use of diagnostic technology may be linked to more treatment.

- Supporting this possibility are data showing that the number of employees per bed (full-time equivalents) in the United States is highest among the countries ranked, whereas they are very low in Japan, far lower than can be accounted for by the common practice of having family members rather than hospital staff provide the amenities of hospital care.

Figure 7.7. Healthcare expenditures as a percentage of GDP Have Skyrocketed

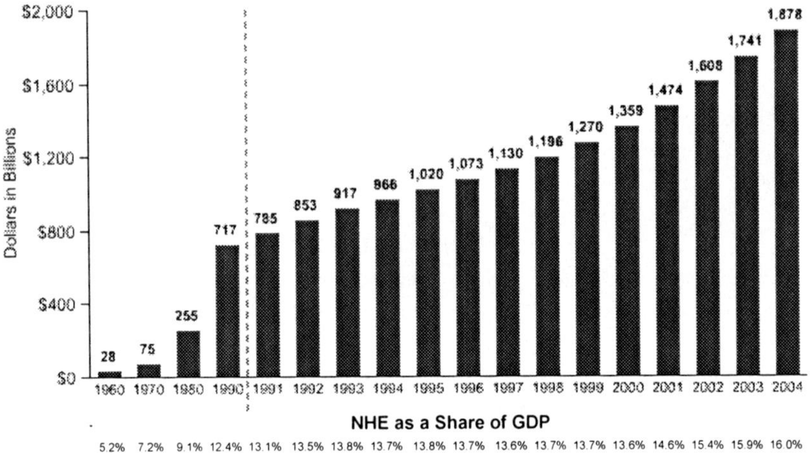

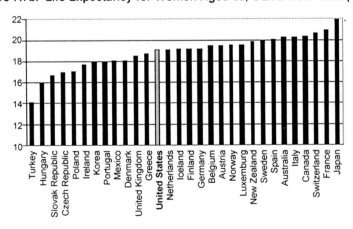

Source: Ibid, The Henry J. Kaiser Family Foundation

Figure 7.7b. Life Expectancy for Women Aged 65, OECD Countries (1999)

Source: OECD (2003). Created by Munnell, Alicia H. Hatch, Robert E. Lee, James G. "Why is Life Expectancy So Low in the United States?" CRR Number 21. Figure 2, August 2004.

Figure 7.7c. Life Expectancy for Men Aged 65, OECD Countries (1999)

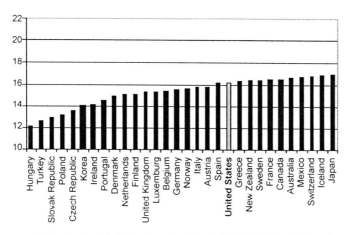

Source: OECD (2003). Created by Munnell, Alicia H. Hatch, Robert E. Lee, James G. "Why is Life Expectancy So Low in the United States?" CRR Number 21. Figure 2, August 2004.

Figure 7.7d. Percentage of Women Classified as Obese (Late 1990s[a])
(Body Mass Index Greater than 30kg/m^2)

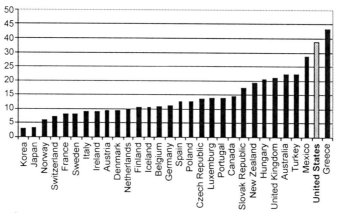

[a] Data for Individual countries are from 1997, 1998, or 1999.
Source: OECD (2003). Ibid, Munnell, Alicia H. Hatch, Robert E. Lee, James G.

Figure 7.7e. Percentage of Men Classified as Obese
(Body Mass Index Greater than 30kg/m^2)

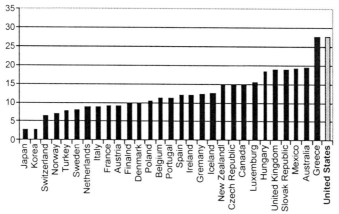

Source: OECD (2003). Ibid, Munnell, Alicia H. Hatch, Robert E. Lee, James G.

410

Figure 7.7f. Percentage of Adults in OECD Nations Who Report Being Daily Smokers, (1990 & 2000)

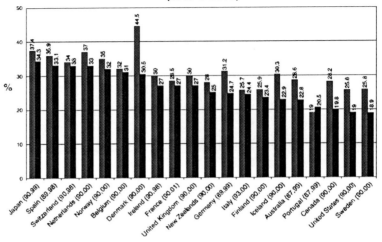

Source: OECD Health Data, 2002

Section 7.8: Medicaid

And the majority of these unanticipated expenses will be passed onto the American consumers. Already, Medicaid services have been eliminated for 2 percent of Medicaid's 47 million recipients and the remaining 46.5 million will face cuts from dropped medical coverage from certain programs. This is a recent list of how states are trying to control Medicaid costs:

- •45 states — Limiting prescriptions; charging new or higher co-payments; requiring use of generic drugs; requiring that Medicaid approve a drug before a physician prescribes it.

- •37 states — Freezing or reducing rates paid to hospitals, nursing homes and doctors.

- •27 states — Toughening eligibility rules.

- •25 states — Reducing benefits, including coverage for dental work and hospitalization.

- •17 states — Increasing co-payments for emergency room visits, ambulances and doctor visits.

Figure 7.8. Projections of Federal Medicaid Spending (2004 to 2010)

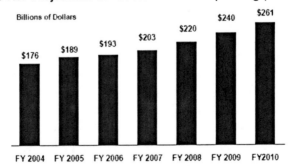

Projections do not reflect baseline spending but include the Bush Administration's policies including proposals with net savings of $13.7 billion within 5 years and $45 billion within 10 years.
Source: OMB, FY2006 Historical Tables

In addition to cutting hundreds of thousands from Medicaid, many states are also eliminating the types of illnesses and amount of benefits as a way to enact further cost cutting measures. Some of the types of coverage eliminated from Medicare include adult outpatient care from eye doctors, dentists, and physical therapists.

Section 7.9: Medicare

Medicare Hospital Insurance (Part A) covers hospital costs, hospice care, and home health care. Medicare Supplementary Health Insurance (Part B) pays for doctor fees, outpatient hospital services, which provides Medicare patients with coverage for physician services, outpatient hospital care, certain home health services, medical equipment and supplies. Beneficiaries pay 25 percent of the cost through premiums ($78.20 per month in 2005). The government pays 75 percent of the cost through general revenues (mainly personal income taxes and borrowing). The Medicare Prescription Drug Benefit (Part D) began in 2006 and provides a 75 percent subsidy for all prescription drugs for the beneficiaries.

Figure 7.9. Medicare Enrollees (millions)

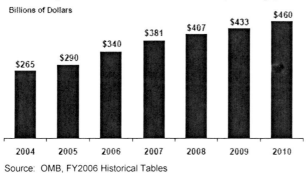

Number Enrolled in Traditional Medicare Program
Number Enrolled in Medicare Managed Care

Source: Ibid, The Henry J. Kaiser Family Foundation

Figure 7.9b. Projections of Federal Medicare Spending (2004 to 2010)

Billions of Dollars

2004	2005	2006	2007	2008	2009	2010
$265	$290	$340	$381	$407	$433	$460

Source: OMB, FY2006 Historical Tables

Section 7.9a: The Medicare Drug Subsidy

If you think fraud has occurred in healthcare thus far, just wait until the scavengers sink their teeth into the President's new Medicare drug subsidy. With an estimated cost of nearly $800 billion over the next decade (eventually growing to over $7 trillion) and an initial outlay of over $350 billion already disbursed since the plan began in January 2006, this is the government's largest social program ever. And while it sounds like a good way to combat the soaring costs of prescription drugs, it is yet another policy failure of President Bush.

President Bush seems to think that you can throw massive amounts of money at a problem and it will go away. The only thing that has go away is tax payer money while increasing fraud. And once fraud is detected, the penalties are so minor that they do not discourage repeat offenders. The accountability offices headed by inspector generals of many of these programs are headed by individuals with either inadequate expertise or resources, sometimes both. And when it comes to prosecuting fraud, the only time individuals are faced with huge penalties and jail time is when they are not affiliated with corporate America.

To date, I can think of not one single healthcare company executive that has gone to jail for the billions of dollars bilked form the U.S. government. And as far as Enron and WorldCom, the only reason executives were found guilty and forced to serve prison time is due to the massive media exposure. Prior to that there has never been anyone from corporate America to my knowledge that has faced jail time for similar crimes.

Section 7.10: The Managed Care Disaster

A couple of decades ago, a dramatic shift was made intended to improve the efficiency of healthcare in America, with the hopes that savings would occur and more people would have access to healthcare. Thus, managed-care organizations sprung up. It was thought that running hospitals like a business would lead to much improved efficiency and benefit everyone. However, this experiment has been nothing short of a disaster. Typically, physicians are only given 10-15 minutes to see patients (or they are compensated for 10 minutes work), leading to very ineffective care. And the pill-popping mentality created by the drug companies has lead physicians and patients alike to the misconception that a pill will make you better, when in fact, in most cases, FDA-approved drugs are toxic and only mask the core health problems.

Figure 7.10. Total Federal Spending for Medicaid and Medicare Under Different Assumptions About Excess Cost Growth

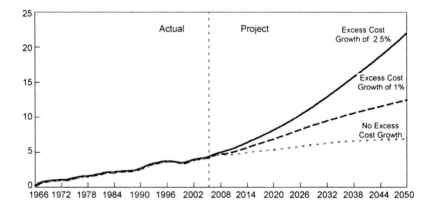

U.S. Health Care Statistics

- 46.6 million Americans without health coverage in 2005 (U.S. Census Bureau).

- 1.2 million individuals lose health coverage with each 1 percent increase in unemployment (Kaiser Commission on Medicaid and the Uninsured)

- 15-20 percent of every premium dollar reflects cost of caring for the uninsured (The nonprofit insurer Blue Shield of California)

- 30 percent of health care cost increases were attributable to rising costs of prescription drugs between 1995 and 2000 (Alliance for Health Reform)

- 0 Number of industrialized nations besides the U.S. lacking a plan for universal health coverage

- Every minute, nearly 5 people lose their health insurance in the U.S.

- 74 percent of those without insurance come from working families.

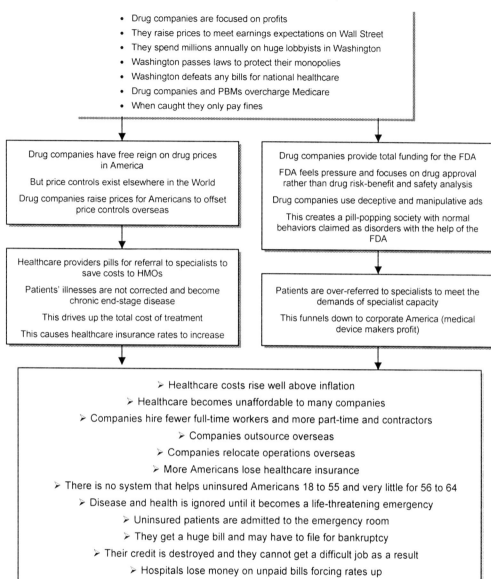

Figure 7.10b. America's Healthcare Spiral

- Drug companies are focused on profits
- They raise prices to meet earnings expectations on Wall Street
- They spend millions annually on huge lobbyists in Washington
- Washington passes laws to protect their monopolies
- Washington defeats any bills for national healthcare
- Drug companies and PBMs overcharge Medicare
- When caught they only pay fines

Drug companies have free reign on drug prices in America

But price controls exist elsewhere in the World

Drug companies raise prices for Americans to offset price controls overseas

Drug companies provide total funding for the FDA

FDA feels pressure and focuses on drug approval rather than drug risk-benefit and safety analysis

Drug companies use deceptive and manipulative ads

This creates a pill-popping society with normal behaviors claimed as disorders with the help of the FDA

Healthcare providers pills for referral to specialists to save costs to HMOs

Patients' illnesses are not corrected and become chronic end-stage disease

This drives up the total cost of treatment

This causes healthcare insurance rates to increase

Patients are over-referred to specialists to meet the demands of specialist capacity

This funnels down to corporate America (medical device makers profit)

> Healthcare costs rise well above inflation
> Healthcare becomes unaffordable to many companies
> Companies hire fewer full-time workers and more part-time and contractors
> Companies outsource overseas
> Companies relocate operations overseas
> More Americans lose healthcare insurance
> There is no system that helps uninsured Americans 18 to 55 and very little for 56 to 64
> Disease and health is ignored until it becomes a life-threatening emergency
> Uninsured patients are admitted to the emergency room
> They get a huge bill and may have to file for bankruptcy
> Their credit is destroyed and they cannot get a difficult job as a result
> Hospitals lose money on unpaid bills forcing rates up
> Discounts to insurance companies are raised due to increasing costs passed on by HMOs

The healthcare establishment preaches preventative medicine, yet they really do not practice it. It is merely a buzz word that makes one think that medicine in America is not the end-stage journey just prior to death. Still, millions cannot afford health insurance and when they have a health problem, hospitals often avoid informing them of charity programs so they can increase their revenues. Because today's private healthcare in America is a for-profit industry, unpaid bills are sold to collection agencies that often place liens on homes, sued them in court and even issued warrants for their arrest when they do not show up for court. And many physicians will not even see uninsured patients unless they have proven means of paying. Of course we always have our credit cards right?

Chapter 8 Supplement

Table 8.1. Total Social Security Beneficiaries: 48,035,000 (June 30, 2005)

Beneficiaries	Number of Beneficiaries	Average Monthly Benefit (2005)
Retired Workers and their Families	33,259,000	
Retired workers	30, 238,000	$959
Wives and husbands of retired workers	2,544,000	$479
Children of retired workers	477,000	$469
Survivors of Deceased Workers	6,641,000	
Widows and widowers and parents aged 60 and older	4,390,000	$925
Children of deceased workers	1,861,000	$627
Widowed mothers and fathers caring for children	178,000	$692
Disabled widows and widowers	212,000	$584
Disabled Workers and their Families	8,135,000	
Disabled workers	6,393,000	$897
Wives and husbands of disabled workers	156,000	$234
Children of disabled workers	1,587,000	$265

Source: http://www.ssa.gov/OACT/FACTS/fs2005_06.html

For 2006, the average monthly benefit in all categories was raised by 4.1 percent, representing the largest annual increase in over a decade.

Figure 8.1. Older Americans Are Somewhat More Likely to Remain in the Workforce
Percentage of Men Age 65 and Older Participating in the Labor Force (1999)

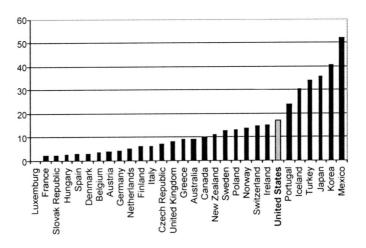

Source: OECD (2003). Created by Munnell, Alicia H. Hatch, Robert E. Lee, James G. "Why is Life Expectancy So Low in the United States?" Figure 9, CRR Number 21. August 2004.

Section 8.1: How Big is the Shortfall?

To put the Social Security issue into perspective, let us compare the shortfalls that will occur up through 2080 for Social Security compared to President Bush's Medicare prescription drug benefit program, the costs of tax cuts in 2001 and 2003 (if made permanent), tax cuts for the top 1 percent (if made permanent), and the shortfall in the Medicare Hospital Insurance Trust Fund. From Table 6-2, you can see that shortfalls in Social Security pail in comparison to these other government programs, which further emphasizes that there is no crisis in Social Security.

Table 8.2. Shortfall in the Social Security Trust Fund Compared to Other Sources of Deficits

	Shortfall or cost as a percent of GDP through 2080	In trillions of dollars through 2080[a]
Shortfall, Social Security Trust Fund (CBO est.) b	0.5%	NA
Shortfall, Social Security Trust Fund (Trustees estimate) c	0.7%	$4.6 trillion
Cost of the new Rx Drug Benefit (Trustees estimate) d	1.1%	$8.0 trillion
Shortfall, Medicare Hospital Insurance Trust Fund	1.6%	$11.0 trillion
Cost of the tax cuts enacted since 2001, if made permanent [e]	2.0%	$13.6 trillion
Tax cuts for top 1 percent, if made permanent [f]	0.6%	$4.1 trillion

a. Measured in present value in 2006 dollars.

b. Source: Calculations from data supporting, Congressional Budget Office, *Updated Long-Term Projections for Social Security*, June 2006. CBO's data show that the 0.5-percent-of-GDP Social Security shortfall is equivalent to a $3.5 trillion shortfall. Because CBO uses GDP and discount rate assumptions that differ from those used by the Trustees, CBO's $3.5 trillion estimate is not comparable to the Trustees' $4.6 trillion estimate. However, CBO's 0.5 percent-of-GDP figure is comparable to the Trustees' 0.7 percent figure.

c. Source: Calculations from the Trustees' report, *2006 Annual Report of the Old-Age and Survivors Insurance And Disability Insurance Trust Funds*.

d. Source: *2006 Annual Report of the Boards of Trustees of the Federal Hospital Insurance And Federal Supplementary Medical Insurance Trust Funds*, page 112. The figure represents the net federal cost of the drug benefit, i.e., the benefit payments minus premium payments from beneficiaries and "clawback" payments from states.

e. Source: Center on Budget and Policy Priorities. The estimate of the cost of the tax cuts enacted since 2001 — 2.0 percent of GDP — is based on cost estimates of the Joint Committee on Taxation for tax cuts enacted to date, and estimates issued by CBO for the cost of extending the 2001 and 2003 tax cuts, as proposed by the President, and continuing relief from the Alternative Minimum Tax.

f. Source: Center on Budget and Policy Priorities. The estimate is based on the cost of the tax cuts, estimated as noted above, and distributional estimates from the Urban Institute-Brookings Institution Tax Policy Center. In 2006, the top 1 percent of households are those with incomes above $400,000.

Table 8.3. Additional Federal Debt and Interest in 2050 Resulting From Proposed Social Security Plans (Over and Above the Levels that Would Otherwise Exist)

Plan	Increase (+)/Reduction (-) in Debt by 2050 Percent of GDP	Increase (+)/ Reduction (-) in Annual Interest Payments in 2050		Reduction (-)/ Increase (+) in 75-Year Social Security Shortfall** Percent Change
		Percent of GDP	$Billions based on 2005 GDP*	
Bush	19.3%	1.1%	$133	-24%
Pozen	3.8%	0.2%	$29	-51%
Hagel	26.5%	1.5%	$182	-8%
Graham	20.8%	1.2%	$145	-49%
Johnson	65.3%	3.7%	$451	+30%
Kolbe-Boyd	1.2%	0.1%	$11	-66%
DeMint (2003)	79.7%	4.4%	$541	+120%
Shaw	40.1%	2.2%	$272	+7%
Sununu-Ryan	93.7%	5.2%	$635	+129%
Diamond-Orszag	-25.9%	-1.4%	-$173	-100%
Ball	-28.2%	-1.5%	-$188	-92%

* This is calculated by multiplying the estimated additional interest payments in 2050 as a percent of GDP by the GDP projected for 2005.

** Excluding the effect of proposed transfers to Social Security from the rest of the budget. These estimates of the effect of plans on solvency are based directly on estimates of each plan (other than the President's) by the Social Security actuaries, without any adjustment to reflect the assumptions of the Social Security Trustee's 2005 report or a delay in the start of private accounts until 2009.   Such adjustments would have little or no effect on the estimated impact of the plans on Social Security solvency over 75 years. The estimate of the effect of the President's plan on solvency is by Jason Furman of the Center on Budget and Policy Priorities.

Chapter 9 Supplement

Section 9.1: Pension Plan Growth and Decline

Table 9.1. U.S. Retirement Assets by Category

Market Value of Assets	1975 (in billions)	1985 (in billions)	1995 (in billions)	1999 (in billions)
Private defined benefit	$186	$814	$1,402	$2,058
Private defined contribution	$74	$417	$1,322	$2,350
State and local	NA	$399	$1,088*	$2,290**
Federal	NA	$172	$512*	$799**

*Figures as of 1994   **Figures as of 2004

Table 9.2. U.S. Retirement Plan Types and Plan Assets

Number of Plans	1980	1990	1995	1999
Single employer DB plans	145,764	111,251	67,682	48,168
Single employer DC plans	340,378	598,153	622,584	681,815
Multiemployer DB plans	2,332	1,812	1,810	1,727
Multiemployer DC plans	427	1,092	1,328	1,285

Market Value of Assets	1980	1990	1995	1999
Single employer DB assets	$354 billion	$798 billion	$1,163 billion	$1,697 billion
Single employer DC assets	$161 billion	$698 billion	$1,295 billion	$2,311 billion
Multiemployer DB assets	$47 billion	$164 billion	$239 billion	$360 billion
Multiemployer DC assets	$1 billion	$14 billion	$27 billion	$39 billion

Chapter 10 Supplement

Figure 10.1. Estimated Increases in Residential Mortgage Debt (Trillions of Dollars)

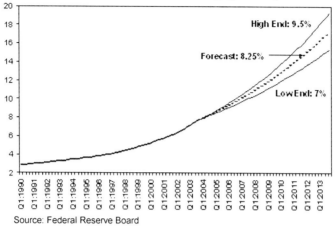

Source: Federal Reserve Board

Figure 10.2. Single-family Housing Investment and Mortgage Debt Will More than Double by 2010

Source: Federal Reserve Board

Figure 10.3. Fannie Mae's Earnings Consistently Met Earnings Targets for Executive Bonuses

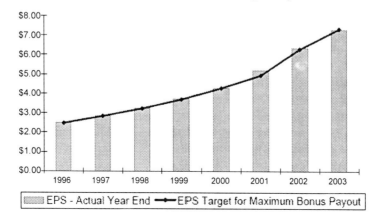

Box 10.1. Brief Summary of the Findings of the OFHEO's Special Report on Fannie Mae

- Fannie Mae senior management promoted an image of the Enterprise as one of the lowest-risk financial institutions in the world and as "best in class" in terms of risk management, financial reporting, internal control, and corporate governance. The findings in this report show that risks at Fannie Mae were greatly understated and that the image was false.

- During the period covered by the OFHEO report—1998 to mid-2004---Fannie Mae reported extremely smooth profit growth and hot announced targets for earnings per share precisely each quarter.   Those achievements were illusions deliberately and systematically created by the Enterprise's senior management with the aid of inappropriate accounting and improper earnings management.

- A large number of Fannie Mae's account policies and practices did not comply with Generally Accepted Accounting Principles (GAAP). The Enterprise also had serious problems of internal control, financial reporting, and corporate governance. Those errors resulted in Fannie Mae overstating reported income and capital by a currently estimated $10.6 billion.

- By deliberately and intentionally manipulating accounting to hit earnings targets, senior management maximized the bonuses and other executive compensation they received, at the expense of shareholders.   Earnings management made a significant contribution to the compensation of Fannie Mae Chairman and CEO Franklin Raines, which totaled over $90 million from 1998 to 2003.   Of that total, over $52 million was directly tied to achieving earnings per share targets.

- Fannie Mae consistently took a significant amount of interest rate risk, and when interest rates fell in 2002, incurred billions of dollars in economic loses. The Enterprise also had large operational and reputational risk exposures.

The Collections Market

On a much smaller scale, another market which you may not know about has grown rapidly due to the ubiquity of credit rating agencies. Virtually every bill you owe, whether it is a monthly phone bill or a service contract with your mobile phone provider makes its way into what I call the asset-lacked securities market. Maybe you have experienced a call from a collection agency at some point, whether it was a mistake or a dispute. Haven't you wondered why you can no longer deal with the company? What happens is this. Companies now sell delinquent bills to collection agencies at a discount in order to secure some revenues instead of getting nothing or devoting efforts towards this. Meanwhile, collection agencies, the sleaze of finance, will try virtually anything to get you to pay, regardless if you really don't owe anything. The problem is that the dispute becomes extremely difficult to remedy since the one who is seeking payment is not connected to the one whose services you paid for.

I do not have any experience in collections but the only reason I know about this silent market is because I have been a victim to the atrocities of this system on many occasions---cell phone, home security, satellite service, and phone bills. In each case, the company either failed to provide services for a long period or never or made some type of promise as in a rebate but never delivered. However, because I signed a contract, this was consider a payable asset and sold to collection agencies, even though I did not obtain my receivables! Needless to say, I refuse to sign any contracts with any service providers. The problem is that there is an epidemic going on in America whereby corporate responsibility for promised services are being ignored and the payment is being sold to collection agencies who use the threat of ruining your credit report as a tool of extortion.

Chapter 12 Supplement

Section 12.1: The FDA

There is now significant evidence that the FDA has been transformed from a consumer protection agency into an agency that protects the interests of the pharmaceutical industry. When the FDA was established in 1906, as a branch of the Health and Human Services Department, it was exclusively funded by the U.S. treasury. This continued up until 1992, when the Prescription Drug User Act (PDUA) was passed by Congress, which called for pharmaceutical companies to pay fees for the drug approval process. According to a former FDA reviewer, when drugs were submitted for approval, the overall feeling by the FDA was that the drug was safe and would be approved. Therefore, FDA officials tended not to look for problems and did not take that extra step to ensure safety, unlike prior to the passage of the PDUFA.

Prior to that time, the FDA served the public's interest by having strict approval and review board process. But today, the FDA looks upon the pharmaceutical industry as their client since they are responsible for what amounts to the full funding of this department. The leaders of the FDA now chose to answer to the pharmaceutical industry and there are no longer any congressional hearings when the FDA has errored, unlike in the past.

> "When I started in 1995, I didn't see the same level of pressure as I did when I left in 2000. So definitely something changed during that five years I was there, and it also coincided with the User Fee Act."
>
> Michael Elashoff, biostatistician and former drug reviewer for the FDA

Prior to the passage of the PDUA, America had the best safety system in place for detecting and removing potentially harmful drugs from the market. However, now that the pharmaceutical industry has exerted control over the FDA and Congress with its strong lobbyists, there are several other countries doing a better job protecting their citizens from harmful drugs. According to a 2002 study by the GAO, the rate of drug recalls has increased since the enactment of the PDUFA in 1992. And although they recommended that the FDA do more to monitor safety even after the drug has been approved, this clearly has not happened. The Journal of the American Medical Association found that over half of all the dangerous side-effects of drugs are only discovered only after the average drug has been on the market for seven years or more.

According to an interview by PBS' Frontline, a former leading candidate for the FDA Commissioner spot stated that he was passed over for another candidate because he wanted to emphasize drug safety more. He concluded that anyone who was seen to focus on drug safety would not be seen as a strong candidate.

Only about 1 to 10 percent of all adverse drug reactions get reported, and most of the reporting by physicians is not to the FDA, as one might imagine, but rather to the pharmaceutical companies, who then pass this information along to the FDA as they see fit. Even when patients in hospitals have adverse drug reactions, this information rarely gets to the FDA or at the very best gets to them at a much later date due to the bureaucracy involved.

According to the Journal of the American Medical Association, from 1976 to 2000, one in five of all approved drugs in the U.S. had to be taken off the market or was subject to a black box warning. Even when these warnings occur, it is often after thousand of illnesses, and many do not become aware of these warnings. Within the climate of many of the FDA reviewers, there is the feeling that many drugs that are approved should have been rejected, and when drugs should be taken off the market, there is too long of a delay, causing more harm to people.

Even the FDA's internal approval process is flawed. When drug candidates are not approved by review boards, the decision is often overturned by upper management. Many former and current FDA employees have stated that upper management silenced them when they did not agree for a drug approval and they were not permitted to speak out during advisory committee meetings for drug approvals or they would receive a backlash. This has caused the rapid exodus of professionals from the FDA over the past decade.

Consequently, according to several FDA employees and watchdog groups, the morale there is the lowest it has been in decades. There have even been dozens from the FDA who have desired to take early retirement or quit to work for watchdog groups.

The FDA has no authority to impose civil penalties on drug companies who send dangerous drugs into the marketplace, creating a "free-for-all" mindset for those companies that have influence and can pursued FDA management to pass drugs that have questionable safety or efficacy. But perhaps the most of the dangerous drugs are the me-too drugs and the drugs that are not life-saving. And because the FDA does a horrendous job of risk-benefit analysis, they basically are ready to approve any drug that appears safe, even from the limited data that they have and especially if a big pharmaceutical company is involved.

> "(people who use prescription drugs) shouldn't have a lot of faith that drugs that are approved have really been demonstrated to be safe and effective to the standards—that they [FDA] were trying to uphold."
>
> Michael Elashoff, biostatistician and former drug reviewer for the FDA

Over the past few years, the number of drugs taken off the market has been higher than any other period in the history of the FDA. And rather than associate this with good safety, it demonstrates that the FDA is not doing good risk-benefit analysis, does a poor job requiring follow up studies by pharmaceutical companies, and is not swift to take action once there are drugs suspected of causing harm.

The healthcare industry has been misguided by its own ignorance and the manipulative tactics of the pharmaceutical industry, which has led them to believe you can treat symptoms and improve a person's overall health from a risk-benefit standpoint. This is simply not true. Treating symptoms is amongst the most indirect evidence for disease prevention or improvement. The most recent example of this was the recommendation for post-menopausal women to take hormone replacement therapy to decrease the incidence of heart attacks.

> "There would be pressure to approve those drugs, or soften the language in the reviews and on the labels, so that they could have a more easy justification for why they're approving it. It was a pretty common practice for those drugs with potential problems."
>
> Michael Elashoff, biostatistician and former drug reviewer for the FDA

One would assume that to make such a claim there would be hard evidence in support of HRT. However, as it turns out, HRT does not decrease heart disease in women and actually has many adverse side effects. When physicians play scientists they often make fools of themselves and harm the public.

Most of the current medication does not attack the core problem, but alters the chemistry in the body, making patients depend on these drugs—a good way to run a business. Meanwhile, there is no drug I am aware of that has 100 percent specificity. Therefore, many healthy tissues in the body are being exposed to the damaging affects of drugs. That is why you hear about the disclaimers that are rattled off in 10 seconds on television commercials. What the FDA has classified as "side-effects" are really toxic effects due to the lack of drug specificity. And because the FDA has turned its back on allowing drug companies to produce life-style enhancing drugs, such as Viagra, or drugs that treat symptoms of complex diseases such as cardiovascular disease, drug efficacy and safety is much harder to determine.

> "In Relenza, when it was ultimately approved, clearly the risks/benefits weren't communicated to people. Relenza was not by any means an isolated incident. I think it was pretty typical for drugs that had problems to get pushed through to approval."
>
> Michael Elashoff, biostatistician and former drug reviewer for the FDA

Section 12.2: Healthcare Fraud

Over the past decade, there have been thousands of examples of fraud by healthcare providers, big pharma, and consumers. For instance, in 2004, Bristol-Meyers Squib was ordered to pay $150 million ($100 million for civil fines and $50 million for accounting violations) by the SEC for improperly booking revenues from drug sales to the tune of $1.5 billion. Yet, this is still the only case of accounting fraud in the pharmaceutical industry discovered by the SEC.

During the same time frame, Pfizer plead guilty to two felony offenses and was ordered to pay $430 million in penalties to settle charges that its Warner-Lambert unit inappropriately promoted its blockbuster epilepsy drug Neurotonin for numerous unapproved uses. The company was alleged to have paid physicians to attend presentations that were focused on unapproved uses for Neurotonin such as bipolar disorder, pain, migraine headaches, and drug and alcohol withdrawal. Since physicians are free to prescribe drugs for uses not specified by the FDA-approved use, it is less expensive and provides a more certain outcome to manipulate or bribe physicians to approve drugs for unapproved uses, known as "off-label" uses.

In addition, many physicians were provided with all-expense paid trips to Hawaii, Florida, and the 1996 Olympics. There was one incident of a single physician receiving $308,000 to push the drug at conferences. Since these activities began in 1995, Neurotonin sales soared from $97 million to $2.7 billion annual by 2003. And many estimates have indicated that as much as 90 percent of the total prescriptions for Neurotonin were for off-label uses. This is not an isolated case and many physicians have been transformed into hired guns for the pharmaceutical industry. And although much of this behavior has been theoretically eliminated, other forms of compensation, bribery, or manipulation continues to occur with the drug rep-physician relationship. It appears as if the FDA does not recognize the effects of these biased behaviors on the deceit and health threats to Americans since it is also controlled by this industry.

In 2003, Bayer was fined $257 million for executing a scheme to overcharge Medicare and Medicaid for its antibiotic Cipro. In 2006, Abbott Labs was found to have overcharged Medicare and Medicaid by $175 million, or as much as ten times the sales price for its prescription drugs. The problem is that drug companies are permitted to hide their pricing practices so it is very easy for them to overcharge one organization while undercharging another, for perhaps some type of favorable treatment. As well, U.S. law regarding the pharmaceutical industry is extremely complex and allows for many types of deceitful activities that are only spotted many years later. These fraudulent and unethical promotional schemes are always one step ahead of the authorities and they serve to corrupt the information process relied upon by physicians in their medical decision making process, putting patients at significant risk.

Tied into the widespread fraud by healthcare providers and big pharma are the pharmacy benefit managers (PBMs), which have recently been attacked by Eliot Spitzer. The PBMs arose not long ago with the goal of keeping drug prices down by negotiating drug discounts from drug manufacturers. While this has helped large providers in many cases, it has also resulted in much higher prices for individuals and corporate clients. The big three PBMs (Medco, Caremark, and Express Scripts) are responsible for controlling prescriptions to around 200 million Americans. There have been numerous allegations that they have overcharged large health plans, partially filled, switched or destroyed the prescriptions of millions of Americans, and reselling returned drugs through mail order businesses.

But the pharmaceutical companies are not the only ones involved in this game of high stakes. Hundreds of physicians, pharmacists, and other providers have been caught over billing Medicare and Medicaid, selling drugs without prescriptions, administering fake flu shots, receiving kickbacks to defraud Medicare and Medicaid, convincing senior citizens to lie about their income in order to receive discounts. And of course the hospitals and HMOs are also involved in fraud, costing American lives and billions of dollars. Amongst a few of the names you may have heard over the past few years are Tenet Healthcare, Pacificare and HCA. Although this short list is by no means exhaustive, HCA alone over billed Medicare by over $1.7 billion, the largest extortion by a hospital management company in the history of America. Finally, there is now significant evidence that many of America's hospitals have been billing private insurers, Medicare and Medicaid for children's vaccinations that are received for free. The list is extensive and it has resulted in losses of billions for Medicare, Medicaid and the private insurers, resulting in even higher costs for insurance. Yet these activities continue because the government has not enacted stiff penalties with prison time for executives of these companies.

Chapter 13 Supplement

Figure 13.1. Percentage of Elder by Country (65 and Over), 2000 and 2050

2000

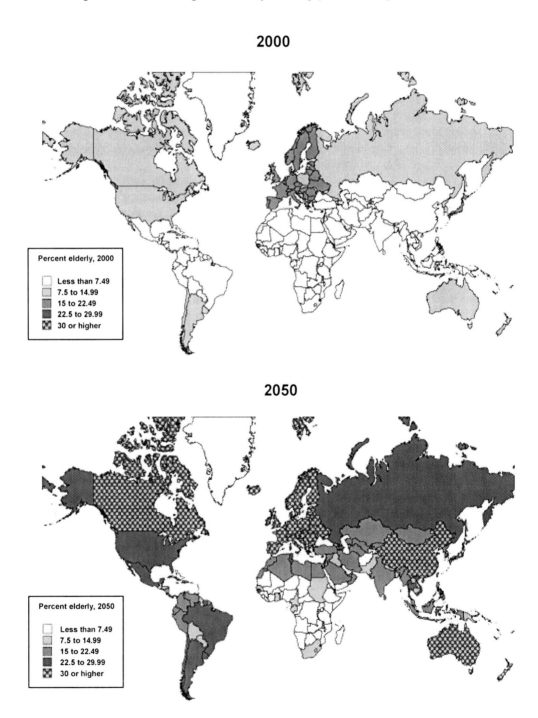

2050

Source: United Nations Population Division, *World Population Prospects: The 2005 Revision* (New York: United Nations, 2005)

Chapter 14 Supplement

www.economyincrisis.org

Section 14.1. Foreign Control of US Industry

Motion Picture and Sound Recording Industry	69%
Plastics and Rubber Manufacturing	47%
Nonmetallic Mineral Product Manufacturing	43%
Pipeline Transportation	38%
Financial Securities Companies	36%
Machinery Manufacturing	32%
Petroleum and Coal Products Manufacturing	30%
Chemical Manufacturing	30%
Mining	29%
Transportation Equipment Manufacturing	27%
Heavy Construction	22%
Publishing Industry	21%
Printing	20%
Food Manufacturing	18%
Computer and Electronic Product Manufacturing	17%
Insurance Carriers	17%
Primary Metal Manufacturing	15%
Total Across All Industries	13%

Oil and Gas; Petroleum Refining

Amoco Corp	British Petroleum Co PLC	United Kingdom	$48.174 B
ARCO	BP Amoco PLC	United Kingdom	$27.224 B
Texaco-US Refining & Marketing	Shell Oil-Western US Business	Netherlands	$3.964 B
Pennzoil-Quaker State Co	Shell Oil Co	Netherlands	$2.909 B
Texaco Inc-Refining Operations	Saudi Refining Inc	Saudi Arabia	$1.280 B
Amerada Hess-St Croix Refinery	PDVSA	Venezuela	$0.932 B
Chevron Corp-Port Arthur,TX	Clark Refining & Marketing Inc	Canada	$0.825 B
Monsanto Oil Co(Monsanto Co)	BHP Petroleum(Americas)Inc	Australia	$0.745 B
CITGO Petroleum Corp	Propernyn BV	Netherlands	$0.662 B
Other			$29.603 B
Total			**$116.317**

Telecommunications

AirTouch Communications Inc	Vodafone Group PLC	United Kingdom	$60.287 B
VoiceStream Wireless Corp	Deutsche Telekom AG	Germany	$29.404 B
AT&T-Worldwide Assets,Ops	British Telecomm-Worldwide	United Kingdom	$5.038 B
GE Americom Communications	SES Global SA	Luxembourg	$4.326 B
Cellular Communications Intl	Kensington Acquisition Sub Inc	Italy	$1.688 B
Loral Space-Satellites(6)	Intelsat Ltd	Bermuda	$1.100 B
QUALCOMM-Land-Based Wireless	Kyocera Corp	Japan	$1.000 B
GE Capital Spacenet Services	Gilat Satellite Networks Ltd	Israel	$0.228 B
Lockheed Martin Corp-World	Intelsat Ltd	Bermuda	$0.120 B
Other			$43.239 B
Total			**$146.429 B**

Transportation Equipment

Chrysler Corp	Daimler-Benz AG	Germany	$40.466 B
ITT Inds-Automotive Electrical	Valeo SA	France	$1.700 B
AlliedSignal Auto-Braking Busn	Robert Bosch GmbH	Germany	$1.500 B
Blue Bird Corp	Henlys Group PLC	United Kingdom	$0.665 B
Motor Coach Industries Intl	Consorcio G Grupo Dina'l'ads	Mexico	$0.335 B
Dana Corp-Driveline Business	GKN PLC-Driveline Assembly	United Kingdom	$0.108 B
Mack Trucks Inc	Renault Vehicules Industriels	France	$0.104 B
Delphi Automotive Sys-Magnaque	San Huan Group Inc	China	$0.070 B
General Motors-Assembly Line	China-General Engine Factory	China	$0.017 B
Dana Corp-Kirkstall Forging	Bharat Forge Ltd	India	$0.006 B
Other			$9.247 B
Total			**$54.217 B**

Printing, Publishing, and Allied Services

Harcourt General Inc	Reed Elsevier Group PLC	United Kingdom	$5.603 B
Simon & Schuster-Educ,Prof	Pearson PLC	United Kingdom	$4.600 B
West Publishing Co	Thomson Corp	Canada	$3.425 B
Macmillan Inc	Maxwell Communication Corp	United Kingdom	$2.522 B
Houghton Mifflin Co	Vivendi Universal SA	France	$2.272 B
Ziff Davis Media Inc	Softbank Corp	Japan	$2.100 B
CBS Records Group(CBS Inc)	Sony Corp	Japan	$2.000 B
Random House Inc	Bertelsmann AG	Germany	$1.300 B
Doubleday-Publishing&Printing	Bertelsmann AG	Germany	$0.500 B
Harper & Row Publishers Inc	News America Holdings Inc	Australia	$0.293 B
Addison-Wesley Publishing Co	Pearson Inc(Pearson PLC)	United Kingdom	$0.273 B
Other			$31.483 B
Total			**$56.371 B**

Mining

Magma Copper Co	BHP	Australia	$2.432 B
NERCO Inc	Kennecott Corp(RTZ Corp PLC)	United Kingdom	$1.162 B
Cyprus Amax-US Coal Mining Ops	RAG International Mining Gmbh	Germany	$1.100 B
Getchell Gold Corp	Placer Dome Inc	Canada	$1.079 B
ASARCO Inc	Nueva Grupo Mexico SA de CV	Mexico	$1.073 B
Other			$12.281 B
Total			**$19.126 B**

Insurance

John Hancock Finl Svcs Inc	Manulife Financial Corp	Canada	$11.063 B
TransAmerica Corp	Aegon NV	Netherlands	$9.691 B
Farmers Group Inc	BATUS Inc(BAT Industries PLC)	United Kingdom	$5.200 B
CIGNA Corp-US & International	ACE Ltd	Bermuda	$3.450 B
American Bankers Ins Group Inc	Fortis AG	Belgium	$2.630 B
Providian Corp-Insurance	Aegon NV	Netherlands	$2.624 B
Other			$51.261 B
Total			**$85.917 B**

Electronic and Electrical Equipment

AMP Inc	Tyco International Ltd	Bermuda	$10.736 B
DII Group	Flextronics International Ltd	Singapore	$2.591 B
Silicon Valley Group Inc	ASM Lithography Holding NV	Netherlands	$1.561 B
ChipPAC Inc	ST Assembly Test Services Ltd	Singapore	$1.459 B
VLSI Technology Inc	Koninklijke Philips Electronic	Netherlands	$1.163 B
GTE Electrical Prods-Sylvania	Osram GmbH	Germany	$1.000 B
Artisan Components Inc	ARM Holdings PLC	United Kingdom	$0.933 B
Exide Electronics Group Inc	BTR PLC	United Kingdom	$0.583 B
Westinghouse Elec-Power Equip	Asea Brown Boveri(ABillion Asea)	Sweden	$0.370 B
Zenith Electronics Corp	LG Electronics Inc	South Korea	$0.186 B
Natl Semiconductor Corp-Bus	VIA Technologies Inc	Taiwan	$0.167 B
Natl Semiconductor-Chip Plant	Matsushita Electric Industrial	Japan	$0.100 B
Other			$40.773 B
Total			**$61.622 B**

Drugs

SmithKline Beckman Corp	Beecham Group PLC	United Kingdom	$7.922 B
Marion Merrell Dow Inc	Hoechst AG	Germany	$7.265 B
Syntex Corp	Roche Holding AG	Switzerland	$5.307 B
Rorer Group Inc	Rhone-Poulenc SA	France	$3.476 B
SICOR Inc	Teva Pharma Inds Ltd	Israel	$3.401 B
Genentech Inc	Roche Holding AG	Switzerland	$1.530 B
Chiron Diagnostics Corp	Bayer AG	Germany	$1.100 B
Other			$30.301 B
Total			**$60.302 B**

Computer and Office Equipment

IBM Corp-Hard Disk Drive	Hitachi Ltd	Japan	$2.050 B
Kingston Technology Corp	Softbank Corp	Japan	$1.071 B
Amdahl Corp	Fujitsu Ltd	Japan	$0.925 B
Maxtor Corp	Hyundai Electn Industries Co	South Korea	$0.228 B
Quantum-Recording-Head Bus	Matsushita Kotobuki Electn Ind	Japan	$0.200 B
Proxima Corp	ASK AS	Norway	$0.083 B
Other			$28.337 B
Total			**$32.894 B**

Machinery

United States Filter Corp	Vivendi SA	France	$6.318 B
Westinghouse-Conven Power Gen	Siemens AG	Germany	$1.525 B
Rexnord Corp	BTR Dunlop Holdings(BTR PLC)	United Kingdom	$0.815 B
Progressive Tool & Industry Co	Fiat SpA	Italy	$0.630 B
Detroit Diesel	DaimlerChrysler AG	Germany	$0.581 B
Pinnacle Automation Inc	FKI PLC	United Kingdom	$0.425 B
Ingersoll-Rand-Drilling Bus	Atlas Copco AB	Sweden	$0.225 B
Other			$13.588 B
Total			**$24.106 B**

Metal and Metal Products

Triangle Industries Inc	Pechiney SA	France	$3.658 B
Lucent Tech-Optical Fibre Unit	Furukawa Electric Co Ltd	Japan	$2.127 B
Inland Steel Co	Ispat International NV	Netherlands	$1.427 B
AlliedSignal Laminate Systems	Rutgers AG	Germany	$0.815 B
Cargill Inc-Cert Steel Asts	Gerdau Ameristeel US Inc	Canada	$0.266 B
Other			$14.722 B
Total			**$23.015 B**

Investment & Commodity Firms,Dealers,Exchanges

PaineWebber Group Inc	UBS AG	Switzerland	$12.243 B
Aetna-Fin'l Svcs & Int'l Bus	ING Groep NV	Netherlands	$4.933 B
PIMCO Advisors Holdings LP	Allianz AG	Germany	$1.930 B
Scudder Stevens & Clark Inc	Zurich Versicherungs GmbH	Switzerland	$1.667 B
AIM Management Group Inc	Invesco PLC	United Kingdom	$1.599 B
Dain Rauscher Corp	Royal Bank of Canada	Canada	$1.354 B
First Boston Inc	Credit Suisse First Boston	Switzerland	$1.100 B
Brinson Partners Inc	Schweizerischer Bankverein	Switzerland	$0.750 B
Warburg Pincus Asset Mgmt	Credit Suisse Asset Management	Switzerland	$0.650 B
Dillon Read & Co(UBS AG)	SBC Warburg(Swiss Bank Corp)	Switzerland	$0.600 B
Other			$39.379 B
Total			**$66.205 B**

Commercial Banks, Bank Holding Companies

Bankers Trust New York Corp	Deutsche Bank AG	Germany	$9.082 B

Republic New York Corp,NY,NY	HSBC Holdings PLC{HSBC}	United Kingdom	$7.703 B
Banknorth Group Inc,ME	Toronto-Dominion Bank	Canada	$3.813 B
Centura Bank Inc,NC	Royal Bank of Canada	Canada	$2.320 B
Mellon Fin-Retail Banking Bus	Citizens Financial Group,RI	United Kingdom	$2.100 B
Other			$18.572 B
Total			**$43.590 B**

Motion Picture Production and Distribution

MCA Inc	Matsushita Electric Industrial	Japan	$7.406 B
Columbia Pictures Entmnt	Sony USA Inc(Sony Corp)	Japan	$4.792 B
MGM/UA Communications Co	Pathe Communications Corp	Luxembourg	$1.709 B
All American Communications	Pearson PLC	United Kingdom	$0.500 B
RCA Columbia Home Video	Columbia Pictures Entmnt	Japan	$0.350 B
Other			$3.546 B
Total			**$18.303 B**

Chemicals and Allied Products

Nalco Chemical Co	Suez Lyonnaise des Eaux SA	France	$4.063 B
American Cyanamid Agri Product	BASF AG	Germany	$3.900 B
Quantum Chemical Corp	Hanson PLC	United Kingdom	$3.220 B
Loctite Corp	Henkel KGaA	Germany	$1.289 B
Merck-Crop Protection Business	Novartis AG	Switzerland	$0.910 B
Other			$37.249 B
Total			**$50.630 B**

Rubber & Miscellaneous Plastic Products

Firestone Tire & Rubber Co	Bridgestone Corp	Japan	$2.533 B
Uniroyal Goodrich Tire Co	Michelin SA	France	$1.500 B
Gates Corp	Tomkins PLC	United Kingdom	$1.400 B
Johnson Controls-Plastic Div	Schmalbach-Lubeca AG(Viag AG)	Germany	$0.650 B
General Tire Inc(GenCorp)	Continental AG	Germany	$0.625 B
Other			$9.716 B
Total			**$16.424 B**

Food and Kindred Products

Bestfoods	Unilever PLC	United Kingdom	$25.065 B
Ralston Purina Co	Nestle SA	Switzerland	$10.479 B
Miller Brewing(Philip Morris)	South African Breweries PLC	United Kingdom	$5.574 B
Pfizer Inc-Adams	Cadbury Schweppes PLC	United Kingdom	$4.200 B
Gerber Products Co	Sandoz AG	Switzerland	$3.686 B
Dr Pepper/Seven-Up Cos Inc	Cadbury Schweppes PLC	United Kingdom	$2.367 B
Slim-Fast Foods Co	Unilever NV	Netherlands	$2.300 B
Snapple Beverage Group Inc	Cadbury Schweppes PLC	United Kingdom	$1.450 B
Beringer Wine Estates Holdings	Fosters Brewing Group Ltd	Australia	$1.447 B
Tropicana Products Inc	Joseph E Seagram & Sons Inc	Canada	$1.200 B
Other			$26.150 B
Total			**$83.917 B**

Credit Institutions

Household International Inc	HSBC Holdings PLC{HSBC}	United Kingdom	$15.294 B
CIT Group Inc	Tyco International Ltd	Bermuda	$9.341 B
AT&T Capital Corp(AT&T Corp)	Investor Group	United Kingdom	$2.129 B
Genstar Corp	Imasco Enterprises(Imasco)	Canada	$2 B
Peoples Bank-Credit Card Bus	Royal Bank of Scotland Group	United Kingdom	$0.518 B
HealthCare Financial Partners	Heller Financial Inc	Japan	$0.485 B
Other			$2.584 B
Total			**$32.193 B**

Electric, Gas, and Water Distribution

PacifiCorp	Scottish Power PLC	United Kingdom	$12.600 B
Niagara Mohawk Holdings Inc	National Grid Group PLC	United Kingdom	$8.048 B
American Water Works Co Inc	RWE AG	Germany	$7.726 B
LG&E Energy Corp	PowerGen PLC	United Kingdom	$5.426 B
New England Electric System	National Grid Group PLC	United Kingdom	$4.217 B
Tejas Gas Corp	Shell Oil Co	Netherlands	$2.166 B
United Water Resources Inc	Suez Lyonnaise des Eaux SA	France	$1.845 B
Gas Transmission NW Corp	TransCanada Corp	Canada	$1.703 B
Other			$11.892 B
Total			**$55.622 B**

Business Services

Ernst & Young-Consulting Bus	Cap Gemini SA	France	$11.774 B
LHS Group Inc	Sema Group PLC	United Kingdom	$4.338 B
Nielsen Media Research Inc	VNU NV	Netherlands	$2.788 B
ACNielsen Corp	VNU NV	Netherlands	$2.341 B
Sensormatic Electronics Corp	Tyco International Ltd	Bermuda	$2.203 B
Shared Medical Systems Corp	Siemens Corp	Germany	$2.058 B
Safety-Kleen Corp	Laidlaw Environmental Services	Canada	$1.804 B
Combustion Engineering Inc	Asea Brown Boveri(ABillion Asea)	Sweden	$1.795 B
MCI Communications Corp-Whl	Cable & Wireless PLC	United Kingdom	$1.750 B
Experian Corp	Great Universal Stores PLC	United Kingdom	$1.700 B
Manpower Inc	Blue Arrow PLC	United Kingdom	$1.328 B
Primark Corp	Thomson Corp	Canada	$1.081 B
Island ECN Inc	Instinet Corp(Reuters Group)	United Kingdom	$0.543 B
Zenith Computer Group(Zenith)	Cie des Machines Bull	France	$0.496 B
Knight-Ridder Information Inc	MAID PLC	United Kingdom	$0.420 B
Pinkerton's Inc	Securitas AB	Sweden	$0.383 B
Other			$72.510 B
Total			**$109.312 B**

Section 14.2. Who is Really Winning the War in Iraq?

Halliburton, the Texan oil company tied to U.S. vice president Dick Cheney, is making a killing on subsidiary contracts to Iraq, doing everything from repairing oil wells to providing housing for U.S. troops. And investors have taken notice, as they have driven the price of the stock up nearly 300 percent since the end of the war in mid-2003. Meanwhile, during the same time period, the Dow Jones Industrial Average has moved by a much lower amount (figure 14.2).

Just two years before the war, a major accounting scandal at Halliburton caused shareholders to dump the stock to multiyear lows. But after Iraq was officially taken in April 2003, the share price of Halliburton began a surge that has not let up. In contrast, during that same time period, the Dow Jones Industrial Average has gained only about 24 percent. From figure 14.2b, it is apparent that Halliburton's troubles began in mid-2001, with accounting fraud that was highlighted by several other companies such as Enron, WorldCom, Global Crossing and many others. After falling by more than 80 percent to a 20-year low in 2001, it appears as if Vice President Cheney was well-positioned to deliver some great news to his former company two years later.

Figure 14.2. Stock Price Chart for Halliburton versus the Dow Jones Index (2003-2006)

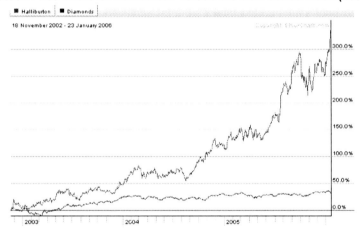

You can see from figure 14.2b that Halliburton's share price really began to take off in early fall 2004, just after the contract awards were being issued. How is it possible that a company involved in fraud only a couple of years ago is receiving large government contracts? I would be interested to know how many of Cheney's friends and colleagues hold Halliburton stock.

Table 14-1 shows the top ten company contract awards in Iraq for 2004. As you can see, with the exception of Lockheed-Martin (which had already experienced a run-up in price prior to the war) each one of these companies has reported gains in share price that are far above the performance of Dow Jones Industrial Average during the same time period. Most notably, the awards increase from 2003 to 2004 was astronomically higher for Halliburton (105%) than the remaining top ten contractors, as was its stock appreciation since the end of the war. Only Humana has appreciated more.

The lack of financial transparency in today's Iraq creates unprecedented opportunities. And it appears as if some U.S. firms have already taken advantage of this system. For instance, Halliburton has already been charged with bilking hundreds of millions of dollars in bogus rebuilding contracts or over billing of expenses, while the integrity of the U.S.-UK controlled fund slated to recover foreign Iraqi assets has been called into question. Despite the fact that the U.S. Department of State has called Halliburton's work in Iraq "Poor" and the fact that over $1 billion remains unaccounted for from its operations in Iraq, Halliburton continues to receive more government contracts.

Figure 14.2b. Stock Price Chart for Halliburton Versus the Dow Jones Index (2000-2006)

Table 14.1. Top Ten Pentagon Contractors in 2004 (Dollars in Millions)

RANK 2004	COMPANY NAME	AWARDS 2003	AWARDS 2004	% AWARDS CHANGE	% CHANGE IN STOCK (04/03 to 01/06)
1	Lockheed Martin Corporation	21,900	20,700	-5%	30%
2	Boeing Company	17,300	17,100	-1%	148%
3	Northrop Grumman Corporation	11,100	11,900	7%	61%
4	General Dynamics Corporation	8,200	9,600	17%	97%
5	Raytheon Company	7,900	8,500	7%	38%
6	Halliburton Company	3,900	8,000	105%	261%
7	United Technologies Corporation	4,500	5,100	13%	83%
8	Science Applications International Corp	2,600	2,500	-3%	Private company
9	Computer Sciences Corporation	2,500	2,400	-4%	52%
10	Humana Inc.1	2,400	2,400	0%	440%

Source: World Policy Institute www.worldpolicy.org

Over and over, Halliburton has been found unable to account for expenses and has even been found to have overcharged the U.S. government for food, gasoline, and other items while doing work in Iraq over the past three years. Most of this fraudulent activity has been conducted through KBR, one of Halliburton's business units.

Since the war, Halliburton has been awarded well over $25 billion in U.S. Army contracts; much of it for work in Iraq. And it has been stated by many insiders that Halliburton was not required to bid on these contracts, but was simply awarded them based on the price they decided to charge after the work was completed. Interestingly, the FBI has begun to investigate the Halliburton-Cheney connection. With big money usually comes corruption and Halliburton is not alone in this activity. Apparently, corruption is widespread and includes U.S. companies, officials, and Iraqis. According to the special inspector general of the U.S. in charge of Iraq's reconstruction, several billions of dollars have gone unaccounted for.

428

Rep. Henry Waxman (Calif.), of the House Government Reform Committee, released a document "Dollars, Not Sense: Government Contracting Under the Bush Administration," reveals significant evidence that in fact Vice President Cheney had a very direct role in awarding several major contracts to his former company even before the war in Iraq began and without the due diligence and competitive bidding process that is required by the government.

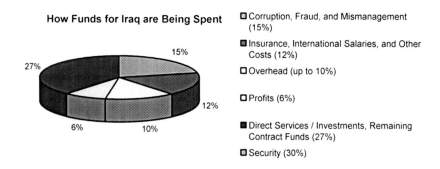

How Funds for Iraq are Being Spent

- ▣ Corruption, Fraud, and Mismanagement (15%)
- ▣ Insurance, International Salaries, and Other Costs (12%)
- ▢ Overhead (up to 10%)
- ▢ Profits (6%)
- ■ Direct Services / Investments, Remaining Contract Funds (27%)
- ▣ Security (30%)

Source: Center for Strategic and International Studies: Progress or Peril? Measuring Iraq's Reconstruction. December 2004.

Chapter 15 Supplement

Figure 15.1. Energy Consumption by Source

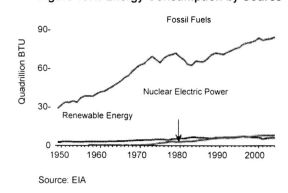

Source: EIA

Figure 15.2. Production as Share of Consumption for Coal Natural Gas, and Petroleum

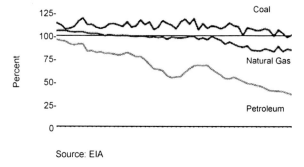

Source: EIA

Chapter 17 Supplement

Perhaps you are familiar with the battle between Microsoft (MSFT), Sony (SNE) and Nintendo for control of the gaming market. But the WAR is between MSFT and SNE for much more than gaming—control of the home digital multimedia market that will soon expand into a huge industry.

AOL Led it But Blew It

The first company with the vision of this new industry was AOL but they failed due to poor leadership, execution, and a buyout of TWX that was done quickly without proper due diligence. Subsequently, this poor oversight led to the largest quarterly write-off in U.S. history at over $54 billion, nearly causing the complete destruction of Time-Warner.

Microsoft Took the Reins

Shortly after the AOL-TWX merger, MSFT announced plans to enter the gaming market. But this would serve as its method to enter the home and eventually be an all-in-one provider of digital media content. Meanwhile, Sony had been in chaos for a few years and only recently posted the first annual loss in the company's history, prompting an unheard of move—hiring a non-Japanese CEO to run this confused company. SNE had grown so large and had so many business units that it was no longer an efficient business. In short, SNE had lost the competitive edge it created over a decade ago through branding and cost synergy.

Sony Finally Figured Things Out

Prior to Microsoft's entry into this war, SNE was the only real player for digital media, having acquired significant motion picture and other media assets from American companies. However, once MSFT indicated its intent to become a player in this battle, SNE took a more aggressive offensive approach despite its managerial disarray. Soon after the release of the Xbox, SNE began to beef up its Playstation with more than gaming in mind. And now consumers have been led to believe that these two powerhouses are vying for the title of the best video console, when in fact they are fighting an intense war for entry of a comprehensive digital multimedia entertainment center within American households, with these game consoles as their "Trojan Horse" so to speak.

The Other Enemies of the War

However, they are not the only players in this war of digital media. Yahoo, ATT, and Comcast are also engaged in this war, but are attacking the competition from different fronts. ATT and Comcast are battling each other as well as the satellite TV providers, while trying to replace recently lost revenues from the telecom shakeout which caused a collapse of telecom services prices due to expansion of wireless telephony and the massive fiber optic build out. Comcast had its sights set on digital content delivery early on with its spin off of Blockbuster Video. However, early in 2005, Comcast completely sold off all ownership. Now Blockbuster is struggling to avoid bankruptcy protection due to poor management and lack of a viable and timely digital strategy.

ATT Made a Great Buy

With its recent acquisition of SBC, ATT is now strongly positioned for the first time in a decade. Actually it was SBC who bought ATT but due to the widespread customer reach of the ATT brand name, SBC chose to retain the ATT name. You may be familiar with SBC's strategic alliance with Yahoo. This has been great for both companies. For Yahoo, it has provided them with a new market—customers needing ISP service.

Yahoo was one of the early players in the Internet and chose not to go with the ISP business model route; a good decision due to the high costs of technology maintenance, upgrade, and customer acquisition costs. The ISP model provides no real sustainable growth, as AOL realized, and should only be used for building a customer base to bundle other services. Yahoo has always had a competitive edge in content, but it did not have an ISP service. But its patience was rewarded and allowed them to avoid the high risks of creating an ISP from the ground floor. Now with Yahoo as a partner, SBC provides DSL at the lowest available prices. Most likely they are not making much money from this, but are relying on selling a bundled package of services—long distance, DSL, cable TV, and wireless. As well, the least expensive DSL subscriber fees require customers to subscribe to its unlimited long distance package, which is a critical move to combat the expected explosive growth of VoIP. But don't expect the ma-bells to start offering VoIP until smaller competitors steal their customers, which is not far off. But they will avoid the low-cost VoIP transition for as long as they can.

In order to take things to the next level, ATT will need a more aggressive approach to compete with MSFT and SNE. Most likely they are not currently in a position of sufficient financial stability to take on such a task. Regardless, the merger with SBC and the existing alliances with Yahoo have positioned ATT to do well relative to its direct competitors over the next several years. The only difficulty will be determining who their direct competitors are since the ma-bells are in a major transition phase.

Yahoo, the Silent Giant

In contrast, Yahoo is the strongest competitor to MSFT and SNE and they already have significant digital content with relationships with major television networks. Yahoo is gradually transforming its once exclusive advertising business model into several fee-based services. Already with an ISP (via ATT), domain name registry, web hosting, and exclusive contracts with major television networks providing broadcast viewing, Yahoo will soon expand its digital content rapidly by leveraging its 100 million plus worldwide customer base. However, one might wonder whether they would benefit from having hardware to help them compete with MSFT and SNE. Yahoo has been the maverick of the Internet and most likely they will not go this route.

The Buyout Game

Most likely, if Nintendo survives it will be bought by ATT, Comcast or other companies that can leverage its brand and customer base. With hardware, either of these two companies will be able to compete better with MSFT and SNE for a share of the digital media market. However, such a move would be considered very expensive and risky and these two companies are typically more conservative. ATT is still licking its wounds from its bad investments in telecom and even ATT wireless was a major problem with its enormous debt.

Most likely, the digital content delivery market will be won by MSFT, although I would never count Yahoo out. Either way, I see MSFT continuing its buying spree for small gaming software companies. And I see the possibility of one or two publicly traded gaming companies being bought by MSFT and SNE in the future. The top gaming software developers are ATVI, TTWO, ERTS, and MWY.

Loyalty Has Power in this Game

MSFT has already invested an enormous amount of money in its Xbox platform. In less than 5 years, MSFT has positioned the Xbox with a 30 to 35% market share, second only to SNE's 45%. This is quite remarkable, given that Sony's Playstation has been around for nearly two decades. As well, due to the ridiculous trade practices in Japan, MSFT has not been able to reach much of this market. Regardless, the most serious gamers will only buy Xbox. Selling the console for as much as 50% off its total costs, MSFT offers a clearly superior console, creating a loyal customer base with which to leverage additional media, and this investment will pay off soon.

The Pie in the Sky

And by the way, you can forget about Sirius Satellite. They have only a very slim chance of survival because not only is the business model for satellite radio poorly designed, but Sirius has all but eliminated any chance to compete with XM Satellite since they have given most of their equity away to Howard Stern and Sirius' CEO, as if company stock had no value. And most likely, unless they get a buyout offer, it probably won't have much value in the future.

Over the long run, the satellite radio market will not be able to compete with the media giants such as Comcast, ATT, Yahoo and others that have business diversity and can withstand financial hardships that will be inevitable in this intense media war. In addition, business diversity provides cross-selling opportunities to leverage the consumer base. The satellite radio companies are in no position to provide these optional services.

Once Internet access becomes a standard feature in automobiles (perhaps within 6 years) Yahoo will most likely eventually provide free radio with an option of paying for no advertisements. Today's consumers want options and they want a host of value-added services.

The fate of these 2 companies will depend on the fate of Sirius. If Sirius is bought out by say Comcast or Yahoo, then XM will most likely be able to stick around for several more years. But most likely, these 2 companies will fight head-to-head as the media giants watch from the outside, waiting for both to collapse. But I will say this, unless both companies form strategic alliances with other media companies, they will not survive. And Sirius will most likely be the first casualty.

References

The Great Depression

Gene Smiley. Rethinking the Great Depression. Ivan R. Dee, 2003.

David Kyvig. Daily Life in the United States, 1920-1940: How Americans Lived During the Roaring 20s and the Great Depression. Ivan R. Dee, 2004.

Robert Mcelvaine. The Great Depression: America 1929-1941. Three Rivers Press, 1993.

Poverty & Wealth

U.S. Bureau of Census

U.S. Department of Labor and Statistics

Greenstein and Shapiro. Poverty Up, Incomes Down for Second Straight Year in 2002. Center on Budget and Policy Priorities, September 23, 2003.

Income Inequality Grew Across the Country Over the Past Two Decades: Early Signs Suggest Inequality Now Growing Again After Brief Interruption. Center on Budget and Policy Priorities, January 26, 2006.

Friedman and Richards. Capital Gains and Dividend Tax Cuts: Data Make Clear that High-Income Households Benefit the Most. Center on Budget and Policy Priorities, January 30, 2006.

Robert Greenstein and Isaac Shapiro. Poverty Up, Incomes Down for Second Straight Year in 2002. Center on Budget and Policy Priorities, September 23, 2003.

Income Inequality Grew Across the Country Over the Past Two Decades: Early Signs Suggest Inequality Now Growing Again After Brief Interruption. Center on Budget Policy and Priorities, January 26, 2006.

Low-Income Children in the United States (2004). National Center for Children in Poverty. http://nccp.org/pub_cpf04.html

Ohlemacher. Calculating Poverty in U.S. Fuels Debate. Associated Press, February 21, 2006.

Robert Frank. The US Led a Resurgence Last Year Among Millionaires World-Wide. Wall Street Journal, June 15, 2004.

Valdas Anelauskas. Discovering America as It Is. Clarity Press, 1999.

Edward Wolff. The Wealth Divide: The Growing Gap in the United States Between the Rich and the Rest. Multinational Monitor, May 2003.

Patrice Hill. Income Gap Grows in U.S. The Washington Times. July 31, 2005.

Bernard Wasow. The New American Economy: A Rising Tide that Lifts Only Yachts. The Century Foundation. 2004.

How Poor is Poor? Associated Press, February 21, 2006.

Jeannine Aversa. Unemployment Rate Climbs to 4.8 Percent. Associated Press, August 4, 2006.

Does Inequality Matter? The Economist, June 14, 2001.

Carl Goldstein. The Gap. Minnesota Public Radio, April 2000.

Barbara Hagenbaugh. Nation's Wealth Disparity. USA Today, January 22, 2003.

Federal Deficit

Lawrence Kotlikoff. Deficit Delusion. The Public Interest (Summer 1986): 53-65.

Lawrence Kotlikoff. From Deficit Delusion to the Fiscal Balance Rule—Looking for a Meaningful Way to Describe Fiscal Policy. National Bureau of Economic Research working paper no. 2841, February 1989.

Lawrence Kotlikoff. Generational Accounts—A Meaningful Alternative to Deficit Accounting. In Tax Policy and the Economy, vol. 5, edited by David Bradford. 1991.

Lawrence Kotlikoff. Generational Accounting: Knowing Who Pays and When for What We Spend. 1992.

Carolyn Lochhead. Deficit cracking GOP's solidarity Party-line votes no longer assured. SF Chronicle, Nov 27, 2005.

Martin Crutsinger. U.S. Aims to Address China Trade Deficit. Associated Press, February 20, 2006.

Martin Crutsinger. U.S. Trade Deficit Hits High on Storms. Associated Press, November 10, 2005.

Peter G. Peterson. Riding for a Fall. Foreign Affairs, September/October 2004.

Julia Boorstin. Maybe Deficits Really Don't Matter. Fortune, November 11, 2005.

www.economyincrisis.com

Pedro Nicolaci da Costa. Big Deficit Looms Behind Revival of 30-yr Bond. Reuters, February 8, 2006.

Dean Baker and David Rosnick. The Forty-Four Trillion Dollar Deficit Scare. Center for Economic and Policy Research, September 10, 2003.

Federal Debt

Interest on the Federal Debt http://www.publicdebt.treas.gov/opd/opdint.htm

Debt to the Penny. http://www.publicdebt.treas.gov/opd/opdpenny.htm

Peter G. Peterson. Riding for a Fall. Foreign Affairs, September/October 2004.

Liqun Liu, Andrew Rettenmaier and Thomas Saving. A Debt is a Debt. Texas A&M University, Private Enterprise Research Center. Perspective on Policy, September 2002.

Dean Baker. Dangerous Trends: The Growth of Debt in the U.S. Economy. Center for Economic Policy Research, September 7, 2004.

Consumer Debt

Dennis Cauchon and John Waggoner. The Looming National Benefit Crisis. USA Today, Oct 3, 2004.

Dean Baker. Dangerous Trends: The Growth of Debt in the U.S. Economy. Center for Economic Policy Research, September 7, 2004.

Jason Zweig. The Oracle Speaks. CNN Money, May 2, 2005.

Deanne Loonin. The Life and Debt Cycle. Part One: The Implications of Rising Credit Card Debt Among Other Consumers. National Consumer Law Center, July 2006.

Kathy Chu. Consumer Groups Blast Fed Credit Card Report. USA Today, July 29, 2006.

Mauricio Soto. Will Baby Boomers Drown in Debt? Center for Retirement Research at Boston College. An Issue in Brief. Just the Facts on Retirement Issues, March 2005, Number 15.

Tamara Draut and Javier Silva. Borrowing to Make Ends Meet: The Growth of Credit Card Debt in the '90s. Demos, 2003.

Bernard Wasow. Rages to Riches? The American Dream is Less Common in the United States than Elsewhere. The Century Foundation, 2004.

Chris Faulkner-MacDonagh and Martin Muhleisen. Are U.S. Households Living Beyond Their Means? Finance & Development, March 2004.

Facts About Consumer Credit Card Debt and Bankruptcy. Consumer Federation of America, Aug. 7, 2006.

Patricia Sabatini. Study: Credit Card Issuers Ensnare Many Debt Traps. Pittsburg Post-Gazette, July 28, 2006.

Carly Zander. Federal Reserve Releases New Statistics About Credit Cards, reports LowCards.com. Send2Press Newswire, March 2, 2006.

Susan Walker. U.S. Consumer Credit Card Debt May Crash Economy. FoxNews.com, December 31, 2004.

Laura Bruce. Low Rates: A Temptation for Deeper Debt. Bankrate.com, April 13, 2005.

The Plastic Safety Net: The Reality Behind Debt in America. Center for Responsible Credit Lending. Demos, Oct. 2005.

Life and Debt: Why American Families Are Borrowing to the Hilt. A Century Foundation Guide to the Issues. The Century Foundation, 2004.

William Mapother. Taming Consumer Debt. Credit Union National Association, April 2004.

Thomas Garrett. Up, Up, and Away: Personal Bankruptcies Soar! Federal Reserve Bank of St. Louis, October 2005.

Martin Bosworth. Higher Minimum Credit Card Payments Add to Consumer Queasiness. ConsumerAffairs.com, Aug 26, 2005.

Martin Bosworth. Congress Passes Bankruptcy Bill. ConsumerAffairs.com, April 14, 2005.

Melody Warwick. Your Credit Card Payment Just Doubled. Bankrate.com

Consumer Credit. Federal Reserve Statistical Release, February 7, 2006.

John Gist and Carlos Figueiredo. Deeper in Debt: Trends Among Midlife and Older Americans. AARP Public Policy Institute, April 2002.

Economic Recovery

Board of Governors of the Federal Reserve System www.federalreserve.gov

Federal Reserve Bank of New York www.ny.frb.org

Federal Reserve Bank of St. Louis www.stlouisfed.org

Federal Reserve Bank of San Francisco www.frbsf.org

United States Bureau of Census www.census.gov

U.S. Department of Commerce: Bureau of Economic Analysis www.bea.gov

National Bureau of Economic Research www.nber.org

Bureau of Labor and Statistics www.bls.gov

Office of Management and Budget, Congressional Budget Office www.whitehouse.gov

Internal Revenue Service

National Association of Manufacturers

www.economyincrisis.com

K. Shapiro and A. Aron-Dine. How Does this Recovery Measure Up? Center on Budget and Policy Priorities, Jan. 9, 2006. Jason Zweig. The Oracle Speaks. CNN Money, May 2, 2005.

Frank Shosak. Making Sense of Money Supply Data. Mises Institute, Dec. 17, 2003 www.mises.org.

John Carlson and Benjamin Keen. MZM: A Monetary Aggregate for the 1990s? Federal Reserve Bank of Cleveland Economic Review, 1996.

No Consensus on Stock Market Valuation. CBS News, July 27, 2005.

Jeffery Wenger. Share of Workers in 'Nonstandard' Jobs Declines: Latest Survey Shows a Narrowing—Yet Still Wide—Gap in Pay and Benefits. Economic Policy Institute, 2006.

Remarks Prepared for Delivery by U.S. Secretary of Labor Elaine Chao, 2005 States & nation Policy Summit Agenda, American Legislative Exchange Council, Marriot Wardman Park, Washington, D.C., Thursday, December 8, 2005.

Rex Nutting. Profits Surge to 40-year High. MarketWatch, March 30, 2006.

Asha Bangalore. The FOMC, Federal Funds Rate, and Unemployment Rate. Northern Trust Daily Global Commentary, April 24, 2006.

Paul Craig Roberts. Where Are the Jobs? Business Week, March 22, 2004.

Let the Dollar Drop. The Economist, May 8, 2005.

Flow of Funds Accounts of the United States. Flows and Outstandings, First Quarter 2006. Federal Reserve Statistical Release, Z1. Board of Governors of the Federal Reserve System, June 8, 2006.

David Walker. The Long-Term Fiscal Challenge and How the Public Perceives It. Government Accounting Office.

Yolanda K. Kodrzycki. Discouraged and Other Marginally Attached Workers: Evidence on Their Role in the Labor Market. New England Economic Review, May/June 2000.

OECD Factbook 2005: Economic, Environmental and Social Statistics. 2006.

Joel Friedman and Robert Greenstein. Administration Proposals to Hide Tax-Cut Costs. Center on Budget Policy and Priorities, February 14, 2006.

Jonathan Gruber. The Cost and Coverage Impact of the President's Health Insurance Budget Proposals. Center on Budget Policy and Priorities, February 15, 2006.

Aviva Aron-Dine and Joel Friedman. The Skewed Benefits of the Tax Cuts, 2007-2016: If the Tax Cuts Are Extended, Millionaires Will Receive More than $600 Billion Over the Next Decade. Center on Budget Policy and Priorities, February 23, 2006.

Robert Greenstein and Isaac Shapiro. Poverty Up, Incomes Down for Second Straight Year in 2002. Center on Budget Policy and Priorities, September 23, 2003.

Robert Parker. Will the Real Economy Please Stand Up? The National Association of Business Economists, 2003.

Paul A. Volcker. An Economy on Thin Ice. MoneyNews (adapted from a speech in February 2005 at an economic summit sponsored by Stanford Institute for Economic Policy Research, April 10, 2005.

Paul A. Volcker. The Most Dangerous Economy Ever. MoneyNews, April 14, 2005.

Jeanne Sahadi. House Passes Bankruptcy Bill. CNNMoney.com, April 14, 2005.

U.S. Senate Committee on Banking, Housing, and Urban Affairs; Hearing on "Risks of a Growing Balance of Payments Deficit." Prepared Testimony of Paul Volcker, Federal Reserve System, July 25, 2001.

Q&A About Bush's $2.77 Trillion Budget. Reuters, February 6, 2006.

Mark Felsenthal. Treasury Says Extending Tax Cuts Would Cost Blns. Reuters, February 6, 2006.

Mary Dalrymple. Bush's Budget Seeks to Preserve Tax Cuts. Associated Press, February 6, 2006.

25-year Record U.S. Inflation Surge Sparks Debate. Agence France Presse, October 15, 2005.

434

United States Senate Budget Committee. FY06 Budget Resolution: Challenges and Opportunities.

Isaac Shapiro and Joel Friedman. Tax Returns: A Comprehensive Assessment of the Bush Administration's Record on Cutting Taxes. Center on Budget and Policy Priorities, April 23, 2004.

Dorothy Rosenbaum. President's Budget Would Cut Food For Over 420,000 Low-Income Seniors. Center on Budget Policy and Priorities, February 14, 2006.

Richard Freeman and William Rogers III. The Weak Jobs Recovery: Whatever Happened to the Great American Jobs Machine? January 2005.

The American Jobs Creation Act of 2003. Summary of H.R. 2896 as Passed by Committee. Committee on Ways and Means, October 28, 2003.

www.bankruptcydata.com

U.S. Budget

United States Bureau of Census www.census.gov

U.S. Department of Commerce: Bureau of Economic Analysis www.bea.gov

National Bureau of Economic Research www.nber.org

Bureau of Labor and Statistics www.bls.gov

Office of Management and Budget, Congressional Budget Office www.whitehouse.gov

Friedman and Greenstein. Administration Proposes to Hide Tax-Cut Costs. Center on Budget and Policy Priorities, February 14, 2006.

J. Gruber. The Cost and Coverage Impact of the President's Health Insurance Budget Proposals. Center on Budget and Policy Priorities, February 15, 2006.

Aron-Dine and Friedman. The Skewed Benefits of the Tax Cuts, 2007-2016: If the Tax Cuts Are Extended, Millionaires Will Receive More than $600 Billion over the Next Decade. Center on Budget and Policy Priorities, February 23, 2006.

J. Horney, A. Sherman and S. Parrott. Program Cuts in the President's Budget: Cuts Grow Deeper Over Time and Will Hit States Hard. Center on Budget and Policy Priorities, February 23, 2006.

Friedman and Aron-Dine. Extending Expiring Tax Cuts and AMT Relief Would Cost $3.3 Trillion Through 2016. Center on Budget and Policy Priorities, February 6, 2006.

D. Rosenbaum. President's Budget Would Cut Food for Over 420,000 Low-Income Seniors. Center on Budget and Policy Priorities, February 14, 2006.

Park and Greenstein. Administration Defense of Health Savings Accounts Rests on Misleading Use of Statistics. Center on Budget and Policy Priorities, February 16, 2006.

Dave Koitz, Melissa Bobb and Ben Page. A 125-Year Picture of the Federal Government's Share of the Economy, 1950 to 2075. A series of issue summaries from the Congressional Budget Office, No. 1, July 3, 2002.

Judd Gregg. FY06 Budget Resolution: Challenges and Opportunities: Summary of 2006 Budget Resolution. The United States Senate Budget Committee.

Basics of the Budget Process: A Briefing Paper. U.S. House of Representatives Committee on the Budget, Majority Caucus, 107th Congress, Washington, DC, February 2001.

Committee on the Budget, U.S. House of Representatives, 107th Congress, Washington D.C. Basics of the Budget Process, A Briefing Paper. February 2001.

Jagadeesh Gokhale and Kent Smetters. Fiscal and Generational Imbalances: New Budget Measures for New Budget Priorities. 2003.

http://www.aaas.org/spp/rd/nih05h.pdf (2005 NIH budget)

http://www.aaas.org/spp/rd/nih06h.pdf (2006 NIH Budget)

http://www.whitehouse.gov/omb/budget/fy2006/nasa.html (NASA 2006 budget)

http://www.whitehouse.gov/omb/budget/fy2005/nasa.html (NASA 2005 budget)

Education, Technology & Research

Frank Bass, Nicole Dizon and Ben Feller. AP: States Omit Minorities' School Scores. Associated Press, April 17, 2006.

CIA World Factbook. www.cia.gov/cia/publications/factbook

National Science Foundation www.nsf.gov

National Institutes of Health www.nih.gov

National Science Board

www.economyincrisis.com

Emily Heffter and Nick Perry. Student Takes on College and Wins. The Seattle Times, February 26, 2006.

Michael Louie, Laila Weir, and Lisa White. State Oversight Lax for Vocational Schools. Sacramento Bee, Aug. 18, 2004.

Ronald Bovich. Lessons from a Scandal. American School Board, May 2006.

Bernard Wysocki. Once Collegial Research Schools Now Mean Business. Wall Street Journal, May 4, 2006.

Juliet Williams. Suit Filed Against High Schools' Exit Exam. Associated Press, February 9, 2006.

A Shortage of Scientists? Science in the News. www.vonews.com May 18, 2004.

William Symonds. America the Uneducated. BusinessWeek Online, November 21, 2005.

Peter Duesberg. Inventing the AIDS Virus. Regnery Publishing: Washington, D.C. 1996.

Baby Boomers

Walter Updegrave. Will Killing Social Security Kill the Markets as Well? CNN/Money, April 1, 2005.

Dean Baker. Dangerous Trends: The Growth of Debt in the U.S. Economy. Center for Economic Policy Research, September 7, 2004.

Jeff Sanford. Dying to Get Out: Will Baby Boomers Cashing Out Crash the Stock Market? Canadian Business Magazine, July 18-August 14, 2005.

Kyung-Mook Lim and David Weil. The Baby Boom and the Stock Market Boom. March 10, 2003.

Population and Migration: Demographic Trends OECD 2005 Factbook.

Alicia Munnell, Robert Hatch, and James Lee. Why is Life Expectancy So Low in the United States? Center for Retirement Research at Boston College, August 2004.

Household and Retirement Savings

Peter G. Peterson. Riding for a Fall. Foreign Affairs, September/October 2004.

The personal saving rate is available from the Bureau of Economic Analysis website. (3-14-2002). http://www.bea.doc.gov/bea/dn1.htm

Milt Marquis. What's Behind the Low U.S. Personal Saving Rate? Federal Reserve Bank of San Francisco, Economic Letter, 2002-09; March 29, 2002.

Personal Financial Education, FederalReserveEducation.org, 2003.

Dean Maki and Michael G. Palumbo. Disentangling the Wealth Effect: a Cohort Analysis of Household Saving in the 1990s. Finance and Economics Discussion Series, Board of Governors of the Federal Reserve System, Washington, DC, 2001-21, page 21.

Bureau of Economic Analysis, data on personal saving as a percentage of disposable personal income. http://www.bea.doc.gov/bea/dn1.htm

Karen Dynan and Dean Maki. Does Stock Market Wealth Matter for Consumption? Finance and Economics Discussion Series, Board of Governors of the Federal Reserve System, 2001-23. http://www.federalreserve.gov/pubs/feds/2001/200123/200123abs.html

Dean Maki and Michael G. Palumbo. Disentangling the Wealth Effect: a Cohort Analysis of Household Saving in the 1990s. Finance and Economics Discussion Series, Board of Governors of the Federal Reserve System, 2001-21. April 2001. http://www.federalreserve.gov/pubs/feds/2001/200121/200121abs.html

Milt Marquis. What's Behind the Low U.S. Personal Saving Rate? Federal Reserve Bank of San Francisco, Economic Letter, 2002-09; March 29, 2002. http://www.frbsf.org/publications/economics/letter/2002/el2002-09.html

James Poterba. Stock Market Wealth and Consumption. Journal of Economic Perspectives 14, no. 2 (Spring), pp. 99-118, 2000.

OECD Factbook 2005. Economic, Environmental and Social Statistics
Maki and Palumbo. Disentangling the Wealth Effect: A Cohort Analysis of Household Saving in the 1990s. Federal Reserve, April 2001.

Michael Ash. Who Got All of the 1990s Boom? Center for Popular Economics, July 2, 2002.

Gist and Figueiredo. Deeper in Debt: Trends Among Midlife and Older Americans. AARP Public Policy Institute, April 2002.

Golub-Sass, Francesca. Varani, Andrew. How Much is the Working-Age Population Saving? Center for Retirement Research at Boston College.

436

Alicia Munnell, Francesca Golub-Sass, and Andrew Varani. How Much Are Workers Saving? Center for Retirement Research at Boston College, October 2005, Number 34.

Barry Bosworth and Lisa Bell. The Decline in Household Savings: What Can We Learn From Survey Data? Center for Retirement Research at Boston College, December 2005.

James Poterba. Population Aging and Financial Markets. MIT and NBER, August 27, 2004.

Marco Terrones and Roberto Cardarelli. Global Imbalances: A Saving and Investment Perspective.

Beverly Goldberg. Inequality, Work, and Retirement: A Downward Spiral. The Century Foundation, August 1, 2006.

Beverly Goldberg. Working Retired: An Idea Whose Time May Never Come. The Century Foundation, April 19, 2006.

Chris Isodore. The Zero-savings Problem. CNNMoney, August 3, 2005.

Outsourcing, Free Trade, and American Workers

World Trade Organization http://www.wto.org/index.htm, http://www.wto.org/English/docs_e/legal_e/legal_e.htm, http://www.wto.org/English/docs_e/legal_e/itadec_e.doc

WTO Rules Cotton Subsidies Unfair. Rural News, April 28, 2004.

EU Scores a Steel Victory Over the US. BBC News, November 10, 2003.

General Agreement on Tariffs and Trade http://www.ciesin.org/TG/PI/TRADE/gatt.html, http://www.wto.org/English/docs_e/legal_e/gatt47_01_e.htm, http://gatt.stanford.edu/page/home

North American Free Trade Agreement http://www.fas.usda.gov/itp/Policy/NAFTA/nafta.html, http://www.mac.doc.gov/nafta, http://www-tech.mit.edu/Bulletins/nafta.html

Paul Craig Roberts. The Harsh Truth About Outsourcing. BusinessWeek, March 22, 2004.

Bob McTeer and Robert L. Formaini. David Ricardo: Theory of Free International Trade. Economic Insights. Volume 9, Number 2. Federal Reserve Bank of Dallas.

John Aldrich. The Discovery of Comparative Advantage. Journal of the History of Economic Thought, Volume 26, Number 3, September 2004.

Bob Powell. A Systems Thinking Perspective on Manufacturing and Trade Policy. Continuous Improvement Associates, December 24, 2003.

J. Haskel, S. Pereira and M. Slaughter. Does Inward Foreign Direct Investment Boost the Productivity of Domestic Firms? NBER Working Papers. 8724, 2002.

Eaton and Kortum. International Technology Diffusion: Theory and Measurement. International Economic Review, August 1999, Vol. 40, No. 3, 537-569.

W. Keller. Geographic Localization of International Technology Diffusion. American Economic Review, March 2002, Vol. 92, No. 1, 120-142.

Coe and Helpman. International R&D Spillovers. European Economic Review, Vol. 39, 1995, 859-887.

Aitken and Harrison. Do Domestic Firms Benefit from Direct Foreign Investment? Evidence from Venezuela. American Economic Review, 1999.

R. Dornbusch, S. Fischer and P. Samuelson. Comparative Advantage, Trade, and Payments in a Ricardian Model with a Continuum of Goods. AER, 1977.

P. Krugman. .Increasing Returns, Monopolistic Competition, and International Trade. JIE, 1979.

Keller, W. and S. Yeaple, Multinational Enterprises, International Trade and Productivity Growth: firm-level evidence from the US. NBER Working Paper No. 9504, 2003.

B. Javorcik. Does Foreign Direct Investment Increase the Productivity of Domestic Firms? In search of spillovers through backward linkages. American Economic Review, 2004.

John Williams. Analysis Behind and Beyond Government Statistics. GRA Archives, October 6, 2004.

Robert Morley. The Death of American Manufacturing. TheTrumpet.com, February 2006.

Kate Randall. US Minimum Wage Remains at $5.15 an Hour: Failed Republican Bill Tied Increase to Inheritance Tax Cuts. World Socialist Website, August 2006 www.wsws.org.

Job Openings and Labor Turnover: November 2005. Bureau of Labor Statistics. United States Department of Labor, January 10, 2006.

Rising Above the Gathering Storm: Energizing and Employing America for a Brighter Future. A Disturbing Mosaic. February 2006.

Craig Barrett. America Should Open Its Doors Wide to Foreign Talent. The Financial Times, Feb. 1, 2006.

Vivek Wadhwa. About That Engineering Gap. BusinessWeek Online, December 13, 2005.

Timothy Aeppel. An Inflation Debate Brews Over Intangibles at the Mall. Wall Street Journal, May 9, 2005.

Private Healthcare

Health System Tweaks Proposed. USA Today, November 19, 2002.

Doctors Find Broken System on Both Sides of the Bed. USA Today, December 25, 2002.

More Patients Get Stuck With the Bills. USA Today, April 30, 2002.

Medical Bills Play Big Role in Bankruptcies. USA Today, April 25, 2000.

Medical Costs Can Add Up To Some Healthy Deduction. USA Today, February 11, 2002.

States Reduce Services, Drop Many From Medicaid Rolls. USA Today, March 12, 2003.

Help Both Uninsured And Seniors. USA Today, February 5, 2003.

Why People File for Bankruptcy Study. USA Today, July 10, 1997.

Top Ten Consumer Needs For The Year 2000. Consumer Union Press Release, Dec. 28, 1999.

Medical Bills Are A Large Factor in Bankruptcy Filings. The Washington Post, April 25, 2000.

The U.S. Spends More Money On Healthcare Than Any Other Country. Consumer Reports, Sept. 2000.

Half of HMOs Lost Money in 1999. USA Today, September 8, 2000.

U.S. Healthcare System Gets a Critical Diagnosis. USA Today, October 16, 2000.

Medical Costs Are Rising and Insurance Premiums Could Jump As High as 20%. USA Today, Dec. 8, 2000.

Report: Health System Broken. USA Today, March 2, 2001.

Insurers' Ability to Manage, Deny Medical Care Will Be Clipped. The Kiplinger Letter, August 3, 2001.

Health Benefits for Retirees Continue Decline. USA Today, August 13, 2001.

Prescriptions Up as Drug Makers Spend More on Ads. USA Today, August 13, 2001.

Insurance Caps Leave Some Struggling To Pay. USA Today, August 13, 2001.

Healthy Individuals Often Turned Down for Coverage. USA Today, August 13, 2001.

Retiree Health Benefits Not Like the Good Old Days. Dallas Morning News, August 19, 2001.

Health Insurance Premiums, Economic Slowdown Listed as Factors in Declining Coverage. Dallas Morning News, August 19, 2000.

Health Insurance Prices To Soar. USA Today, August 27, 2001.

Millions of Americans Lack Health Insurance. USA Today, October 11, 2001.

More HMOs to Drop Patients. USA Today, October 25, 2001.

Prescription Drug Costs Rise by $21 Billion. USA Today, October 25, 2001.

U.S. Study, Medical Bills Main Culprit in Bankruptcies. Common Dreams News Center, Nov. 15, 2001.

Health Care Spending Rose 6.9% In 2000. USA Today, January 7, 2002.

Healthcare Crisis in America. United Service Association For Health Care, 2003.

Christopher Snowbeck. Medical Bills Figure in Personal Bankruptcy. Pittsburg Post-Gazette, Aug. 06 2004.

Christopher Snowbeck. Unisured Waiting in Line. Pittsburg Post-Gazette, July 16, 2004.

Christopher Snowbeck. Foregoing Health Insurance Can Be a Costly Gamble. Pittsburg Post-Gazette, February 22, 2004.

Christopher Snowbeck. How Those With the Least are Charged the Most. Pittsburg Post-Gazette, March 24, 2004.
Why Congress Should Subsidize Health Insurance Coverage for Laid Off Workers. Consumers Union Press Release, October 22, 2001.

http://www.ufcw.org/working_america/august_2003/health_care_stats.cfm

C. DeNavas-Walt, B. Proctor, and R. J. Mills. Income, Poverty, and Health Insurance Coverage in the United States: 2003. U.S. Census Bureau, August 2004.

Number of Americans Without Health Insurance Reaches Highest Level on Record. Center on Budget and Policy Priorities, August 26 2004.

The Henry J. Kaiser Family Foundation. The Uninsured: A Primer, Key Facts About Americans without Health Insurance, November 10, 2004.

U.S. Department of Labor, Bureau of Labor Statistics. December 22, 2005. www.bls.gov/oco/cg/cgs035.htm

The Henry J. Kaiser Family Foundation. Access to Care for the Uninsured: An Update, September 29, 2003.

The Henry J. Kaiser Family Foundation. Employee Health Benefits: 2004 Annual Survey, September 9, 2004. http://www.kff.org/insurance/7148/index.cfm

The Henry J. Kaiser Family Foundation. The Uninsured: A Primer, Key Facts About Americans Without Health Insurance. November 10, 2004.

The Henry J. Kaiser Family Foundation. Health Care Worries in Context with Other Worries. Oct 4, 2004.

Health Care Expectations: Future Strategy and Direction 2005. Hewitt Associates LLC, November 17, 2004.

M. Dalrymple. Senators Seek Tax Credit for Unemployed. Associated Press, October 9, 2003.

Institute of Medicine. Insuring America's Health - Principles and Recommendations. The National Academies Press, 2004.

Institute of Medicine. Care Without Coverage - Too Little, Too Late. The National Academies Press, 2002.

The Urban Institute. Key Findings from the 2002 National Health Interview Survey, August 9, 2004.

How Many People Lack Health Insurance and For How Long? Congressional Budget Office, May 12, 2003.

Employee Benefit Research Institute, "Sources of Health Insurance and Characteristics of the Uninsured: Analysis of the March 2004 Current Population Survey." Issue Brief No. 276, December 2004.

J. Smith. Healthy Bodies and Thick Wallets: The Dual Relation Between Health And Economic Status. Journal of Economic Perspectives 13(2): 145-166.

Institute of Medicine. Hidden Costs, Values Lost: Uninsurance in America. The National Academies Press, June 17, 2003.

Smith, Cowan, Sensenig and Catlin. Health Spending Growth Slows in 2003. Health Affairs 24:1 (2005): 185-194.

Centers for Medicare and Medicaid Services, Office of the Actuary, National Health Statistics Group; and U.S. Department of Commerce, Bureau of Economic Analysis and Bureau of the Census. 2003. http://www.cms.hhs.gov/statistics/nhe/projections-2003/t2.asp

California Health Care Foundation. Health Care Costs 101. March 2005.

R. Pear. U.S. Health Care Spending Reaches All-Time High: 15% of GDP. The New York Times, January 3, 2004.

Simmons and Goldberg. Charting the Cost of Inaction. National Coalition on Health Care, May 2003.

Michael Chernew. Rising Health Care Costs and the Decline in Insurance Coverage. Economic Research Initiative on the Uninsured, ERIU Working Paper, September 8, 2002.

J. Appleby. More Insured Workers Unable to Pay Medical Bills. USA Today, April 29, 2005.

The Commonwealth Fund. Wages, Health Benefits, and Workers' Health. Issue Brief, October 2004.

Committee on the Consequences of Uninsurance. Health Insurance is a Family Matter. Washington, D.C.: The National Academies Press, 2002.

Prescription Drug Trends 2004. The Henry J. Kaiser Family Foundation, October 25, 2004.

Cost Sharing Cuts Employers' Drug Spending but Employees Don't Get the Savings. RAND, 2002.
Trends in the Health of Americans. National Center for Health Statistics. Hyattsville, Maryland. 2004.

Ahman and Gold. Average Out-of-Pocket Health Care Costs for Medicare and Choice Enrollees Increase 10 Percent in 2003. The Commonwealth Fund, August 2003.

Marilyn Moon. Growth in Medical Spending: What Will Beneficiaries Pay? The Commonwealth Fund, May 1999.

Steve Sellery. The Uninsured Healthcare Crisis in America. Econ-Atrocity Bulletin, July 6, 2005.

John Iglehart. The Challenges Facing Private Health Insurance. Health Affairs, November/December 2004. http://content.healthaffairs.org/cgi/content/extract/23/6/9

Sarah Reber and Laura Tyson. Rising Health Insurance Costs Slow Job Growth and Reduce Wages and Job Quality. Unpublished paper, quoted in http://www.csls.ca/events/nylabor/freeman_rodgers.pdf Aug 19, 2004.

Gary. Growing Health Care Concerns Fuel Cautious Support for Change. ABC News, October 20, 2004.

Uninsurance Facts and Figures. The Institute of Medicine, drawn from Coverage Matters, 2001; Insuring America's Health, 2004.

Trends in U.S. Health Coverage, 2001-2003. Center for Studying Health System Change, August 2004.

Families USA, One in Three: Non-Elderly Americans Without Health Insurance. 2002-2003.

Health Insurance Coverage in America, 2003 Data Update. The Henry J. Kaiser Family Foundation. November 2004.

Tiffany Ray. Law Changes Health-Care Bankruptcies. Birmingham Business Journal, Nov. 11, 2005.

The Effects of Congressional Proposals on Prescription Drug Costs for Medicare Beneficiaries. Department of Health and Human Services, Office of the Assistant Secretary for Public Affairs. June 19, 2002.

Assessment of Approaches to Evaluating Telemedicine. Prepared by the Lewin Group for the office of the Assistant Secretary for Planning and Evaluation, Department of Health and Human Services, December 2000.

Cathi Callahan and James Mays. Working Paper: Estimating the Number of Individuals in the United States Without Health Insurance. Prepared for the Office of the Assistant Secretary for Planning and Evaluation, Department of Health and Human Services, March 31, 2005.

Western Europe, Not the US, Ranks as World's Healthiest Region. Reuters London, March 25, 2002.

Rising Healthcare Costs Making Employers and Employees Sick. PricewaterCoopers, Trendsetter Barometer, Apr 1, 2004.

Employer Health Benefits 2003 Annual Survey. The Henry J. Kaiser Family Foundation.

U.S. Census Bureau.

Medical Cost Reference Guide. BlueCross BlueShield, 2002.

J. Cohen. Design and methods of the Medical Expenditure Panel Survey Household Component. Rockville (MD): Agency for Health Care Policy and Research; 1997. MEPS Methodology Report No. 1. AHCPR Pub. No. 97-0026.

S. Cohen. Sample design of the 1996 Medical Expenditure Panel Survey Household Component. Rockville (MD): Agency for Health Care Policy and Research; 1997. MEPS Methodology Report No. 2 AHCPR Pub. No. 97-0027.

Marcia Angell. The Truth About Drug Companies: How They Deceive Us and What to Do About It. Random House: New York. 2004.

Bernadette Tansey. Huge penalty in drug fraud Pfizer settles felony case in Neurontin off-label promotion. SF Gate, May 14, 2004.

Largest Health Care Fraud Case in U.S. History Settled HCA Investigation Nets Record Total pf $1.7 Billion. U.S. Department of Justice. June 26, 2003.

U.S. Intervenes in $175 Million Drug Fraud Suit Against Abbott Labs. Thompson West. Find Law, May 2006.

Melody Peterson. Bayer Agrees to Pay U.S. $257 Million in Drug Fraud. New York Times, April 2003.

Malcolm Sparrow. License to Steal: Why Fraud Plagues America's Health Care System. Westview Press, 1996.

Albany Oncologists to Repay Medicaid $1.2 Million: Physicians Group Overbilled for Drugs Dispensed to Patients. New York Attorney General Press Release, December 5, 2005.

Blount County Couple Arrested for TennCare Fraud. Department of Finance and Administration, Tennessee State Government Office, April 6, 2006.

Sheila Berke. Doctor convicted of health-care fraud. The Tennessean, April 12, 2005.

Doctor convicted in AIDS clinic fraud scheme. South Florida Business Journal, June 2, 2006.

Rx for Fraud. Forbes, June 20, 2005.

Health Care Compliance Association. http://www.hcca-info.org

Mathias Consulting

U.S. Department of Justice

Dangerous Prescription. Frontline, PBS.

Mark Sue Coleman. A Report on the Institute of Medicine Committee on Uninsurance. Keynote Address to the "Voices of Detroit Initiative" Annual Meeting, May 19, 2003.

Theresa Agovino. Young Adults Lacking Health Insurance. Associated Press, May 24, 2005.

Joanne Laurier. 82 Million Americans Lacked Health Insurance in 2002-2003. World Socialist Website, June 23, 2004.

The U.S. Health Care System: Best in the World, or Just the Most Expensive? Bureau of Education, U. of Maine, 2001.

Jessica Fraser. Statistics Prove Prescription Drugs Are 16,400% More Deadly Than Terrorists. News Target, July 5, 2005.

Doctors Are the Third Leading Cause of Death in the US, Causing 250,000 Deaths Every Year. Journal of the American Medical Association, July 26, 2000; 284(4) 483-5.

Susan Starr Sered and Rushika Fernandopulle. Uninsured in America: Life and Death in the Land of Opportunity. The University of California Press, 2005.

Matthew Harper and Peter Kang. The World's Ten Best-Selling Drugs. Forbes, March 22, 2006.

Leif Wellington Haase. A New Deal For Health: How to Cover Everyone and Get Medical Costs Under Control. The Century Foundation. June 1, 2005.

Insuring America's Health: Principles and Recommendations. The National Academy of Sciences, 2004.

Medicaid

Carolyn Lochhead. Speeches Ignore Impending U.S. Debt Disaster. SF Chronicle, September 12, 2004.

National Coalition on Health Care.

Centers for Medicare and Medicaid Services (CMS).

Leighton Ku and Bethany Kessler. The Number and Cost of Immigration on Medicaid: National and State Estimates. The Urban Institute, December 16, 1997.

Kaiser Commission on Medicaid and the Uninsured

Medicare

Andrew Rettenmaier and Thomas Saving. With an Eye to the Future. Texas A&M University, Private Enterprise Research Center. Perspective on Policy, May 2004.

Liqun Liu, Andrew Rettenmaier, and Thomas Saving. A Debt is a Debt. Texas A&M University, Private Enterprise Research Center. Perspective on Policy, September 2002.

Andrew Rettenmaier and Thomas Saving. Just What the Doctor Ordered? Texas A&M University, Private Enterprise Research Center. Perspective on Policy, August 2002.

Dennis Cauchon and John Waggoner. The Looming National Benefit Crisis. USA Today, Oct 3, 2004.

Centers for Medicare and Medicaid Services (CMS).

Medicare.org

U.S. Department of Health and Human Services.

Cathi Callahan and James Mays. Estimating the Number of Individuals in the United States Without Health Insurance. Working Paper. Prepared for the Office of the Assistant Secretary for Planning and Evaluation, Department of Health and Human Services, March 31, 2005.

The Effects of Congressional Proposals on Prescription Drug Costs for Medicare Beneficiaries. Department of Health and Human Services. Office of the Assistant Secretary for Public Affairs, June 19, 2002.

Medicare Premiums Hike. LA Times, September 7, 2004.

D.R. Francis. Medicare Reform Carries Huge Fiscal Toll. Christian Science Monitor, October 17, 2003.

Medicare HMOs Cutting Coverage, Increasing Rates. USA Today, November 23, 2001.

Paul Van de Water and Joni Lavery. Medicare Finances: Findings of the 2006 Trustees Report. National Academy of Social Insurance, No.13, May 2006.

Medicare Sourcebook. National Academy of Social Insurance. www.nasi.org

Statistical data on Poverty, Medicare and Social Security. National Committee to Preserve Social Security and Medicare (NCPSSM). www.ncpssm.org

The Privatization of Medicare. National Committee to Preserve Social Security and Medicare (NCPSSM), June 2006.

The Future of Social Security and Medicare: Demographics vs the Cost of Health Care. National Committee to Preserve Social Security and Medicare (NCPSSM), May 2006.

Martin Crutsinger. Social Security Financial Health Declining. Associated Press, May 2, 2006.

Leif Wellington Haase. Taking Stock in the Medicare Drug Benefit. The Century Foundation, May 18, 2006.

Leif Wellington Haase. The Senate's Medicare Drug Bill: Where It Works, Where It Falls Short. The Century Foundation, June 19, 2003.

Shannon Jones and Barry Grey. Medicare Bill Marks Major Step in Destruction of Government Health Plan for U.S. Seniors. World Socialist Website, November 26, 2003.

Ricardo Alonzo-Zaldivar and Joanna Neuman. Give and Take in New Rules for New Year. LA Times, January 1, 2006.

Medicare Premiums Jumps 13.5%. CBS/Associated Press, October 16, 2003.

Scott Burns. Costs of Medicare Snowball. Dallas Morning News, April 9, 2005.

Increase in Medicare Payments to Doctors This Year Will Raise Beneficiaries' Part B Premiums More Than Expected Next Year, Officials Say. Medilexicon.com, April 2, 2005.

Food Industry Additives and Morbidity

Russell L. Blaylock, MD. Excitotoxins: The Taste that Kills. Health Press, 1995.

B. Yastag. Obesity is Now on Everyone's Plate. *JAMA*. 291 (10): 1186-1188, March 10, 2004.

S.G Bouret, S.J. Draper, and R.B. Simley. Trophic Action of Leptin on Hypothalamus Neurons that Regulate Feeding. Science. 2; 304 (5667), 108-110, April, 2, 2004.

B. Frieder and V. E. Grimm. Prenatal Monosodium Glutamate (MSG) Treatment Given Through the Mother's Diet Causes Behavioral Deficits in Rat Offspring. Intern J Neurosci. 23: 117-126, 1984.

Centers for Disease Control, National Center for Chronic Disease Prevention and Health Promotion. Physical Activity and Good Nutrition: Essential Elements to Prevent Chronic Diseases and Obesity 2003. Nutr Clin Care. 6(3):135-8. Review.,Oct - Dec, 2003.

J.W. Olney. Brain Lesions, Obesity, and Other Disturbances in Mice Treated with Monosodium Glutamate. Science. 164(880):719-21, May 9, 1969.

J.W. Olney and O.L Ho. Brain Damage in Infant Mice Following Oral Intake of Glutamate, Aspartate, or Cysteine. Nature (Lond). 227: 609-611, 1970.

Edwin Park and Robert Greenstein. Administration Defense of Health Savings Accounts Rests on Misleading Use of Statistics. Center on Budget Policy and Priorities, February 16, 2006.

FDA and Big Pharma and Healthcare Fraud

PBS Frontline Feature: Dangerous Prescription, 2005.

Marcia Angell. Research for Sale. The New England Journal of Medicine, May 18, 2000; 342.

Thomas Bodenheimer. Uneasy Alliance—Clinical Investigators and the Pharmaceutical Industry. The New England Journal of Medicine, May 18, 2000; 342, No. 20.

Brian Vaszily. Spin and the Pharmaceutical Industry: Proudly Protecting Profits by Scaring You. www.mercola.com July 26, 2003.

Bernadette Tansey. Huge Penalty in Drug Fraud Pfizer Settles Felony Case in Neurotonin Off-label Promotion. SFGate.com May 14, 2004.

Most Media Coverage of Drugs Highly Biased. June 10, 2000. www.mercola.com

U.S. Intervenes in $175M Drug Fraud Suit Against Abbott Labs. FindLaw, June 14, 2006.

Melody Peterson. "Bayer Agrees to Pay U.S. $257 Million In Drug Fraud." The New York Times, April 17, 2003.

Blount County Couple Arrested for TennCare Fraud." WATE Channel 6. April 7, 2006.

Robin Mathias. Local Doctor Convicted on Healthcare Fraud Charges. NewsNet5.com, January 13, 2006.

Robin Mathias. Pharmacist Arrested for Fraud. Jan. 6, 2006. http://mathiasconsulting.com/cases/prescriptions

Robin Mathias. Albany Oncologists to Repay Medicaid $1.2 Million. December 7, 2005. http://mathiasconsulting.com/cases/prescriptions

Robin Mathias. Pharmacy Owner Receives Jail in Medicaid Fraud. December 7, 2005. http://mathiasconsulting.com/cases/prescriptions

John Dorschiner. Four Arrested in AIDS Drug Scam. Herald.com, December 6, 2005.

Flu Shot Fraud Indictment in Texas. Press Release: US Department of Justice, US Attorney, Southern District, Chuck Rosenberg, November 17, 2005.

Texas Conviction of Physical Therapist. Press Release: US Department of Justice, US Attorney, Southern District, Chuck Rosenberg, November 17, 2005.

Waging War on Prescription Drug Abuse: New Medco Analysis Reveals Prescription Drug Abusers Engage in Doctor Shopping and Script. PRNewswire-FirstCall, September 29, 2005.

Computers Blamed for Billing Woes. Republican American, January 9, 2005.

TX Attorney Sues Fraudulent Mail-order Prescription Drug Service. May 31, 2005. http://mathiasconsulting.com/cases/prescriptions

MyRxForLess Owners Guilty of Importing Phony Pharmaceuticals from Mexico. January 28, 2005. http://mathiasconsulting.com/cases/prescriptions

CT Pediatricians Settle in Operation Free Shot. Jan. 3, 2005. http://mathiasconsulting.com/cases/prescriptions

Another Lupron Guilty Plea. November 22, 2004. http://mathiasconsulting.com/cases/prescriptions

Maine Urologist Receives Light Sentence for Lupron Scam. Oct 7, 2004. http://mathiasconsulting.com/cases/prescriptions

$4.7 Million Injectable Drug Fraud in Florida. October 7, 2004. http://mathiasconsulting.com/cases/prescriptions

Operation Free Shot. September 5, 2004. http://mathiasconsulting.com/cases/prescriptions

Doctor Indicted in Chemotherapy Scam. July 7, 2004. http://mathiasconsulting.com/cases/prescriptions

Serostim Fraud Ring Busted in Florida. Feb. 24, 2004. http://mathiasconsulting.com/cases/prescriptions

James Hood. Pharmacy Benefit Managers Scrutinized. Consumer Affairs. October 28, 2004.

Sheila Burke. Doctor Convicted of Health-care Fraud. Tennessean.com, December 13, 2005.

Doctor Convicted in AIDS Clinic Fraud Scheme. South Florida Business Journal, June 2, 2006.

Former Hospital Secretary Sentenced. Press Release, February 9, 2006.

Doctor Sentenced. Press Release, June 16, 2006. http://www.usdoj.gov/usao/txs/

Health Center Guilty of Fraud. Press Release, June 13, 2006.

Pensions and Retirement

Marcy Gordon. Pension Agency Reports $22.3 B Shortfall. Associated Press, November 15, 2005.

Andrew Bridges. Nearly One in 10 Pension Plans Said Frozen. Associated Press, December 21, 2005.

Nanette Byrnes. Rising Tensions Over Pensions. BusinessWeek, May 16, 2005.

Susan Cornwell. Delphi Senn Moving Pensions to US Agency. Reuters, October 10, 2005.

Matt Krantz. Stocks Rebound, But Pensions Haven't. USA Today. July 17, 2005.

Corporate America's Legacy Costs: Now for the Reckoning. The Economist, Oct. 13, 2005.

Pension Plan Funding Under Social Security. Forbes, June 10, 2005.

Jonathan Elsberg. Underfunded Pensions and Perverse Incentives. Center for Popular Economics, August 17, 2005.

PBGC Releases Fiscal Year 2004 Financial Results. PBGC No. 05-10. PBGC Public Affairs, Nov. 15, 2004.

Pension Benefit Guaranty Corporation Performance and Accountability Report. Fiscal Year 2004, Nov. 15, 2004.

Yvonne Sin. Minimum Pension Guarantees. The World Bank, Washington. Presented at the Russian Federation, Moscow, 3-5 July 2003.

Jim Abrams. Pensions Moving Slowly in Congress. The Associated Press, October 23, 2005.

Albert Crenshaw. Panel Votes for Higher Pension Insurance Fees. The Washington Post, Oct. 27, 2005.

David John. America's Pensions: The Next Saving and Loan Crisis? Testimony Before the Select Committee on Aging, United States Senate. The Heritage Foundation, October 14, 2003.

Stephen McCourt. Defined Benefit and Defined Contribution Plans: A History, Market Overview, and Comparative Analysis. Benefits Compensation Digest. Vol. 43, No.2 February 2006.

U.S. Chamber of Commerce

David John. Treasury Department Proposal for Defined Benefits Includes Important Reforms. The Heritage Foundation, August 7, 2003.

Lawrence Bader. Pension Deficits: An Unnecessary Evil. Financial Analysts Journal, 2004.

Roger Lowenstein. The End of Pensions. New York Times, 2006.

Craig Smith. Retired Seniors Find Little Security. Pittsburg Tribune-Review, June 5, 2006.

David Francis. Tension Over Pensions: Can They Be Saved? Christian Science Monitor, Jan. 23, 2006.

Richard Johnson, Gordon Mermin, and Cori Uccello. How Secure are Retirement Nest Eggs. Center for Retirement Research, Boston College. Number 45. April 2006.

Alicia Munnell, Francesca Golub-Sass, Mauricio Soto and Francis Vitagliano. Why are Healthy Employers Freezing Their Pensions? Center for Retirement Research, Boston College. Number 44. Mar. 2006.

Alicia Munnell, Anthony Webb and Luke Delorme. A New National Retirement Risk Index. Center for Retirement Research, Boston College. Number 48. June 2006.

Alicia Munnell and Annika Sunden. 401(k) Plans Are Still Coming Up Short. Center for Retirement Research, Boston College. Number 43. March 2006.

Alicia Munnell. A Bird's Eye View of the Social Security Debate. Center for Retirement Research at Boston College. Issue in Brief Number 25 December 2004.

Alicia Munnell, Robert Hatch, and James Lee. Why is the Life Expectancy So Low in the United States? Center for Retirement Research at Boston College. Number 21. August 2004,.

Alicia Munnell. Population Aging: It's Not Just the Baby Boom. Center for Retirement Research at Boston College. An Issue in Brief. Number 16. April 2004.

Alicia Munnell, Annika Sunden and Elizabeth Lidstone. How Important Are Private Pensions? Center for Retirement Research at Boston College. An Issue in Brief. Number 8, February 2002.

Gary Burless and Joseph Quinn. Is Working Longer the Answer for an Aging Workforce? Center for Retirement Research at Boston College. An Issue in Brief. Number 11, December 2002.

Courtney Coile and Kevin Milligan. How Portfolios Evolve After Retirement: The Effect of Health Shocks. Center for Retirement Research at Boston College, December 2005.

Barbara Butrica, Joshua Goldwyn, and Richard Johnson. Understanding Expenditure Patterns in Retirement. Center for Retirement Research at Boston College, January 2005.

Mauricio Soto. Will Baby Boomers Drown in Debt? Center for Retirement Research at Boston College. Number 15. March 2005.

Francesca Golub-Sass and Andrew Varani. How Much Are Workers Saving? Center for Retirement Research at Boston College. Issue in Brief Number 34 October 2005.

Richard Johnson, Gordon Mermin and Cori Uccello. How Secure Are Our Nest Eggs? Center for Retirement Research at Boston College, Number 45. April 2006.

Courtney Coile. Milligan, Kevin. How Portfolios Evolve After Retirement: The Effect of Health Shocks. Center for Retirement Research at Boston College, October 2005.

Barry Bosworth and Lisa Bell. The Decline in Household Saving: What Can We Learn From Survey Data. Center for Retirement Research at Boston College, October 2005.

Richard Johnson, Gordon Mermin and Cori Uccello. When the Nest Egg Cracks: Financial Consequences of Health Problems, Marital Status Changes and Job Layoffs at Older Ages. Center for Retirement Research at Boston College, October 2005.

James Lee. Changing 401(k) Defaults on Cashing Out: Another Step in the Right Direction. Center for Retirement Research at Boston College. Just the Facts Number 12, September 2004.

Robert Triest and Natalia Jivan. How Do Pensions Affect Actual and Expected Retirement Ages? Center for Retirement Research at Boston College. Working Paper. November 2004.

Cori Uccello. Are Americans Saving Enough for Retirement? Center for Retirement Research at Boston College, Number 7, July 2001.

Mike Orszag, The Shortcomings of 401(k) Plans. European Pensions and Investment News.

Report of the Working Group on Defined Benefit Plan Funding And Discount Rate Issues. U.S. Department of Labor, Employee Benefits Security Administration, February 14, 2006. www.dol.gov/ebsa

Mark Glickman and Charles Jeszeck. PBGC and the Current Challenges Facing the U.S. Defined Benefit Pension System. U.S. Government Accountability Office, April 4, 2005.

An Analysis of Frozen Defined Benefit Plans. Pension Benefit Guaranty Corporation, December 21, 2005.

August Cole. U.S. Pension Peril Grows with Bankruptcies. MarketWatch, June 20, 2006.

August Cole. Rising Rates Ease Pressure on Pension Plans. MarketWatch, June 22, 2006.

William Watts. Legislation Won't Save Defined Benefit Pensions. MarketWatch, June 22, 2006.

Andrea Coombes. Dis-United in Outlook for Retirement. MarketWatch, June 20, 2006.

Andrea Coombes. Retirement Outlook? Poor. MarketWatch, June 6, 2006.

Milliman 2006 Pension Study

Bush Signs Massive Pension Overhaul. Associated Press, August 17, 2006.

Sue Kirchhoff. Pension Act: Does It Add to Instability? USA Today, August 9, 2006.

Ellen Hoffman. Is Your Pension Plan Retiring Before You? BusinessWeek Online, April 21, 2006.

Pension Publications Fact Sheets. Pension Rights Center. www.pensionrights.org

Tom Shean. Even Healthy Companies Are Killing Pension Plans. The Virginian-Piloy, June 18, 2006.

Daniel Gross. The Big Freeze. American Association of Retired Persons, March 2006.

Mary Williams Walsh. I.B.M. to Freeze Pension Plans to Trim Costs. New York Times, Jan. 6, 2006.

Geoffrey Colvin. The End of a Dream. Fortune, June 22, 2006.

Ellen Schultz, Charles Forelle and Theo Francis. Forecast: More Pension Freezes on the Way. WSJ.com.

Mary Williams Walsh. More Companies Ending Promises for Retirement. New York Times, Jan 9, 2006.

Adam Geller. Even Healthy Companies Are Freezing Pensions. Associated Press, December 10, 2005.

Interview with Alicia Munnell. Retirement's Risky for Many Americans. Boston Globe, July 2, 2006.

The Shortcomings of 401(k) Plans. European Pensions and Investment News, June 21, 2004.

David Francis. Tension Over Pensions: Can They Be Saved? The Christian Science Monitor, Jan 23, 2006.

Lawrence Thompson. The Predictability of Retirement Income. National Academy of Social Insurance. Social Security Brief No.5.

Clifford Asness. Fight the Fed Model: The Relationship Between Stock Market Yields, Bond Market Yields, and Future Returns. AQR Capital Management, LCC, December 2002.

Pension Benefit Guarantee Corporation www.pbgc.gov

Charles R. Morris. Apart at the Seams: The Collapse of Private Pension and Health Care Protections. A Century Foundation Report, 2006.

Mark Glickman and Charles Jeszeck. PBGC and the Current Challenges Facing the U.S. Defined Benefit Pension System. U.S. Government Accountability Office, April 4, 2005.

An Analysis of Frozen Defined Benefit Plans. PBGC, December 21, 2005.

Report of the Working Group on Defined Benefit Plan Funding And Discount Rate Issues. Employee Benefits Security Administration. U.S. Department of Labor, February 14, 2006.

Susan Cornwell. Airlines Could Get More Relief from Pension Bill. Reuters, November 10, 2005.

Joanna Lahey. Do Older Workers Face Discrimination? Center for Retirement Research at Boston College. An Issue in Brief. Number 33, July 2005.

Eileen Powell. Workers Have Retirement Overconfidence Associated Press, April 4, 2006.

Brandt Urban. GM Earnings Announcements Knocks $2.9 Billion from Market Cap. The Monroe Street Journal, March 21, 2005.

Can You Afford to Retire? PBS Frontline Feature, 2006.

Steven Kandarian, Executive Director, Pension Benefit Guaranty Corporation. Government Affairs Subcommittee on Financial Management, The Budget, and International Security. September 15, 2003.

David John. Treasury Department Proposal for Defined Benefits Includes Important Reforms. The Heritage Foundation, August 7, 2003.

Caroline Daniel and Stephanie Kirchgaessner. US Pension Body Reform Key to Savings. Financial Times. Feb. 6, 2006.

Real Estate Bubble

Board of Governors of the Federal Reserve System www.federalreserve.gov

Federal Reserve Bank of New York www.ny.frb.org

Federal Reserve Bank of St. Louis www.stlouisfed.org

Federal Reserve Bank of San Francisco www.frbsf.org

United States Bureau of Census www.census.gov

U.S. Department of Commerce: Bureau of Economic Analysis www.bea.gov

National Bureau of Economic Research www.nber.org

Bureau of Labor and Statistics www.bls.gov

Office of Management and Budget, Congressional Budget Office www.whitehouse.gov

National Home Equity Mortgage Association www.nhema.org

National Mortgage Association of America (Fannie Mae) www.fanniemae.com

Mortgage Bankers Association of America www.mbaa.org

National Association of Realtors www.realtor.org

Office of Federal Housing Oversight www.ofheo.gov

Office of Federal Housing Enterprise Oversight www.ofheo.gov

National Reverse Mortgage Lenders Association www.reversemortgage.org

Federal Depository Insurance Corporation www.fdic.gov

Federal Home Loan Mortgage Corporation (Freddie Mac) www.freddiemac.com

Sallie Mae www.salliemae.org

Government National Mortgage Association (Ginnie Mae) www.ginniemae.gov

Department of Housing and Urban Development (HUD) www.hud.gov

Federal Housing Finance Board www.fhfb.gov

Bond Market Association www.bondmarkets.com

U.S. Social Security Administration

Dean Baker. Dangerous Trends: The Growth of Debt in the U.S. Economy. Center for Economic Policy Research, September 7, 2004.

Dean Baker. The Run-Up in Home Prices: Is It real or is It Another Bubble? Center for Economic Policy Research, August, 5, 2002.

Dean Baker. Too Much Bubbly at the Fed?: The New York Federal Reserve's Analysis of the Run-Up in Home Prices. Center for Economic Policy Research, June 12,, 2004.

Maya MacGuineas. Homeowner Tax Breaks are Breaking the Budget. Fiscal Policy Program at the New America Foundation, October 30, 2005.

Peter Coy. The Home Vexing Greenspan. News Analysis, June 10, 2005.

Dana Dratch. Bubble Fear? Rethink Your Mortgage. Bankrate.com, March 10, 2006.

Noelle Know. Some Homeowners Struggle to Keep Up With Adjustable Rates. USA Today, April 3, 2006.

Jason Zweig. The Oracle Speaks. CNN Money, May 2, 2005.

Gary Shilling. The Housing Bubble Will Probably Burst. January 2006.

Scott Wright. Real Estate Bubble 3. May 27, 2005.

Peter Miller. Will There Be a Real Estate Bubble? April 23, 2002.

Michael House. Oversight on Government Sponsored Enterprises: The Risks and Benefits to Consumers. Testimony to Senate Government Affairs Committee, July 21, 2003.

Lew Sichelman. Is Household Wealth Rising or Falling? Realtytimes.com.

Les Christie. Take This House and Shove It. CNNMoney.com, December 8, 2005.

Fred Foldvary. Real Estate Cycles. The Progress Report, 2004.

Nicholas von Hoffman. Pop Goes the real Estate Bubble. October 5, 2005.

Forrest Pafenberg. Single-Family Mortgages Originated and Outstanding: 1990-2004. Office of Federal Housing Enterprise Oversight, July 2005.

Richard Freeman. Fannie and Freddie Were Lenders': U.S. Real Estate Bubble Nears Its End. Executive Intelligence Review, June 21, 2002.

Dider Sornette. Is the Real Estate Bubble ready to Burst? UCLA Today, 2004.

Frank Nothaft. The Next Decade for Mortgage Finance. Special Commentary from the Office of the Chief Economist, Freddie Mac, June 23, 2004 http://www.freddiemac.com/news/finance/commentary/sp-comm_062304.html

http://calculatedrisk.blogspot.com/

A Supervisor's Perspective on Mortgage Markets and Mortgage Lending Practices. Remarks by Governor Susan Schmidt Bies at the Mortgage Bankers Association Presidents Conference, Half Moon Bay, California. June 14, 2006.

Federal National Mortgage Association Form 8-K, The United States Securities and Exchange Commission, Mar. 21, 2006.

New Home Sales Drop in the West. East Bay Business Times, March 24, 2006.

Michael Corkery. Hot Homes Get Cold in Once-Booming Markets. The Wall Street Journal, Apr. 22, 2006.

Predatory Appraisal Stealing the American Dream. The National Community Reinvestment Coalition.

John Bellamy Foster. The Household Debt Bubble. May 2006.

Mike Wells. Local Mortgage Firms Searched by Federal Agents. Columbia Daily Tribune, April 2, 2005.

Peter Coy. Buyer (And Seller) Beware. BusinessWeek Online, April 4, 2006.

Noelle Knox. Some Homeowners Struggle to Keep Up With Adjustable Rates. USA Today, Apr. 3, 2006.

Larry S. Levy. The Fraud of Appraisal Regulation. Financial Sense, July 2004.

Bob Burnitt. Appraisal Fraud: So What Else is New, Pal? Financial Sense, March 2005.

Richard Freeman. Fannie and Freddie Were Lenders': U.S. Real Estate Bubble Nears Its End. Executive Intelligence Review, June 21, 2002.

Greenspan Calls for Curbs on Fannie Mae, Freddie Mac Growth. Bloomberg, April 6, 2005.

Oversight on Government Sponsored Enterprises: The Risks and Benefits to Consumers. Testimony of W. Michael House, July 21, 2003.

Robert Tanner. Property Taxes Questioned As Prices Zoom. Associated Press, May 22, 2006.

Social Security

Social Security Administration

Seniorjournal.com

Craig Smith. Retired Seniors Find Little Security. Pittsburg Tribune-Review, June 5, 2006.

Gar Alperovitz. Time for Moral Outrage About Social Security. CommonDreams.org, January 31, 2005.

Social Security Primer. National Committee to Preserve Social Security and Medicare, February 2006.

The Truth About Social Security. National Committee to Preserve Social Security and Medicare.

National Committee to Preserve Social Security and Medicare. Myths and Realities About Social Security and Privatization. March 2005.

Personal Retirement Accounts are a Recipe for Benefit Cuts. National Committee to Preserve Social Security and Medicare, February 2006.

An Op-ed on Social Security: Risks Far Outweigh Benefits of Privatized Social Security. National Committee to Preserve Social Security and Medicare, September 30, 2004.

Sylvester Schieber. Social Security: Past, Present and Future. National Academy of Social Insurance. Social Security Brief No 5. March 1999.

Marie Smith. The Future of Social Security. Social Security Conference, Menendez Pelayo Conference, Santander, Spain. July 18, 2005.

2004 Report of the OASDI Board of Trustees and Social Security Office of the Chief Actuary.

E. J. Dionne. Why Social Insurance? National Academy of Social Insurance. Social Security Brief No 6. January 1999.

What is Social Security Disability Insurance? National Academy of Social Insurance.

Social Security Finances: A Primer. National Academy of Social Insurance, April 2005.

Virginia Reno and Anita Cardwell. Social Security Finances: Findings of the 2006 Trustees Report. National Academy of Social Insurance. Social Security Brief No 21. May 2006.

Virginia Reno and Joni Lavery. Can We Afford Social Security When Baby Boomers Retire? National Academy of Social Insurance. Social Security Brief No 22. May 2006.

Virginia Reno and Joni Lavery. Options to Balance Social Security Funds Over the Next 75 Years. National Academy of Social Insurance. Social Security Brief No 18. February 2005.

Virginia Reno and Joni Lavery. Social Security: What Role for Life Annuities in Individual Accounts? Issues, Options, and Tradeoffs. National Academy of Social Insurance. Social Security Brief No.5.

Lockhart versus the United States, Supreme Court of the United States. http://www.law.cornell.edu/supct/html/04-881.ZO.html

Evaluating Issues in Privatizing Social Security. The Report of the Panel on the Privitization of Social Security. National Academy of Social Insurance.

Richard Kogan and Robert Greenstein. President Portrays Social Security Shortfall as Enormous But His Tax Cuts and Drug Benefit Will Cost at Least Five Times as Much. Center on Budget and Policy Priorities, 2005.

Board of Trustees. 2005. The 2005 Annual Report of the Board of Trustees of the Federal Old-Age and Survivors Insurance and Disability Insurance Trust Funds. Washington, D.C.: U.S. Government Printing Office.

U.S. Social Security Administration (SSA). 2005. Income of the Population 55 or Older, 2002. Washington, D.C.: Social Security Administration.

Alicia Munnell. A Bird's Eye View of the Social Security Debate. Center for Retirement Research at Boston College, An Issue in Brief 25.

U.S. Social Security Administration (SSA). 2004. *Effect* of COLA on Social Security Benefits. Washington, D.C.: Social Security Administration. www.ssa.gov/OACT/COLA/colaeffect.html.

Robert Clark and Joseph Quinn. The Economic Status of the Elderly. National Academy of Social Insurance. Medicare Brief No 4. May 1999.

Leonesio and Vaughan. Increasing the Early Retirement Age Under Social Security: Health, Work, and Financial Resources. National Academy of Social Insurance. Health and Income Security for an Aging Workforce. No. 7. December 2003.

Robert Clark and Joseph Quinn. The Economic Status of the Elderly. National Academy of Social Insurance. Medicare Brief No.4 May 1999.

Jason Furman and Robert Greenstein. What the New Trustees' Report Shows about Social Security. Center on Budget and Policy Priorities, June 15, 2006.

Jason Furman. Does Social Security Face a Crisis in 2018? Center on Budget and Policy Priorities, January 11, 2004.

Greg Anrig. Ten Myths About Social Security. The Century Foundation, January 25, 2006.

Max Sawicky. Collision Course: The Bush Budget and Social Security. Economic Policy Institute, March 2005.

Jagadeesh Gokhale. Why America Needs Social Security Reform. CATO Institute, November 30, 2004.

Jagadeesh Gokhale. The Future of Retirement in the United States. CATO Institute, January 22, 2004.

Peter G. Peterson. Riding for a Fall. Foreign Affairs, September/October 2004.

Thomas Saving. The 2004 Report of the Social Security Trustees: Social Security Shortfalls and the Prospect for Reform. Texas A&M University, Private Enterprise Research Center. Perspective on Policy, September 2004.

Social Security and Medicare from a Trust Fund and Budget Perspective. ASPE issue Brief. April 2005.

Liqun Liu, Andrew Rettenmaier and Thomas Saving. A Debt is a Debt. Texas A&M University, Private Enterprise Research Center. Perspective on Policy, September 2002.

Andrew Rettenmaier and Thomas Saving. With an Eye to the Future. Texas A&M University, Private Enterprise Research Center. Perspective on Policy, May 2004.

James Horney and Richard Kogan. Private Accounts Would Substantially Increase Federal Debt and Interest Payments. Center on Budget and Policy Priorities, August 2, 2005.

The Outlook for Social Security: Potential Range of Social Security Outlays and Revenues Under Current Law. Congressional Budget Office, June 2004.

Greg Anrig and Bernard Wasow. Twelve Reasons Why Privatizing Social Security is a Bad Idea. The Century Foundation, February 14, 2005.

Greg Anrig and Bernard Wasow. What Would Really Happen Under Social Security Privitization? Part III: IRAs and 401(k)s You Can Not Control or Leave to Heirs. The Social Security Network, The Century Foundation.

Greg Anrig and Bernard Wasow. What Would Really Happen Under Social Security Privatization? The Social Security Network, December 10, 2001.

Michael Leonesio, Denton Vaughtan and Bernard Wixon. Increasing the Early Retirement Age Under Social Security: Health, Work, and Financial Resources. National Academy of Social Insurance. Health and Income for an Aging Workforce. No. 7 December 2003.

DeWitt, Larry. The Social Security Trust Funds and the Federal Budget. Research Note #20. Social Security Administration Historian's Office, March 4, 2005.

Social Security Sourcebook. National Academy of Social Insurance. www.nasi.org

Social Security Reform. A Century Foundation Guide to the Issues, Revised 2005 edition. The Century Foundation, 2005.

Supreme Court of the United States, No. 04-881. James Lockhart, Petitioner v. United States et al. On Writ of Certiorari to the United States Court of Appeals for the Ninth Circuit, December 7, 2005.

Public Policy in an Older America. A Century Foundation Guide to the Issues. The Century Foundation, 2006.

Austan Goolsbee. The Fees of Private Accounts and the Impact of Social Security Privatization on Financial Managers. University of Chicago, September 2004.

Alicia Munnell. Social Security's Financial Outlook: The 2006 Update in Perspective. Center for Retirement Research at Boston College, Number 46. April 2006.

Alicia Munnell. Social Security's Financial Outlook: The 2005 Update and a Look Back. Center for Retirement Research at Boston College, Number 16. March 2005.

Douglas Holtz-Eakin. The Outlook for Social Security. Congressional Budget Office, June 2004.

Statement of Hal Daub, Chairman, Social Security Advisory Board at the Nationwide Public Policy Forum on Retirement Security. June 28, 2004.

Michael Leonesio, Denton Vanghan, and Bernard Wixon. Increasing the Early Retirement Age Under Social Security: Health, Work, and Financial Resources. National Academy of Social Insurance. Health and Income Security, No. 7. December 2003.

Max Sawicky. Collision Course: The Bush Budget and Social Security. Economic Policy Institute, March 2005.

Richard Johnson and Rudolph Penner. Will Health Care Costs Erode Retirement Security? Center for Retirement Research at Boston College. An Issue in Brief. Number 23. October 2004.

448

Charles Hurt. Illegals Granted Social Security. The Washington Times, May 19, 2006.

Thomas Saving. The 2004 Report of the Social Security Trustees: Social Security Shortfalls and the Prospect for Reform. Texas A&M University, Private Enterprise Research Center, September 2004.

Larry DeWitt. Social Security Administration, Agency History, Research Notes & Special Studies by the Historian's Office. Research Note #20. March 4, 2005.

The World's Dependence on Oil

U.S. Energy Information Administration www.eia.gov

CIA World Factbook www.cia.gov

Society of Petroleum Engineers. www.spe.org

Association for the Study of Peak Oil and Gas. www.peakoil.net

American Petroleum Institute www.api.org

Chevron Inc. www.cheveron.com

Exxon-Mobil Inc. www.exxon.com

U.S Department of Energy. http://www.fe.doe.gov/programs/reserves/spr/spr-facts.html

Jean Leherrere. Estimates of Oil Reserves. Paper presented at the EMF/IEA/IEW Meeting IIASA, Laxenburg, Austria, June 10, 2001.

Wood, Long and Morehouse. Long-Term World Oil Supply Scenarios: The Future is Neither as Bleak or Rosy as Some Assert. EIA, August 18, 2004.

R. W. Bentley. Global Oil & Gas Depletion: An Overview. Energy Policy 30 (2002) 189-205.

Alfred Cavallo. Oil: The Illusion of Plenty. Bulletin of the Atomic Scientists, January/February 2004, Vol. 60, no 01.

William Engdahl. Iraq and the Problem of Peak Oil. Current Concerns, No 1, 2004.

Bamberger, Robert. Strategic Petroleum Reserve. CRS: Issue Brief for Congress: Resources, Aug. 2, 2001.

Matthew Simmons and King Hubbert. The World's Giant Oilfields. Center for Petroleum Supply Studies, Colorado School of Mines, January 2002.

Samsam Bakhtiari. 2002 to see birth of New World Energy Order. Oil and Gas Journal, January 7, 2002.

Kenneth Deffeyes. Peak of World Oil Production. paper No. 83-0, Geological Society of America Annual Meeting, November 2001.

King Hubbert. Nuclear Energy and the Fossil Fuels. Publication No. 95, Shell Development Company Exploration and Production Research Division. Presented before the Spring Meeting of the Southern District, Division of Production, American Petroleum Institute. Plaza Hotel, San Antonio, Texas, March 7-9, 1956.

Kjell Aleklett. International Energy Agency Accepts Peak Oil: An Analysis of Chapter 3 of the World Energy Outlook 2004. Association for the Study of Peak Oil and Gas (ASPO).

www.peakoil.net/uhdsg/weo2004/TheUppsalaCode.html

Rudolf Rechsteiner. Adding Fuel to Fire? The Role of Petroleum and Violent Conflicts. Presented at the swisspeace annual conference, October 30, 2003.

Bengt Soderbergh. Canada's Oil Sands Resources and Its Future Impact on Global Oil Supply. Masters of Science Degree Project, Systems Engineering, Uppsala University, 2005.

T. Ahlbrandt. The USGS World Petroleum Assessment 2000.

T. Quinn. Turning Tar Sands into Oil. Cleveland Plain Dealer, July 22, 2005.

David Greene, Janet Hopson and Jia Li. Running Out of and Into Oil: Analyzing Global Oil Depletion and Transition Through 2050. Prepared by the Oak Ridge national Laboratory for the U.S. Dept of Energy, October 2003.

Robert Hirsch, Roger Bezdek and Robert Wendling. Peaking of World Oil Production: Impacts, Mitigation, and Risk Management. February 8, 2005.

James A. Paul. The Iraq Oil Bonanza: Estimating Future Profits. Global Policy Forum, January 28, 2004.

James A. Paul. Oil Companies in Iraq: A Century of Rivalry and War. Global Policy Forum, Nov. 2003.

James A. Paul. Oil in Iraq: the heart of the Crisis. Global Policy Forum, December 2002.

Iraq: Setting the Record Straight. New American Century, April 2005. www.newamericancentury.org

US Dept of Energy Office Supports Peak Oil Theory. U.S. Department of Justice, Dec. 17, 2004.

A. Naparstek. The Coming Global Energy Crunch: A $2 Gallon of Gas is Just the Beginning. New York Press, June 1, 2004.

T. Appenzeller, T. End of Cheap Oil. National Geographic, June 2004.

A. Cavello. Oil: Caveat Empty. Bulletin of the Atomic Scientists, May 25, 2005.

W. Youngquist. Survey of Energy Resources: Oil Shale. World Energy Council, April 24, 2005.

US: Caution Warranted on Oil Shale. Denver Post Editorial, April 18, 2005.

T. Sykes. Staring Down a Barrel of a Crisis. Australian Financial Review, January 15, 2005.

D. Ross. Plan War and the Hubbert Curve, An Interview with Richard Heinberg. ZNet Venezuela, April 17, 2004.

E.J. Schultz. Billionaire Microsoft Corp. Chairman Bill Gates is Investing in a Fresno Ethanol Company. Environmental News Network, November 17, 2005.

J. R. Healey. Alternate energy not in cards at ExxonMobil. USA Today, October 28, 2005.

National Democratic Committee. Americans' Pain at the Pump a Boom for Oil Companies. U.S. Newswire, Oct. 27, 2005.

Stocks Slump Despite Exxon's Staggering Profit. CNBC Market Dispatches, October 27, 2005.

Dean Baker. Taxing Exxon's Windfall From Hurricane Katrina. Center for Economic Policy and Research, Sept. 2005.

B. Hamilton. Automotive Gasoline. Open Press, January 18, 1995.

Small Business Association

Mystery Chinese Outfit Eyes Exxon. BBC News, October 31, 2005.

Ben Berkowitz. Exxon Dismisses Chinese Buyout Bid. Reuters, October 31, 2005.

Timothy Gardner. Green Energy Sales Seen Quadrupling in Decade. Reuters, March 6, 2006.

Grace Wong. Sorting Through the Ethanol Hype. CNNMoney.com, June 12, 2006.

Shell to Invest $17B in Canadian Oil Production. International Market Insight Report, December 2005.

Wealth of Major Projects for Alberta's OILSANDS. International Market Insight Report, December 2005.

Husky's $10B Sunrise Oil Sands Project Approved. International Market Insight Report, December 2005.

CO2 Oil Injections Boost Oil Recovery Efficiency. International Market Insight Report, December 2005.

Garance Burke. Groups Set to Profit From Ethanol Shipping. Associated Press, February 22, 2006.

International Energy Outlook 2006. Chapter 3: World Oil Markets. Energy Information Administration. June 2006.

Power and Fraud in Corporate America

Corporate Share of US National Income Increases at Faster Rate than at Any Time Since 1945. Finfacts Team, Jun 5, 2006.

The American Jobs Creation Act of 2003. Summary of H.R. 2896 as passed by Committee. Committee on Means and Ways. October 28, 2003. http://waysandmeans.house.gov/media/pdf/fsc/fscsummary.pdf

Kim Clark. A Parade of Profitability. U.S. News and World Report, July 9, 2006.

Christopher Swann. US Groups Boost Share of Economic Pie. June 4, 2006.

Chris Fishman. The Wal-Mart You Don't Know. Fast Company, December 2003.

Tim Hamilton. Study Finds Low Gasoline Inventories Unreasonably Driving Up Pump Prices. May 24, 2006.

Rx for Fraud. Forbes, June 20, 2005.

United States Senate Committee on the Judiciary. Consolidation in the Energy Industry: Raising Prices at the Pump? Testimony of Tim Hamilton, February 1, 2006.

Ian Fried. Al Gore Joins Apple's Board. News.com, March 20, 2003.

Tim Hamilton. Running on Empty in the West: Low Gasoline Inventories Set the Stage for $4 at the Pump in 2006. The Foundation for Taxpayer and Consumer Rights, May 23, 2006.

S&P 500 Constituents Spent $100.2 Billion on Stock Buybacks During the First Quarter, Up 22.1% on Q1 2005. Finfacts.com, June 12, 2006.

Kathleen Pender. Write-offs Remove Excess Inventory from Books—Not Shelves: Accounting Move Can Often Distort Firms' Financial Data. San Francisco Chronicle, May 8, 2001.

Ed Wolff and Jared Bernstein. Inequality and Corporate Power. Global Policy Forum, June 2003.

Marcy Gordon. SEC Requires More Executive Pay Disclosure. Associated Press. July 26, 2006.

Declan McCullagh. Behind the Stock Options Uproar. News.com, July 26, 2006.

Randall Heron and Erik Lee. What Fraction of Stock Option Grants to Top Executives Have Been Backdated or Manipulated? July 14, 2006.

Adam Lashinsky. Options Gone Wild! Fortune, June 30, 2006.

Adam Lashinsky. Why Options Backdating is a Big Deal. Fortune, July 26, 2006.

Geoffrey Colvin. A Study in CEO Greed. Fortune, March 30, 2006.

Troy Wolverton. Options' Deluding Effect. TheStreet.com, June 7, 2006.

Jonathan Stempel. Halliburton Accused of Accounting Fraud. Reuters, August 6, 2004.

Carl Osgood. Cheney's Halliburton Paradigm for Fraud. Executive Intelligence Review, July 6, 2006.

Willie Green. Bayh Wants Study of Dangers Posed by Foreign Ownership of U.S. Debt. Chesterton Tribune.

Elisabeth Bumiller. Make Industries' Tax Cuts Permanent, President Urges. New York Times, Feb. 3, 2006.

Lynnley Browning. Richest & Largest U.S. Corporations Paying Less and Less Taxes. New York Times, Sept. 23, 2004.

Iman Anabtawi. Secret Compensation. UCLA School of Law & Economics Research Paper Series. Research Paper No.04-9.

Government Waste and Deception

Larry Margasak. FEMA Funds Spent of Divorce, Sex Change. Associated Press, June 14, 2006.

Tamar Gabelnick and Anna Rich. In Focus: Globalized Weaponry. Federation of American Scientists. Volume 5, Number 16. May 2000.

Timothy Aeppel. An Inflation Debate Brews Over Intangibles at the Mall. Wall Street Journal, May 9, 2005.

Sidney Dean. Transatlantic Armament Cooperation: Washington Open for Business. Centre for SouthEast European Studies, February 11, 2005.

International Action Network on Small Arms. Undermining Global Security: the European Union's Arms Exports, 2003.

Rosario-Malonzo, Jennifer del. US Military-Industrial Complex: Profiting from War. IBON Features. Special Report, 2002.

Senator John McCain's Floor Statement on Defense Authorization Bill. May 23, 2003.

Jack Triplett. Some Objections to Hedonic Indexes. Brookings Institution, July 3, 2004.

Paul R. Liegey. Developing an Hedonic Regression Model For DVD Players In the U.S. CPI. U.S. Department of Labor Statistics, October 16, 2001.

Antal E. Fekete. The Supply of Oxen at the Federal Reserve. Financial Sense, January 20, 2005.

Measurement Issues in the Consumer Price Index. Bureau of Labor Statistics, U.S. Dept of Labor, June 1997.

Paul Liegey and Nicole Shepler. Adjusting VCR Prices for Quality Change: A Study Using Hedonic Methods. Bureau of Labor Statistics, Monthly Labor Review, September 1999.

Lee Russ. How the U.S. Measures Employment and Unemployment. Section News, January 8, 2006.

Jennifer del Rosario-Malonzo. US Military-Industrial Complex: Profiting from War. IBON Features.

Mary Kokoski, Keith Waehrer, and Patricia Rozaklis. Using Hedonic Methods for Quality Adjustment in the CPI: The Consumer Audio Products Component. Bureau of Labor Statistics, U.S. Department of Labor, October 16, 2001.

Steven Landefeld and Bruce Grimm. A Note on the Impact of Hedonics and Computers on Real GDP. Survey of Current Business, December 2000.

How the Government Measures Unemployment. U.S. Department of Labor, Bureau of Labor Statistics, Labor Force Statistics from the Current Population Survey, July 2001.

Undermining Global Security: the European Union's Arms. Amnesty International, 2003.

Charles Paul Freund. Government Smokes: The Tobacco Settlement. KeepMedia, June 1, 2002.

Tamar Gabelnick and Anna Rich. In Focus: Globalized Weaponry. Federation of American Scientists. Volume 5, Number 16, May 2000.

Earl Baxter. Overseas Markets Upturn on the Near Term Horizon. Military Training Technology. Volume: 9, Issue 2. April 22, 2004.

Christopher St. John. How Should Maine Spend the Tobacco Settlement? Thoughts on a Federal Balanced Budget Amendment. Maine Center for Economic Policy. Volume V, No. 4, May 6, 1999.

Lester Brickman. Want to Be a Billionaire? Sue a Tobacco Company. Citizens Against Lawsuit Abuse, Oct. 23, 2004.

Analysis of the 2002-03 Budget Bill, Health & Social Services, State of California, Legislative Analyst's Office. Tobacco Settlement Fund.

Curtis Kirk. Tobacco Funds Protecting Our Land, Air, and Water. Kentucky Natural Resources and Environmental Protection Cabinet, Division of Conservation. Fall 2002, Vol. 13, No. 4.

Daniel Fisher. Smoke This. Forbes, September 2, 2002.

Daniel Fisher. Why Are the Lawyers Getting $3.3 Billion in Fees from the Texas Tobacco Settlement Trying to Avoid a State Investigation? Forbes, September 2, 2002.

Dan McGraw and Julian E. Barnes. Junkyard Dogs for Hire. U.S. News and World Report, June 2, 1997.

Pamela Sherrid. Class Action Crumbs. U.S. News and World Report, March 25, 2002.

Lou Whiteman. Pa. Uses Tobacco Settlement to Fund Biotech. The Deal, April 17, 2002.

Susan Sanders. Tobacco Fund Only a Fraction of Health Costs. American Medical Association News, May 6, 2002.

Spending Tobacco Settlement Money. American Cancer Society, May 1, 2001.

Christine Hall. States Spend Tobacco Settlement on Budget Shortfalls. Budget & Tax News, May 1, 2004.

Andrew McKinley, Lee Dixon, and Amanda Devore. "State Management and Allocation of Tobacco Settlement Revenue 2003." National Conference of State Legislatures, September 2003.

Tobacco Settlement: States' Allocations of Fiscal Year 2003 and Expected Fiscal Year 2004 Payments. Report to Congressional Requesters. GAO. March 2004.

The War in Iraq and the Reconstruction

O'Neill: Bush Planned Iraq Invasion Before 9/11. CNN.com, January 14, 2004.

Peter G. Peterson. Riding for a Fall. Foreign Affairs, September/October 2004.

Erik Eckholm. Halliburton Unit's Work in Iraq Is Called 'Poor.' New York Times, April 12, 2005.

FBI Interviews Halliburton Whistleblower. The Associated Press, November 25, 2004.

New Audit Slams Halliburton for Work in Kuwait. Reuters, October 28, 2004.

Vicki Allen. Halliburton Gave U.S. Troops Foul Water, Workers Say. Reuters, January 23, 2006.

Jason Leopold. Halliburton Sold Iranian Oil Company Key Nuclear Reactor Components, Sources Say. World News Trust, August 6, 2005.

James Sterngold. Casualty of War: The U.S. Economy. San Francisco Chronicle, July 17, 2005.

Fraud Rampant in Iraq: Report. The Australian. January 18, 2006.

China

Special Feature-China. The Economic Review, November 2003.

Jen Lin-Liu. Catering to China's Fashionistas. Wall Street Journal, September 30, 2005.

Busy Signals. Economist.com, September 8, 2005.

Randeep Ramesh. Silk Road to Riches for China and India. Taipei Times, October 5, 2005.

Bian Yi. Nation Needs Renewable Energy Sources. China Daily, October 6, 2005 www.chinadaily.com

Paul Roberts. Our Post-Oil Future Needs a Push. Washingtonpost.com, July 14, 2005.

Vivek and Subramanian. Why Global Oil Prices are Rising. Rediff.com, September 1, 2005.

Doug Tsuruoka. China's Ever-Growing Oil Needs May Result in a Global Shortage. Globalsecurity.org, Jan. 26, 2005.

Dream Machines. The Economist, June 2, 2005.

Charolette Windle. Luxury Cars Inspire China's Dreamers. BBC News, April 27, 2005.

James Laurenceson and Fengming Qin. China's Exchange Rate Debate. School of Economics, University of Queensland, August 2005.

Annual Report to Congress: The Military Power of the People's Republic of China 2005.Office of the Secretary of Defense.

China's Oil Imports Rise to Hit Record High. Shenzhen Daily, November 23, 2004.

Jon D. Markman. How China is Winning the Oil Race. MSN Money, April 27, 2006.

Richard Hallorar. Conventional Wisdom Overlooks China's Troubles. Real Clear Politics, April 14, 2006.

Stephanie Hoo. China Cuts Currency Link to U.S. Dollar. Associated Press, July 21, 2005.

David Berman. Base Metal Prices in 'Unchartered Territory:' Huge Chinese Demand. Financial Post, February 1, 2006.

OECD Finds That China is Biggest Exporter of Information Technology Goods in 2004, Surpassing US and EU. OECD, December 12, 2005.

David Lague. China Sees Foreign Cash Pile as Possible Peril. International Herald Tribune, Jan. 16, 2006.

China's Currency Manipulation and U.S. Trade. Economic Policy Institute, Economic Snapshots. October 30, 2003.

Peter Goodman. China Set to Reduce Exposure to Dollar. Washington Post Foreign Service, Jan. 10, 2006.

Eswar Prasad. Next Steps for China. International Monetary Fund, September 2005, Volume 42, Number 3.

India

India's Tata Group Buying Tyco Network at Bargain Price. TechWeb.com InformationWeek, Nov. 1, 2004.

Zubair Ahmed. India's Car Market is Revving Up. BBC News, July 19, 2005.

Engardio, Hamm, and Kripalani. The Rise of India. BusinessWeek Online, December 8, 2003.

Miscellaneous

www.truthinlabeling.org

www.opensecrets.com

Center for American Progress

Eugene Yeboah and Stephen Boxer. Structured Credit Products: Finding New Ways to Spread Credit Risk and Capture Return. The Babson Staff Letter, September 24, 2004.

Jeff Huther. Treasury Debt Instruments. U.S. Department of Treasury, 2005.

U.S. Department of Labor http://www.bls.gov

Stephan Ohlemacher. State Tax Burdens Jump Across the Nation. Associated Press, 2005.

Karen Lee. Lawyers Listening for retirement Plan Dissatisfaction. KeepMedia, April 1, 2001.

Hirsch Organization. <u>Stock Trader's Almanac 2006</u>. Wiley, October 2005.

About the Author

Mr. Stathis applies his expertise in finance and healthcare as a business consultant with a focus on early-stage high technology companies. He also provides consulting services to venture capital firms, hedge funds and money managers. He previously worked for several years at two of Wall Street's largest and most prestigious investment firms. In his spare time, he continues to remain active in the public markets as an investment strategist and research analyst for a successful investment newsletter.

Prior to his career in finance, he was involved in research projects ranging from alternative energy systems, material science, solid-state chemistry, and human disease. He is a member of the New York Academy of Sciences and formerly a National Science Foundation Research Fellow. He received an M.S. in biological chemistry in addition to several years of graduate level coursework in the biosciences.

Speaking Engagements and Consulting

If your company has an interest in hiring Mr. Stathis to speak or provide educational instruction on investment- or business-related topics, serve as a consultant for your fund or early stage company, please inquire about availability, topics and rates by emailing info@apexva.com.

Upcoming Books by this Author

To receive advance notification about future books or other publications by this author, send an email to info@apexva.com. If you are a financial professional, a member of academia, or an accomplished author and would be interested in providing a review of future publications by this author, please email your CV for consideration.

Printed in the United States
87343LV00003B/2/A